Advances in
Intrinsic Motivation
and Aesthetics

Advances in
Intrinsic Motivation and Aesthetics

Edited by
Hy I. Day
York University
Downsview, Ontario, Canada

Plenum Press · New York and London

Library of Congress Cataloging in Publication Data

Main entry under title:

Advances in intrinsic motivation and aesthetics.

Bibliography: p.
Includes index.
1. Motivation (Psychology). 2. Curiosity. 3. Aesthetics — Psychological aspects. 4.
Berlyne, D. E. I. Day, Hy I., 1925-   .
BF503.A35   153.8   81-2766
ISBN 0-306-40606-3   AACR2

© 1981 Plenum Press, New York
A Division of Plenum Publishing Corporation
233 Spring Street, New York, N.Y. 10013

Printed in the United States of America

Contributors

FRANK AULD, Department of Psychology, University of Windsor, Windsor, Ontario, Canada

IRVIN L. CHILD, Department of Psychology, Yale University, New Haven, Connecticut

J. B. CROZIER, Department of Psychology, Glendon College, York University, Toronto, Ontario, Canada

GERALD C. CUPCHIK, Division of Life Sciences, Scarborough College, University of Toronto, Toronto, Ontario, Canada

HY I. DAY, Department of Psychology, York University, Downsview, Ontario, Canada

H. J. EYSENCK, Department of Psychology, Institute of Psychiatry, De Crespigny Park, Denmark Hill, London, England

CHRISTINE P. FUREDY, Division of Social Sciences, York University, Downsview, Ontario, Canada

JOHN J. FUREDY, Department of Psychology, University of Toronto, Toronto, Ontario, Canada

FRANCIS G. HARE, Department of Psychology, Ryerson Polytechnical Institute, Toronto, Ontario, Canada

HEINZ HECKHAUSEN, Institute of Psychology, Ruhr University, Bochum, West Germany

R. WALTER HEINRICHS, Department of Psychology, University of Toronto, Toronto, Ontario, Canada

J. McVICKER HUNT, Department of Psychology, University of Illinois, Champaign, Illinois

CORINNE HUTT, Late Reader in Psychology, University of Keele, Keele, Staffordshire, England

SUZANNE C. KOBASA, Department of Behavioral Sciences, University of Chicago, Chicago, Illinois

SALVATORE R. MADDI, Department of Behavioral Sciences, University of Chicago, Chicago, Illinois

K. B. MADSEN, The Royal Danish School of Educational Studies, Copenhagen, Denmark

ALBERT MEHRABIAN, Department of Psychology, University of California, Los Angeles, California

FRANÇOIS MOLNAR, Institut d'Esthétique et des Sciences de l'Art, Université de Paris, Paris, France

CHRISTY MOYNIHAN, Department of Psychology, University of California, Los Angeles, California

RICHARD M. NICKI, Department of Psychology, University of New Brunswick, Fredericton, New Brunswick, Canada

JUM C. NUNNALLY, Department of Psychology, Vanderbilt University, Nashville, Tennessee

KLAUS SCHNEIDER, Department of Psychology, Philipps University, Marburg, West Germany

PETER SUEDFELD, Department of Psychology, The University of British Columbia, Vancouver, British Columbia, Canada

EDWARD L. WALKER, 3041 Lopez, Pebble Beach, California

JOACHIM F. WOHLWILL, College of Human Development, Pennsylvania State University, University Park, Pennsylvania

Preface

It has been both a pleasure and an honor to edit this book. The pleasure has been in interacting with the gifted authors who wrote the chapters for this volume and the honor has been in knowing that the book is dedicated to a great man and a brilliant psychologist—Daniel E. Berlyne.

All the contributors to this book have been touched, at some time, by Dan Berlyne and his ideas. Whether as his teachers, his colleagues, his peers, his students, or his friends and arguing partners, we have all felt his presence and been improved by it.

The list of contributors to this volume is large and could have been much larger, for a number of people, in fact, contacted me for the opportunity to contribute when they heard about the purpose of this book. It is also an international list, for Dan Berlyne's contacts were international.

The diversity in content and style is also intentional. The authors were invited to contribute an original paper in the field in which they are presently engaged, whether theoretical or a report of empirical work, and to indicate the contribution that Dan Berlyne had made to their work. As the reader will note, contributions range from personal and contact in a laboratory to ideas that elicit controversy, argument, and intensive research.

Daniel Ellis Berlyne was born in Selford, England, a suburb of Manchester, in 1924, and died in Toronto, Canada, on November 2, 1976. During his fifty-two years of life he managed to write or coedit seven books and over 150 articles and papers. His books were translated into seven languages, and he lectured in eight languages over five continents.

Dan was, in every way, a scholar. His interests ranged far and wide. He worked at decoding German messages during the Second World War, was a fair pianist, and loved going to the cinema. As a psychologist he did his research with animals as well as humans and conducted cross-cultural studies across the continents. He took an active role in psychological societies and was, in turn, president of The Canadian Psychological Association, Division 1 (General Psychology) of the APA, Division 10 (Psychology and the Arts) of the APA, and president of the International Association of Empirical Aesthetics.

More than anything else, Dan was curious. It was as if he chose to study curiosity and exploratory behavior more as a response to his own phenomenology than for any other reason. But lest one might think that his was a diversive and superficial curiosity, it should be noted that one of the strong influences on him was Clark Hull, and that Dan always tried to pursue his investigations with the same meticulous care.

Dan also had a dry British sense of humor, which he often displayed by inventing new words and phrases. Thus he titled an article in the Canadian Psychological Review (1975) "Behaviorism? Cognitive Theory? Humanistic Psychology?—To Hull with Them All!" He named his laboratory at the University of Toronto the Laboratory for the Study of Aplopathematic and Thelematoscopic Pneumatology, and from this came the title for one chapter in a book he edited (Berlyne, 1974), "The Vicissitudes of Aplopathematic and Thelematoscopic Pneumatology (or the Hydrography of Hedonism)."

Dan's journey through exploratory behavior was not a simple one. His first publications, prior to the awarding of his Ph.D., were based on animal studies in the area of attention and curiosity as a drive. In fact, he insisted that he had pioneered the concept of curiosity in the literature. After earning his Ph.D. at Boston University, he shifted his research emphasis to human subjects and gradually abandoned drive theory for arousal theory (although he never completely relinquished some of the drive-theory concepts and often called himself a neo-Hullian).

Arousal theory and exploratory behavior can be a large pond, and within its parameters Dan Berlyne swam freely: fixation in human infants, physiological and other orienting responses, Piaget translated into S–R theory, epistemic behavior, decision theory, learning and retention, and education. But all the while Dan kept drifting relentlessly toward aesthetics—probably his true love. He spent the only sabbatical he ever had at the Institut d'Esthétique et des Sciences de l'Art in Paris in 1968–1969, and really found his true vocation. From this stay emerged his most complex and advanced book, *Aesthetics and Psychobiology* (1971), and numerous articles and chapters. He gradually reduced his study of specific exploration for that of diversive exploration—the hunt for the hedonic homeostasis and the explanation of aesthetic behavior.

When we planned to organize the conference at the Ontario Institute for Studies in Education in 1969, Dan and I discussed the concepts of Curiosity and Intrinsic Motivation. He was reluctant to equate them, but bowed to the fact that so many in the field were already using these concepts interchangeably. He feared that adopting the title "Intrinsic Motivation" might dilute his position and blur the differences that he felt existed between his own ideas and those of other psychologists. But in the end the conference was called "Intrinsic Motivation" rather than "Curiosity," and the proceedings were published under the title *Intrinsic Motivation: A New Direction in Education.* I felt that Dan did not care greatly whether people would use the term "curiosity" or "intrinsic motivation," for his concerns were already with the study of aesthetics. Although some of his students' papers still dealt with arousal, learning, and attention, his own works were mainly in the area of "The New Experimental Aesthetics."

This volume to some extent parallels Dan Berlyne's journey along the path leading from Arousal and Curiosity to Aesthetics. The diversity of the chapters reflects the diversity of the man this book honors, so that to some extent I have attempted to order the papers to parallel the sequence of his own interests. The first paper, written by two of his colleages and friends, describes Dan as a psychologist and a human being, and the last paper, by one of his students, summarizes the final research of his laboratory.

All the papers are original and written for the volume. Some report one or more studies in a field, whereas others strike out into new uncharted courses. Most do both. We hope that the papers will lead to new ideas, new research, and new contributions to science.

But most of all we all hope that the reader will recognize the contribution of Daniel Ellis Berlyne and honor his memory in reading the book.

HY I. DAY

Contents

1

"My First Interest Is Interest"

Berlyne as an Exemplar of the Curiosity Drive

JOHN J. FUREDY AND CHRISTINE P. FUREDY

The quotation of the title is not simply a young man's clever aphorism. It became, for Daniel E. Berlyne, a motto for a life of scientific research. It cannot be found in the voluminous published works which Berlyne completed in his tragically truncated academic career, but we know that he repeated it many times at the outset of his career from the independent recall of academic friends. There is every reason to believe that it continued to be a guiding maxim for the rest of his life. We can regard it as one modern psychologist's equivalent of the dictum of Socrates that "the unexamined life is not worth living."

There is more to Berlyne's motto than first appears, once we consider the context in which it was coined and the implications which his early interest in interest and curiosity had for the rest of his career. In this chapter we will explore some of the possible origins of Daniel Berlyne's intellectual "drive" and some manifestations of it in his later interactions with colleagues at the University of Toronto. Our thesis is that, besides studying curiosity as a scientist, Berlyne exemplified, from his youth, some of the more fruitful or "higher-order" elements of scientific curiosity. His work was characterized by independence of thought, and the rare ability to play the role of a disinterested critic for colleagues and students, even for ideas outside his many areas of research and specialization.

This interpretation is not derived from an analysis of Berlyne's writings or from the published principles of motivational theory, for we think

JOHN J. FUREDY • Department of Psychology, University of Toronto, Toronto, Ontario M5S 1A1, Canada. CHRISTINE P. FUREDY • Division of Social Sciences, York University, Downsview, Ontario M3J 2R3, Canada. Preparation of the paper was facilitated by a grant from the Social Science and Humanities Research Council of Canada to both authors.

that Berlyne did not so much publicly advocate[1] a Socratic approach to an investigatory life as he lived it. We wish, rather, to explicate the origins and nature of Berlyne's intellectual style and his mode of operation as an academic, as revealed by his interactions with colleagues and friends rather than by his scholarly publications. Our major sources, then, comprise: (1) a number of letters which Berlyne wrote to a lifelong friend between 1942 and 1950; (2) interviews we have conducted since 1977 with Berlyne's colleagues, relatives, and friends; (3) an interview conducted by R. C. Myers in 1973 with Berlyne as part of the former's historical work with eminent Canadian psychologists; (this Berlyne-with-Myers interview has been transcribed, and will here be cited as BMI);[2] and (4) recollections by the first author of academic interactions with Berlyne during his period at the University of Toronto.

When a colleague dies relatively suddenly, and prematurely, one is inclined to "summarize" the person on the basis of personal recollection, however limited that may be. When Daniel Berlyne died, the characterization that immediately occurred to the first author was the concept of the "disinterested critic," the Socrates-like scholar (cf. Furedy, 1979). Later, when we embarked on our research into Berlyne's life and career (cf. Furedy & Furedy, 1978), we were struck just as forcefully by another characteristic: his great independence of mind. This was perhaps most strikingly evident in his career-long engagement with the Hullian S–R approach to psychology. Independently of his peers and teachers and without meeting Hull, he, as a Cambridge undergraduate, espoused the approach simply through reading the 1943 *Principles* for himself. Then, in a move that made him seem too "cognitive" to the dominant S–R psychologists of the fifties and early sixties, he began his career by arguing for the "nonbiologically" based motive of curiosity, rather than sticking to

---

[1]The one possible exception to this is his brief foray into applying the principles of intrinsic motivation to education (cf. esp. Berlyne 1965). In this paper (entitled "Curiosity and Education"), he notes that even such a supposedly pragmatic and "relevant" theorist as John Dewey appreciated the importance of curiosity and interest in ideas for their own sake. He cites Dewey as one who "condemned the misunderstanding that makes 'interest' mean 'merely the effect of an object upon personal advantage or disadvantage, success or failure' " and who considered that " 'to secure attention and effort by offering a bribe of please' is a 'procedure that is properly stigmatized as soft pedagogy, as a soup kitchen theory of education' " (p. 78). However, as another commentator has noted, "somehow education never became a fruitful ground for his ideas and by 1968, when G. S. Lesser invited him to write a chapter for a textbook on psychology for teachers, he turned over the burden of writing it to someone else" (Day, 1979, p. 381).

[2]We have tried to honour Berlyne's expectation at the time of making this taped interview that it would not be published for at least 10 years by avoiding the use of any material that might be construed as unfavorable to persons still living. Permission to make use of the interview was obtained from both Dr. Myers and Hilde Berlyne.

the orthodox Hullian and more scientifically respectable biological drives like hunger and thirst. Finally, at the close of his life, in his "To Hull with Them All" paper (Berlyne, 1975), he continued to argue for a return to the Hullian emphasis on the importance of motivational factors and unified theories to explain behavior, at a time when experimental psychology or "psychonomy" (Furedy & Furedy, 1978, p. 203) had become cognitive, amotivational, and no longer interested in the "grand theory" approach.

So we became intrigued by these characteristics. What evidence could we find of the development of independence of thought and the ability to be disinterestedly critical in Berlyne's early education and career? How were these qualities displayed in aspects of his later life? We present here some hypotheses which at least to some extent help to explain a scholar whom we regard as exemplifing the curiosity drive of a scientist. We hope, also, that this examination will prompt thought about the life of the scientist and the education which shapes a scientific mind.

CURIOSITY IN YOUTH AND EARLY CAREER

Curiosity and independence of mind are readily apparent in Berlyne's early childhood. By his own account (BMI), Berlyne was something of a loner. The son of a Jewish small manufacturer, he was conscious of being better off than most of the neighboring families in Salford, Manchester. It was clear very early that he lacked good motor-skills coordination and functioned poorly in most boys' games. "When it came to kicking balls, catching balls, I was always butterfingers," he recalled, "I just couldn't do it and I wasn't particularly interested in it." But he was intellectually precocious, being able to read before entering school at age six. He was the eldest of three children. His sister and brother were younger by five and ten years, respectively, and Daniel appears to have enjoyed a certain intellectual status in the family, derived both from his scholastic achievements and from a certain judicial quality. He was called, within the family, "the judge." His sister in particular often looked to him rather than to their parents for arbitration in intellectual and artistic matters.

His mother recalls an anecdote which suggests that Daniel had an inquiring and empirical frame of mind as a young boy. Noticing the destination sign on a Manchester bus, he asked where it was going. His mother told him. "How do you know that it will go there?" he asked. He was satisfied with the reply that "the sign says so." He insisted that they should get on the bus and ride to the terminal as this was the only way to be sure that the bus would, in fact, go there. Mrs. Berlyne indulged this

whim: she must have reinforced on many other occasions such manifestations of intrinsic motivation and empirical curiosity.

In the interview with Dr. Myers, Berlyne recalled the first three times
that he heard the words "psychology" or "psychoanalysis." His teacher
in elementary school explained one day that some boys who did not want
to go to school told their mummies that they had a tummyache, and very
soon they actually developed a tummyache. She asked the class if they
knew who it was who studied such things, and told them that they were
called "psychologists." The second occasion was in high school. A history teacher was talking about Vienna. He said that the city had made
many contributions to culture, especially through musicians, and then
asked if they knew what science had been founded in Vienna. He referred
to psychoanalysis. The third time was at the end of his high-school days.
The day after Poland was invaded in September, 1939, a vast evacuation
programme was implemented for English schools. Dan's school was sent
to Blackpool, where they shared a school with local students. The visiting
students went to classes for only half a day, leaving much spare time for
(in Dan's case) reading and discussion. Later that month, Sigmund Freud
died in London, and the papers carried obituaries. A classmate went to
the Blackpool library and took out Freud's *Introductory Lectures.* He
showed the book to Dan and some friends:

> We found this very interesting. There obviously was salacious appeal which
> was part of it, but apart from that, this was a new world of ideas, interesting
> ideas. Whether they were true or not, we couldn't help finding them interest-
> ing. And so we talked about these and when we got back, I read more about it.
> (BMI, p. 40)

Thus Berlyne's first encounters with the concept of psychology as a
field of study shared some features: in each case there was an enquiring,
experiential aspect in the discussion of the word. The Blackpool incident
seems to us to demonstrate a high degree of intrinsic motivation.

Berlyne's high school was Manchester Grammar, a highly selective
school which "creamed off" 1,400 of the best male students in and around
Manchester. Entrance was through an intensely competitive examination. Within the school, streaming by achievement was continuous and
all-pervasive. That is, in every grade and every subject, pupils were
placed in classes A, B, C, D, etc. on the basis of examination performance
in the previous year. Among the students, the "Scholarship boys" (of
which Berlyne was one) felt they were "an elite of the elite" (BMI p. 18). In
such a streamed system an intelligent, independent student can go forward without developing skills of getting on with others. We think that
this is related to Berlyne's later ability to pursue ideas independently of
the approval of colleagues and dominant "schools" in psychology.

Berlyne believed that the vast majority of the students did not have intellectual values (BMI p. 25). He identified closely with the serious scholarship boys, but still felt isolated. The pressure of the examination system did not narrow his focus. He did extremely well, particularly at languages, but he never saw examinations as ends in themselves. When the routine of school life was broken as it was in 1939, he was not at a loss for intellectual pursuits. Whereas many boys simply wasted time during the Blackpool period, Berlyne was greatly stimulated, his excitement being enhanced by the fact that this was his first time "away from home" (BMI, p. 39).

It seems, then, that Berlyne's high-school experience reinforced his interest in subjects for their own sakes. He learned the joy of mastery of languages while recognizing that he could never perform more than adequately in art or even mathematics (BMI, pp. 19–20). Significantly, he remained interested in both these subjects throughout his life, despite his relatively low level of aptitude for them.

At age 16 Berlyne won four separate scholarships to Cambridge University: the Trinity College modern languages, a United Kingdom government scholarship, a Manchester city, and a Salford city one. He went up to Cambridge in 1941, a young student among 17- and 18-year-olds, to study modern languages. This initial Cambridge period lasted until he was called up in the fall of 1942. Toward the end of it he began to recognize that he was dissillusioned with the prospect of becoming a scholar of modern languages for the rest of his life. The main reason that he gave, rather casually in conversation with Roger Myers, is important:

> But then I was asking myself: Do I really want to spend the rest of my life writing about Goethe and Schiller or reading books about them? I didn't mind reading Goethe and Schiller, but literary criticism . . . didn't seem to be what I wanted to do. (BMI, p. 53)

Literary criticism held no prospect for really original work, and consequently he no longer regarded it as stimulating in the long term.

Concurrently, Berlyne reveled in the intellectual life of Cambridge. He enjoyed exploring ideas outside the classroom and beyond his specialism in university clubs and coffee houses with a group of close friends pursuing differing courses of study. Within this intellectual circle Berlyne was regarded as a wit, a vivacious and accomplished conversationalist. He saw this period of intense social interaction as an important change in his life, in distinct contrast with his relative isolation in high school (BMI, p. 52).

This stimulating intellectual life and his doubts about his future career were suspended abruptly in 1942 by military service. He became a private in the Intelligence section of His Majesty's Armed Forces.

His three years in the army were ultimately instructive for him. He was obviously not "cut out" for the military life. He had no strong desire to rise within the ranks, and in fact only reached the status of lance corporal (equivalent to private first class in the United States). But what impressed him, and distressed him, about work in the Intelligence Corps (IC) was the logical absurdities of, and lack of genuine purpose in, the assigned tasks, and the consequent boredom they induced.[3]

He noted that he got into the IC and coding work because of his expertise in foreign languages, but the actual work required no such knowledge, consisting rather of fiddling with symbols in the hope of breaking codes, a task for which the main qualification seemed to be a high tolerance for boredom. It was a tolerance Berlyne did not possess; throughout his life he required a high level of stimulation and variety in both his work[4] and his recreational pursuits. His unhappiness was intensified by the fear that his intellect would atrophy with lack of challenge. It is not unreasonable to suggest that his later emphasis on the importance of information, curiosity, and intrinsic motivation owed much to his military period of (intellectual) "sensory deprivation."

The return to Cambridge in 1946 was, of course, welcome. But almost immediately he had to face one of the most serious decisions of his life: whether to switch from modern languages to psychology. He suffered one "very, very bad week." Predictions were difficult to make, vocational guidance "very hard to find." He felt that there was no one readily available to give advice. He recalled that he "got through this week by getting as much information as possible and by taking aspirin." He was not completely sure that he was "doing the right thing," but by the end of the week he felt sure enough "to take the plunge" (BMI, p. 78).

We have noted that Berlyne's independent interest in psychology began at high school. While he was at Cambridge, before he entered the Army, this interest was fostered by many discussions with fellow students, often of the "Freudian interpretation" variety. By 1946, however,

[3]For material on this period of 1941–1947 we have relied heavily on Berlyne's correspondence with J. Goldberg, a contemporary pupil at Manchester Grammar who went to Oxford to study law when Berlyne went to Cambridge. Berlyne wrote to him about once a week during his army period, and quite frequently before and after. We are much indebted to Mr. Goldberg, now a solicitor in Manchester, for giving us access to this correspondence.

[4]For example, during his period at Toronto he was quite notable for the willingness and ability to pursue several projects simultaneously, and to interrupt such tasks as book writing either with delivering an undergraduate lecture or talking with a colleague without any difficulty in getting back to the book writing after the interruption. Again, contrasting his year as a full-time teaching faculty member at Berkeley with the immediately preceding year as a fellow at Stanford with no teaching duties, he says that he got more work done at Berkeley, where "I found I was able to do more work on the book (*Conflict, Arousal, and Curiosity,* 1960), when I had other things to do. I've always found that, that to have nothing to do but one thing isn't the most efficient way" (BMI, p. 150). His immediately succeeding remark that, "I'm sure a lot of people find this too," suggests that he overestimated the degree to which most people prefer variety.

his knowledge of psychology as an academic field had widened. It seemed to promise the student a stimulating range of possible future careers to choose from upon graduation. However, Berlyne was not attracted to the sort of psychology espoused by the field's representatives at Cambridge in the 1940s. F. E. Bartlett, the Professor, dominated psychology at the University. It was a psychology confined to cognitive-perceptual issues. No work was done with animals, and the faculty showed little interest in motivational factors. Indeed, there was no attempt to account for behavior in its totality. Even as an undergraduate Berlyne was to write to a friend: "I feel sceptical and irritated by the limitations of Cambridge psychologists." Bartlett became his research supervisor. Berlyne respected his intellectual abilities, but he could not respect the approach to psychology which Bartlett represented. Berlyne thus found little to stimulate him in the undergraduate lectures, but while preparing for his last undergraduate psychology exams he read, among other books, Clark Hull's *Principles of Behavior* (1943). He was electrified and "converted."

This conversion was an isolating experience, for Berlyne pursued Hullianism through a decade of British indifference before interest was expressed there in Hull's ideas. It is a very significant illustration of his intellectual independence and his relative indifference to the opinions of his academic superiors and his peers. The British psychological establishment, and especially the "Cambridge School," headed by Bartlett, regarded the Hullian, "Yale school" approach to the field, with its emphasis on grand theory building designed to explain all behavior, as unfeasible, not to say ridiculous. To Berlyne, however, "the Americans . . . were using scientific method" to deal "with the vital questions" (BMI, p. 83). He was aware that his enthusiasn for Hull and his lack of interest in "that musty Cambridge stuff" (BMI, p. 91) might carry a high cost in career terms. However, Bartlett showed his integrity by giving Berlyne a research scholarship, although Berlyne was not and clearly would not become one of his disciples. But between them there was no touch of the "warm student–teacher relation" which Bartlett had with followers keenly interested in his work.

It is important to understand, at this point, that, in pursuing his interest in Hull, Berlyne was not merely switching from one "school" to ally himself with another. His thinking also did not closely fit the paradigms of the American S–R theorists. They thought that only scientifically respectable "biological" drives like hunger and thirst were worth the attention of a truly behavioral science. Berlyne's interest in the areas of interest and curiosity would have led them to dismiss him as a loose thinker or a "cognitive type." But it is a mistake to see Berlyne as a one who sought merely to be different, to be an intellectual loner. Rather, it appeared to him from his reading (and discussions with others) that the logic of the subject matter of psychology made interest not only exciting, but also a reasonable, if not necessary, target of enquiry. The Yale school had succeeded in synthesizing the Hullian and Freudian approaches into what

> seemed . . . a convincing theoretical system that was just about in the finishing stages . . . and it struck me that problems like attention and interest and curiosity were a few minor things that the present state of that theory hadn't taken care of sufficiently. I thought that just a few finishing touches would take care of it. (BMI, p. 112)

Later, of course, in the 60s, Berlyne, together with many other psychologists, recognized that the "plausibility" of this sort of "synthesis can be very deceptive" (BMI, p. 113) and that the "natural scientific" character of the Hullian system was more apparent than real. But in the 1940s it was reasonable to accept the Hullian system as fully scientific, one which would provide a sound base for the study of interest, and which would, in turn, benefit from having these "few minor things" "taken care of." Thus the young Berlyne would declare to his friends that "my first interest is interest." His first published paper was a theoretical analysis of the concept (Berlyne, 1949).

In 1948 Berlyne took his "first interest" with eagerness to his first appointment at the University of St. Andrews, where, through Bartlett's good offices, he was appointed to a full rather than an assistant lectureship after only a year of postgraduate work. His initial reaction to the appointment at this small, traditional institution was highly enthusiastic. In a letter to Goldberg (June 17, 1948) he judged the job to be

> as good as anything I could hope for, being the oldest university in the country, after Oxford and Cambridge, which has a specially good and long standing reputation for psychology and a department who are extremely go ahead . . . I shall be able to fulfill my ambitions to work on animals."[5]

But only a few weeks after arriving at St. Andrews he was writing in a very different vein, in a November 3 letter, about the staff life being "dead," referring to the senior staff as "old, petty-minded incredibly crustly old cusses" and the junior staff as "mostly browned off." He concluded this letter with the hope that he could "get away from here in a year or two."

So intense were his feelings that he did not confine them to private letters, but started to ask people how long it was "decent" to "stay in a

---

[5]Berlyne was almost the only British experimental psychologist to work with animals following the war. This lack of interest in animal work at the time contrasts starkly with the burst of American experimentation, in which the Hullians and their opponents (Tolman and his students) used the laboratory rat almost exclusively in their empirical disputes.

place." He recalled that "people gave me the idea that two or three years was decent" (BMI, p. 114).

Berlyne was prepared for the fact that St. Andrews was a small community. He had anticipated in his June 17 letter that "one snag" in going there "is the fact that the town is so small and isolated. It is picturesque and historical enough but Edinburgh is two hours away by train, Glasgow three by coach, and Dundee (a hole!) 20 minutes." What he was not prepared for and quickly found intolerable was that the academic community did not provide the intellectual stimulation he needed. He missed the "endless conversations" with his Cambridge friends. He found no comparable group at St. Andrews. Perhaps, too, this sudden "sensory isolation" was uncomfortably reminiscent of his Army service period.

All these difficulties were exacerbated by another unexpected source of frustration. He soon discovered that, contrary to his prior impressions, psychology at St. Andrews was not "well viewed" within the university, and was not "allowed to flourish" (BMI, p. 106). Berlyne attributed this to the fact that the department was under the control of the Philosophy Board of Studies. The dominant figure on that Board, the professor of moral philosophy, was a Hegelian who was "bitterly opposed to experimental psychology" and who considered that topics such as behavior and motivation were the concern of moral philosophy and not psychology. In the many curricular arguments that followed, Berlyne and the professor found that they had little in common.[6] The moral philosopher was not the only senior staff member to object to Berlyne's concept of his subject matter: "The professor of Greek would say—I mean literally, I'm not exaggerating at all—'I see that you have here something about the psychology of language and I think that until people have done sufficient Latin and Greek, they shouldn't learn the psychology of language.' " Berlyne's general dismay was deepened by his conclusion that this was the way of academia: "I had no way of knowing how peculiar this was; I thought all universities were like this. I didn't realize what an odd place St. Andrews was, especially with regard to psychology" (BMI, p. 106).

Nevertheless, Berlyne enjoyed his teaching, and he sought solace in what he had looked forward to greatly—research on animals. In January, 1949, he began to get estimates of costs, anticipating "another tussle with the powers of darkness." By April he could report that he had started

[6]In fact, as Berlyne was fond of saying at the time, according to Peter McKellar (one of the two new arrivals to the department, and now Professor of Psychology at the University of Otago, New Zealand), the only thing he and the Hegelian had in common was that "they both disliked tomatoes." One is reminded here of the lesson of the Socratic dialogues that intellectual argument is possible only if the parties share a reasonable amount of common ground!

taming two rats, "which requires a good deal of patience and daring."[7]
So, he announced to Goldberg, "rat psychology will soon be launched
again in the U.K." He describes how he visited the Bethlhem Hospital in
London where there was an "outgrowth of Eysenck's Maudsley department." Roger Russell was a visiting American Fulbright professor. Here
Berlyne saw his first "experimental rat," and "for the first time in my life I
saw a Lashley jumping stand and a maze, in the flesh. . . . I had read
about these things in books . . . they had a certain glamour. . . . This
was very exciting" (BMI, p. 108). One can imagine how stimulating this
trip to London was for Berlyne. He regarded Russell as "an emissary from
the parts where all this work went on" (BMI, p. 109). It was great contrast
to interacting with a faculty predominantly interested in "golf and church
affairs."

By the beginning of his second academic year, in the fall of 1949, he
was in a more optimistic frame of mind, writing of looking forward to
being able to "get back to my rats," and relieved to hear that two young
lecturers were joining the staff. (This "not only means less work, but also
a little less isolation.") He expected to feel "more settled" in the coming
year, but he was "still not sufficiently enamored of St. Andrews to want
to stay here much longer." It is not surprising that he began to think of
going to the United States,

> because the type of psychology I was interested in was going on in the United
> ⁻tates. We very much got the impression, which I think was accurate, that
> psychology in the United States was 20 or 30 years ahead of British psychol-
> ogy. I don't just mean that as a value judgment. I mean they were doing things
> in Great Britain that they had done in the United States 20 or 30 years
> ago. . . . So I had to go to the United States temporarily, that was my idea,
> just temporarily to learn what was going on and come back. (BMI, p. 114)

He applied for a Commonwealth Scholarship to get there, but was unsuccessful.

In the meantime he proceeded with his rat research and sought out
young faculty with stimulating ideas. It was at this time that he became
firm friends with Laurence Goddard (now professor of mathematics at
the University of Salford) and Peter McKellar.

[7]If not foolhardiness, since Berlyne not only had no experience with rats, but had access to
few advisors. One of them, a psychologist who had done some work with rats before the
war, advised him "never handle the rats with gloves." "Which I didn't," noted Berlyne,
"and, of course, I've still got some scars—I'm quite proud of them—rat bites. But since
then, my students who handle rats handle them with gloves and there has never been any
evidence that it makes any difference to their experiments, and it certainly makes a
difference to their fingers" (BMI, p. 110). This "daring" in one untrained and ill-suited (on
account of poor motor coordination) to deal with such animals provides another illustration of the strength of his curiosity drive. His "interest in interest" seemed to require, at the
time, that sort of "patience and daring."

Goddard used to remark to McKellar that "after a conversation with Daniel Berlyne, one felt that one's mind had been thoroughly exercised." To them Berlyne propounded his "theory of adventure," according to which "one should do something different, preferably exciting." Among many excursions, for instance, was one which involved going down a coal mine with McKellar and his wife. (McKellar, personal communication, 1978). Incidentally, McKellar recalls that when he first met Berlyne in a coffee shop and asked him about St. Andrews he was convinced from Berlyne's account that he was talking to a "paranoid," and was stunned to find out for himself later that what Berlyne said about the staff was essentially correct.[8]

It was not until 1950–1951 that Berlyne succeeded in "getting out," with a one-year fellowship to Yale to work with Hull. As it turned out, his sojourn in the United States was not temporary, although it was for many years uncertain and unsettling, if also exciting.[9] We shall not discuss this period here, since our intention was simply to trace some of the early elements in the development of Berlyne's approach to psychology and to the life of a scholar. We have shown what we think are some of the important factors which shaped his independent and far-ranging mind. It is obvious, from the articles by Konecni (1978), and Day (1979), that his interests changed and multiplied over the subsequent years; but we think it true to say that it was interest or curiosity that was the dominant force in his exploration of ideas.

The Disinterested Critic

In this section we examine the characterization of Berlyne in the last decade of his life as a disinterested critic (Furedy, 1979). We maintain that the dynamic force of such characteristics derives from curiosity and intrinsic motivation.

The key term—"disinterested"—does not mean the same as "uninterested." A disinterested approach to an issue can be a vitally concerned

[8]Imagine, for example, what a "paranoid" impression would be given by hearing a new colleague tell you that one professor (not in psychology) had objected to Berlyne's *seminars* (as versus lectures) on the grounds that "male and female knees might touch under the table!" But McKellar reports having found later that this "moral" objection had, in fact, been made.

[9]The sources of excitement were not purely academic. Berlyne always preferred the "city lights," and disliked small, parochial towns. To the old Roman saying that it was better to be King of Etruria than the second man in Rome, he recalled that "I used to say that the last man in Rome for me anytime was my preference" (BMI, p. 134). Sojourns in Berkeley, Washington, and Geneva must have appealed greatly in comparison with the "Etrurian" town of St. Andrews.

one, but the concern is solely with the issue *per se,* rather than with any implications the issue may have for others with a vested interest in it. Disinterestedness, then, when correctly used, is a term denoting an interest (or *curiosity,* or even "mere" curiosity) in phenomena for their own sakes, independent of any personal benefits that might be gained from understanding (and presumably controlling) those phenomena. In motivational terms, disinterested interest is intrinsically rather than extrinsically motivated.

The concept of disinterestedness is a relatively new one in civilization. The notion of disinterested inquiry, or "considering X for its own sake," first arose among a group of Ionian philosophers who are generally known as the Pre-Socratics. It is this Greek influence, this "thinking about the world in the Greek way" (Burnet, 1930, p. v), that epitomizes Western science, rather than such correlated but noncriterial features as the carrying out of many observations or the developing of a complex system of quantification.

Socrates is taken to be the model or "ideal type" of the disinterested enquirer. His passion for inquiry is summed up both in his dictum on the worthlessness of the "unexamined" life, and in his willingness to die by that dictum when all that would have been required of him was to cease that sort of examination which the Athenians held was "corrupting the youth."

The concept of disinterested criticism grows naturally out of a life of inquiry, it being the essence of inquiry that propositions be subjected to *critical* appraisal in any "examined" life. The outstanding characteristic of the disinterested critic is that he is neither hostile nor sympathetic to the proponent of the position under examination, because his attention is on the position alone, and not the proponent.

Another feature of disinterested criticism is that it transcends areas of expertise. This feature is more relevant for the contemporary era of increased specialization than for the times of Socrates (although Socrates showed the same willingness to "step outside" his purported domain and criticize Euthyphro on the nature of piety). In contemporary terms, the disinterested critic is both willing and able to criticize the experts in areas in which the critic himself has no qualifications. This attitude contrasts with that of many contemporary academics, who are willing to criticize only those positions that relate to their own area of specialization.

The first author's paper (Furedy, 1979), which characterized Berlyne as a curiosity-driven individual, referred to the "Socratic" mode of many of his academic interactions and gave some examples. Here we would like to elaborate on the first of those three examples. Because this elaboration is a personal one, it will, for convenience, be told from the point of view of the first author.

The example pertained to the area of human Pavlovian autonomic conditioning. According to one "expert" view, the predominant mechanism was that of *contingency* between the conditional stimulus and unconditional stimulus (e.g., Rescorla, 1967), whereas the work of my laboratory (e.g., Furedy & Schiffmann, 1971) had led us to attack the contingency position (cf., e.g., Furedy, Poulos, & Schiffmann, 1975a). In the spring of 1972 I was preparing an oral presentation of our position for an audience in Hungary who were not really specialists in this problem. I decided to ask for a joint meeting of my and Berlyne's labs as a "sounding board" for my ideas. We held joint lab meetings about once a year, in spite of the fact that our respective areas were barely related. I valued these meetings because of the disinterested criticism that Berlyne and his lab members provided and provoked at them.

In this particular case, as we shall see, I got much more than I bargained for! What happened illustrates a subtle but important facet of the disinterested critic: his ability to force the "expert" to consider *definitional distinctions* that the specialists have not thought to be important. I expected Berlyne and his lab to be emotionally neutral with respect to our attack on the contingency position as applied to human Pavlovian autonomic conditioning, if only because his lab was not researching any form of Pavlovian conditioning at the time. Even those members of my lab who were not directly involved in the contingency controversy could not provide such a "neutral" base, because they were, of course, aware of my convictions regarding the issue.

Accordingly, and not for the first time (for I had talked to other generalist, nonexpert audiences before on this subject), I began by briefly indicating the nub of the problem by a slide which spelled out the "contingency prediction" which can be derived from the contingency position (for derivation details, see Furedy, 1971). In essence, the "contingency prediction" states that a conditional stimulus (CS) that is "explicitly unpaired" with the unconditional stimulus (US) would produce inhibition relative to a CS that is "truly random" in relation to the US. The terms "explicitly unpaired" and "truly random" were taken directly from Rescorla's (1967) influential contingency paper, although the respective abbreviations of euCS- and trCS- on my slides were my own. In previous talks I had found that I was able to dispatch this preliminary section in a couple of minutes, after which my audience, having learned what the slide abbreviations stood for, was prepared to follow my anticontingency evidence (presented on subsequent slides) to the effect that there was no autonomic performance difference between euCS- and trCS-.

This time, however, one member of my audience proved difficult, not to say disruptive. Berlyne asked me to explain again what I meant by the terms euCS- and trCS- on the first slide. I was a little surprised by his apparent slowness in following Pavlovian conditioning terminology. Other people outside the field seemed to pick up quickly the talk of various "CSs" and "USs." I went over the distinction by reminding him that, whereas the more traditional euCS- was negatively correlated with US occurrence, the correlation between the trCS- and US occurrence was random or zero. I could see that there was something that Berlyne did not like about my terminology, but I turned to the issue of more general interest, that is, just how the contingency prediction was faring in our lab experiments. This more general issue had quite wide significance, for the same reason that Rescorla's (1967) original paper was so influential. For, to the extent that the newer contingency position was correct, the traditional euCS- control was not "proper" (Rescorla, 1967), and classical conditioners were ignoring inhibitory factors in their areas of investigation. The message I wanted to get across was that Rescorla and other contingency theorists were wrong insofar as human Pavlovian autonomic responses were concerned, and hence graduate students and others did not have to worry about running "truly random" controls in their conditioning experiments.

But Berlyne kept me from getting to my "message" with what seemed to be very nitpicking interruptions concerning my terminology. At first I thought he did not approve of my abbreviations on aesthetic grounds. But that was not Berlyne's problem. Then, I thought that he was arguing for the contingency camp against my "message." Even by then we had become aware that the experts in the field were not at all happy with what seemed to us to be perfectly straightforward assessments (Furedy et al., 1975a) of the contingency position (Furedy, Poulos, & Schiffmann, 1975b; Prokasy 1975a,b). Surely, I thought, it was more appropriate for him to hear me out before questioning me.

It was only then that I realized that he was criticizing the "explicitly unpaired" and "truly random" terminology itself, independently of whether the pairings or the contingency position was correct. I was taken aback, because if there was one thing that had not been questioned by my fellow specialists in the area and my previous generalist audiences, it was our terminology. The meaning of "explicitly unpaired" and "truly random" was quite clear to all, even though then and later there was much argument about whether the randomization procedures in certain experiments (cf. Furedy et al., 1975b, Prokasy, 1975a,b) were adequate. But Berlyne questioned the use of the terms themselves. Why, he asked, did I use the adjective "explicitly" in qualifying "unpaired"? Surely this qualifier was as inappropriate as its antonym, "implicitly," in describing an unpairing operation. Again, he asked, did the qualifier "truly" make any sense, given that the notion of "falsely random" seemed to make none?

It is hardly surprising that I should have taken so long to understand the nature of his criticisms. As an expert in this area explaining terminology to a group of generalists, I hardly expected them to argue about my usage of terminology, given their unfamiliarity with it. What I was forgetting, of course, was that such unfamiliarity when combined with a critical, disinterested consideration of the issue in question often leads to the uncovering of experts' definitional absurdities. In this case, though I and other classical conditioners may not have been favorably disposed to the Rescorla (1967) contingency claims, we accepted his "explicitly unpaired" and "truly random" terminology without question. Yet, on examination, the terminology was clearly inappropriate, and we acknowledged this by changing our terminology in subsequent papers (Furedy & Schiffman, 1973, p. 210).

One essential dimension of the disinterested critic's contribution should be obvious from this example. Berlyne disrupted the dress rehearsal, but he raised important definitional problems. The parallel between this case and that described in the Socratic Euthyphro dialogue seems close, although no doubt the negative emotions that Euthyphro felt were stronger than mine on being shown by Socrates that his definition of piety was not as satisfactory as he so confidently thought at the beginning of the conversation, when he, as the expert, was ready to give all sorts of advice to the "generalist" Socrates. It is in this way that the experts can be instructed by generalists about important definitional distinctions and problems in the field of expertise under consideration.

Another aspect of this sort of disinterested criticism is that the generalist, by the force of his arguments, actually changes the focus or direction of the discussion, and again the Socratic Euthyphro dialogue has parallels. In my case I was moved to consider the terminological problem of using expressions like "explicitly unpaired," whereas my original intention was to focus on whether or not the contingency position was sound. Similarly, Euthyphro was forced (before finally leaving the field in a huff) to consider the definitional problems involved in using such definitions of piety as "what is pleasing to the Gods," whereas his original intention was simply to give a few helpful hints, in his role as expert on piety, to Socrates to enable the latter to "beat" the corruption-of-the-youth "rap."

More generally, the disinterested critic's contribution in academic interaction is to question the unquestioned, to refuse to accept what is assumed, in short, to challenge the specialists and experts. And in connection with the concept of disinterestedness, it is worth noting that nowadays one frequently hears the word "disinterested" misused to mean "uninterested." The incident recounted here in some detail demonstrates, we think, that, on the contrary, disinterestedness is a sophisticated manifestation of the intellect which is fired by curiosity and "pure" interest. From this vantage it is not surprising that a scholar whose "first interest is interest" would, in pursuit of this interest, naturally in formal and informal interactions play the role of disinterested critic for his colleagues.

CONCLUSION

Berlyne was an eminent and influential figure in experimental psychology, but he was not, in his time, a dominant one. Whether he will eventually become one through his published works is of less interest to us here than the fact that his life as an academic appears to serve as a clear example of the power of curiosity and intrinsic motivation. We end, therefore, with a quotation from his 1973 discussion with Dr. Myers as exemplifying the attitude and drive which sustained his life as a scholar and researcher:

> When I was in Manchester Grammar School, before the Sixth Form, I was very much of an auto-didact. I read a lot of stuff on my own. I read economics and I read philosophy; I even read some psychology. And this is one thing I suppose that makes me less capable of understanding our present students who say, "We want courses on this, that, and the other." When we wanted to know something, we didn't ask for courses, we read it. (BMI, p. 47)

ACKNOWLEDGMENT

The authors wish in particular to acknowledge help in gathering the biographical background from Hilde Berlyne, Jack Goldberg, and Roger Myers.

REFERENCES

BERLYNE, D. E. "Interest" as a psychological concept. *British Journal of Psychology*, 1949, *39*, 186–195.

BERLYNE, D.E. *Conflict, arousal and curiosity*. New York: McGraw-Hill, 1960.

BERLYNE, D. E. Curiosity and education. In J. D. Krumboltz (Ed.), *Learning and the educational process*. Chicago: Rand-McNally, 1965, pp. 67–89.

BERLYNE, D. E. Behaviorism? Cognitive theory? Humanistic psychology?—To Hull with them all! *Canadian Psychological Review*, 1975, *16*, 69–80.

BURNET, J. *Early Greek philosophy*. London: Adam & Charles Black, 1930.

DAY, H. I. Daniel Ellis Berlyne (1924–1976). *Motivation and Emotion*, 1979, *1*, 377–383.

FUREDY, J. J. Explicitly-unpaired and truly-random CS- controls in human classical differential autonomic conditioning. *Psychophysiology*, 1971, *8*, 497–503.

FUREDY, J. J. Berlyne as a disinterested critic: A colleague's account of some academic interactions. *Canadian Psychological Review*, 1979, *20*, 95–98.

FUREDY, J. J., & FUREDY, C. P. Daniel Berlyne and psychonomy: The beat of a different drum. *Bulletin of the Psychonomic Society*, 1978, *13*, 203–205.

FUREDY, J. J., & SCHIFFMANN, K. Test of the propriety of the traditional discrimination control procedure in Pavlovian electrodermal and plethysmographic conditioning. *Journal of Experimental Psychology*, 1971, *91*, 161–164.

FUREDY, J. J., & SCHIFFMANN, K. Concurrent measurement of autonomic and cognitive processes in a test of the traditional discriminative control procedure for Pavlovian electrodermal conditioning. *Journal of Experimental Psychology*, 1973, *100*, 210–217.

FUREDY, J. J., POULOS, C. X., & SCHIFFMANN, K. Contingency theory and classical autonomic excitatory and inhibitory conditioning: Some problems of assessment and interpretation. *Psychophysiology*, 1975, *12*, 98–105.(a)

FUREDY, J.J., POULOS, C. X., & SCHIFFMANN, K. Logical problems with Prokasy's assessment of contingency relations in classical skin conductance conditioning. *Behavior Research Methods and Instrumentation*, 1975, *7*, 521–523.(b)

HULL, C. L. *Principles of behavior*. New York: Appleton-Century, 1943.

KONECNI, V. Daniel E. Berlyne: 1924–1976. *American Journal of Psychology*, 1978, 91, 133–137.

PROKASY, W. F. Random control procedures in classical skin conductance conditioning. *Behavior Research Methods and Instrumentation*, 1975, *7*, 516–520.(a)

PROKASY, W. F. Random controls: A rejoinder. *Behavior Research Methods and Instrumentation*, 1975, *7*, 524–526.(b)

RESCORLA, R. A. Pavlovian conditioning and its proper control procedures. *Psychological Review*, 1967, *74*, 71–80.

We can summarize our metatheory in the form of a diagram (see Figure 1).

The Metalevel of Berlyne's Theory

Introduction

Modern psychologists have, for a long period (from about 1935 to 1960), not been interested in an explicit formulation of their philosophical presuppositions. During this period, the influence of logical empiricism was so dominant—at least amongst American psychologists—that they regarded the ontological problems as "pseudoproblems," or at least as problems belonging to speculative, "metaphysical" philosophy—not to science (and "scientific philosophy"). Therefore, we have to reconstruct these philosophical presuppositions on the basis of an interpretation of the text (and therefore a discussion with the author of the text was of special value for this point).

Psychologists were in this period more often explicit in their formulation of their philosophy of science, and Berlyne was especially explicit and clear in his exposition.

Berlyne's Philosophy of the World

Berlyne has no explicit formulations about his conception of the mind–brain problem. But from the more explicit part of his metalevel, we can infer that Berlyne presupposed a neutral-monistic theory about the psychophysical relationship between mind—or consciousness—and brain. There were some doubts left in the present author's mind, but after some discussion with Berlyne it became clear that he adopted the neutral-monistic theory (and not a materialistic theory which was the other possibility).

Similarly, with Berlyne's conception of man there are no explicit formulations, but here there is no doubt that Berlyne presupposed a biological Darwinian conception, like most American psychologists. Thus he made use of experiments with animals—as well as men—and inferred, without any discussion, results from animal experiments to a general theory of motivation. But it must be added that Berlyne does not underestimate the difference between man and other animals. Thus he

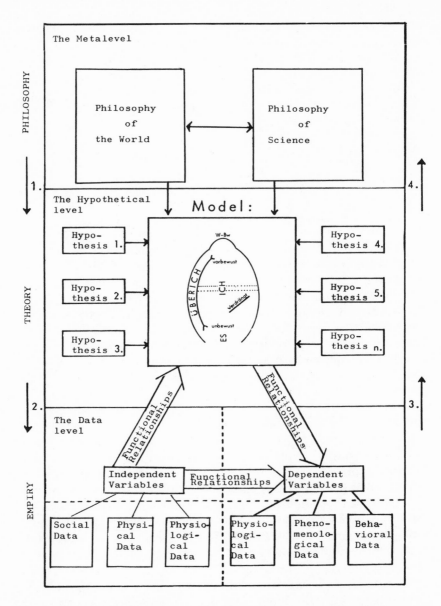

FIGURE 1. The hierarchical structure of a theory. This diagram illustrates the three strata of a scientific text: M = M-level or metastratum; H = H-level or hypothetical stratum; D = D-level or descriptive stratum. The four arrows (1,2,3,4) indicate that the top level influences the formation of the next level, which, in turn, influences the bottom level. But there is also a feedback of influence from the D-level to the H-level and the M-level. (Otherwise, it would not be a scientific theory.)

stresses symbolic activity ("epistemic behaviour") as being special for man.

On the third ontological problem, the problem of determinism, Berlyne is not explicit. But from the text as a whole we can infer that he presupposed a causal determinism. There are no formulations in favour of a probabilism, and a free-will indeterminism would have been in contradiction with Berlyne's whole scientific philosophy.

Thus Berlyne's philosophy of the world can be summarized as a neutral-monistic, biological, and causal-deterministic philosophy.

Berlyne's Philosophy of Science

The epistemological presuppositions of Berlyne's theory are not formulated explicitly, but it is rather obvious from the whole text that Berlyne presupposes a rationalistic empiricism à la "logical empiricism." And Berlyne confirmed this in our discussions.

In accordance with this, Berlyne had a naturalistic (physicalistic) ideal of science. Thus he used the word *psychobiology* in the title of his last book, and it was my impression that he was eager to defend the naturalistic conception of psychology against the growing humanistic school. It is also in accordance with this naturalistic conception that neurophysiological data as well as neurophysiologically inspired hypothetical constructs are applied freely in Berlyne's hypotheses. This is especially true for his motivational theories about curiosity (1960) and aesthetics (1971). The theory about thinking (1965) contains more "intervening variables" (in the narrow sense without any "surplus meaning"), but this "integrative neoassociationism"—as Berlyne called it—is also a naturalistic (physicalistic) type of psychology.

Although Berlyne thus has a clear naturalistic ideal of science, he is not in favor of a narrow logical-empiricist conception of "theory" as a deductive system, like his teacher, C. L. Hull. Thus, he wrote that he would prefer applicability to precision in theory construction.

Berlyne is explicit and clear in his formulations about methodological problems. Thus, he favored and used himself the experimental method. And he also explicitly preferred a behavioral datalanguage. He even warned against a phenomenological datalanguage. Thus he wrote about the psychology of behavior and the psychology of consciousness, "both of these may be legitimate pursuits, but it is important not to confuse the two" (Berlyne, 1965, p. 14).

We can summarize Berlyne's philosophy of science as a logicalempiricistic, naturalistic (physicalistic) experimental and behavioral philosophy of science.

THE HYPOTHETICAL LEVEL OF BERLYNE'S THEORY

Introduction

In this section we concentrate on Berlyne's theory of motivation, because it is much better known and important than his theory of thinking. Furthermore, the present author has specialized in comparative studies of theories of motivation (see Madsen, 1959, 1973 and 1974).

The most important book by Berlyne is his *Conflict, Arousal and Curiosity*. In addition to this, he has written about motivation in several papers and chapters in handbooks. Among these, his chapter (1963) in S. Koch (Ed.), *Psychology: A Study of a Science* (Vol. V) is of special relevance. Its title is "Motivational Problems Raised by Exploratory and Epistemic Behavior." Also his book *Psychobiology and Aesthetics* (1971) can be regarded as an elaboration and application of his theory of curiosity presented in his main work (the 1960 book).

Summary of the Hypotheses

We shall presently turn to the contents of Berlyne's explanatory system. But before we go into a deeper analysis, we present here a very short summary of the contents of the theory as a whole. It is very easy to do, because Berlyne has given us an excellent summary of the whole book in his title *Conflict, Arousal and Curiosity*. In other words, curiosity behaviour (which will be described further and classified later) is caused by various conflicts (which also will be described under the analyses of the descriptive level). The causal link, the mediating or intervening variables between conflict and curiosity, is "arousal." This is the most important explanatory term or *H*-variable in Berlyne's theory. It is a very well-defined variable, which is introduced after a very thorough analysis of the concept of "drive" in general. As this analysis is one of the most rewarding the present author has found, we will consider it at some length in the next paragraph. But before leaving this summary of the theory, we shall present a summarizing diagram representing the hypotheses in Berlyne's theory (Figure 2).

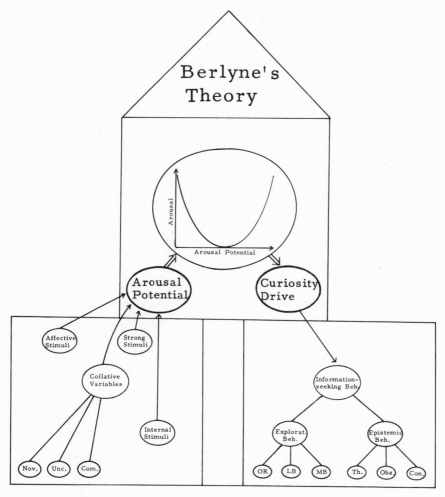

FIGURE 2. Berlyne's theory of curiosity. See explanation in text.

The Hypothetical Terms (H–Terms)

Berlyne (1960) confesses in the preface that

the book has two features that would have surprised me when I first set out to plan it. One is that it ends up sketching a highly modified form of drive-reduction theory. . . . The second surprising feature is the prominence of neurophysiology. (p. VIII)

Later in the more theoretical part of the book (Chapters 7 to 11) Berlyne makes "a very thorough analysis" of the concept of drive:

The concept of drive, which dominates contemporary discussions of motivation, resolves itself into three logically distinct concepts. We may distinguish
them as $drive_1$, $drive_2$ and $drive_3$.

$Drive_1$. There is first the notion of drive as a condition that affects the level
of activity. It is customary to speak of the "energizing effect of drive" in this
connection. . . . The close resemblance between the manifestations of $drive_1$
and those of arousal will hardly have escaped to the reader. . . . So it will
require no great temerity to regard $drive_1$ and arousal as intimately related.
Nor will it require great originality, as several writers have been drawn
towards the same step. . . .

$Drive_2$. The second notion represents drive as an internal condition that
makes certain overt responses more likely than others. It differs from $drive_1$ in
its selectivity.

$Drive_3$. The third notion identifies drive as a condition whose termination
or alleviation is rewarding, that is, promotes the learning of an instrumental
response. (pp. 165–167)

After this thorough analysis of the drive concept Berlyne continues:

One of the working assumptions of S–R reinforcement theory as developed
especially by Hull . . . and his associates has been that $drive_1$, $drive_2$ and
$drive_3$ can be identified. (p. 168)

The rest of the two most theoretically significant chapters (7 and 8)
contains an extensive argument for identifying "$drive_{1,2,3}$" with
"arousal," which is a function of the "recticular arousal system" (RAS).
But with this argumentation we move on to the next part of our analysis
(the hypotheses).

Classifications of the Hypotheses

We are now naturally led to the next part of our analysis: the hypotheses in Berlyne's explanatory system. We will first look at some S–H
hypotheses, which formulate the causal or functional relationships between arousal and its antecedents.

Berlyne (1960) discusses the independent variables, which are "determinants of arousal" (especially pp. 170–179). They are: (1) intensive
variables, (2) affective variables, and (3) "collative variables" (the special
curiosity-motivating variables, which will be dealt with later). He presents considerable experimental evidence for every class, and then coins a
new term: "We shall henceforth refer to all these properties of incoming
stimuli with power to affect arousal as *arousal potential*" (p. 179).

This "arousal potential" is perhaps not an H-variable, but rather a
very general descriptive term standing for abstract properties processed
by independent variables of stimuli. It is one of those variables, which
makes it extremely difficult to draw a sharp boundary between D-level
and H-level, between the descriptive and explanatory contents of a
theory.

But we have come to the conclusion that "arousal potential" should be regarded as an "intervening variable" in the narrow sense, that is, "arousal potential" is an H-term without any surplus meaning. As discussed in Chapter 2 of Madsen (1974), "intervening variables" can be conceived of as belonging to the "lowest" or least abstract part of the H-level.

Berlyne discusses two possible hypotheses about the relationship between "arousal potential" and "arousal."

One hypothesis is set forth by Hebb and other psychologists. It postulates "that the conditions that make for boredom will produce exceptionally low arousal, and that low arousal, as well as high arousal, must therefore be aversive." (Berlyne, 1960, pp. 188–189). The other hypothesis is set forth by Berlyne himself. He writes: "When arousal potential is inordinately low, arousal may mount" (p. 193). Berlyne prefers this hypothesis to the first one, because "a state of low arousal is a state of drowsiness characterized by high-amplitude, low-frequency EEG waves" (p. 189).

But he is in agreement with Hebb and others that low arousal potential "boredom," as well as high arousal potential, is aversive, and that the optimal arousal potential is preferred or striven for:

> Our hypotheses imply, therefore, that for an individual organism at a particular time, there will be an *optimal influx of arousal potential*. Arousal potential that deviates in either an upward or a downward direction from this optimum will be drive inducing or aversive. The organism will thus strive to keep arousal potential near its optimum. (p. 194)

This apparently paradoxical part agreement and part disagreement between Berlyne and Hebb is a consequence of Berlyne's special hypotheses (best elaborated in his 1963 paper). Whereas Hebb and others presuppose a linear, increasing relationship between arousal potential and arousal, Berlyne presupposes a U-shaped relation between arousal potential and arousal. In other words, Berlyne presupposes that only a medium strength of arousal potential causes a low arousal. But it is a low arousal which is preferred, not a medium (which Hebb postulates).

This makes clear that Berlyne and Hebb are in agreement about the fact that medium arousal potential is optimally attractive.

All these confusing agreements and disagreements are perhaps cleared up by Berlyne's own diagram (Figure 1(a) and 1(b) and Figure 2) from his "Koch-paper" (see Figure 3).

The agreement between Hebb's and Berlyne's hypotheses can here be noted.

Although Hebb's hypotheses are the simpler, I think that Berlyne's are the more adequate empirically. We have already mentioned that his

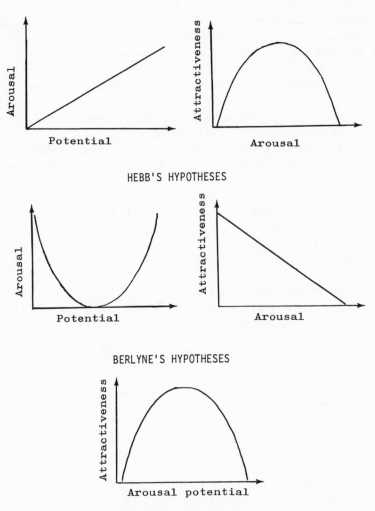

FIGURE 3. Berlyne's theory.

hypotheses can explain the paradoxical simularities and differences between "sleepiness" (low arousal), which is preferred, and "boredom"
(high arousal, but low arousal potential), which is avoided. Berlyne's
hypotheses also explain how high arousal caused by high arousal potential is avoided. This "high-high-condition" exists in all drives (except
boredom). And "curiosity" is thus a drive which is caused by conflicting
stimuli-conditions (called "collative variables") which we will deal with
later.

     Thus Berlyne could formulate a very general H–R hypothesis: all
high-arousal conditions or "drives" determine arousal- and drive-

reducing behavior. This drive-reducing behavior must be different in "boredom" and other "drives" (including curiosity). In "boredom" (high arousal, but low potential) the behavior of the organism consists of a seeking for increased stimulation (increasing potential, but reducing arousal). In "curiosity" (and other drives with high potential and high arousal) the behavior of the organism consists of a striving for reducing stimulation (and potential, which reduces arousal). Berlyne assumes that the reducing of arousal, or drive reduction, is always rewarding or "reinforcing." He thus accepts the "drive$_3$" concept as valid for curiosity drive (without necessarily accepting a general reinforcement theory of learning).[2]

Berlyne also accepts the "drive$_2$" concept as valid for curiosity drive,[3] as he supposes that curiosity drive has a selective effect upon several other processes. These hypotheses may be classified as H–H hypotheses. He elaborates on them in Chapter 3 of his 1960 book under the title of "Attention." He concludes the Chapter with the following summary:

> the evidence we have to go on tends to favor the view that the determinants of attention in performance, attention in learning, and attention in remembering are similar. They seem to include many of the factors that affect response strength in general. Moreover the collative variables that are a special concern of ours seem to play a part in all three. (p. 77)

What Berlyne here calls "attention" is a selective function of the reticular system (RAS). He—especially in his 1963 paper—mentions several investigations which present evidence for a specific activating function in the thalamic part of the RAS. Even the brain-stem part of the RAS has not only a general but also a specific activating function, according to some experiments by the Soviet psychophysiologist P. K. Anokhin:

> He has shown that different chemical substances will block the normal reticular reaction to some kinds of stimuli while leaving the potency of other stimuli unaffected. Anokhin concludes from these and other facts . . . qualitatively different biological reactions (orienting reaction, defensive reaction and alimentary reaction) excite in the reticular formation different complexes of neural elements which are specific to them. These neural elements, in their turn, exert a specific activating influence on the cerebral cortex mobilizing in it intracortical connections adequate to the given reaction. (Berlyne, 1963, p. 309)

As "learning" and "remembering" may be classified as H-variables, it is correct to describe the hypotheses about the relationship between

---

[2] In later works Berlyne modifies his hypothesis about reinforcement. According to the new version of his reinforcement hypothesis, reinforcement or reward is the result of either reduction of high arousal or increase in low arousal. (See Berlyne, 1967, 1969.)

[3] The reader may be reminded that Berlyne logically accepts the "drive$_1$" concept too, because "drive$_1$" is identical with "activation" or "arousal."

"attention" (specific activating arousal) on the one side and "learning" and "remembering" on the other side as H–H hypotheses. As "performance" must be classified as a dependent, empirical variable ("R-variable"), we must describe the hypothesis about the relationship between "attention" (RAS) and "performance" as an H–R hypothesis.[4]

Basic Classification of Hypotheses

Having presented the most important of Berlyne's hypotheses, we now turn to the basic classification into S–H, H–H, and H–R hypotheses. Before doing this we shall make our systematic reconstruction of the hypotheses and reformulate them in partially symbolic formulas.

In this reconstruction we have finally decided to regard "arousal potential" (A.P.) as an H-term representing the variable which determines "arousal" (A). Thus we have the following hypotheses:

1.   Hypothesis: S(intensive, external stimuli)$\rightarrow$H$_{A.P.}$
2.   Hypothesis: S(affective stimuli)$\rightarrow$H$_{A.P.}$
3.   Hypothesis: S(collative variables)$\rightarrow$H$_{A.P.}$
4.   Hypothesis: S(internal stimuli from needs)$\rightarrow$H$_{A.P.}$
5a. Hypothesis: H$_{A.P., low}\rightarrow$H$_{A., high}$ ("boredom")
5b. Hypothesis: H$_{A.P., high}\rightarrow$H$_{A., high}$ ("curiosity")
5c. Hypothesis: H$_{A.P., high}\rightarrow$H$_{A., high}$ ("other drives")
5d. Hypothesis: H$_{A., medium}\rightarrow$H$_{A., low}$ ("optimally preferred state")
6.   Hypothesis: H("boredom")$\rightarrow$R(stimulus seeking)
7.   Hypothesis: H("other drives")$\rightarrow$R(stimulus reduction)
8.   Hypothesis: H("curiosity")$\rightarrow$R(explorative, epistemic)
9.   Hypothesis: H$_{A.(specific, "attention")}\rightarrow$H(acquisition, learning)
10. Hypothesis: H$_{A.(specific, "attention")}\rightarrow$H(remembering)
11. Hypothesis: H$_{A.(specific, "attention")}\rightarrow$R(performance)

After having made this partially symbolic reformulation of the hypotheses, we conclude this section with our basic classification:

1. *Purely theoretical hypotheses (H–H):*
   Hypothesis Nos. 5, 9, and 10. In all: 3 hypotheses.
2. *Partly empirical hypotheses:*
   a. S–H hypotheses: Numbers 1, 2, 3 and 4. In all: 4 hypotheses.
   b. H–R hypotheses: Numbers 6, 7, 8 and 11. In all: 4 hypotheses.

[4]Berlyne has dealt with the problems of attention in later works; see especially Berlyne (1968).

THE DATA LEVEL

The Abstract D–Level

We are now going to analyze the independent variables and later on the dependent variables in Berlyne's theory.

Berlyne deals with the independent empirical variables in Chapter 2 of his 1960 book. These variables are:

1. "Novelty" is a basic characteristic of many stimuli. This stimulus variable can be classified in several ways. Thus stimuli can be "completely novel," when they have never been perceived before. They can have a "short-term-novelty," when they have been perceived recently, and a "long-term-novelty," when they have been perceived a long time ago (without being completely novel).

The stimulus pattern can be classified as "absolutely novel" or "relatively novel." In the latter case, there are some elements in the pattern which are familiar.

Related to novelty are "change," "surprisingness," and "incongruity." All these characteristics—like novelty itself—are, of course, relative to an organism.

2. "Uncertainty" is another basic characteristic of stimuli. Berlyne defines this stimulus variable in accordance with "information theory," but it would take too long to present it here.

3. "Complexity" is a third basic characteristic of stimulus patterns. These stimulus variables depend on the number of elements in the stimulus pattern, on the dissimilarity of the elements, and on the degree of "cohesion" of the pattern.

Some of these stimulus variables can be defined in terms of information theory, with uncertainty as the basic variable (called *entropy* in information theory). Then "complexity" is "content of information," and "novelty" is "amount of information."

From a psychological point of view, these variables can all be described as having elements of conflict. But to distinguish this conflict between stimuli from conflict between responses, Berlyne calls them *perceptual conflicts*. Besides these, Berlyne later notes another sort of conflict between symbolic stimuli, which he designates *conceptual conflict*.[5]

---

[5]It is possible to regard "conflict"—just like "arousal potential"—as an intervening variable (without surplus meaning), rather than a descriptive, independent variable.

For all these independent empirical variables Berlyne coins the common term "collative variables."

These collative variables contribute to the "arousal potential," which is also determined by "affective stimuli" (associated with reward and punishment), all intensive external stimuli, and internal stimuli arising from needs. We thus have a hierarchical system of more or less generalized independent empirical variables in Berlyne's theory (see Fig. 4).

We now turn to the dependent empirical variables in Berlyne's theory. He has himself made a very systematic classification of these behavior- or R-variables in his 1960 book, and elaborated it further in his 1963 paper.

One of his main classifications is into *exploratory behavior* and *epistemic behavior*.

He gives us a short definition in the 1963 paper: "Exploratory responses have the function of altering the stimulus field" (pp. 286–287).

"Exploratory behavior" can be classified in several ways (pp. 288–290):

1. Classification in accordance with the form it takes.
    a. "Receptor—adjusting responses" (to these belongs the "orienting reflex")
    b. "Locomotor exploration"
    c. "investigatory responses" (mostly manipulative)

These three classes are dealt with in Chapter 4–6 of Berlyne's 1960 book.

2. Classification in accordance with its motivation:
    a. "Intrinsic exploration" (motivated by curiosity)
    b. "Extrinsic exploration" (other motives than curiosity)

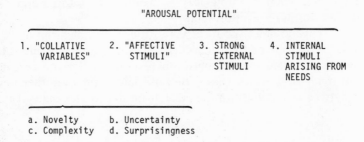

FIGURE 4. Schematic representation of the independent empirical variables in Berlyne's theory. ("Arousal potential" can be regarded as an "intervening variable.")

3. Classification in accordance with the object:
    a. "Specific exploration," which has the function of providing stimulation from a specific source (often motivated by curiosity)
    b. "Diversive exploration," which has the function of providing stimulation in general (often motivated by "bordeom") and is named "recreation," "entertainment," etc.

"Epistemic behavior" is defined in this way in the 1963 paper: "The term *epistemic behavior* refers to behavior whose function . . . is to equip the organism with *knowledge*, by which we mean structures of symbolic responses" (p. 322).

Epistemic behavior is classified into:

1. Epistemic observation—which includes the experimental and other observational techniques of science
2. Epistemic thinking—which is a sort of directed and productive thinking
3. Consultation—which includes asking other people questions or consulting reference books

As we already know, Berlyne has made the empirical generalization (S–R sentence or "law"), that exploratory and epistemic behavior is determined by perceptual and conceptual conflicts. It was in order to explain this "law" that he elaborated the hypotheses about arousal with which we are now familiar.

The Concrete D–Level

It goes without saying that Berlyne employs numerous protocol sentences as the basis for his empirical generalizations and hypotheses. The protocol sentences are used in all the experiments about curiosity which Berlyne presents in his books and papers. Many of these experiments were made by Berlyne and his co-workers. Others were made by diverse American, European, and Soviet psychologists. Many of these experiments have an interest both for general psychologists and for educational psychologists, but it would lead us too far afield to review them in this paper.[6] It is sufficient to state that, in the present author's opinion, Berlyne's theory is based on firm empirical ground.

---

[6]It is also impossible to discuss here Berlyne's application of his theory to "Art" and "Humor" (1960, 1971).

The protocol sentences themselves are, of course, not quoted in reviews of the experiments, which are, as is usual in a book of this sort, presented in a generalized form.

THE THEORY AS A WHOLE

In this final section, we shall make an overall evaluation of Berlyne's theory.

First, we shall evaluate the "explanatory power," or the testability, of the theory. According to modern philosophers of science—especially those influenced by Karl Popper—testability is the main criterion for the distinction between scientific theories and other, nonscientific theories (e.g., philosophical, metaphysical, religious, ideological, and political theories).

Testability (i.e., verification and/or falsification) is not an easy quality to estimate, because it is a quality of degree rather than a all-or-nothing quality (at least for whole theories—a single hypothesis may be classified as testable or not testable). If testability is a quality of degree, it must be possible to estimate—or measure—it quantitatively. Therefore, we have designed a formula for the quantitative estimation of testability (or "explanatory power"). The formula consists of the ratio between the number of theoretical hypotheses and the number of partly empirical hypotheses.

"Theoretical hypotheses" are hypotheses about the functional relationships between pure hypothetical constructs or other unobservable intervening variables. In our former classification of Berlyne's hypotheses, these were classified under the label "H–H hypotheses". These are not directly testable, only indirectly through their connection with the "partly empirical hypotheses." These are hypotheses about the functional relationships between at least one empirical variable and at least one hypothetical variable (hypothetical construct or intervening variable). The empirical—or descriptive—variables are independent, or stimulus variables (S-variables) and dependent or reaction variables (R-variables). (It is at least so in psychological theories based on a behavioural datalanguage—such as Berlyne's and most modern American theories.) Therefore, we have classified these empirical hypotheses under the labels S–H hypotheses and H–R hypotheses. The partly empirical hypotheses are directly testable. Thus our formula for testability consists of the ratio between the number of H–H hypotheses and the sum of the S–H and the H–H hypotheses. The ratio is named the "Hypotheses Quotient" (H. Q.). We have calculated the H. Q. for Berlyne's theory and several other theories. Berlyne's theory's H. Q. is:

$$H.Q. = \frac{\Sigma(H-H)}{\Sigma[(S-H) + (H-R)]} = \frac{3}{4+4} = 0.38$$

As may be seen from the table below, the H. Q. varies from 0.09 to 1.43. It must be remembered that, the lower the H. Q., the higher the degree of testability. Thus Berlyne's theory has a rather high degree of testability.

TABLE I. Hypotheses Quotients for 14 Modern and 10 Earlier Theories in Psychology.

Modern theories	H.Q.	Earlier theories	H.Q.
Cattell	0.09	Tinbergen	0.11
Maslow	0.13	Hebb	0.13
Duffy	0.14	McClelland	0.14
Miller (I)	0.20	Hull	0.36
Pribram	0.29	McDougall	0.43
Bindra	0.30	Lewin	0.50
Atkinson and Birch	0.33	Murray	0.71
Berlyne	0.38	Young	0.82
Brown	0.38	Allport	1.00
Konorski	0.54	Tolman	1.43
Woodworth	0.57		
Miller (II)	0.60		
Festinger	0.84		
Atkinson	0.86		

Second, we shall try to evaluate the practical utility of Berlyne's theory. Unfortunately, we do not have a quantitative estimation of the practical utility of theories. A possible solution to this problem could be to make a statistical enumeration of quotations of references to Berlyne's theory in educational literature or other applied-science literature. Without such exact data, we must rely on our subjective evaluations. And it is my subjective evaluation that Berlyne's theory is one of the most influential psychological theories in education—at least as seen from the Danish viewpoint (see Olsen, 1970).

REFERENCES

BERLYNE, D. E. *Conflict, arousal and curiosity*. New York: McGraw-Hill, 1960.
BERLYNE, D. E. Motivational Problems Raised by Exploratory and Epistemic Behavior. In S. Koch (Ed.), *Psychology: A study of a science* (Vol. V). New York: Wiley, 1963.
BERLYNE, D. E. *Structure and direction in thinking*. New York: Wiley, 1965.
BERLYNE, D. E. Arousal and reinforcement. In D. Lewine (Ed.), *Nebraska symposium on motivation*. Lincoln: Nebraska University Press, 1967.

BERLYNE, D. E. Attention as a problem in behavior theory. In D. Mostofsky (Ed.), *Attention*. New York: Appleton, 1968.

BERLYNE, D. E. The justifiability of the concept of curiosity. *Proceedings of the XIX International Congress of Psychology*, London, 1969.

BERLYNE, D. E. *Psychobiology and asthetics*. New York: McGraw-Hill, 1971.

BERLYNE, D. E. & MADSEN, K. B. (Eds.). *Pleasure, reward, preference*. New York: Academic Press, 1973.

HABERMAS, J. *Knowledge and human interests*. Boston: Beacon 1968; English edition, 1971.

KUHN, T. S. *The structure of scientific revolutions*. Chicago: The University of Chicago Press, 1962.

MADSEN, K. B. *Theories of Motivation* Copenhagan: Munksgaard, 1959.

MADSEN, K. B. *Theories of motivation* (4th ed). Copenhagen: Munksgaard, 1968.

MADSEN, K. B. Theories of motivation. In B. B. Wolman (Ed.), *Handbook of general psychology*. Englewood Cliffs, N.J.: Prentice-Hall, 1973.

MADSEN, K. B. *Modern theories of motivation*. Copenhagen: Munksgaard, 1974.

OLSEN, T. P. *Indlaering og Nysgerrighed, D. E. Berlyne's Teori*. Kobenhavn: Munksgaard, 1970.

POPPER, K. & ECCLES, J. *The self and its brain*. New York: Springer, 1977.

PRIBRAM, K. *The languages of the brain*. Englewood Cliffs, N.J.: Prentice-Hall, 1971.

3

The Quest for the Inverted U

Edward L. Walker

The quest for the inverted U, although not without historical precedents, received its major modern impetus with the publication of Daniel E. Berlyne's *Conflict, Arousal and Curiosity* (1960). In this and in later volumes Berlyne developed a conception of motivation that was in sharp contrast to the prevailing formulations of psychiatry, psychology, and behavior theory.

A key concept in Berlyne's theoretical work is that of an optimal arousal level. An implication is that the organism prefers to be at such a level and will behave in a manner that will serve to maintain an optimal level of arousal. Arousal level in Berlyne's theory is affected by a number of structural variables, referred to by him as collative variables. This conception of motivation envisions an optimal level of activity as the normal state of the organism. Suboptimal activity will lead to a seeking of means to increase the arousal level to optimum, and superoptimal arousal will lead to the seeking of means of reducing arousal to optimum.

Berlyne's conception of motivation is in sharp contrast to the dominant formulations that prevailed prior to 1960. In these theories, the normal state of the organism was seen as inactivity and quiescence. In psychoanalytic theory, behavior was motivated by conflict. Successful therapy reduced or removed conflict, which produced zero motivation and an inactive state. Homeostatic mechanisms in physiology were conceived in terms of an optimal state, with activity occurring whenever there was a displacement from optimum. When optimum was restored, the organism ceased to be motivated and therefore ceased to be active. In behavior theory, the major motivational concept was that of the biological

Much of the material in this chapter is drawn from Edward L. Walker, *Psychological Complexity and Preference: A Hedgehog Theory of Behavior*. Monterey, Calif.: Brooks/Cole Publishing Co., 1980.

EDWARD L. WALKER • 3041 Lopez, Pebble Beach, California 93953.

or social drive. Activity occurred only when there was a positive value of the drive present. When all drives were satisfied, the organism ceased to behave.

Berlyne, in contrast, saw the optimum as involving normal physical and cognitive activity. The idea of the active state as both normal and ideal has far more intuitive appeal than any ideal that specifies torpor or quiescence.

PSYCHOLOGICAL COMPLEXITY AND PREFERENCE THEORY

My own quest for the inverted U has been guided by what I have called *Psychological Complexity and Preference: A Hedgehog Theory of Behavior*. This theory was inspired positively by Dember and Earl (1957) and by Berlyne (1960). The reference to the hedgehog comes from classical comparisons of the behavior of hedgehogs and foxes. The fox is a clever animal with more solutions than he has problems. The hedgehog has survived for many thousands of years with a single trick. Whatever happens, the hedgehog curls up into a ball. Psychological Complexity and Preference Theory is a simple theory that is applicable in all situations. It is for this reason that I refer to it as a Hedgehog theory of behavior. This designation implies an intellectual strategy. The simple elegance of the theory is to be preserved as long as possible. The theory is not to be modified with each new finding, but is to be preserved intact until it is necessary to abandon it altogether in the face of irrefutable evidence.

There are two basic postulates of theory:

1. There is an optimal level of psychological complexity for a psychological event that will be preferred to either simpler or more complex events.
2. Repeated experience of an event will lead to progressive simplification of that event.

The first is the preference postulate, and the second is the learning postulate. They are presented graphically in Figure 1.

The quest for the inverted U within the Hedgehog is a search for an optimal complexity level, rather than for an optimal arousal level as suggested by Berlyne. Variables in behavior theories can be divided into three classes: structural variables, such as psychological complexity, affective variables, such as pleasure–pain, and energetic variables, such as arousal. Berlyne (1971) and Kreitler and Kreitler (1972) choose energetic variables. Berlyne chose arousal and the Kreitlers chose tension. It cannot be argued strongly that one choice, structural or energetic, is right, and

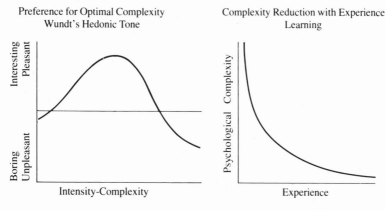

Preference for Optimal Complexity
Wundt's Hedonic Tone

Complexity Reduction with Experience
Learning

FIGURE 1

the other wrong. However, the Hedgehog, being true to its nature, chooses the simpler of the two concepts. Stimuli have only structural properties, and it is the structural aspects of psychological events that have logical and temporal priority. If some aspect of the energetic variable is to be optimized in order to result in an affective experience, then all three concept realms are involved in a logical chain with a logical order. The first is the structural effect, that in turn induces an energetic effect (arousal or tension), which then results in an affective effect (an aesthetic experience). This logical order implies a three-step temporal order in reaction. It is also implied that all three steps must occur and be congruent on all occasions. The arousal condition cannot occur without appropriate prior structural conditions, and it must always occur when those structural conditions occur. The affective effect can occur only when the arousal conditions are those specified by the theory, and must occur when the arousal conditions are appropriate. By this logic, and under most circumstances, the quest for the inverted U in terms of psychological complexity is nearly identical with the search for optimal arousal level.

The search for the inverted U has been sufficiently successful to justify maintaining the hunt, yet there are a great many experimental studies in which the results do not fully support the simple character of the original conception. Some results are inconsistent with other results, some appear contradictory, some are difficult to replicate, and some cannot be said to arise from the theory without elaborate post hoc explanation. In the remainder of this paper I shall cite empirical results which seem to support the theory. I shall demonstrate the generality of the theory across species and problems, and then I shall provide a partial list of circumstances in which Figure 1 could represent the true state of affairs even though some other function was obtained empirically.

The Preference Postulate

The preference postulate says that there should be an inverted U-shaped relation between the structural variable, psychological complexity, and any affective variable resulting in preference. The Wundtian curve in Figure 1 is the prototype. However, Wundt (1874) was expressing what he believed to be the relation between stimulus intensity and hedonic tone. It is an important question whether and to what extent stimulus intensity, independent of some structural quality of the stimulus, produces an inverted U when plotted against an affective variable.

Intensity and Complexity

There is some reason to expect intensity to function as a complexity variable. Heat would seem to be an intensity dimension, and there are clearly optimum temperatures that are pleasant, and lower and higher temperatures that are unpleasant. On the other hand, Stevens found it necessary to make a distinction between two kinds of continua. Metathetic continua refer to what kind and where and yield equal jnds. Prototothetic continua refer to the question of how much and yield jnds which increase systematically with increases in the magnitude of the stimulus. Complexity could be associated with metathetic continua, and intensity with protothetic continua.

Some of the most challenging and difficult data to deal with from a theoretical standpoint are shown in Figure 2. The Engle (1928) data are rather primitive from a psychophysical standpoint. However, I consider them good enough that they must be dealt with. For some years I thought that all four curves could be brought together to form an inverted U if they

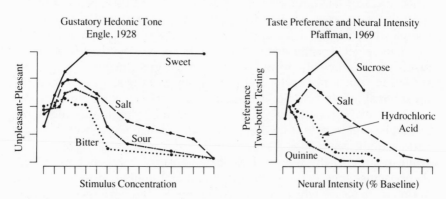

FIGURE 2

were plotted against neural intensity, and that the differences resided in the different effects of the various substances on the neural-intensity variable. Unfortunately for this belief, Pfaffman (1969) did two experiments with squirrel monkeys. One was a two-bottle preference test, and the other a measurement of the neural-intensity change induced by the various concentrations of the four substances. He used different concentrations of substance in the two studies, and it was therefore necessary to interpolate and extrapolate to generate the curves on the right side of Figure 2.

Several points are obvious in the figure. The four curves do not coalesce into a single inverted-U-shaped function, at least when intensity is measured in the chorda tympani nerve. Two of the curves show no value of positive preference. Unlike the human curve, the squirrel-monkey curve shows a concentration of sugar that is too sweet.

A very foxlike way to react to these data would be to decide that the Wundtian hedonic curve applied to complexity as a metathetic continuum, while the protothetic function of intensity required a family of functions ranging from the quinine curve in Pfaffman's data to the sweet curve in Engle's. A Hedgehoglike way to respond would be to say that the results might be different if neural intensity were to be measured at an appropriate central site rather than in the sensory nerve. I have not found a way to resolve this issue to my own satisfaction.

The Language of Experimental Subjects

There are many studies in this area of research in which the results appear to hinge on the particular set of descriptive terms employed to scale the stimuli. Do such terms as "liking" and "pleasantness" mean the same thing to experimental subjects? One approach to this problem is to investigate the way in which the typical experimental subject associates the usual terms employed in experimental work, but in the absence of experimental stimuli. This has been done in a series of studies of the semantic space of experimental subjects. In one set of studies, Walker (1980) asked subjects to scale each of six dimensions frequently employed in relevant research in order to determine how typical subjects saw these terms to be related.

Figures 3 through 6 show the results of some of these studies. Figure 3 shows the relation between two major structural variables, complexity on the one hand and a scale of relative difficulty on the other, as they were determined in two different studies. In the absence of experimental stimuli or tasks, these two are seen as being essentially equivalent.

Figure 4 depicts the relations seen between three evaluative or affective variables, pleasantness, interestingness, and approach–avoidance

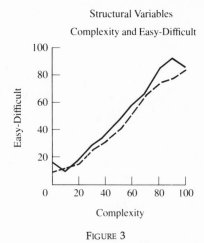

Structural Variables

Complexity and Easy-Difficult

FIGURE 3

behavior. Experimental subjects see these three dimensions as highly correlated.

Figure 5 shows the results obtained when subjects were asked to relate two structural variables, complexity and difficulty, to the three affective variables, pleasantness, interestingness, and approach–avoidance behavior. In all six instances, including replications of three of them, an inverted U appears. It is clear that the quest for the inverted U has found some success in the semantic space of college students.

Figure 6 contains a somewhat surprising result. These people see the energetic dimension, as represented by the word arousal, to be so per-

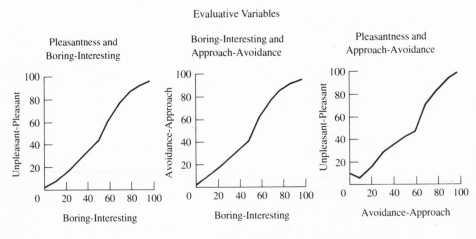

Evaluative Variables

FIGURE 4

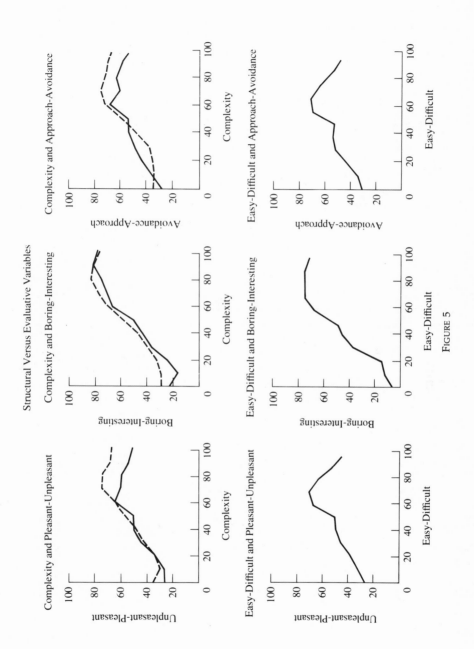

FIGURE 5

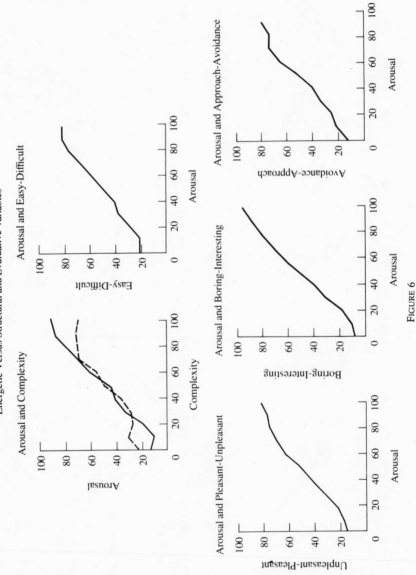

FIGURE 6

fectly correlated with all structural and evaluative dimensions that few if any distinctions can be made.

There are a number of implications of these data. I shall point out only three.

These interesting-looking data were obtained without the involvement of any experimental stimuli. They therefore suggest that we take great care to insure that we are theorizing about subjects' reactions to pictures or musical stimuli rather than to the language we have used in instructing our subjects.

Second, the results in Figure 4 seem to indicate that there is little difference between the pleasantness dimension and the interestingness dimension. These results suggest considerable caution in implying that the two dimensions represent functionally different kinds of exploration, as has been suggested by Berlyne.

Third, while there are clear indications of an inverted-U relationship between structural and evaluative variables in the semantic space of experimental subjects, these same subjects see no level of arousal as being too high or too great. High arousal is not associated with unpleasantness or any other negative evaluative or affective state.

Incomplete Processing of Complex Stimuli

There can be situations in which the range of complexity values of the physical stimulus can be quite large while the range of psychological complexity values can be considerably restricted. This can occur when the subject fails to process all of the material present in the physical stimulus, especially of the more complex stimuli. A result could be an inverted U when all of the information is processed, but an essentially linear rising pattern when it is not. Some of the theoretical possibilities, along with the results of an illustrative empirical study (Olson, 1977), are shown in Figure 7.

The stimuli in the Olson study were 12 black-and-white graphic prints from well-known artists. The prints represented a wide range of stimulus complexity values. The subjects were instructed to study the pictures until they were certain that they could recognize them in a later recognition test.

The theoretical figure on the left represents two hypothetical behaviors. Subjects might increase their study time in exact proportion to the complexity of the stimulus and thus generate a straight-line relationship between study time and the complexity of the stimulus. Alternatively, they might fail to process all the information in the more complex stimuli leading to the curved line in the figure. The empirical curve on the

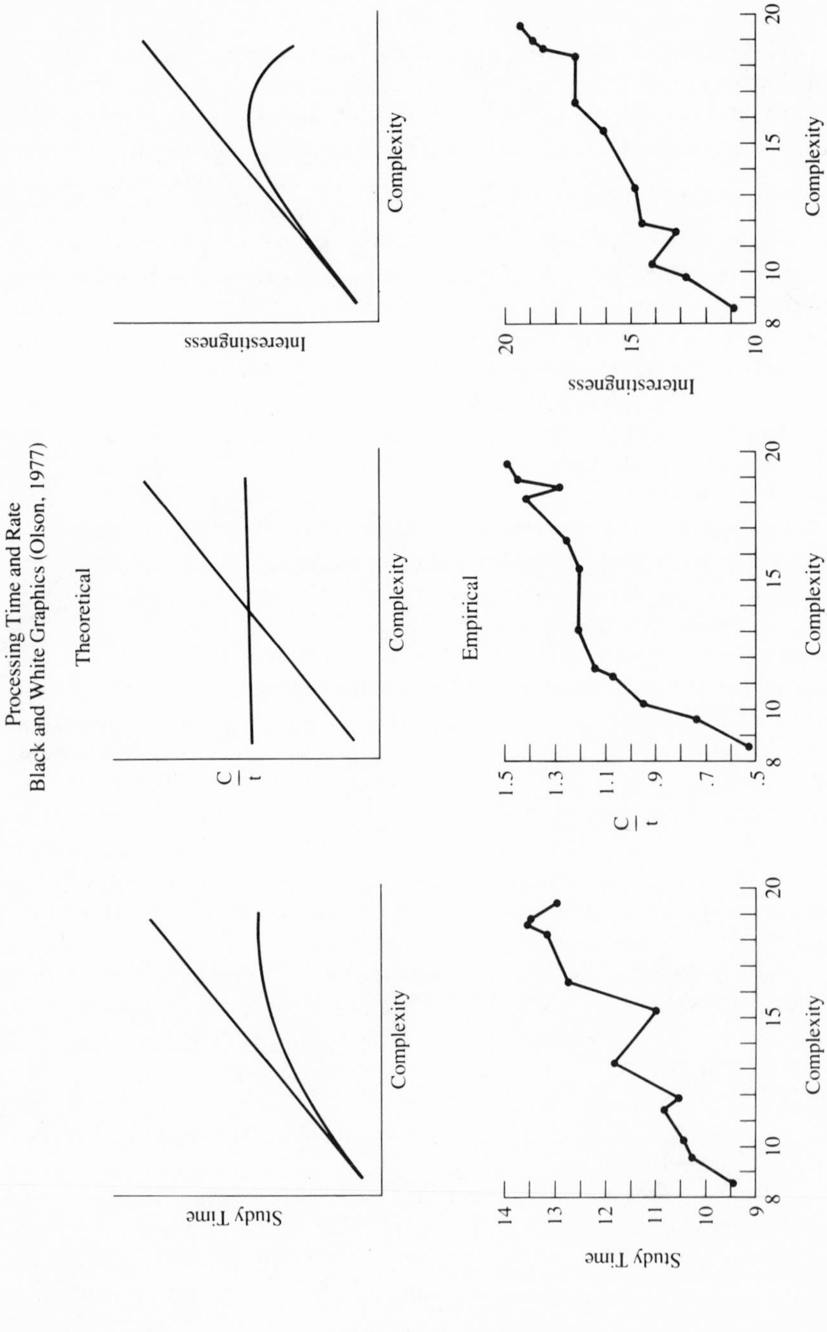
Processing Time and Rate
Black and White Graphics (Olson, 1977)
Theoretical
Study Time
Complexity
C/t
Complexity
Interestingness
Complexity
Empirical
Study Time
14
13
12
11
10
9
8
10
15
20
Complexity
C/t
1.5
1.3
1.1
.9
.7
.5
8
10
15
20
Complexity
Interestingness
20
15
10
8
10
15
20
Complexity

FIGURE 7

left shows that in this instance there was a general increase in study time as the complexity of the pictures increased.

One cannot determine from the results above whether the rate of information processing is constant or is adjusted in response to the amount of information in the stimulus. A rough index of information-processing rate can be calculated by dividing the complexity value of the pictures (C) by the study time (t) to produce a rate $(\frac{C}{t})$. The middle theoretical figure shows a hypothetical case in which processing rate is independent of complexity and therefore constant, and a case in which the processing rate increases as the complexity of the stimulus increases. The empirical result shown in the middle of the lower set of figures indicates a very substantial increase in the rate of processing information, thus tending to refute the hypothesis that the rate of information processing remains constant as shown by the horizontal line in the figure. Study time increased with increases in the complexity of the stimulus, but the rate of information processing increased as well.

The theoretical curves on the right show two possible relations between interestingness and complexity. The straight line would be expected if none of these graphics were so complex as to be uninteresting. The inflected curve would indicate the beginnings of an inverted U. The empirical curve at lower right shows no evidence of inflection and thus indicates that none of these graphics was above the optimal complexity level for interestingness for visual materials of this kind. It is to be noted, however, that an inverted U was obtained from this same set of prints when preference judgments were asked in another study. This result is shown later in Figure 15.

In this instance, it appears fairly clear that the failure to obtain an inverted U was not attributable to a failure on the part of the subjects to process all the available information in the stimulus. The instructions to study the materials long enough to provide for later recognition was sufficient to produce an exhaustive search. Had a fixed study time been a part of the procedure, the result might have been quite different.

Visual Complexity—Animal Studies

Figure 8 shows the results of five different studies of response to visual complexity in animals. Each involves an array of stimuli varying in stimulus complexity, placing the animals in choice situations and determining which they prefer, usually in terms of the amount of time the animals spend in the presence of each. The variety of results permits an interpretation based on the range of stimulus complexity presented to the animal.

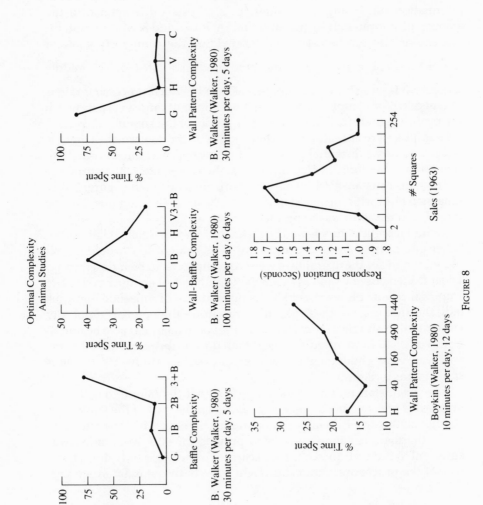

FIGURE 8

such materials should be predictable (as demonstrated in Walker, 1980), and it might even be possible at some point to invoke principles of motivation in accounts of human verbal behavior.

Complexity and Auditory Stimuli

The results of the several studies shown in Figure 12 are to be interpreted as reflecting different portions of the inverted-U preference curve. The figure is to be read clockwise beginning at the lower left. The first figure shows ratings of four short musical compositions composed by Heyduk (1972, 1975). They were played on a piano and sounded like familiar jazz compositions. His most experienced subjects showed little liking for the simplest of these and rated the composition composed to be the third most complex as the one they liked the most. The least experienced subjects, as shown in the second figure, agreed on the optimum but showed more liking, as expected, for the simpler compositions.

Arkes (1971) generated stimuli in the laboratory with an oscillator and a computer. He varied stimulus complexity in chunked sets by varying the number of chunks and by varying the number of tones within a chunk. When the responses to these rather strange sounding stimuli are analysed by number of chunks, there is an optimum, and preference falls off rapidly down the right side of the inverted U. When he increased complexity by adding tones to the chunks, the simplest stimuli were liked best, as shown in the top figure.

The three figures on the right come from studies by Aeschbach (1975) and by Ayres (1974, 1975). They involve ratings of two-note chords, which were generated by an oscillator in the Aeschbach study and by a synthesizer in the Ayres studies. All three of these studies show that subjects preferred the intervals which they judged to be the simplest and most consonant.

Preference Postulate Summary

This long list of studies that are relevant to the preference postulate was selected and organized to indicate the breadth of applicability of the postulate. The range of human behavior covered includes visual and auditory perception, verbal behavior, and cognitive behavior represented by problem solving. The applicability of the postulate was extended to animals in studies of preference for visual and spatial complexity.

This set of studies was also selected to demonstrate three of the many methodological problems associated with the quest for the inverted U. The results one might expect are highly dependent on the language one chooses to use in instructing experimental subjects, and our assumptions concerning what the language means to subjects is not always correct. It

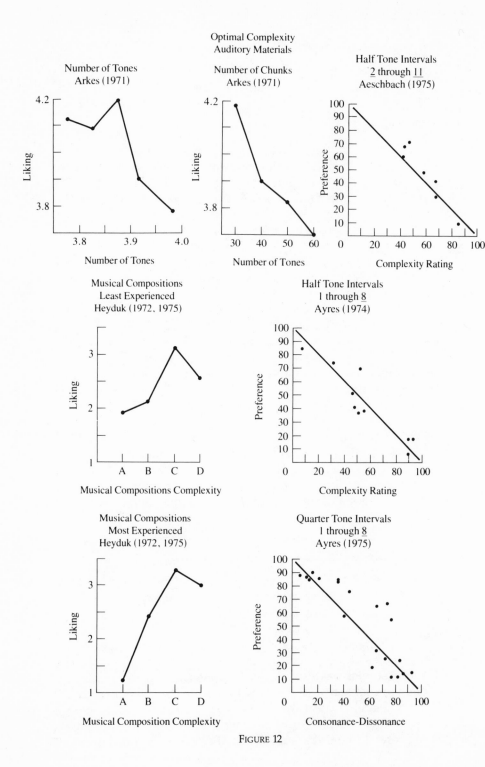

FIGURE 12

has been demonstrated repeatedly that an increasing function, an inverted U, or a decreasing function can result from the range of complexities presented to the subjects. In addition, there is some evidence that even when a full range of stimulus complexities is presented to the subject there may be instances in which subjects fail to process all the information presented. Other methodological issues will be presented in a later section of this paper.

The Learning Postulate

The learning postulate of Psychological Complexity and Preference Theory says that, with repeated experience of a particular psychological event, that event will undergo simplification. Simplification will manifest itself through a reduction in errors, reduced latency of response, and so-called improvement in other manifestations of learning. It should be obvious that the learning postulate and the preference postulate are closely related. The change in complexity with experience shown in the figure on the right side of Figure 1 could result in a psychological event being too complex to be comfortable, then simplifying to optimum, passing to the simple end of the scale and becoming boring. Thus it would move from the right end of the complexity scale to the left end in the left figure of Figure 1. Such effects can be demonstrated in a variety of experience or learning paradigms with both animal and human subjects.

Animal Experience

Figure 13 shows some of the results of five different animal studies. A basic problem with animal studies is that it is difficult to ask an animal how complex a stimulus appears, independently of asking it which stimulus it prefers. As a consequence, the usual practice is to construct stimuli that appear to the experimenter to constitute a range of stimulus complexity for the animal. If the range of stimulus complexity is sufficient, the animal should show an initial preference for simple stimuli, and with prolonged or repeated exposure it should shift its preference to more complex members of the set.

In the left panel of Figure 13 are data from four studies of the preferences of rats carried out by Bruce Walker (Walker, 1980). Other aspects of these studies were plotted in Figure 8. The four studies differed in the stimuli involved, in the length of time the animals spent in the choice situation, and in the number of days they experienced the stimuli involved. Averaged over five or six days, each of the curves indicates that there was a gradual shift in preference for more complex stimuli within any given exposure period. This effect of experience within days should

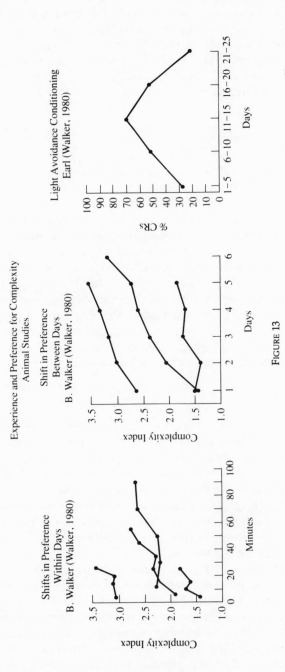

FIGURE 13

be the result of a combination of temporary habituation effects and more permanent effects of experience or learning. The middle panel indicates the progressive shift in preference for more complex stimuli between days. These effects should be attributable exclusively to learning, the simplification of the relevant psychological events through experience, if one assumes that habituation effects have dissipated between the daily experiences.

When the organism does not have a free choice among responses but must either choose to respond or not to respond, then progresive simplification of the psychological event involved should lead to first an increase and then a decrease in the tendency to make the response. The panel on the right in Figure 13 is a classic example. This is a light-avoidance response. It is one sample from our laboratory which stands for a large number of such curves that I have collected in order to demonstrate that the true learning curve, as generated from the Hedgehog, is one which first "improves" and then "deteriorates" under continued reward (see especially Walker, 1964, 1969).

Human Experience

Similar effects of experience on psychological complexity and preference can be shown in human behavior. Figure 14 shows the effects of 18 repetitions of one of Heyduk's (1972, 1975) four musical compositions. It reveals that complexity ratings fall progressively, whereas liking ratings first rise and then fall. This is the effect one would expect if the initial complexity value was just above optimum at the beginning. There is some

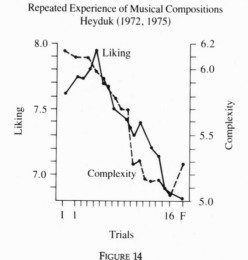

Repeated Experience of Musical Compositions
Heyduk (1972, 1975)

FIGURE 14

question of the extent to which these data represent a semipermanent change, and thus learning, or reflect a temporary change, and thus habituation. In any case, the results conform to theoretical expectations.

In many of our studies involving visual and auditory stimuli, information has been obtained from the subjects concerning the extent of their prior backgrounds with the class of stimulus materials. In at least one case, subjects were selected to have different amounts of relevant experience. The data were then analysed to determine whether the experienced subjects gave different ratings than inexperienced subjects. In most instances, no differences were found that were statistically significant. However, whenever a difference was found, it was always in the direction predicted by the theory. Figure 15 (Sinclair, 1967) is a good example. Art students preferred more complex graphics than did law students, who had had much less experience with such materials. There was even some difference between the more experienced art students as compared with the less experienced art history students. A similar effect of prior experience can be seen in comparing the two figures based on Heyduk's data in Figure 12.

The effects of prior experience on the psychological complexity and preference for verbal materials are easily shown. Figure 16 demonstrates a high correlation between the complexity ratings of letters of the alphabet and the frequency with which they occur in the English language.

The four sets of data in Figure 17 relate complexity ratings to either ease of learning or to association value which is closely related to ease of learning. The measure of learning is the mean number of items correct in a fixed number of paired-associates trials. In each instance, the more complex the item is judged to be, the more difficult it is to learn.

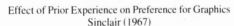

Effect of Prior Experience on Preference for Graphics
Sinclair (1967)

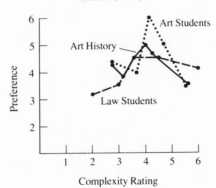

FIGURE 15

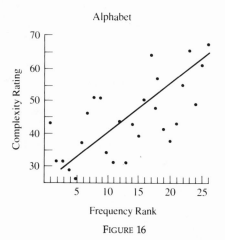

Alphabet

FIGURE 16

Complexity and Ease of Learning

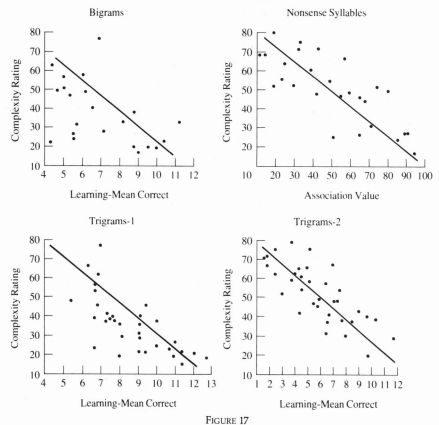

FIGURE 17

A large number of three-letter items are compared in Figure 18 in terms of their comparative psychological complexities. Words are rated as less and less complex as their frequency of occurrence in English increases. High-association nonsense syllables receive ratings close to the rarest words, and trigrams are rated as the most complex of all.

These studies demonstrate the viability of the learning postulate in its declaration that learning can be seen as progressive simplification of the material experienced, and that there is an intimate relation between the degree of simplification of the material and the degree of preference for it.

SOME OBSTACLES TO A SUCCESSFUL QUEST

The pursuit of the inverted U is beset with a great many obstacles. Earlier I made an effort to document three of them. It is not always clear that the language of experimental subjects is the same as the language used by an experimenter in instructing his subjects. Often the range of stimuli presented is sufficient to tap only a portion of the preference curve. There are some instances in which experimental subjects do not process all the information in the complex stimuli presented to them, with a consequent foreshortening of the range of complexity values. There are many other problems which can stand in the way of obtaining an inverted U in empirical data, even if that function represents the true state of affairs. I should like to document a few of them.

Three-letter Combinations

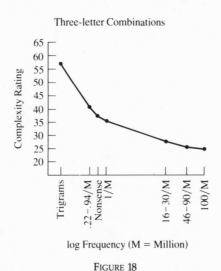

log Frequency (M = Million)

FIGURE 18

Motivational Problems

Considerable confusion arises because of the ambiguity in the meanings of the terms *intrinsic* and *extrinsic* motivation. The motivation to perform a task may be intrinsic to the task, intrinsic to the person but extrinsic to the task, or it may be extrinsic to both the task and the person. Many studies purporting to involve intrinsic motivation utilize operations which produce a complex of motives for performing a given task, and for this reason yield results which are difficult to interpret. As a step in the direction of clarification, I should like to distinguish three classes of motivation that could result in the performance of the same task, but that have different sources. I shall give these classes of motivation new names because of the confusion involved in the use and misuse of the terms intrinsic and extrinsic.

Autarkic Motivation

The word autarkic means self-sufficient. The source of autarkic motivation is the task itself. Autarkic motivation involves performance of the task for the sake of that performance alone, unsupported by motivation from any other source. Behavior that is autarkically motivated will result in what Berlyne (1960, p. 79) called *intrinsic exploration.* Autarkic motivation is automatic, autonomous, and spontaneous. It is intrinsic to the task being performed.

Idiocratic Motivation

This label refers to motivation the source of which is the individual. It is motivation characteristic of a given person. Idiocratic motivation is a stable aspect of the personality. Its essential feature is that idiocratic motivation is not dependent on any external source of support. The performance of a given task can be motivated idiocratically if its performance is seen by the individual to serve some personal motive. Behavior that is idiocratically motivated can result in what Berlyne (1960, p. 79) called *extrinsic exploration,* in which the individual seeks cues for guidance for some succeeding response with an independent source of biological value. Idiocratic motivation is autogenous and endogenous to the person. It is extrinsic to the task performed, but its source is intrinsic to the person performing the task.

Extraneous Motivation

This class of motive has its source outside the individual. It is not essential, it is not intrinsic in any sense, it is foreign. The essential feature of extraneous motivation is that behavior which is motivated extraneously will occur only when the source of that motivation is present and operating. The behavior will cease when the source of that motivation is removed.

The Impurity of Motivational Operations

It should be obvious from a consideration of this set of definitions that what is purported to be activity motivated only by autarkic factors (intrinsic motivation) in many studies in the literature is actually motivated by a complex of factors including both idiocratic and extraneous sources of motivation. It is difficult to induce a person to become a subject in an experiment without invoking extraneous motivation. Any instruction intended to entice subjects to work on a task carries with it an implication that the experimenter will be pleased if the subject does so and displeased if the subject does not. If the subject works in the absence of overt instructions from the experimenter, the subject may be self-instructed to please the experimenter on the basis that the person is a subject and is in a laboratory setting. Furthermore, many subjects see such tasks as a personal challenge, thus invoking idiocratic motivation to add to the complex.

Some theories confine the expectation of an inverted U to behaviors motivated only by intrinsic motivation. For them this set of distinctions is critical. In the Hedgehog an inverted U is postulated to be universal and therefore to be expected regardless of the source of motivation. The distinctions do, however, have practical importance. The persistent association of idiocratic motivation with the autarkic motivation for educationally relevant tasks leads to scholarship. The persistent association of extraneous motivation to the same tasks leads to poor academic persistence.

Evaluation of Something Other Than the Intended Quality

There are circumstances in which subjects may evaluate a set of stimuli on a dimension other than the one intended by the experimenter. Suppose that a set of paintings is evaluated for complexity by one group of subjects. Then suppose that another group of subjects is asked to rate the paintings for pleasantness. Suppose that this group of raters knows the monetary value of each of the paintings and rates them for pleasant-ness in terms of this value. Since they would not be rating the paintings in terms of the intrinsic properties of the stimuli, complexity and preference ratings would not be related.

Individual versus Group Data

Most psychological theories refer to mechanisms that operate within an individual and to characteristics of an individual. There is an almost universal assumption that what is true of the group is true of the indi-vidual. Therefore, a plot of the results of group performance reflects what goes on within each of the individuals within the group. This assumption about the relation of group and individual results is often quite false.

Suppose we have five stimuli that vary in complexity, and we ask five subjects to rank them for preference. If the stimuli are ordered in complex-ity from 1 to 5, it is not inconceivable that the five subjects could give us the following orders: 12345, 21345, 32145, 43215, and 54321. Each of these five has an optimum and an orderly decrease in preference from the optimum. Each is either an inverted U or, in two instances, the first and last, could be a part of an inverted U if the range of stimuli had been larger. Yet, if we average the five ranks assigned to each stimulus, the averages are 3.0, 2.4, 2.4, 3.0, and 4.2. The group result appears to be a U-shaped function that would refute an inverted-U theory. Thus, the theory would be confirmed in each of the five individual subjects and refuted by the group results. The group results are suspect, unless they can be shown to correspond to individual results by some means.

The Number of Experimental Stimuli

The number of experimental stimuli to be used in an experiment is critical. In order to simplify the problem, let us assume that the theoretical expectation is that the optimal complexity level of an individual may be above all the stimuli in the set, below all the stimuli, or somewhere between the simplest and the most complex. Assume further that the data are nonmetric and consist of preferential orders given by subjects. If we had used three experimental stimuli, which might be labeled, C, M, and S for Complex, Medium, and Simple, then there are only six preferential order relationships that the subjects could provide. Of these, four ($C > M > S$, $S > M > C$, $M > C > S$, and $M > S > C$) represent monotonically increasing, monotonically decreasing, and inverted-U-shaped functions, and are thus acceptable preference order relationships within the theory.

Only two of the six possible orders are unacceptable. These are $C > S > M$ and $S > C > M$, which yield U-shaped functions which violate the theory. Therefore, if the results were truly random, two-thirds of the results would agree with the theory and only one-third would not. It is obvious that it would be exceedingly difficult to test the theory with only three stimuli, and the literature contains the reports of many studies which employ only two values of the stimulus dimension. In that case the theory cannot be tested at all.

Table I shows the number of possible combinations of stimuli, $N!$, that arise from various number of stimuli, N. It is obvious that 3 stimuli are infinitely better than 2, 4 are better than 3, 5 are better than 4, etc.

The techniques of analysis of ordinal data of the kind usually obtained in complexity and preference research come largely from the work of Coombs (1964), where it is largely unintelligible to me. A version which I find somewhat easier to understand appears in Coombs, Dawes, and Tversky (1970). Basically, Coombs refers to a preference order, such as 34215 as an *I–scale*. An *I–scale* can be *unfolded* to determine whether there is an underlying *J–scale*, a unidimensional scale on which each of the stimuli as well as the ideal position of the subject can be arrayed. Given the I–scale 34215, one can reason that such a preference order can be unfolded into a J–scale with the individual occupying a position between stimulus 2 and 4 and nearer to stimulus 3 than to either 2 or 4. The I–scale 34215, is an acceptable preference-order relationship because it can be unfolded into a J–scale. The preference order 31542 is an unacceptable preference-order relationship because it cannot be unfolded into a unidimensional J–scale. When a subject gives such judgments, one can only appeal to errors of measurement, conclude that the subject is not responding exclusively to

TABLE I. Effects of Numbers of Experimental Stimuli

Number of stimuli (N)	N!	Number of acceptable preference order relationships	Percentage
1	1	1	100.00
2	2	2	100.00
3	6	4	66.67
4	24	8	33.33
5	120	16	13.33
6	720	32	4.44
7	5,040	64	1.33
8	40,320	128	.32
9	362,880	256	.07
10	3,628,800	512	.01

the experimental dimension (in this case complexity), or that the theory is wrong or inapplicable in the situation.

A much more elegant and detailed exposition of some of the problems of testing theories of complexity and preference using Coombs' scaling procedures is given by Thomas (1971). It is worthy of note that Thomas is somewhat pessimistic concerning the problem of testing bimodal curves from ordinal data. Bimodal curves are expected from Adaptation Level Theory (Helson, 1959) and discrepancy theories of motivation such as those of McClelland (1953) and Hebb (1949). Thomas shows that any result involving three stimuli can fit a bimodal discrepancy prediction. Thus a much larger number of stimuli would be required to verify a bimodal distribution than is required for the inverted-U-shape, as indicated in Table I.

The Problem of Nonmetric Data

It is very doubtful if scales of either complexity or preference meet the requirements of metric scales. That is, there is little reason to suppose that units on either of two dimensions characteristic of a study of complexity and preference involve equal units. The point can be illustrated even within studies in which a physical scale is used as a dimension of complexity. Let us take for an example a study in which the ubiquitous random polygon is employed. It is typical practice to choose a set of random polygons that vary in the number of independent sides. In a study by Day and Crawford (1971), complexity was varied by using random polygons of 20, 24, 28, 34, 40, and 48 sides. The results were then plotted on a linear scale of the number of sides. The results obtained with the 40-sided polygon were discrepant on all four of the dimensions used in the study: simplicity, liking, pleasing, and interesting. After establishing the statistical significance of the discrepancy, Day and Crawford eliminated results for this polygon and reported results for the remaining five figures. It is obvious that the number of sides for this set of polygons did not form a metric scale, and in this case, judging by the ratings of simplicity, did not even form an ordered scale.

The Occultation Effect

Occultation occurs whenever the act of determining the value of a variable either distorts or changes the character of the event and thus hides the true value. The occultation effect is widespread in psychology, and usually goes totally unrecognized. A concrete example will illustrate the point. In psychological complexity and preference theory, the psychological complexity of an event can be expected to decrease progressively with repeated exposure to the same stimulus. A temporary decrease in complexity can be expected from simple habituation. A semi-permanent decrease in complexity constitutes the learning which occurs. In any measurement technique which requires repeated measurements from the same subject, each judgment the subject makes represents a different psychological event with a different psychological complexity value, even though the stimulus remains constant. Thus, if one uses a paired-comparison technique to order eight stimuli on a complexity dimension, each stimulus will be exposed a minimum of seven times by being paired at least once with every other stimulus. Each exposure will produce some degree of complexity reduction, and depending on the interval between exposures and the rate of recovery from habituation there will be a partial restoration. Depending on the character of the individual stimuli and the amount of prior experience with them, the amount of complexity reduction and the amount of recovery from habituation may be different. The final result is thus a mean of seven different values for each stimulus, and represents neither the initial nor the final value. The true psychological complexity of the event at initial exposure has been occulted. What may originally have been the basis for an inverted U may now produce a quite different shape.

How Successful the Quest?

I have recounted some of the adventures of the little Hedgehog through a jungle of data and a mountain of experiments in quest of the inverted U. It is now time to assess the relative success of that journey.

The learning postulate appears to have been sustained without any contrary evidence, despite the fact that it predicts such unexpected phenomena as the rising and falling learning curve. We grow to love moderately complex music and art, and then grow bored with that which we formerly loved.

When the preference postulate is applied to qualitative or structural differences between stimuli, there is no convincing contrary evidence. Within any one class of materials, one might argue for a contrary interpretation, but no alternative interpretation exists which will handle all of the preference data from such diverse materials. We do tend to show preference for an optimal level of complexity in art and music as well as in other areas, and to show less preference for stimuli or events either above or below that optimum.

Somewhere in the thicket of the intensity variable, the Hedgehog may have sustained a grievous wound. Sugar which can't be too sweet, the odor which is pleasant in any concentration, substances which taste bad in any concentration, may require the Hedgehog to accept a family of related functions, of which the Wundtian hedonic curve is one, in order to handle intensity. It remains to be seen whether the wound will heal by itself, or whether the Hedgehog will have to learn some variations on his one trick.

REFERENCES

AESCHBACH, S. *Ratings of dichords along the continua of complexity–simplicity, consonance–dissonance, and pleasing-displeasing.* Honors dissertation, University of Michigan, 1975.

ARKES, H. R. *The relationship between repetition and organization and the role of organization in psychological complexity.* Unpublished doctoral dissertation, University of Michigan, 1971.

AYRES, T. *Exploratory behavior in musical intervals as related to measures of consonance and dissonance.* Research paper, Amherst College, 1974.

AYRES, T. *Psychological and physiological factors in the consonance of musical intervals.* Honors dissertation, Amherst College, 1975.

BERLYNE, D. E. *Conflict, arousal and curiosity.* New York: McGraw-Hill, 1960.

BERLYNE, D. E. *Psychobiology and aesthetics.* New York: Appleton-Century-Crofts, 1971.

BOYKIN, A. W., JR. *Verbally expressed preference and complexity judgments as they relate to levels of performance in a problem-solving situation.* Unpublished doctoral dissertation, University of Michigan, 1972.

BOYKIN, A. W., JR. Verbally expressed preference and problem-solving proficiency. *Journal of Experimental Psychology: Human Perception and Performance.* 1977, *3*, 165–174.

COOMBS, C. H. *Theory of data.* New York: Wiley, 1964.

COOMBS, C. H., DAWES, R. M., & TVERSKY, A. *Mathematical psychology.* Englewood Cliffs, N.J.: Prentice-Hall, 1970.

DAY, H. I., & CRAWFORD, G. C. *Developmental changes in attitudes toward complexity.* Paper read at the meetings of The Society for Research in Child Development, Minneapolis, 1971.

DEMBER, W. N., & EARL, R. W. Analysis of exploratory, manipulatory, and curiosity behavior. *Psychological Review,* 1957, *64*, 91–96.

ENGLE, R. Experimentelle Untersuchungen über die Abhängigkeit der Lust and Unlust von der Reizstärke beim Geschmacksinn. *Archis fuer die Gesamte Psychologie,* 1928, *64*, 1–36. Cited in Woodworth, R. S., & Schlosberg, H. *Experimental psychology.* New York: Holt, 1954.

HEBB, D. O. *The organization of behavior.* New York: Wiley, 1949.

HELSON, H. Adaptation-level theory. In S. Koch (Ed.), *Psychology: A study of a science.* New York: McGraw-Hill, 1959.

HEYDUK, R. G. *Static and dynamic aspects of rated and exploratory preference for musical compositions.* Unpublished doctoral dissertation, University of Michigan, 1972.

HEYDUK, R. G. Rated preference for musical compositions as it relates to complexity and exposure frequency. *Perception and Psychophysics,* 1975, *17*, 84–91.

KREITLER, H., & KREITLER, S. *Psychology of the arts.* Durham: Duke University Press, 1972.

McCLELLAND, D. C., ATKINSON, J. W., CLARK, R. A., & LOWELL, E. L. *The achievement motive.* New York: Appleton-Century-Crofts, 1953.

OLSON, M. H. *Complexity and preference and information processing rate.* Unpublished doctoral dissertation, University of Michigan, 1977.

PFAFFMAN, C. Taste preference and reinforcement. In Tapp, J. T. (Ed.), *Reinforcement and behavior*. New York: Academic Press, 1969.

SALES, S. M. Stimulus complexity as a determinant of approach behavior and inspection time in the hooded rat. *Canadian Journal of Psychology/Review of Canadian Psychology*, 1968, 22, 11–17.

SINCLAIR, K. *Optimal complexity and aesthetic preference*. Honors dissertation, University of Michigan, 1967.

THOMAS, H. Discrepancy hypotheses: Methodological and theoretical considerations. *Psychological Review*, 1971, 78, 249–259.

WALKER, E. L. Psychological complexity as a basis for a theory of motivation and choice. In D. Levine (Ed.), *Nebraska symposium on motivation*. Lincoln: University of Nebraska Press, 1964.

WALKER, E. L. Reinforcement: "The one ring." In J. T. Tapp (Ed.), *Reinforcement and behavior*. New York: Academic Press, 1969.

WALKER, E. L. *Psychological complexity and preference: A Hedgehog theory of behavior*. Monterey, Calif.: Brooks/Cole, 1980.

WUNDT, W. *Grundzüge der physiologischen Psychologie*. Leipzig: Englemann, 1874.

4

Environmental Restriction and "Stimulus Hunger"

Theories and Applications

PETER SUEDFELD

Throughout much of the history of psychology, theorists concerned with motivation have focused on constructs having to do with internal states. Certainly toward the middle of the twentieth century most professional psychologists agreed that the major sources of motivation lay either in tissue deficits (drive-reduction theory) or in the combination of physiological and psychic needs for various kinds of gratification (psychodynamic theory). In both instances, the basic thrust was that a variety of physiological processes gives rise to sets of intense stimuli that, monitored and interpreted within the body, engage some sort of behavioral regulator which leads to the emission of appropriate responses. To a degree, the stimuli are unpleasant; behavior is directed toward their elimination, which is reinforcing. Biological concepts of instincts, homeostasis, and general drive (D) all share this basic underlying orientation (Cannon, 1932; Freud, 1915; Hull, 1943).

Of course, most people recognized that this picture is oversimplified. Theorists realized that intensification of stimuli is not necessarily aversive, and that certain events are reinforcing even though they have no clearly discernible drive-reducing consequences. Among such events are sexual arousal even without subsequent copulation (Sheffield, Wulff, & Backer, 1951), the ingestion of sweet but nonnutritive substances (Sheffield & Roby, 1950), and the exploration and manipulation of novel stimulus environments and objects (Harlow, 1950). It was at this point

PETER SUEDFELD • Department of Psychology, The University of British Columbia, Vancouver, British Columbia V6T 1W5, Canada.

that research on "perceptual isolation" conducted at McGill University under the direction of Donald O. Hebb introduced a new point of view (Bexton, Heron, & Scott, 1954), and Daniel Berlyne's theoretical contributions began to elucidate a dramatic set of findings.

MOTIVATIONAL EFFECTS OF STIMULUS RESTRICTION

In the McGill work on perceptual isolation, internal stimulation was presumably maintained by the satisfaction of identifiable physiological needs. At the same time, external stimulation was supposedly reduced through the use of immobilization, constant white noise and diffuse light, and coverings over the hands and the body. As is well known, the consequences of this situation during the course of two or three days included intense negative affect, performance decrements on many kinds of cognitive and perceptual/motor tasks, reported visual and auditory sensations without identifiable external cause, increased desire to be exposed to even boring and repetitive stimuli, greater persuasibility in response to propaganda messages, and changes in psychophysiological functioning (see Heron, 1961). Thus, the data appeared to indicate that a lowering of both internal (drive) and external stimuli did not lead to the quiescent, inactive state predicted by previous theories.

According to Berlyne (1960), these symptoms could be explained by the concept of arousal potential. The argument was that the unpleasantness of low stimulus levels is based on the curvilinear relationship between arousal potential, which is a function of stimulus complexity (cf. deCharms, 1968), and the level of reticular arousal. The latter in turn is negatively related to the hedonic positiveness of the situation. Both low and high levels of stimulus complexity lead to increases in the state of arousal of the reticular activating system (see Lindsley, 1961). Such increases are experienced as unpleasant, and motivate the organism to initiate attempts to restore more acceptable arousal levels. The tactic for achieving this goal may be to move the collative properties of environmental stimuli (novelty, surprisingness, change, ambiguity, incongruity, blurredness, and power to induce uncertainty—Berlyne, 1963) toward such moderate levels.

Naturally, this explanation was not unchallenged. Fiske and Maddi (1961) argued that monotonous environments, both in natural situations and in the laboratory, result in low levels of activation, which the individual attempts to raise by seeking change and action. These authors also emphasized the variability of arousal level over time, and suggested that future research pay attention to such fluctuations. This formulation is quite compatible with that of Hebb (1955), who also explained the purported aversiveness of monotonous environments by the argument that such environments lead to low arousal, which is affectively unpleasant, at least until it becomes low enough to produce sleep. Schultz (1965) agreed that low levels of stimulation lead to low arousal, which motivates the organism to try to restore "sensoristasis" —a term analogous to homeostasis, but related to a drive state of cortical arousal rather than one of physiological need. One problem, of course, is that almost any behavioral phenomenon may be interpreted in either direction. For example, increased activity may be viewed as a sign that arousal is high and expresses itself in the expenditure of muscular energy, just as it does when an anxious or hungry person or animal paces back and forth. On the other hand, the same behavior can be interpreted as a sign that the arousal level is low, and that the behavior is being emitted in order to raise it, as when a drowsy individual deliberately stimulates himself by fidgeting.

Compared to its rivals, Berlyne's explanation of the phenomena emerging from research with what is now usually called the restricted environmental stimulation technique (REST) seems to have held up quite well. In fact, it has held up better than the original data themselves. Many of the latter have been nonreplicable, or at best inconsistently replicable, and may in fact have been to some unknown degree the consequences of procedural details and of experimenter or subject expectancy rather than of any intrinsic aspect of stimulus reduction itself (Zubek, 1973). Recent studies have demonstrated that REST is frequently perceived as a relaxing, calming, and enjoyable environment. There is even some question as to whether the original perceptual isolation technique used at McGill in fact leads to any reduction in stimulus level (Suedfeld, 1980). Of course, a reduction in the collative properties of stimuli did occur beyond any reasonable doubt, so that the variables upon which Berlyne rested his theoretical case were indeed appropriate. They remain appropriate throughout the entire REST literature, which has expanded to include such widely differing methodologies as confinement in a dark, soundproof room, immersion in a tank of water, floating in a gel-like liquid, immobilization in an iron lung respirator or a wooden box, and so on (Zubek, 1969a).

The Effects of REST

Research performed in stimulus-poor environments after the early McGill studies has shown a more complex picture than was painted at first. It appears that many of the bizarre phenomena reported in the early days may have been the consequences of some now unclarifiable combination of specific procedural, experimenter, and subject variables (see

Zubek, 1973). For example, the occurrence of hallucinations, in the sense of a clinically defined perceptual disturbance, is extremely rare; and certain types of performance, including some aspects of cognitive process, show improvements rather than decrements (Suedfeld, 1980; Zubek, 1969a).

Even what has been considered the most reliable characteristic of "sensory deprivation," its aversive and unpleasant nature, has been challenged by recent evidence. This was perhaps the issue on which most people agreed in the earlier literature. Stimulus restriction was supposedly experienced as stressful, tolerable for relatively short periods at best, and a source of anxiety, boredom, and other unpleasant emotions. In one early review, for example, this aspect of the effects was summed up as follows:

> In general, the affective response to sensory deprivation includes boredom, restlessness, irritability, and occasionally anxiety and fear of panic proportions. Descriptions of post-isolation affective states have referred to fatigue, drowsiness, and feelings of being dazed, confused and disoriented. (Kubzansky & Leiderman, 1961, p. 229)

This general picture was accepted and widely transmitted by secondary sources, and is still the modal description of the effects in the vast majority of undergraduate-level psychology textbooks (Adams, 1979). It is in fact the case that many studies have reported subjects terminating the experiment before its scheduled end (Myers, 1969), that confined subjects have often said that the experience was relatively unpleasant compared to the ratings of control subjects (Myers, 1969), and that subjects in REST have been shown to emit operant responses not only to obtain stimulation but also to shorten the period of confinement (Jones, 1969; Rossi & Solomon, 1964).

But the findings are not so monolithic as they appear on the surface. To begin with, there are significant differences among subjects, procedures, and measures. Myers (1969) has shown that tolerance for REST is very much a function of such variables as whether the dependent variable is time spent in the condition, an operant response to modify this situation, or one of several affect scales; whether the programmed (expected) duration is known or unknown, short or long; whether the subject is immersed in water, immobilized, or put into a dark and silent room as opposed to a homogeneously stimulating environment; and so on.

Subject set seems to be extremely important (e.g., see Jackson & Pollard, 1962); and the procedures that in the early years surrounded REST experimentation without at all being substantively related to it (e.g., panic buttons, mysterious equipment, legal release forms) were certainly sufficient in themselves to lead to the anxiety-laden affective responses that were so widely interpreted as showing the effects of REST itself (Orne & Scheibe, 1964; Suedfeld, 1977). By the same token, more neutral procedures lead to a great reduction in the level of stress and anxiety expressed by participants, frequently to the point of evaluations that are indistinguishable from those of control subjects, and evidence for any kind of serious disturbance is minimal (Suedfeld, 1977; Tarjan, 1970). The monotonous stimulation (homogeneous light and white noise) procedure appears to be reliably less pleasant and also less therapeutically effective than the stimulus-reduction methods of darkness and silence. Even the most extreme version of the latter—water immersion—has frequently been perceived as beneficial and enjoyable by participants with the appropriate set of expectations and orientations (Lilly, 1977).

Evidence Concerning Arousal

One aspect of this newly recognized complexity is that it turns our attention to the issue of differential effects and responses. It has become clear that the various techniques of implementing stimulus restriction are not in fact interchangeable. Some of the parametric work reported in Zubek's (1969a) book demonstrates the range of effects that can be obtained to a greater or lesser degree by using different combinations of reduced or monotonous stimulus arrays in the sensory modalities, as well as by varying the extent of output restriction (e.g., by immobilizing the subject). In the argument as to what the arousal effects of sensory restriction really are, the empirical evidence is inconclusive.

Performance on intellectual tasks is compatible with Berlyne's theory of relatively high activation level. Complex cognitive processes reliably deteriorate, whereas simple ones frequently improve in efficiency. This finding is compatible with data using more traditional arousal-increasing procedures, such as electric shock and food deprivation: when arousal is high, responses that are dominant in the subject's learned hierarchy become even more likely to be emitted. This phenomenon should lead to improved efficiency on simple tasks, such as memorization and recall, where the appropriate solution modes have been overlearned, so that the correct approach is likely to be the dominant one. In contrast, complex tasks (such as telling a story integrating several prescribed elements) are not so familiar, and the lack of a clear-cut dominant solution leads to response competition and reduced performance effectiveness when arousal is too high (Landon & Suedfeld, 1972, 1977; Suedfeld, 1969).

One problem with this literature is that most studies draw conclusions based on two, or at most three, points along the two axes (task complexity and arousal level). For example, the effects of stimulus restriction on high-level creative activity have never been adequately tested, since most experiments use tasks that cover only a small segment of the complexity continuum. We do have subjective reports that the environment is conducive to vivid fantasy and imagery, and that some creative artists and scientists have used the technique to generate new ideas and cognitively explore older ones (Lilly, 1977). Whether these anecdotal instances would be supported by systematic, objective studies, and what implications such studies might have for the relationship between stimulus reduction and arousal, are questions that await further research.

Along the dimension of arousal most researchers have used only a control and a confinement condition. Obviously, in such cases no curvilinear function could possibly be demonstrated to exist. A few other studies have incorporated social-isolation groups without global environmental restriction, but it is difficult to place these along the continuum. Only a few experiments have involved other manipulations, such as combining REST with other motivational factors, or using different durations of confinement as a parametric variable. Another flaw in this regard is that the level of arousal is almost never directly measured. This is understandable in view of the difficulty of identifying an appropriate index of arousal, but obviously critically damaging to the effort to establish whether arousal is in fact a mediating variable between stimulus reduction and cognitive performance.

Noncognitive data have been quite inconsistent. For example, it appears that subjects sleep less as time in REST increases, which may again show increasing arousal; but this may be a function of the type and duration of confinement as well as of individual differences, and it is also mediated by diurnal cycles. Myers, Murphy, Smith and Goffard (1966) reported that motor movement, obviously related to wakefulness, showed similar variability. Restlessness went up across several days of confinement, remaining high during the daytime but dipping at night. Subjects who eventually quit the experiment before the scheduled end of the session were considerably more restless than those who managed to stay throughout the planned period. This last datum reminds us of the finding of Vernon and McGill (1960) that eventual quitters were significantly higher than stayers in the rate of button-pressing to view an unstructured visual stimulus. Zuckerman and Haber (1965) also showed that tolerance for reduced stimulation, this time measured by GSR responsivity, was negatively related to operant responding for stimulation.

Psychophysiological measures also fail to answer this basic question. Although there is evidence that boredom leads to high arousal (London, Schubert, & Washburn, 1978), such data do not serve to identify direct environment–arousal links. For instance, many subjects find the REST experience to be anything but boring. A review of the relevant studies leads to the conclusion that REST appears to cause cortical deactivation coupled with high peripheral arousal (Zuckerman, 1969). One of the most stable findings is a progressive decrease in mean alpha frequency as confinement time goes on, but there are great individual differences in the pattern. Furthermore, the change is not found consistently when EEG is measured cross-sectionally rather than longitudinally, and the magnitude of change varies greatly as a function of the type of sensory restriction being employed. Studies using GSR as the dependent variable typically show decreases in skin resistance (indicating high peripheral arousal), but other measures, such as skin temperature, blood pressure, metabolic rate, and a number of biochemical analyses, show no consistent significant changes (Zubek, 1973).

These reports point to a more complicated explanation of what may erroneously be considered a REST–arousal relationship. One possibility is that many of the arousal data are unduly affected by whatever proportion of subjects finds stimulus reduction particularly stressful. It may be that changes in arousal are found only among this subgroup, and that such changes are a direct result of stress. This would explain the finding that the adverse behavioral effects of stimulus restriction are more consistently related to indices of relatively high arousal than to low or normal activation levels (e.g., Zuckerman, 1969). As we know (Suedfeld, 1980), a negative reaction to environmental restriction may be owing to a wide number of sources, including subject expectancy, personality variables (e.g., sensation-seeking), and aspects of the experimental procedure other than the reduction of stimuli. Even a relatively few highly reactive subjects may exhibit enough change for a significant intergroup difference in arousal to be found; but any conclusion that REST itself has a reliable affect on arousal would be unwarranted from such data.

The specific question of the arousal effects of REST cannot be answered. Both behavioral and physiological measures show inconsistent results, which is perhaps not surprising. After all, stimulus restriction covers a great variety of specific experimental environments, durations, manipulations, types of orientation, subject and experimenter expectancies, and personality differences; and the term arousal stands for almost as wide a variety of measures (Lacey, 1967). Although it is true that the global relationship being sought would be a very useful one if we could find it, the failure of the search is understandable. Perhaps the best tactic, then, is to turn to a more focused, and possibly more useful, line of inquiry.

The Motivational Consequences of REST

Because of the confusion about the most appropriate measure of arousal, and in fact about whether arousal is in any meaningful sense a unitary concept, it seems better at least for the time being to lay the issue aside. Instead, attention should be paid to the consequences of REST for motivation. We may accept the principles of sensoristasis (Schultz, 1965) and optimal levels of stimulation (Zuckerman, 1969), that there is some moderate stimulation range or level. Deviations from this level result in behavioral changes tending to rectify the situation. When stimulus level is excessively low, the individual may seek several ways to increase it. One way is to change environments. Another is to produce actual stimulation in any of the sensory modalities (by talking to oneself, making noise, moving about, etc.). A third is to exploit the residual stimulation in the environment more effectively. This can be accomplished by lowering sensory thresholds, by focusing more intensely on stimuli that might normally be processed only superficially and casually, or conversely by scanning the stimulus array more widely to attend to aspects that would normally be filtered out. Another class of solutions is to attend to and/or generate more of the total stimulus load internally. That is, the individual may become aware of thoughts, emotions, and physical processes that are normally unconscious, or intensify the level of fantasizing, intense dreaming, concentrated thought, and emotional experience above that characterizing processing in the normal environment (Budzynski, 1976; Lilly, 1977; Suedfeld, 1979, 1980).

Considerable research has been performed on the motivational aspects of stimulus reduction. Perhaps the most widely accepted concept is that of "stimulus-action hunger" (Lilly, 1956). The need for "action" arises from the restriction of movement involved in most REST situations, and probably also from the interference with feedback from one's own behavior which the situation imposes (Miller, Galanter, & Pribram, 1960; Suedfeld, 1980). As has been mentioned, motor behavior tends to increase over time in REST, and individuals who are the most stressed by the reduced-stimulation environment tend to move the most (Myers et al., 1966). These findings imply that response restriction is one of the contributors to the motivational consequences of REST. This hypothesis is supported by evidence that extreme immobilization even when there is no interference with input modalities has the same effect as global stimulus reduction (Zubek, 1969b), and that physical exercise can counteract some of the negative effects of REST (Zubek, 1973).

However, most of the evidence is concerned with the stimulus-hunger aspect of motivation. The evidence is overwhelming that REST does increase the desire for stimulation. In the very first studies (Scott, Bexton, Heron, & Doane, 1959), confined subjects continued to request repetitious presentations of extremely boring material, such as excerpts from children's primers and old stock market reports. Such material was avoided by control subjects. More recently, Leckart and his colleagues have shown that even a brief period of stimulus deprivation in a given modality increases the subject's operant rate for prolonging stimulation in that modality. Leckart's team established this phenomenon with auditory (Levine, Pettit, & Leckart, 1973) and tactile (Yaremko, Glanville, Rofer, & Leckart, 1972) deprivation and stimulation. Several studies, both by this group and by others, have demonstrated the same phenomenon in the visual modality (Bearwald, 1976; Drake & Herzog, 1974; Leckart, Glanville, Hootstein, Keleman, & Yaremko, 1972; Leckart, Levine, Goscinski, & Brayman, 1970).

In contrast with Leckart, who used complex visual stimuli, a series of experiments by Jones and others (reviewed in Jones, 1969) used sequences of lights varying in color and tones varying in pitch. Once again, the subjects' desire to see a light sequence was a function of preexposure REST duration. But Jones and his colleagues went beyond this to look at specific stimulus variables affecting the motivational consequences of REST. After several experiments, they drew the conclusion that the most important variable is predictability. Maximum incentive value was associated with the least predictable sequences. Furthermore, high levels of exposure to unpredictable sequences resulted in greater preference for predictable ones, another finding that was constant in various modalities (Jones, 1969; Rogers, 1975). Evidence for central mediation also appeared. For example, satiation with visual information reduced the desire for auditory information, and the converse was true as well. Jones's definition of information value as the inverse of predictability has become standard in the field. Unfortunately, the incentive value of other collative variables was not investigated.

However, the term "information" is perhaps even more useful in thinking about the response to meaningful inputs than in the purely formal sense used by Jones. I have already referred to the early McGill findings concerning information deprivation and consequent desire for information; later research has shown that the incentive values and positive ratings of stimuli are related to predictability and meaningfulness in somewhat complex ways. There was one study using only two hours of stimulus restriction, in which the relationship was the same as with Jones's meaningless stimuli (Rossi, Nathan, Harrison, & Solomon, 1969). In an experiment lasting 24 hours, scrambled words that presented a challenging cognitive puzzle were preferred to both standard meaningful phrases and highly randomized assortments of letters (Landon & Suedfeld, 1969). In studies of individual differences, personality variables related to global stimulus need (Gale, 1969; Lambert & Levy, 1972) and to more specific information orientation (Levin & Brody, 1974; Suedfeld, 1964; Suedfeld & Vernon, 1966) significantly mediated the motivational consequences of stimulus reduction.

Nonexperimental Stimulus Restriction

In environments of monotonous and/or reduced stimulation other than experimental settings, such as long-duration confinement in prison cells, hospitals, submarines, polar stations, or spacecraft, or in such less dramatic circumstances as performing a boring and repetitious job (e.g., on an assembly line), performance decrements may result from stimulus hunger (which may be conceptualized in these cases as the need for variation, challenge, and novelty). It has been argued that impaired task performance, interpersonal conflict, and even deliberate violence, sabotage, and malingering may result (Frankenhaeuser & Johansson, 1974; Suedfeld, 1978). Job enrichment, task rotation, work teams, and the introduction of new and varied stimuli into the working and off-duty environment are all methods whose goal is to avoid such adverse affects. This can be done by introducing new social and physical configurations, by providing higher levels of stimulation in off-duty facilities, by making the diet and other ancillary factors more varied, or by coupling more optimal stimulation levels with improved performance. However, most people even in total institutions or other generally restricted environments are probably able to restore approximately optimal levels of stimulation through their own efforts.

APPLICATIONS OF REST: THE USES OF STIMULUS HUNGER

Information need has been invoked in a number of studies that explored the effects of REST on persuasibility, and more recently in research testing the usefulness of environmental restriction as a therapeutic technique.

Effects on Persuasion

Besides the willingness to listen to normally boring and aversive material, the earliest McGill studies demonstrated that confined subjects, who requested to hear propaganda messages about the reality of psychic phenomena more frequently than controls, also came to accept the arguments presented in those messages (Bexton, 1953). Similar data were obtained by a number of other researchers (reviewed in Suedfeld, 1969, 1980). For example, Myers, Murphy, and Smith (1963) found a generally greater desire for hearing persuasive messages (in this case concerning

Turkey) on the part of restricted subjects. However, only the less intelligent members of this group showed increased persuasibility. Suedfeld and Vernon (1966) presented each of their messages only once, but made the presentation of the next message contingent on stated agreement with the previous one. REST subjects showed more compliance than controls. Among the experimental group, subjects who were relatively high in information orientation (conceptual complexity) were particularly compliant, but showed no more actual attitude change than their less information-directed fellows.

Therapeutic Uses

A large number of other studies have presented various types of messages to patients in stimulus-impoverished environments and have reported positive results. Improved self-concept, lower scores on clinical scales of the MMPI, and similar changes among psychiatric patients have been found (Adams, 1980). More successful smoking cessation, greater adherence to dieting and exercise, better rapport and communication with therapists, more adaptive social interaction and learning among autistic children, and other such phenomena, have been reliably observed (Suedfeld, 1980). Some of the researcher–therapists involved in this work have proceeded explicitly from the hypothesis that clinical progress would result as a function of stimulus hunger arising from sensory reduction (e.g., Adams, 1980; Gibby, Adams, & Carrera, 1960). However, the hypothesis that the therapeutic effect is in fact mediated by this particular type of motivational arousal has not been unequivocally upheld (Suedfeld, 1972).

There is, however, one series of studies clearly supporting the view that stimulus hunger facilitates therapy. Here, rather than verbal messages, slides depicting snakes were shown to snake-phobic subjects. Not only did the REST participants emit operant responses in order to see the slides (which in the normal environment tended to be aversive), but both verbal and behavior signs of snake fear and aversion showed significant reductions at the end of the session. These reductions were accompanied by appropriate psychophysiological changes (Suedfeld & Hare, 1977). Furthermore, in agreement with Jones's (1969) theory, positive effects were significantly greater when the slides were presented in a random order of verisimilitude. In contrast, increasing realism was more effective among control subjects, in accordance with the general procedure used by behavior therapists using desensitization (Suedfeld & Buchanan, 1974).

Arousal and the Applications of REST

To bring the discussion full circle, alternative explanations of thera-peutic effects of REST include the proposition that increased arousal is the, or at least one, crucial mediating variable. The argument is that superoptimal arousal leads to the impairment of cognitive performance, as has already been discussed; that resistance to persuasion is one kind of complex cognitive task; and that such resistance is therefore impaired by REST, leading to greater persuasibility both in purely experimental and in therapeutic settings (Suedfeld, 1972).

This hypothesis is supported by data that other sources of high arousal increase openness to therapeutic intervention (e.g., Hoehn-Saric, Liberman, Imber, Stone, Pande, & Frank, 1972). As usual, however, other workers have argued that the potency of clinical techniques is increased by low arousal (Wickramasekera, 1978). Once again we may resurrect the familiar U-shaped function, a tactic that leaves the question of the relationship between REST and arousal level still unanswered; or, from a more pragmatic point of view, we may suspend the debate and carry on with the empirical research.

SUMMARY

There is no doubt that environments that are either monotonous or low in stimulation lead to important motivational changes in human beings. Under some circumstances, these phenomena may have undesir-able consequences. These changes may be summarized by the term "stimulus–action hunger." Alterations of arousal level may be a mediat-ing variable. However, the data are mixed as to the direction of such alterations, and different indices of arousal show inconsistent results.

Researchers have found that changes in the reaction to various kinds of stimuli, and resultant effects on cognitive processes and persuasibility, can be put to use in improving the effectiveness of therapeutic interven-tions. A wide variety of such applications has been reported with both children and adults, ranging from the treatment of psychotic inpatients to facilitating self-management of behavior patterns that affect health maintenance (Suedfeld, 1980). It is probable that the motivational shifts caused by environmental restriction play a crucial role in such changes. At this moment, the actual scope and potency of this technique have not yet been established. Nor has there been any theoretical formulation that comes even close to giving an adequate explanation of the motivational changes mediating the findings. A more specific elucidation of the concepts of arousal and arousal potential, and the application of some of Berlyne's ideas about these variables and about collative stimulus factors, may be one promising step in this direction.

References

ADAMS, H. B. *Reduced environmental stimulation: Positive research findings vs. negative stereotypes.* Unpublished manuscript, Area C Community Mental Health Center, Washington, D. C., 1979.

ADAMS, H. B. The effects of reduced stimulation on institutionalized adult patients. In P. Suedfeld, *Restricted environmental stimulation: Research and clinical applications.* New York: Wiley, 1980.

BEARWALD, R. R. *The effects of stimulus complexity and perceptual deprivation or stimulus overload on attention to visual stimuli.* Unpublished doctoral dissertation, Indiana University, 1976.

BERLYNE, D. E. *Conflict, arousal, and curiosity.* New York: McGraw-Hill, 1960.

BERLYNE, D. E. Motivational problems raised by exploratory and epistemic behavior. In S. Koch (Ed.), *Psychology: A study of a science* (Vol. 5). New York: McGraw-Hill, 1963.

BEXTON, W. H. *Some effects of perceptual isolation in human subjects.* Unpublished doctoral dissertation, McGill University, 1953.

BEXTON, W. H., HERON, W., & SCOTT, T. H. Effects of decreased variation in the sensory environment. *Canadian Journal of Psychology,* 1954, *8,* 70–76.

BUDZYNSKI, T. H. Biofeedback and the twilight states of consciousness. In G. E. Schwartz & B. Shapiro (Eds.), *Consciousness and self-regulation: Advances in research* (Vol. 1). New York: Plenum, 1976.

CANNON, W. B. *The wisdom of the body.* New York: Norton, 1932.

deCHARMS, R. *Personal causation: The internal affective determinants of behavior.* New York: Academic Press, 1968.

DRAKE, G. L., & HERZOG, T. R. Free-looking time for randomly generated polygons with experimenter present: Effects of content and duration of foreperiod. *Perceptual and Motor Skills,* 1974, *39,* 403–406.

FISKE, D. W., & MADDI, S. R. (Eds.). *Functions of varied experience.* Homewood, Ill.: Dorsey, 1961.

FRANKENHAEUSER, M., & JOHNSSON, G. *On the psychophysiological consequences of understimulation and overstimulation.* Reports of the Psychological Laboratories, University of Stockholm, Supplement No. 25, 1974.

FREUD, S. Instincts and their vicissitudes. In J. Strachey (Ed.), *The collected papers of Sigmund Freud.* London: Hogarth, 1957. (Originally published, 1915.)

GALE, A. "Stimulus hunger": Individual differences in operant strategy in a button-pressing task. *Behaviour Research and Therapy,* 1969, *7,* 265–274.

GIBBY, R. J., ADAMS, H. P., & CARRERA, R. N. Therapeutic changes in psychiatric patients following partial sensory deprivation. *Archives of General Psychiatry,* 1960, *3,* 33–42.

HARLOW, H. Learning and satiation of response in intrinsically motivated complex puzzle performance by monkeys. *Journal of Comparative and Physiological Psychology,* 1950, *43,* 289–294.

HEBB, D. O. Drives and the CNS (Conceptual Nervous System). *Psychological Review,* 1955, *62,* 243–254.

HERON, W. Cognitive and physiological effects of perceptual isolation. In P. Solomon, P. E. Kubzansky, P. H. Leiderman, J. H. Mendelson, R. Trumbull, & D. Wexler (Eds.), *Sensory deprivation.* Cambridge: Harvard University Press, 1961.

HOEHN-SARIC, R., LIBERMAN, B., IMBER, S. D., STONE, A. R., PANDE, S. K., & FRANK, J. D. Arousal and attitude change in neurotic patients. *Archives of General Psychiatry*, 1972, *26*, 51–56.

HULL, C. L. *Principles of behavior*. New York: Appleton-Century-Crofts, 1943.

JACKSON, C. W., JR., & POLLARD, J. C. Sensory deprivation and suggestion: A theoretical approach. *Behavioral Science*, 1962, *7*, 332–342.

JONES, A. Stimulus-seeking behavior. In J. P. Zubek (Ed.), *Sensory deprivation: Fifteen years of research*. New York: Appleton-Century-Crofts, 1969.

KUBZANSKY, P. E., & LEIDERMAN, P. H. Sensory deprivation: An overview. In P. Solomon, P. E. KUBZANSKY, P. H. LEIDERMAN, J. H. MENDELSON, R. TRUMBULL, & D. WEXLER (Eds.), *Sensory deprivation*. Cambridge: Harvard University Press, 1961.

LACEY, J. I. Somatic response patterning and stress: Some revisions of activation theory. In M. H. Appley & R. Trumbull (Eds.), *Psychological stress*. New York: Appleton-Century-Crofts, 1967.

LAMBERT, W., & LEVY, L. H. Sensation-seeking and short-term sensory isolation. *Journal of Personality and Social Psychology*, 1972, *24*, 46–52.

LANDON, P. B., & SUEDFELD, P. Information and meaningfulness needs in sensory deprivation. *Psychonomic Science*, 1969, *17*, 248.

LANDON, P. B., & SUEDFELD, P. Complex cognitive performance and sensory deprivation: Completing the U–curve. *Perceptual and Motor Skills*, 1972, *34*, 601–602.

LANDON, P. B., & SUEDFELD, P. Complexity as multi-dimensional perception: The effects of sensory deprivation on concept identification. *Bulletin of the Psychonomic Society*, 1977, *10*, 137–138.

LECKART, P. T., LEVINE, J. R., GOSCINSKI, C., & BRAYMAN, W. Duration of attention: The perceptual deprivation effect. *Perception and Psychophysics*, 1970, *7*, 163–164.

LECKART, P. T., GLANVILLE, B., HOOTSTEIN, E., KELMAN, K., & YAREMKO, R. M. Looking time, stimulus complexity, and the perceptual deprivation effect. *Psychonomic Science*, 1972, *26*, 107–108.

LEVIN, J., & BRODY, N. Information-deprivation and creativity. *Psychological Reports*, 1974, *35*, 231–237.

LEVINE, J. R., PETTIT, A., & LECKART, B. T. Listening time and the short-term perceptual deprivation effect. *Bulletin of the Psychonomic Society*, 1973, *1*, 11–12.

LILLY, J. Mental effects of reduction of ordinary levels of physical stimuli on intact, healthy persons. *Psychiatric Research Reports*, 1956, *5*, 1–9.

LILLY, J. *The deep self*. New York: Simon & Schuster, 1977.

LINDSLEY, D. B. Common factors in sensory deprivation, sensory distortion, and sensory overload. In P. Solomon, P. E. Kubzansky, P. H. Leiderman, J. H. Mendelson, R. Trumbull, & D. Wexler (Eds.), *Sensory deprivation*. Cambridge: Harvard University Press, 1961.

LONDON, H., SCHUBERT, D. S. P., & WASHBURN, D. Increase of autonomic arousal by boredom. *Journal of Abnormal Psychology*, 1978, *80*, 29–36.

MILLER, G. A., GALANTER, E., & PRIBRAM, K. H. *Plans and the structure of behavior*. New York: Holt, 1960.

MYERS, T. I. Tolerance for sensory and perceptual deprivation. In J. P. Zubek (Ed.), *Sensory deprivation: Fifteen years of research*. New York: Appleton-Century-Crofts, 1969.

MYERS, T. I., MURPHY, D. B., & SMITH, S. *The effect of sensory deprivation and social isolation on self-exposure to propaganda and attitude change*. Paper read at the meeting of the American Psychological Association, September 1963.

MYERS, T. I., MURPHY, D. B., & SMITH, S., & GOFFARD, S. J. *Experimental studies of sensory deprivation and social isolation*. Washington, D. C.: Human Resources Research Office Technical Report 66–8, George Washington University, 1966.

Orne, M. T., & Scheibe, K. E. The contribution of non-deprivation factors in the production of sensory deprivation effects: The psychology of the panic button. *Journal of Abnormal and Social Psychology*, 1964, *68*, 3–12.

Rogers, D. L. *Information-seeking behavior in the tactile modality*. Unpublished doctoral dissertation, Arizona State University, 1975.

Rossi, A. M., & Solomon, P. Button-pressing for a time-off reward during sensory deprivation. *Perceptual and Motor Skills*, 1964, *18*, 211–216.

Rossi, A. M., Nathan, P. E., Harrison, R. H., & Solomon, P. Operant responding for visual stimuli during sensory deprivation: Effect of meaningfulness. *Journal of Abnormal Psychology*, 1969, *74*, 188–192.

Schultz, D. P. *Sensory restriction: Effects on behavior*. New York: Academic Press, 1965.

Sheffield, F. D., & Roby, T. B. Reward value of a non-nutritive sweet taste. *Journal of Comparative and Physiological Psychology*, 1950, *43*, 471–481.

Sheffield, F. D., Wulff, J. J., & Backer, R. Reward value of copulation without sex drive reduction. *Journal of Comparative and Physiological Psychology*, 1951, *44*, 3–8.

Scott, T. H., Bexton, W. H., Heron, W., & Doane, B. K. Cognitive effects of perceptual isolation. *Canadian Journal of Psychology*, 1959, *13*, 200–209.

Suedfeld, P. Conceptual structure and subjective stress in sensory deprivation. *Perceptual and Motor Skills*, 1964, *19*, 896–898.

Suedfeld, P. Changes in intellectual performance and in susceptibility to influence. In J. P. Zubek (Ed.), *Sensory deprivation: Fifteen years of research*. New York: Appleton-Century-Crofts, 1969.

Suedfeld, P. *Attitude manipulation in restricted environments: V. Theory and research*. Paper read at the International Congress of Psychology, Tokyo, July 1972.

Suedfeld, P. Using environmental restriction to initiate long term behavior change. In R. B. Stuart (Ed.), *Behavioral self-management: Strategies, techniques and outcomes*. New York: Brunner/Mazel, 1977.

Suedfeld, P. Characteristics of decision-making as a function of the environment. In B. King, S. Streufert, & F. E. Fiedler (Eds.), *Managerial control and organizational democracy*. Washington, D. C.: Winston, 1978.

Suedfeld, P. Stressful levels of environmental stimulation. In I. G. Sarason & C. D. Spielberger (Eds.), *Stress and anxiety* (Vol. 6). Washington, D. C.: Hemisphere, 1979.

Suedfeld, P. *Restricted environmental stimulation: Research and clinical applications*. New York: Wiley, 1980.

Suedfeld, P., & Buchanan, E. Sensory deprivation and autocontrolled aversive stimulation in the reduction of snake avoidance. *Canadian Journal of Behavioural Science*, 1974, *6*, 105–111.

Suedfeld, P., & Hare, R. D. Sensory deprivation in the treatment of snake phobia: Behavioural, self-report, and physiological effects. *Behavior Therapy*, 1977, *8*, 240–250.

Suedfeld, P., & Vernon, J. Attitude manipulation in restricted environments: II. Conceptual structure and the internalization of propaganda received as a reward for compliance. *Journal of Personality and Social Psychology*, 1966, *3*, 586–589.

Tarjan, G. Sensory deprivation and mental retardation. In L. Madow & L. H. Snow (Eds.), *The psychodynamic implication of physiological studies on sensory deprivation*. Springfield, Ill.: Charles C. Thomas, 1970.

Vernon, J., & McGill, T. E. Utilization of visual stimulation during sensory deprivation. *Perceptual and Motor Skills*, 1960, *11*, 214.

Wickramasekera, I. *Psychophysiological stress reduction procedures and a suggestion hypothesis: Sensory restriction and low arousal training*. Paper read at the meeting of the American Psychological Association, Toronto, September 1978.

Yaremko, R. M., Glanville, B., Rofer, C. P., & Leckart, B. T. Tactile stimulation and the short-term perceptual deprivation effect. *Psychonomic Science,* 1972, *26,* 89–90.

ZUBEK, J. P. (Ed.). *Sensory deprivation: Fifteen years of research.* New York: Appleton-Century-Crofts, 1969.(a)

ZUBEK, J. P. Sensory and perceptual-motor effects. In J. P. Zubek (Ed.), *Sensory deprivation: Fifteen years of research.* New York: Appleton-Century-Crofts, 1969.(b)

ZUBEK, J. P. Behavioral and physiological effects of prolonged sensory and perceptual deprivation: A review. In J. E. Rasmussen (Ed.), *Man in isolation and confinement.* Chicago: Aldine, 1973.

ZUCKERMAN, M. Theoretical formulations: I. In J. P. Zubek (Ed.), *Sensory deprivation: Fifteen years of research.* New York: Appleton-Century-Crofts, 1969.

ZUCKERMAN, M., & HABER, M. M. Need for stimulation as a source of stress response to perceptual isolation. *Journal of Abnormal Psychology,* 1965, *70,* 371–377.

Explorations of Exploration

JUM C. NUNNALLY

Initially let me rapidly dispense with some matters concerning human (more generally, mammalian) exploratory activity that would not be worth extensive discussion. First, it would be no feat at all to find long quotations from famous men in antiquity, such as Plato or Confucius, who bespoke the importance of exploratory activity (by the same or other names) in man and animals, illustrated the phenomena with their observations, and stated some straightforward principles which are still at the heart of "modern" theory on the topic.

Second, I shall not preach about a "shameful neglect" of exploration as a topic for theory and research, because if I did I would be lying. As will be mentioned more fully later in a brief historical summary of the last 140 years, the topic was neglected for a while; but, since about 1955, numerous prominent psychologists and persons in kindred fields have sounded the clarion call regarding the prominent place of exploratory activity in the overall lives of men and other animals; and many researchers have been busy since that time performing experiments, and writing extensively on the topic in diverse places. This is evidenced in the bibliography for this chapter, the more extensive bibliographies in some of the articles listed there by myself and my colleagues, and the bibliographies throughout this book.

Third, it would be both trite and somewhat illegitimate with respect to the rules which govern the game of science to attempt inversely to aggrandize the importance of exploratory activity by going into great detail as to why such activity cannot be explained by simplistic theories of classical and instrumental conditioning. Most typically, this attack has been by way of mentioning activities that apparently cannot be explained by, or that apparently contradict, the theory(s) being attacked—examples

---

JUM C. NUNNALLY • Department of Psychology, Vanderbilt University, Nashville, Tennessee 37240.

being as follows. Why do people rack their brains solving crossword puzzles when they could just relax? Why would a person spend hours searching a shoreline for interesting bits of flotsam and jetsam, when the objects obtained are almost always of no monetary value? Why would a person take the equivalent of a month's pay from hard work to drive with his family one thousand miles just to gaze at the Grand Canyon? Why would a hungry child stave off going home for dinner while he is taking apart and exploring each piece of a discarded alarm clock?

The fourth matter that I shall not belabor is that of giving a tight, data-bound definition of exploratory activity. I am purposely using the word "activity" rather than the word "behavior," because I am as much concerned with the covert aspects of exploration as with the overtly observable aspects, if not more so. To escape criticism, most scientists who fall into the trap of trying to give a brief but comprehensive definition of a complex topic do so by couching their definition in terms at one or the other extreme of a continuum relating to specificity versus generality. The eventual definition either is so specific in terms of data-related language that it gets at only a very limited aspect of the topic, or, at the other extreme, the definition is so general and abstract that it covers everything possible in the topic under consideration, but really says nothing that the experimentally minded scientist can lay his hands on. Exploratory activity is not *one* circumscribed form of overt behavior that can be neatly defined; rather, the term "exploration" refers to a variety of kindred psychological processes that must be picked apart and studied individually. Distinctions among such activities, illustrations of them, and relevant experimental methods and results will be discussed throughout this chapter.

Before getting at the meat and bones of exploratory activity, let me say a word about Daniel Berlyne; then, at the end of the chapter, I shall pay a most warmly-felt tribute to this great man. Unquestionably, Dan was the "father" of modern theory and experimentation concerning exploratory activity. Although I admired him deeply and maintained a long comradeship with him, we frequently disagreed, in direct conversation and in print, about theories concerning exploration and the interpretation of extant experimental findings. Some of these disagreements will become evident in the pages ahead. What I should like to mention here is that it was only several years before his death that he and I came to realize that, right or wrong, frequently we were talking about different aspects of the problem. Subsequently, I shall discuss in detail a comprehensive scheme that includes the major constructs that were important in Berlyne's theorizing about exploratory behavior, my points of view, and the salient constructs in the theoretical positions of other people.

SOME HISTORICAL MILESTONES IN THE STUDY OF EXPLORATORY BEHAVIOR

Ignoring the many individuals who have made observations about and written about exploratory behavior through the centuries, we shall pick up the scene circa 1850, and mention briefly the impact of a number of lines of theory and research that are epitomized by well-known proponents (so well-known that no references will be required). In 1850, Gustav Fechner was working away on the development of a new subdiscipline, *psychophysics*, the goal of which was the development of scientifically acceptable measurement methods for probing the human mind. In the course of this work, he developed or refined numerous techniques for gathering data (e.g., the method of paired comparisons), with simple mathematical models for transforming the results into unidimensional scales of measurement, and demonstrated the applicability of emerging knowledge about statistical methods to data obtained from his own experiments. As is usually the mark of a creative innovator, Fechner's technical developments during his own lifetime are not nearly so important as the immense impact that he had on psychology and kindred emerging disciplines. Fechner's vision of scientifically acceptable mental measurement and his demonstration of workable technology laid the groundwork for modern psychometrics, which is important in the development of both independent and dependent variables in the study of exploratory behavior, as well as in the behavioral sciences more generally.

The second reason why it is important to remember Fechner in discussing the historical roots of exploratory behavior is that he was very much interested in the study of aesthetics; but, unlike so many persons going back many hundreds of years before him, he also made an effort to do something about it through actual research. Even though his efforts in this regard were on a rather small scale and he never found much of a substantial nature, his work did encourage future generations to attempt further scientific investigations of the topic. This is important for exploratory behavior, because aesthetics is closely related to exploratory behavior.

At approximately the same time that Fechner was developing "from scratch" the field of psychophysics, Charles Darwin was gathering massive evidence for organic evolution, and trying to explain it by a mechanism of "natural selection." Because of his impressive work in this regard, it is easy to forget the much wider array of contributions that he made as a naturalist, for example, the study of facial expressions and other overt signs of emotion in man and other animals; also, although he made no frontal attack on the problem, one can find throughout his writings numerous mentions of the phenomena that we would classify today as types of exploratory behavior. Regarding the latter consideration, he pondered why some animals spent considerable time playing and exploring the environment in ways that did not obviously relate to "survival of the fittest." As with Fechner, perhaps as important as his own personal contributions was the interest that he kindled in scholars for the study of animal behavior. During the last decades of the nineteenth century, many gentlemen scholars became naturalists rather than invest their energies in other scientific pursuits or the humanities. In turn, this interest in the natural behavior of animals evolved into the ethology of this century, one aspect of which is the study of exploratory behavior.

Darwin had a marked influence on psychology, but this was largely related to inspiring Sir Francis Galton and others to take the first steps toward developing a technology of mental testing and to apply such tests on behalf of the systematic investigation of individual differences in human traits. Galton was very much interested in the heritability of human traits, and, as the reader knows, he founded the eugenics movement in England. Of primary interest to Galton and his colleagues (e.g., Karl Pearson) was the heritability of various types of mental traits. The tests concerned very simple sensory, perceptual, and motor functions; and the persons who followed Galton in such studies of individual differences also worked with such simple processes up to the first decade of the twentieth century. Then Binet, Spearman, and others began to develop a wide variety of measures relating to richer human mental processes. However, even to this day the study of individual differences has had very little to say or do about intrinsic motivation or exploratory behavior as a part thereof. (We have found some interesting correlations among individual differences in exploration as incidental results in experiments; for example, males tend to look longer at *all* of our stimuli than females do.) Even in modern times very little is being done about studies of individual differences with respect to amount and style of exploratory activity.

Many introductory textbooks speak of Wilhelm Wundt as the first true experimental psychologist—which, of course, one could dispute. The man was so extremely prolific and broad in his interests and writings that, were I to read some of the thousands of pages that he put into print, I surely would find something quite directly related to exploratory behavior; however, his actual experimentation consisted of studies concerning simple sensory, motor, and perceptual functions, as, for example, reaction time under various circumstances. Most of the persons who worked in his laboratory (and this included many men who later became famous as experimental psychologists in their own right) picked up this interest and technical know-how of "brass instrument" research rather than following Wundt's many other diverse interests and theories (e.g., he had many interesting ideas about psycholinguistics). However, there was nothing in this form of research that directly concerned intrinsic motivation or exploratory behavior as a subpart; and the same has remained true to this day of many persons who work with simple processes concerning memory, reaction time, sensation, elementary forms of learning, and perceptual judgment.

Partly in antipathy to the "brass instrument" approach, and the subsequent effort to resolve conscious states into elementary components, as typified by Titchener and his followers, there developed a variety of forms of psychological theory which were more holistically concerned with the psychology of how man adjusts to his environment. This movement began in the 1880s and was identified in the early days with such persons as Stout in England and Dewey in the United States. During the first twenty years of the current century, there was considerable research as well as psychologizing about the matter, as evidenced in the education-related studies of problem solving in cats and other animals by E. L. Thorndike, studies of education by Dewey, and, along with Dewey and others, the overall research activity of the so-called "functionalist school" that was centered at the University of Chicago at the time. Much of the theorizing and subsequent research by the functionalists (held together more by a name than a unified point of view) was relevant to exploratory behavior and vice versa, but I have never seen any writings specifically on the topic, and little if anything was done to study either overt exploratory behavior or the underlying covert processes.

Circa 1920, both introspectionism and functionalism were shoved from the scene by the behaviorist movement, which, oddly enough, was championed by John Waltson, who did his graduate training under the foremost of functionalists at Chicago. He advocated a psychology that would expunge all introspective analyses and mentalistic constructs; instead, all data must be codified as directly observable, overt behavior (which construed broadly is a scientific must), and all theories about such data must contain no constructs which themselves are not semantically "tied down" directly to simple observable events (a standpoint which is oppositional to the necessities and ultimate purpose of all science). This hyperoperationalism dominated the scene in experimental psychology from about 1920 until the early fifties. Only those studies were performed that concerned simple, observable events in motor skills, sensation, perception, and the "queen" of activities during this period—rat-running.

Many famous men emerged during this period of "behaviorism," such as the greatest rat-runner of them all—Clark Hull. In this research, there was an emphasis on all the scientific niceties of careful design, measurement, and analysis; and many of the findings were valuable, and served as foundation stones for more comprehensive theories and modes of investigation later. But, in retrospect, it is hard to see how we took all this so seriously as representing inquiries into the things that we most want to know about human thought and action.

There were dissenters to this reductionistic make-believe: for example, Tolman explicitly included constructs concerning intrinsic motivation in his theories of learning, and directly studied exploratory behavior at choice points in mazes; and Kurt Lewin studied exploratory behavior, and promoted the research of one of his doctorial students in documenting the now famous Zeigarnick effect, which is directly related to my own conceptual scheme for exploratory behavior. However, all throughout the forties and lingering into the fifties, if you were a "real" experimental psychologist you were following in the Watson–Hull footsteps of reductionistic hyperoperationalism (which in turn had borrowed much from the work many years before of Pavlov).

Although there had been many dissenters to this behaviorist elementarianism, the revolt became widespread in the 1950s. Part of this was because most of the "rat learning" experimentalists became disillusioned with their own findings and their limited horizons for future experimentation. (Now, the rat-runner's paradigm is dead—it has become a source of independent variables for people interested in various aspects of physiological psychology.) Some of those who still clung to the ultrabehaviorist mentality "fled" into other fields that permitted the same type of theorizing and experimental modus operandi, such as in certain areas of perception, memory, verbal learning, and others—nearly all of this work being done with human beings. Some of the other "refugees," and many good psychological researchers who had never been card-carrying Hullians, opened up exciting new areas of research in human learning, motivation, and adjustment. A concern for intrinsic motivation, and exploratory activity as a part of it, was important in this set of new directions in psychology.

Hebb (1955), whose reputation as a solid experimental psychologist was immense, broke the ice by speaking of the "conceptual nervous system." His thesis was that the brain is an "acting" system rather than a "reacting" system, and he spoke of many forms of motivation that could not be explained by simple need reduction. He mentioned many types of intrinsic motivation that are required to explain human and animal activity. Near the same time, Dan Berlyne reawakened the field of psychology from its dormancy regarding the importance of exploratory behavior (e.g., 1954, 1957). In Berlyne's 1960 book, he placed exploratory activity (freely interchanging the term with curiosity as the underlying motive) in perspective with the field of psychology as a whole, made many important distinctions that are still with us, borrowed heavily from information theory and physiological psychology, demonstrated simple but workable procedures of experimentation, and described the interesting results that had been obtained to date. This is when the psychological investigation of exploratory activity really got under way—with Dan's 1960 book. Everyone who is reading these pages knows the story from that point on. Many psychologists became interested in methods of investigation, numerous theoretical positions have appeared in print, and much research has been undertaken. Let us turn now and look at what has happened since that 1960 milestone in terms of theory, data-gathering techniques, experimental paradigms, results, and, finally, fruitful directions for the future.

COMPONENTS OF EXPLORATORY BEHAVIOR

One of the major impediments to developing theories regarding exploratory behavior and formulating experiments to test those theories has been the absence of any comprehensive classification scheme for the subprocesses involved. As is usually the case with a new scientific problem, there has been a tendency to put into one category a wide variety of phenomena and refer to them all as constituting exploratory behavior. Then, as is usually the case in science, several simple notions were proposed to explain this wide variety of behaviors.

Berlyne (1960) made an important distinction, namely that between *specific* and *diversive* exploratory behavior. The former refers to exploratory behavior in relation to a particular stimulus, for example, a fox encountering a red balloon blown from a backyard to some faraway field. Diversive exploratory behavior is concerned with seeking stimulus change motivated by boredom with the present environment. I would like to add a third category which involves exploratory activity and other processes as well, namely that of *searching activity*. Examples are a dog searching for a bone that he has buried, a man looking around the house for a misplaced set of keys, and the more covert searching of a composer for the most appropriate next notes of a song. These are important distinctions, because, as will be seen later, these types of behavior relate to different theoretical propositions and different types of experimentation. Other investigators have made subdivisions of these important distinctions and have added other categories (e.g., those proposed by Hutt, 1970).

What has been lacking in the efforts to subdivide all exploratory behavior into meaningful categories is a temporal scheme that articulates the various processes in relation to one another. An attempt to do that for some types of exploration is depicted in Figure 1. Presented here is a series of observed classes of behaviors and correlated covert processes that are intended to cover in a broad way the domain of what is involved in exploratory behavior. It is proposed that throughout life there is an endless cycle of encountering a stimulus that initiates the sequence depicted in Figure 1. When a different stimulus configuration is encountered and elicits attention, the cycle starts over again, runs itself out, and so on, endlessly. Of course, it must be recognized that such sequences interact in very complex ways with other sequences, such as (1) cycles of sleep and alertness, (2) socially induced patterns of activity, such as the routine aspects of the daily life of a school child, and (3) cycles of waxing and waning tissue needs. Also, there are many activities under the rubric of exploration that either do not fit the scheme at all, or that do not proceed in the stepwise fashion which is depicted. The scheme is particularly relevant to an encounter with a novel object.

In Figure 1 the presumed covert processes purposefully are shown to overlap the various stages concerning observed behavior. Thus, the first phase of encoding extends beyond the behavioral phase of perceptual investigation, into the phase of manipulatory behavior. Similarly, the phase of behavior concerning play activity goes beyond the covert process of autistic thinking, into the covert process of boredom.

In Figure 1 not all stimuli encountered by the organism elicit exploratory behavior. The stimulus must have certain properties (e.g., some type of novelty) before the proposed sequence of behaviors will be relevant. Later in this chapter, considerable attention will be given to the stimulus attributes that tend to instigate this temporal sequence of responses. The discussion here will use novel objects as examples of stimuli that instigate the processes depicted in Figure 1. Examples of such novel objects are the red balloon to a fox, a very unusual automobile for an adult, and a box that makes strange noises when a button is pushed by a child. On such encounters, typically the first behavior to be noted is related to orienting. This is seen in terms of orienting receptors toward the novel source of stimulation, for example, turning of the head toward the object and fixation of the eyes on the object. Here orienting behavior is meant to refer only to the first several seconds of behavior—the immediate state of activation described by Sokolov (1963), as manifested in heart rate, changes in brain waves, and other processes relating to providing an overall, immediate heightening of attention to the presence of the object.

Following, and blending into, the stage of orienting behavior is the stage of perceptual investigation. This would consist behaviorally of such acts as staring at the object, circling it to obtain different perspec-

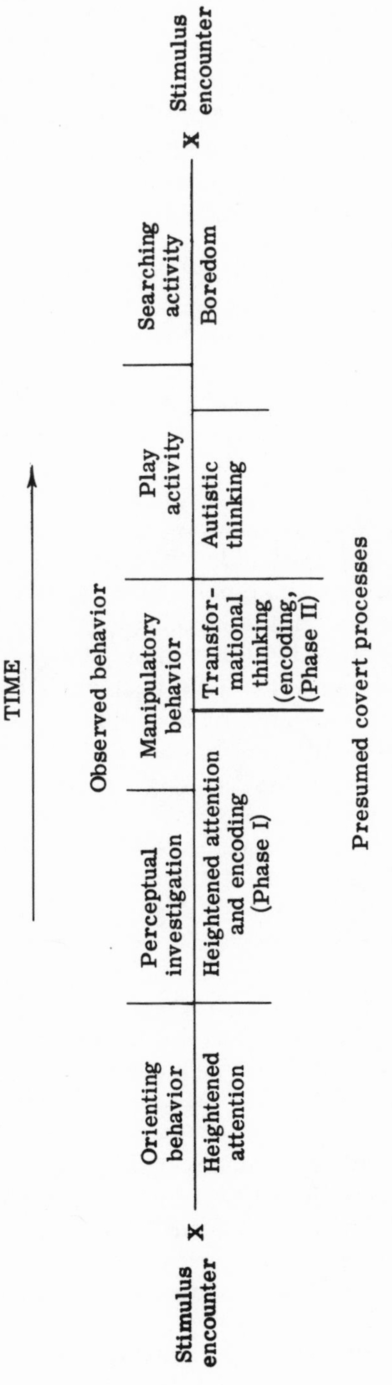

FIGURE 1. A temporal scheme of exploratory behavior.

tives, and putting an ear to a sound source. The covert processes corresponding to perceptual investigation are continued attention, and, more important, the beginning of a process of encoding. As the term is being used here, encoding consists of a hierarchical process that concerns the attributing of meaning to a stimulus, which will be discussed in detail later. The first stage—heightened attention corresponding to orienting behavior—is defined in terms of the sheer recognition of the object's presence. In the subsequent stage of perceptual investigation, the heightened attention is in relation to giving meaning to the stimulus, in the sense of identifying and categorizing the object. For example, the man who encounters a strange automobile categorizes it as being a custom-built vehicle made in Italy. The child who encounters a tangle of wires and variously colored small parts categorizes it as probably being a much abused pocket radio or something of the like. If the covert process in this stage is not successfully terminated, subsequent behavioral stages do not occur. This would be the situation if the early part of the perceptual investigation evoked fear. An example would be a cat rounding the corner of a house and meeting a bulldog that had been clothed by children in a green hat, pink bootees, and other unusual garments. This certainly would be a novel stimulus, but the aspects of the stimulus configuration relating to the bulldog would be sufficient to put the cat in retreat before any continued efforts at perceptual investigation were made. However, as will be argued more fully later, most stimuli that evoke exploratory behavior are capable of dominating emotional states, and thus maintain the animal through at least the first two stages of observed behavior listed in Figure 1.

After perceptual investigation leads to a partial encoding of the stimulus, frequently a stage of manipulatory behavior ensues. The man encountering the unusual automobile might circle it, noting special features, open the door to look inside, sit down and try the gears, and engage in other such manipulatory behavior. On first encounter with a large ball of clay that bounced when dropped, the manipulatory phase for a child might consist of taking the clay apart and making small pieces, testing to see if they also bounced, smelling the clay, and making various figures with it.

During the stage of manipulatory behavior, the covert process of encoding continues. This in turn changes to a broader mental speculation about the object in terms of its origin, its usefulness, its relation to other objects in the environment, and other such distal speculations regarding the place of the object in the overall cognitive domain of the individual. This can be referred to as transformational thinking or "Phase II" of encoding.

Blending into the end of the stage of manipulatory behavior is a set of activities which is best referred to as play. No hard and fast distinction can be made between these two phases, but play activity gives the appearance of being far less directed toward learning about the object in any sense, and more toward using the object for some pleasant activity. For the child, this might consist of rebounding the ball of bouncing clay off a wall and catching it. For the child who encountered the remains of a transistor radio, play activity might consist of idly pulling apart the different pieces, stacking them into groups of objects of the same color, and subsequently tossing the pieces at a nearby bucket.

In play activity, as contrasted with manipulatory behavior, the covert process is referred to as autistic thinking because it is not largely concerned with cognizing the object in terms of elementary encoding processes or in terms of what was referred to as transformational thinking. Rather, during this time either the organism is pleasantly distracted from thinking about the object at all, or the object enters into fantasies. Typically, in this stage of exploratory behavior boredom begins before the play activity ends. The play activity becomes more stereotyped and more monotonous. The adult human, the child, or the lower animal begins to feel ill at ease and "itchy" for new stimulus configurations and new activities (this stage has been referred to by various authors as boredom and/or "need for stimulus change").

As boredom grows in intensity, restlessness leads to searching behavior. The more mature the organism, the less random such searching behavior tends to be; for example, the mature dog has learned that something different probably is occurring in one location rather than another. Regardless of the extent to which the search is random rather than structured in terms of prior learning, eventually the animal encounters another stimulus which has the properties to evoke exploratory behavior, and the sequence is reinstigated.

Obviously, the temporal sequence depicted in Figure 1 must be augmented and further specified in many ways. First, only some objects in the environment induce exploratory behavior. Most investigations of exploratory behavior to date have concerned the stimulus characteristics that initiate this sequence of activities. Second, not all objects that elicit the initial stages of the sequence elicit subsequent stages of manipulatory behavior or play activity. An example was mentioned previously of how a stimulus that had cues for danger would tend to cut short this sequence. In other cases, the stimuli that elicit the earlier parts of the sequence simply do not lend themselves to subsequent parts of the sequence; for example, manipulatory behavior and play activity are not possible with an object that is out of reach. Third, the amount of time spent in each of the successive phases, and the probability of moving from one phase to the next, depend upon the nature of the stimulus, the other stimulus impingements in the environment, organismic states, maturity of the animal, and possibly many other factors. Investigation of all these relations, however, constitutes the challenge to which researchers have addressed themselves—eventually determining the place of exploratory behavior in relation to human behavior in general.

EXPLORATION THROUGH VOLUNTARY VISUAL ATTENTION

By far the largest number of experiments on specific exploration have concerned some aspect of visual attention. Traditionally, most investigations of vision have concerned *directed attention*, in which the subject is instructed to look at a target object and make a judgmental response of some kind. Studies of visual reaction time to various types of words, effects of stimulus intensity on binocular rivalry, and perceived visual motion are some examples. In these and other traditional studies of directed attention, the subject is usually told where to look, what to look for, and how to respond. Allied with this important tradition of studies of directed attention, a new subarea of research has developed—that of *voluntary visual attention* (VVA).

One type of VVA experiment concerns the amount of time spent looking at different objects within a visual field when there are no instructions regarding how attention should be distributed. In other approaches, subjects view displays one at a time, and are allowed freely to control the time looking at each. In essence, VVA concerns "visual browsing," or the "natural" distribution of attention when the subject is not under instructions to look at particular objects, to make judgments about them, or to distribute his or her attention in any other prescribed way.

Studies of VVA are part of an emerging interest in exploratory behavior that has developed over the last 20 years and has been evidenced by a moderate amount of research. Nunnally and Lemond (1973) summarized the place of VVA in an overall model concerning the components of exploratory behavior and presented a theoretical scheme for VVA.

A very simple example from one part of a major investigation (Wilson, 1973) will serve to illustrate a typical study of VVA. The study concerned the effect of the homogeneity versus the heterogeneity of objects. In the most homogeneous display, ten copies of the same face appeared. In the most heterogeneous display, ten different faces appeared. Essentially the subject was allowed to look at each slide as long as he elected, then push a button to move to the next slide. The dependent variable was amount of time in seconds spent viewing each picture. As was expected, heterogeneous displays were viewed longer than homogeneous displays. More complex equipment, procedures, and visual displays are employed in the studies of VVA, but in all cases the subject controls the distribution and duration of attention.

Numerous psychometric issues have been encountered in our studies of VVA. Many of our independent variables concern characteristics of the visual stimuli, such as the effect of novelty on VVA. In earlier studies, simple comparisons were made of drawings of a novel object with drawings of a banal counterpart, for example, a distorted shape of a cow as compared to an ordinary cow. In order to understand more fully the effects of novelty and other stimulus characteristics on VVA, scales were developed to measure degrees of the stimulus characteristic in question. For example, we developed scales to measure novelty at five different levels, and scales to measure physical complexity at many different levels. The development of such scales involved numerous psychometric issues and experiments on scaling.

MAJOR THEORETICAL CONSTRUCTS

By now there are numerous theoretical positions regarding the major determinants of voluntary visual attention, among which are Berlyne (1960, 1966), Dember and Earl (1957), Fiske and Maddi (1961), Fowler (1965), and Nunnally and Lemond (1973). The author and his colleagues began their investigations about ten years ago on the basis of a loosely conceived cognitive point of view which emphasized the *encoding* of the visual stimulus as being primarily important in determining amount of VVA. By the term "encoding" are meant all the subprocesses involved in making sense out of a stimulus—detecting, identifying, recognizing, naming, and associating the visual stimulus with other stimuli "in the mind" of the viewer. Broadly speaking, this is referred to as a *meaning-processing* point of view, which concerns the activity of subjects in attributing meaning to the stimulus regardless of its characteristics.

This essentially cognitive point of view has been opposed to a *motivational* point of view in a variety of experiments. The motivational point of view emphasizes variables such as specific emotional states, general arousal, and tedium. Both the cognitive and the motivational points of view have much to contribute; but a rapprochement is required if VVA is to be investigated productively. The following represents an abbreviated version of our present point of view concerning the major cognitive and motivational constructs relating to VVA.

Cognitive Variables

Information Conflict

Information conflict refers to competing cues for encoding, as we defined encoding above. An example is a drawing of a cow with the trunk of an elephant. To a lesser extent, information conflict occurs at any place in daily life where a visual stimulus, such as a horse standing in the lobby of a hotel, simply does not "fit" into the scheme of what we already know or are accustomed to seeing. It is our hypothesis that information conflict is a powerful determinant of VVA, and usually will dominate any other variable that is present. Discussions of this point of view are given in Nunnally (1972), Nunnally and Lemond (1973), and Nunnally, Lemond, and Wilson (1977).

Number of Representational Elements

A second cognitive variable concerns the number of thinglike objects that can be recognized in a visual display. In studies of random polygons, it became apparent that people were seeing all kinds of things in what had been intended to be random jumbles of lines that varied only in terms of sheer physical complexity. In various psychophysical scalings of these geometrical forms we obtained association hierarchies, naming responses, and ratings of the number of things that could be seen. Highly reliable differences were found among the stimuli in number of things seen, and this variable correlated highly with the complexity of the stimuli as defined in information-theoretic terms. In randomly constructed geometrical forms and in some other materials used to study complexity (e.g., dot patterns), it is best to speak of the thinglike elements as quasi-representational, because they are much like the elements that can be seen in ink-blot tests—that is, portions of the figures remind people of things (e.g., a bird) rather than being directly representative of them. Frequently these quasi-representational elements in visual displays produce some information conflict, which, according to our hypotheses, would further enhance amount of visual exploration.

Complexity of Physical Attributes

In much of our theorizing, the major emphasis was placed on the meaningful components of the visual stimulus as evidenced in the two variables mentioned above, and the purely physical characteristics of the stimuli were deemphasized. This is in contrast to some other authors, who rely heavily on the purely information-theoretic properties of the stimuli rather than on meaning-processing. However, it became apparent that there are some purely physical dimensions of stimuli that are determinants of visual exploration. An example is in our extensive collection of geometrical forms, where it was found that some variance in VVA could be explained by sheer complexity, but not by our other cognitive variables. By sheer complexity we mean physical complexity that one can measure in terms of length, angles, and number of parts, and that can thus be expressed in information-theoretic terms.

Other Physical Attributes

We recognize the possibility that there are other purely physical attributes of stimuli that may be important in determining VVA. Such variables are symmetry, distribution of details in the stimulus configuration, contrast within the stimulus, and others. For example, VVA may be elicited by sharp borders in terms of changes from black to white or from one color to another.

Associations, Cognitive

Part of our overall concept of meaning-processing is that amount of VVA depends on the associates the individual has to the stimulus. Visual displays can be investigated by the typical method of free association, and association hierarchies can be obtained. It was hypothesized that information conflict is present in any display where there are two or more strongly competing associates, a hypothesis which proved subsequently to be the case. However, there are probably many other cognitive aspects of association that are important. For one example, the number of definite associates should act like the number of representational elements to hold VVA. Also, the nature of these associates should be important; for example, the associates themselves might vary in difficulty of encoding. This category is specifically labeled "cognitive" because later we want to mention the importance of affectual associations on VVA.

Signal Characteristics, Cognitive

The term *signal* is being used in its traditional sense to refer to the information that an object supplies about other objects or events. The primary examples are words, as on stop signs, billboards, store fronts, and other places. Nonverbal signals are such as stone or wood markers used by primitive hunters to signal directions, distances, presence of game, or dangers that lay ahead. Berlyne (1971) presents an extensive discussion of the place of such signals in exploratory behavior generally, which includes VVA. Here we distinguish between the cognitive components of such signals and the motivational components (discussed below). We hypothesize that any object with signal characteristics draws and holds VVA. For example, it seems that people are compulsively drawn to read almost any written material that comes before their eyes, notice arrows indicating one-way streets, or gaze at the movements of people that signal some type of activity (e.g., many people crowding into the door of a store). We regard these cognitive aspects of signals as another part of the overall meaning-processing point of view about VVA.

Motivational Variables

The major motivational variables that are considered in our overall conceptual scheme are as follows.

Arousal

The construct of arousal (or activation) is usually indexed in terms of physiological variables, such as electrical activity of the brain, heart rate, cortico-steroid levels in the blood, GSR, and pupillary response. Berlyne (1971) built a theory of exploratory behavior around the concept of arousal. Essentially the major proposition relating to VVA is that there are optimum levels of arousal produced by visual configurations which enhance amount of attention. This optimum level depends on the maturity of the organism, various types of individual differences, organic states at the moment, and numerous characteristics of the stimulus itself. Similar positions have been advocated by Fiske and Maddi (1961), Dember and Earl (1957), and others. All these points of view are discussed well by Berlyne (1971, 1974) in relation to aesthetics.

Specific Emotions

It is hypothesized that the emotions evoked by visual stimuli are important determinants of amount and kinds of VVA. For example, in addition to the other variables that influence VVA, it probably makes a difference whether the visual configuration enduces anger, joy, disgust, sadness, surprise, or some other emotion. Effects of such specific emotions on VVA have not been investigated to date, but will be in the future.

Tedium

Various authors have emphasized the influence of *tedium* or boredom in relation to VVA (e.g., Cantor & Cantor, 1966; Fowler, 1965). It would be more proper to say that tedium potentially explains why a stimulus is *not* afforded much VVA, or why visual exploration wanes. In its simplest form, tedium is expressed as a direct function of exposure time to a particular stimulus. So, the theory goes, tedium becomes conditioned to the stimulus and obeys laws of classical conditioning as regards repeated exposures, intertrial intervals, and extinction over a period of non-reinstatements of tedium. Although earlier studies by the author and his colleagues attempted to explain away any effects of tedium on VVA (e.g., Faw & Nunnally, 1970, 1971), in subsequent investigations (e.g., Lemond, 1973) it gradually became apparent that the concept of tedium might be important, particularly in studies of prior familiarization of stimuli.

Signal Characteristics, Motivational

As has been mentioned, some of the variables that have cognitive implications can also have definite motivational implications. By motivational aspects of signals we mean information that will help the individual safeguard himself from unpleasant events and/or lead him to desired outcomes. The sign on the highway that says "Gas and Restaurant Two Miles Ahead" provides information of potential motivational importance. Nonverbal signals, such as cars backed up on the road ahead or physical signs of ill health, can also have motivational implications. We certainly hypothesize that these motivational implications of signals are important as determinants of VVA.

Associations, Motivational

In addition to their cognitive implications, the motivational implications of visual displays potentially are important in amount of visual exploration. For example, in a painting not only is there information to process, numbers of objects to view, arousal, and the various other determinants of attention, but also what is depicted in the display frequently has motivationally significant associations. There may be reminders of events in childhood, a face resembling an important person in one's life, or an object that brings old memories that induce strong emotions of one type or another. It is probably the case that many of these motivation-related associations are at low levels of consciousness, such as cues that induce feelings relating to sex, disgust, or personal aggrandizement. This is a difficult category in which to perform operationalized research; but such motivationally-relevant associations potentially are important in certain aspects of VVA, particularly in aesthetic preferences.

MEASUREMENT OF DEPENDENT VARIABLES IN STUDIES OF VVA

Visual exploration refers to any behavior which results in a stimulus being fixated on, brought into view, maintained in view, or voluntarily brought back into view after it is gone. Although the methods of investigation differ in terms of formal operations, all methods present the subject with one or more visual configurations and, by one method or another, allow him to view the stimuli for varying amounts of time. The major difference among methods is that in some cases the individual is shown a number of different visual configurations at the same time on a screen, whereas in others he is shown visual configurations serially one at a time. Visual configurations include randomly constructed geometrical forms, patterns of dots, drawings of novel animal-like things, drawings of furniture or other objects, and pictures of real-life objects and social scenes. The major methods employed in studies of VVA are the following.

Gross Head Movements

Methods for the study of gross movements of the head involve simultaneously exposing the subject to several stimuli and forcing him or her to make a head movement in order to focus on a stimulus. For example, Faw and Nunnally (1968b) presented stimuli on two viewing screens separated by about three feet, and each child was seated in a chair facing the screens. This forced the child to make a gross head movement in order to bring either of the two stimuli into view. Looking behavior was monitored through a one-way looking screen from a separate room. The amount of time spent viewing each stimulus in each pair provided an index of VVA. The primary advantage of this response measure is that it can be employed in seminaturalistic settings which make visual exploration "natural."

Visual Fixations

A popular method of measuring visual fixations has been employed by Berlyne (1958) and Nunnally and his associates (e.g., Faw & Nunnally,

1967). The details vary, but essentially a small number of stimuli are presented at a short distance (e.g., 60 cm) from the subject's face. A chin rest or other device is used to prevent gross head movements. The stimuli are separated by enough distance to require the subject to make gross eye movements in order to view any particular stimulus. Visual fixations are either judged by a hidden rater (e.g., Berlyne, 1958) photographed (e.g., Faw & Nunnally, 1967), or videotaped (e.g., Lemond, 1973).

The primary advantage of studying visual fixations is that the procedure is rather simple, and requires little understanding or physical effort from the subject. Lemond (1973) reported an interjudge agreement of 97% on the scoring of videotaped records of the visual fixations of adults. Another advantage is that it is very easy to disguise the purpose of the investigation in such a manner that the subject is unaware that the amount of time spent looking at different stimuli is important. In post-experimental testing, it has been found that subjects are unaware of which parts of the visual display they viewed longer (e.g., Durham, Nunnally, & Lemond, 1971).

Instrumental Viewing Responses

A third approach to the measurement of VVA concerns instrumental responses made by the subject to bring a stimulus into view or to keep a stimulus in view. This includes such responses as button pushing, bar pressing, and lever pulling. Many different types of apparatus have been employed for this purpose. For example, Berlyne (1957) used a tachistoscope to present visual stimuli to subjects. When the subject pressed a key, a stimulus became visible for .14 second. Subjects were allowed to view each stimulus as many times as they wished. Various types of "looking boxes" have also been employed, in which the subject pushes buttons to light up different screens on a box. Each screen illuminates a different visual configuration (e.g., Nunnally, Duchnowski, & Knott, 1967). The data of interest in these instrumental viewing procedures are the number of times or the amount of time the subject looks at each stimulus.

By far the most popular procedure for studying instrumental viewing responses has been that of "free looking time" (e.g., Leckart & Bakan, 1965). With this procedure, subjects are allowed to view a series of stimuli one at a time through the use of a remote-control slide projector. A stimulus remains in view until the subject pushes a button which advances the projector to the next stimulus. An example from one of our experiments is in studying viewing time as a function of different levels of complexity of geometric forms. Sixty slides, each containing a geometric form at a particular level of complexity, are randomly ordered in the tray of a slide projector. Subjects are shown how to operate the remote-control switch, and are left to view the stimuli, freely distributing their viewing time. The data of interest are amount of time spent viewing each stimulus.

The primary advantages of studying free looking time over other types of responses is that it is very simple and economical, and allows one to gather large amounts of data in rather short periods of time. A potential disadvantage of investigating free looking time is that the task may appear rather trivial to adults. Also, children may get lost in the sheer fun of manipulating the projector, to the detriment of any findings regarding visual investigation. Neither of these has appeared to be a major disadvantage in our investigations so far.

Absolute and Comparative Measures

An important distinction is between *absolute* and *comparative* viewing time. The use of a free-looking-time procedure is a cardinal example of the former. Although there are subtle constraints on time spent viewing the stimuli, the subject is under the impression that he can spend as much time as he likes viewing each stimulus. Thus, the stimuli are not obviously in competition with one another as regards amount of looking time. Several other methods involving instrumental viewing responses are measures of absolute looking time. In contrast, gross head movements, visual fixations, and some instrumental viewing responses obviously involve comparative looking time. This is the case in any situation where the individual is shown two or more stimuli at the same time and the response measure concerns the percentage of the time spent looking at one stimulus rather than others. One might expect that there would be important differences in VVA in these two conditions, but no important differences have been found to date (see Nunnally & Lemond, 1973).

Instructions

The instructions given the subject have been shown to play an important role in determining visual investigation (see Nunnally & Lemond, 1973). For example, data frequently are different if instructions emphasize pleasantness of the stimuli rather than remembering or otherwise encoding the stimuli. In spite of the proven importance of instructional sets, the specific instructions frequently are described in scanty detail in research articles, which makes it difficult to interpret the results of many studies of VVA.

SELECTION, CONSTRUCTION, AND SCALING OF VISUAL STIMULI

The theoretical scheme given earlier requires the employment of a very wide variety of visual stimuli. This is for two reasons. First, the nature of the problem frequently dictates the type of visual stimuli that are employed in the investigation. For example, if one is investigating cognitive and emotional associations, copies of a wide variety of paintings will be needed. Second, many of the independent variables concern the characteristics of the stimuli. To investigate the effects of physical complexity, for example, one must construct stimuli that vary systematically in that regard.

Types of Stimuli Employed

Statistically Formed Displays

In some cases the visual stimuli are constructed on the basis of probability models. This is the case for randomly constructed polygons, dot patterns, and checkerboard patterns. Such displays are constructed by a set of statistical rules rather than by an intentional effort to depict representational objects. A simple example is that of manipulating the "grain" of checkerboard patterns. All the patterns occupy the same amount of space, that is, 10 × 10 inches. The grain of the figure can be manipulated by the number of blocks into which the square is divided, varying from only four blocks up to a very large number. Specified percentages of blocks can be filled in either randomly or with some probabilistic contingency restraints. An example is a coin being flipped to decide whether each block is left vacant or blackened. There are many types of stochastic models that can be employed to construct stimuli with respect to some of the purely physical properties mentioned in our theoretical scheme.

Drawings

For many purposes, it has been necessary to hire artists to construct figures specifically related to particular stimulus variables. An example is in our studies of information conflict. We specified for the artist the cardinal features that an object should have at each level of information conflict (novelty), and he drew versions of the stimuli until they met our satisfaction. In the study of pleasantness it was necessary to have a series of outline drawings on a 5-step continuum composed of female faces varying from very ugly to very pretty. (Of course all such sets of stimuli necessarily were subjected later to psychophysical scaling studies, prior to their employment in studies of VVA.)

There are advantages and disadvantages of employing outline drawings. One disadvantage is that they are time-consuming and relatively expensive. On some occasions it has been necessary for the artist to draw several versions of the same picture before it appeared suitable. The second disadvantage is that there are many kinds of stimuli that would be prohibitively complex and would require the use of colors.

The major advantage of working with outline drawings is that one can manipulate the particular stimulus variable in question and attempt to hold constant possible confounding stimulus variables. For example, there is so little detail in some of the outline drawings that amount of detail is not likely to be important in VVA. Since they are all in black and white, obviously colors and distributions of colors would not have an influence. By having the pictures drawn, one can emphasize the particular feature being investigated, for example, the novel component. Also, with drawings one can depict impossible things, as in pictures we employ in studies of information conflict.

Posed Scenes

On a number of occasions we have photographed posed scenes, such as a parent spanking a child or a young man and woman embracing. These were used to investigate various affectual states. The advantage of posed scenes over drawings is that, obviously, they are much more lifelike, and thus may have stronger effects than outline drawings. However, posed scenes have their problems also, particularly in controlling for unwanted and frequently unsuspected confounding stimulus characteristics.

Sample Pictures from Daily Life

Studies of VVA have used many pictures of scenes from daily life, ones that either were photographed specifically to meet some purpose, or cropped from magazines and other printed matter. We presently are investigating 38 categories of real-life scenes (with five pictures in each category). The categories were formed in terms of our hypotheses about some of the determinants of VVA mentioned earlier. In many cases we photographed these in our environment; in other cases they were taken from magazines.

Works of Art

Particularly for investigations into variables relating to aesthetics it is useful to employ photographic reproductions of works of art. One can do this either by making slides for a very broad "sample" of paintings, or by collecting slides with respect to specified categories of paintings which are intended to represent one or more of the theoretical constructs mentioned previously.

Psychometric Requirements

Only persons who have one foot in psychometric theory and one foot in experimental psychology can appreciate the demands that these two subdisciplines place on one another. What sounds perfectly logical from one perspective proves to be patently impractical from the standpoint of the other, and vice versa. Some of the salient principles whereby these two subdisciplines have been wedded in our research are as follows:

Multiple Levels

Theories concerning VVA speak of various aspects of looking behavior as being a function of certain treatment conditions or characteristics of stimulus variables. The pioneering work in this area (e.g., Berlyne, 1960) primarily involved showing pictures that represented only two levels of the variable in question. For example, a comparison would be made of the amount of time spent looking at a picture of an ordinary house and at a novel drawing of a house. In other instances, only several levels of a stimulus variable were investigated, such as several levels of complexity.

Another problem relating to number of levels concerns the range of stimuli employed in the investigations. When we started investigating the physical complexity of random polygons, it was not uncommon to see reports in journal articles in which the highest level represented was 40 random sides. Now we are working with random polygons that have up to 200 sides. A major effort on our project has been to develop sets of stimuli that varied widely and at numerous points on the continuum of the particular stimulus characteristic being investigated. This permits us to make firmer, more general statements about the nature of functional relationships.

Scaling Data

For the development of stimulus scales, we relied on two types of data. First, in some instances we could rely on the physical properties of the stimuli. One example is with our random polygons, in which complexity could be measured in terms of the number of random sides used to generate the figure. Another example was in the number of different encodable stimuli in a display, which was indexed quite simply in terms of the proportions of elements of different kinds that were shown. Such physical properties served directly to develop interval or ratio scales.

With most of the stimuli that we have employed, it is logically impossible to use as scaling data any measurable physical properties. This is illustrated with our drawings of incongruous juxtapositions of animal parts with other elements, such as an outline drawing of a cow with symmetrical polka dots. Actually, in information-theoretic terms, the splotches on an ordinary cow would represent a higher level of complexity than would the polka dots, but, of course, the polka-dotted cow is responded to as being much more novel. In the outline drawings that we employ to depict various motivational states, for example, a child receiving a spanking, there is nothing that can be measured physically by ruler, photoelectric cell, or any other physical process that would index the variable in question. The only way to index novelty, motivational states, associations, and most of the important stimulus variables is in terms of subjects' reactions. Consequently, a large part of our research effort has been dedicated to gathering responses to our stimuli, which then could be employed for psychophysical scaling. These scales were subsequently used in studies of VVA. For this purpose, we obtained subject reactions of many kinds. We relied heavily on rating scales, as, for example, for the measurement of pleasantness. Free associations were obtained to scale stimuli in terms of some of the variables relating to meaning processing. In our studies of incongruous drawings, children were asked to rank-order the pictures within each set from the most usual to the most unusual. In these and in other ways it not only was practicable to employ subjects' reactions as data for scaling stimuli, but logically there were no other type of data that could possibly have served that purpose.

Need for Replicate Stimulus Sets

In the investigation of any variable in our conceptual scheme, it was necessary to employ more than one set of materials in each study. In a study of effects of sets of incongruous drawings on amount of looking time, we typically would employ four or more different sets, each of which involved four or more levels of novelty. Similarly, in investigating effects of different levels of complexity as evidenced in randomly constructed geometrical forms, we typically employed four or more sets of stimuli that varied on as many as six levels.

The reason for employing replicate sets of this kind is to give the overall results a form of content generality, much as is traditionally involved in the construction of psychological tests. We could not trust the results that we obtained from one set alone, simply because there may have been something peculiar about the picture used to represent a particular level, or even about a whole set of pictures. Looking through the literature on visual exploration over the last ten years or so, one can find authors making much out of a particular dip in a curve or a final downturn; but frequently these curves are based on one set of stimuli only. One should employ multiple sets of stimuli for any variable, and these should be scaled psychophysically before studies of VVA are undertaken.

Need for Minimal Overlap

Our investigations require levels of stimuli that barely overlap in terms of scale properties. A cardinal example is in respect to information conflict. We cannot employ such scales unless nearly all subjects agree on the way in which stimuli should be rank-ordered with respect to novelty. Similarly, in our scales that are constructed in terms of physical principles, it is necessary to employ stimuli at each level (e.g., of complexity) that do not overlap with other levels. Without these clean-cut differences between stimuli at adjacent levels on each scale, we could not expect to obtain clear results in VVA.

Floor and Ceiling Effect

In developing stimuli, we frequently encounter natural floors in which either one is working with a logical zero point or one can not obtain a lower level on the stimulus continuum in scales based on subjects' ratings. One cannot obtain a polygon with fewer than three sides, or a collection of objects less heterogeneous than one in which all the objects are alike. Similarly, in our scales obtained primarily from the pretesting of subjects' reactions to pictures rather than in terms of physical properties, we frequently found floor effects or logical zero points. For example, we cannot draw a picture of a cow that will be rated clearly as more "usual" than the picture of the cow that we presently employ in that set. Similarly, in many efforts we have been unable to construct a more bizarre concatanation of cow, elephant, and airplane parts than the most incongruous stimulus in that series. Logically, then, we have covered the range from the bottom to the top, which leaves little argument about what would happen if stimuli were more extreme in either direction. Some of our sets constructed in terms of physical properties have been made so complex, or so extreme in terms of some other physical property, that it is doubtful that any practicable increases in scale values would result in different findings regarding VVA.

Scaling Techniques

We have found it necessary to rely on only some very simple approaches to scaling. For example, we have encountered no case in which multidimensional scaling would have been useful. Such scaling methods are used when stimuli are expected to differ from one another prominently on more than one dimension and/or the cardinal dimensions cannot be specified in advance. Neither has been the case in our investigations. Rather, we have worked from a hypothesis-testing model, in which our effort is to measure each theoretical variable separately, for example, information conflict or complexity. We make efforts to purify our stimulus materials of any other psychological dimensions that might intrude themselves. Also, the employment of replicate sets as mentioned above helps to average out any confounding stimulus variables that might by chance be represented in one of the sets but not in others.

As mentioned above, some of our unidimensional scales were developed directly from their physical properties, such as levels of complexity in geometrical forms and relative homogeneity of elements of visual displays. The numerical characteristics of the displays themselves provide sensible scales, although in some circumstances we found that the overall nexus of lawful relations among independent variables and with dependent variables was simplified by systematic modifications of the intervals; for example, we found it mathematically convenient to work with logarithmic values concerning complexity in random polygons.

For our scales based on data obtained from human impressions it was not necessary to apply any complex scaling techniques. All the scaling methods that have grown out of Thurstone's law of comparative judgment did not apply, because the research required nearly nonoverlapping distributions of individual differences. Consequently, where stimuli were based on ranking we simply used the average ranks over subjects as though they constituted an interval scale. With scales based on ratings, for example, 9-step scales concerning judged pleasantness of pictures, we simply took the average ratings to form interval scales.

Not all the materials that we use in studies of VVA constitute ordered scales as produced by the procedures described above. A primary example is our investigation of VVA with respect to 190 pictures of real-life objects and scenes. In such cases, we essentially are "sampling" broadly from a domain of content. Another domain in which we are studying a broad sample of pictures is with respect to works of art. (Of course, such "sampling" does not precisely match the process as it is defined in mathematical statistics.) When performing such sampling, it greatly helps if a conceptual scheme is available for ensuring that an adequate coverage of the domain is obtained, as in our use of 38 categories to obtain a broad collection of 190 pictures.

ILLUSTRATIVE FINDINGS

Space permits only the summarizing of some of the most pervasive and conclusive findings from our investigations of VVA. More extensive summaries and numerous references to particular experiments are given in Lemond (1973), Nunnally (1977), Nunnally and Lemond (1973), Wilson (1973), and Nunnally, Lemond, and Wilson (1977).

Information Conflict

There is a monotonically increasing relationship between degree of information conflict (an important type of novelty) and amount of VVA. A typical set of pictures used in such investigations is shown in Figure 2. A typical set of results is shown in Figure 3.

Representational Elements

There is a monotonically increasing relationship between the number of different representational elements (thinglike objects) in visual displays and the amount of VVA (evidence summarized by Wilson, 1973). An example is in studying visual displays that range on the lower end to a display containing 16 copies of the same face, varying in degree of heterogeneity up to a display containing 16 different faces. Although the exact shapes of the relationships are not identical, we find the same monotonic trend between the number of different elements in a picture and the amount of time spent in visual exploration.

Physical Complexity

There is a monotonically increasing relationship between physical complexity (e.g., as manifested in number of random sides of a polygon

FIGURE 2. Examples of stimuli containing various degrees of information conflict.

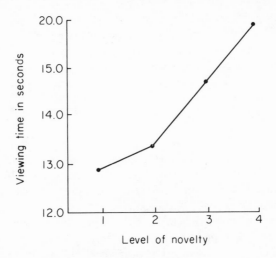

FIGURE 3. Relationships among four levels of stimulus novelty (information conflict) and viewing time (from Faw & Nunnally, 1968a).

or number of random dots in a pattern) and amount of VVA. A typical set of 4 ordered stimuli varying from 3 to 200 random sides is shown in Figure 4. A typical set of results is shown in Figure 5. The levels of complexity shown there are 3, 10, 20, 40, and 80 random sides expressed in terms of

FIGURE 4. Examples of randomly generated geometric forms (3,40,80, and 200 random sides).

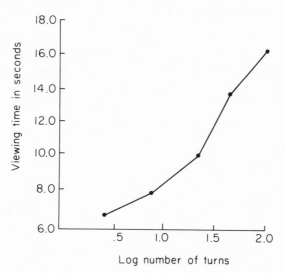

FIGURE 5. Relationship between stimulus complexity and viewing time.

log 10. We have unpublished data showing that the monotonically increasing trend continues up to 200 random sides.

Pleasantness

There is *no* general relationship between subjects' ratings of pleasantness of stimuli and amount of VVA. Theory and research results on this matter are discussed in detail in Nunnally, 1977. Findings with one type of stimuli do not hold with other types of stimuli; for example, rated pleasantness of female faces versus outline drawings of scenes showing various types of social interactions. There has been a tendency throughout our studies (by no means entirely consistent) for pleasant pictures to dominate neutral pictures, but VVA with respect to various levels of negative affect evidenced in ratings is unpredictable. There is some evidence from our studies (e.g., Faw & Nunnally, 1971) that people compulsively stare at some types of unpleasant pictures, particularly those concerning any type of human harm.

Familiarization

With various experimental approaches, numerous studies have been performed on the effects of prior familarization of stimuli on subsequent VVA. It is quite conclusive that familiarization reduces subsequent VVA, both when stimuli are subsequently viewed separately and when a familiarized stimulus is paired in the same display with an unfamiliarized stimulus. However, there are many puzzling features regarding these investigations which do not fit any simple generalization beyond the observed major effect; for example, our studies show no effects of such prior familiarization on subsequent ratings of pleasantness, and the effects of amount of familiarization in our studies level off after only a few seconds rather than increasing monotonically.

Other Findings

Many findings by us and others on numerous experimental treatments are referenced in the summary articles mentioned above. These include effects of various physical characteristics of stimuli, of amounts and kinds of sensory isolation, of instructional sets, and of interposing various types of vigilance tasks between trials of VVA. Some of the findings from these investigations have been clear-cut, but they have not been replicated or studied as broadly as those in the five categories discussed above.

COVERT ASPECTS OF EXPLORATION

Although it sometimes is arguable which is being investigated, it is important to make a distinction between the overt aspects of exploratory behavior and the covert, or more purely mental aspects. A look back at Figure 1, a temporal scheme of exploratory behavior, will remind the reader that for each overt behavior in the sequence there is a hypothesized covert attendant process. A great deal of research has been performed on the overtly behavioral aspects of exploratory activity, particularly specific exploration in the study of VVA, but very little actual research has been performed on the covert components. Rather, what has been done is to presume that certain covert processes were in operation while stimuli were being presented in studies of VVA. In addition to the covert processes that correlate in time with observable aspects of exploratory behavior, some of the most interesting forms of exploration are purely mental. In such cases, there may be no observable, external behavior at all; but the mental processes relating to exploration may be quite important for the individual, and quite important for scientists to investigate. An example of specific covert exploration would be scanning with the "mind's eye" the scene of an automobile accident witnessed earlier in the day. An example of covert search as a form of exploration would be simply rambling through one's mind as to the most logical location of a misplaced set of keys. An example of diverse exploration, one that is highly familiar to us all, is simply having the mind wander in chains of free association of symbols, words, mental pictures, and related tinges of emotion.

For the investigation of covert aspects of exploration one runs into the perpetual dilemma that is found throughout psychology in studying through scientifically acceptable means what goes on in the mind. Of course the radical behaviorists claimed that this was not possible at all (even going back to the great philosopher Kant). However, the revolt against such radical behaviorism and the rekindled interest in human thinking and feeling has made the rubric Cognitive Psychology quite popular (and for some reason that I do not understand, this switch in names solves all the problems of dealing with unobservable, mental processes). We cannot give up on the study of human feeling and thinking as mental phenomena even if they do pose severe problems with respect to the logic of science. Subsequently I shall discuss some inroads into such investigations, but let me first illustrate the problem with some covert processes that have been highly important in my own theorizing about exploratory behavior.

Meaning Processing of Incongruity

Earlier in this chapter I gave an extensive list of constructs that I and others have mentioned as being important in the study of exploratory behavior, some of which are rather easily tied down in terms of overt activity, and others of which are almost wholly related to covert activity. My major theorizing and research activity has been with respect to the *meaning processing* of specific exploration of visual displays. In Figure 1 I refer to this as encoding, and earlier in the text I talked about some of the major components of encoding or "making sense" out of the displays. Some of the separate constructs in this overall interest in meaning processing were information conflict, number of representational elements, and others. Here let me go into some detail about the construct of information conflict as a prelude to analyzing some of the approaches to studying covert exploration.

Considering the many places in which information conflict occurs and the many interesting impacts on human behavior, it is very surprising that no one (in so far as I know) has pointed out the widespread nature of the phenomenon and attempted to state general principles concerning the impact of information conflict on human behavior. Perhaps the phenomenon of information conflict has been largely overlooked because it is so very rudimentary. Animals, from protozoa to man, sense and respond selectively to the diverse stimuli that impinge on them. Protozoa will move from the dark to the light side of a container. Bees have a large repertoire of specific responses to specific actions by other bees. More by dint of learning than by wired-in proclivities, men respond selectively to myriad stimuli in the social and in the material environment. For example, other than for lunatics and pranksters, the greeting "Good morning" is predictably met with a similarly pleasant reply. In all herdlike animals, including man, at least some highly predictable stimulus–response relations are required for maintenance and survival of the herd.

In order to respond appropriately to any stimulus, it is necessary, in a very general sense of the term, to attribute meaning to the stimulus. The master's whistle signals that dinner is ready for the dog. A particular flapping of the wings signals to the bee that honey is to be found in a specific direction. The astringent effects of a particular chemical signal to the protozoan that he should move in the opposite direction. The crouching behavior of a timber wolf signals to a more dominant male that he should not attack. The examples are legion, to say the least, of needs in the animal kingdom for appropriate responses to stimuli. This does not mean, however, that everything in the sensorium is an object of intimate attention, prolonged curiosity, or dread. It is probable that the vast majority of all stimuli are simply classified as harmless, biologically irrelevant, highly familiar, or for some other reason uninteresting. In connection with stimuli that do prove to be of interest and importance to the organism, however, organisms perish or survive in terms of the appropriateness of the responses they make. An animal cannot make an appropriate response to a stimulus if the cues for encoding, or attributing meaning to, the stimulus are in conflict.

There obviously are some differences in the way that conflicting information of different kinds is handled. Information conflict is involved in dichotic listening, where different messages are going to the two ears, but attention in this situation apparently is very much under the control of the subject. In contrast, the information conflict involved in binocular rivalry apparently is influenced almost not at all by conscious efforts of a person to keep one of two competing percepts in view. As another example of differences in the way that different types of information conflict are handled, there apparently is much more disturbance caused by certain types of information conflict than by others. For example, whereas the information conflict inherent in delayed feedback of speech and air sickness tends to be quite disturbing to people, the information conflict inherent in dichotic listening and the viewing of incongruous pictures of animals tends not to be very disturbing. In spite of these differences in the way that different types of information conflict are handled, it is thought that there are at least two general principles that hold for all information conflict.

The first principle, the one that I am forced to treat more tentatively, is that, with any type of information conflict, the emotional response varies with the degree of conflict. Mild levels of conflict are experienced as pleasant; moderate levels of conflict are experienced as producing giddiness, dizziness, and a tolerable feeling of unreality; and extreme levels of conflict tend to produce anxiety, feelings of hopelessness, confusion, and nausea. This principle tends to hold most fully when there is neither an automatic nor a consciously controllable mechanism for selecting among the conflicting cues for meaning. In binocular rivalry images flip-flop automatically, and rarely is there a mixture of the two images. The individual has practically no control over which image comes into view. Apparently there is an on-off switching mechanism that prevents the information conflict from disturbing the organism. Consequently, no one reports strain or distress in experiments on binocular rivalry. For a very different reason, little strain is experienced in studies of dichotic listening. In that case, subjects apparently are quite adept at switching their attention from the information coming into one ear to that coming into the other ear. In real life situations, individuals are able largely to tune in on one conversation or other source of sound and thus diminish the salience of competing sources of sound. Because people can and do select from the available competing auditory stimuli, the individual does not experience strong information conflict or the stress that would be attendant upon it.

With most forms of information conflict, however, there is no on-off switching mechanism to protect the organism from the impact of competing information. This is the case, for example, in response to vertigo, weightlessness, conflicting components of verbal messages, and novelty in the form of incongruous pictures. In such situations, it is proposed that the degree of stress induced by information conflict varies with the degree of the conflict. As was mentioned previously, it is hypothesized that very mild levels of conflict actually are experienced as pleasurable. This is the case, for example, in jokes, and in the relatively mild vertigo experienced in carnival rides. (As is true of almost everything else, there probably are very large individual differences, relating to age, sex, subculture affiliation, and other differences among people.) The distress that is inherent in highly incongruous stimulations is thought to result from a general state of vertigo, or dizziness, that attends highly conflicting information. This certainly is the case with air sickness, and it may also be the case in less obvious circumstances. For example, personally I get dizzy while looking at some of the incongruous pictures of animals and other objects that we employ in our studies of selective visual attention. Also, although people will laugh at those pictures, they also rate them as somewhat unpleasant—not highly unpleasant, but less pleasant than pictures of normal objects and animals.

The second principle regarding situations that concern information conflict—the principle that intrigues me far more than the first principle—is that information conflict elicits and sustains attention. In the same way that a tropism draws a moth to the flame, I propose that a tropism draws all animals to look at, or otherwise attend to, objects or circumstances that induce information conflict. It should be obvious why it is biologically useful for stimuli that elicit information conflict to dominate attention. One can envision the animal moving through its environment, checking out, giving meaning to, and subsequently ignoring the stimuli it encounters. The fox wanders through its woodland domain, encountering a familiar rock, passing a tree, chasing but failing to catch a rabbit; but suddenly here is something new—a red balloon bobbing through the trees, bouncing off rocks, and bursting with a loud bang. Now the balloon lies limp on the side of a boulder. The fox is faced with a welter of information conflict. All birds fly, but they do not make a loud sound when they land. Big round things do not suddenly become small, limp things. In this and in other ways the fox is experiencing considerable information conflict. The fox would attend very acutely to the balloon, and if the information conflict was not too much for him to stand he would continue to investigate until most of his curiosity regarding the object was satisfied.

An experience of my own may help to illustrate the tropism that I have hypothesized regarding the attention-getting properties of incongruous stimuli and the related covert processes. One day while walking near my office I encountered what appeared to be a Rolls Royce station wagon. The front end of the vehicle was unquestionable a Rolls Royce, and the rear end of the vehicle was a gawky, highly unusual looking wooden aspect of a station wagon. This represented a high degree of information conflict for me because (1) the awkward looking rear end of the vehicle was in strong contrast with the classic lines of the front part of the vehicle, and (2) whereas I obviously was looking at a Rolls Royce station wagon, at the same time I felt sure that Rolls Royce had never routinely manufactured station wagons. The information conflict in this situation was sufficiently strong that I could not take my eyes off the strange contraption. I am sure that my attention was sufficiently drawn to the object that a good friend would have passed by unnoticed. Had the vehicle not lumbered off, I probably would have gaped at it for some time. My "mental" attention to the object persisted after it passed over a nearby hill. I could not get the incongruous object out of my mind until I made up a little story for myself, most probably highly erroneous, regarding the origin of the vehicle and its presence outside my office. My little story concerned how an English country gentleman had wanted something special in which to bring guests from a nearby train station to his baronial estate, and how he had requested that the Rolls Royce company design and construct a special vehicle for the purpose. Then, having satisfied myself that someone could have had such a vehicle constructed in England, I compulsively went on to make up further stories about how the vehicle got to Nashville, Tennessee. Viewing the incongruous vehicle had set up a tension in me, one that would not lessen until I resolved the information conflict, even if the resolution was more fantasy than fact. I refer to such activity as tropistic, because it is highly motivating and end-directed in the same way as other animal tropisms are.

THEORETICAL POSITIONS REGARDING COVERT ASPECTS OF EXPLORATION

Many of the constructs mentioned previously that are thought to be important in determining extent of VVA and perhaps other forms of specific exploration are either partly or wholly "in the mind" rather than in terms of overt activities. A primary example is the possible influence of specific emotions while exploration is under way; another consists of the associations that occur during that period. Exploration in the form of covert search, for example, looking for misplaced keys, may occur while the person is sitting inert in an armchair and not doing or saying anything that can be observed. Similarly, the mental ramblings that constitute diverse exploration, "in the mind," need not be accompanied by any consistent observables.

The list of constructs described previously spawns numerous specific hypotheses that are ripe for testing. Also, these constructs and other covert, cognitive, and affective variables combine into more complex theoretical positions regarding exploratory behavior. A simple example was illustrated previously of the hypothesized tendency of people to "make up a story" to explain an incongruous stimulus or message. The validity of the hypothesis is then "checked out" by overt exploratory behavior and covert thinking about the plausibility of the hypothesis. Frequently this first hypothesis is formed in a split second, because humans have a tropism for not only paying attention to incongruous stimuli but for resolving them quickly into something meaningful. If as is usually the case the first attempt at encoding does not meet with what is seen and thought, then a second hypothesis is formed and subsequently "checked out." A chain of such hypothesis formulations and testings goes on until either the object is made to fit in a meaningful way into what the person knows about the world, or his principles concerning reality are altered to incorporate the incongruous object. (Of course, this simple theoretical illustration is very similar to other cognitive theories concerning learning and perception, for example, Piaget's concepts of *assimilation* and *accommodation*, Broadbent's concept of *template matching*, and other cognitive theories.)

Many theoretical principles could be given regarding covert search activity, which would represent the purely mental counterparts of overt theories of problem-solving—in mentally searching for the lost keys, the person could employ the problem-solving heuristic of retracing his steps mentally to the places that he had gone since the last location in which he was sure that the keys were in his possession. This aspect of the search activity would be joined with considerations regarding those places in which it would have been appropriate to remove the keys. By homing in this way with subsets of principles regarding probabilities as to where the keys might be, the search could be narrowed to several locations which would be inspected overtly (and if the keys were not there, the hierarchy of converging mental operations in the research would start over).

As a theoretical point of view underlying diverse exploratory behavior, such overt behavior has been theorized to be motivated by boredom (or tedium). This should be manifested in verbal reports of boredom and restlessness, and in physiological arousal corresponding to the "itchiness" that is hypothesized to be involved. One could elaborate this theoretical scheme considerably.

The foregoing are meant to be bare-bones examples of the possibilities of building rather elaborate theories regarding the covert aspects of all forms of exploratory behavior; but the purpose of the examples is not to offer elaborate explanations in the limited space that is available here, but rather to illustrate the theoretical developments that could emerge—if only adequate methods of gathering scientifically acceptable data with respect to the related forms of mental activity were currently available for the purpose.

Data-Gathering for Covert Exploration

As many authors have discussed it (e.g., Nunnally, 1978), the gathering of scientifically acceptable data is tantamount to measurement. Of course, there is a hierarchy of measurement in terms of the amount of information supplied, ranging from lowly categorical data of the form of present-absent to the ratio scale at the top of the hierarchy. Viewed in this way, the major problem of studying covert aspects of exploratory activity is to adequately measure variables that permit theories to be tested. Before going into some of the particular methods that have been tried to date and some that I will advocate for the future, it is well to recognize that nearly all scientists have contented themselves with the need for rather indirect measurement in most research. Actually, nothing other than the measurement of length is done purely in terms of ostensive characteristics, that is, one can actually see whether one stick is longer than another. The zero point on the scale can be seen as the empty space at the lower end of a ruler; and the equality of intervals may actually be observed by sawing the inch-long wooden strips into pieces and examining their equality visually. Unfortunately, no other characteristic in nature can be fully justified as measuring what it is supposed to measure; and no other scale except length permits one to see directly the scale properties, in this case a ratio scale. Even weight is measured indirectly with a balance or other devices. Most measures in the physical sciences are much further removed from the actual attribute being measured; for example, the Fahrenheit thermometer, the Richter scale for earthquakes, and the pollution index given by the nightly TV "weatherman." The situation is much the same in psychology—most methods of measurement only indirectly quantify the attribute in question, and the degree of intuitive convincingness without additional supporting evidence varies considerably from measure to measure, as, for example, measures of reaction time as opposed to measures of "rigidity."

Because many newly developed measures do not convincingly quantify what they are purported to quantify, it is necessary to *validate* such methods, by procedures that are familiar to most behavioral scientists (see Nunnally, 1978). In particular, those measures that are rich in explanatory power for the formulation of theories require a rather complex type of *construct validity*, which can either be explicated in terms of a ponderously proper formal logic or simply kept in mind as a necessary type of commonsense accruing of circumstantial evidence regarding how well a proposed measure works in practice. Looked at in either way, this boils down to the extent to which a measure "acts" as it should in situations where the results of experiments relating to the construct follow from highly agreed-on principles, and when the new measure proves valuable in explaining experimental results in the domain of inquiry where it was intended to be employed. All this applies to the development of adequate measurement methods for the covert aspects of exploratory behavior, and the problems here are no easier or no worse than they are in many other areas of psychology and kindred sciences where questions regarding human thoughts and feelings are at issue. However, far too little has been done to develop the measurement tools that are needed for testing existing theories of covert aspects of exploratory behavior and, in turn, encouraging the development of much more comprehensive theories in this regard. Following are some of the types of measures that either have been used for this purpose or could be used in the future.

Measurement Methods for Covert Exploration

Unfortunately, many theories regarding covert concomitants of various aspects of overt exploratory behavior and purely covert exploratory behavior are very difficult to affirm or deny because of the paucity of scientifically acceptable methods of measuring the variables involved in the theories. Of course, this is not an idiosyncratic problem for the study of exploration, but rather it is a problem that is common throughout all aspects of psychology and kindred fields that concern covert processes. Following are some methods that we currently employ or could employ in the future.

Physiological Measures

Many psychologists have a real "hang-up" on the possibility of using physiological measures as a mind-reading machine. Attempts of this kind have been made with respect to the covert aspects of exploratory activity, but with scant success. Among the measures that have been employed while subjects viewed stimuli that varied in terms of one or another characteristic are heart rate, GSR, EEG, pupillary dilation, and others. If the reader will glance back at Figure 1, concerning hypothesized covert activities relating to their overt counterparts in specific exploration, hypotheses can be formulated regarding the physiological concomitants of the various stages. However, the actual use of such physiological measures in VVA has proved to be very "messy" and has produced very little of substance. All such measures tend to be very volatile and easily influenced by artifacts. For example, GSR tends to decrease throughout the experiment no matter what the subject is viewing. With respect to the orienting response, Sokolov argued that heart rate increased, but most American psychologists find that heart rate decreases during this period. Whereas earlier it was thought that pupillary response was bipolar, in the sense that dilation occurred in viewing pleasant pictures and constriction occurred with respect to unpleasant pictures, this proves not at all to be the case. What was found instead was that any stimulus that activated (aroused) the person caused dilation—pictures of pleasant or unpleasant objects, physical strain as in lifting weights, and the purely mental strain of performing complex arithmetic problems. The EEG is of little use in most studies of VVA, because the transduced waves "go flat" when the subject is alerted by viewing stimuli that are novel or interesting in any other manner. Efforts to use autonomic measures and products of the central nervous system to index particular emotions (e.g., anger, disgust, and happiness) have utterly failed.

The only place in which physiological measures have proved useful is in the indexing of overall activation (or arousal). For example, pupillary response has proven to be an excellent measure of arousal. Because Dan Berlyne and others have placed such a heavy emphasis on arousal as a covert process underlying exploratory activity, it is useful to employ some of these physiological measures to investigate the theories. For example, when subjects are viewing one picture at a time in the study of VVA, it is rather easy with some of our equipment to measure simultaneously pupil size. Although physiological measures may be useful for studying overall states of arousal, there is no evidence now and very little hope on the horizon that physiological measures will ever by useful for determining the *content* of what people are feeling and thinking.

Association Methods

One very important approach to getting at the covert processes that are involved in exploration is through changes in association toward the explored object or event from before to after the encounter. If my overall meaning-processing point of view is correct with respect to what occurs in exploratory behavior, then one would make numerous predictions regarding changes in association hierarchies as a function of the exploration. We usually make studies of association as part of the indexing of stimulus characteristics of visual displays. Our most typical approach is to have the individual list up to ten ideas that come to mind while looking at the display as it is projected on a screen. This formation of association hierarchies is done prior to our subsequent investigations of looking behavior, and with different subjects than are included in the latter. Such association hierarchies have proved very valuable to us in selecting stimuli that vary in terms of the extent to which there are highly agreed-on representational elements in the display. For example, in studying randomly constructed geometrical designs, purely by accident one of the designs will have a rather obvious appearing birdlike object present which most of the subjects will see. Thus one finds a rather "steep" association hierarchy with the word bird appearing as the foremost associate. In other circumstances, no salient thinglike object is present, and consequently the association hierarchy is rather flat. Although we mainly have employed such association hierarchies to index stimuli prior to investigating VVA, we have begun to investigate changes in such hierarchies as a function of viewing behavior. If our meaning processing point of view has credibility, then predictable changes should occur in these association hierarchies. For example, if there is a birdlike object that occurred perchance in the random construction of geometrical forms, then the number of associations in that regard should increase as a function of VVA. In addition, highly idiosyncratic associations should drop out after the stimuli have been viewed.

Rating Methods

Associations can be investigated either by the typical method of association or by a more structured approach, such as the Semantic Differential or other rating methods (see discussion in Nunnally, 1978). The use of the SD in that respect would not only allow one to investigate a very wide variety of associations, but would also force the subject to respond with respect to some dimensions that have proved quite elusive in previous research. Such uses of Semantic Differential and other rating methods would be particularly useful with respect to the study of specific emotional reactions to visual stimuli, which have proved quite difficult to measure in any other way. This could have a very important place in the study of specific emotions generated by viewing works of art.

Content Analysis of Verbalization

As we move from more to less structured techniques, there is an important place for the study of the manner in which both adults and children freely explore objects that vary in terms of the characteristics discussed previously (e.g., incongruity, aesthetic value). The principle is quite old, namely the subject is required to describe his thoughts while viewing a stimulus. Methods of content analysis can be developed that require either the simple counting of words of a particular kind or judges' ratings of expressed feelings. Although the study of such impressionistic reactions of subjects has been out of style for many years, it has come to be realized that we were overly compulsive in castigating data that are either directly informative or that suggest hypotheses for subsequent investigation. A quick example will suggest what I mean in this regard. I frequently have asked students to recall some incident in which they witnessed an apparently quixotic event. Many of them have told me that momentarily they made up an illogical rationale for a seemingly incongruous event; but after rechecking the matter, discovered that the mistaken incongruity was not there. Such intuitive analyses of individuals' responses to apparently incongruous situations have led me to the postulation of a type of drive or "tropism" for resolving information conflict. I think that other intuitive analyses of free verbalizations regarding exploratory activity would provide valuable hypotheses for future testing as well as being informative in their own right.

A Tribute to Dan

Daniel Berlyne had the courage to speak cogently about exploratory activity and other aspects of intrinsic motivation during a time when psychologists were gradually escaping from a long slumber of hyper-behavioristic nonsense. Dan fitted the term "gentleman scholar" as much or more so than anyone I have known. He would have felt perfectly at home in the company of such great gentleman scholars of the past as William James, Sir Francis Galton, and Charles Darwin. Very few persons manage to be so intellectually gifted yet so humbly kind. Like me, many persons have profitted from Dan's writings and friendship. I have carried that friendship on to study many aspects of intrinsic motivation; but there simply is no one to replace him—we have lost a leader.

Acknowledgments

Appreciation is expressed to three publishers for permission to quote liberally, paraphrase, and borrow figures and tables from three of my own writings. The writings and publishers are (1) Nunnally (1977), *Journal of Applied Psychological Measurement;* (2) Nunnally (1972), Teachers College Press, Columbia University; and (3) Nunnally and Lemond (1973), Academic Press.

REFERENCES

BERLYNE, D. E. An experimental study of human curiosity. *British Journal of Psychology,* 1954, *45,* 256–263.

BERLYNE, D. E. Conflict and information-theory variables as determinants of human perceptual curiosity. *Journal of Experimental Psychology,* 1957, *53,* 399–404.

BERLYNE, D. E. The influence of complexity and novelty in visual figures on orienting responses. *Journal of Experimental Psychology,* 1958, *55,* 289–296.

BERLYNE, D. E. *Conflict, arousal and curiosity.* New York: McGraw-Hill, 1960.

BERLYNE, D. E. Curiosity and exploration. *Science,* 1966, *153,* 25–33.

BERLYNE, D. E. *Aesthetics and psychobiology.* New York: Appleton-Century-Crofts, 1971.

BERLYNE, D. E. *Studies in the new experimental aesthetics.* New York: Wiley, 1974.

CANTOR, J. H., & CANTOR, G. N. Functions relating to children's observing behavior to amount and recency of stimulus familiarization. *Journal of Experimental Psychology,* 1966, *72,* 859–863.

DEMBER, W. N., & EARL, R. Analysis of exploratory, manipulatory, and curiosity behaviors. *Psychological Review,* 1957, *64,* 91–96.

DURHAM, R. L., NUNNALLY, J. C., & LEMOND, L. C. The effects of levels of information conflict on visual selection. *Perception and psychophysics,* 1971, *10,* 93–96.

FAW, T. T., & NUNNALLY, J. C. The effects on eye movements of complexity, novelty and affective tone. *Perception and Psychophysics,* 1967, *2,* 263–267.

FAW, T. T., & NUNNALLY, J. C. The influence of stimulus complexity, novelty, and affective value on children's visual fixations. *Journal of Experimental Child Psychology,* 1968, *6,* 141–153.(a).

FAW, T. T., & NUNNALLY, J. C. A new methodology and finding relating to visual stimulus selection in children. *Psychonomic Science,* 1968, *12,* 47–48.(b).

FAW, T. T., & Nunnally, J. C. Effects of familiarization with incongruous stimuli on their dominance in visual selection. *Psychonomic Science,* 1970, *19,* 359–361.

FAW, T. T., & NUNNALLY, J. C. The influence of stimulus incongruity on the familiarity effect in visual selection. *Perception and Psychophysics,* 1971, *9,* 150–154.

FISKE, D. W., & MADDI, S. R. *Functions of varied experience.* Homewood, Ill.: Dorsey Press, 1961.

FOWLER, H. *Curiosity and exploratory behavior.* New York: Macmillan, 1965.

HEBB, D. O. Drives and the C.N.S. (conceptual nervous system). *Psychological Review,* 1955, *62,* 243–254.

HUTT, C. Specific and diversive exploration. In H. W. Reese & L. P. Lipsitt (Eds.), *Advances in child development and behavior* (Vol. 5). New York: Academic Press, 1970.

LECKART, B. T., & BAKAN, P. Complexity judgments of photographs and looking time. *Perceptual and Motor Skills,* 1965, *2,* 16–18.

LEMOND, L. C. *The influence of degrees of complexity, incongruity, and pre-exposure on the familiarity effect in visual selection.* Unpublished doctoral dissertation, Vanderbilt University, 1973.

NUNNALLY, J. C. A human tropism. In S. R. Brown & D. J. Brenner (Eds.), *Science, psychology, and communication: Essays honoring William Stephenson*. New York: Teachers College Press, 1972.

NUNNALLY, J. C. Meaning-processing and rated pleasantness: Effects on aesthetic preference. *Scientific Aesthetics*, 1977, *1*, 161–181.

NUNNALLY, J. C. *Psychometric theory* (2nd ed.). New York: McGraw-Hill, 1978.

NUNNALLY, J. C., & LEMOND, L. C. Exploratory behavior and human development. In H. W. Reese (Ed.), *Advances in child development and behavior* (Vol. 8). New York: Academic Press, 1973.

NUNNALLY, J. C., DUCHNOWSKI, A. J., & KNOTT, P. D. Association of neutral objects with rewards: Effects of massed versus distributed practice, delay of testing, age, and sex. *Journal of Experimental Child Psychology*, 1967, *5*, 152–163.

NUNNALLY, J. C., LEMOND, L. C., & WILSON, H. W. Studies of voluntary visual attention: Theory, methods, and psychometric issues. *Applied Psychological Measurement*, 1977, *1*, 203–218.

SOKOLOV, E. N. *Perception and the conditioned reflex*. New York: Macmillan, 1963.

WILSON, W. H. *The influence of stimulus complexity on exploratory behavior: Implications for a meaning-processing model*. Unpublished doctoral dissertation, Vanderbilt University, 1973.

Arousal, Intrinsic Motivation, and Personality

H. J. EYSENCK

AROUSAL AND MOTIVATION

The notion of intrinsic motivation, and the associated concepts of collative properties of stimuli and the arousal potential which they mediate, have played a large part in the thinking of D. Berlyne (1969, 1971). Thinking along these lines began with Wundt (1874) over a hundred years ago, and his famous Figure 141 (p. 558) illustrates the way in which the argument linking arousal potential and intrinsic motivation has proceeded. Figure 1 reproduces Wundt's diagram. The logarithmic ascending line represents E (*Empfindung:* subjective experience) as a function of R (*Reizstärke:* stimulus strength). The abscissa marks the point where E becomes conscious (at point a), and at height y (point m on the abscissa) E reaches its maximum, regardless of further growth of R. Wundt then goes on to say that we can represent the dependence of hedonic tone on R in terms of the stippled curve. He represents positive hedonic tone as lying above the abscissa and negative hedonic tone as lying below it, and shows that maximum hedonic tone is reached at a medium strength of R, as point c. At point e (the indifference point) positive hedonic tone changes into negative hedonic tone. Thus, increasing stimulus intensity from zero values of E first increases, then decreases, hedonic tone.

Berlyne took issue with the interpretation of R in purely physical terms of intensity; he prefers the term *arousal potential*, by which he means to refer to all the properties of stimulus patterns that tend, on the whole, to raise arousal; he defines it as the "psychological strength of a stimulus pattern, the degree to which it can disturb and alert the organism, the

H. J. EYSENCK • Department of Psychology, Institute of Psychiatry, De Crespigny Park, Denmark Hill, London SE5 8AF, England.

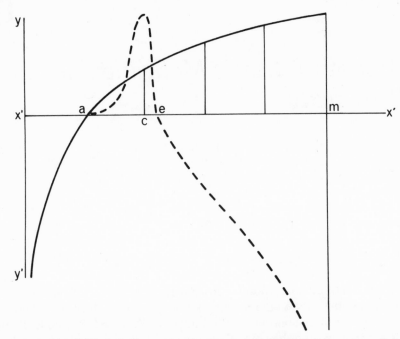

FIGURE 1. Wundt's (1874) original arousal-hedonic tone curve *(redrawn)*. See text for explanation.

ease with which it can take over control of behaviour and overcome the claims of competing stimuli" (1971, p. 70). The term refers to properties of stimuli, and not to their effects on the arousal system; this leaves us with the unsolved problem of how to quantify the arousal potential objectively and uniquely. Fiske & Maddi (1961) use the term "impact" instead of "arousal potential"; they define it as "the property of the stimulus which affects activation level" (p. 18), and analyze this property into three main classes: intensity, meaningfulness, and variation.

Berlyne has attempted to rephrase Wundt's hypothesis in modern physiological and neurological terms. He starts out from a consideration of Olds's work on the primary and secondary reward system and the aversion system (Olds & Olds, 1965), suggesting that, although the primary reward and punishment systems are antagonistic to each other (in the sense that the latter, if activated, inhibits the former), and though stimulation of either system produces signs of increased arousal, the secondary reward system is more or less identical with the trophotropic or dearousal system, in the sense that its activation coincides with dearousal. The suggestion is that the secondary reward system produces rewarding effects indirectly, by inhibiting the aversion system, which, in turn, disinhibits the primary reward system. Activation of the secondary rewarding system produces reward by releasing the primary rewarding system from inhibition. Thus, one of the brain mechanisms involved produces reward when arousal is *lowered* after rising to an uncomfortably high level, and the other works through arousal increase rather than arousal reduction, and comes into play when arousal is *raised* to a moderate extent. The former mechanism, Berlyne suggests, depends on the secondary reward mechanism; the latter, on the primary reward mechanism.

Berlyne arrives at a Figure similar to Wundt's by making two assumptions. One is a Gaussian distribution of the firing thresholds of the neurons involved in the primary reward and the aversion systems. The other is that the average threshold for neurons is higher in the aversion system than in the primary reward system. From these assumptions he deduces a situation rather like that in Figure 2, where the horizontal axis represents arousal potential, and the vertical axis represents degree of activity (number of neurons excited) in the primary reward and aversion systems. The solid curve represents the way in which activation of the primary reward system varies with arousal potential. The broken curve does the same for the aversion system. The two curves are drawn in opposite directions because the two systems are antagonistic. The aversion-system curve is displaced to the right to take account of the assumption that it takes more arousal potential to activate it. Finally, the figure incorporates the assumption that the distance between the base line and the asymptote is greater in the aversion curve (Y_A) than in the primary reward curve (Y_R). Taking the algebraic sum of the two curves gives the Wundt curve in Figure 1.

Berlyne adds one refinement to his figure. Between the points marked X_1 and X_2, arousal will be mild enough to fall within the pleasant range, but nevertheless high enough to activate the aversion system partially. Consequently, anything that then reduces arousal and thus

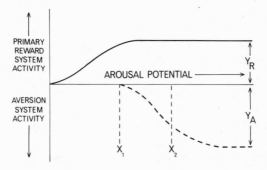

FIGURE 2. Berlyne's (1971) attempt to deduce arousal potential as a function of the activity of the primary reward and the aversion systems *(redrawn)*. See text for explanation.

inhibits the aversion system should add to the pleasure that is already present, by disinhibiting the primary reward system further. Berlyne discusses sexual activity and aesthetic pleasure in this connection.

THE SYSTEM AND ITS PROPOSITIONS

This theory of arousal increase and decrease as intrinsic motivation through hedonic tone changes will be taken up again later on; it is part of a wider setting to which we must turn next. The general conceptual framework to be used has been proposed by Fiske & Maddi (1961), and although there has been much experimental work done in relation to the propositions which they put forward, this has tended on the whole to strengthen their model. In the following paragraphs some of their propositions will be presented in paraphrased form; this is done in order to integrate the use of terms such as "arousal" with that adopted throughout this chapter.

Proposition 1 is: *An organism's level of arousal varies directly over time with the total impact of current stimulation.*

Proposition 2 is: *For any task, there is a level of arousal which is necessary for maximally effective performance.* This is simply a statement of the Yerkes–Dodson Law (Broadhurst, 1959) and Hebb's (1955) inverted-U relation between drive and performance; it also brings together Pavlov's law of strength and his law of transmarginal (protective) inhibition. These propositions are general in nature; we now come to propositions which are relevant to the concept of intrinsic drives.

Proposition 3 reads as follows: *The behavior of an organism tends to modify its arousal level toward the optimal zone for the task at hand.* As Fiske and Maddi point out, since the behavior of an organism provides stimulation, behavior can modify impact and alter arousal level. When confronted with a task, the organism can maximize the effectiveness of its performance by taking advantage of this potentiality. This capacity of an organism to modify its level of activation makes a major contribution to its flexibility, adaptability, and efficiency. However, as Proposition 4 tells us: *In the absence of specific tasks, the behavior of an organism is directed toward the maintenance of arousal at the characteristic or normal level.* In the absence of specific motivation requiring the performance of some specific task, the organism is still active. This activity can be viewed as motivated in the sense that the organism is faced with the need to maintain the level of arousal normal for its particular stage of wakefulness. Hebb and Thompson (1954) have expressed a similar view when saying that organisms "act so as to produce an optimal level of excitation" (p. 551), and Leuba (1955) similarly stated that "the organism tends to acquire those reactions which, when overall stimulation is low, are accompanied by an increasing stimulation; and when overall stimulation is high, those which are accompanied by decreasing stimulation" (p. 29). Similarly, Berlyne (1960): "For an individual organism at a particular time, there will be an *optimal influx of arousal potential.* . . . The organism will strive to keep arousal potential near its optimum" (p. 194). The picture is rounded off by Proposition 5, which tells us: *Negative affect is ordinarily experienced when arousal level differs markedly from normal level; position affect is associated with shifts of activation toward normal level.* The concept of characteristic level of arousal thus has relevance for affect; marked discrepancies from this norm are associated with negative affect, whereas positive affect accompanies or follows the process of reducing such discrepancies.

Arousal, Personality, and Hedonic Tone: Lemma I

These five propositions require to be supplemented by two further propositions the evidence for which has been accumulating since the publication of the Fiske and Maddi book. The first proposition relates to the systematic relation of personality to level of arousal (Eysenck, 1967); it may be worded thus: *The habitual (resting) level of extraverts is significantly lower than that of ambiverts, which, in turn, is significantly lower than that of introverts.* There is ample physiological evidence for this proposition (Eysenck, 1978). We shall not here go into detail on the nature of this evidence, but shall rather explore the implications of the proposition, taken in conjunction with the other propositions already listed. We shall refer to this proposition as the *personality postulate.*

Our seventh and eighth propositions refer to circadian rhythms of arousal (Blake, 1971). Proposition 7 states: *Arousal levels show a circadian rhythm, arousal increasing from morning to evening.* This is a very clear trend which can be monitored, as, for example, through measurements of body temperature. And the final proposition states: *Introverts have a higher level of arousal than extraverts in the morning, but their rate of increase during the day is less than that of extraverts, so that late in the evening extraverts have a higher level of arousal than introverts.* The work referred to showed that changes in body temperature, which provided the initial suggestion for this proposition, mirrored the performance on various tasks of extraverts and introverts during the day quite neatly, and "could therefore be considered a reasonably valid indicant of variations in arousal, and in resultant levels of efficiency, in both types" (Blake, 1971, p. 145). (The terms extraversion and introversion are used in many different senses; they are used in this chapter in the psychometrically and experimentally validated sense given them by Eysenck, 1967, and Eysenck & Eysenck, 1969.)

Propositions 6, 7, and 8 indicate that the other propositions cannot be properly tested, or used for applied purposes, without taking into account such factors as personality and time of day. As most experimental work in psychological laboratories is carried out at times which precede the switchover time (afternoon), we have far more data on that part of the circadian rhythm which favors introverts, and hence we shall concentrate on proposition 6; the final two propositions will only be mentioned in passing. We shall first of all consider Figure 3, which brings together proposition 6 and proposition 3; it should be compared with Figure 1, being in essence an extension of Wundt's original insight. Figure 3 relates level of stimulation on the abscissa ("impact" in Fiske and Maddi's terms; "arousal potential" in Berlyne's terms; not Wundt's simple R concept!) to hedonic tone on the ordinate (Eysenck, 1963). The broken line parallel with the abscissa indicates the indifference level, with the area below being characterized by negative hedonic tone, and the area above by positive hedonic tone.

The solid curved line indicates schematically the relationship involved; $O.L._P$ denotes the optimum or preferred level of stimulation for the population. Levels of stimulation higher or lower than this reduce the positive hedonic tone, and if departure from $O.L._P$ is too marked, the curve cuts the indifference level and hedonic tone becomes negative. There is one obvious departure from the Wundt curve; very low levels of sensory stimulation are considered not, as in his case, indifferent, but actively aversive. The work on sensory deprivation, boredom, and "sensation seeking" suggests that too low levels of sensory stimulation can be as aversive as too high levels, and consequently it is felt that this change from the Wundt/Berlyne picture is fully justified. The curve is skewed in order to indicate the obvious fact that it is easier to increase level of stimulation beyond the indifference points, and into the aversive region,

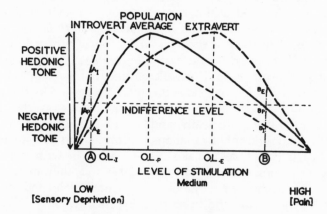

FIGURE 3. Eysenck's (1963) diagrammatic representation of the relation between arousal potential and hedonic tone, with particular reference to personality differences in arousal.

than to do the same for decrements in stimulation, and that the range is greater on the right side of the diagram than on the left. In reality, the skew should probably have been much more marked, but from our point of view this is not an important point in so far as the demonstration of the personality theory is concerned.

Separate curves are drawn for introverts and extraverts, to take account of proposition 6. Introverts have high resting levels of arousal, and hence need little stimulation to produce their optimum level ($O.L._I$); extraverts, on the other hand, have low resting levels of arousal, and hence need a good deal of stimulation to produce their optimum level ($O.L._E$). In accordance with this argument, the curve for introverts has been displaced toward the left, that for extraverts to the right; the actual distances involved are of course purely notional. Consider now points A and B on the level of stimulation dimension. Given the amount of stimulation symbolized by A, introverts would be located at a point A_I on the ordinate, extraverts at point A_E, and ambiverts (or random samples of the population) at point A_P. Thus, introverts would react with a positive hedonic tone to this level of stimulation, extraverts with a negative tone, and ambiverts would be near the indifferent point. Conversely, at point B we would find that extraverts (B_E) would show a mildly positive hedonic tone, ambiverts would again show indifference (B_P), but introverts would suffer discomfort or pain (B_I). Thus, outwardly (objectively) identical levels of stimulation would produce quite different hedonic tones (and consequently behavior) in extraverts, ambiverts, and introverts. With particular reference to the diagram, we can see that introverts would tolerate sensory deprivation better, extraverts pain. The experimental evidence is in line with these predictions (Eysenck, 1967, 1978).

Among other deductions from the general theory, we may list just a few. It has been deduced, and verified, that extraverts like women with large breasts, introverts women with small breasts (Eysenck & Wilson, 1978a.) (The argument is that large breasts are more arousing than small breasts.) It has been deduced, and verified, that extraverts prefer brighter colors, introverts duller colors (Götz & Götz, 1975). It has been deduced, and verified, that extraverts opt for strong visual and auditory stimuli, introverts for weak stimuli (Weisen, 1965). These and other experiments (see Eysenck, 1978) suggest that our first lemma results in large numbers of testable deductions, many of which have been tested and supported by the empirical results.

AROUSAL AND DRUGS: LEMMA II

Eysenck (1963) has suggested that experimental changes in arousal level through the administration of drugs might be used to test the predictions mediated by the general theory under consideration, and much work has been done to substantiate this prediction (Eysenck, 1967.) Here we shall consider just one recent (unpublished) experiment to illustrate the possibilities of this approach. This study, carried out by K. O'Connor, used extraverts and introverts as subjects, selected according to their scores on the E.P.Q. (Eysenck Personality Questionnaire; Eysenck & Eysenck, 1975), and nicotine, administered through the smoking of a standard cigarette, under standardized conditions, as the stimulant drug. According to hypothesis, a stimulant drug should increase cortical arousal, and hence have an introverting effect. The index of arousal chosen was the *CNV* (contingent negative variation), or "expectancy wave"; this is a slow negative-going potential elicited when the subject is expecting or preparing for a forthcoming event. In the experimental paradigm, a preparatory signal (S_1) is followed by a second signal, S_2, which informs the subject that he should now press a button, or whatever the agreed performance may be. Usually there is a 1 sec interval between S_1 and S_2, but a 4 sec interval may be preferred, as the longer interval of anticipation allows clearer separation of waveform components, the earlier components relating to alerting and the later to information-processing aspects of the *CNV*. Both intervals were used in the experiment.

Figure 4 shows the predicted results. *E* and *I* denote extraverts and introverts, respectively. *S.S.* and *R.S.* refer to sham smoking and real smoking conditions; under the *S.S.* conditions the subject "smokes" an unlit cogarette, and hence absorbs no nicotine. According to hypothesis, the $I_{S.S.}$ condition is near the arousal peak, and hence shows a strong *CNV* which becomes smaller when arousal is increased under the $I_{R.S.}$ condition. The $E_{S.S.}$ condition is at a lower point of arousal, and hence smoking shifts the *CNV* nearer to the high arousal part of the curve. The actual positions indicated should of course not be taken too literally.

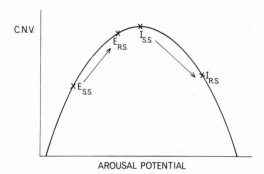

FIGURE 4. Predicted effects on *CNV* of smoking (R.S. = real smoking; *S.S.* = sham smoking) in introverts and extraverts.

The results, for both the 1 sec *I.S.I.* and the 4 sec *I.S.I.*, bear out predictions with considerable fidelity. During sham smoking, introverts show greater *CNVs* than extraverts; smoking increases the *CNV* for extraverts and decreases the CNV for introverts, so that under the smoking condition extraverts have greater *CNVs* than introverts. In the 4 sec *I.S.I.* condition, the *EC* (alerting component) shows results similar to those for the 1 sec *I.S.I.* condition. As regards the *LC* (information processing component), this is clearly elevated for the smoking extraverts and lowered for the smoking introverts. These results too follow prediction very closely.

We may conclude that these results, taken together with those of many other experiments, support the psychopharmacological lemma (Eysenck, 1967); examples of such other work are the studies by Gupta (1974) on figural aftereffects, Franks and Trouton (1958) on eye-blink conditioning, and Martin (1960) on adaptation.

External Manipulation of Arousal: Lemma III

It is possible to manipulate cortical arousal by manipulation of sensory input; thus, white noise, delivered over earphones, would serve to increase arousal, in much the same way as stimulant drugs would increase arousal, although by a different route, and using a quite different mechanism. Two experiments will here be discussed, one dealing directly with a measure of arousal, and the other with a perceptual task, namely, sensory thresholds. The first experiment was carried out by Frith (1967) as part of our general research program. Critical flicker fusion was used as the reaction measured; this has been shown physiologically to be an index of cortical arousal in cats and humans. C.F.F. was studied under conditions of noise and quiet in extraverts and introverts, and the expectations tested are shown in Figure 5. According to the diagram, we would expect improved performance in the C.F.F. task under noisy conditions in the extravert group only, with little change in the introvert group; had the noise level actually been increased well beyond the level used, then we might have expected a *decline* in performance of the introvert group. Going even beyond that level, we should ultimately find a decrement in performance even for extraverts. The predicted interaction effect (personality × noise level) was actually found, at an acceptable level of significance, and the mean C.F.F. values demonstrated that the direction of the observed difference was as predicted.

The other studies to be noted in this section are Shigehisa & Symons (1973) and Shigehisa, Shigehisa, and Symons, (1973.) These studies were concerned with the effect on sensory thresholds in one modality of sensory stimulation in another modality. Shigehisa performed two exper-

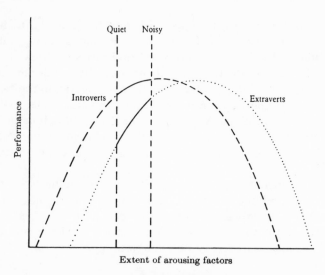

FIGURE 5. Hypothesized relationship between the extent of arousing factors, personality, and performance on the C.F.F. (critical flicker fusion) test. (After Frith, 1967.)

iments; in the first he varied the intensity of visual stimulation and studied the effects on auditory thresholds, and in the second he varied the intensity of auditory stimulation and studied the effects on visual thresholds. As results were similar in both experiments, only the first will be discussed. His prediction can best be illustrated by a diagram (Figure 6), which shows on the abscissa differing and increasing amounts of visual stimulation (in ten ascending steps), and on the ordinate auditory thresholds, with high thresholds at the top and low at the bottom. The theory tested predicts that sensory stimulation in one modality will increase cortical arousal, and hence lower sensory thresholds in other modalities. However, there would not be any purely linear decrease, in view of the inverted-U relation; at some stage transmarginal inhibition (to use Pavlov's useful concept) would set in and reverse the relationship.

This reversal should occur at a relatively low level of sensory stimulation for the high-arousal introverts; at a somewhat higher level for the intermediate ambiverts; and at a relatively high level for the low-arousal extraverts. These relationships are indicated in the figure, which of course is purely diagrammatic; the results actually came out very much as predicted. When the alternative experiment was carried out, that is, when auditory stimulation was employed to change visual thresholds, the same result was obtained. Shigehisa has carried out several other experiments, always obtaining results favoring the hypothesis illustrated in Figure 6, and we may conclude that this lemma too has been empirically supported.

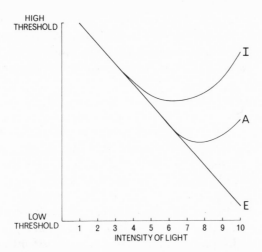

FIGURE 6. Dependence of auditory threshold (ordinate) on intensity of visual stimulation (abscissa), for introverts, ambiverts, and extraverts. Diagrammatic representation of results reported by Shigehisa and Symons (1973).

TASK AND AROUSAL: LEMMA IV

If conditions external to the task (e.g., white noise) can modify the arousal level of the subject, and accordingly his performance, it should be possible to specify conditions of the task itself which would also have predictable consequences in so far as arousal level and performance are concerned. The most obvious example is the set of tasks referred to as *vigilance* tasks, that is, monotonous tasks requiring long-maintained high arousal when the stimulation provided is minimal (Mackie, 1977). Such conditions are known to lower arousal, and low arousal leads to errors of omission and commission which should discriminate between introverts and extraverts toward the later stages of the task performance. Usually performance is perfect or nearly perfect at the beginning of the task, which is typically very easy; it is the lowering in arousal consequent to the boring continuation of the stimulation involved which produces the errors, and, according to hypothesis, this lowering should proceed more quickly in extraverts than in introverts.

A whole series of studies has been published supporting this lemma. Davies, Hockey, and Taylor (1969), Keister and McLaughlin (1972), Krupski, Raskin, and Bakan (1971), Thackray, Jones, and Touchstone (1974), and Tune (1966) are only a few of the many authors who could be cited. Krupski *et al.* (1971), for instance, used a signal detection task and correlated errors of commission with a variety of physiological and psychological measures; the correlation with extraversion was .33, and the correlation with several indices of arousal (all derived from the GSR) was between −.3 and −.4. Thus, high arousal correlated negatively with the commission of errors, extraversion positively; this is precisely what is predicted. Vigilance tasks are among the most reliable measures of extraversion in the whole literature.

Vigilance tasks illustrate the point that low arousal leads to poor performance, and high arousal (up to the point where transmarginal inhibition sets in) to good performance. Some tasks, such as eyeblink conditioning, contain a task-related stimulus which produces changes in arousal level, namely, the UCS; one would predict that with less intense stimulation (weak UCS) introverts would perform better than extraverts, but that with (transmarginal) intense stimulation (strong UCS) extraverts would perform better than introverts. This hypothesis has been tested by Eysenck and Levey (1972), and the results are shown in Figures 7 and 8. The former shows the rate of eyelid conditioning for introverts, ambiverts, and extraverts under conditions of weak UCS, and the latter

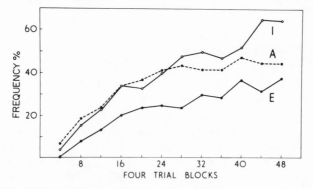

FIGURE 7. Eye-blink conditioning in extraverts, ambiverts, and introverts under weak intensity UCS conditions. (After Eysenck & Levey 1972.)

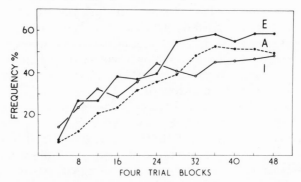

FIGURE 8. Eye-blink conditioning in extraverts, ambiverts, and introverts under strong intensity UCS conditions. (After Eysenck & Levey, 1972.)

shows the rates of eyelid conditioning of these three groups under conditions of strong UCS. It will be seen that, though the ambivert group is intermediate under both types of conditions, there is a switchover for the E and I groups, very much as predicted.

Many more examples of the influence of task conditions on performance, acting through the arousal-introversion paradigm, will be found in the literature (Eysenck, 1978). Thus, for example, Eysenck (1971) has shown that we may regard a typical intelligence test in part as a measure of vigilance; he predicted and found that, although introverts and extraverts showed no difference in performance at the beginning or toward the middle of the test, the extraverts showed a significant decline toward the end. This is typical of the universality of task-related changes in arousal level; the motivational properties of these changes are only too frequently neglected in orthodox experimental designs.

AROUSAL AND MEMORY: LEMMA V

In order to apply the arousal and personality propositions to the memory field, we need connecting theories which can specify concrete predictions. Two of these will be briefly mentioned, and some results discussed. The first link between propositions and deductions is Walker's (1958) action-decrement theory. According to this view, psychological events establish a perseverative trace lasting for some length of time, during which long-term memory is laid down. During this consolidation period there is a temporary inhibition of retrieval ("action decrement") which preserves the trace and protects it against disruption. It is further assumed that high arousal has the effect of producing a longer lasting active trace, with the result that high levels of arousal should lead to greater long-term memory, but a larger initial inhibition of retrieval. Howarth and Eysenck (1968) tested the derived deduction that introverts should have poor immediate recall, but should show reminiscence and much better recall after a lengthy period of time, whereas extraverts should show good immediate recall, but poor retrieval after some extended period of time. Figure 9 shows the results of the experiment; clearly the predicted crossover has occurred after around 5 min. Each point in the graph is the mean score of 11 subjects, and of course no subject was used more than once. The recall task was a paired associates test, with a maximum score of 14.

The other link is provided by an hypothesis due to Broadbent (1971), and in a physiological form to Walley and Weiden (1973). In a grossly simplified form, this hypothesis states that a crucial characteristic of an aroused CNS is that it devotes a higher proportion of its time to the intake

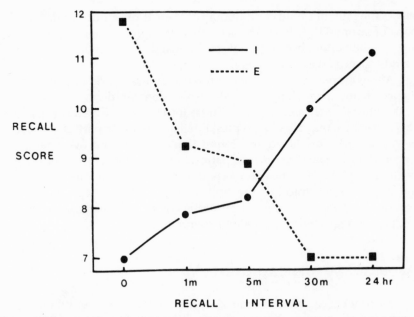

FIGURE 9. Mean recall scores of extraverts and introverts at the recall interval stated. (After Howarth & Eysenck, 1968.)

of information from dominant sources than does the unaroused system. M. W. Eysenck (1977) has argued that a large number of deductions can be made from this hypothesis regarding the retrieval of information by extraverts and introverts, and has conducted a series of experimental studies which, on the whole, have verified these deductions. He summarizes his conclusions as follows:

> Extraverts show more rapid learning than introverts on difficult tasks, such as those involving response competition; extraverts tend to recall better than introverts at short retention intervals, whereas the opposite is the case at long retention intervals; and extraverts retrieve information faster than introverts from episodic and semantic memory. Furthermore, there are clear parallels between the results obtained by investigators concerning themselves with arousal and learning and those dealing with introversion–extraversion and learning. There is some important link between introversion–extraversion and arousal. . . . a reasonable assumption is that the optimal level of physiological arousal is lower in introverts than in extraverts. (p. 218)

AROUSAL AND SOCIAL BEHAVIOR: LEMMA VI

It is one of the more potent aspects of the system of motivation here under discussion that it extends well beyond the experimental laboratory, and into the social lives of individual extraverts and introverts. Links with social behavior are either direct, as when the low arousal typical of the extravert triggers off sensation-seeking, risk-taking and stimulation-producing behavior, or indirect, as when introverts form more easily, more quickly, and more strongly the conditioned responses which are the causes of neurotic symptoms on the one hand, and socialized behavior on the other (Eysenck, 1977; Eysenck & Rachman, 1964). Introverts, according to this paradigm, are predisposed to neurotic, extraverts to antisocial (criminal) dysfunctions; there is much evidence to support these predictions. The social side of the extravert, on this hypothesis, can be explained in terms of the strong arousal produced by other people; such arousal is not welcomed by the introvert, already in a state of arousal compared with the extravert. The impulsivity of the extravert would be explained in terms of the lessened power of the cortex to exert a proper control over the lower centres; introverts, with their strongly aroused cortex, show more control and less impulsivity.

Sexual behavior in particular has been studied in some detail in connection with the set of propositions detailed in the opening paragraphs of this chapter. Eysenck (1976) predicted that extraverts would have intercourse earlier than introverts; that they would have intercourse more frequently than introverts; that they would have intercourse with more different partners; that they would have intercourse in more different positions than introverts; that they would show more varied sexual behavior outside intercourse; and that they would indulge in longer precoital love play than introverts. All these predictions were verified at satisfactory levels of statistical significance, and in several different studies in the United States, the United Kingdom, and Germany. We may accept the proposition that differences in sexual behavior among human beings are to a predictable extent mediated by differences in arousal, linked with the personality dimension of extraversion-introversion.

Going beyond these varied applications of our paradigm to social behavior, we may even extend it to the development of social attitudes and value judgments (Eysenck & Wilson, 1978b). Tough-minded attitudes are more frequently found in extraverts, tender-minded attitudes in introverts. This mediation through personality factors may explain why, like other aspects of personality, social attitudes are strongly determined by genetic factors (Eaves & Eysenck, 1974). The determination of social conduct and social attitudes, in so far as they are not influenced directly or indirectly by biological factors, may be attributed to evaluative conditioning (Martin & Levey, 1978); cognitive theories in this field have not received much experimental support.

SUMMARY AND CONCLUSIONS

In this chapter an effort has been made to argue that the biologically determined, innate differences in resting arousal level constitute intrinsic motivating factors which, directly or indirectly, produce personality differences (extraversion–introversion), which in turn mediate many different types of behaviors. These differences go well beyond differential reactions to collative properties of stimuli, and powerfully influence social behavior as well as reactions in the laboratory. An attempt has been made to spell out a series of propositions which constitutes the general background of the system here developed, and then to derive a series of lemmas which can be experimentally tested; some of the resulting laboratory investigations have been briefly discussed, and found to give positive results on the whole. We conclude that it is possible to develop a rational, testable system of propositions in the field of intrinsic motivation, and that such a system extends into many areas of experimental and social psychology. The system has a firm biological underpinning, and relates psychophysiological concepts to psychological behavior patterns. Further development of the system seems eminently worthwhile.

REFERENCES

BERLYNE, D. E. *Conflict, arousal, and curiosity.* New York: McGraw-Hill, 1960.

BERLYNE, D. E. *Aesthetics and psychobiology.* New York: McGraw-Hill, 1971.

BLAKE, M. J. F. Temperament and time of day. In W. P. Colquhoun (Ed.), *Biological rhythms and human performance.* London: Academic Press, 1971.

BROADBENT, D. E. *Decision and stress.* London: Academic Press, 1971.

BROADHURST, P. L. The interaction of task difficulty and motivation: The Yerkes–Dodson Law revised. *Acta Psychologica,* 1959, *16,* 321–338.

DAVIES, D. R., Hockey, G. R. J., & TAYLOR, A. Varied auditory stimulation, temperament differences and vigilance performance. *British Journal of Psychology,* 1969, *60,* 453–457.

EAVES, L. J., & EYSENCK, H. J. Genetics and the development of social attitudes. *Nature,* 1974, *249,* 288–289.

EYSENCK, H. J. (Ed.). *Experiments with drugs.* New York: Pergamon, 1963.

EYSENCK, H. J. The biological basis of personality. Springfield, Ill.: Charles C Thomas, 1967.

EYSENCK, H. J. Relation between intelligence and personality. *Perceptual and Motor Skills,* 1971, *32,* 637–638.

EYSENCK, H. J. *Sex and personality.* London: Open Books, 1976.

EYSENCK, H. J. *Crime and personality.* London: Routledge & Kegan Paul, 1977.

EYSENCK, H. J. (Ed.). *The measurement of personality.* Baltimore: University Park Press, 1978.

EYSENCK, H. J., & EYSENCK, S. B. G. *Personality structure and measurement.* London: Routledge & Kegan Paul, 1969.

EYSENCK, H. J., & EYSENCK, S. B. G. *Manual of the E.P.Q.* London: Hodder & Stoughton, 1975. San Diego: EdITS, 1975.

EYSENCK, H. J., & LEVEY, A. Conditioning, introversion–extraversion and the strength of the nervous system. In V. D. Nebylitsyn & J. A Gray (Eds.), *Biological bases of individual behavior*. New York: Academic Press, 1972.

EYSENCK, H. J., & RACHMAN, S. *The causes and curses of neurosis*. New York: Pergamon, 1964.

EYSENCK, H. J. & WILSON, G. D. *The psychology of sex*. London: Dent, 1978.(a)

EYSENCK, H. J., & WILSON, G. D. *The psychological basis of ideology*. Baltimore: University Park Press, 1978.(b)

EYSENCK, M. W. *Human memory*. New York: Pergamon, 1977.

FISKE, D. W., & MADDI, S. R. *Functions of varied experience*. Homewood, Ill.: Dorsey Press, 1961.

FRANKS, C. M., & TROUTON, D. Effects of amobarbital sodium and dexamphetamine sulphate on the conditioning of the eyelid response. *Journal of Comparative and Physiological Psychology*, 1958, *51*, 220–222.

FRITH, C. D. The interaction of noise and personality with initial flicker fusion performance. *British Journal of Psychology*, 1967, *58*, 127–131.

GÖTZ, K. O., & GÖTZ, K. Colour preferences, extraversion, and neuroticism of art students. *Perceptual and Motor Skills*, 1975, *41*, 919–930.

GUPTA, B. S. Stimulant and depressant drugs on kinaesthetic figural after-effects. *Psychopharmacologia*, 1974, *36*, 275–280.

HEBB, D. O. Drives and the C.N.S. (Conceptual nervous system). *Psychological Review*, 1955, *62*, 243–254.

HEBB, D. O., & THOMPSON, W. R. The social significance of animal studies. In G. Lindzey (Ed.), *Handbook of social psychology*. Cambridge, Mass.: Addison-Wesley, 1954.

HOWARTH, E., & EYSENCK, H. J. Extraversion, arousal, and paired-associate recall. *Journal of Experimental Research in Personality*, 1968, *3*, 114–116.

KEISTER, M., & MCLAUGHLIN, R. J. Vigilance performance related to Extraversion–Introversion and caffeine. *Journal of Experimental Research in Personality*, 1972, *6*, 5–11.

KRUPSKI, A., RASKIN, D. C., & BAKAN, P. Physiological and personality correlates of commission errors in an auditory vigilance task. *Psychophysiology*, 1971, *8*, 304–311.

LEUBA, C. Toward some integration of learning theories: The concept of optimal stimulation. *Psychological Reports*, 1955, *1*, 27–33.

MACKIE, R. R. (Ed.). *Vigilance*. New York: Plenum, 1977.

MARTIN, I. The effects of depressant drugs on palmar skin resistance and adaptation. In: H. J. Eysenck (Ed.), Experiments in Personality. New York: Praeger, 1960.

MARTIN, I., & LEVEY, A. B. Evaluative conditioning. *Advances in Behaviour Research and Therapy*, 1978, *1*, 57–101.

OLDS, J., & OLDS, M. Drives, rewards and the brain. In *New directions in psychology II*. New York: Holt, Rinehart & Winston, 1965.

SHIGEHISA, T., & SYMONS, J. R. Effect of intensity of visual stimulation on auditory sensitivity in relation to personality. *British Journal of Psychology*, 1973, *64*, 205–213.

SHIGEHISA, P. M. J., SHIGEHISA, T., & SYMONS, J. Effects of intensity of auditory stimulation on photopic visual sensitivity in relation to personality. *Japanese Psychological Research*, 1973, *15*, 164–172.

THACKRAY, R. I., JONES, K. N., & TOUCHSTONE, R. M. Personality and physiological correlates of performance decrement on a monotonous task requiring sustained attention. *British Journal of Psychology*, 1974, *65*, 351–358.

TUNE, G. S. Errors of commission as a function of age and temperament in a type of vigilance task. *Quarterly Journal of Experimental Psychology*, 1966, *18*, 358–361.

WALKER, E. L. Action decrement and its relation to learning. *Psychological Review*, 1958, *65*, 129–142.

WALLEY, R. E., & WEIDEN, T. D. Lateral inhibition and cognitive masking: A neurophysiological theory of attention. *Psychological Review,* 1973, *80,* 284–302.

WEISEN, A. Differential reinforcing effects of onset and offset of stimulation on the operant behavior of normals, neurotics and psychopaths. University of Florida, 1965. Unpublished doctoral dissertation.

WUNDT, W. M. *Grundzüge der physiologischen Psychologie.* Leipzig: Engelmann, 1874.

7

Subjective Uncertainty and Task Preference

KLAUS SCHNEIDER AND HEINZ HECKHAUSEN

INTRODUCTION

Humans as well as other animals face the problem of orienting themselves to their environment. Action potentialities of all living beings are a
function of the objective opportunities of the environment as well as of
the behavioral limitations of the living being. Both have to be explored
(Lorenz, 1969). The adaptive value of a behavioral disposition to explore
both the environment and one's own possibilities is not so evident as in
such "homeostatic drives" as hunger and thirst. Thus the tendency to
explore was generally not considered an original motive by students of
animal and human motivation in the first half of this century.

At the time when Daniel Berlyne started his lifelong study of
exploratory behavior of humans and animals the prevalent mode of
theorizing was not at all sympathetic to such a biologically oriented point
of view. All the more then we should be grateful to him, in that he not
only took seriously what he called "ludic behavior," but also demonstrated creative ways to do experiments and to theorize in this area of
motivational research.

Starting from a different tradition, students of achievement motivation also studied a kind of self-exploratory behavior in achievement-
oriented situations. Although similar concepts, such as subjective uncertainty (cf. Atkinson, 1957), were discussed in both areas, the programs
were done in "splendid isolation" from each other. The point we want to
make here is that both, the phenomenon of exploring the world as

KLAUS SCHNEIDER • Department of Psychology, Philipps University, Marburg 3550, West
Germany. HEINZ HECKHAUSEN • Institute of Psychology, Ruhr University, 4630 Bochum,
West Germany.

studied by Berlyne and his students, and the phenomenon of exploring one's own performance potentialities as studied by students of achievement motivation, can be explained most parsimoniously by using Berlyne's informational way of theorizing.

EXPLAINING TASK PREFERENCE IN THE LEWIN–ATKINSON TRADITION

When individuals have a choice among several levels of a skill task varying in difficulty, they prefer tasks of an intermediate level. The phenomenon has been observed both in level-of-aspiration studies and in risk-taking studies by Lewin and associates, and more recently by students of achievement motivation (cf. Atkinson & Feather, 1966; Heckhausen, 1967; Lewin, Dembo, Festinger, & Sears, 1944). The explanation given for this behavior by Lewin and associates (Lewin *et al.*, 1944) and Atkinson (1957) is based on the assumption that valences of success and failure are weighted by the probabilities—success probabilities (P_s) and failure probabilities (P_f)—that the individual assumes for these outcomes.

According to these models, valences of success and failure (anticipated positive and negative affects after success and failure) are monotonic functions of the perceived difficulty: the lower the subjective success probability, the higher the positive valence of anticipated future success and the lower the negative valence of anticipated failure. Hence, weighted valences of success and failure reach a maximum anywhere in the intermediate difficulty range, depending on the exact form of the functional relation between P_s and valences (cf. Schneider, 1973). According to Atkinson's more specific model, this relationship is a linear inverse relationship: $Va_s = k(1-P_s)$ and $Va_f = k(-P_s)$. Therefore the maximum of weighted valences of success and failure has to be predicted at a P_s of .50. The constant term k stands for a dispositional personality variable in Atkinson's model, that is, motive strength. Valences are assumed to be functions of the achievement motives, the motives to seek success (M_s) and to avoid failure (M_f), as well as of the difficulty-dependent incentives of success (I_s) and failure (I_f). The complete formulas for expected valences of success and failure therefore are functions of motives, incentives, and subjective probabilities. In the following discussion we shall deal only with weighted (expected) incentives of success (EI_s) and failure (EI_f): (1) $EI_s = (1-P_s) \times P_s$; (2) $EI_f = (-P_s) \times P_f$ when P_s and P_f add to 1.0. Adding a constant, which represents the difference between M_s and M_f, does not change the maxima and minima of these functions.

Consequently, success-oriented subjects should prefer an intermediate difficulty level, whereas failure-oriented subjects should avoid this difficulty level and preferably select tasks that are either very easy or very difficult.

However, it has been found that failure-oriented subjects normally show only a somewhat reduced preference for intermediate task difficulty levels compared with success-oriented subjects. Besides this, success-oriented subjects do not maximize positive affect by selecting only tasks of intermediate difficulty, but do a kind of matching instead, that is, they generally prefer intermediate difficulty levels, but select easier and more difficult tasks as well—although in decreasing numbers. This problem has been hushed up so far by students of achievement motivation.

Finally it was found that success-oriented subjects select task-difficulty levels where objective and also subjective success probabilities are lower than .50 (cf. Heckhausen, 1968; Schneider, 1973). The most preferred difficulty levels were those where one trial out of three was a success.

In order to explain this consistent deviation from the prediction of the model, Heckhausen (1968) proposed a revision of the model, which shifted the maximum of weighted success incentive into the more difficult range and the maximum of weighted failure incentive into the easier range. This can be achieved by several possible modifications of the inverse linear relationship between P_s and I_s, as assumed in Atkinson's model.

In three studies (Schneider, 1973) in which subjects were free to select among nine difficulty levels of a psychomotor task it was found that the rank-preference order of groups of success- and failure-oriented subjects could be better predicted with such an asymmetric modification of the model than with Atkinson's original model (cf. Table I).

Subjective Uncertainty and Task Preference

In the task used here, subjects had to push a steel ball through a gap of nine different widths at the end of the table (Schneider, 1973, p. 126). They were given 10 practice trials at each width, their objective probabilities being written on a blackboard in front of them. Subjective probabilities were assessed post-experimentally (in some experiments before the free choice of difficulty levels, to check for sequence effects). Predictions were given either in respect to one further trial at each gap $(P_{s\,1})$ or in respect, to 10 trials $(P_{s\,2})$. A previous study had shown that motivated "biasing up" of objective probabilities is different with these two response modes (Schneider, 1972). However, after subjects had extensive practice before estimating their success probabilities, both scaling techniques yielded quite similar results. P_s estimates were used in order to compute theoretical values of expected incentives of success and failure according to Atkinson's original formula and according to a revised formula. Assuming that the relationship between P_s and incentives was downwardly concave, power functions [$I_s = (1-P_s)^{.5}$ and $I_f = (-P_s)^{.5}$] were postulated.

In all three studies, both success-oriented subjects and failure-oriented subjects showed a clear preference for task-difficulty levels where subjective success probability was lower than .50. Maximal preference was found at difficulty levels where subjects believed their chances to be between .30 and .40. At the same difficulty levels, however, subjects needed maximal time to predict success or failure by saying "yes" or "no." Thus, group-preference orders of task-difficulty levels could be predicted as well with mean decision times (DT) as with the revised asymmetric model.

Figure 1 illustrates the results of the first of these studies. After 10 practice trials at each difficulty level, decision time in predicting success or failure for each difficulty level was measured. Decision time (DT) was measured in these studies without the knowledge of the subjects. To achieve this a screen was lowered in front of the gap. The subject raised the screen by pushing a button in the middle of a panel at the front end of the game table and then predicted success or failure by pushing either one of two buttons (labeled "yes" and "no") at either side of this panel.

Free choice behavior was assessed by giving subjects the possibility of choosing 15 games at any difficulty level they wanted. Free choices were allowed after the procedure in which decision time was measured. Subjective probabilities were measured post-experimentally. Subjects estimated their chance of success out of one trial (P_{s1}) or out of 10 trials (P_{s2}) for every difficulty level.

Subjects in this study were 45 first-year male college students. Heckhausen's TAT measure (Heckhausen, 1963; cf. Heckhausen, 1968) had been given first in group sessions. As success- and failure-oriented subjects behaved alike in these three studies, their data were pooled in Figure 1.

Figure 1 demonstrates that subjects tended to select gap 3. At this difficulty level their objective success probability was .23 on average and their mean estimated subjective success probability was still .32 (P_{s1}) and .35 (P_{s2}). The maximum of the weighted success incentives computed from objective success probabilities is therefore to be found at difficulty level 6, and even the maxima of the more appropriate ones, based on P_s estimates, are to be found at difficulty levels 5 and 4, depending on the P_s measure. However, the maximum of averaged DT and the 50% criterion of the distribution of yes answers is to be found at the most preferred

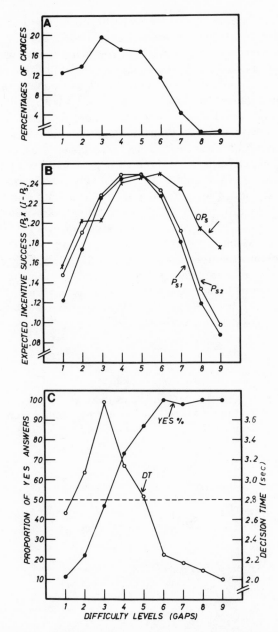

FIGURE 1. (A) Percentages of choices of objective task-difficulty levels. (B) Averaged expected incentives of success, computed from objective probabilities for success (OP_s), and from P_{s1} and P_{s2} estimates. (C) Averaged decision time (DT) and proportions of yes answers. Incentives of success were computed according to Atkinson's formula: $P_s \times (1-P_s)$. (Data from Schneider, 1973, Chapter 4, Exp. I.)

difficulty level 3. The same results were found in the following two studies, in which high-school students, aged 16–18, served as subjects. Table I shows Kendall rank-correlation coefficients among the three predictor variables and group preference order for all three studies.

Several authors have successfully used DT as a behavioral measure of subjective uncertainty (cf. Cohen, Hansel & Walker, 1960; Crandall, Solomon, & Kellaway, 1955). Thus, an alternative to an asymmetric revision of Atkinson's model seemed to be adequate, based on the assumption that subjects prefer task-difficulty levels where the outcome is perceived as maximally uncertain. Following Berlyne's (1960) interpretation of preference for intermediate difficulty levels in skill situations, and a related phenomenon, the preference for intermediate probabilities in chance games (Edwards, 1953, 1954), Schneider (1973, 1974, 1977) assumed that individuals select intermediate difficulty levels at skill tasks in order to receive maximum information in respect to their task competence. Maximum information can be ascertained at intermediate difficulty levels, where subjective uncertainty in respect to task outcome is greatest and where success and failure cannot be explained by task ease or task difficulty (Weiner, Frieze, Kukla, Reed, Rest, & Rosenbaum, 1971; Weiner, Heckhausen, Meyer, & Cook, 1972).

TABLE I. Kendall Rank-Correlation Coefficients Between the Expected Incentive Values of Atkinson's Original Model, an Asymmetric Modification, and Mean Decision Time (DT) as Predictor Variables and Group Preference Functions for Difficulty Levels.

Study	Subjects[a]		Atkinson model	Asymmetric model	DT
Experiment I	45 male college students	HS>FF	.72	.79	.83
		FF>HS	−.50	−.78	.67
Experiment II	45 male high school students	HS>FF	.29	.44	.53
		FF>HS	−.39	−.67	.56
Experiment III	30 male high school students	HS>FF	.46	.92	.86
		FF>HS	−.60	−.92	.86

[a]Subjects were divided into success-oriented and failure-oriented subjects at the respective medians of the distributions of "Netto–Hope" score of Heckhausen's achievement motive TAT (Heckhausen, 1963; cf. Heckhausen, 1968).

The reduction of maximal uncertainty, built up and reduced in a short while, is also a thrill, that is, a positive affective experience (Berlyne, 1960)—and this positive affective experience holds for skill as well as for chance games. So we think that the affective component and not the informational component of uncertainty reduction is the common element in skill and chance situations and can explain similar findings in both situations, whereas achievement-motivation theory is only valid in situations where individuals have some control on task outcome (Lewin et al., 1944).

Information Search in Achievement Situations

The ultimate goal of selecting intermediate difficulty levels in achievement-oriented situations, as conceived here, is information concerning one's own task competence. Experimental analysis of behavioral and experiential phenomena do not allow for an easy decision for or against such an assumption, because ultimate goals very often are not experienced by subjects themselves. In an evolutionary perspective, however, the functional value of such a goal can be shown. Lorenz (1943, 1969) has convincingly argued that an innate tendency to explore the environment as well as the potentialities of the organism ("self-exploration," Lorenz, 1969) must have been of a high adaptive value in the evolution of species living in large and variable habitats, most prominently among them rat and man.

The immediate cause for the search for competence information, however we believe, is subjective uncertainty; in this case, self-created subjective uncertainty. The state of self-created subjective uncertainty in a context of playful behavior, as well as the sudden relief from it, is experienced as a positive affect (Berlyne, 1960), and may guide the behavior of subjects as well by its cue function (this is the game you should play!) as by its positive feedback function (this is the game which gives fun!). Unlike comparative concepts, subjective uncertainty as an explanatory concept has the advantage that in principle three classes of indicators can be assessed (Berlyne, 1960, 1966): (1) the experience of the subjects of their state of uncertainty; (2) behavioral conflict indicators as decision time; and (3) peripheral and central physiological indicators (cf. Higgins, 1971; Sutton, Braren, Zubin, & John, 1965).

So far only a general assumption has been made. However, the model can be supplemented easily by an individual-differences hypothesis, which has been around in achievement-motivation research

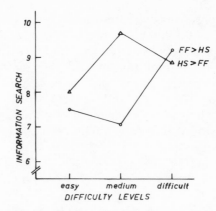

FIGURE 2. Mean frequencies of feedback search in 3 difficulty conditions for success- and failure-oriented subjects ($HS > FF$ and $FF > HS$). There are 20 subjects in each of the 6 conditions. (From Butzkamm, 1972.)

from its very beginning (McClelland, 1961). Success-oriented subjects can be characterized by an eager search for valid competence feedback, whereas failure-oriented subjects tend to avoid such feedback—at least under circumstances where their self-evaluation is being threatened (Schneider & Meise, 1973).

A similar individual-differences hypothesis was proposed on the basis of an attribution-theoretical reinterpretation of achievement motivation by Weiner and associates (Weiner et al., 1971).

Butzkamm (1972) tested the individual-differences hypothesis by giving subjects a chance to ask for performance feedback after each series of quantity-estimation trials. Randomly distributed numbers of dots were shown for brief periods with a slide projector, objective difficulty being varied so that three difficulty levels resulted: high difficulty (objective success probability approximately 10%), medium difficulty (50%), and low difficulty (10%). Subjects had to estimate the number of dots, and could ask for immediate performance feedback. Figure 2 shows the mean numbers of performance-feedback search. Subjects were 80 male high-school students, 12–16 years of age. Whereas success-oriented subjects had on an average the highest request at the intermediate difficulty level, failure-oriented subjects tended to avoid the intermediate range. The difference between success- and failure-oriented subjects at this difficulty level is significant ($p < .001$).

Therefore an informational interpretation of incentives in achievement-oriented situations appears to be an attractive, that is, heuristically valuable, alternative to Atkinson's affect-maximation theory. However, there remains a puzzling fact in these studies. According to commonsense considerations (cf. Brim, 1955) as well as to the logic of Shannon's and Weaver's calculus for objective uncertainty "H," subjective uncertainty should be maximal where the subjective probabilities for both possible events (exhausting and excluding events!) are equal. Yet equal subjective probabilities for success and failure were found in these studies to be one or even two difficulty levels higher than where maximum DT was measured.

Different Indices of Subjective Uncertainty

A series of studies was planned in order to find out why these different indices of subjective uncertainty diverge in an achievement-oriented context. In these studies, a further index of subjective uncertainty was assessed—*confidence* in one's prediction of success and failure. In addition, the informational value of task outcome at every difficulty level was estimated by subjects in two studies, and the importance of the four causal factors for success and failure of the Heider–Weiner causal attribution scheme was ascertained in two other studies.

All studies were done with first-year male and female students; no individual-differences measures were given, as the general relations had to be ascertained first. The same psychomotor task was used as in the first study mentioned above (see p. 151), and the same general procedure was followed.

Figure 3 shows the relationship found between DT and confidence (C) in the first of these studies (Schneider, 1974, Exp. 1). Confidence estimates were given orally after the subjects had predicted success or failure by pushing one of two buttons. To help subjects in giving this estimation, a bipolar 21-step scale ("No," "100," "90," . . . "0," . . . "90," "100," "Yes") was displayed on the wall in front of the subjects.

Mean confidence estimates were symmetrically related to mean DT (Figure 3a), although the relationship was not exactly linear (Figure 3b). On the average, subjects had their lowest confidence estimates at the same difficulty levels where they needed the longest time to predict success or failure. However, they needed more time at higher difficulty levels than at lower ones, even when their mean confidence was roughly similar. The apparent reason is that subjects tended to predict success even when their chances were very low, but did not predict failure in cases where chances for success were high (Figure 3a) as much. Prediction of improbable success took subjects longer, whereas the prediction of very likely success could be done in a short time. The point biserial correlation coefficients between the prediction of success and DT consequently move from positive to negative from the highest to the lowest difficulty level (DL) where failures are still predicted (DL 1 to 6: .43, .24, .33, $-.21$, $-.41$, and $-.41$; $r_{.05;24} = \pm.33$, one-sided). The overprediction of success at the more difficult range influences DT more than confidence.

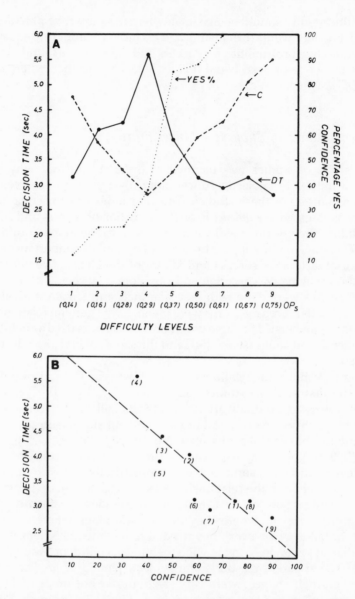

FIGURE 3. (A) Averaged decision times (*DT*) and confidence estimates (*C*) and percentages of yes answers (yes %) at the 9 difficulty levels of the task. Objective success probabilities (OP_s) are given in brackets in respect to all difficulty levels. (B) The average decision times as a function of the averaged confidence estimates. Numbers of difficulty levels are given in brackets. Subjects were 26 male and female first-year students. (From Schneider, 1974, p. 154–155.)

The correlation coefficients between mean DT and C estimates as well as between H values based on subjective probability estimates are shown in Table II for this and all following studies. The relationship between confidence and DT was generally high, yet not higher than the relationships found between confidence and P_s-based uncertainty measures. Only the relationships including DT were generally lower.

The most straightforward reason for the lower relationships between DT and the other indicators of uncertainty may be found in the fact that DT, the way we measured it here, had a low internal consistency. Internal consistency was estimated by an analysis of variance technique (Winer, 1962). Only the estimated reliability coefficients for the means of measurements were acceptable for all three variables (Table III). P_s estimates, however, are most reliable.

Although the overall relationships between P_s based uncertainty measures are even higher than those between confidence estimates and DT, the fact remains that mean DT and mean C indicate maximum subjective uncertainty at higher difficulty levels than P_s-based uncertainty measures.

Schneider and Posse (1978a,b) tried to explain this divergence of different response modes of subjective uncertainty in a Lewinian framework:

1. In skill-oriented situations expectations of future outcomes are generally optimistic, that is, individuals anticipate more success than may be warranted in view of the history of success and failure a person has had with a task.

TABLE II. Product-Moment Correlation Coefficients between Averaged Decision Time (DT), Averaged Confidence (C), and Averaged P_s-Based Uncertainty Measures (H).

Study	N^a	DT vs. C	DT vs. H	C vs. H
Schneider (1974)				
Exp. I	26	−.84	.47	−.78
Exp. II	32	−.86	.76	−.97
Schneider & Posse (1978a)	27	−.91	.93	−.96
Schneider & Posse (1978b)				
Exp. I	21	−.87	.64	−.88
Exp. II	20	−.78	.60	−.93

[a] Subjects in all studies were first-year male and female psychology students.

TABLE III. Internal Consistency Coefficients for Mean Measurements (r_k) and Single Measurements (r_1) of Subjective Probability (P_s), Confidence (C), and Decision Time (DT).

Study	r_k			r_1		
	P_s	C	DT	P_s	C	DT
Schneider (1974)						
Exp. I	.99	.96	.83	.89	.47	.15
Exp. II	.99	.95	.83	.87	.37	.13
Schneider & Posse (1978a)	.99	.91	.92	.83	.27	.30
Schneider & Posse (1978b)						
Exp. I	.99	.95	.75	.90	.50	.13
Exp. II	.99	.90	.74	.85	.29	.12

2. In all studies with the psychomotor task used here it was found that subjects gave P_s estimates which were 10–15% higher than their objective success probabilities, especially in the intermediate and easy range. Figure 4 shows the typical results from one study. Similar results have been reported with other tasks by Howell (1972) and Langer (1975).

3. P_s estimates do not indicate the complete extent of overconfidence in a skill-oriented situation. The divergence between the direct indices of uncertainty, DT and C, and P_s-based uncertainty H, dem-

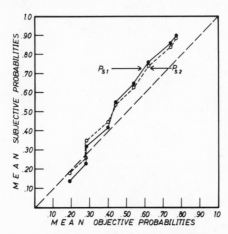

FIGURE 4. Averaged P_{s1} and P_{s2} estimates in relation to averaged objective probabilities of success. Subjects were 45 male college students. (From Schneider, 1973, p. 134.)

onstrates that individuals are still more optimistic in such a situation than they disclose by their P_s estimates. Such optimism holds for skill tasks only. In a similarly structured chance game, we measured the same indices of uncertainty. Figure 5 shows mean decision times in predicting the critical event and the proportions of estimates in this prediction as well as the means of estimated confidence in the prediction and the means of the estimated probabilities of the critical event at all positions. No biasing of expectancies in the middle range of the objective probability scale is shown here. Maximum DT and minimum confidence were to be found at subjective probabilities between .50 and .60 (Figure 5).

In this study (Schneider & Rieke, 1976) subjects had to predict a random event. Two rows of pairs of bulbs, yellow and green, were arranged horizontally. Subjects had to predict the occurrence of the yellow light. The objective probability of this event increased in equal steps from .10 to .90 from the first to the ninth position. After 10 learning trials at every position, subjects had to predict the critical event once again at every position. Decision time was measured and confidence assessed concurrently. The perceived probabilities of the event at the 9 positions were also scaled.

Alternately, true expectancies in skill situations may be still 10–15% higher than stated P_s estimate, at least in the intermediate difficulty range.

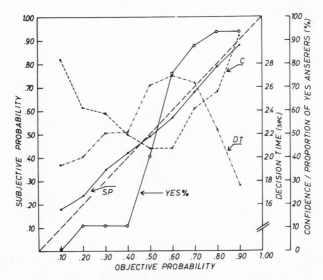

FIGURE 5. Averaged decision time (*DT*), confidence estimates (*C*) and percentages of yes answers (yes%) and subjective probabilities (*SP*) of the critical event at nine objective probability levels of a chance game. Subjects were 17 male and female first-year students. (From Schneider & Rieke, 1976.)

DT and C estimates are probably less influenced by reality constraints against being overconfident than P_s estimates are, because only the latter can be checked later with additional trials. Furthermore, the expression of overconfidence of DT and C estimates was facilitated by the fact that in most studies success had to be predicted with pushing a button labeled "yes" and failure by pushing a button labeled "no." Also, subjects were allowed to play one game after every prediction, whereas P_s estimates were given postexperimentally. Changing both conditions in two of these studies shifted the maximum DT and the minimum confidence in the direction of that difficulty level, where subjects estimated their success probability on the average of .50 (Schneider & Posse, 1978a, 1978b, Exp. 2): However, the overall relationships between DT, C estimates, and P_s-based uncertainty measures were no closer in these studies than in the former ones.

The Prediction of Individual Preference Orders

The more optimistic true expectancies and the state of subjective uncertainty created by them and expressed in DT and confidence are obviously the basis for the subjects' choice behavior, and not the stated P_s estimates. Thus, the rank correlations between mean DT and/or mean confidence and group-preference order are, except in one study, closer than the relationships between group-preference orders and the subjective uncertainty H, and Atkinson's expected incentive of success variable (Table IV).

In spite of this, individual preference orders, deduced from the distributions of 15 (or in some studies, 10) choices each subject was given, could not be better predicted with the two direct and apparently more genuine indices of subjective uncertainty, DT and C, than with the P_s-based uncertainty values. This is not so astonishing in view of the lower reliability coefficients of DT and C as compared with P_s estimates. To summarize the results of five studies, in which all three variables were assessed under similar conditions, individual preference order could be predicted better than by chance ($p < .05$) in 22% of all cases ($N = 126$) with DT, in 35% with C estimates, and in 32% with P_s-based uncertainty measures.

The perceived information value of task outcome for one's own task competence which was asked in one study (Schneider & Posse, 1978a) did not predict individual preference functions better than either C estimates or P_s-based uncertainty measures. The medians of the distributions of the Kendall rank-correlation coefficients in this study ($N = 27$) were .56 for information value and .51 and .58 for confidence and subjective uncertainty respectively; significant rank correlations were 44%, 44%,

TABLE IV. Kendall Rank-Correlation Coefficients of Group and Individual Preference Orders with Subjective Uncertainty and Expected Incentive of Success, Respectively, (H/EI_s), Confidence (C), and Decision Time (DT).

Study	Group preference orders[a]			Individual preference orders		
	H/EI_s	C	DT	H/EI_s	C	DT
Schneider (1974)						
Exp. I	.22	−.67	.47	.15(15%)	−.27(19%)	.11(15%)
Exp. II	.83	−.78	1.00	.49(44%)	−.39(41%)	.30(13%)
Schneider & Posse (1978a)	.83	−.67	.56	.58(58%)	−.51(44%)	.42(44%)
Schneider & Posse (1978b)						
Exp. I	.50	−.78	.78	.25(19%)	−.44(29%)	.20(14%)
Exp. II	.56	−.44	.83	.31(25%)	−.43(40%)	.30(25%)

[a]In the case of group-preference orders, averaged predictor variables were used to compute rank-correlation coefficients; in the case of individual preference orders, the given coefficients are the medians of the individually computed rank correlations between individual preference orders and the single measurement of the predictor variables. Besides the medians percentages of significant ($p<.05$) individually computed Kendall coefficients in each study are given in brackets.

and 48%, respectively. Mean information values had a maximum at gap 2, the second highest difficulty level. The product-moment correlations between mean information values and the indices of subjective uncertainty were high (1. DT: .88; 2. C: −.91; 3. H: .96). However, the reliability of this variable was lower than for P_s estimates ($r_k = .93$; $r_1 = .33$). In a later study with the same task (Schneider, unpublished observations) mean information values were monotonically related to task difficulty. In both studies, some subjects estimated the information value of task outcome with increasing task difficulty increasingly higher, whereas others estimated information value highest at intermediate task-difficulty levels. Although we believe that information on one's own task competence is the ultimate goal in choice behavior, it is unlikely that this variable regulates behavior, as individuals vary so much in how to evaluate information.

OTHER STRATEGIES IN TASK SELECTION

C estimates as well as P_s-based uncertainty measures do not do better than predict roughly one-third of all individual cases significantly. This does not seem very much. One may wonder whether the reduction of uncertainty is the only strategy individuals use in selecting task-difficulty levels. Observing the actual choice behavior of the subjects in our setup revealed that quite a number of them behaved in a similar way as has been described as the typical behavior in a level-of-aspiration paradigm (Lewin et al., 1944).

Many of our subjects started with medium or even very easy tasks, moving up to more difficult tasks when they were successful, and staying or even dropping back when they failed. This happened in spite of the fact that subjects had considerable experience with task-difficulty levels before they could select a task on their own. Although selecting tasks of intermediate difficulty would be the best strategy in order to learn one's own task competence in such a case (cf. Schmidt, 1966), subjects may rely on a second-best strategy, that is, moving stepwise from the easier to the more difficult task, and trying again as long as one succeeds at least once.

In order to test this hypothesis, a study was run in which subjects (first-year psychology students) were allowed to select task-difficulty levels on their own from the beginning. They were allowed to play 50 times in the difficulty levels they had chosen themselves. In one condition, subjects received the standard instruction, just telling them they could play where they wanted. In the second condition, they were asked to select tasks in such a way that they would learn as much as possible about how good their competence was for this task. In this condition, subjects generally started with easy tasks, as predicted, and moved stepwise to the more difficult ones. The distribution of individually computed Kendall rank-correlation coefficients between the rank order of trials (1 to 50) and the increasing numbers of task-difficulty levels had a median of .52 in the standard situation, and .83 in the situation where learning was stressed ($p < .10$).

In summary, we have to conclude that the selection of task-difficulty levels in a free-choice and achievement-oriented context is an expression of several overlapping strategies. From an informational point of view, subjects select all difficulty levels in a stepwise manner, starting with the easiest and going to the most difficult, and show a preference for intermediate task-difficulty levels, where competence information is maximum and success and failure must not be devalued because success is not ascribed to task ease and failure to task difficulty (Weiner et al., 1971). The stronger hypothesis of Weiner and associates, that subjects prefer intermediate task difficulty because at such levels success and failure are attributed most strongly to internal causal factors (ability and effort), could not be supported by our experimental paradigm (Schneider & Posse, 1978a,b,c). Among the four causal attribution factors (ability, effort, task difficulty, and luck) only task difficulty differentiated between task levels as an explanation for success and failure. Such an attribution to entities (task-difficulty levels) instead of to persons (ability and effort) should be obtained, according to Kelley's (1967) covariation model. The feedback information our subjects received was highly consistent (repeated trials within each task-difficulty level), highly distinctive (between task-difficulty levels), and without any information whatsoever about the performance level of other subjects (low consensus information). Such information of cause-and-effect covariation should (and did) lead to an attribution of success and failure to entity and not to person (cf. Heckhausen, Schmalt, & Schneider, 1978).

In so far as a situation without social-comparison norms is the typical achievement-oriented situation, at least in early years (cf. Veroff, 1969), the attribution model cannot be used in explaining achievement behavior. The fact that individual preference orders could be predicted as well with task-ease and task-difficulty attributions as with C estimates and P_s-based uncertainty measures (Schneider & Posse, 1978a,b) was owing to the fact that subjects showed a clear preference for the higher difficulty levels (DL 1 and 2), where subjective uncertainty, as indicated by C and P_s estimates, was not higher than at the easier difficulty levels 4 and 5. This can be understood as a consequence of that second strategy of going stepwise from the easy to the difficult games and remaining only as long as one succeeds at lower difficulty levels.

The assumption of two overlapping main strategies in choice behavior in a skill-oriented situation can also explain the fact that subjects do not maximize either subjective uncertainty or expected incentive of success, but match the proportions of their choices to the strength of these assumed predictor variables (see p. 57). Although they have a tendency to prefer maximum uncertain outcomes, they also sample all difficulty levels.

The informational interpretation of choice behavior in an achievement-oriented context proposed here should not be misunderstood as an absolute antimodel to an affectional interpretation. First P_s-based uncertainty H in two outcome situations is numerically identical with the expected incentive variable of Atkinson's original model.

Even if we give priority to cognitive processes and variables as those variables which control subjects' choice behavior, affective determinants cannot and should not be excluded. Such affects may be effective as well in the sense of Berlyne's notion of affective uncertainty reduction as in the sense of Atkinson's concept of anticipated success and failure affects by sustaining or bringing to an end certain behaviors. Besides this, in the longer perspective, a stabilizing effect of such emotions on achievement motives was supposed (Heckhausen, 1972). The absolute dissociation between information (without affect) and affect (without information) is an armchair distinction. Neither self-experience nor neurophysiological results support such a distinction (Arnold, 1970). Among psychologists, Daniel Berlyne has cogently laid open inherent relations between information and affect, and has demonstrated to motivation theorists a way of theorizing in which justice is done to phenomenological, behavioral, and physiological observations.

REFERENCES

ARNOLD, M. B. Perennial problems in the field of emotion. In M. B. Arnold (Ed.), *Feelings and emotions*. New York: Academic, 1970.

ATKINSON, J. W. Motivational determinants of risk-taking behavior. *Psychological Review*, 1957, *64*, 359–372.

ATKINSON, J. W., & FEATHER, N. T. (Eds.). *A theory of achievement motivation*. New York: Wiley, 1966.

BERLYNE, D. E. *Conflict, arousal, and curiosity*. New York: McGraw-Hill, 1960.

BERLYNE, D. E. Curiosity and exploration. *Science*, 1966, *153*, 25–33.

BRIM, O. G. Attitude content-intensity and probability expectations. *American Sociological Review*, 1955, *20*, 68–76.

BUTZKAMM, J. *Informationseinholung über den eigenen Leistungsstand in Abhängigkeit von Leistungs- und von Aufgabencharakteristika*. Unpublished diploma thesis, Psychologisches Institut, Ruhr-University, Bochum, W. Germany, 1972.

COHEN, J., HANSEL, C. E. M., & WALKER, D. B. The time taken to decide as a measure of subjective probability. *Acta Psychologica*, 1960, *17*, 177–183.

CRANDALL, V. J., SOLOMON, D., & KELLAWAY, R. Expectancy statements and decision times as functions of objective probabilities and reinforcement values. *Journal of Personality*, 1955, *24*, 192–203.

EDWARDS, W. Probability-preferences in gambling. *American Journal of Psychology*, 1953, *66*, 349–364.

EDWARDS, W. The reliability of probability-preferences. *American Journal of Psychology*, 1954, *67*, 68–95.

HECKHAUSEN, H. *Hoffnung und Furcht in der Leistungsmotivation*. Meisenheim: Hain, 1963.

HECKHAUSEN, H. *The anatomy of achievement motivation*. New York: Academic Press, 1967.

HECKHAUSEN, H. Achievement motive research: Current problems and some contributions towards a general theory of motivation. In W. J. Arnold (Ed.), *Nebraska Symposium on Motivation* (Vol. 16). Lincoln: University of Nebraska Press, 1968.

HECKHAUSEN, H. Die Interaktion der Sozialisationsvariablen in der Genese des Leistungsmotivs. In C. F. Graumann (Ed.), *Handbuch der Psychologie* (Vol. 7 [2]). Göttingen: Hogrefe, 1972.

HECKHAUSEN, H., SCHMALT, H.-D., & SCHNEIDER, K. Fortschritte der Leistungsmotivationsforschung. Unpublished manuscript, 1978.

HIGGINS, J. D. Set and uncertainty as factors influencing anticipatory cardiovascular responding in humans. *Journal of Comparative and Physiological Psychology*, 1971, *74*, 272–283.

HOWELL, W. S. Compounding uncertainty from internal sources. *Journal of Experimental Psychology*, 1972, *95*, 6–13.

KELLEY, H. H. Attribution theory in social psychology. In D. Levine (Ed.), *Nebraska Symposium on Motivation* (Vol. 5). Lincoln: University of Nebraska Press, 1967.

LANGER, E. J. The illusion of control. *Journal of Personality and Social Psychology*, 1975, *32*, 311–328.

LEWIN, K., DEMBO, T., FESTINGER, L., & SEARS, P. S. Level of aspiration. In J. McV. Hunt (Ed.), *Personality and behavior disorders* (Vol. 1). New York: Ronald, 1944.

LORENZ, K. Die angeborenen Formen möglicher Erfahrung. *Zeitschrift für Tierpsychologie*, 1943, 5, 235–409.

LORENZ, K. Innate bases of learning. In K. H. Pribram (Ed.), *On the biology of learning*. New York: Harcourt, 1969.

McCLELLAND, D. C. *The achieving society*. Princeton, N. J.: Van Nostrand, 1961.

SCHMIDT, H. D. *Leistungschance. Erfolgserwartung und Entscheidung*. Berlin: VEB Deutscher Verlag der Wissenschaften, 1966.

SCHNEIDER, K. *Leistungs- und Risikoverhalten in Abhängigkeit von situativen und überdauernden Komponenten der Leistungsmotivation: Kritische Untersuchungen zu einem Verhaltensmodell.* Doctoral Dissertation, Ruhr-University Bochum, W. Germany, 1971. Partly reprinted in K. Schneider, *Motivation unter Erfolgsrisiko*. Göttingen: Hogrefe, 1973, Chapters, 1,2,4,5, and 6.

SCHNEIDER, K. The relationship between estimated probabilities and achievement motivation. *Acta Psychologica*, 1972, 36, 408–416.

SCHNEIDER, K. *Motivation unter Erfolgsrisiko*, Göttingen: Hogrefe, 1973.

SCHNEIDER, K. Subjektive Unsicherheit und Aufgabenwahl. *Archiv für Psychologie*, 1974, 126, 147–169.

SCHNEIDER, K., & MEISE, C. Leistungs- und anschlussmotiviertes Risikoverhalten bei der Aufgabenwahl. In K. Schneider, *Motivation unter Erfolgsrisiko*. Göttingen: Hogrefe, 1973.

SCHNEIDER, K., & POSSE, N. Subjektive Unsicherheit, Kausalattribuierungen und Aufgabenwahl I. *Zeitschrift für experimentelle und angewandte Psychologie*, 1978, 25, 302–320. (a)

SCHNEIDER, K., & POSSE, N. Subjektive Unsicherheit, Kausalattribuierungen und Aufgabenwahl II. *Zeitschrift für experimentelle und angewandte Psychologie*, 1978, 25, 474–499. (b)

SCHNEIDER, K., & POSSE, N. Der Einfluss der Erfahrung mit einer Aufgabe auf die Aufgabenwahl, subjektive Unsicherheit und die Kausalerklärungen für Erfolge. *Psychologische Beiträge*, 1978, 20, 228–250.(c)

SCHNEIDER, K., & RIEKE, K. Entscheidungszeit, Konfidenz, subjektive Wahrscheinlichkeit und Aufgabenwahl bei einem Glücksspiel. Unpublished report, Psychologisches Institut, Ruhr-University, Bochum, W. Germany, 1976.

SUTTON, S., BRAREN, M., ZUBIN, J., & JOHN, E. R. Evoked potential correlates of stimulus uncertainty. *Science*, 1965, 150, 1187–1188.

VEROFF, J. Social comparison and the development of achievement motivation. In C. P. Smith (Ed.), *Achievement-related motives in children*. New York: Russel Sage Foundation, 1969.

WEINER, B., FRIEZE, I., KUKLA, A., REED, L., REST, S., & ROSENBAUM, R. M. *Perceiving the causes of success and failure*. New York: General Learning Press, 1971.

WEINER, B., HECKHAUSEN, H., MEYER, W.-U., & COOK, R. E. Causal ascriptions and achievement behavior: A conceptual analysis of effort and reanalysis of locus of control. *Journal of Personality and Social Psychology*, 1972, 21, 239–248.

WINER, B. J. *Statistical principles in experimental design*. New York: McGraw-Hill, 1962.

8

Experiential Roots of Intention, Initiative, and Trust

J. McVicker Hunt

Intention, initiative, and trust have been considered to be developmental products of the first two years of living in human infants by widely disparate schools of thought. Since evidences of plasticity have weakened the traditional belief that early development is essentially predetermined in course and rate by heredity, an influential role in it may properly be attributed to experience, and especially early experience (Hunt, 1979a). It is common to call this influence "environmental." Yet it is the functioning of the infant organism rather than the environment per se which modifies the course and rate of its development. Environmental circumstances are only indirectly of influence as they serve in the control of an infant's functioning. Recent evidence has turned up hitherto unsuspected evidences of specificity between kinds of experience and the kinds of developmental achievements affected (see Hunt, 1977). These evidences of such specificity make it important for both the science of developmental psychology and the technology of early education to know as definitely and accurately as possible what kinds of experience are important for the various developmental achievements. The substance of this paper has been suggested by an unexpected consequence of an intervention in the infant rearing at an orphanage in Tehran (Hunt, Mohandessi, Ghodssi, & Akiyama, 1976). This intervention was planned to foster vocal imitation and, through it, language achievement (Hunt, 1979a). When the intervention turned out to produce also radical improvements in initiative, mood, and trust, it, combined with other new findings in the literature, suggested a need to revise my formulation of the role of intrinsic motivation in early psychological development.

J. McVicker Hunt • Department of Psychology, University of Illinois, Champaign, Illinois 61820.
 The research reported in this paper was supported by grants (MH–11321 and MH–K6–18567) from the Public Health Service.

Perhaps an equally appropriate title for this paper would be "Intrinsic Motivation and the Genesis of Intention, Initiative, and Trust." It is highly fitting that this discussion should appear in a book organized in the honor and memory of Daniel Ellis Berlyne, for probably no one has contributed more to this innovation in the theory of motivation than has Dan Berlyne. His investigation of the motivational influence of what he has termed "*collation*" has the two aspects of *comparison* and *synthesis*. It was to a considerable degree the findings of Berlyne's experiments that encouraged me to take seriously the idea that there might be a fundamental system of *affect* and *conation*, in a classical sense, within *cognition*. In modern terms, this is to say that there must be a system of motivation within the discriminated and coordinated meanings of perceived events and of plans for which the modern term is *information processing*.

I must admit that the findings from Berlyne's (1960) beautifully designed experiments influenced my thinking about such motivation more than did his theorizing. Because we shared a faith in Hull's (1943) drive theory when most of his experiments were done, I took the findings seriously. Despite the evidences of the importance of Berlyne's "collative variables" on emotional arousal, his own theorizing focused on his concept of "*arousal potential*." By adopting this concept, he was able, at least in language, to make his findings consonant with drive theory. Thus, he failed to go on to the view that it is the meanings that control emotional arousal and motivate actions (see Hunt, 1963a, 1971a,b).

Even though Berlyne became very much concerned about the structure of thought (1965) and the significance of curiosity in education (1971), his focus continued to differ in yet another way from mine. His experiments focused on the immediate antecedents of collation for the learning process. Also, his theorizing concerned the intrinsic motivation of the developed individual, rather than the role of intrinsic motivation in the process of development, which has been my own focus. It saddens me that Dan Berlyne is no longer available for consultation and discussion. I am glad for an opportunity to contribute to this volume in his honor and his memory.

In this paper, I wish to synopsize (1) the way I have previously conceived of how motivation inheres in information processing and action, (2) my formulation of how such motivation figures in psychological development, (3) the evidence for the unexpected outcome of the intervention in the child-rearing practices at the orphanage in Tehran originally planned to foster the development of vocal imitation and language acquisition, (4) the evidence from other investigators which lends meaning to my own serendipitous findings, and finally (5) the change suggested by these findings in my hypothesis about the role of early experience in the development of intentional behavior, initiative, and trust in human infants.

MOTIVATION INHERENT IN INFORMATION PROCESSING

The idea of a system of intrinsic motivation, or motivation inherent in information processing and action, originated in evidence showing the limitations of what in the 1950s had become a traditional drive theory. This theory had its beginnings in the attempt of Descartes to explain the behavior of animals. For Descartes, the forces which move the bodies of animals were external stimuli, and they remained so until Claude Bernard's (1859) discovery of disturbances in the homeostasis of the internal milieu as springs of action, but they continued to remain extrinsic, at least to cognition and action per se. The drive theory of recent tradition came to us through the writings of Sigmund Freud. Freud put the irrationalism of Schopenhauer into his concept of *Trieb*, and synthesized with it something akin to Bentham's "hedonic calculus" in his aim of action through the functioning of the ego. Beginning with his *The Interpretation of Dreams* (1900/1938), in his *Three Contributions to the Theory of Sex* (1905/1938), and his classic paper entitled "Instincts and Their Vicissitudes" (1915/1950), Freud put together the essentials of drive theory. Freud's term *Trieb* got translated into English by A. A. Brill (1912) as "instinct," and it is Woodworth (1918) who appears first to have introduced the term "drive." What are essentially Freud's motivational conceptions became cornerstones of Hull's (1943, 1952) neobehavior theory, which was applied to social learning by Miller and Dollard (1941), and to the theory of personality development by Mowrer and Kluckhohn (1944) and Dollard and Miller (1950). The publications within this tradition include the writings of Kenneth W. Spence (e.g., 1956), J. S. Brown (1953), I. E. Farber (1954), and a tremendous list of papers on experimental investigations testing aspects of Hull's theory.

According to this traditional drive theory, organisms become active only as they are driven by the strong stimuli originating from pain, from the organismic needs of hunger and thirst, and from the innocuous stimuli which had previously been associated with such strong drive stimuli. Such stimuli produce arousal in the brain-stem reticular formation (see Lindsley, 1951; Pribram, 1958). Behavior is supposed to be instigated with the onset of aversive stimuli which have produced arousal, and it stops with the cessation of such stimuli. According to the theory, moreover, the cessation of such arousal is rewarding, and those actions which lead to drive reductions are reinforced. It should probably be noted that Freud (1905, 1915) included sexual arousal among the aversive drives because the orgasm terminates such arousal. This was clearly an error, because sexual arousal is inherently pleasurable. Moreover, as the investigations of James Olds (1955) have shown, even direct stimulation of the septal area, a subcortical structure in the middle of the brain which has much to do with both olfaction and sex, will reinforce actions. Such dissonant facts, however, are tangential to the message of this paper. Although drive theory is a conceptual edifice of many dimensions and complexities of structure, and many of the propositions comprising the edifice show rather nice correspondence with observables,[1] the central presumptions that organisms should become quiescent in the absence of drive and that what reinforces patterns of action is their capacity to reduce drive have severe limitations.

It was evidence dissonant with these fundamental propositions of drive theory that suggested the need for reformulations. Evidence dissonant with the proposition that organisms will become quiescent unless driven by pain, the threat of pain, hunger, thirst, or sex is fairly voluminous (see Hunt, 1963a). A few illustrations will serve here. The apparent delight that young animals and children take in highly active play has long been obvious to observers (see Groos, 1896/1905). After surveying reports of such observations, Beach (1945) arrived at the conclusion that young animals are most likely to exhibit playful activities in the absence of painful stimulation, threats of pain, homeostatic need, or sex. Harlow, Harlow, and Meyer (1950) observed that "monkeys would learn to unassemble three-device puzzles with no other 'drive' and no other 'reward' then the privilege of unassembling it." In another study, moreover, Harlow (1950) found that two monkeys worked repeatedly at unassembling a six-device puzzle for ten consecutive hours, even though they were quite free of painful stimulation, and were well-fed and well-watered. At the tenth hour of testing, Harlow reported that they were still "showing enthusiasm for their work" as Harlow went home to dinner. As a final example, consider one that involves human subjects. In the now famous McGill studies of stimulus deprivation, students who were well fed, free of pain and strong stimulation of any sort, and without any allusions to sex, refused to remain quiescent in a room where stimulus variation was minimized, even though they were paid the then munificent sum of $20 a day (Bexton, Heron, & Scott, 1954; Heron, Doane, & Scott, 1956).

Such evidence has suggested to some the idea of an exploratory drive or need for stimulation, but such attempts to explain the behavior are purely circular (see Hunt, 1963a, p. 41ff). It suggested rather that there must be one or more systems of motivation which are inherent in information processing and action. Various investigations have produced evidence which points toward the nature of these systems. For instance, Pavlov early noted the capacity for abrupt changes in the characteristics of ongoing receptor input or of encounters with unexpected things in famil-

---

[1] Elsewhere I have described the way in which drive theory has answered each of the eight questions that I have found to be implicit in theorizing about motivation (see Hunt, 1963a, 1965, 1971a).

iar circumstances to elicit the "what-is-it?" reflex or the "orienting response" (Razran, 1961). In human beings, moreover, abrupt changes in a wide variety of receptor inputs have been known to elicit indications of arousal ever since the galvanometer was first utilized to measure the conductivity of the skin (see Landis, 1932). The irrational fears of chimpanzees are evoked by "familiar things in an unfamiliar guise" (Hebb, 1946; Hebb & Riesen, 1943). A basis for anxiety has been suggested in the inconsistency or dissonance of perceived evidence about self with one's self-concept (Kelly, 1955; Rogers, 1951). Leon Festinger (1957) formulated a cognitive theory of motivation with considerable explanatory value out of such "cognitive dissonance" generalized. Thus, on the one hand, abrupt changes and discrepancies between the constructions of reality already established and the information from encounters with reality can be disagreeable.

On the other hand, in an extended series of studies beginning in 1950, Berlyne (1960) found not only that rats will explore areas new to them if only given an opportunity, but that the more varied and numerous the objects within the region to be explored, the more persistently the rats explored it. Berlyne also found that variations in innocuous receptor inputs will not only instigate and sustain looking or listening, but such collative variables as *novelty*, *incongruity*, and *complexity* will reinforce learning behavior in both rats and human beings. In a similar vein, Montgomery (1955) and Montomery and Segall (1955) showed that rats will learn actions merely for an opportunity to explore unfamiliar territory; and Premack (1965) has evaluated this to a fairly general principle by contending that making an opportunity for an activity high in an organism's hierarchy contingent upon engaging in an act lower in the hierarchy will reinforce the latter. Such evidence suggests that lesser degrees of discrepancy between information encountered and ready-made constructions is hedonically attractive.

From the kinds of evidence in the two foregoing paragraphs, it seemed that positive interest and concern for information and action must be a matter of an optimal degree of discrepancy in something which, for lack of anything better, I called "incongruity." "Incongruity" was my term for this discrepancy between the information available in observations of situations and expectations, beliefs, and understandings already construed out of past experience. It was to be a generic construct for all Berlyne's various "collative" variables. It was to cover both action and information processing. Yet, from rereading the paper (Hunt, 1963a), it seems clear in retrospect that I got the term "incongruity" from the Test-Operate-Test-Exit (TOTE) model (Miller, Galanter, & Prigram, 1960), which concerns discrepancies between the existing state of affairs and that intended. In a mistaken attempt to generalize it, I also attempted to make incongruity fit Helson's (1964) theory of the "adaptation level." Such was the urge for generality, apparently, that this mistaken attempt to generalize was made despite the evidence reviewed of two separate sets of anatomical thalamocortical systems in the brain. When Rose and Woolsey (1949) discovered these separate systems, they termed them "intrinsic" because they lack fiber tracts connecting them with either receptors or effectors. Thus, they correspond to what Hebb (1949) termed the "associative" portion of mammalian brains to differentiate them from the "sensory" portion with connections to receptors. The paper also made use of Pribram's (1960) argument that these systems constitute the central neuroanatomical counterparts of the components required in computers to permit programming for the solution of logical problems (see Newell, Shaw, & Simon, 1958).

One of these "intrinsic" systems, the posterior, consists of fibers connecting what have been termed the association areas of the brain posterior to the central sulcus, that is, those of the occipital, parietal, and temporal lobes, with the pulvinar nucleus of the thalamus and also with the brain-stem reticular formation which is especially involved in emotional arousal (see Lindsley, 1957). The other such system, the frontal, consists of fibers connecting the frontal lobes with the dorsomedial nucleus of the thalamus. Cutting the fibers of the posterior system interferes with the recognitive intelligibility of receptor inputs, and this suggests that the posterior intrinsic system is concerned with information processing per se and with the energization evoked by encounters with abrupt changes of input and with the unexpected. Cutting the fibers of the frontal system, on the other hand, results in deficiencies in the formulation of plans and the ordering of information to test the meaning of incongruities between such dispositional states and expectations based on past experience and recent perceptual impressions (see Pribram, 1960). Thus, with the essentially established existence of an anatomical basis for these two separate systems, one for information processing and the other for the executive functions based on intentional behavior, it should have been clear that no single generic construct such as "incongruity" could serve adequately for discrepancies between the organizations of action and the perceptual and conceptual constructions established from past experience, on the one hand, and for the demands upon coping or upon recognition and understanding, on the other hand.

In fact, the single construct of "incongruity" failed to serve adequately even within the domain of information processing. The idea that there might be something akin to a Helsonian "adaptation level" for "incongruity" of neutral hedonic value with moderate discrepancies from it in both directions having positive hedonic value (after the Haber, 1958, "butterfly curve"; see Hunt, 1963a, p. 74) turned out to be quite wrong. A study by Unikel (1971) one of my own students, demonstrated that once a given level of perceptual complexity becomes hedonically neutral, only increases in it are attractive. Similar evidence for rat subjects has been reported by Dember and Earl (1957). It should be noted that as the level of complexity beyond that which has become neutral increases, the positive hedonic value becomes negative. This exemplifies what Dan Berlyne (1971) referred to as "inverted U-shaped functions continually cropping up . . . [for which] it is by no means clear that those who talk about U-shaped functions are always talking about the same one" (p. 191).

Suffice it to conclude here that the system of motivation inherent in information processing may be expected to differ from that inherent in action, and that fifteen years after "incongruity" was proposed, a generic construct for the nature of the discrepancy between the achieved and the encountered still appears to be premature.

RECOGNITIVE FAMILIARITY AS THE ORIGIN OF INTENTIONS

Even though the newborn human infant exhibits spontaneous movements, there is no evidence that these are intentional acts in the sense that the infant anticipates the effect or outcome of its movements. These movements have been observed, by Piaget (1936/1952) and others, to include sucking, grasping, looking, listening, vocalizing, and moving the limbs and body, but to most observers they not only occur without evidence of any anticipation of outcome, but appear to be essentially independent systems. Skinner's (1953) behavior theory, with emphasis on what is most directly observable, has termed those movements "operants," and has been concerned with the contingent effects that reinforce them and thereby increase the frequency of their occurrence. Piaget, on the other hand, with less concern with immediate observables, has been concerned with the modifications in the structures of behavior that come about through the accumulative effects of experience in what he terms the invariant processes of "accommodation" and "assimilation." Although I have never doubted an important role for heredity in the developmental process also, the focus of my own investigations has been concerned with the influence of experience on development, and with the importance of various kinds of experience for the rate of development in specific behavioral organizations. From the literature, and especially from Piaget's (1936/1952) observations of the development of his own three infants, and from observing our own infants, I came to believe that intentional behavior, defined as behavioral organizations in which the infant clearly anticipates the outcome of his action, seldom or never appears until human infants are nearly six months of age. Thus, even though the newborn may have the system of connections between frontal lobes and dorsomedial nucleus of the thalamus for intentional action, I presume that it must take half of the first year of postuterine life to get this system programmed.

The experiences that appeared to be important for this programming were those described by Piaget (1936/1952, 1937/1954) and by the ethologists for the following behavior they termed "imprinting" (see Hunt, 1963b, 1970; Lorenz, 1937). The important causal aspects of these experiences appeared to be on the side of information processing. Ready-made at birth is the "orienting respose" to changes in the intensity, increase or decrease, or quality of receptor input. Orienting responses lead, as Piaget (1936/1952) has described, to the coordinations between the several motor systems, so that "something heard becomes something to look at," "something seen becomes something to grasp," "something grasped becomes something to suck," etc. This I described as the first form of intrinsic motivation.

The second form came as many things became recognizable through repeated perceptual encounters. Recognition appeared to be a perceptual source of pleasure evidenced by the smile of recognition (Piaget, 1936/1952, p. 71) and by looking longer at familiar visual patterns or sounds than at those unfamiliar and novel (Greenberg, Uzgiris, & Hunt, 1970; Hunt, 1965; Weizmann, Cohen, & Pratt, 1971; Wetherford & Cohen, 1973). The pleasurableness of what is becoming recognizable appeared to be a special case of Hebb's (1949) theory that "sensory conditions are called pleasant, then, which contribute to the current development in the cerebrum" (p. 232). The fact that the earliest of acts clearly intentional appeared to consist of efforts to regain or to gain perceptual contact with what has become recognizable through repeated encounters led me to what I now consider the mistaken inference that intentional behavior is a direct effect of the achievement of perceptual recognition.

Within information processing, as distinct from intentional behavior, the orienting response continues to appear to me to be the original form, the attractiveness of what is recognizable the second form, and the attractiveness of what is new and novel within a familiar context the third form. I continue to suspect that, as repeated encounters with the objects, persons, and places within an infant's life space occur, a learning set that "things should be recognizable" develops. It is probably this "set" that comes to motivate longer looking at novel patterns than at familiar ones (see Greenberg et al., 1970, and the other studies cited above).

AN UNEXPECTED OUTCOME OF AN INTERVENTION IN INFANT-REARING

When situations encountered yield information expected, that information constitutes established knowledge. Yet it is from the unexpected that one learns, for it indicates that the beliefs about reality on which the expectations are based are in some way wrong. When an intervention in the rearing practices at a Tehran orphanage (see Hunt *et al.*, 1976) designed to foster vocal imitation and language unexpectedly resulted in spectacular increases in initiative and trust, it provoked a rethinking of the role of intrinsic motivation in early psychological development (Hunt, 1963b; 1965, 1971c).

The program of successive interventions in the rearing of infants at the Orphanage of the Queen Farah Pahlavi Charity Society in Iran was originally undertaken to test my hypothesis about the kinds of experience that would foster psychological development as measured by the Piaget-inspired ordinal scales of Uzgiris & Hunt (1975). The subjects in this program were five groups of foundlings (termed "waves") who were selected, because they were without detectable pathology, from those available at the Municipal Orphanage of Tehran when they were less than a month old. The strategy of the research was longitudinal in the sense that the development of foundlings in each wave was assessed every other week during their first year, and every fourth week thereafter, with Uzgiris–Hunt scales. For the first wave of 15 foundlings, the only intervention consisted of the repeated examining. These were the controls. We avoided the use of simultaneous control and treatment groups for a combination of strategic and ethical reasons (see Hunt *et al.*, 1976). The second wave of 10 foundlings got an intervention consisting of audiovisual enrichment. At the beginning, the nature of this intervention was dictated by the hypothesis outlined above, that variations in input would activate the orienting response and thereby sustain the interest and alertness of the infants. The inputs provided consisted of tape-recorded music and mother-talk that came on and off. Later, the infants were provided with an intentional means of obtaining this music and mother-talk by tugging on a plastic bracelet attached by a spring to a switch that turned on the speaker attached to the side of the crib. The visual portion consisted of mobiles, each with four dangles hung at appropriate distances above the eyes of the infants as they lay on their backs in their cribs. The dangles could be activated by body shaking. Unfortunately, this attempt at audiovisual enrichment proved abortive because the then resident director of the project failed to maintain the apparatus in operating condition.

The third wave of ten foundlings received untutored human enrichment which consisted of a reduction in the infant–caretaker ratio from something in the order of 30/3 to 10/3. As a control for tutored enrichments to come, the caretakers for the infants in this third wave were allowed to do whatever came naturally.

A fourth wave of 20 foundlings received the audiovisual enrichment originally planned for the second wave. In the meantime, however, evidence that the prevalence of noise, and especially vocal noise, that is irrelevant to an infant's spontaneous actions, had been found to show negative correlations with infant development (Wachs, Uzgiris, & Hunt, 1971). This prompted us to drop the first kind of audio "enrichment" consisting merely of tape-recorded mother-talk and music that came on and off without the infant's voluntary control. For this third wave, the apparatus was kept in working order, and the execution followed the plan quite well.

The intervention to be emphasized here, however, was that for the fifth wave of 11 foundlings which consisted of human enrichment in which we taught the caretakers what to do. This intervention was launched after it had become evident that the controls and those in Wave II had failed to achieve expressive or even receptive language by the time they were nearly three years old. Badger's teaching guides for infants learning (1971a) and toddler learning (1971b) were translated into Farsi, the language of Persia.

The Badger programs, when used with the caretakers in a day-care program for the infants from uneducated parents of poverty at the Parent and Child Center of Mt. Carmel, Illinois, served to advance the mean age (73 weeks) in infants born to these uneducated parents of poverty, some 25 weeks ahead of the mean age (98 weeks) at which the top step on the scale of Object Permanence was obtained by 12 home-reared children from predominantly professional families at Worcester, Massachusetts, but unfortunately left the mean age (114 weeks) at which the former attained the top step on the scale of Vocal Imitation 20 weeks behind that (94 weeks) at which this landmark was attained by the latter (see Hunt, Paraskevopoulos, Schickedanz, & Uzgiris, 1975; Hunt et al., 1976). This serendipitous finding of a discrepancy of nearly a year in the age of attaining the top steps on the scales of Object Permanence and Vocal Imitation, which are ordinarily attained at about the same age by home-reared children from educated families, illustrates the specificity in the kinds of experience which foster development along the separate branches (see Hunt, 1977). This finding also demonstrated a need to improve the Badger programs with experiences calculated to foster vocalization, vocal imitation, and language.

In view of my belief that the phonological aspect of language comes about through vocal imitation, this serendipitous finding suggested the need to augment the Badger manuals with instructions for the fostering of vocal imitation. The instructions added followed my hypothesis concerning the developmental epigenesis in intrinsic motivation. On the presumption that familiar sounds would first interest infants, the caretakers were instructed to imitate the spontaneous vocalizations of the infants in their charge. The aim was to get interactive vocal games going. The caretakers were also instructed to initiate such games by vocalizing sounds that they had heard their infants make repeatedly. Getting a response in kind from an infant constitutes what Piaget (1936/1952) has termed "pseudoimitation," and is the critical reaction for Step 4 on the Uzgiris–Hunt Scale of Vocal Imitation. Once an infant had been heard to vocalize repeatedly several different sounds, the caretakers were to introduce a new game of "follow the leader." In such games, they were to utter one of the sounds in the infant's repertoire. When the infant manifested pseudoimitation by repeating it, and the interchange had gone through several repetitions, the caretaker was to shift to another of the familiar sounds from the infant's repertoire, and get a vocal interchange going on this new sound, and then to a third and a fourth. Gradually, the caretaker was to reduce the number of times that each successive familiar pattern was to be repeated in such interchanges, and to approach getting the infant to follow immediately from the modeling of one pattern to another and to another. Once the infant had acquired facility in this game of "follow the leader," the caretaker was instructed to introduce new vocal patterns from the Persian language, new in the sense that she had never heard the infant make them. The caretaker was to utter these unfamiliar sounds repeatedly as the infant, through successive approximations, came closer to the sounds modeled.

Such vocal games were to be part of the caretaker–infant action during each stint of bathing, dressing, feeding, toileting, etc. Once an infant had begun to copy the sounds of novel phonemes, the caretaker was instructed to include in each stint of caretaking experiences designed to foster the beginning of naming, or semantic mastery. The procedures described are based on the assumption that semantic mastery can be fostered by heightening the palpability of the experiences of the objects to be named. On the assumption that the most palpable experiences would be parts of the body touched by washcloths during bathing, I instructed the caretakers to say, "Now, I am going to wash your *ear*." As the caretaker's vocal emphasis on the word *ear* occurred, she was to have her washcloth make contact with the anatomical ear. The choice of *ear* may not have been the most fortunate, because it is invisible to the infant. In the development of gestural imitation, which is based largely on visual experience, an infant imitates gestures involving visible parts of the body well before beginning to imitate parts that are invisible (see Uzgiris & Hunt, 1975, pp. 182–185). In choosing the ear, I neglected this fact. I might better have chosen for the start of my paradigm such visible parts of the body as the hand, the arm, the leg, the knee, and the foot.

This is as far as explicit instructions in the fostering of vocal imitation went, except for the instruction to talk about the caretaking operations as they conducted them. Were I to repeat the experiment, I would add a request for the caretakers to touch various parts of the infant's body and ask, "What is this?" I would also suggest that they ask of each infant in their charge such questions as whether he or she might need to go to the toilet, which of two or three games he or she might wish to play, which food he and she wish to eat first, etc.

Results

The results of this intervention as obtained with the Uzgiris–Hunt Scales have come in terms of the means and standard deviations of the ages in weeks at which these foundlings of Wave V attained an intermediate step and the top step on each of the scales as compared with the means and standardizations for those of the earlier four samples or "waves" (see Hunt et al., 1976, pp. 200–201). Suffice it here to indicate the general nature of these findings. Each successive wave, except Wave II that got the abortive attempt at audio-visual enrichment, attained the top steps on these scales at average ages younger than did the infants in all preceding waves. Reducing the infant–caretaker ratio to 10/3 permitted those for the infants in Wave III time for more than the most necessary care. At one year of age, these infants were substantially ahead of those in Waves I and II in the mean age of sitting and standing while holding on to the rails of their cribs, but they were not advanced at all on any of the Piaget-inspired scales. The caretakers had used the extra time to carry the infants in their care about and put them in strollers. Being carried about enabled them to use their balancing mechanisms. Presumably it was this use that advanced the ages at which they sat up. Experience in strollers enabled them to put weight on their legs, and the combination of these two experiences advanced the age of standing. But such advances in posture and locomotion occurred without these infants showing any gains over those in Waves I and II in attaining steps on the Piaget-inspired scales.

The audiovisual enrichment provided for the infants in Wave IV enabled them to attain the intermediate steps on the Uzgiris–Hunt Scales at mean ages considerably ahead of those of Waves I and II, also well ahead of those in Wave III who got the untutored human enrichment. It was, however, the infants in Wave V who showed by far the greatest gains in mean ages of attaining the top steps on all the Uzgiris–Hunt scales. In fact, on five of the seven scales, they attained the top steps at somewhat earlier ages than did the home-reared infants from predominantly professional families of Worcester, Massachusetts. Even so, they were substantially behind the Worcester children in attaining the intermediate steps. In fact, they were only slightly ahead of those infants in Wave IV who got only the audiovisual enrichment in attaining the intermediate steps. When one compares the infants of Waves I and II with those of Wave V, who received the tutored human enrichment, in mean ages of attaining the top steps on the seven scales, these differences range from 34 weeks to 87 weeks. The mean of these mean differences for the seven scales is 65 weeks. This transforms to a mean of approximately 47 points of IQ ratio. Since performance on composites of Piagetian tasks show high correlation with performances on standard tests of intelligence (Humphreys & Parsons, 1979), this gain of 47 points of IQ ratio probably approximates what would have been found with a standard psychometric test.

Even more dramatic is the difference between the foundlings of Wave I and Wave II from those of Wave V in the attainment of language. This shows on the scale of schemes for relating to objects. Whereas only one of the foundlings in Wave I and only one of those in Wave II ever spontaneously named an object before they were 169 weeks of age, all 11 of those in Wave V spontaneously named objects, and did so at an average age of 90 weeks, which is only four weeks later on the average than this landmark was attained (86 weeks) by the home-reared infants from predominantly professional families in Worcester. In fact, when these infants of Waves I and II were between two and three years of age, they used their voices only for crying and yelling in anger. Moreover, they showed no appreciation of the meaning of even the simplest of verbal requests, although many of them showed an appreciation of these requests in gesture. When, for instance, I invited them to approach me (one at a time), about half would come hesitatingly, but the other half would screw up their faces in tearful fear and withdraw further. Either reaction implied an appreciation of the meaning of the gesture (see Hunt et al., 1976).

The foundlings in Wave V, on the other hand, greeted me when I entered their playroom for the first time by saying "Hello" in unison at a signal from one of their caretakers. Before being shown to the playroom, I had been held inordinately long for the customary tea ceremony in the office of the directress. It turned out that the delay was occasioned by an effort to get these infants of Wave V, then between 17 and 22 months of age, to say in unison "Hello, Dr. Hunt." That was too much. The caretakers and examiners had to settle for "Hello."

Perhaps the contrast of Wave V with Waves I and II in both language and initiative can best be communicated with vignettes of individual behavior. After "Hello" had been said, Cambiz, the oldest of the foundlings in Wave V, surprised me with an exhibition of initiative and trust by requesting with both speech, which I could not understand, and gesture, which I could understand, to be picked up. None of those in Waves I and II had ever shown anything like this behavior. As Cambiz resisted being put down when the chief examiner invited me to the examining room, I carried him along. Through the window opposite the door of entry was a sprayer. Cambiz immediately began an excited utterance of "ab, ab, ab." *Ab* is the Farsi word for water. This was a beautiful example of spontaneous naming as well as initiative.

As the chief examiner was demonstrating that Shabnam, then somewhat less than 18 months of age and the youngest of the 11, could imitate the names of all of the infants in the group, she came to Yaz. I had no opportunity to see Yaz, because she was adopted and taken away from the orphanage the week before I arrived for this last planning visit. Shabnam had been uttering clear approximations of the names modeled. As the examiner uttered the name, "Yaz," however, Schabnam twisted in my arms, reached and looked toward the door, and said, "Yaz rafteh." This is a sentence meaning, "Yaz gone." No one had deliberately schooled her in such sentence construction, yet she reflected in speech a state of affairs of which she had full appreciation. Suffice it here to add that every one of these 11 infants in Wave V showed semantic mastery of the parts of their bodies, their garments, and other things involved in the caretaking operations by naming them in response to the question, "What is it?" asked by me in my best imitation of the Farsi. No attempt was made to test their receptive vocabularies, but their naming vocabularies were of the order of at least 50 words, and one of the older infants showed perfect semantic mastery of the elementary abstraction of colors by naming the reds, yellows, greens, and blues pointed to in pictures along the wall. Several others also showed imperfect semantic mastery of colors (see Hunt, 1979b). When one considers that only about a quarter of the four-year-olds in Head Start programs show semantic mastery of the elementary abstraction of colors (Kirk, Hunt, & Lieberman, 1975), this must be considered no mean achievement for orphanage-reared foundlings. These linguistic achievements, however, were expected from the tutoring given the caretakers in fostering vocal imitation and semantic mastery. On the other hand, the degree of success was beyond expectations.

What was quite unexpected was the effect of this intervention on facial expression, and on the behavioral evidences of initiative and trust. Unfortunately, no scales or metrics exist for measuring such phenomena. Nevertheless, the contrast was exceedingly sharp. It was sharpest in the domain of action. It would be great to have got sound cinemas of the interactions between the children in these contrasting groups with adults in standard situations. Unfortunately, this was not planned and would probably have been unfeasible. I can, nevertheless, report what I observed. The children of Waves I and II wore glum expressions, initiated no interactions with adults and seldom with other children, failed to play with toys, and tended to be wary or withdrawn from anyone but their accustomed caretakers. The children of Wave V, on the other hand, regularly initiated interactions with adults, preoccupied themselves with activities of their own choice, and exhibited an interested approach toward any adult who came within view or earshot. Although Cambiz was somewhat more forward than others in demanding that I pick him up the first time he saw me, all of the others endeavored to show me what they were doing or could do. Moreover, all those in Wave V readily understood such verbal requests from their caretakers as had been tried with the children in Waves I and II. They all approached me without hesitation when a caretaker or examiner suggested verbally that they should. When I spread my arms and motioned one of them to come, none hesitated to comply with my gestured request.

Although sound cinemas with which to document these statements are lacking, I did take color snapshots of the children. Those of Waves I and II had to be taken without flash to avoid frightening them. When I got out the slides in order to identify children in Wave V whose language behavior I wished to discuss, I noted the tremendous contrast of their facial expressions with those of children from Waves I and II. Figure 1A shows four of the children representative of Waves I and II for contrast with four others (Figure 1B) from Wave V.

The glum or distressed expressions of the children from Waves I and II are obvious. The most attractive expression that I can find among my pictures of the children in Waves I and II is that of the child on the bottom, right in Figure 1A. This picture was taken while I was vocalizing my imitation of cooing sounds in an attempt to elicit pseudoimitation. This accounts for his expression of mild interest, which differed from that when I was simply talking to him in adult fashion. It is of interest that I do not recall his name or those of any children in Waves I and II, but I readily recall the names of nearly all those in Wave V. Children who are unresponsive and lacking in communication skills seem to acquire no identity.

The happy, interested expressions of the four children in Wave V contrast sharply with the glum expressions of those in Waves I and II. The top, left picture in Figure 1B is Cambiz. Note his enthusiasm in striking the ball hung from a ring in the ceiling. In the same group, the top, right is Parvis. Note his interested preoccupation with the stacking toy. The bottom, left in this group is Monee. Note the evidence of initiative in his

FIGURE 1A. Waves I and II.

gesture of request or demand of the adult standing by. The bottom, right is Shabnam, the youngest one, when somewhat less than 18 months old, who turned in my arms when the examiner modeled the name, "Yaz," and said in Farsi, "Yaz gone." Note her unsolicited wave to me as I took her picture.

You will probably agree that these infants from Wave V are much more attractive than those from Waves I and II. If so, you may be interested to know that your judgment was confirmed by several childless couples of Tehran who chose seven of these eleven foundlings of Wave V for adoption. Of the 57 foundlings who served in the preceding waves, only two were ever adopted, and these two were adopted before they were six months old because they were pretty babies. These seven were adopted because they were attractively responsive two-year-olds.

My inclination is to attribute the attractive characteristics of the children in Wave V to the nature of the intervention designed to foster vocal imitation, and, indirectly, language. But another factor deserves consideration. The caretakers of Wave V developed a bond of affection for

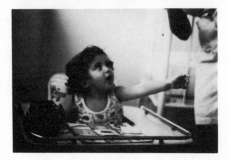

FIGURE 1B. Wave V.

the infants in their charge not evident in the caretakers of those in Waves I and II nor in the caretakers of those in Wave III where the infant–caretaker ratio (10/3) was not much higher than that for Wave V (2 or 3/1). The caretakers of Wave V claimed that they could not love an infant to whom they gave birth more than they loved those in their care. Evidence of the validity of their claim came in the tearful signs of separation grief following the departure of each child with its adoptive parents. To what degree caretaker affection rather than their imitative responsiveness to the vocalizations of the infants in their charge is responsible for their attractive characteristics is a moot question. My inclination to favor the importance of the imitative responsiveness that they were taught gets some support from other evidence to be summarized.

There is yet another nagging question. Did the caretakers of Wave V develop the strong bond of affection for the infants in their charge simply because they were responsible for only the two or three in their charge? Or was the bond a result of their interacting imitatively and intimately with them? Consider the other evidence.

OTHER RELATED EVIDENCE

Other related evidence has helped to construct the still hypothetical meaning of these unexpected effects of the interventions designed to foster vocal imitation and language. One kind consists of the correlations of measures of rearing conditions in homes, ones which control the imitate, proximal experiences of infants, with measures of their developmental advancement. Some of these are both negative and substantial, and their nature is theoretically instructive. For instance, when "there is a high level of adult activity in the home," or when "mother and infant go visiting almost daily," both presumably bases for mothers being inattentive and unresponsive to their infants, the correlations with assessments of development in several branches range from $-.39$ to $-.82$. Such negative correlations are already present at age seven months, and continue to exist through testings at 11, 15, 18, and 22 months with a modified version of the Uzgiris–Hunt scales (Wachs et al., 1971). In other words, when no one responds to the spontaneous actions of infants, they show retardation in the development of Object Permanence $(-.6)$, the Development of Means for Obtaining Desired Events $(-.39)$, the Development of Gestural Imitation $(-.59)$, Vocal Imitation $(-.46)$, Object Relations in Space $(-.49)$, and Schemes for Relating to Objects $(-.46)$. Similar evidence of damage to the rate of early development from the unresponsiveness of the social and inanimate conditions have appeared in other studies (see Bradley & Caldwell, 1977; White, 1978; White & Watts, 1973).

Conversely, the degree of prevalence of conditions indicative of the responsiveness of human beings and materials to the spontaneous actions of infants correlates positively with developmental advancement. For instance, in the study by Wachs et al. (1971) positive correlations with level of development occurred in the case of "Child given training in one or more skills," "Home contained an adequate supply of small manipulatable items that child is allowed to play with," and "Mother spontaneously vocalizes the names of objects examined by child in observer's presence." A condition in which "Father helps take care of the infant" also showed a positive correlation with development in several branches, as might be expected if prevalence of responsiveness helps to hasten the rate of development. These correlations are of substantial size; they range from $+.35$ to $+.76$ with most of them between $+.4$ and $+.6$. Especially interesting are the findings from a study by Yarrow, Rubenstein, and Pedersen (1975) in which assessments of home conditions, based on two three-hour periods of observation, were correlated with measures of psychological development with the Bayley scales. Among the highest of the correlations found $(+.58)$ was that between the responsiveness of the inanimate materials available to the infants with their persistence of goal-striving at age six months. It is of interest that ordinary paper turns out to be the most responsive of inanimate materials. Paper not only changes in visual shape, but makes crackling sounds as it is manipulated. Such immediate and direct perceptual effect of manipulation clearly serves to interest young infants, and helps to explain why infants are often less interested at first in a toy received as a present than in the paper in which it was wrapped.

Several theoretical interpretations of this behavioral phenomenon have been made. If one wishes to emphasize only the immediate observables, one may say with Skinner (1938, 1953) that the perceptual feedback reinforces the manipulative action. Persistence in manipulation is also, however, a function of the perceived feedback; if it is aversive, the manipulative action stops. Since neither changes of shape nor crackling have any obvious hedonic value in themselves, one can well say with Robert White (1959) that it is "a sense of having an effect" or "effectance" that is pleasant. Here the hedonic value appears to be a function of the immediateness and directness of the effect. Thus far, only the effect on persistence in manipulative action is being considered. To explain the positive correlation of developmental advancement with the prevalence of such experience, I believe it wrong to say that this is a mere product of the reinforcement. With repeated encounters with paper an infant comes to express delight, and may be seen to move toward the paper with active hands. The child anticipates the effect that he or she can have the joy therefrom. Anticipation is a subjective term; it can only be implied by the nature of behavior, but it can readily be explained by the fact that the central brain processes constituting the memory of such events run off faster than do the events. It is the anticipation which is learned, and it is this anticipation that motivates the approach to paper, or what not, that has been encountered with interesting effect earlier. In at least a limited sense, the child *intends* to recapture the earlier experience. He or she will try the means first used, namely, manipulative action. If the expected effect does not come, then he or she will modify the action. It is thus that infants whose mothers or caretakers are slow in responding to the efforts of their infants to elicit their attention learn to cry louder and louder. That fact that infants learn what will elicit their intended consequence helps to confirm the implication that it is failure to attain the anticipated consequence that motivates continued action and modifications in the form or intensity of that action. This corresponds to the TOTE model (Miller, Galanter, & Pribram, 1960).

The nature of another negative correlate of infant development is also instructive. It consists of highly prevalent auditory input, and particularly human vocal input, which is irrelevant to the infant's functioning. In the study by Wachs *et al.* (1971), the examples of this negative correlate included "High sound level in the home," and "Television on most of the time." For these conditions, negative correlations with assessments of development are already evident by seven months of age. At ages of 18 and 22 months, they range from −.37 (with Vocal Imitation) to −.81 (with Foresight) and are substantial for all branches of development involving appreciations of meaning. Also, that home condition described as "child never restricted," which indicates lack of adult attention to whatever the infant does, shows a high negative correlation (−.64) with the measure of development of Vocal Imitation and negative correlations between −.4 and −.5 with the development of Foresight and of Means of Obtaining Desired Events, at age 22 months. Conversely, conditions suggesting that the parents have interacted vocally and instructively with their infant show substantial positive correlations with assessments of both Vocal Imitation (+.4) and with such indications of developing understanding as Foresight (+.7).

With vocal noise prevalent and irrelevant to an infant's developing expectations and interests, his or her inclination to orient and attend to adult speech might well be expected to become habituated or extinguished. Receptor inputs to which the orienting response is weak serve poorly as either conditional stimuli or cues in learning (Maltzman & Raskin, 1965). Since irrelevant vocal noise tends to be considerably more common in homes of the uneducated poor than in those of the educated middle class, it is hardly surprising that children of the former aged 4 and 5 years have proved to be less attentive to and understanding of adult talk and less discriminative of vocal patterns than children of the latter (see Hunt, 1969, pp. 202–214). Moreover, there is evidence that this inimical influence on early development persists through the high-school years. In a cross-lagged panel analysis of cognitive measures for four grade levels, a correlation (+.73) of a measure of listening and comprehension at grade five with an intellectual composite at grade 11 stood out (Atkin, Bray, Davison, Herzberger, Humphreys, & Selzer, 1977). Such evidence highlights the importance of vocal communication in intellectual development, leading to knowledge and intellectual skills with motivation to know and learn. Now, in retrospect, these relationships of irrelevant and relevant vocal noise to development lend credence to the idea that it is of importance for the events responsive to an infant's action to be not only contingent in time, but of a piece with his or her expectations. Events responsive to an infant's actions, if one is concerned with only the immediate observables, may seem to reinforce those particular actions, but, what is more important, they give rise to expectations, intentions, and plans that generate goal striving. As the anticipated outcomes of actions are elaborated, they become the basis for initiative, and as they include collaborative assistance from adults and peers, they become trust. As, for instance, repeated encounters with objects, persons, and places made those within an infant's life space recognizable, the infant comes to expect that the things he encounters should be recognizable. This expectation, or learning set, becomes a kind of goal, so that novelties evoke prolonged scrutiny. Such learning sets appear to be ubiquitous in development. One has long been evident in the acquisition of the semantic aspect of language. From associating heard vocal patterns with a number of perceived things, an infant achieves the "rule" or "set" that "things have names." Achieving this set leads him or her to ask, sometimes ad nauseam, "What's that?" in a variety of ways. If the thing's name is the child's goal, supplying it or them will temporarily stop the asking. When such questions begin, the rate of vocabulary building takes off at a rapid rate (see McCarthy, 1954).

But the process appears to continue indefinitely. As children form rules or sets that constitute "epistemic" understandings, they, as do mature men and women of science, encounter information through either perception or language that is dissonant with these understandings. It was Nathan Isaacs (1930/1974) who first pointed to children's "why" questions as epistemic quandaries in which they call for help in their attempts to cope with their puzzlements. There are, of course, "whys" that are merely delaying tactics, but many are serious. Isaacs has suggested, and I am inclined to agree, that the fate of children's "why" questions is highly important for both intellectual development and self-esteem. If adult responses to children's "whys" lead them to more accurate understandings of the operations of things and people, these understandings constitute intellectual development. If a child's "why" questions are taken seriously, it gives him a sense of confidence in his own thought and a sense of self-worth. If the answers encourage the child to investigate for himself, they encourage his curiosity. For the domain of what has been termed discipline, moreover, it is worth noting that honest and candid treatment of children's "why" questions opens the channel of communication to include discussions of ethics, sex, values, and the meaning of life. If the answers are honest, are within the grasp of the child, and involve no hidden agenda of arbitrary control, parental discipline becomes a matter of discussing the consequences of choices and courses of action in terms not only of the objective but also of the subjective feelings of all concerned. Parents may thereby become consultants on living for their young.

Such evidence and considerations suggest that it is the responsiveness of both inanimate materials and human beings to children's spontaneous actions that is important for their development of intentionality, initiative, and trust. The affection on the part of parents and caretakers is probably only indirectly of importance, in that it helps to guarantee their responsiveness and understanding of the child's efforts.

The First Appearance of Intentional Behavior

Piaget (1936/1952) did not observe the first signs of goal anticipation in the behavior of his own three children before they were somewhat more than four months old. The first examples consisted of "procedures" to gain or regain perceptual contact with "interesting spectacles." Even though I was assembling the evidence against it (Hunt, 1961), the idea that the rate of psychological development is genetically predetermined still influenced my thought. Because Piaget's children would presumably be among the genetic elite, I inferred that the initial appearance of intentional behavior would be early for them, so that age four or five months would be its lower limit. Because the "interesting spectacles" were largely those recognitively familiar through repeated encounters, I inferred that intentional action was initiated by recognitive familiarity. Thus, despite my knowing that separate anatomical equipment must exist at birth for action as well as for information processing, this inference led me to infer that information processing is the source of intention. With evidence that the beginnings of intentional behavior may, under proper conditions, appear much earlier than age four or five months, and with the consideration that it is the repeated experience of producing an effect that leads to the anticipation of that effect and acting to obtain it, it becomes clear that the source of intentionality resides in the effects obtained through action itself.

The evidence that the beginnings of intentional behavior appear much earlier than age four or five months has come from three sources: first, the investigations of learning processes in newborn infants (see Lipsitt, 1966, 1967); second, studies of the precocious neonatal capacities of infants (see Bower, 1974; Haith & Compos, 1977; Meltzoff & Moore, 1977); and third, recent investigations of the neonate–mother relationship by a number of pediatricians (Brazelton, Tronick, Adamson, Als, & Wise, 1975; Papousek & Papousek, 1977; Schaffer, 1977; Trevarthen, 1974, 1977). The work of Lipsitt and his collaborators has shown that newborns show something akin to what Skinner has termed "operant conditioning" during the first four or five days of postuterine life. From the theoretical interpretation of the effects of persistence in actions that have effects, or are "reinforced," this evidence of early operants suggest that the beginnings of intentionality are early indeed. The investigations of perception and cognition seem to have uncovered evidences of precocious neonatal capacities that are still a matter of debate. It is the evidence of the third type from the pediatric investigations of the neonate–mother relationship that helps most directly to indicate the theoretical significance of the unexpected findings from the orphanage in Tehran for the origins of intention in action.

This latter evidence has come from evaluative studies of the effects of the new practice of leaving newborns with their mothers continuously during their stay in the lying-in hospital. This new practice is a radical break with the tradition of keeping newborns in cribs in a mass nursery except when they are nursing. There is suggestive evidence that the new practice fosters maternal attachment to their young in a surprisingly enduring fashion (Klaus, Jerauld, Kreger, McAlpine, Steffa, & Kennel, 1972), and also gives the infant a "cognitive head start" (Papousek & Papousek, 1977). This evidence is also changing the conception of the neonate–mother relationship. In place of a one-sided chain of mother actions and infant reactions, this evidence suggests reciprocality of interaction. It has led to such metaphorical terms as "communication," "conversation," "dialogue," and "dance" (see Brazelton et al., 1975; Schaffer, 1977; Trevarthen, 1974, 1977; Uzgiris, 1978). In cinematic records, neonates at ages as young as two or three weeks have shown differing patterns of interaction with their mothers than with inanimate objects. With their mothers, they show cycles of interaction in which they act and then hesitate, apparently waiting for a maternal reaction (Trevarthen, 1974, 1977). With inanimate objects, they act on the object persistently. The hesitation in the neonate's interaction with its mother suggests the beginnings of intentionality in the sense that the infant acts with anticipation of its mother's reaction.

This evidence suggests that in the course of as few as two or three weeks of intimate, responsive interaction with their mothers infants acquired fairly generalized anticipations of maternal reactions to their spontaneous acts. It is, I suspect, these anticipations of maternal responses which motivate the infant's actions and the hesitations. In so far as I know, no one has made any studies of such infant behavior as a function of maternal imitative responsiveness. Would actions followed by hesitations occur in infants whose mothers did not react imitatively to their infants' spontaneous movements and vocalizations? My guess is negative. A major share of mothers, when they are not otherwise preoccupied, appear to be inclined to imitate the expressions and vocalizations of their infants. By virtue of their similarity to the neonate's action, imitative responses are inclined to have the positive hedonic value of recognitive familiarity. This provides the neonate with a pleasureable effect of its actions. This comes about because memorial records of sequences of infant action and mother's imitative response would presumably be established in the neonate's brain. Since these memorial records typically run off faster than the sequences of events, they would lead to anticipation of the mother's imitative reaction. The anticipated maternal reaction would establish the goal-standard of the TOTE unit (Miller, Galanter, & Pribram, 1960), and thereby provide the beginnings of intentionality. This hypothetical scenario is readily testable, although, to the best of my knowledge it has not been properly put to test. A related attempt in our laboratory by Schickedanz (1974) failed. It consisted, however, of an attempt to test Watson's (1967) hypothesis of an acquired set to discern contingencies between actions and effects by looking for progressively fewer reinforced acts to achieve the criterion of acquisition in successive operants.

Now let us consider the nagging question about the source of the deep caretaker affection for foundlings that was present in those of Wave V but absent in those of Wave III. The evidence that having their newborns left with them in the lying-in hospitals fosters mothers' affectional attachment for them suggests that it may be the opportunity afforded for intimate and uninterrupted interaction that is important. Once mothers return home from the hospital, a myriad other obligations typically interfere with such interaction. In such intimacy, it is probably in coming to recognize patterns of infant action and becoming able to elicit some of them that affection develops. At the Iranian orphanage, the caretakers of Wave V probably developed affection for the foundlings in their charge through imitating their cooings and babblings. The instructions for such imitating served to foster an intimacy that was not called for in the caretakers of Wave III, where they were allowed to do whatever came naturally. Had each caretaker had charge of three specific infants, there would have been greater likelihood of intimacy and the development of affection, but each having responsibility for all 10 combined with the tradition of casual care at the orphanage mitigated against such intimacy. Apparently carrying the infants about and putting them in strollers fostered less intimacy of interaction than imitating the infant's cooings and babblings to get vocal games going. A capacity to elicit predictable responses from the infants appears to be highly rewarding and endearing. It is highly rewarding to a mother, and also to a father, as I can testify. It is of interest that women of the poverty sector who have participated in training for parenting which enables them to elicit predictable responses have very commonly acquired a new level of ambition, improved their skills, and become leaders in their neighborhoods (see Badger, 1972; Klaus & Gray, 1968). Such evidence suggests that the motivational consequences of such experiences for adults as well as infants is quite broad.

Papousek and Papousek (1977) have emphasized the "cognitive head start" that they find following early establishment of conversationlike interaction between mother and neonate. Learning to anticipate maternal reactions early would be expected to lead to early achievement of the landmarks in the development of gestural and vocal imitation, and particularly that of "pseudo-imitation." This is Piaget's term for infants' responding in kind to familiar patterns of gesture or vocalization when these are modeled by another person. It is an intermediate step on the Uzgiris–Hunt scales of both gestural and vocal imitation. Vocal pseudo-imitation was achieved at a mean age of eight weeks by the home-reared infants from predominantly professional families in Worcester, Massachusetts (see Hunt *et al.*, 1976), where presumably mothers would be fairly highly reactive to their infants' vocalizations. On the other hand, only about two-thirds of the infants of Waves I and II ever achieved this landmark, and they at an average age of 90 weeks ($SD = 29$ weeks). Even those of Wave V failed to achieve it until their average age was 38 weeks ($SD = 7$ weeks), yet such is the plasticity in early development that all of the foundlings of Wave V achieved the top step on the scale of Vocal Imitation at an average of 93 weeks ($SD = 5$ weeks), and this average is one week younger than this landmark was achieved by the home-reared infants from predominantly professional families in Worcester. Presumably, by having caretakers trained to foster vocal imitation and without the conflicting obligations of household and social duties of middle-class mothers, the infants of Wave V were enabled to make up for their earlier retardation even though those of the professional families had the advantage of earlier intentionality.

Establishing intentionality early permits an infant to become a somewhat independent and active agent in his own development. The importance of intentions in motivation and in learning is supported by abundant evidence (see Ryan, 1970). The earlier and better established an infant's intentionality has become, the more independent of caretaker and maternal reactions he or she will be, and also the more able to foster his or her own development through interaction with inanimate materials. The acquisition of language, and social norms, however, are very heavily dependent on interaction with other human beings who use language to mediate understanding and appreciation of standards of conduct.

INTENTIONAL ACTION AND INFORMATION PROCESSING

Separating the genesis of intentional action from that of information processing appears to me to leave the accuracy of my description (Hunt, 1965) of the epigenesis of the latter essentially unchanged. It still appears to me to begin with the orienting response to abrupt changes in the characteristics of receptor input, to move with repeated encounters to interest in what is recognizable, and to lead to a learning set that "things should be recognizable," which motivates the scrutiny of what is not recognizable. This sketch of the epigenesis in the development of information processing suggests the nature of the changes in that information which interest infants and foster, or "reinforce" in the language of behavior theory, their intentional behavior. On the other hand, within the domain of action there are challenges to skills which seem to be roughly equivalent to the challenges to understanding within the domain of information processing. These challenges demand adaptive modifications of the means of both action and information processing used to achieve the intentional ends. These adaptive modifications are what Piaget (1936/1952) has termed "accommodations."

The adaptive modifications in those sensorimotor organizations concepts or skills already achieved which are demanded by the challenging goals provided by models for imitation or by encounters with information and problems that are unfamiliar and complex must be within the coping capacity of the child if he or she is to make them. This is what Piaget (1936/1952, 1977) has considered under his concept of "equilibrium" or "equilibration." Whereas Piaget has limited his consideration to cognition and cognitive grasp, however, my own concerns for the implications of the discrepancy between situational demands and the understandings or skills already attained have been motivational. Development occurs only in encounters with situations which pose demands that engage the concern of a child and call for adaptive modifications of his existing attainments that are within his capacity for coping and modification. Encounters with already mastered demands tend to become boring. Those entirely beyond the cognitive appreciation of the child fail to engage his or her attention and concern. As I have often said, they are like talking to a pig about Sunday. Those encounters with situations that pose demands for adaptive modifications in a child's existing attainments with which he can cope are not only interesting, but a source of joy. But those for which the child has sufficient cognitive appreciation to engage him or her, but which pose demands for adaptive modifications beyond his or her limits, are a source of emotional distress. If parental demands through either threat of punishment or promise of reward prevent withdrawal from such situations, the consequence is a sense of failure, which can become a chronic sense of worthlessness if repeated and repeated. Because providing infants and young children with games and models for imitation with which they can cope is a problem for caretakers, parents, and teachers, I have termed it the "problem of the match" (Hunt, 1961, 1965, 1966, 1971b).

In responding to the calls for help from infants inevitably dependent, it is essential for the development of trust that the response match the nature of the source of the need for help. When the source is one of the homeostatic needs, the response should obviously meet the need. What is less well recognized is that infants and young children seek both information and challenges to the skills that they have already attained. When children seek new information, it is important for them to obtain information with which they can cope. Responding to "why" questions with rewards other than information is distracting. In questioning first-grade children of classes managed by token-rewards about what they are learning, for example, I have all too commonly received answers such as "how to get stars." In questioning first-grade children in classes where the emphasis is on the information and skill at hand, on the other hand, I have typically received answers in kind. For instance, when I asked a group of six first-graders from Spanish-American families, who were listening to their own dictations of stories about one of their projects in the Tucson program of Marie Hughes, what they were doing, two answered almost in unison, "We are learning to talk English good." Token-rewards may be useful as therapy for missed opportunities to develop that motivation inherent in action and information processing, but they can also distract those children who are already "on track."

INITIATIVE AND TRUST

Initiative appears to come into being through success in achieving intended goals, but not necessarily easy success. Here the increased resistance to extinction of actions intermittently reinforced, often referred to as the Humphreys (1939) effect for his work on the eyelid reflex but repeatedly demonstrated (see Jenkins & Stanley, 1950), has suggestive theoretical significance. So also does the evidence from the effects of effort (Solomon, 1948). The suggestive value is based on assuming that what is learned is not the operant action from attaining the intended goal but rather confidence that striving will bring about attainment. Once a young child has developed intentional behavior and has experienced the attainment of his goals only after persistent striving with effort and by modifying the pattern of his or her action, an increase in motivational readiness to undertake new goals is probably acquired. Moreover, as the child's repertoire of means for achieving his or her goals develops, these lead to competencies and a readiness to use them in an increasing variety of situations. By definition, such readiness for striving combined with competencies is the basis for what we call "initiative."

Trust appears to result from the manner in which the relevant adults in an infant's experience respond to his or her difficulties in achieving his or her intentional goals. Trust appears to consist of confidence in the inevitably dependent relationship of an infant and his mother or caretakers. This has been most directly investigated by Ainsworth (1972) and her collaborators (Ainsworth, Bell, & Stayton, 1971, 1972). These investigations have discovered not merely differing degrees of attachment, but also differing kinds of attachment. These kinds include "avoidant attachment" in which toddlers and young children avoid being close to their mothers, "ambivalent attachment" where they show high scores on scales of both resistance to contact and the seeking of proximity, and "secure attachment," which is an equivalent of trust, and in which toddlers and young children, following a separation, greet their mothers happily, seek proximity to them, and show no tendency to avoid contact. Secure attachment, or trust, was characteristic of toddlers and young children whose mothers showed a high degree of acceptance of their infants, accessibility to them and their demands, cooperation with them, and sensitivity to their wishes. In other words, trust appears to develop in infants who have experienced help from their mothers or caretakers in attaining their intentional goals and their homeostatic needs.

These hypothetical scenarios for the acquisition of intentionality, initiative, and trust are obviously different from those to be found in more traditional theories of early learning, motivation, and development. They are obviously not predeterministic. Unlike J. B. Watson's (1928) they consider imitation to have an important role. Watson's deriding the importance of imitation in psychological development because it is mothers who imitate their infants rather than the opposite showed a lack of appreciation of the epigenetic character of the development of imitation and of development in general. In taking into account and attributing importance to such subjective elements as anticipation of outcome, expectation, and intentionality, which are justified in neuropsychological terms, they differ radically from the exclusive concern with the direct observables in Skinner's (1938, 1953) analyses of behavior. Yet the research on operant conditioning sometimes has suggestive relevance. In their emphasis on that motivation inherent in action and information processing, the hypothetical scenarios differ from those of Freud (1905) and Erikson (1950), and are less vague from a standpoint of early education. They also differ in the same way from and are, I believe, less vague than those of Dollard and Miller (1950) or of Mowrer (1960) with respect to procedures for early education. They also differ from J. S. Watson's (1967) in placing more emphasis on anticipation of the outcomes of spontaneous actions and intention in the explanation of learning in infancy. The theory on which these scenarios are based owes much to the observations and theorizing of Jean Piaget (see all references), but it is less concerned with cognitions per se and much more concerned with the emotion, motivation, and interpersonal relationships in which cognitive development participates.

SUMMARY AND CONCLUSION

In this reinterpretation of the experiential roots of intentions, I have relinquished my contention that they originate during the second stage of information processing with efforts to attain perceptual contact with objects, persons, and places that have become recognitively familiar in favor of one in which intentions come into being through anticipations of the outcomes of spontaneous actions. Intentional action, by definition, is action with anticipated outcome.

This change of view has its origin in an unexpected finding from an intervention in infant rearing at an orphanage in Tehran. In this intervention, caretakers were taught how to foster vocal imitation as a means of helping the foundlings to acquire language. They were taught to imitate the cooings and babblings of the infants in their charge to get vocal games going, to extend these games to vocal "follow the leader" with familiar vocal patterns, then to copy unfamiliar vocal patterns from the Persian language modeled by the caretakers, and finally how to sharpen the conditions for associating parts of their bodies with the sounds of the names of the parts. This intervention was dramatically successful in fostering the acquisition of language. Unexpectedly, however, it was also dramatically successful in fostering intentionality, joy in living, initiative, and trust.

The theoretical significance of this unexpected result of this intervention gets considerable clarification and enhancement from recent findings of the effects of leaving newborns with their mothers in the lying-in hospital during the days immediately following their births. Such infants develop very early a mutuality of interaction in which they act and then hesitate as if waiting for their mothers to react. Such hesitations suggest that these infants have come to anticipate their mothers' responses. Such anticipations might be expected from repeated sequences of interaction because the representative central processes which constitute memory typically run off more rapidly than do events. The fact that mothers who are free from distractions and are concerned with their infants commonly imitate their expressions and vocalizations suggests that such imitative responses to spontaneous actions of infants constitute the experiential roots of intentions.

Separating the genesis of intentions from the epigenesis of information processing appears to leave the plausible accuracy of my hypothetical description of the latter intact.

Initiative appears to come about through success in achieving anticipated or intentional goals, but not necessarily easy success. Success with effort after instances of failure combined with the resulting achievement of competencies is suggested as the experiential root of initiative.

Trust appears, from such considerations and from recent evidence, to come about experiences of acceptance, assessibility, and sensitive and cooperative help from mothers or caretakers in achieving difficult intended goals.

ACKNOWLEDGMENT

The writing of this paper has been supported by a grant from the Waters Foundation of Framingham, Massachusetts, and I wish to acknowledge it with gratitude.

REFERENCES

AINSWORTH, M. D. S. Attachment and dependency: A comparison. In J. L. Gewirtz (Ed.), *Attachment and dependency*. Washington, D. C.: Winston, 1972.

AINSWORTH, M. D. S., BELL, S. M., & STAYTON, D. J. Individual differences in strange-situation behavior of one-year-olds. In H. R. Schaffer (Ed.), *The origins of human social relations*. New York: Academic Press, 1971.

AINSWORTH, M. D. S., BELL, S. M., & STAYTON, D. J. Individual differences in the development of some attachment behaviors. *Merrill-Palmer Quarterly*, 1972, *18*, 132–143.

ATKIN, R., BRAY, R., DAVISON, M., HERZBERGER, S., HUMPHREYS, L., & SELZER, U. Cross-lagged panel analysis of sixteen cognitive measures at four grade levels. *Child Development*, 1977, *48*, 944–952.

BADGER, D. *Teaching guide: Infant learning program*. Paoli, Pa.: The Instructo Corporation (subsidiary of McGraw-Hill), 1971.(a)

BADGER, E. D. *Teaching guide: Toddler learning program*. Paoli, Pa.: The Instructo Corporation (subsidiary of McGraw-Hill), 1971.(b)

BADGER, E. D. A mothers' training program—A sequel article. *Children Today*, 1972, *1* (3), 7–12.

BEACH, F. A. Current concepts of play in animals. *American Naturalist*, 1945, *79*, 523–541.

BERLYNE, D. E. *Structure and direction of thinking*. New York: Wiley, 1965.

BERLYNE, D. E. What next? (Concluding summary). In H. I. Day, D. E. Berlyne, & D. E. Hunt (Eds.), *Intrinsic motivation: A new direction in education*. Toronto & Montreal: Holt, Rinehart & Winston of Canada, 1971.

BERNARD, C. *Leçons sur les propriétés physiologiques et les altérations pathologiques des liquides de l'organisme*. (2 vols.). Paris: Ballière, 1859.

BEXTON, W. H., HERON, W., & SCOTT, T. H. Effects of decreased variation in the sensory environment. *Canadian Journal of Psychology*, 1954, *8*, 70–76.

BOWER, T. G. R. *Development in infancy*. New York: W. H. Freeman, 1974.

BRADLEY, R. H., & CALDWELL, B. M. Home observation for measurement of the environment: A validation study of screening efficiency. *American Journal of Mental Deficiency*, 1977, *81*, 417–420.

BRAZELTON, T. B., TRONICK, E., ADAMSON, L., ALS, H., & WISE, S. Early mother–infant interaction. In *Parent–infant interaction*, Ciba Symposium No. 33. Amsterdam: Associated Scientific Publishers, 1975.

BRILL, A. A. *Psychoanalysis*. Philadelphia: Saunders, 1912.

BROWN, J. S. Problems presented by the concept of acquired drives. In M. R. Jones (Ed.), *Current theory and research in motivation: A symposium*. Lincoln: University of Nebraska Press, 1953.

DEMBER, W. N., & EARL, R. W. Analysis of exploratory, manipulatory and curiosity behaviors. *Psychological Review*, 1957, *64*, 91–96.

DOLLARD, J., & MILLER, N. E. *Personality and psychotherapy: An analysis in terms of learning, thinking, and culture*. New York: McGraw-Hill, 1950.

ERIKSON, E. H. *Childhood and society*. New York: Norton, 1950.

FARBER, I. E. Anxiety as a drive state. In M. R. Jones (Ed.), *Nebraska symposium on motivation* (Vol. II). Lincoln: University of Nebraska Press, 1954.

FESTINGER, L. *A theory of cognitive dissonance*. Evanston, Ill.: Row, Peterson, 1957.

FREUD, S. *The interpretation of dreams*. In A. A. Brill (transl. & ed.), *The basic writings of Sigmund Freud*. New York: Modern Library, 1938. (Originally published, 1900.)

FREUD, S. *Three contributions to the theory of sex*. In A. A. Brill (trans. & ed.), *The basic writings of Sigmund Freud*. New York: Modern Library, 1938. (Originally published, 1905.)

FREUD, S. Instincts and their vicissitudes. In *Collected papers* (Vol. 4). London: Hogarth, 1950. (Originally published, 1915.)

GREENBERG, D. J., UZGIRIS, C., & HUNT, J. McV. Attentional preference and experience: III. Visual familiarity and looking time. *Journal of Genetic Psychology*, 1970, *117*, 123–135.

GROOS, K. *The play of man* (1896). (E. L. Baldwin, trans.) New York: Appleton, 1905. (Originally published, 1896.)

HAITH, M. M., & CAMPOS, J. J. Human infancy. In M. R. Rosenzweig & L. W. Porter (Eds.), *Annual Review of Psychology*, 1977, *28*, 274–293.

HARLOW, H. F. Learning and satiation of response in intrinsically motivated complex puzzle performance by monkeys. *Journal of Comparative and Physiological Psychology*, 1950, *43*, 289–294.

HARLOW, H. F., HARLOW, K., & MEYER, D. R. Learning motivated by a manipulation drive. *Journal of Experimental Psychology*, 1950, *40*, 228–234.

HEBB, D. O. On the nature of fear. *Psychological Review*, 1946, *53*, 259–276.

HEBB, D. O. *The organization of behavior*. New York: Wiley, 1949.

HEBB, D. O., & RIESEN, A. H. The genesis of irrational fears. *Bulletin of the Canadian Psychological Association*, 1943, *3*, 49–50.

HELSON, H. *Adaptation-level theory*. New York: Row, 1964.

HERON, W., DOANE, B. K., & SCOTT, T. H. Visual disturbances after prolonged perceptual isolation. *Canadian Journal of Psychology*, 1956, *10*, 13–18.

HULL, C. L. *Principles of behavior*. New York: Appleton-Century-Crofts, 1943.

HULL, C. L. *A behavior system*. New Haven: Yale University Press, 1952.

HUMPHREYS, L. G. The effect of random alternation of reinforcement on the acquisition and extinction of conditioned eyelid reactions. *Journal of Experimental Psychology*, 1939, *25*, 141–158.

HUMPHREYS, L. G., & PARSONS, C. K. Piagetian tasks measure intelligence and intelligence tests assess cognitive development: A reanalysis. *Intelligence*, 1979, *3*, 369–382.

HUNT, J. McV. *Intelligence and experience*. New York: Ronald, 1961.

HUNT, J. McV. Motivation inherent in information processing and action. In O. J. Harvey (Ed.), *Motivation and social interaction: The cognitive determinants*. New York: Ronald, 1963.(a)

HUNT, J. McV. Piaget's observations as a source of hypotheses concerning motivation. *Merrill-Palmer Quarterly*, 1963, *9*, 263–275.(b)

HUNT, J. McV. Intrinsic motivation and its role in psychological development. In D. Levine (Ed.), *Nebraska symposium on motivation* (Vol. 13). Lincoln: University of Nebraska Press, 1965.

HUNT, J. McV. Toward a theory of guided learning in development. In R. H. Ojemann & K. Pritchett (eds.), *Giving emphasis to guided learning*. Cleveland: Educational Research Council, 1966.

HUNT, J. McV. *The challenge of incompetence and poverty: Papers on the role of early education.* Urbana: University of Illinois Press, 1969.

HUNT, J. McV. Attentional preference and experience: I. Introduction. *Journal of Genetic Psychology,* 1970, *117,* 99–107.

HUNT, J. McV. Intrinsic motivation: Information and circumstance. In H. M. Schroder & P. Suedfeld (Eds.), *Personality theory and information processing.* New York: Ronald, 1971(a)

HUNT, J. McV. Intrinsic motivation and psychological development. In H. M. Schroder & P. Suedfeld (Eds.), *Personality theory and information processing.* New York: Ronald, 1971.(b)

HUNT, J. McV. Toward a history of intrinsic motivation. In H. I. Day, D. E. Berlyne, & D. E. Hunt (Eds.), *Intrinsic motivation: A new direction in education.* Toronto: Holt, Rinehart & Winston of Canada, 1971.(c)

HUNT, J. McV. *Specificity in early development and experience.* Annual Lecture in Development Pediatrics. Omaha: Meyer Children's Rehabilitation Institute, University of Nebraska Medical Center, 1977.

HUNT, J. McV. Developmental psychology: Early experience. *Annual Review of Psychology,* 1979, *30,* 103–143.(a)

HUNT, J. McV. *Language acquisition and experience.* (G. Stanley Hall Award Address, Meetings of the APA, San Francisco, August 1977).

HUNT, J. McV., Mohandessi, K., Ghodssi, M., & Akiyama, M. The psychological development of orphanage-reared infants: Interventions with outcomes (Tehran). *Genetic Psychology Monographs,* 94, 1976, 177–226.

HUNT, J. McV., Paraskevopoulos, J., Schickedanz, D., & Uzgiris, I. C. Variations in the mean ages of achieving object permanence under diverse conditions of rearing. In B. L. Friedlander, G. M. Sterritt, & G. E. Kirk (Eds.), *The exceptional infant* (Vol. 3.): *Assessment and intervention.* New York: Brunner/Mazel, 1975.

ISAACS, N. Children's "why" questions in *Children's ways of knowing: Nathan Isaacs on education, psychology, and Piaget.* New York: Teachers College Press, 1974. (Originally published, 1930.)

JENKINS, W. P., & STANLEY, J. C., JR. Partial reinforcement: A review and critique. *Psychological Bulletin,* 1950, *47,* 193–234.

KELLY, G. A. *The psychology of personal constructs* (2 vols.). New York: Norton, 1955.

KIRK, G. E., HUNT, J. McV., & LIEBERMAN, C. Social class preschool language skill: II. Semantic mastery of color information. *Genetic Psychology Monographs,* 1975, *91,* 299–316.

KLAUS, R. A., & GRAY, S. W. The early training project for disadvantaged children: A report after five years. *Monographs of the Society for Research in Child Development,* 1968, *33*(4), 1–66.

KLAUS, M., JERAULD, R., KREGER, N., MCALPINE, W., STEFFA, M., & KENNEL, J. Maternal attachment: Importance of the first post-partum days. *New England Journal of Medicine,* 1972, *286,* 460–463.

LANDIS, C. Electrical phenomena of the skin. *Psychological Bulletin,* 1932, *29,* 693–752.

LINDSLEY, D. B. Emotion. In S. S. Stevens (Ed.), *Handbook of experimental psychology.* New York: Wiley, 1951.

LINDSLEY, D. B. Psychophysiology and motivation. In M. R. Jones (Ed.), *Nebraska symposium on motivation* (Vol. V). Lincoln: University of Nebraska Press, 1957.

LIPSITT, L. P. Learning processes of human newborns. *Merrill-Palmer Quarterly*, 1966, *12*, 45–71.

LIPSITT, L. P. Learning in the human infant. In H. W. Stevenson, R. Hess, & H. L. Rheingold (Eds.), *Early behavior: Comparative and developmental approaches*. New York: Wiley, 1967.

LORENZ, K. The companion in the bird's world. *Auk*, 1937, *54*, 245–273.

MALTZMAN, I., & RASKIN, D. C. Effects of individual differences in the orienting reflex on conditioning and complex processes. *Journal of Experimental Research in Personality*, 1965, *1*, 1–16.

MCCARTHY, D. Language development in children. In L. Carmichael (Ed.), *Manual of child psychology* (2nd ed.). New York: Wiley, 1954.

MELTZOFF, A. N., & MOORE, M. K. Imitation of facial and manual gestures of human neonates. *Science*, 1977, *198*, 75–78.

MILLER, N. E., & DOLLARD, J. *Social learning and imitation*. New Haven: Yale University Press, 1941.

MILLER, G. A., GALANTER, E., & PRIBRAM, K. H. *Plans and the structure of behavior*. New York: Holt, Rinehart and Winston, 1960.

MONTGOMERY, K. C. The relation between fear induced by novel stimulation and exploratory behavior. *Journal of Comparative and Physiological Psychology*, 1955, *48*, 254–260.

MONTGOMERY, K. C., & SEGALL, M. Discrimination learning based upon the exploratory drive. *Journal of Comparative and Physiological Psychology*, 1955, *48*, 225–228.

MOWRER, O. H. *Learning theory and behavior*. New York: Wiley, 1960.

MOWRER, O. H., & KLUCKHOHN, C. Dynamic theory of personality. In J. McV. Hunt (Ed.), *Personality and the behavior disorders* (Vol. 1). New York: Ronald, 1944.

NEWELL, A., SHAW, J. C., & SIMON, H. A. Elements of a theory of human problem solving. *Psychological Review*, 1958, *65*, 151–166.

OLDS, J. Physiological mechanisms of reward. In M. R. Jones (Ed.), *Nebraska symposium on motivation* (Vol. 3). Lincoln: University of Nebraska Press, 1955.

PAPOUSEK, H., & PAPOUSEK, M. Mothering and the cognitive head-start. In H. R. Schaffer (Ed.), *Studies in mother–infant interaction*. New York: Academic, Press, 1977.

PIAGET, J. *The origins of intelligence in children* (M. Cook, trans.) New York: International Universities Press, 1952. (Originally published, 1936.)

PIAGET, J. *The construction of reality in the child* (M. Cook, trans.) New York: Basic Books, 1954. (Originally published, 1937.)

PIAGET, J. *Play, dreams, and imitation in childhood* (C. Gattegno & F. M. Hodgson, trans.) New York: Norton, 1951. (Originally published, 1945.)

PIAGET, J. Problems of equilibration. In M. H. Appel & L. S. Goldberg (Eds.), *Topics in cognitive development* (Vol. 1): *Equilibration: Theory, research and application*. New York: Plenum, 1977.

PREMACK, D. Reinforcement theory. In D. Levine (Ed.), *Nebraska symposium on motivation* (Vol. 13). Lincoln: University of Nebraska Press, 1965.

PRIBRAM, K. H. Neocortical function in behavior. In H. F. Harlow & C. N. Woolsey (Eds.), *Biological and biochemical bases of behavior*. Madison: University of Wisconsin Press, 1958.

PRIBRAM, K. H. A review of theory in physiological psychology. *Annual Review of Psychology*, 1960, *11*, 1–40.

RAZRAN, G. The observable unconscious and the inferrable conscious in current Soviet psychophysiology: Interoceptive conditioning, semantic conditioning, and the orienting reflex. *Psychological Review*, 1961, *68*, 81–147.

ROGERS, C. R. *Client-centered therapy*. Boston: Houghton Mifflin, 1951.

ROSE, J. E., & WOOLSEY, C. N. The relations of thalamic connections, cellular structure and evocable electrical activity in the auditory region of the cat. *Journal of Comparative Neurology*, 1949, *91*, 441–446.

RYAN, T. R. *Intentional behavior: An approach to human motivation.* New York: Ronald, 1970.

SCHAFFER, H. R. (Ed.). *Studies in mother–infant interaction.* New York: Academic Press, 1977.

SCHICKENDANZ, D. I. *An investigation of the human infant's acquisition of internal control.* Unpublished doctoral dissertation, Department of Psychology, University of Illinois, 1974.

SKINNER, B. F. *The behavior of organisms: An experimental analysis.* New York: Appleton-Century-Crofts, (1938).

SKINNER, B. F. *Science and human behavior.* New York: Macmillan, 1953.

SOLOMON, R. L. The influence of work on behavior. *Psychological Bulletin,* 1948, *45,* 1–20.

SPENCE, K. W. *Behavior theory and conditioning.* New Haven: Yale University Press, 1956.

TREVARTHEN, C. Conversations with a two-month old. *New Scientist,* 1974, *62,* 230–235.

TREVARTHEN, C. Descriptive analyses of infant communicative behavior. In H. R. Schaffer (Ed.), *Studies in mother–infant interaction.* New York: Academic Press, 1977.

UNIKEL, I. P. Effects of changes in stimulation upon preference for stimulus complexity. *Journal of Experimental Psychology,* 1971, *88,* 246–250.

UZGIRIS, I. C. Die Mannigfaltigkeit der Imitation in der frühen Kindheit. [The Many Faces of Imitation in Infancy.] In L. Montada (Ed.), *Brennpunkte der Entwicklungspsychologie.* Stuttgart: W. Kohlhammer, 1979.

UZGIRIS, I. C., & HUNT, J. McV. *Assessment in infancy: Ordinal scales of psychological development.* Urbana: University of Illinois Press, 1975.

WACHS, T. D., UZGIRIS, I. C., & HUNT, J. McV. Cognitive development in infants of different age levels and from different environmental backgrounds: An exploratory investigation. *Merrill-Palmer Quarterly,* 1971, *17,* 283–317.

WATSON, J. B. *Psychological care of infant and child.* New York: Norton, 1928.

WATSON, J. S. Memory and "contingency analysis" in infant learning. *Merrill-Palmer Quarterly of Behavior and Development,* 1967, *13,* 55–76.

WEIZMANN, F., COHEN, L. B., & PRATT, R. J. Novelty, familiarity, and the development of infant attention. *Developmental Psychology,* 1971, *4,* 149–154.

WETHERFORD, M., & COHEN, L. B. Developmental changes in infant visual preferences for novelty and familiarity. *Child Development,* 1973, *44,* 416–424.

WHITE, B. L. *Experience and Environment: Major influence on the development of the young child* (Vol. II). Englewood Cliffs, N.J.: Prentice-Hall, 1978.

WHITE, B. L., & WATTS, J. *Experience and environment: Major influences on the development of the young child.* Englewood Cliffs, N.J.: Prentice-Hall, 1973.

WHITE, R. W. Motivation reconsidered: The concept of competence. *Psychological Review,* 1959, *66,* 297–333.

WOODWORTH, R. S. *Dynamic psychology.* New York: Columbia University Press, 1918.

YARROW, L. J., RUBENSTEIN, J. L. & PEDERSEN, F. A. *Infant and environment: Early cognitive and motivational development.* Washington, D. C.: Hemisphere Publishing Company, 1975.

9

A Theory Deriving Preference from Conflict

FRANK AULD

A THEORY OF PREFERENCE

The breadth of Daniel Berlyne's interests is suggested by the title of his early book *Conflict, Arousal, and Curiosity* (1960). Just as the title expresses a breadth of interest, the content of the book demonstrates Berlyne's ability to make connections between concepts that many other psychologists keep apart. For him, thinking and motivation, physiological arousal and aesthetics, curiosity and information theory have important linkages—linkages that he brought to our attention, reflected on, speculated about, and did research on.

The present paper was stimulated by Berlyne's writings on arousal, conflict, and preference. I make use of some of Berlyne's ideas about arousal, conflict, preference, expectation, and incentive, applying his formulations in the analysis of a newly devised test of personality, and in the study of how a name helps or hinders the sale of a particular make of car. Although the research reported here was not originally stimulated by Berlyne's theorizing, I believe that we can understand this research more deeply if we reflect about it within the framework of Berlyne's ideas.

Statement of the Theory

In his writings Berlyne came back again and again to the concept *arousal*. To Berlyne, "arousal" meant activity and alertness. He defined "arousal potential" as a grouping of those properties of stimuli that

FRANK AULD • Department of Psychology, University of Windsor, Windsor, Ontario, Canada.

produce an increase in arousal, that is, roughly, as stimulus strength. According to Berlyne (1973), stimulus intensity is related to hedonic value (pleasantness or unpleasantness) in the following ways: (1) At low and moderate levels of stimulus intensity, as the stimulus increases in intensity, activity of the primary reward system also increases; activity of this reward system reaches a maximum at some moderate level of intensity. (2) At a low level of stimulus intensity, the aversion system is inactive. Beginning at a moderate level of stimulus intensity, the aversion system becomes active; and its activity increases, according to a function of ogival shape, until it reaches a maximum at some fairly high level of stimulus intensity. (3) Hedonic value is the net result of the summation of positive reward and aversion. If positive reward is greater than aversion, the hedonic value is positive; if less, the hedonic value is negative. The relationship between stimulus intensity and hedonic value is a curve like that described by Wundt, in which with increasing stimulus intensity hedonic value rises from a neutral value to a high, positive level at a moderate intensity of the stimulus, then falls until, at very high intensities of the stimulus, the hedonic value is strongly negative.

In discussing how stimulus strength determines hedonic value, Berlyne hoped to lay down principles applying to the first part of a theory of behavior—the part that specifies the determinants of hedonic value. Part 2 of the theory would explain how, given that a stimulus has a particular hedonic value, the individual guides his behavior so as to take account of this. As Berlyne (1973) put it, Part 2 is the area of research concerned with "the role of hedonic value in the determination of behavior."

In discussing this problem of how hedonic value influences behavior, Berlyne relied upon an expectancy theory. Briefly stated, this theory says: (1) that the person has learned that a particular consequence follows a particular action; (2) that the individual wants such a consequence to occur; and (3) that he or she therefore makes the particular response in order to bring about the desired consequence.

THE PICTURE-PREFERENCE TEST

We can now apply these ideas to a picture-preference test originally devised by Lawrence Cowan (1967/1971). In its original version this test comprised 106 pairs of pictures. The person taking the test is asked to look at each pair of pictures, which is presented to him for 10 sec by means of a slide projector, and then to choose either the left-hand picture (called "A") or the right-hand picture (called "B") as the one he likes better. Cowan selected the 106 items of his test with the aim of measuring ten personality traits associated with a predisposition to becoming addicted to alcohol or to other drugs. Thus, one picture of each pair was intended to appeal more strongly to an addicted person than to a person who is not addicted. A tendency of addicts to prefer this picture to the other more often than nonaddicts do would make the picture pair a valid measure of the traits characterizing addicts.

Cowan expected that the addicts would more often choose the picture that he had designated as the "addictive choice," either because this picture evoked in them an expectation of a gratification that addicted people very much want, or because the other picture bestirred a response that addicted people find it necessary to avoid. The tendency to choose Picture A over Picture B is the result of the difference between (1) the positive valence of A, less its negative valence, and (2) the positive valence of B, less its negative valence. The positive valence is aroused by the rewarding events provided by, promised by, or suggested by the picture; the negative valence is evoked by aversive events suggested by the picture. We assume that *each* picture evokes some positively valent tendencies and some negatively valent tendencies. The pull toward choosing Picture A, we repeat, is the result of the net positive valence that Picture A has.

As an example of our analysis of the choice between two pictures, let us consider Cowan's pair of pictures that has as Picture A, "A baby with a pacifier in his mouth," and as Picture B, "A baby looking at a mobile." This picture is included in Figure 2. Cowan postulated that addicts have a stronger oral-incorporate need than other people do. He believed that Picture A, evoking imagery and fantasies associated with oral gratifications, would appeal to people in proportion to their level of need for such gratifications. It would also be aversive to people in proportion to the level of fear that they had about allowing themselves oral gratifications. In using these assumptions, Cowan adopted the system for explaining conflict behavior that Neal Miller (1959) had developed.

Cowan reasoned that, on the other hand, Picture B should appeal less to the viewer on the basis of his motivation to obtain oral gratifications, because it does not picture the baby obtaining such gratifications. The baby, looking at a mobile that is suspended above his crib, is gratifying his curiosity. Cowan assumed that a viewer of this picture who possessed some degree of exploratory drive would, through identification with the baby watching the mobile, experience some partial gratification of this exploratory drive. Quite possibly some persons would be fearful about exploring the environment, even with their eyes; for such people, Picture B would also arouse aversive tendencies. The net of the imagined gratifications and the aversive forces would, Cowan reasoned, determine the tendency to chose Picture B.

Whereas Berlyne focused on properties of the stimulus—"stimulus strength," for example—that would be expected to produce arousal in a person, and then attempted to forecast the hedonic value on the basis of an opposition between the primary reward system and the aversion system, Cowan allowed for a more diverse set of determinants of attraction or repulsion. In what follows, I too take this broader view. Instead of directing our attention to the stimulus intensity of the picture, Cowan and I consider the primary or learned drives and rewards that are *represented* in the picture. We take for granted that the picture is not so dim that if fails to register or so bright that it hurts the eyes. Stimulus intensity of the picture itself is not at issue, therefore; we are considering what is represented by the picture. Now, within the framework of visually represented drives and rewards, again we direct our attention beyond the issue of representation of stimulus intensity, even though this is one of the qualities that a picture can represent. We consider a rather diverse set of drives and rewards that are, in our opinion, represented by our pictures. Where we follow the same reasoning as Berlyne is in assuming, as he does, that liking something or disliking it, finding it pleasant or unpleasant, is a resultant of opposing forces. Berlyne called these forces "reward system" and "aversion system"; we would call them "approach tendency" and "avoidance tendency," or "positive valence" and "negative valence."

But what is rewarding to one person is not necessarily rewarding to another; and what frightens one may not frighten another. People differ in their desires, and in what can gratify them. It is the aim of our picture-preference test to measure the ways in which people do, in fact, differ in their motivations.

If we knew what rewards were represented by the pictures and what aversive qualities were represented; and if we also knew the strength of the relevant motives in a particular person; then we could forecast how this person would respond to our pair of pictures. In using the test to measure people's personality traits, we attempt to reverse this sequence: knowing the individual's choice between Picture A and Picture B, and making some assumption about the rewards and dangers represented by the pictures, we draw an inference about the strength of the individual's motivations and fears.

In doing this, we are following a well-trodden path. Henry Murray made the assumption that needs direct behavior (Murray, 1938, pp. 61–66). He cited evidence that hunger influences a child's completion of unfinished pictures (Sanford, 1936), and that fear changes a child's interpretations of photographs (Murray, 1933). McClelland and Atkinson (1948) showed that, as the hours of food deprivation increased, subjects gave more food-related responses to a blank slide. After reviewing a mass of evidence about the relationship between personality and perception, Zubin, Eron, and Schumer (1965) expressed the judgment that the same stimulus under seemingly similar mental set produces one type of projective response in one individual and a different one in another. These individual differences in overt response are the data from which we attempt to make valid inferences about the internal dispositions of the subjects.

I assume, as Cowan did, that each picture stirs up both approach and avoidance tendencies. In making this assumption, I am making use of Miller's (1959) model of conflict. At least one investigation of projective testing—that of Minuchin (1950/1965)—has shown that accurate prediction of overt behavior requires taking into account the inhibitory forces in a conflict, as well as the pressure toward expression of impulse. Minuchin studied the relationship between TAT stories and the overt behavior of mental-hospital patients. She found no relationship between the number of themes of aggression on the test and the patient's overt aggression. But she was able to predict from the qualifications, denials, and expressions of guilt about aggression—in other words, from signs of the inhibitory tendencies—whether the patient would be overtly aggressive on the hospital ward. She also found that very strong verbalizations—for example, descriptions of blood and gore—were predictive of aggression on the ward.

Minuchin's findings are consistent with the general principle (stated by Auld, 1954) that whether an overt response occurs or not depends on the balance between approach and avoidance tendencies. In our use of the Picture-Preference Test, the choice of Picture A or Picture B is, according to this analysis, dependent on the net resultant of approach and avoidance tendencies evoked by each of the pictures.

Given that we know which picture the viewer chose, we can infer something about the relative net attractiveness (approach minus avoidance tendencies) of the two pictures. If we are successful in excluding unwanted determinants of net attractiveness—that is, in keeping other factors from influencing, differentially, Picture A and Picture B, thereby biasing the choice—then we can assume that the rewarding or aversive qualities of each picture, which we intended the picture to have, determine its net attractiveness.

Here is an example of an unwanted determinant of net attractiveness: The tendency to choose a picture because the choice is viewed as socially desirable, rather than because of the balance between the picture's specific appeals and specific aversive qualities, would disturb the measurement of the specific appeals and aversions. Amin (1974/1976), in devising a picture-preference scale to measure "avoidance of sexual intimacy," took care to pretest the general social desirability of each of the separate pictures. Using a nine-point scale taken from Edwards (1970), he had a group of 30 subjects rate the social desirability of each picture proposed for the new scale. Where the pictures that had been intended as members of a pair were sharply discrepant in their social desirability ratings, he eliminated this pair of pictures. For example, one proposed item included, as Picture A, "A shower room with several nude men; a partition conceals their genitals," and, as Picture B, "A soldier in fatigues peeling potatoes." The social desirability rating of Picture A was 5.69 ("moderately desirable"), and of Picture B, 3.30 ("moderately undesirable"). Thus there would be a bias to choose Picture A because of the social desirability response tendency, even if one were rather high in the tendency to avoid sexually explicit or sexually embarrassing situations. In any event, individual differences in the tendency to respond in a socially desirable way would influence the response to such an item, thereby obscuring the intended basis for choice between the two pictures.

Finding it necessary to abandon this item, Amin was able nevertheless to use these two pictures, paired with two other pictures. The soldier on KP was paired with "Woman having a tooth drilled by a dentist" (which gave ratings of 3.30 and 3.53 for Pictures A and B), and the shower-room scene (now A) was paired with "Woman ironing near a child with a rattle" (which yielded ratings of 5.69 and 5.23 for Pictures A and B). By such reassignments of pictures Amin achieved a balance between the social desirability ratings of pictures whose choice was to indicate avoidance of social intimacy (mean rating for these was 5.84) and those whose choice was to indicate acceptance of explicit representations of sexual intimacy (mean rating was 5.93). Pictures belonging to the same pair fell within 0.5 of a scale-unit of each other 89% of the time, and within 0.81 of a unit for the remaining 11%. An intraclass correlation between the pairs of pictures was computed; r is .94. (By comparison, in developing his Personal Preference Schedule, Edwards achieved an intraclass r of .85.)

Collative Properties and Preference

In his writings on aesthetic preferences, Berlyne laid considerable stress on the collative properties of artistic stimuli. He believed that the variety and complexity of a stimulus pattern has an important effect on its aesthetic appeal (Berlyne, 1971, 1974). Monotonous and oversimple patterns would be expected to lack the capacity to evoke interest. On the other hand, patterns that lacked all sense of order or regularity, patterns that were close to random, would be expected to place so great a demand on the observer for organizing and coping with the disorder that such patterns would provoke displeasure (Day, 1967). In summary, a fairly high level of complexity of pattern would be optimal in interest, and would produce greatest pleasure.

Although the research cited by Berlyne is surely sufficient to verify the correctness of this line of reasoning, it is of some interest to see how these ideas could be used to explain a part of the bias toward one or another of the items of Cowan's Picture-Preference Test. Of the 272 items that have been developed for the Picture-Preference Test (Cowan's original 106 items and 166 items subsequently devised by others), seven present a clear choice between a less complex and a more complex picture, with other aspects of the pictures besides complexity having less saliency than usual. None of the items includes a picture of such great disorder that we would expect the viewer to reject it because of extremely high complexity.

Let us consider these seven items. (Six of the seven are shown in Figure 1.) The first item shows four Ms increasing in size from left to right, as Picture A, and four Ms all of the same size, as Picture B. In a sample of 309 university students (Berek, 1975/1976), 44% preferred the left-hand picture of the increasing Ms, which I would consider to be more complex in the sense of information theory because the Ms are more heterogeneous in appearance. The remaining 56%, of course, preferred the same-sized Ms. The second item compares $+ 0$ with $+ +$; 62.8% preferred $+0$, which I consider to be more complex. The third item shows at the left four swans and one vulture, at the right, five vultures; 34.7% preferred the left-hand, "more complex" picture. The fourth item shows at the left a circle and square just touching each other, at the right the two figures intersecting; 53.8% preferred the intersecting figures, which I consider "more complex." The fifth item presents an arithmetic progression and a geometric progression; 56.7% preferred the geometric progression, which is more complex. The sixth item presents a neat, orderly room at the left, and a cluttered, disorderly room at the right; 9.13% preferred disorder, which, of course, is more complex. Finally, the seventh item shows at the left eight true–false items on an examination paper, all marked "true," and at the right eight items, four of them marked "true," four marked "false"; 60% preferred the right-hand, true-and-false picture.

On the hypothesis that greater complexity is more interesting, that it arouses curiosity, and that therefore it should be preferred, we would be right about five of the seven items but wrong about two, the increasing Ms and the four swans and one vulture. One can only speculate about why the expectations were not borne out for these two items, and what other determinants worked against the complexity factor. Is it that the rapidly increasing letters threaten to take over the whole world—the problem of too-much-intensity to which Berlyne has called our attention? Is it that we feel that a vulture doesn't belong among swans, that he should stay among his own nasty kind? I have no data to answer these questions.

FIGURE 1. Picture-preference items presenting a clear choice between more complex and less complex pictures. The six items are used with the permission of Dr. Lawrence Cowan, who developed them; © 1980 by Lawrence Cowan.

Attempts to Create Trait Scales

Of course, the Picture-Preference Test was not developed to demonstrate the influence of collative properties on preference; it was developed to measure individual differences in dispositions. Although some would say that attempts to measure personality traits are doomed to failure, and would call me wrongheaded for trying to measure such traits, I agree with Stagner (1976) that any theory of personality requires an assumption that there are enduring dispositions in human beings. As Whiting and Child (1953, p. 20) have pointed out, an enduring behavioral disposition is not activated by any or every situation; instead, it is a readiness to respond whenever a particular kind of situation arises.

Most of the Picture-Preference items demand a choice between pictures that represent different interpersonal situations or different objects. The items were devised on an a priori basis, being intended to measure traits such as "compulsiveness," "impulsiveness," "avoidance of sexual intimacy," and "magical thinking." Cowan, who devised the first 106 items, and other researchers who, following him, created the remaining 166 items (see Amin, 1974/1976; Bégin, 1975; Morrison, 1973/1975), realized that each of the pictures they created would provoke a certain degree or arousal together with a certain level of aversive motivation. The trick is to achieve the right balance between provocation to arousal and provocation to avoidance, so that the dispositions of the subject can be measured by his choice of Picture A or Picture B of a pair.

I have already given an example of a picture-preference item, one that was intended to measure Oral Incorporative Trends—the item with "A baby with a pacifier in his mouth" as Picture A and "A baby looking at a mobile" as Picture B. This item is shown, along with four others, in Figure 2. These other four items belong to scales intended to measure Impulsiveness, Avoidance of Sexual Intimacy, Damaged Self-Esteemed, and Antisocial Tendencies. The rationale for Item 50 is that a person intolerant of delay and frustration—an impulsive person—will tend to choose the left-hand picture of the bumpy road. For Item 31 we reason that choosing the picture showing one person in the bed indicates a tendency toward avoidance of sexual intimacy. We assume that the picture of the woman having a fantasy about a gravestone will be more often chosen by those who suffer from damaged self-esteem and depression. And, finally, we believe that the choice of the picture showing a man with mask and gun is an expression of antisocial tendencies.

Although it was hoped that the scales would measure the traits that they were devised to measure and that research would quickly provide evidence for the reliability and validity of the scales, it has turned out that few of the proposed scales are as reliable as we could wish, and that validation is a long and laborious task.

First, as to reliability, I can report that test–retest reliabilities (with a three-week interval between first and second testings) for the scales we have been considering are as follows: Oral-Incorporative Trends, .62; Impulsiveness, .42; Avoidance of Sexual Intimacy, .79; Damaged Self-Esteem, .58; and Antisocial Tendencies, .75. These reliability coefficients come from a study by Fuerth (1977) involving 105 university students (75 women, 30 men).

The strongest evidence for validity of any of the Picture-Preference scales was obtained by Amin (1974/1976) in his study of the Avoidance of Sexual Intimacy scale that he developed. Scores on this scale correlated substantially ($r = .64$) with a measure of the tendency to sexual inhibition that was based on responses to five TAT pictures. Because the scoring of the TAT stories was done with complete independence, with high scorer reliability ($r = .86$), and with a rationale based on psychoanalytic hypotheses about the source of women's fears of sexuality, it is impressive that the TAT ratings show such a close correspondence to the Picture-Preference scores that were derived by a different approach.

Some evidence for validity is available also for the Antisocial Tendencies scale. Ryan (1976/1977), correlating various picture-preference scales with the scales of Jackson and Messick's (1964) Differential Personality Inventory, using a sample of 192 university students, found modest but statistically significant correlations between Morrison's (1973/1975) Antisocial Tendencies scale and three Differential Personality Inventory (hereafter called DPI) scales: Cynicism ($r = .29$), Impulsivity ($r = .30$), and Socially Deviant Attitudes ($r = .24$). We can surely accept the correlation with Socially Deviant Attitudes as a modest support of the proposition that the picture-preference scale measures what its name would lead one to expect. The correlations with Cynicism and Impulsivity are not alarming, but they do indicate that this picture-preference scale is less specific in what it measures than Jackson and Messick's scales are.

Additional evidence for the validity of the Antisocial Tendencies scale is provided by data obtained by Bégin (1975) in the course of his doctoral research. Bégin gave the Picture-Preference Test to 83 alcoholic men, 35 alcoholic women, 80 normal men, and 35 normal women. Comparing scores of the alcoholics and the normals of Bégin's sample on Morrison's Antisocial Tendencies scale, Dennis Ratner and I (see Auld, Ratner, & Begin, 1977) found that, for both sex groups, the alcoholics have mean scores that are significantly higher. For men, $t(161) = 3.58, p < .001$; for women, $t(68) = 1.85, p < .05$. Because the group differences are as expected, these findings strengthen our confidence in the validity of this scale.

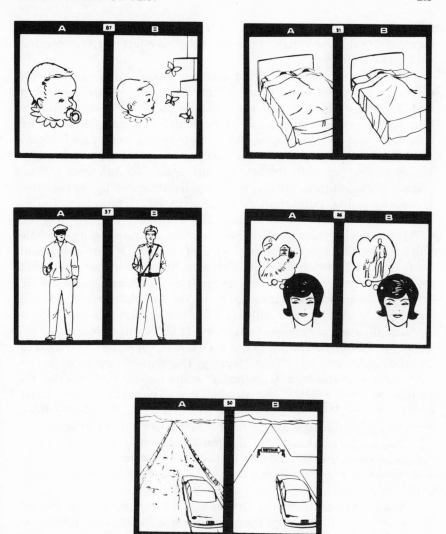

FIGURE 2. Items illustrating trait scales of the Picture-Preference Test. Taken in order from left to right and top to bottom, the items illustrate the following scales: Oral Incorporative Trends, Avoidance of Sexual Intimacy, Antisocial Tendencies, Damaged Self-Esteem, and Impulsiveness. These items are used with the permission of Dr. Lawrence Cowan; © 1980 by Lawrence Cowan.

From the same set of data we also have some indication of the validity of Cowan's Oral-Incorporative Trends scale. Although male alcoholics and male normals have mean scores that are substantially the same, female alcoholics have a significantly higher mean than female normals; $t(68) = 3.88$, $p < .001$. I should point out that in analyzing these data

Ratner and I adjusted the scores for the effects of age and of social class. It happened that these variables have a negligible effect on the dependent variables we studied.

Evidence for the validity of the two other scales we are considering—Damaged Self-Esteem and Impulsiveness—is much more limited. In a study by Cowan, Auld, and Bégin (1974), mean scores on Impulsiveness were higher for alcoholics than for normals, but the difference fell short of significance. When Ratner and I compared Bégin's alcoholics with his normals on this scale, we found the alcoholics to have higher scores, especially the women; but, again, the difference was not statistically significant. We are, of course, handicapped by the brevity of the scale; it has only eight items. Fuerth (1977) found its Kuder–Richardson reliability to be only .11 and its test–retest reliability to be .42.

Although the Damaged Self-Esteem scale has an appealing rationale, although for all subjects (male and female combined) it correlates significantly ($r = .17$) with one of the DPI scales, Impulsivity (see Ryan, 1976/1977), although for male subjects it correlates significantly with the DPI scales for Neurotic Disorganization ($r = .36$), Impulsivity ($r = .35$), and Irritability ($r = .28$), and although for female subjects it correlates significantly—negatively—with 11 of the 12 DPI content scales, the evidence for differential validity of this scale is not clear-cut enough so far for us to be sure exactly what it is measuring. The markedly different correlations for men and women with the DPI scales make it plausible that this picture-preference scale measures a trait that is central to character differences of men and women, perhaps a trait that we might call "confident narcissism" (in the male direction, i.e., with lower scores on the scale) or "inhibition of aggression" (in the female direction, i.e., with higher scores). Ryan (1976/1977) did find that women have higher scores on this scale (mean of 4.18) than men (mean of 3.00), a difference that is statistically significant.

Ryan's research demonstrated one of the strengths of the Picture-Preference Test: its freedom from saturation with social desirability response bias. For his total sample of 192 university students, none of the 28 picture-preference scales he studied correlated significantly with the DPI social desirability scale. We should point out, however, that among the women of his sample several of the picture-preference scales—particularly those we would understand as measuring aggressive tendencies—had significant negative correlations with DPI Desirability scale. We interpret this finding as an indication that women believe that it is inappropriate for a woman to be aggressive, and as evidence that this belief influences, to some extent, their responding on the relevant picture-preference scales.

Factor Analysis of the Picture-Preference Test

Feeling some disappointment at the heterogeneity of many of the trait scales developed for the Picture-Preference Test, I decided to factor-analyze all of the picture-preference items, with the hope of creating factorially pure and homogeneous scales. John Berek joined me in this enterprise, and it is his doctoral research (Berek, 1975/1976) that provides the data now to be cited. Berek analyzed all 196 of the items that had been devised at the time he undertook his study. He split the item pool into two parts, in order to make possible an evaluation of the reliability of the factors he would discover, and the two item sets (which I will call Set A and Set B) were separately factor-analyzed; then the subjects' scores on the factors from Set A were correlated with their scores on the factors from Set B. The correlations between the factor scores of Set A and Set B should tell us how dependable, how generalizable, our factor solution is.

Berek administered the Picture-Preference Test to 309 university students (207 women, 102 men), computed G-coefficients (cf. Holley and Guilford, 1964, 1966), and then extracted factors by the principal axes method, with squared multiple correlations in the diagonal of the correlation matrix. The original factor solution was rotated to simple structure by the indirect oblimin method (setting gamma equal to $\frac{1}{2}$, which gives a biquartimin solution). In all of these computations Berek made use of the BMD–08M program (Dixon, 1974).

Only the first three factors accounted for enough of the variance of the test, and had salient loadings on enough items, to be interpretable. The first factor of Set A correlated strongly, $r = .96$, with the first factor of Set B. The two second factors had a correlation with each other of .54, and the two third factors had a correlation of .50. There was also a substantial correlation ($r = .54$) between the first factor of Set A and the second factor of Set B. On this evidence, then, there is substantial psychometric reliability of the factors obtained from the two independent factor analyses. I should point out that the two sets of items were created by randomly assigning half of the items of each a priori scale to Set A and half to Set B. Because this assignment was done by randomization, Berek could not have biased the selection toward showing an agreement between the factors of Set A and those of Set B.

It is disquieting, however, that Factor 1 of Set A correlates so highly with Factor 2 of Set B. We suspect that the oblique rotations have so oriented the reference axes that the axis defining Factor 2 of Set B is allowed to move too close to the axis defining Factor 1. When we examine the factor-correlation matrix, we find that in Set B, Factor 1 and Factor 2 correlate .35. In set A, Factor 1 and Factor 2 are virtually independent; $r =$ .04.

Turning now to the task of interpreting the factors, we can say with reasonable confidence that the first factor of either set is an *evaluative* one, related to the social desirability response set and to the first factor of the MMPI. Berek called this factor "Social Dysfunction." Another label for this factor might be "Maladjustment." Berek called the second factor of each set "Antisocial Activity." I would prefer to call it "Masculine Aggressiveness," leaving the evaluative connotations to the first factor. Berek called the third factor "Passive Orientation." Another name for it, which I suggest, is "Inward/Outward Orientation," because the items that load on this factor seem to be related to taking an *active*, outgoing attitude toward the world, or a reflective, *passive* attitude.

The three factors bear some similarity to the dimensions of meaning found by Osgood and by others (see Berlyne, 1971, p. 72): *evaluation*, *potency*, and *activity*. The third factor may be related to introversion/extraversion as Jung originally defined that dimension. In his *Psychological Types* (1921/1971) he defined extraversion as follows: "Extraversion is an outward turning of the *libido*. I use this concept to denote a manifest relation of subject to object, a positive movement of subjective interest towards the object" (1971, p. 427). In the same book Jung defined introversion as "an inward turning of *libido*, in the sense of a negative relation of the subject to object. Interest does not move toward the object but withdraws from it into the subject" (1971, p. 452).

Our third factor is probably not related to sociability, the more specific meaning that "extraversion" has come to have. Jung himself (1936/1971) pictured the extravert as a more sociable person than the introvert, writing:

> Extraversion is characterized by interest in the external object, responsiveness, and a ready acceptance of external happening, a desire to influence and be influenced by events, a need to join in and get "with it," the capacity to endure bustle and noise of every kind, and actually find them enjoyable, constant attention to the surrounding world, the cultivation of friends and acquaintances, none too carefully selected, and finally by the great importance attached to the figure one cuts, and hence by a strong tendency to make a show of oneself. [The introvert] holds aloof from external happenings, does not join in, has a distinct dislike of society as soon as he finds himself among too many people. . . . He is not in the least "with it," and has no love of enthusiastic get-togethers. He is not a good mixer. (1971, pp. 549–550)

Eysenck (1970), Cattell, Eber, & Tatsuoka (1970), and other writers have considered extraversion to be roughly equivalent to "social ease," and introversion to "social withdrawal." I do not intend so specific a meaning of sociability for this third factor.

In Figure 3 the first three items, starting from the top left, are exam-

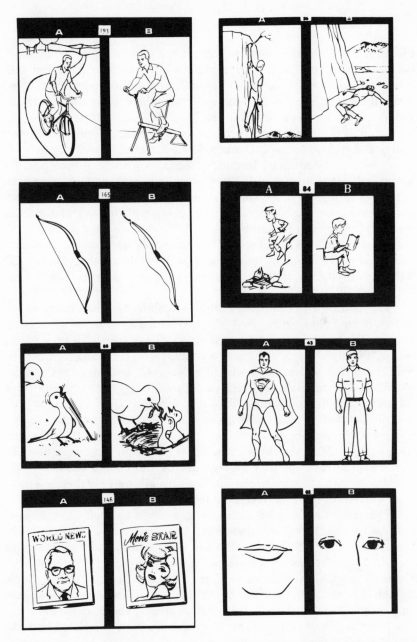

FIGURE 3. Items defining the three factors found by Berek in his factor analysis of the Picture-Preference Test. First three, Social Dysfunction; second two, Antisocial Activity (or Masculine Aggressiveness); last three, Passive Orientation (or Inward/Outward Orientation). All but one of these items were devised by Dr. Lawrence Cowan and are used with his permission; © 1980 by Lawrence Cowan. The right-hand item of the second row, "A boy jumping off a high rock, rubble below; boy sitting and reading," was devised by Dr. Barry Morrison and is used with his permission.

ples of items that have large loadings on the evaluative factor. For such items, a choice that seems to express ineffectiveness, damaged self-esteem, or depressive mood is keyed for Maladjustment. With these items the keyed choices are: the exercycle, the man crumpled on the ground at the foot of a cliff, and the bow with slack string.

Berek (1975/1976) found correlations of this factor with the a priori trait scales as follows: with Damaged Self-Esteem, .69; with Impulsiveness, .50; with Antisocial Impulses, .62; and with Oral-Incorporative Trends, .49. I would conclude that Cowan, attempting to measure these various, supposedly somewhat distinct traits, in fact devised items that overlap in measuring a general sense of being maladjusted, of not doing well in adpating to life's problems.

Ryan (1976/1977) found small but statistically significant correlations between the evaluation factor and several DPI scales: with Cynicism, .30; with Impulsivity, .22; with Rebelliousness, .23; and with Socially Deviant Attitudes, .20.

We turn now to examples of the Masculine Aggressiveness factor, shown further along in Figure 3. Choices scored as showing aggressiveness are the boy jumping off a rock onto a pile of rubble and the young bird pulling up a worm. The aggressiveness factor correlates significantly with these trait scales: Antisocial Impulses, .42, and Magical Omnipotence, .51. Among male subjects Ryan found the aggressiveness factor to correlate with the following DPI scales: Neurotic Disorganization, .30; Socially Deviant Attitudes, .30; Impulsivity, .27; Rebelliousness, .26; and Cynicism, .25. Among female subjects it correlated only with the Desirability scale, $-.30$. I should point out that, although the correlation of a factor with a DPI scale may be regarded as an external validation, the correlation with a picture-preference scale usually may not, because there is an overlap of items between the factor scale and the trait scale.

Examples of the third factor, which we may well call "Inward/Outward Orientation," are presented at the bottom of Figure 3. The inward choices are: Superman, the movie magazine, and the picture of a mouth. Factor scores on the inward/outward factor correlate .44 with Cowan's original Avoidance of Close Personal Contact scale, which, though it is the precursor of the Avoidance of Sexual Intimacy scale, emphasizes social withdrawal rather than anxiety about sexual intimacy. The introversive direction of this factor is negatively correlated with the DPI Irritability scale; $r = -.20$.

Is there any connection between the ideas in the back of Auld's head—ideas about conflict, about impulses striving for expression and defenses keeping these impuses in check—and the gritty, practical task of developing the Picture-Preference Test? I believe that there is, even though the concept of conflict is a "deep" one, not one that can be identified with a particular empirical datum. One infers the presence of conflict from a rather complex pattern of responses. For instance, I would guess that many women have to repress their awareness of their aggressiveness, especially their competitiveness with men; that they find it necessary to affirm a positive image of themselves as passive, nonaggressive beings; that as a result these women reject the aggressively oriented pictures of the Picture-Preference Test—and at the same time show their need for a positive self-presentation by scoring high on the DPI Desirability scale. Such a complex pattern would account for the relationships that were found. But, of course, other explanations could also account for these correlations.

CHOOSING A NAME FOR A CAR

Let us consider now some data from a survey conducted by the Campbell–Ewald Company more than 15 years ago, in the summer of 1962, to give guidance to the Chevrolet Division in its choice of names for new cars. I need hardly say that research like this is only one source of guidance for the executives who decide what to call a new car.

The Effects of Naming on Preference

Before presenting the data, may I present several points of theory. Like many other authors, Berlyne drew a distinction between (1) learning by contiguity that gives the organism a store of knowledge (of "what follows what") and (2) decision about action, a process that seems to be guided by incentives. That is to say, the organism on the basis of rewards chooses, during performance, what will then meet its needs. For a statement of Berlyne's views on expectations and incentives, the reader can do no better than consult his discussion of these matters in the book edited by Berlyne and Madsen (1973).

Obviously, Berlyne's formulation is related to the common distinction between learning and performance. Two papers by Egger and Miller (1962, 1963) also bring out interesting points bearing on the learning–performance distinction. It is my view that these ideas can fruitfully be applied to the task of understanding what difference it makes what we call a car.

I start by assuming that the consumer—the prospective purchaser of a car—has a set of values already. For example, he wants a car that is powerful enough to enable him to emerge safely from the entrance ramp into freeway traffic. Or he wants a car that will be recognized by his neighbors as a "luxury car," thereby conferring prestige on him. Or he wants a car that will save him money on purchases of fuel during his long and frequent business trips. These preexisting values determine what can gratify the consumer.

Second, I assume that the manufacturer by naming the car attaches certain expectations to it, that is, leads the consumer to expect that certain needs will be gratified. Some of the names, for instance, suggest what the car can do (names suggesting power and speed, like "Typhoon" or "Sprint"), others suggest how one can express aggression (e.g., "Buc-caneer") or sexual motives (e.g., "Spitfire"). If the manufacturer chooses a name that is relevant to the needs that the consumer has, and if to a sufficient degree the car can in fact meet these needs, attaching the name to the car will increase the sales of the car.

If the car cannot in fact satisfy the consumer's needs—for example, if the name promises power but the car lacks good performance—the value of the name will at best be temporary, and in the long run the name will hurt the manufacturer.

It is frequently true, however, that the competing cars from which the consumer must choose differ little in their actual ability to meet his needs. In such a situation, a name that promises to provide what the consumer wants will be helpful to the manufacturer, because it will give the car a distinctiveness it would otherwise have lacked. The consumer will be comparing the car to other makes that, although they might meet his needs as well, do not inform him (through their names) that they can do so.

The Campbell–Ewald Study

The research done on names for cars was designed to throw light on what qualities would be suggested by each of the tested names, and on how these connotations might influence the respondents' reactions to a car having that name. Working with the research department of the Campbell–Ewald Company, I prepared a questionnaire that asked for free associations to each of a list of 12 possible names for a new car. The questionnaire also asked for judgments about 48 possible names. These judgments were obtained in two ways: by ratings on a five-point scale, and by paired comparisons. The lists of names were worked up by a member of the advertising agency's staff, Mr. David E. Davis, Jr. We arranged to have the questionnaire filled out by 100 employees of Campbell–Ewald. We hoped that the association data would tell us what expectations would be created by attaching a particular name to a car, and that the paired-comparisons and ratings data would at least in a rough way tell us whether this expectation was an appropriate one for a "performance car" and whether it would, therefore, increase the preference for a car of that name.

In the research that we have just described, we found from the association data that "Sprint" and "Spitfire" suggest speed and that "Typhoon" suggests great strength. We found that "Scorpion," "Mustang," "Torpedo," and "Buccaneer" all suggest aggression. Our respondents associated the names "Spitfire," "Panther," "Torpedo," "Cougar," and especially "Firefly" with femininity. Finally, "Monte Carlo" suggested prestige to our respondents.

Even if we should agree that a "new high-performance car" that "will be powerful and responsive and will handle exceptionally well" (as we described the proposed car to our respondents) should have a name that makes one think of power and speed—and perhaps of aggression also—we must keep in mind that *too much* power, speed, or aggression might be aversive. Berlyne's writings make us sensitive to this issue, and Neal Miller's theory of conflict warns us that we must take account of both approach and avoidance tendencies. It should come as no surprise, therefore, that the ratings and paired comparisons do not always give the prize to the name with the most "strength" or "speed" associations. In rating or expressing preference for these names as names "for a new high-performance car," our respondents considered "Sprint" to be a "fair" name (rating = 2.0) and "Spitfire" a good name (2.6). The average rating for "Typhoon" was only 1.8, despite the strong associations with strength, whereas "Panther" and "Cougar," which suggest strength (but not to the degree that "Typhoon" does), got better ratings, 3.0 and 2.4, respectively.

During the presentation of this paper at the Canadian Psychological Association meeting (Vancouver, 1977), the late Professor Glenn Macdonald pointed out that the name "Toronado," which suggests a violent and dangerous wind, does not seem to have hampered the sales of that car, produced by the Oldsmobile division of General Motors. I could only respond that a multiplicity of factors influence the sales of a car, which makes it quite difficult to disentangle the effects of the name from the effects of other factors.

"Scorpion," "Mustang," "Torpedo," and "Buccaneer" all suggest aggression, but some were slightly more acceptable as names than others: "Scorpion" was at 1.7, "Mustang" at 2.4, "Torpedo" at 2.4, and "Buccaneer" at 1.8 on the rating scale. Considering now the names to which our respondents had associations indicative of femininity, women gave "Firefly" a mean rating of 2.7 ("good"), whereas men gave it a rating of only 1.8. Finally, "Monte Carlo," which suggested prestige to our respondents, got a rating of 2.3 ("fairly good").

Concluding Remarks on Choosing a Name

I have presented these fragments of data from a rather extensive study—a study that was intended more as a demonstration of method than as a means of choosing good names—in order to illustrate the kinds of incentives that can be symbolized by a name. If the two hypotheses are correct, attaching an evocative name to a car should make the customer more likely to choose it, if what it evokes fits with what he wants from a car. The expectancy–incentive paradigm enables us, therefore, to make a prediction about the customer's behavior. The sales figures may help us to tell whether the paradigm is a correct one.

FINAL THOUGHTS ON CONFLICT AND PREFERENCE

There is no psychological situation that puts theory to the test quite so dramatically as the challenge to predict which of two choices a person will make. If a therapist can accurately predict, "In the next session my patient wil recoil from the intense sexual feelings he is having toward me and, rather than continuing therapy, will declare his intention to quit therapy," we are rightly impressed. If a tester can predict that a young woman whose TAT stories show her to be more than usually afraid of abandonment by a man will also show by her choices from pairs of pictures that she is afraid of sexual intimacy, we are impressed. If a market researcher can tell us, "This young man who yearns so to assert his masculinity, if given the choice between a wildly impractical Corvette and a tame but practical Chevelle, will take the Corvette," and if the market researcher is right, we are impressed.

And so preference and choice have a great fascination for us. As psychologists, we keep trying to find out how to predict human choices accurately.

Throughout this chapter I have asserted my belief that paying attention to conflict—to the interplay of positive and negative forces—will help us to make predictions that are more accurate. Although I have given examples of the contending forces that influence human choice, and have from time to time demonstrated successes of the conflict model, I was not able to drive my point home by demonstrating remarkably successful prediction. The conflict model remains an article of faith rather than an amply proved assumption. But—is there a better theory for predicting the choices that human beings will make?

REFERENCES

AMIN, S. A picture-preference test to measure the trait of avoidance of sexual intimacy in females (Doctoral dissertation, University of Windsor, 1974). *Canadiana*, June 1976, 67. (National Library of Canada order no. 23852)

AULD, F. Contributions of behavior theory to projective testing. *Journal of Projective Techniques*, 1954, *18*, 421–426.

AULD, F., RATNER, D., & BÉGIN, P. E. Personality traits of alcoholics. Unpublished manuscript, University of Windsor, 1977.

BÉGIN, P. E. An oral dependency trait-scale for the picture-preference test of addictiveness (Doctoral dissertation, University of Windsor, 1975). *Dissertation Abstracts International*, 1975, *36*, 1911–B. (National Library of Canada order no. 23859)

BEREK, J. J. A factor reliability study of a picture-preference test (Doctoral dissertation, University of Windsor, 1975). *Dissertation Abstracts International*, 1976, *36*, 4677–B. (National Library of Canada order no. 29112)

BERLYNE, D. E. *Conflict, arousal, and curiosity.* New York: McGraw-Hill, 1960.

BERLYNE, D. E. *Aesthetics and psychobiology.* New York: Appleton-Century-Crofts, 1971.

BERLYNE, D. E. The vicissitudes of aplopathematic and thelematoscopic pneumatology (or the hydrography of hedonism). In D. E. Berlyne & K. B. Madsen (Eds.), *Pleasure, reward, preference.* New York & London: Academic Press, 1973.

BERLYNE, D. E. (Ed.). *Studies in the new experimental aesthetics: Steps toward an objective psychology of aesthetic appreciation.* Washington, D. C.: Hemisphere Publishing Corporation, 1974.

CATTELL, R. B., EBER, H. W., & TATSUOKA, M. M. *Handbook for the Sixteen Personality Factor Questionnaire.* Champaign, Ill.: Institute for Personality and Ability Testing, 1970.

COWAN, L. A picture-preference test to measure the trait of addictiveness in personality (Doctoral dissertation, Wayne State University, 1967). *Dissertation Abstracts International*, 1971, *31*, 6894–B. (University Microfilms No. 71–12,024)

COWAN, L., AULD, F., & BÉGIN, P. E. Evidence for distinctive personality traits in alcoholics. *British Journal of Addiction*, 1974, *69*, 199–206.

DAY, H. Evaluations of subjective complexity, pleasingness and interestingness for a series of random polygons varying in complexity. *Perception & Psychophysics*, 1967, *2*, 281–286.

DIXON, W. J. (Ed.). *BMD: Biomedical computer programs.* Berkeley: University of California Press, 1974.

EDWARDS, A. L. *The measurement of personality traits by scales and inventories.* New York: Holt, Rinehart and Winston, 1970.

EGGER, M. D., & MILLER, N. E. Secondary reinforcement in rats as a function of information value and reliability of the stimulus. *Journal of Experimental Psychology*, 1962, *64*, 97–104.

EGGER, M. D., & MILLER, N. E. When is reward reinforcing? An experimental study of the information hypothesis. *Journal of Comparative and Physiological Psychology*, 1963, *56*, 132–137.

EYSENCK, H. J. *The structure of human personality* (3d ed.). London: Methuen, 1970.

FUERTH, A. B. *A test–retest reliability study of the picture-preference test scales.* Unpublished master's thesis, University of Windsor, 1977.

HOLLEY, J. W., & GUILFORD, J. P. A note on the G index of agreement. *Educational and Psychological Measurement*, 1964, *24*, 749–753.

HOLLEY, J. W., & GUILFORD, J. P. Note on the double centering of dichotomized matrices. *Scandinavian Journal of Psychology*, 1966, *7*, 97–101.

JACKSON, D. N., & MESSICK, S. *Differential personality inventory, Form L.* Goshen, N.Y.: Research Psychologists Press, 1964.

JUNG, C. G. *Psychologische Typen*. Zürich: Rascher, 1921. English translation: *Psychological types*. In *The collected works of C. G. Jung* (Vol. 6). A revision by R. F. C. Hull of the translation by H. G. Baynes. London: Routledge & Kegan Paul, 1971.

JUNG, C. G. Psychologische Typologie. *Sueddeutsche Monatschefte*, 1936, *23*, 264–272. English translation: Psychological typology. In *The collected works of C. G. Jung* (Vol. 6), R. F. C. Hull trans. London: Routledge & Kegan Paul, 1971.

MCCLELLAND, D. C., & ATKINSON, J. W. The projective expression of needs: I. The effect of different intensities of the hunger drive on perception. *Journal of Psychology*, 1948, *25*, 205–222.

MILLER, N. E. Liberalization of basic S–R concepts: Extensions to conflict behavior, motivation and social learning. In S. Koch (Ed.), *Psychology: A study of a science* (Vol. 2). New York: McGraw-Hill, 1959.

MINUCHIN, P. P. The relation between aggressive fantasy and overt behavior (Doctoral dissertation, Yale University, 1950). *Dissertation Abstracts*, 1965, *26*, 2324. (University Microfilms No. 64–11877)

MORRISON, M. B. Evidence for distinctive personality traits in alcoholics using a picture-preference test for addictiveness (Doctoral dissertation, University of Windsor, 1973). *Canadiana*, September 1975, *75*. (National Library of Canada order no. 19939)

MURRAY, H. A. The effect of fear upon estimates of the maliciousness of other personalities. *Journal of Social Psychology*, 1933, *4*, 310–339.

MURRAY, H. A. *Explorations in personality*. New York: Oxford University Press, 1938.

RYAN, P. K. A construct validation study of a picture-preference test (Doctoral dissertation, University of Windsor, 1976). *Dissertation Abstracts International*, 1977, *38*, 1903–B.

SANFORD, R. N. The effects of abstinence from food upon imaginal processes: A preliminary experiment. *Journal of Psychology*, 1936, *2*, 129–136.

STAGNER, R. Traits are relevant: Theoretical analysis and empirical evidence. In N. S. Endler & D. Magnusson (Eds.), *Interactional psychology and personality*. Washington, D.C.: Hemisphere Publishing Corporation, 1976.

WHITING, J. W. M., & CHILD, I. L. *Child training and personality*. New Haven: Yale University Press, 1953.

ZUBIN, J., ERON, L. D., & SCHUMER, F. *An experimental approach to projective techniques*. New York: Wiley, 1965.

10

Play

A Ludic Behavior

HY I. DAY

When Berlyne reviewed the status of play in 1969 and pessimistically concluded that psychology should give up the category of play as a concept, little did he anticipate the explosion of interest that would follow soon after publication of his article. Even more interesting is that much of this new literature is concerned directly with motivational aspects of play and, in fact, is strongly influenced by Berlyne's theory of exploration and maintenance of optimum level of arousal potential (surprisingly, this literature rarely cites his 1968 paper).

In this chapter, I wish to show that taking Berlyne's advice does not necessarily lead to abandonment of research into the concept of play but rather leads to establishing new approaches to it. Two of these will be proposed and examined, one viewing play from a typological approach and the other looking at it as a descriptive phenomenon, studying playfulness as a characteristic of all behaviors.

A DEFINITION OF PLAY

Dan Berlyne's contribution to the *Handbook of Social Psychology* (Lindzey & Aronson, 1969) was a chapter entitled "Laughter, Humor and Play" (Berlyne, 1969). In this chapter, Berlyne pointed out the difficulties in identifying an adequate definition of play. Introducing the section of his paper dealing with play, he stated that "there is, however, obvious

HY I. DAY • Department of Psychology, York University, Downsview, Ontario M3J 2R3, Canada.

disagreement on what ought to be regarded as the salient defining characteristics of play" (p. 814). He went on to suggest, following Valentine (1942), that "play is any activity which is carried out entirely for its own sake" (p. 814), and is therefore an intrinsically motivated behavior, one of a class that includes exploration and aesthetic behavior. Then, trying to distinguish play from other behaviors in the class, he argued that play, unlike exploration, may be reinforced by the activity itself rather than by the receipt of satisfying sensory, emotional, or ideational consequences. Aesthetic behavior, Berlyne felt, was more "serious" than play; that is, more likely to bring extrinsic rewards from the activity, thus acceding to the socially accepted norm that play is frivolous. Finally, Berlyne summed up the section with the acknowledgment that "it seems highly likely that our ignorance has caused a great variety of activities, with widely differing functions, to be lumped together under the heading of 'play' " (p. 816).

Following this pessimistic introductory section, Berlyne, with his usual thoroughness, reviewed most of the available information in the field and emerged with the conclusion that the field is a "discordant polyphony" (p. 840). Despite this, he extracted the following recurrent motifs and consonances:

1. It is repeatedly asserted that playful activities are carried on "for their own sake" or for the sake of "pleasure." They are contrasted with "serious" activities, which deal with readily identifiable bodily needs or external threats, or otherwise achieve specifiable practical ends.

2. Many writers stress the "unreality" or "quasi-reality" of play. "Reality" presumably refers to the forms of interaction between the organism and its environment that occupy most of its waking hours.

3. Several, but not all, of the writers we have reviewed have noted the admixture of "tension" and unpleasant excitement in play, and have attached importance to it.

4. The final question is how reduction of arousal, relaxation of tension, relief from conflict, occurs in the course of play.

Finally, Berlyne's parting shot is that there is "little support to the view that *play* is a useful category for psychology . . . it looks as if psychology would do well to give up the category of *play* in favor of both wider and narrower categories of behavior" (p. 843).

Somewhat over 10 years later, we find that Berlyne's pessimistic advice has been honored largely in the breach. A dozen books and hundreds of articles since 1969 have shown that Berlyne was one of the few psychologists interested in children's behavior who failed to concern themselves with play behavior.

Furthermore, under the rubric of leisure and recreation rather than play, researchers are investing time and money toward an understanding of the phenomenon. Possibly as a result of the leisure-time explosion in America, the importance of recreation and other leisure activities has increased immensely. Governments have set up ministries to concern themselves with the quality and quantity of recreational activities indulged in by voters. Private enterprise has sensed a gold lode in creating recreational environments, manufacturing and selling equipment and clothing for recreation, and teaching skills that might increase pleasure obtained from recreational pursuits.

It may be because of the huge investments of time and money that adults spend on recreational activities that they have tended to stress the differences between adult recreation and children's play, the former being considered less frivolous than the latter. But whether golf is taken more seriously than sandcastle building or mountain climbing is considered more worthwhile than Frisbee tossing, one may wonder whether the differences between recreation and play are real or imaginary. Webster's Third New International Dictionary, for example, defines to play as "to engage in a recreational activity," whether to amuse or to divert oneself.

Those who stress differences between the two activities focus on the goals of each and argue that recreation is to "re-create", to restore one's physical and mental health between periods of work; and, since children are not considered to work, they cannot recreate. Instead of recreating, they play—an activity which, they argue, prepares the child for adulthood (and work). (Almost like contrasting the wine drunk between courses at dinner with the predinner aperitif.) Ignoring these differences, this paper will treat recreation as a synonym for play, acknowledging all the problems and pitfalls in the former that play theorists have recognized in the latter.

A review of the literature since Berlyne's chapter of 1969 attests to the proliferation of research in the area of play and recreation, including a number of books and papers that begin with a review of all the theories to date and end by introducing a new variation. Interestingly, most of these new theories incorporate Berlyne's theory of intrinsic motivation somewhere in their formulations, and argue that play is primarily a self-rewarding activity that incorporates arousal-inducing as well as arousal-reducing qualities and has affective components associated with these qualities (cf. Ellis, 1973; Levy, 1978). But most of these writers fall into the trap that Berlyne had warned against, and treat play as a single unitary concept. Having fallen into the trap, they can only try to establish a definition through painfully drawn-out attempts to refute the equally inadequate definitions of play proposed by others and to exclude from their conceptualization the many instances of play stressed by other authors that do not fit their own formulations.

PLAY AS A TYPOLOGICAL CONCEPT

Like the blind men and the elephant, these researchers have been sensing different aspects of the beast and conceptualizing different animals. Like most hypothetical constructs, play is multifaceted, with numerous antecedents, many uncorrelated or poorly correlated concomitants, and a plethora of variations in overt response styles.

To play is to whitewash a fence as Ben Rogers did for Tom Sawyer, and to gamble at Las Vegas. To play is to hit a small white ball into a cup on a golf course, as well as to dress up like a doctor and explore the anatomy of a friend. One plays piano, the stock market, and around; one plays with dolls, with one's life, and with a baseball team. Like anxiety, play means all things to all people, and very little to a scientist.

Clearly, the error has been in trying to compress all this variability into one concept. It is obvious that if we want to preserve the concept of play we must subdivide it into various categories and reintroduce it as a typology.

As such, we can accept the complexity of the concept, the varied antecedents and differences in behaviors associated with play, and yet we can unite all this diversity into a single construct. We can also recognize the differences in affective states during play, and the many short-and long-term goals that play leads to. Thus we can treat Berlyne's caveat with the honor it deserves, while still acknowledging that the world conceives of play as if it were a unitary concept.

Suppose we were to reexamine the recurrent motifs and consonances as Berlyne did in 1969, but from the vantage point of an additional hundred papers and books that report research in the area of play. We would find that the language has altered somewhat, but the motifs are still the same.

Play as a Voluntary Activity

Theorists seem to want to believe that one initiates, continues, or ceases to play, at will, with complete disregard for the external world. Another way of expressing this is that the locus of control is internal—one feels oneself to be the master, the origin of the behavior. One can destroy one's sandcastle, or quit the bowling team, or stop gambling at will. Attribution theorists argue that this willfulness can be destroyed by the intrusion of an extrinsic reward (cf. Lepper, Greene, & Nisbett, 1973). Interestingly, this attitude of free will exists side by side with a plethora of research that measures the effect on quality and duration of play of environmental conditions such as playgrounds and toys.

Play Is Intrinsically Motivating (Autotelic)

Even though the first motif seemed to argue that one does not expect a reward for play, there are many who acknowledge that the activity is controlled by various forces, some intrinsic to the individual and others intrinsic to the activity. Thus, one plays because the situation is conducive to it, or because there is some ultimate gain in playing. But, either way, the activity is self-reinforced. A player is an amateur, not a professional. (Interestingly, in cricket a "player" is a professional cricketer as distinguished from the amateur who is called a "gentleman.") The question will arise later as to what "intrinsic" means, for there are two interpretations: task-intrinsic, and person-intrinsic.

Play Is Pleasurable

There is little controversy about this motif. Play is considered to be fun, enjoyable, and pleasurable. This is clear from the first motif, which stated that the activity could be abandoned at will; and so one must expect that, if one continues to play, one must be enjoying it. But this motif can also be questioned when we look at children in "play" therapy who seem to be angry, upset, and suffering, while "playing." We see it too in the college football player who appears to be in considerable pain and anguish while "playing" a game with his team.

A number of other motifs have appeared in the literature, but these do not seem to be held so ubiquitously. For example, some argue that play is highly imaginative, and includes some degree of reality suspension. But others speak of concrete play and do not attribute a high level of imaginativeness to it. Others stress a "peak-experience" in play, as if it is a unique event that comes and goes during an activity.

These three motifs, so similar to those formulated by Berlyne in 1969, can be translated into measurable variables or dimensions. These may be labelled control (voluntariness), arousal (telicity), and affect (pleasure). But more of this later.

At this point we need only recognize that there are certain characteristics that describe play or playfulness, characteristics that are commonly, but not unanimously, held to be necessary conditions for the designation of an activity as play. But what about the concept of playfulness?

PLAYFULNESS

Heeding Berlyne's admonition to give up the category of play in favor of both wider and narrower categories, we could consider switching our study from play to the characteristics that make play unique—*playfulness*. Playfulness could then be defined as qualities of voluntariness, pleasure, and autotelicity. It is what makes people describe play as giving the feelings of freedom, control, fun, and excitement. Lieberman (1977) came close to this when she defined playfulness operationally as "physical, social, and cognitive spontaneity, manifest joy, and sense of humor" (p. 23).

The antithesis of play is commonly held to be work, and we tend to ascribe the opposite characteristics to it—obligatory, serious, tiring, and instrumental. These characteristics may be termed *workfulness*.

Play is a behavior that is usually associated with children, and it is presumed that if adults play, they are being childlike. Work is the main occupation of adults, and when they do not work they may spend their leisure time recreating, which, though one recognizes it to have playful qualities, is denied equivalence to play. In fact, adult play is frowned on, for it is conceived as a frivolous or ludic behavior and undignified for a cultured person. Only the very rich admit to indulging in playful activities, and this is generally viewed with a jaundiced (though envious?) eye.

It has been the contention of this author that both playfulness and workfulness are characteristics of all, or nearly all, behaviors, and that activities can be located on a continuum in which the proportion of playfulness to workfulness varies (Day, 1971/1973, 1972, 1979). Furthermore, since playfulness depends on intrinsic motivational characteristics such as Berlyne had subsumed under the rubric of collative variability, over time and with experience the proportion of playfulness in an ongoing or repetitive activity should gradually wane.

But before we examine the concept and measurement of playfulness, let us digress somewhat and examine the concept of work in historical perspective.

Over the ages, a negative view of work has generally persisted. The source book of Western values, the Bible, points out that our first humans, Adam and Eve, were expelled from the Garden of Eden as punishment for their transgressions. Genesis (3:17) tells us that Adam was told that he would eat of earth's yield in pain (note that in the Gideon

Bible translation, the word is "sorrow" rather than "pain"), and two sentences later "in the sweat of thy face shall thou eat bread" (Genesis 3:19). Work, to the early Hebrews, was clearly associated with pain and sorrow.

Similarly, we find that in the Greek language the word for work was *ponos*, which seems to have the same root as the word for punishment—*poine*. The Greek style of life reflected this—free men did not work, they recreated. Only slaves worked.

From time to time, attitudes to work vacillated. When a new religion arose (as, for example, Christianity or Islam) it tended to view work as uplifting and godly, for its early adherents were peasants and slaves. As the religion became more acceptable to the establishment, attitudes changed to acknowledge that work was not the only way to achieve godliness, or the ultimate reward. The Industrial Revolution, requiring the availability of motivated workers, called on earlier Protestant teachings and assigned a positive role to work. But, not wanting to pay excessively for services rendered, the industrialists presented work as instrumental to the receipt of consummatory rewards in heaven. Thus the necessity for work was emphasized while the conditions of work were downplayed, and industrialists argued that, regardless of its unpleasant, obligatory, and demeaning nature, work yielded ultimate satisfactions.

Psychologists, interested in the motivation to work, but taking an areligious stance, have identified various less ultimate reward systems to account for the facts that people are generally obligated to work, and that there are, indeed, satisfactions associated with this enterprise. One example of a motivational theory is that of Vroom (1964), who identifies five motivations to work:

1. Work provides wages to the role occupant in return for his services.

2. Work requires from the role occupant expenditures of mental or physical energy.

3. Work permits the role occupant to contribute to the production of goods and services.

4. Work permits or requires the role occupant social interaction with other persons.

5. Work defines at least in part the social status of the role occupant.

W. C. Menninger, in the introduction to a standard textbook for vocational counselors (Menninger, 1964), suggests that the ability to work is an essential activity of a mentally healthy person. He argues that work satisfies psychological needs which cannot be met by other activities, such as an outlet for hostile and aggressive drives, satisfaction derived from the feeling of worthwhileness of work, pleasant personal relations with fellow workers, a chance to be a member of a team, and satisfaction derived from allegiance with a superior. All these are clearly task-extrinsic motivations, and merely serve to rationalize why one should perform what may be an undesirable and unenjoyable task. No mention is made of fun, enjoyment, feelings of overcoming complexities, learning, and decision making. Work is serious business and is not to be confused with ludic behavior.

Philosophers have reflected on the negative attitudes to work with its implications of serious obligatoriness. Schiller, for example, described work as a world of burdensome impositions compared with play, a world of freedom and spontaneity.

More recently, articles in national magazines and newspapers continue to remind us that "normal Americans" hate work and pursue it only for the task-extrinsic gain. Swados (1959/1966), for example, states:

> In the case of work, if we grant the possibility that millions of American workers may in truth be terribly discontented with their jobs, doesn't this arouse a consequent suspicion; that the growing white collar classes are reluctant to admit this likelihood, not only because it would disturb the comfortable mass media concept of America as a land of blissful togetherness, but even more importantly because it would do violence to their own self-esteem, the basic worth and individuality of what they themselves are doing to earn a living?. . . The hidden bonds of boredom and frustration that link the lives—if they only knew it—of the professional man and the working man are close to the surface in the working pattern of the burgeoning millions of clericals and technicians, which is so similar to that of the numerically declining working class. (pp. 14–15)

Yet, we find that people who, for one reason or another, are unable to work have difficulty in discovering equally satisfying alternatives. Like old work horses set free, they chafe from too much leisure and disrupt the normal activities of others about them.

As Weiss and Riesman (1961/1963) point out:

> A study of the impact of the four-day week in a situation where it was too unpredictably scheduled to permit other employment on the additional day off, indicates that this additional day was less of a boon for the workers than they had originally anticipated. The extra day off was not a day off for the children, so there was an empty house during school hours; nor was it a day off for the wife, so there was house-cleaning and vacuuming, with the man in the way. In this plant, a small aircraft manufacturing company in Southern California, the four-day week was scheduled for one week out of four. Though originally anticipated with high hopes, it was soon disliked: television, loafing, ballgames, all these were felt to be week-end activities, and fell flat during the work week. (pp. 172–173)

The distinction between work and play is made early in life. We learn that the former is expected to have characteristics of workfulness and the latter characteristics of playfulness. In a recent experiment (Day & Forteath, 1976), nine-year-old children clearly tagged 23 of a list of 25 activities as either work or play. Moreover, they defined play as an activity that is fun, something chosen, not difficult, exciting, and social but not boring or tiring. The concept of work was defined as an activity that is not chosen but, interestingly, is also not boring.

This dichotomy is reflected by attribution theorists who not only distinguish work and play but also argue that, having attributed one motive to an activity, one must discount all other motivations to perform that activity. Kelley (1971) named this the *discounting principle* and argued that one could not accept the presence of more than one motive force for an activity at any time. In fact, most attribution theorists argue that when an activity that has been considered intrinsically motivated (voluntary, interesting) is extrinsically reinforced it becomes work and, following cessation of the reward, will extinguish for lack of motivation to continue.

In fact, there is no way of knowing, from an examination of the published literature, in how many studies the cessation of a reward failed to be followed by extinction of the behavior, for the literature tends to be biased toward positive results. In two studies conducted at my laboratory (Romanuk, 1975; Russon, 1975), subjects continued to occupy themselves at the task long after withdrawal of extrinsic reinforcement. Perhaps the tasks were so interesting that the extrinsic reward served only as a supplement to, rather than a displacement of, the intrinsic reward. Kennaley (1979), working in our laboratory, and Ross (1976) found that young children often tended to use an additive rather than a discounting principle.

But the repeated finding of the operation of a discounting principle may also be a methodological artifact foisted on us by the style of questioning in which subjects are asked to identify a single motive force for an activity. What would happen if people were asked to list as many motivational forces as they wished?

Some of the motive forces that would be identified would be intrinsic but others, extrinsic. No doubt the intrinsic motives would be those associated with the playfulness of the activity, and the other motives with the workfulness. One could then recognize the concurrent existence of both characteristics. For example, an artist painting a portrait may be working for the money, prestige, and acclaim, but also enjoying the creative act of juxtaposing colors and manipulating form and balance on a canvas, clearly playfulness characteristics. The artist may be motivated by the challenge of creating a good aesthetic composition, the uncertainty of the task demands, and the complexity of the situation, as well as by the need to produce a saleable product and become better known among his peers.

Two common forums for activities in our society are jobs and games. We tend to call the activity at a job, work and that at a game, play. Yet, most jobs have playful aspects to them in the form of decision-making situations, conflict resolution, and responding to difficulty, ambiguity, and uncertainty, and most games have workfulness characteristics in the form of rules, formal structure, obligations, competition, and serious-ness. These two activity sets, motivationally speaking, really vary only in the proportion of playfulness in them—games tend to be highly playful, and jobs less so.

Two people "playing" golf together may seem to be doing the same thing. Yet, close inspection of the situation finds one using the activity as a means of selling the other a life-insurance policy. The former is work-ing, and the latter is playing. The total amount of playfulness in the activities may be equal, but the amount of workfulness may be more for the former than for the latter.

The proportion of playfulness in an activity may change during its performance. Our hero spends Tuesday nights bowling with the boys in a team. He considers this activity as recreation, fun, and voluntary. Asked about it, he would probably describe it as "going out to play with the boys." However, one Tuesday night he chooses to stay home to watch something on television and discovers that he really does not have a choice. As the best bowler on his team, the boys put pressure on him and insist that he participate, for it is an important game. He bridles against the obligatoriness, and his feelings of lack of control diminish his percep-tion of bowling as "fun," "enjoyable," etc. Grumbling, he goes to work, and, miraculously, bowls a perfect game. Forgotten is his feeling of workfulness and his joy knows no bounds. In the space of a few hours the activity has shifted back and forth from one with a predominance of playfulness to one with a predominance of workfulness and, despite attribution theory, back again.

In a recent study in our laboratory, Day and Murray (1978b) ap-proached the classification of activities using a Multidimensional Scaling (MDS) method. A list of 30 activities, commonly performed by adoles-cents, was presented to 31 students, 15 in grade 8 and 16 in grade 12. They were asked to group the activities into discrete sets on the basis of perceived similarity. They also rated the activities along nine semantic differential scales selected as relevant to an understanding of the MDS dimensions that were hypothesized to appear.

A three-dimensional solution was selected as most appropriate and was interpreted. The first dimension described the extent to which the activities were school- or home-related. The second was clearly a work-fulness–playfulness dimension, and the third reflected the amount of energy expended in the act.

The workfulness–playfulness dimension correlated with seven of the nine differential scales: work/play, difficult/easy, compulsory/voluntary, dislike/like, dull/exciting, reward/self-satisfaction and not interesting interesting. As seen from the factor analysis of the rating data, the seven scales form a very discrete cluster. Consideration of names suggested by the students shows that workfulness is appropriate.

Figure 1 thus becomes a scale of workfulness to playfulness on which any activity can be located. The limitation is that each activity is placed in relation to the other 29, and to use the MDS method requires the researcher to compare a set of activities. Another approach is to study each

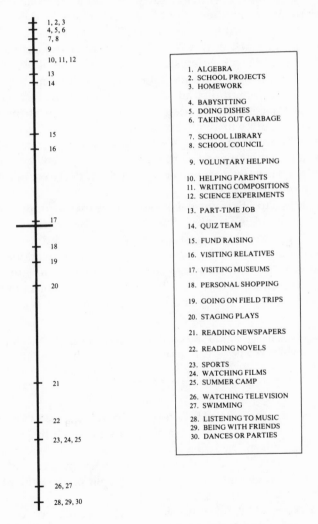

| 1, 2, 3 |
| 4, 5, 6 |
| 7, 8 |
| 9 |
| 10, 11, 12 |
| 13 |
| 14 |
| 15 |
| 16 |
| 17 |
| 18 |
| 19 |
| 20 |
| 21 |
| 22 |
| 23, 24, 25 |
| 26, 27 |
| 28, 29, 30 |

1. ALGEBRA
2. SCHOOL PROJECTS
3. HOMEWORK

4. BABYSITTING
5. DOING DISHES
6. TAKING OUT GARBAGE

7. SCHOOL LIBRARY
8. SCHOOL COUNCIL

9. VOLUNTARY HELPING

10. HELPING PARENTS
11. WRITING COMPOSITIONS
12. SCIENCE EXPERIMENTS

13. PART-TIME JOB

14. QUIZ TEAM

15. FUND RAISING

16. VISITING RELATIVES

17. VISITING MUSEUMS

18. PERSONAL SHOPPING

19. GOING ON FIELD TRIPS

20. STAGING PLAYS

21. READING NEWSPAPERS

22. READING NOVELS

23. SPORTS
24. WATCHING FILMS
25. SUMMER CAMP

26. WATCHING TELEVISION
27. SWIMMING

28. LISTENING TO MUSIC
29. BEING WITH FRIENDS
30. DANCES OR PARTIES

FIGURE 1. Distribution of 30 activities along a Workfulness–Playfulness dimension from an INDSCAL solution.

activity independently of any others and locate it on a workfulness–playfulness continuum.

THE WHY SCALE

MDS was demonstrated as one method of locating activities along a workfulness–playfulness continuum. Had the subjects been required to place the 30 activities into either-or categories, as had the subjects in the Day and Forteath study, they might have been forced to discount some motive factors. By allowing free choice, a different picture was obtained. But the MDS approach only fixes relative locations of activities on a continuous scale. We were interested in the proportion of playfulness to workfulness for any activity, and that required a different approach.

We asked subjects to list all the reasons for their participation in activities, but their answers varied with the eloquence of the respondents, with their ability to identify and name motivations, and with their willingness to introspect freely. We also found it impossible to equate synonyms or near synonyms and fit them into discrete categories. At the same time we discovered that subjects were always very cooperative and tried to be honest and open.

So we shifted to a fixed formal questionnaire that required subjects to respond on preselected scales. Five motives that represented task-intrinsic motivational factors most commonly found in the previous questioning were used, together with five task-extrinsic motivational factors. The 10 statements were staggered in a set order and identified as 10 reasons for performing an activity. Table I shows the items of the WHY scale. As an internal reliability check, one more question was added, as follows:

> People do things for two kinds of reasons. Split the reasons why you do
> this activity into two percentages totaling 100.
> (a) Because *you enjoy the activity itself* _____%
> (b) Because *you get something out of doing it* _____%
> Total = 100%

Subjects were then asked to complete the WHY scale twice, once for their job and once for any recreational activity in which they participate regularly. Other questions on the WHY scale relate to time spent, amount of change in the activity, etc., but these are not relevant here, and only the data from the 10 scales and the percentage split on enjoyment versus instrumentality will be discussed.

The total score of the five intrinsically motivated reasons for performing an activity could be termed a playfulness scale, and the other five, a workfulness scale. The two scales are independent of each other. The

TABLE I. Items from the WHY Scale

We are interested in understanding why people do things. Choose an activity that you do fairly regularly and answer the following questions as honestly as you can.

Activity: _____

Is this activity a job or recreation (Underline one).

Please put a number from 1 to 10 in each box that represents the degree to which each reason answers why you do it.

(0 means *not at all,* 1 means *very, very little,* and so on until 10 meaning *very, very much.*)

	Number 0–10
Because you are learning something	☐
Because of the money	☐
Because it is interesting	☐
Because of recognition or respect	☐
Because you feel like it	☐
Because you get to be somebody	☐
Because of the challenge	☐
Because you have to	☐
Because it is exciting	☐
Because it is expected of you	☐

proportion of playfulness in any activity can be ascertained by looking at $P/(P + W)$. This proportion can be compared with the percentage of enjoyment in the other question.

Over a number of studies with different populations the data show that most jobs vary about 50% playfulness, with undergraduate students scoring at 46%, clerical workers 47%, teachers 53%, and rehabilitation counsellors 59%. Recreational activities, as expected, have a higher percentage ($P = 76\%$), and vary from continuing education ($P = 69\%$) through hobbies ($P = 74\%$) and sports ($P = 76\%$) to relaxation ($P = 80\%$).

Rarely does a subject score 100% on either scale, and results clearly show that the few people who indicated that they wanted to quit their jobs had extremely low proportions of playfulness.

When we developed the WHY scale, we hypothesized that, over time, playfulness would diminish, for activities, with experience become familiar, controlled, and lose their collative variability. Interestingly, we did not find this result and realized that people generally have the opportunity to change jobs and abandon recreational activities fairly easily. It was unusual to find someone who said that he wanted to leave his job, and not one respondent declared that he wanted to quit a recreational activity. In an upcoming study, we expect to ask people to indicate their degree of satisfaction with an activity, and then correlate this with proportion of playfulness.

Thus we see that playfulness exists to some extent in all activities.

Playfulness is characterized by those qualities of intrinsic motivation that we call fun, enjoyment, challenge, interest, excitement, and voluntariness. It can be operationalized, and the proportion of playfulness in any activity can be measured.

VARIETIES OF PLAY

It was noted earlier that even the "recurrent motifs" that were identified cannot be considered as the common denominator in definitions of play. Definitions are often contradictory and antagonistic. Furthermore, even when writers use similar phrases to describe play, the shades of meaning are often subtly different.

For example, Lazarus, in 1883, argued that "play is activity which is itself free, aimless, amusing or diverting," a suggestion that play is voluntary, freely chosen and need not rely on deterministic motivational theories. On the other hand, Gulick (1920, p. 125) said that play is "doing that which we want to do, without reference to any ulterior end, but simply for the joy of the process." Again this argues that play is a voluntary behavior, but this time it seems to suggest that there is some intrinsic motivation, however obscure, for the choice, and seems to predate the position of the attribution theorists who, while determinists, accept their inability to locate a source of control extrinsic to the player.

But this divisiveness is not unusual in psychology and is merely one illustration of the multiplex of definitions, philosophies, and methodological styles in this science.

Some of the main differences warrant our attention. The first is in the approach to play as a dependent or independent variable. In the former instance, play is treated as a consummatory behavior, as a dependent variable, and the direction of this research focusses mainly on the content, style, or location of play, on motivational and personality factors, and on environmental conditions that determine the quality and quantity of the behavior. The alternative approach is to view play as an instrumental act in which one participates to achieve an eventual goal. Style, content, quality, and quantity of play are manipulated and predictions are made on other variables such as creativity, learning, and personality development.

One of the main reasons for the differences in approach lies in the definition of *intrinsic motivation*. Although most, if not all, theorists agree that play is intrinsically motivated, the question of "intrinsic-to-what" is important. To Berlyne, the answer was clear cut—intrinsic meant *task-intrinsic*. Play was an activity which was self-reinforcing and autotelic. Using an arousal theory and a homeostatic approach, Berlyne viewed play as an activity the goal of which is to help maintain an optimum level of arousal. To Berlyne, then, play was a task-intrinsic, consummatory behavior. Other optimum-level theorists (e.g., Fiske & Maddi and Hunt) would perforce agree with this approach, while quibbling over minor (?) issues such as what is being kept at an optimum level, arousal level, information processing level, or activation level. But regardless of these distinctions, play was dependent on the interaction of the player and his immediate environment. Research was designed to show how changes in the environment, such as complexity and novelty, affect the quality and duration of play.

On the other hand, "intrinsic" has been defined by various theorists as *person-intrinsic;* that is, the individual as a self-rewarding agent. This allows for a definition of play either as an activity that is immediately reinforced, or as one in which the reinforcement can be delayed for hours, days, or years. But, in any case, the reward comes from the person himself, rather than from other people.

White (1959), for example, treats play as an activity that is instrumental to the attainment of competence. Research following this line would be interested in measures of competence as the dependent variable, and characteristics of the play situation and style of play as variables to be manipulated, or at least observed, so that their contribution to eventual competence can be measured.

This is in line with Piaget and others who view play as a developmental stepping stone toward maturity and adulthood. Even more, this is the approach taken by play therapists such as Axline (1969) who consider that "healthy" play reflects a "healthy" child, and that one can utilize play situations as a means of reducing anxiety and working through unconscious feelings as well as promoting growth, creativity, and self-actualization.

A strong thrust into the intrinsic-motivation literature was made in the seventies when the attribution theorists began publishing (cf. Deci, 1975). Influenced by the work of Rotter and deCharms, these theorists seek to identify the causal agent for an activity, locating it either in the extrinsic world, or failing this, intrinsically. The concept of volition is sometimes introduced as an explanation of the cause of an activity for which no extrinsic motivation can be perceived. This is clearly a person-intrinsic approach. Yet, when research is mounted in which situational conditions are varied in order to measure persistence of a task and evaluation of it, one recognizes that a task-intrinsic approach is being used.

Other theorists also ignore the distinction between task- and person-intrinsic motivation. Herzberg (1966), for example, speaks of motivational factors (as opposed to hygienic) that lead to enjoyment and satisfaction with a task, such as a job. These include challenge, achievement, recognition, responsibility, and advancement. Clearly, some of these factors are extrinsic, in the control of other agents; foremen, bosses, etc. Achievement and responsibility are person-intrinsic factors. One need not be dependent on others to derive satisfaction from the performance of a task. One can recognize the worth of one's work and be self-laudatory. Challenge tends to be a characteristic that is task-intrinsic. One interacts with the complexities, incongruities, and difficulties of the job, and is reinforced by overcoming them.

Thus, we find that play activities can be studied as dependent or as independent variables, affecting personality development and maturation directly or indirectly. Furthermore, we have noted that play is seen as autotelic (task-intrinsically motivated), person-intrinsic, or both.

Finally, we should note that research in play can be directed in the main to content or style of play, or to motivational variables that affect the initiation, direction, intensity, and cessation of the behavior.

Those interested in content and style of play have developed classification systems of their own, and are mainly concerned with play materials and companions, games, locations of play, and style of interaction. Parten (1933), for example, identified six categories of social play: unoccupied behavior, solitary play, onlooker play, parallel play, associative play, and cooperative play. Although motivational approaches to play concentrate mainly on why peeple play, they are also concerned with motivational effects on style and content. For example, Hutt (1970) was concerned with the effects of familiarity on choice of toys, Eifermann (1971) with complexity on toy preference, and Gilmore (1964) and Gold (1976) on the effects of the emotional state of the children on their style of playing.

Thus, these fields overlap while remaining diverse and often use the same nomenclature to refer to different concepts. No wonder Berlyne was unable to find a unifying principle in the concept of play.

In fact, it seems clear that if one wants to study play, one must identify subcategories rather than try to discover a lowest common denominator. We have, therefore, postulated the existence of five types of play, each with its own motivations and goals.

It is difficult, of course, to identify any particular play activity as being only of a single type, and, in fact, close study suggests that the nature of the activity changes over time, so that at one time one could classify a play behavior into one category, but as it continues, its style, direction, and goals may change. For example, at first encounter, play may be mainly in the nature of exploration of a novel toy or situation, but as familiarity increases, the style, content, and goal of the play activity may alter considerably.

On the basis of a review of the literature and personal observation, we conclude that one should be able to identify at least five different kinds of play, and distinguish them along various motivational and content criteria (Day, 1979).

Table II outlines the five categories of play, suggests whether they are task- or person-intrinsic, and tentatively describes the characteristics of the activity.

Exploratory play is the same as Berlyne's specific exploration. It is motivated by the presence of a high level of collative variability in the environment and uncertainty in the player. The player seeks to explore the environment to gain information and understand it. Overt forms of activity tend to include locomotion and orientation of the body toward the object or event that has induced the state of uncertainty, curiosity manipulation of the object (toy), and possibly questions about the object or situation, mainly of the factual variety. If allowed to continue, this form of play may wane in favor of other activities or other forms of play, or attention may shift to other novel, complex, or surprising elements in the environment. The player may appear to be somewhat tense, and tends to concentrate on the source of uncertainty. Given that the motivation to

TABLE II. Play Typology

Type	Initiating mechanisms	Characteristics	Goals	Telicity
Exploratory	Novelty Uncertainty Curiosity	Stimulus-oriented Locomotion Body orientation Concentrated Factural-type questions	Factual information	Task-intrinsic
Creative	Interesting environment Familiarity	Stimulus-oriented Symbolic, fantasy Free, undirected Explanatory-type questions	Explanatory information Mastery Integration	Task-intrinsic
Diversive	Boredom	Aimless Easily disrupted Relaxed, fun	Hedonic homeostasis	Task-intrinsic
Mimetic	Needs Dispositions	Structured, formal Repetitive Often social	Competence	Person-intrinsic
Cathartic	High tension Anger Hostility Anxiety	Deliberate Symbolic, fantasy Often destructive	Tension reduction	Task-intrinsic

explore (play) arises, at least in part, in environmental conditions, one should expect that the person would be somewhat constrained in his activities, and less distractible. Changes in the environment would be reflected in changes in the player's concentration, direction of attention, intensity of play, and willingness to sustain the activity.

In time Exploratory play may change to *Creative play*. Creative play requires an environment with a high level of familiarity (Kurtz, 1977). Uncertainty and intensity of behavior are more under the control of the player who can manipulate the environment to a greater extent. Overt behavior should reflect less involvement with the external environment but greater internalization of exploration and information search. Questions may shift to the explanatory type as the level of collative variability drops (Evans, 1969). Fantasy and imagination may become more predominant, and the goal of the activity shifts from reduction of uncertainty to maximization of hedonic pleasure.

Although *Diversive play* may seem to resemble Creative play, they differ in many respects. Like Creative play, Diversive play involves a high degree of imagination and fantasy. But, unlike the former, it tends to be more aimless. Diversive play is an outgrowth of extreme familiarization and boredom, and thus is a search for diversion.

One can notice the aimlessness and restlessness of a bored person playing with old, familiar, worn-out toys, or switching stations on a television set. The person tends to be distractible, and one can sense that he is not feeling great pleasure. Diversive play is easily disrupted, and the player is quite willing to direct his attention to other activities.

Mimetic play is a common form of play, especially in adolescents and children. They dress up, act roles, imitate grown-up behavior, and mimic emotions of others. It is the play that psychologists have described as being so important for mastery or the attainment of competence. Young animals also engage widely in this form of play, mimicking behaviors and affects of their adults. The behavior appears to be pleasurable and tends to persist with a high level of intensity (witness the amount of time and effort expended by a novice tennis player on the courts perfecting his serve). Although some of the reward is task-intrinsic, most of it lies in personal satisfaction gained from a feeling of control, mastery, and competence.

Cathartic play is the activity we recognize as play therapy. It is usually initiated by a therapist and is assumed to be a way of releasing anxiety and a high level of tension. (Whether the play itself is initiated by the high level of tension or the opportunity to play, is debatable. One might argue that at least on the first session the play is largely exploratory.) Cathartic play tends to be imaginative, with a high level of fantasy. Depending on the environment created by the therapist and the style of play he induces, Cathartic play can be destructive, creative, or even imitative. Although many play therapists try to be objective, unbiased, and aloof, they often control the form of play through instruction, making available a limited selection of toys and articles of play, and by their tacit invitation to be destructive and act out. Cathartic play is initiated by an external agent, and stopped when that agent decides. But often the form of play changes in the alotted time from Cathartic to Mimetic or Creative play. For, though the original goal may be to reduce tension, there are obvious drives to gain competence in coping with external and internal stresses and to maximize hedonic pleasure in a play environment.

Following this, we designed a study to test some of the ideas arising from the theory.

Ten brief scenarios were written, each one attempting to depict a situation which would represent as clearly as possible one of the categories in the classification table. There were two situations for each of the five categories, and we attempted to make them as terse and succinct as possible. The 10 paragraphs are listed in Table III.

Each paragraph was put at the top of an answer booklet in which the Mehrabian and Russell (1974) semantic differential type scales were listed. These scales have been constructed so that the respondent can indicate the level on each of 18 bipolar adjectives that best represents his feelings in a situation. Among the adjective sets are happy-unhappy; excited-calm; and controlled-controlling. Factor analysis of the scales has shown that they represent three dimensions: Pleasure, Arousal, and Dominance; the same three factors that seem to identify the three recurring motifs in the definitions of play (and the three factors that Osgood identified as Evaluative, Activity, and Potency).

A number of undergraduate students were asked to read the scenarios and to respond for each one along the 18 scales.

The results are presented in Figure 2.

It is interesting to note how close some of the data come to the predictions.

Looking at the Pleasure dimension we note that Cathartic play is viewed (at least through the imagination of undergraduate students) as being low in pleasure compared with the others, and Creative play as the most pleasurable. A test of significance showed significant differences for the five groups ($F = 2.57$, $p < .05$). One interesting result that appeared was a large difference in means for the two Diversive play situations (5.12 and 7.19). Apparently an afternoon in one's own room seems to be less pleasurable than an afternoon at the beach. Maybe one's room is more boring.

TABLE III. Play Scenarios

Exploratory

You are 5 years old and have come to Kindergarten for the first time. There are lots of strange games and toys and you are allowed to explore the whole place. You go over to the first thing you see and start to play with it.

You are 4 years old and have been given a new toy for Christmas. It is a most wonderful strange toy and you sit right down and take it apart to see how it works.

Creative

You are 4 years old and alone with your Lego blocks. They are your favorite because you can create anything you like with them.

You are 5 years old, it's Sunday morning and everyone is still asleep. You take out your construction set and build strange and wonderful things with it.

Diversive

You are 5 years old and have nothing to do. It's a warm day and your parents have just gone to take a nap and left you in your own room for an hour to play.

You are 4 years old and have gone to the beach with the family. Everybody is just sitting around relaxed and talking while you are near them on the sand playing.

Mimetic

You are 5 years old and together with your best playmate are playing doctor. In your game you are grownups and do all the things you have seen doctors do with patients.

You are 5 years old and looking through the family storage closets. You come across some of your parents' old clothes and dress up in them, imitating their walk and talk.

Cathartic

You are 5 years old and a psychiatric problem. Your mother has taken you to the psychiatrist because she doesn't know what else to do. Your behavior is always wild and destructive. You meet the doctor who takes you into a therapy playroom and invites you to play with any of the toys. You start to play with the building blocks.

You are 4 years old and in a psychologist's office. You have had a lengthy history of disturbed, neurotic behavior. You are introduced to the psychologist, a very pleasant person, who takes you into a play-therapy room and lets you play with the toys there. You choose a Mommy, Daddy, and child to play with.

Significant differences among the five forms of play were also found on the Arousal dimension. Exploratory play is clearly the most tense, and Diversive play the most relaxed ($F = 5.89$).

Cathartic and Mimetic play give one the greatest feelings of control, and Exploratory play the least. Again group differences were significant ($F = 6.82$).

Looking across the scales for the varieties of play, we can note that Exploratory play is highly arousing, with a concommitant feeling of low control. Creative play seems to be characterized as highly pleasurable, arousing, and dominant. Diversive, on the other hand, is low on all these. Mimetic play is highly pleasurable, and Cathartic play arousing but low on pleasure and dominance.

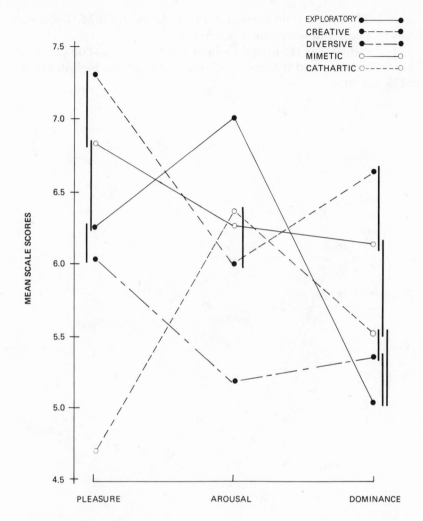

FIGURE 2. Scale values of five types of play on three dimensions. (Vertical lines join points not significantly different.)

Perhaps when we visualize play in general terms, and describe it as joyful, intrinsically controlled, and highly active, we tend to imagine Creative play rather than the others.

In a second part of the same study we examined the perceived motivations to engage in these activities as measured by responses on the WHY Scale. Of the 10 individual motivation scales and two general motivation scales (intrinsic as fun and extrinsic as getting something out of it), significant differences were found on six. These are displayed in

Figure 3. The results tend to confirm the findings on the Mehrabian and Russell scales, and show the following:

  1. Creative play is fun and challenging. It is very low on obligation. This can be compared with its profile on the MR scales: high in pleasure and dominance.

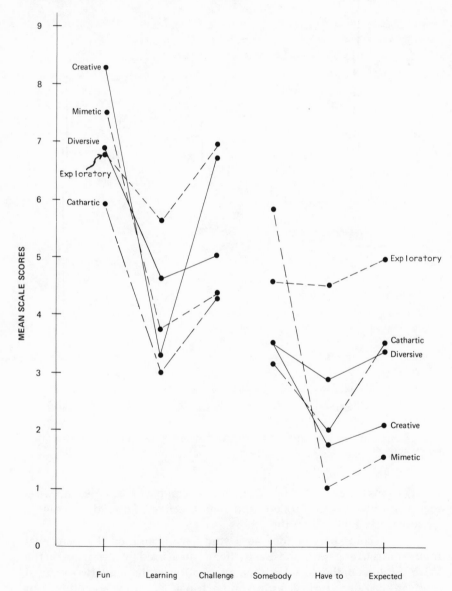

FIGURE 3. Scale values of five types of play on three autotelic and three exotelic dimensions.

2. Mimetic play is fun (high on the pleasure dimension). One does it to get to be somebody, and does not feel that it is expected or obligatory.

3. Diversive and Exploratory play are moderately fun (and moderately pleasurable). Cathartic play is least fun and not at all pleasurable.

4. Exploratory play is challenging (arousing), and one does it to learn. It is relatively high on the extrinsic motivators of getting to be somebody, having to, and being expected to, and thus one feels aroused and dominated.

5. Diversive play tends to be intermediate on most scales—moderately fun (pleasure), learning, challenge, etc. Its only outstanding feature is a comparatively low level of arousal.

6. Cathartic play is least fun (low in pleasure), and is not done to learn or for the challenge.

From this exploratory beginning we can now begin to study the different forms of play in order to examine their motivations and their characteristic styles.

It is clear that the autotelic components of different activities we consider play are not always the same, and that even the different types of play are distinguishable along the various motive forces and in the effects they have on us. Although other attempts have been made to distinguish kinds of play by their overt characteristics, we have tied the typology down to motive forces and goals.

Postscript

We have come a long way from Dan Berlyne's 1969 pessimistic review. We have heeded his advice and reexamined the concept of play from a number of points of view. Having reviewed Dan's "recurrent motifs," we have discovered that they described play along three variables: voluntariness, pleasure, and telicity. Then, when we look at the literature, we find numerous instances of either the external world being described along three dimensions, or the internal response to the environment being measured along three variables. Thus, Berlyne (1963) refers to psychophysical, ecological, and collative properties, whereas Osgood proposes three dimensions of potency, evaluation, and activity (Osgood, Suci, & Tannenbarum, 1957) and Walker (see Chapter 3) speaks of structural, affective, and energetic variables. Mehrabian and Russell (1974) translate Osgood's external variables into a scale that measures their impact along three dimensions: dominance, pleasure, and arousal. It would be presumptuous to equate all the different classifications, but Day and Murray (1978a) demonstrated that some of these are indeed comparable. There is mounting evidence that psychophysical (structural, potency?) properties seem to be the source of control (dominance) or lack of it, ecological (affective?) properties the source of pleasure, and collative (energetic?) properties the source of arousal and activity.

We cannot help but note that play activity is also describable along these same three qualities. Even more, when we define play in a typology we find that the five varieties are distinguishable along these three qualities.

But another approach to the study of play, possibly more useful, was suggested. Playfulness, as a concept, deserves concentrated study. One surely cannot polarize work and play in the way they are treated now. One must recognize that these represent extreme forms of activity at the ends of a workfulness–playfulness dimension that can be characterized by three qualities: voluntariness (obligatoriness), telicity (intrinsic or extrinsic motivation), and affect (pleasure or fun). Given the three instruments of Multidimensional Scaling, the Mehrabian and Russell scales, and the WHY scale, we can attack the question of proportion of playfulness in all activities and look at individual differences in the perception of each activity as playful. We can predict suspension of an activity when it loses its playfulness, and, possibly some day, choice of activities on the basis of their contributing to preferred levels of these three dimensions. We might even want to examine environments or objects for properties which can contribute toward supplying preferable levels of playfulness.

ACKNOWLEDGMENTS

The help of two people is acknowledged here: Michael Murray, my student, who provided much of the statistical expertise, and my son, Moishe, who in our frequent Sunday trips to the ski hills served as the inspiration to investigate play behavior.

REFERENCES

AXLINE, V. M. Play therapy (Rev. ed.). New York: Ballantine, 1969.

BERLYNE, D. E. Motivational problems raised by exploratory and epistemic behavior. In S. Koch (Ed.), Psychology: A study of a science. (Vol. 5). New York: McGraw-Hill, 1963.

BERLYNE, D. E. Laughter, humor and play. In G. Lindzey & E. Aronson (Eds.), Handbook of Social Psychology (2nd ed., Vol. 3). Boston: Addison-Wesley, 1969.

DAY, H. I. A new look at work, play and job satisfaction. The School Guidance Worker, 1971, 27, 4–11. Reprinted in Recreation Review, 1973, 3, 4–11.

DAY, H. I. Work and leisure: Two sides of the same coin. The Canadian Counsellor, 1972, 6, 251–259. Reprinted in Recreation Review, 1972, 2, 10–16.

DAY, H. I. Why people play. Loisir et Société, 1979, 2, 129–147.

DAY, H. I. & FORTEATH, C. *Children's understanding of work and play.* York University Psychology Report #34, York University, Toronto, Canada, 1976.

DAY, H. I., & MURRAY, M. *Complexity and novelty: Equal but different.* Paper read at the Canadian Psychological Association Annual Meeting, Toronto, June 1978(a).

DAY, H. I., & MURRAY, M. *Work and play: A classification of activities.* Paper read at the Second Canadian Congress on Leisure Research, Toronto, April 1978(b).

DECI, E. L. *Intrinsic motivation.* New York: Plenum, 1975.

EIFERMANN, R. *Determinants of children's game styles.* Jerusalem: Israel Academy of Sciences and Humanities, 1971.

ELLIS, M. J. *Why people play.* Englewood Cliffs, N. J.: Prentice-Hall, 1973.

EVANS, D. R. *Conceptual complexity, arousal and epistemic behavior.* Unpublished doctoral thesis, University of Toronto, 1969.

GILMORE, J. B. *The role of anxiety and cognitive factors in children's play behavior.* Unpublished doctoral dissertation, Yale University, 1964.

GOLD, R. *The effect of cognitive set on the manipulatory play behavior of grade two and three boys.* Unpublished M. A. thesis, York University, 1976.

GULICK, L. H. *Philosophy of play.* New York: Scribner, 1920.

HERZBERG, F. *Work and the nature of man.* New York: World, 1966.

HUTT, C. Specific and diversive exploration. In H. W. Reese & L. P. Lipsitt (Eds.), *Advances in child development and behavior* (Vol. 5). New York: Academic Press, 1970.

KELLEY, H. H. *Attribution in social interaction.* New York: General Learning Press, 1971.

KENNALEY, R. *Young children's use of the discounting principle.* Unpublished B. A. honor's thesis, York University, Toronto, 1979.

KURTZ, S. R. *Assimilative exploration and accommodative exploration: Two complementary channels to creative thinking.* Unpublished doctoral thesis, University of Toronto, 1977.

LAZARUS, M. *Über die Reize des Spiels.* Berlin: Dümmler, 1883.

LEPPER, M. R., GREENE, D., & NISBETT, R. E. Undermining children's intrinsic interest with extrinsic rewards. *Journal of Personality and Social Psychology,* 1973, *28,* 129–137.

LEVY, J. *Play behavior.* New York: Wiley, 1978.

LIEBERMAN, J. N. *Playfulness: Its relationship to imagination and creativity.* New York: Academic Press, 1977.

LINDZEY, G., & ARONSON, E. *Handbook of social psychology* (2nd ed., Vol. III). Boston: Addison-Wesley, 1969.

MEHRABIAN A., & RUSSELL, J. A. *An approach to environmental psychology.* Cambridge: M.I.T. Press, 1974.

MENNINGER, C. The meaning of work in western society. In H. Borow (Ed.), *Man in a world at work.* Boston: Houghton Mifflin, 1964.

OSGOOD, C. E., SUCI, G. S., & TANNENBAUM, P. H. *The measurement of meaning.* Urbana: University of Illinois Press, 1957.

PARTEN, M. B. Social play among preschool children. *Journal of Abnormal and Social Psychology, 28,* 1933, 136–147.

ROMANUK, F. W. *Performance, persistence, and satisfaction as a function of reinforcement and the trait of intrinsic motivation.* Unpublished doctoral dissertation, York University, 1975.

ROSS, M. The self-perception of intrinsic motivation. In J. H. Harvey & W. J. Ickes (Eds.), *New directions in attribution research* (Vol. 1). Hillsdale, N.J.: Erlbaum, 1976.

RUSSON, A. E. *The effects of salient extrinsic incentives on the quality of intrinsically motivated activity.* Unpublished M. A. thesis, York University, 1975.

SWADOS, H. Work as a public issue. *Saturday Review,* December 12, 1959, pp. 13–15, 45. Reprinted in H. J. Peters & J. C. Hansen (Eds.), *Vocational guidance and career development.* New York: Macmillan, 1966.

VALENTINE, C. W. *The psychology of early childhood.* London: Methuen, 1942.

VROOM, V. H. *Work and motivation.* New York: Wiley, 1964.

WEISS, R. S., & RIESMAN, D. Some issues in the future of lesiure. *Social Problems*, 1961, *9*(1), 78–86. Reprinted in E. O. Smigel (Ed.), *Work and leisure: a contemporary social problem* New Haven: College & University Press, 1963.

WHITE, R. W. Motivation reconsidered: Concept of competence. *Psychological Review*, 1959, *66*, 297–333.

11

Toward A Taxonomy and Conceptual Model of Play

Corinne Hutt

Introduction

The study of play has a longer history than the study of psychology itself, but the ideas about the phenomenon have shown remarkable changes according to the prevailing climate and conditions.

The social historian Aries (1973) recounts how, in medieval society, play was limited to a very short period of infancy—the first three years. The uncertain future of the infant precluded too close a scrutiny of its needs, but, were it to survive, it immediately became part of the adult community. By the age of four, the Dauphin of France in the early seventeenth century was fully occupied reading or being read to, playing music, dancing, and playing adult games with the pages of the King's Chamber. From the age of five, he participated increasingly in adult activities and amusements. Although the Dauphin was probably most atypical, the diary of his physician illustrates the lack of distinction made between children's and adults' pastimes—games, music, stories were shared by young and old alike. Even toys and miniature replicas were common to both adults and children, serving as knickknacks for both.

Dr. Corinne Hutt died November 25, 1979. The chapter was produced by her husband, John Hutt, from her unpublished notes and papers. Professor Hutt has no illusions but that Corinne's own account would have been different (and better). It is likely, however, that it would have contained some of the present material, and hopefully the present chapter conveys something of the flavor of Corinne's thinking at the time of her death. Professor Hutt offers it as a tribute to the memory of his wife as well as to that of Daniel Berlyne, whose work Corinne revered.

Corinne Hutt • Late Reader in Psychology, University of Keele, Keele, Staffordshire ST5 5BG, England. S. J. Hutt • Department of Psychology, University of Keele, Keele, Staffordshire ST5 5BG, England.

Many of the games too that eventually became children's games were derived from the festive rituals of the adults. Not until the eighteenth century does there seem to have been anything that was distinctly *child's* play. Even then it was somewhat frowned upon—especially by Protestants. John Wesley warned that "he who plays as a boy will play as a man."

Furthermore, Aries suggests that play is a behavioral phenomenon more characteristic of the prosperous industrial peoples of the Western Hemisphere than of the agrarian and nomadic communities of the East. It is salutory to recall this distinction when ascribing functions and uses to play, since it will be necessary to account for a very large number of healthy and well-adapted individuals who nevertheless were deprived of opportunities to play when they were young.

Play is one of those omnibus terms that is used to cover a multitude of activities and pursuits—from the frolics and gambols of young animals to the fantasies and intricate problem solving of man. This is particularly evident with reference to children's activities where all behaviors except those fulfilling vegetative functions may be encompassed by the term (Müller-Schwarze, 1971).

Of much value to students of children's play is Dearden's (1967, p. 81) illuminating discussion. Most of an adult's activities are *serious*, argues Dearden, in that they further some purpose or fulfil some obligation; "play" he argues "is neither the pursuit of purposes dictated by common prudence, nor is it the fulfilling of an obligation to anybody." "Serious" here means subject to the demands and constraints of reality; thus, "nonserious" implies freedom from such restraint. "A child at the sink, for example," says Dearden, "may or may not be playing, depending on how he regards his activity. If he does just as he pleases, then he is playing." Most children over the age of two years are able to recognise this distinction and indicate it in their behavior. Thus Dearden's definition of play is at least a useful working definition. "Play . . . is a nonserious and self-contained activity which we engage in just for the satisfaction involved in it." This formulation, he believes, covers the three chief types of children's activities—role play, object play, and physical play—as well as adult games.

THEORIES OF PLAY

Perhaps the most conceptually elaborate theory of play and one that is uniquely applicable to human behavior is that of Jean Piaget. Piaget's theory (1951) revolves around his two invariant functions of assimilation and accommodation. Imitation and play are seen as particular sorts of relationships between accommodation and assimilation: if accommodation dominates assimilation the result is imitation, and if assimilation of reality dominates accommodation the result is play.

> Intelligent adaptation, imitation and play are thus three possibilities and they result according as there is a stable equilibrium between assimilation and accommodation or primacy of one of these two tendencies over the other. (p. 86)

Sutton-Smith (1966) has taken Piaget to task over what he calls his "implicit copyist epistemology." Play and imitation, he argues, are not dialectical opposites in Piaget's conceptualization: whereas accommodation is given a key role in the formation of concepts by virtue of its representation of external reality, play has only a secondary role in the structure of the intellect—it can only repeat or reproduce the images created by the accommodatory process. Sutton-Smith contends that even in the course of ontogeny Piaget has undermined the significance of play by characterizing it as both an effective buttress to the cognitive process of accommodation and a transient and primitive stage in the emergence of thought, a stage which becomes increasingly unimportant as intellective functioning becomes more efficient. This view of childhood play, maintains Sutton-Smith, is in accordance with his view of adult thought, where he is more concerned with directed and logical structures than with the less directed aspects like reverie, imagination, or divergent thinking—aspects which have great affinity with play.

In a prompt rebuttal of this critique, Piaget (1966) argues that: his conception of intellectual operations and the symbolic function have been misconstrued by Sutton-Smith. "All concepts are derived first from the action and then from the operation. . . . Play is an exercise of action schemes and therefore part of the cognitive component of conception" (p. 111). At the same time the essential property of the play is the deformation and subordination of reality to the individual's desires, but since it is symbolic it needs signifiers, which it borrows from language or the only other source of symbols—interiorized imitation. Thus, in this system play is not necessarily subordinated to accommodative imitation.

The theory of Piaget (1951) is the one truly cognitive exposition of play. As such, however, it has little to say regarding the motivation of play. A number of psychological theories more particularly concerned with motivational issues were formulated in the 1950s and early 1960s. Much of the empirical work that prompted these theories came from Harlow's laboratory in Wisconsin, and sought to explain why monkeys opened windows to explore the scene outside, why they manipulated devices with such persistence for no other reward apparently than their solution, why even rats would choose to go into a maze arm that was novel or learn to press a bar for changes of light or sound. The earliest theories were classical drive theories (Harlow, 1950; Harlow & McClearn, 1954; Montgomery, 1954). The explanatory or predictive power of these theories was minimal, and they invited criticism such as that of Bolles (1958): "Where little is known about the conditions that control some behavior (e.g., exploratory behavior), the inference of a causal drive does little more than restate the facts to be explained" (p. 23). The principal reason for this theoretical impasse was that these early workers failed to distinguish between unconditioned and consummatory responses to an unconditioned novel stimulus and those appetitive and instrumental responses which were strengthened by a contingent stimulus. Berlyne (1960, 1963) dealt with this distinction in discussing specific and diversive exploration, but it was not until 1965 that it was explicitly formulated by Fowler. The distinction between response *to* a stimulus change and response *for* a stimulus change proved to be a theoretical catalyst, for we then had a spate of theories which were evocatively described by O'Connell (1965) as theories of tedium and titillation. These theories will be referred to later.

It is, however, the dedicatee of the present volume who has made the most substantial contribution both theoretically and empirically to this area of intrinsically motivated behaviors. He was the first worker who really encompassed relevant animal data as well as a number of diverse human phenomena within the same conceptual framework (Berlyne, 1963). Since it is essentially his theoretical position that is pursued here, a brief outline of it will be presented.

Berlyne's central construct is that of *arousal*—a psychophysiological energy dimension mediated by the activity of the reticular system that has "sleep" as its low point and "excitement" of one kind or other as its high point. Despite many inadequacies, the viability of such a unitary dimension within Berlyne's theory rests on the unique predictions that it permits, and on its psychological meaningfulness insofar as integration of a wide variety of experimental findings is concerned. Fluctuations in arousal are reflected in changes in brain activity (EEG), cardiovascular indices (ECG), in respiration, in muscular tension (EMG), and so on, thereby yielding objective and independent measures of *level of arousal*. *Arousal tonus* is a level of arousal an individual characteristically maintains when awake and alert, a level which is intermediate between the higher and lower extremes of the arousal dimension. This tonus is maintained by a particular influx of *arousal potential*. Arousal potential of a stimulus is dependent on three types of property—psychophysical, collative, and ecological. *Collative* variables are those properties of stimuli which depend on a comparison of information from different sources for their effects—novelty, complexity, incongruity, ambiguity, etc. To understand

the relationship between arousal level and arousal potential, it is necessary to consider models of the orienting reaction first.

The orienting reaction is elicited by new stimuli or changes in stimulation. Both Thompson and Spencer (1966) and Horn (1967) have
suggested that relatively simple processes at a cellular level can account
for this reaction in most instances, and for its habituation. For stimuli with
collative properties or with meaning, however, the comparator system of
the cortex is essential (Sokolov, 1963). Such a stimulus produced nonspecific excitatory effects, via the axon collaterals, upon the reticular
formation (the amplifying system). As the cortical analyzers cease to
register the stimulus as significant, corticoreticular excitatory impulses
cease and simultaneously the nonspecific excitatory impulses are blocked
and thereupon habituation of the response occurs.

Similarly activation of the reticular activating system (RAS) sends
facilitatory impulses down to motor units and activating impulses up to
the cortex. In animals whose cortex was frozen, excitation of the RAS and
motor facilitation persisted upon elicitation of a monosynaptic reflex
(Hugelin & Bonvallet, 1957). Hence the level of arousal and corticoreticular inhibition (Berlyne, 1960). During the orienting reaction there is
transient escape of the arousal system from cortical control. On being
confronted with stimuli high in arousal potential, this disinhibition of
arousal is protracted; and it is returned to its former level only when the
cortical analyzers have assigned the source of stimulation to a neuronal
model. When there is a lack of stimulus input, that is, when arousal
potential is low, cortical activation is minimal, and hence corticoreticular
inhibition is weakened, allowing the arousal system again unbridled
activity. Thus stimuli both high and low in arousal potential result in
elevations of arousal. (This is contrary to Hebb's, 1955, position that low
stimulation or boredom represents a low level of arousal.) If arousal
potential is such that arousal rises above the tonus level, "a return to the
tonus level will be rewarding and responses that promote such a return
. . . will be reinforced" (Berlyne, 1960, p. 194). It may be seen that Berlyne
therefore only conceives of *decreases* in arousal toward tonus as rewarding. The subjective states associated with high and low arousal potential
are respectively *uncertainty* and boredom.

Thus, when an individual is confronted by stimuli which are novel,
complex, incongruous, etc., arousal is increased as a result of the uncertainty, and he engages in those responses (inspection, investigation)
which will reduce the uncertainty and thereby lower arousal. This motivation is what is colloquially known as *curiosity*, and the behavior is
specific exploration. There are other circumstances, however, when an
animal or individual will seek out stimulation, irrespective of its source,

which will provide the optimum arousal potential to maintain arousal tonus, as when a sensorily deprived subject gives himself mild electric shocks rather than remain devoid of stimulation. This behavior is what Berlyne has termed *diversive* exploration. It is a category which includes playful behavior. Thus, play in Berlyne's conceptualization would be that behavior which is elicited in conditions of low stimulus input, and which serves to optimize influx of arousal potential and thereby return arousal to its tonic level.

Apart from its parsimony and predictive power, this theory has the virtue of being able to synthesize a wide variety of nonutilitarian behaviors in animals and humans—attention, exploration, research, laughter, humor, play, aesthetics, and hedonism (Berlyne, 1966, 1969, 1971, 1973).

TYPES OF PLAY

Physical Play

Physical play is perhaps given more emphasis by students of animal behavior than by students of children. Although the sweeping generalizations of Aldis (1975)—"Most play is chasing and play fighting; these are the two most fundamental kinds of play" (p. 11)—seem unsupported by evidence, in ontogeny physical play is perhaps the form of play that is manifest earliest, with the kicking of legs and flailing of arms. Loizos (1967) notes that play involving bodily activity, such as arm waving, kicking, locomotion, and acrobatics, is evident in the chimpanzee within the first two months of life. Young spider monkeys run and jump from branch to branch, and chimpanzees engage in sequences of climbing, swinging, and dropping (Loizos, 1967). Van Lawick-Goodall (1968) describes other varieties of locomotor play in young chimpanzees—galloping, somersaulting, pirouetting, leaping. Rhesus monkeys repeatedly fall 30 feet into the water (Dolhinow & Bishop, 1970). Van Lawick-Goodall (1968) vividly describes the "play walk" of the chimpanzee: "with rounded back, head slightly bent down and pulled back between shoulders, and [he] takes small almost 'stilted' steps. Often there is a side-to-side movement as he moves forward, rather like a seaman's roll" (p. 258). And Millar (1968) remarks "Looking at the world upside down through one's legs" (p. 111) is a favorite pastime just after infants have learned to stand.

Much of what Piaget calls "practice play" consists of varieties of physical play—running, jumping, skipping, vaulting, hopping, cycling, hooping, and so on. During the process of acquiring these particular motor skills, children appear to be in deadly earnest and serious in intent, and it is only when they are proficient in a skill that they become playful in it. Furthermore, many children over the age of three years are aware of this distinction: once, having watched our five-year-old son completing one dizzy figure-of-eight route after another on his cycle, we inquired of him whether the activity was "play." "Now it is" was his reply, "but it was jolly hard work when I was learning." Thus, as Miller (1973) points out, contrary to Groos's view that play is exercise and practice for skills to be used later, these skills are played with after they are acquired. Many of these physical play activities have, in Miller's term, a quality of "galumphing"—derived from "an onomatopoeic description of a baboon's flailing in play fights . . . [and is] a shorthand term for 'patterned, voluntary elaboration or complication of process, when the pattern is not under the dominant control of goals' " (p. 92).

The protracted engagement in the rehearsal of these physical activities must result in increasing agility, dexterity, and sense of balance and body image, as a consequence of the varied proprioceptive reafferent stimulation fed back to the motor control centres. One is reminded of the two kittens of Held & Hein (1963), one of whom actively walked past a vertically striped wall, while the other was passively moved past the stripes; when the animals were subsequently required to negotiate a split-level similarly striped area, only the animal who had performed the active movements was able to do so. The reafferent stimulation from the active movements enabled the animal to build a stable model of its perceptual world.

Aldis (1975) recounts a number of other physical play activities— rotation, sliding, swinging, and even passive transportation on water or moving branches in children and other species—the common element in all being vestibular stimulation, which, Aldis argues, is reinforcing. In the absence of a direct measure of such stimulation, this interpretation must remain conjectural. These forms of physical play decrease with age, so that in late childhood they have given way to much more structured games. Other forms of physical play, like chasing and rough-and-tumble play which require a social context, will be discussed under the heading of Social Play.

Manipulative Play

As soon as infants are able to reach out, grasp, and hold, manipulative play is much in evidence. To an immobile infant, such contact and manipulation serves to provide and maintain a level of sensory input adequate for keeping awake and alert. A nice example of this need for stimulation is given by Millar (1968): "A girl of four when told not to fidget with the crockery on the table replied that her arm would get bored if she stopped!" (p. 128). The infant is also capable of showing a distinct preference for those responses on which some change in stimulation is contingent (Friedlander, McCarthy, & Soforenko, 1967; Leuba & Friedlander, 1968; Rheingold, Stanley, & Doyle, 1964). As manual efficiency increases, the child is able to investigate and control the greater part of his immediate environment. Infants lose attention and drop their toys as the latter lose novelty (Hutt, 1967c), but this practice can also be used to good effect in controlling adults: as the adult picks up and replaces the toy, out it goes again—the obliging adult simply reinforces the response and delights the child. Much manipulative play in infancy falls into the Piagetian category of practice play in the sensorimotor period, and such play constitutes the categories of primary and secondary circular reactions. The primary circular reaction involves the repetition of a motor pattern, like thumbsucking, usually initially elicited as a reflex; it involves reproductive assimilation, recognitory assimilation, and generalizing assimilation—successive stages in the development of the reaction. There is also gradual accommodation so that the infant tries different ways of sucking or grasping, opposition of fingers one to another, etc., and there is also the coordination of two patterns, for example, prehension and sucking.

The secondary circular reaction involves procedures to make interesting events last, as when an infant kicks his cot and finds that the mobile moves, whereupon he repeats the action to reproduce the effect. During the development of this reaction the infant may, incidentally, involve a number of different actions, and in so doing effect variations in the contingent events. In this manner he not only maintains adequate levels of sensory input, but also learns about the results of his movements. One is reminded of the chimpanzees whom Nissen, Chow, & Semmes (1951) reared with their upper limbs immobilized in splints from soon after birth. When the splints were removed after six months, the animals were seen to have little idea of their body image, and were unable at first to use their limbs for reaching.

The tertiary circular reaction concerns the "discovery of new means through experimentation"; the child no longer seeks to reproduce the identical action just performed, but now introduces innovations—to see what happens. Means and ends are now clearly differentiated. Thus, within Piaget's system, forms of manipulative play are the primitive origins of intelligence.

Köhler (1925) in a classic work described how chimpanzees played with sticks they were given and subsequently were able to combine such tools and use them to procure food placed out of their reach. Schiller

(1957) describes similar incidents with two sticks, one of which was hollowed at one end so that the other could fit into it. Not all chimpanzees learned to do this, nor did all the animals who did succeed use the combined sticks to pull in their food. But of those that did succeed, all had made the connection during play.

In attempting to see how a taboo might develop in a colony of primates, Bernstein (1976) had poles and electric grids fitted into each outdoor compound. He expected that some animals would learn to avoid the grid by experiencing the shocks themselves, whereas others would learn by observation, and so eventually there would emerge a taboo. What he did not expect was that every pole would be destroyed and every grid dismantled, so that, far from being avoided, the "toys" were particularly attractive as far as the monkeys were concerned. Bernstein interprets the failure of the monkeys to be deterred by quite high shocks as evidence of the "power of play."

Young chimpanzees used sticks or blades of grass to insert into termite holes (Van Lawick-Goodall, 1968), and were also able to use poles in a compound as ladders, which they placed against a tree or wall in order to peep through a window (Menzel, 1972).

The analysis of manipulative play in children has been taken to a very sophisticated level by Greenfield and her colleagues, and demonstrates that patterns of cognitive organization are common to both language and other action modes. In the first experiment (Greenfield, Nelson, & Saltzman, 1972), infants from 11 to 36 months of age were presented with five seriated nesting cups and, after a demonstration of nesting, were expected to do the same. A developmental sequence of three rule-bound (i.e., consistent) action strategies were observed. These strategies, Greenfield argues, are "formally homologous to certain grammatical constructions . . . and are acquired in the same developmental order as the corresponding grammatical structures" (p. 735). In a more recent study with two- to six-year-olds, Goodson & Greenfield (1975) demonstrated that three structural principles derived from studies of language development were also applicable to manipulative play, thereby accentuating the parallelism between language and action.

Symbolic Play

This is the type of play which seems quintessentially human. It is variously referred to as make-believe play, fantasy play (Klinger, 1971; Smith, 1977), imaginative play (Singer, 1973), thematic play (Feitelson & Ross, 1973), sociodramatic play (Smilansky, 1968), and symbolic play (Piaget, 1951; Sutton-Smith, 1966). It is the type of play that involves an element of pretence. Singer (1973) tells us that probably the earliest and most vivid accounts of make-believe play were provided by Mark Twain in *Tom Sawyer, Huckleberry Finn* and *The Prince and The Pauper*. Singer comments that it was unlikely that imaginative play only started in the nineteenth century, but that before this time it went unnoticed and unrecorded by an adult world uninterested in childhood experience. He emphasizes the role adults' storytelling and narrative has in eliciting imaginative play, a role which was acknowledged by Mark Twain.

Imaginative play may involve many different imaginary constituents: the child may play the role of another, be it mother, engine driver, or bird, and use as a prop a broom, a hose, or a tree branch. Or the whole incident may be imaginary, with no props whatsoever. The distinctive feature of fantasy play is its lack of constraints; the sequence of actions is fluid, and reflects the child's experiences. In commenting on the similarity between play and fantasy, Klinger (1971) remarks:

> until adolescence, play and fantasy develop in parallel in important respects; and as the incidence of play subsides, fantasy continues and perhaps becomes more frequent.
>
> Throughout his lifespan both fantasy and play reflect the individual's current focal concerns, and . . . the content of fantasy at any given point in development corresponds at least roughly to the content of play. The data strongly suggest structural and functional continuity between children's playful activity and adult's playful fantasy. (p. 32)

The thematic content of imaginative play may range from common themes like mummy-and-daddy, schools, and doctors-and-nurses to space travel, monsters, or an ancient warrior riding to battle. But, whatever the theme, the child gives some indication by act or word that "this is pretending"—the metasignal which is equivalent to the chimpanzee "playface."

Psychologists and educationalists tend to be concerned with the *quality* of play—an elusive attribute at any time—and have attempted to stimulate "better" imaginative play when this is found to be lacking. Perhaps the best known work in this respect is that of Smilansky (1968). Concerned with the scholastic failure of Israeli children whose parents were immigrants from Middle Eastern or North African countries, Smilansky paid especial attention to their behavior, and found in it a tendency to be rigid and repetitious, and an inability to relate and organize different experiences. These children also played very little. She decided to use sociodramatic play to help the children relate their experiences one to another and to enable them to develop coherent conceptual schemes. Smilansky expected that by participating in sociodramatic play the child would learn to concentrate on a given theme, constrained by his peers. Our own observations, however, are of the fluid—and often inconsequential—nature of much fantasy play: a fireman, at the drop of a hat, is transformed into a driver, or a mother into a nurse. Children also seem to move into and out of such play with great ease: a Dalek[1] will stop to ask a matter-of-fact question of a companion and continue in conversation but return to being a Dalek several minutes later. Klinger (1971) supports this view:

> Structurally, play and dreams unfold erratically, easily distracted from one focus to another, their sequence fractionated and seemingly often jumbled. . . . Play and dreams vary in coherence, and under some conditions their abrupt shifts in content or their fusion of elements in unexpected combinations gives rise to strikingly symbolic forms. (p. 348)

Again, Smilansky (1968) believes that through involvement in such play a child "learns vicariously from the experience and knowledge of other children" (p. 15), and cites the example of a girl learning that policemen sometimes work in jails as well as conducting traffic, etc. Such information, however, may equally well be erroneous, as when one boy told another that he was being a spider and that his web would have only four threads, since each thread of a spiderweb was spun by a different leg.

Smilansky rightly argues that the make-believe element relies heavily on verbalisation—whether for changing the identity of object or person, or for constructing an action or a situation. Thus it follows that children deficient in language will be less likely to engage in play demanding communication, or which may be recognized by an observer as symbolic. Moreover, Smilansky contends that sociodramatic play stimulates emotional, social, and intellectual development, the latter by the fact that much problem solving and learning in school involves make-believe; for instance, in history and geography, lands and people and events which have never been experienced by the child have instead to be imagined. But this argument entails a number of unwarranted assumptions: that ability to visualize presented information is directly correlated with ability to organize and enact a theme of fantasy, or that the encoding of conceptual information is dependent on a vivid imagination. There is no evidence that children who engage in much fantasy play in their early years necessarily do well in these scholastic spheres later on.

Smilansky's comparison of the sociodramatic play of children from a "middle and high sociocultural background" (A children) with that of those from a low sociocultural background (D children—largely of immigrants from the Middle East) is essentially subjective:

---

[1] A Dalek is a character in a popular British television series for children "Dr. Who." Resembling an animated pepper pot in appearance, and speaking with a peculiar accent readily imitated by children, the Dalek is an inhabitant of a distant planet that is at war with Earth.

In the *A* kindergarten and nursery-school classes many more sociodramatic games are being played at any given time than there are in the *D* classes. The general impression is of many small groups (from 2 to 6 children), each involved in a lively game. It is difficult for the observer to decide what to record in the *A* classes, for he has to choose one group from the many playing simultaneously. In contrast, it is usual in the *D* classes to see only one or two sociodramatic games going on at any given time, and even these tend to break up very quickly. (p. 20)

The significant difference between the sociodramatic play of the *A* children and that of the *D* children thus lies not in the theme of subject matter that they choose to play but in the diversity and variety of roles undertaken, in the range and the depth of relationships portrayed, and in the dynamic developing process of the play episode through a greater understanding of the main factors involved in a given social situation. (pp. 22–23)

With the *D* child the toy and the activity with the toy constitute the play, whereas with the *A* child the toy has only secondary importance, is easily replaced by any undefined objects, and often verbal description substitutes for toy-connected activity. (p. 26)

Smilansky's emphasis on speech as indicative of "better" socio-dramatic play is very evident from these extracts, and leads her to the conclusion that *D* children are "act- and object-minded," not "concept- and word-minded" (p. 27). The value judgment which remains implicit in such a conclusion is also made explicit:

We regard verbal imitation and verbal make-believe as an essential supplement to imitative action and make-believe movements. . . . We believe, therefore, that role- and theme-related speech during play enriches the play and adds sources of satisfaction that are absent in action-oriented play. (pp. 27–28)

In Smilansky's evaluation, a child who utters the following is at the highest "developmental stage":

Let's pretend that I'm Mommy and let's pretend that I cut the bread with a knife and fed my baby and now I really must go to lie down because we're having guests this evening. (p. 24)

A child who picks up a mop and uses it as a guitar while singing, "playing," gesturing, and cavorting in the manner pop singers do, would only qualify for a lower stage. Yet it is difficult to see why imitative speech is preferable to and better than imitative action.

The only quantitative measures that were obtained in the comparison of *A* and *D* children are those relating to speech. Some of the differences reported seem very small indeed, but in the absence of any statistical appraisal it is not possible to say which of the differences are reliable. Despite this limitation, Smilansky concludes:

We may summarize the analysis of speech by stating that culturally advantaged children speak more, in longer sentences; and in longer utterances; use a higher percentage of nouns, adverbs, and numbers; use fewer adjectives, conjunctions, and pronouns; and have a richer vocabulary. (p. 46)

But in no account of the comparison of these two groups of children is there any clue as to how characteristic these portrayals are of the two groups—are they true of 95% of the group or only of 55%, or are these patterns seen in *most* children of either group, but with differing frequencies? For teachers of young children it is imperative that such information qualifies the vivid pen portraits. Else this characterization of the "action-bound" lower-class child and the "concept-bound" middle-class child will seep into and become part of the pedagogic dogma, just as at one time it was claimed that the speech of middle-class children is characterized by an "elaborated code" and that of working-class children by a "restricted code" (Bernstein, 1971).

Smilansky went on to introduce different methods of adult intervention in the children's play in order to assess their effects. Three methods or "treatments" were carried out. In the first, A, the intervention consisted of attempts to improve the children's observations and to give them a better understanding of their daily experiences; this was done by visits to places like clinics, shops, etc., and discussions about such visits. This treatment was based on the assumption that disadvantaged children look but do not see—"*they do not understand* what they see and experience" (p. 87).

In the second treatment, B, children were taught how to play, but how this was accomplished is unclear, since all we are told is that children were taught "the techniques by which they can utilize their past experiences and convert them into play material" (p. 97). The third treatment, C, consisted of a combination of both A and B. Three experimental groups were exposed to each of these treatments during a daily hour-and-a-half period of sociodramatic play over a period of three weeks for each of three play themes.

The results demonstrated that treatment A had no effect, treatment B resulted in significant improvement, and treatment C had the greatest effect. Since the evaluative factors place great emphasis on speech, it is likely that "improvement" in play consisted of a greater facility in the use of language, and, in fact, Smilansky did obtain evidence of an increased vocabulary and more use of contextual (play-related) verbalizations. What is surprising is that there is no measure of the originality or the complexity of such play. Play that is sustained and therefore scores on persistence may also be extremely stereotyped and unoriginal. Originality and inventiveness are after all what we look for in encouraging imaginative and dramatic play. A boy of four years who with the aid of a piece of blanket became a snail that crept, then curled up in his shell, then became a wailing ghost, then a butterfly, and finally, spreading the blanket on the ground, rolled himself up tightly in it while saying to a girl companion "I'm a sausage—now fry me," would score low on Smilansky's evaluative scale because of the lack of verbalization. His activities, however, were most graphic, and on any index of originality he would surely score high.

There is a tacit assumption among educationalists, both theorists and practitioners, and among many developmental psychologists, that engaging in dramatic, imaginative, fantasy play is somehow *good* for children. No one seems to be very clear as to wherein such merit may lie, but there is some notion that a child who engages in much fantasy play is of a creative turn of mind, and that this creativity spills over into other areas of intellectual function. In fact, there is no evidence that such creativity is related to superior performance in any other intellectual skill.

In contrast to the Freudian drive-reduction view of fantasy, Singer (1973) sees it as a constructive and useful cognitive skill. He also suggests that opportunity for regular contact with at least one parent whose actions and speech patterns are available for imitation is important, as is the attitude of the parents and the subculture toward imagination.

When Singer's colleagues instituted a program of training for lower-class children (Freyberg, 1973), they found that there was some improvement, in that there was better verbal communication, more creativity, and increased attention span. Nevertheless, these lower-class children were unable to function at a comparable level with the middle-class children. In summary, Freyberg makes this cautious statement:

> Modelling effects and direct teaching by adults can be very effective at certain points in children's development, by serving as a catalyst to develop skills that are basically within the resources of the child. These modelling and teaching effects can result in marked changes in the child's functioning despite some long-term lacks in experiential background and cognitive development. (p. 145)

In Singer's view, fantasy is inherent in the normal functioning of the brain, which requires constant recording and rehearsal of stored material; information is not simply stored inactively. Two principles determine what contents come to mind on a regular basis and which of these are stored effectively. The first of these is *current unfinished business:*

> As we store new material, we label it as more or less relevant to particular urgent issues. In a sense, we "ticket it" for replay as part of a more general plan. (p. 195)

The second principle is a *set* toward attention to inner activities, toward processing and reprocessing. Thus, Singer sees make-believe play as a normal outgrowth of information-processing activity.

Many studies have now replicated the finding that disadvantaged children show less fantasy play than advantaged children, and that play tutoring not only helps remedy this deficit, but also potentiates improved functioning in problem solving (Rosen, 1974), in exploration, innovation, and creativity (Feitelson & Ross, 1973), in I.Q. tests, memory skills, and verbalization skills (Saltz & Johnson, 1974), and associative fluency in tests of creativity (Dansky & Silverman, 1973). Marshall and Hahn (1967) found improvement in peer interaction, and thereupon regarded imaginative play as a vehicle for promoting social development. What is unsatisfactory about these studies, dramatic though their results may be, is the lack of a mechanism or process whereby these results are achieved.

In an original analysis of pretend play, Fein (1975) notes that when objects or materials are prototypical, even two-year-olds perform a transformation—for example, the cup treated as if it were full. When objects are less prototypical, the child must extend his transformational activity so that the object can be treated as something else. Fein's findings suggest that an easy transformation (toy animals to living animals) can support a more difficult one (empty shell to full cup), thereby maintaining a functional relationship between two objects. In other words, "The process whereby one thing is used to symbolise another initially requires a relatively prototypical context which serves to anchor the transformation" (p. 295).

It is generally accepted that the less structured a toy, the less explicit its function(s), and hence the more successful a prop in fantasy play. Feitelson, however, gives a salutory warning concerning this generalization: for children who have not previously engaged in much symbolic play, such props or toys are unsatisfactory, and these children benefit more from literal representations; it is only children who "know how to play" that make the most of the unstructured materials.

Piaget (1951) regards symbolic play as egocentric thought in its pure stage, deriving essentially from the structure of child's thought, which is still prelogical. Emphasizing the distinctions between "signs" and "symbols," Piaget argues that

> the symbolic schema is in no way a concept, either by its form, "the signifier" or by its content, the "signified." In its form it does not go beyond the level of the imitative image or deferred imitation . . . In its content, it is not adapted generalization, but distorting assimilation. (pp. 99–100)

Thus, the symbolic image, the ludic symbol, lies intermediate between sensory-motor schema and the logical concept. "Symbolic play is to representational intelligence what practice play is to sensory-motor intelligence" (p. 163).

Vygotsky (1966), on the other hand, sees both the motivation and the function of (symbolic) play as distinct from those of other activities:

Imagination is a new formation which is not present in the consciousness of
the very young child, is totally absent in animals, and represents a specifically
human form of conscious activity. Like all functions of consciousness, it
originally arises from action. The old adage that child's play is imagination in
action can be reversed: we can say that imagination in adolescents and
school-children is play without action. (p. 8)

Vygotsky uses Sully's now classic example of two sisters "playing" at
being sisters to illustrate and emphasise the rule-bound nature of play—
for example, a girl playing "mother" will have *rules* of maternal behavior
in enacting the role; leading him to conclude that "In play a child is free,
(i.e., he determines his own actions, starting from his own 'I'). But this is
an illusory freedom" (p. 17). Such a conclusion, however, is the result of
Vygotsky's undue emphasis on the structure, as opposed to the *content*,
of role play.

Social Play

Most animal play is social play, and of this perhaps the most popular
is chasing play. Aldis (1975) gives a graphic description of chasing play in
many primates: invitations to play are proffered by one animal "tagging"
another, or, as in the case of gibbons, by "dangling." This play is easily
distinguished from real pursuit and flight by its pace (as when one animal
pauses for the other to catch up), accompaniment of the playface, and
being interspersed with other behaviors, like fighting and rolling. "Ma-
neuvering" is a frequent play activity in predator species like the canids,
and consists of circling and zig-zagging round another (Aldis, 1975).
"Wrestling" in stumptail monkeys is often preceded by "sparring," when

both partners are sitting or squatting and fence with open or partly open
hands, slapping and cuffing at each other. In "king of the castle" one animal
occupies an elevated support and prevents one or several partners coming
from below to displace or join him by slapping, pushing, play biting, and
wrestling. (Bertrand, 1976, p. 323)

Bertrand also notes eight different varieties of rough-and-tumble
play that may be observed in primate species: simple chase, tag, ring-
round-the-bush, hide-and-seek, wrestling and sparring, king-of-the-
castle, tug-of-war, and tickling. Tickling and hide-and-seek were not
often seen, but all the other varieties were observed in many species.
These varieties of play fall into one or other of two categories—*contact play*
(i.e., wrestling, sparring), or *distance play*, involving chasing.

The description of serious and play chase in the chimpanzee by
Loizos (1967) is most evocative:

During a serious chase, the pursuer rarely takes his eyes off the pursued animal. His fur is erect and bristling, his lips are pursed and protruded in the aggressive manner. His movements are rapid and economical; if he catches the animal he is pursuing, the sequence of events will be snatch, grab, pull-towards-mouth and bite, at whatever portion of the offender is most readily available. Such interactions are often ended by the pursued animal's renewed escape, accompanied by loud screams and possibly by the fear grimace, in which both rows of teeth are bared, often including the gums.

A play-chase, one the other hand, takes place at an altogether different tempo. The initiator may approach another animal by walking or trotting towards him with a highly characteristic bounce to the gait; the head bobs up and down, his gaze may not be directed at the animal he approaches, he is often wearing a playface, and soft guttural exhalations may be audible. (The playface is a special expression indicating playful intent in which only the lower teeth show. It appears to occur most often at the beginning of a playful interaction, the point at which it is most necessary to avoid being misunderstood.) As he reaches the animal he is approaching and gains his attention he turns around and makes off at a slow lolloping pace in the opposite direction, looking back over his shoulder to see if the other animal is following. His head is still bobbing, he is still wearing the playface. If the other animal responds and takes up the chase the tempo may quicken slightly and the playface become less evident. (pp. 182–83)

Mother–infant play is readily observable in chimpanzees (Van Lawick-Goodall, 1968), and is at its most frequent when the infant is between four and six months old. Play is generally initiated by the mother, and Dolhinow and Bishop (1970) suspect that often the mothers are using it as a distraction—instead of punishing or restraining an infant, the mother initiates play. This is in contrast to monkey mothers, who do restrain and punish their infants physically, and only tolerate, rather than reciprocate, their infant's approaches.

The commonest type of play between mother and infants is the game of peek-a-boo. In a neat analysis, Bruner and Sherwood (1976) have shown that this game has a "syntax" which is governed by a set of rules. The four basic rules are: Initial contact; Disappearance; Reappearance; Reestablished contact. Once these rules have been mastered, any one of several variants may be "generated." One feature of the game that is severely constrained is the duration of disappearance, but it seems to be a constraint of which the mother is very aware. This seems to be the earliest example in the development of rule-governed games.

Harlow and Harlow (1962) described rough-and-tumble play in rhesus monkeys; this involved play activities resulting in bodily contact. Blurton-Jones (1967), on the other hand, uses the term to refer to seven assorted behavior patterns of children, namely, running, chasing, fleeing, wrestling, jumping up and down with both feet together, beating at each other but not hitting, and laughing. It seems unlikely that for much of the time all, or most, of these seven patterns cluster together motivationally. For instance, we have found the incidence of running and chasing to be far greater than that of wrestling; moreover, whereas running and chasing may involve familiar acquaintances, wrestling occurs only between siblings, or children who know each other extremely well.

The contrasting preferences for toys and peers is nicely illustrated in a study by Scholtz and Ellis (1975). With repeated exposure to a play setting with play equipment and objects, four- and five-year-old children became increasingly bored with the toys, and showed increasing preference for playing with their peers.

A most original analysis of social play was made recently by Garvey (1974), who defines such play as "a state of engagement in which the successive, nonliteral behaviors of one partner are contingent on the nonliteral behaviors of the other partner" (p. 163). This definition thus excludes those episodes in which the participants do not modify or influence each other's behavior. Having recorded the behavior and utterances of child dyads (ranging in age from 3½–5½ years), Garvey extracted the ritual play sequences, that is, those composed of repetitive, rhythmic exchanges. She described the structure of interactions in terms of the rules governing alternation of participation (turns), the substantive and formal relations of the behaviors, and the manner in which sequences are built up (rounds). The first speaker is identified as X and the second as Y. In the following examples from Garvey, (p. 167), A is the most ritualized; it is marked as nonliteral by singsong intonation and so forth. In A the rule is that all aspects of the second turn must be identical. In B, however, there is a sequential relation—assertion followed by counterassertion.

	X's Turn	Y's Turn
A	Bye, mommy	Bye, mommy
	Bye, mommy	Bye, mommy
B	Hello, my name is Mr. Donkey.	Hello, my name is Mr. Elephant.
	Hello, my name is Mr. Tiger.	Hello, my name is Mr. Lion.
C	I have to go to work.	You're already at work.
	No, I'm not.	
	I have to go to school.	You're already at school.
	No, I'm not.	

Patterns A and B have a symmetrical distribution of turns, but C's turns are asymmetrically distributed. Garvey argues that certain abilities must be assumed if such structures are to be explained. The first of these is the ability to make a Reality/Play distinction. Children give ample evidence of being able to make such a distinction, as in this example (p. 170):

(X sits on 3-legged stool that has magnifying glass in its center)
X   I've got to go to the potty.

                    Y   (turns to him) Really?

X   (grins) No, pretend.

                    Y   (smiles and watches X).

The use of words like "pretend" or "really" or role assignment, such as "I'll be the Indian and you be the Cowboy," are explicit lexical markers for the state of play.

A second ability that is required is the ability to abstract rules, and the most basic rule in this case is reciprocity, that is, taking turns. Other rules may apply to the content of the roles, for example, "No, Daleks don't speak like that." The third ability required for social play is the ability to construct jointly the theme of the activity and to develop it in accordance with a *shared* image. Garvey's example again illustrates this well (p. 174):

(X is busy cooking at the stove: Y watches)
X   OK, dinner is ready. Now what do
    you want for dinner? (turns to Y)

                    Y   Well . . . (indecisively)

X   Hot beef?

                    Y   OK, hot beef.

X   Coffee, too?

                    Y   No, I'm the little boy. I'll have some
                       milk.

X   OK, you can eat now.

                    Y   (moves closer to stove)

X   Kid, we're going to get some milk from
    the store. Come on in the dunebuggy.

                    Y   OK, I'm in the dunebuggy.

(Dunebuggy is a small toy car; X pushes it and Y moves beside it.)

Garvey's formal analysis of episodes of social play is instructive, and could well be extended to other forms of dyadic interaction.

Play with Language

From early infancy children may be heard to play with sounds, the repetition of syllables being the commonest form—da-da, goo-goo. Repetitive, rhythmic vocalizations also accompany states of pleasure. Onomatopoeic sounds are also repeated—beep-beep, brmm-brmm. Garvey (1977) gives the example of a three-year-old girl who played with the word "yesterday," varying its syllabic structure. This excerpt (p. 87) shows primary and secondary stress transcription:

                yéster yéster yèsterdáy
                yésterdày yès tóo . . .
                yèster díy yéster yèsterdáy . . .
                yés tér yéster . . .

Garvey distinguishes three types of social play with language: spontaneous rhyming and word play; play with fantasy and nonsense; play with speech acts and discourse conventions. Examples of each type will be informative. Rhyming and word play reflect the child's fondness for alliteration—*high/sky* or *sparky/darky,* as in the following ritual (p. 89):

Girl	Boy
(wandering)	(moving ironing board)
'cause it's fishy too	
'cause it has fishes	
	and it's snaky too, 'cause it has snakes
	and it's beary too because it has bears
and it's and it's hatty	
'cause it has hats	

In fantasy and nonsense play there may be nonsense syllables, such as poopaw, splishsplash, or funny names or words introduced (p. 90):

Mrs. Fingernail (smiles and looks expectantly at partner)	
	Toop poop (laughs)
	Hey, are you Mrs. Fingernail?
Yes, I'm Mrs. Fingernail (said proudly)	
	Poop! Mrs. Fingernail.

Other nonsense play may consist of outrageous statements or stories. Play with speech acts consists of contravening implicit assumptions, for example, play threats, or a refusal to take up invitation to a conversation.

Weir's (1962) recordings and analyses of her two-year-old son's monologues as he prepared to sleep are a classic in the literature of language development, and also illustrate well forms of language play. The sequence (p. 109):

> What colour
> What colour blanket
> What colour mop
> What colour glass

for instance is an exercise in noun substitution. Another favorite transformation of Anthony's was the question to nonquestion or vice versa (p. 112):

> Step on the blanket
> Where is Anthony's blanket

Such play with language gives us some insight into what may well be the rehearsal-and-consolidation function of play.

Cazden (1974) makes some profound observations in the course of discussing developmental stages in linguistic awareness. She regards play with language as a normal part of language development. Speaking and listening are primary linguistic activities, whereas reading is a secondary type of activity (Kavanaugh & Mattingly, 1972). During these activities, Cazden remarks, the language itself is *transparent*, that is, the speaker, listener, or reader is not paying attention to the words themselves, but to their meaning. But language can be made *opaque*, or become the focus of attention, and this is what Cazden calls metalinguistic awareness:

> Metalinguistic awareness, the ability to make language forms opaque and attend to them in and for themselves, is a special kind of language performance, one which makes special cognitive demands, and seems to be less easily and less universally acquired than the language performances of speaking and listening. (p. 13)

Cazden gives examples (from Gleitman, Gleitman, & Shipley, 1972) of the difficulty experienced by an eight-year-old child in trying to analyze sentences deliberately constructed to sound "funny":

a. LG: *I saw the queen and you saw one.*
   C: No, because you're saying that one person saw a queen and one person saw a one—ha ha—what's a one?

b. LG: How about this one: *I am knowing your sister.*
   C: No: *I know your sister.*
   LG: Why not *I am knowing your sister?* You can say *I am eating your dinner.*
   C: It's different! (shouting) You say different sentences in different ways! Otherwise it wouldn't make sense.

(Cazden, 1974, p. 15).

Play with words—with their phonetic, syntatic, or semantic aspects—is an indication of this metalinguistic awareness. As we shall see later, children can be playful only with the known and the familiar; they must become proficient in the utilitarian, that is, communicative, function of language before they are able to use language in a ludic manner. Thus it is only late in childhood that we observe play with the meanings of words as in puns and riddles:

> Police: You can't park here.
> Driver: Why not?
> Police: Read that sign.
> Driver: I did. It says, "Fine for parking."
>
> Q. What did Tenne-see?
> A. The same thing Arkan-saw.
> (Cazden, 1974, p. 19)

Games

As children pass into late childhood and toward puberty, fantasy and other forms of social play decline and are replaced by games, the characteristic features of which are explicit rules and conventions. Games form the last of Piaget's three categories of play. Piaget (1932) believes that much may be learned about the child's understanding of morality by observing his acceptance and adherence to the rules and the sanctions he may see as operative. He thus made a very careful study of the manner in which children played the game of marbles. He distinguished between the *practice* of rules and the *consciousness* of rules. He observed four stages in the practice of rules:

1. Motor and individual stage—since play is largely solitary and idiosyncratic there can be no collective rules.
2. Egocentric stage—between the ages of two and five years, play is still solitary or parallel at best; rule is only imitated, not codified.
3. Stage of incipient cooperation—at about seven or eight years, each player tries to win and, although some consensus is achieved, ideas about the rules are still vague.
4. Codification of rules—at 11/12 years, details of procedure are fixed and code of rules known and accepted by everyone.

The consciousness of rules consists of three stages:

1. Rules are not coercive or obligatory.
2. Rules are regarded as sacred, emanating from adults (authority) and any variation is a transgression.
3. Rules are arrived at by mutual consent and may be altered by agreement.

Thus Piaget sees the child's application and appreciation of the rules of a game as a reflection not only of socialisation but also of the development of morality or conscience.

The work of Eifermann (1971a, 1972, 1976) made a substantial contribution, both theoretically and empirically, to our understanding of children's games. With 150 observers she made systematic observations of several thousand children of all age groups, socioeconomic classes, geographical areas, and type of home circumstance in Israel. She questions Piaget's statement that, as practice and symbolic play decline, games with rules increase, and continue to do so with age. She found that participation in rule-governed games increased until the age of 10 years and then declined. The peak for *competitive* rule-governed games was slightly later—at 11 years. Eifermann (1971b) also disputes Piaget's assumption that all rule-governed games are competitive, and his belief that in solitary games rules would be useless. She argues that cooperative games too have rules, and that even in individual games rules and sanctions may be applied, as when the contravention of a rule carries the sanction, say, that the player *must* start again. Piaget's interpretation of games entirely in terms of assimilation and social accommodation is not acceptable to Eifermann, for whom the critical factor in maintaining such games is that of *challenge,* which is a function of the individual's competence and his culture:

> Thus, a game will present a meaningful challenge to the child only if the degree of skill and understanding required for playing it, or for fulfilling a certain role in it, is both within the child's capacities, and is at the same time such as not to predetermine completely the outcome of a particular round of this game. (p. 287)

The challenge in competitive games is self-evident, but there is a challenge in cooperative and solitary games as well, which is that of achieving excellence in performance. Eifermann also attributes the different patterns of games (Steady, Recurrent, Sporadic, or One-Shot) to the nature of the challenges inherent in them:

> A game is steady if it allows each participant to adjust the extent of the challenge to his abilities at that time, while still leaving the outcome of an individual round of such a game sufficiently undetermined. A game is recurrent, if, after the hierarchy of the players has become stabilized, the outcome of any particular round has become predictable and independent of the extent of challenge the players are ready to take upon themselves. A game is sporadic if there is little variation in the extent of the challenge. One-shot games (of which the only clear-cut instance known to me is hulahoop) are games with considerable initial challenge, but such that the mastery obtainable in them after some time is of a kind which the child has no hope of increasing even if he were to take it up again after a lapse of a year or two. (p. 454)

Having studied games in kibbutz children, Eifermann (1976) concludes that cooperation and competition cannot be regarded as opposite poles of the same dimension. Wholly cooperative games are hardly played at all, neither are individual competitive games. The games most commonly played are those which demand cooperation between players to achieve a common aim—in other words, cooperative games within a competitive context. Kibbutz children also "insist that in singleton games there should be as few overprivileged or underprivileged participants as possible, so that egalitarianism be preserved" (p. 586). In this manner, the styles of preferred games appear to reflect the social organization and ethos of the society in which the participants live.

Sutton-Smith and Rosenberg (1971) have documented the changes that have taken place in the game preferences of boys and girls over the period from 1896 to 1959. The data show a marked shift in girls' preferences toward those of the boys, resulting in greater similarity between the sexes. Surprisingly, however, the girls' preferences for symbolic, make-believe games has not changed similarly:

> Apparently, in becoming more masculine, girls have not been concerned to identify themselves with these fantasy roles which are so important to boys. This raises an important question: Why should girls show an increasing preference for the minor and major sports of boys (e.g., Marbles and Swim-

ming), but not for these dramatized male games? The simplest interpretation
is that girls are following the lead of women, that while women have shown
increased interest and participation in men's sports, they have not so extensively taken over the warrior-like activities of men (Soldiers, Cops, Cowboys).
It would be of interest to know whether girls' play is similar in those cultures
where the women have, in recent years, been assuming warrior-like functions
(Israel and China). (p. 36)

Nevertheless, the symbolic play preferences of boys have changed in
that they show a shift away from those games preferred by girls. As
Sutton-Smith and Rosenberg interpret it: "because girls have encroached
upon the play preferences of boys . . . boys have attempted to clarify
their own distinctness by lowering their preference for any games that are
not obviously masculine" (p. 37), thus leaving boys with a much more
circumscribed choice of games. The increased interest of girls in
Dressing-up play is attributed to a "shift in interest from the feminine
domestic to the feminine glamour role" (p. 38). In terms of individual skill
contemporary children are less rough in their play, possibly due to
greater supervision and control. There has been a reduction, too, in
formal group play, and Sutton-Smith and Rosenberg surmise that this
trend will continue in our more permissive, egalitarian latter twentieth-
century society.

EXPLORATION AND PLAY

Exploration is the activity which is most often confused with play,
and it therefore requires especial elucidation.

In his admirable review of the subject, Fowler (1965) has described
the historical and conceptual development of formulations in the domain
of exploratory behavior. Proceeding from the stage where exploration
was "the behavior without a definition," we have reached a point where
both increasing specificity in conceptualization and increasing generality
in terms of empirical findings are possible.

Fowler (1965) described two groups of theory which are in apparent
antithesis—the "curiosity" group and the "boredom" group. The advo-
cates of the former group are notably Berlyne (whose original statement
was made in 1950), Montgomery (1951, 1953), and Harlow (1950, 1953). To
oversimplify, this theory (titillation) postulated that novel stimuli would
evoke an exploratory drive, the strength of which would wane with
continued exposure to the stimulus. The "boredom" (tedium) theorists,
on the other hand, (e.g., Glanzer, 1953; Myers & Miller, 1954), proposed
that continued exposure to the same stimuli would result in satiation to
these stimuli (boredom); thus, subjects would consequently attend to or
explore any change in the stimulus configuration. Fowler conceded that

aspects of both these theories might be applicable—presumably to the same set of empirical data. The difference in emphases of the two theories does, however, generate rather different predictions. In terms of the "curiosity" theory, strength of exploratory drive, and hence response strength, should be a direct function of the novelty or complexity of the stimulus, the degree of familiarity of the rest of the situation having little effect. On the basis of the "boredom" theory, exploratory strength would be primarily a function of the familiarity of the situation rather than of the degree of stimulus change, provided there was a stimulus change. (These predictions were in fact tested and will be referred to later on.) In other words, the titillation theorists were concerned with "specific" exploration, and the tedium theorists with "diversive" exploration.

Thus, it seems that both these theories are valid insofar as they apply to different sets of antecedent conditions. This distinction will become more apparent if we consider results pertaining to the temporal course of exploration. There is a progressive decrement in exploratory activity with continued exposure to the source of stimulation; this decrement has been interpreted in terms of Hullian principles of response inhibition (Berlyne, 1950, 1955), in terms of stimulus satiation (Glanzer, 1958), and in terms of the decrease in drive strength (Montgomery, 1953). On the other hand, workers from the Wisconsin Laboratory emphasized the prepotency of exploration and "curiosity drive" in interpreting the persistent and non-decremental temporal pattern of exploratory activities (Butler & Alexander, 1955; Butler & Harlow, 1954; Harlow, Blazek, & McClearn, 1956). The interpretation of the latter sets of results, however, needs some qualification in view of the nature of the experimental situation utilized. In these studies, the animals were typically restrained in small bare cages with no alternative source of stimulation. Thus, the character of the response elicited is radically different—in the case of the "curiosity" studies it is a consummatory response to a stimulus change, in the "boredom" studies it is an instrumental response *for* a stimulus change (Fowler, 1965). Confusion is worse confounded by the frequent failure to describe accurately the subjects' responses—we are more often told *how much* the animal did than *what* it did. For example, in the Butler and Harlow (1954) study, the monkey was said to be visually exploring when the trap door was held upon for relatively long periods of time. Symmes (1959), however, reported that, in a similar situation, the monkeys "very commonly sat near the door holding it open with one hand, and moving it against the spring resistance, and only occasionally turning to look through the opening" (p. 186). The animals continued to do this even if there was complete darkness outside the door. Thus, there is no equivalence in the responses, *qua* responses, of the "curious" animals and the "boredom-alleviating" animals.

Apart from differences in antecedent conditions, we are also concerned in the one case (specific) with those stimulus attributes that *elicit* attention, and in the other (diversive) with those attributes that *maintain* attention; and they are very unlikely to be the same. Many workers have shown that stimulus changes that are made contingent on such instrumental responses are able to reinforce them (Barnes & Kish, 1961; Butler, 1957; Harlow & McClearn, 1954; Kish & Antonitis, 1956; Moon & Lodahl, 1956); Kish (1955) has formulated this: "A perceptible environmental change . . . will reinforce any response that it follows" (p. 261). But whereas specific exploration is greater the greater the stimulus change, instrumental responses seem best reinforced by moderate stimulus changes (see Fowler, 1965; Leuba & Friedlander, 1968). Nuttin (1973) has recently suggested that the *stimulus change* explanation of reinforcement be replaced by an *event production* explanation. Thus, specific and diversive exploratory activities may be distinguished from each other on a number of grounds.

Selective attention is largely under the control of the "collative" properties of stimuli (Berlyne, 1960). In infancy this attention generally consists of visual inspection, and stimuli high in novelty, complexity, ambiguity, and contrast elicit the greatest attention. In early development such selective attention is important, since it invests the stimuli that elicit it with an affective component. In other words, children say that they "like" or "prefer" those stimuli and objects which hold their attention longest (Aitken & Hutt, 1974; Hutt & McGrew, 1969); and will even work to obtain such stimuli (Aitken & Hutt, 1975; Hutt, 1975). This dependence of liking on attention was most clearly manifest in a study which compared attention to pleasant, unpleasant, and neutral pictures (Hutt, Forrest, & Newton, 1976). Irrespective of their affective tone, five-year-old children claimed to like those pictures which they looked at most, whereas this dependency was not so evident at the age of seven. It is the confluence of these perceptual and affective response modes which we refer to as *interest*.

For our own studies of exploration in preschool children, we designed a new "toy" (see Figure 1) (Hutt, 1966). Into this toy were built sounds and lights which were contingent on certain operations on the toy. For instance, pushing a lever in one direction might work a bell (or an orange light), and in another a buzzer (or a green light.) In doing this we hoped to find out, quite precisely, how much a child learned about the properties of the toy through exploration.

In the course of our studies we saw altogether 128 three- to five-year-olds, and the pattern of specific exploration was fairly similar in all children (Hutt, 1967b). First the children would approach and inspect the toy, and then investigate it, some more tentatively than others. During

FIGURE 1. The new "toy."

this period of active investigation and manipulation the child's posture and expression were of concentration; the child closely watched as he investigated all aspects of the toy. Having done so, he then began to use the toy "playfully." Such behavior was readily distinguished from the specific exploration which preceded it: the child's posture and expression were now relaxed, he did not need to watch closely as he handled and manipulated it, and there might follow any one of a variety of responses. Having learned the properties of this new toy, he was using that knowledge in his play. The quest changed from inquiry to invention, and the child no longer asked himself "What does this *object* do?" but "What can *I* do with this object?" And though investigation declined with time, playful activity increased to a peak before declining (Hutt, 1967a). The distinctive features of investigation and play as we observed them in this series of studies are given in Table I (A) and formalized as laws pertaining to specific and diversive exploration in Table I (B). It may be seen that, though specific exploration is obligatory, diversive exploration is optional and idiosyncratic.

Most surprisingly, we found that if children engaged in play with this toy prematurely, that is, before they had learned all there was to know about it, they might not acquire any further information during

TABLE I. Characteristics of Investigation and Play, and More Generally of Specific and Diversive Exploration[a]

A. Investigation	Play
1. Synchrony of visual and tactile receptors	Desynchrony, or only transient synchrony of receptors
2. Intent facial expression	Relaxed facial expression
3. Stereotyped sequence of behavioral elements	Variable and idiosyncratic sequence of elements
4. Elements of relatively long duration	Elements essentially brief
5. Elicited by novel stimuli	Never manifest in the presence of novel stimuli
6. Implicit query: "What does this *object* do?"	Implicit query: "What can *I* do with this object?"
7. Shows linear decrement with time	Is quadratic function of time
B. Specific exploration	Diversive exploration
1. Concerns those inspective, investigative responses directed to a particular source of stimulation, i.e., *stimulus-oriented*	Concerns those activities which seem to increase stimulation irrespective of source, i.e., *response-oriented*
2. Occurs in *presence* of highly stimulating (by virtue of novelty, complexity, etc.) set of environmental factors	Occurs in *absence* of specific environmental stimulation
3. Consists of consummatory response *to* stimulus change	Consists of instrumental response *for* stimulus change
4. Attention governed by external cues	Attention dependent on internal state
5. Characterized by response stereotypy	Characterized by response variability or entropy
6. Occupies superordinate position in motivational hierarchy in that it can inhibit most tissue-preserving activities	Low in motivational hierarchy and can be inhibited by almost any other drive state

[a] From Hutt, 1970.

their play. Thus, a boy, having found the bell and incorporated it in a game in which he ran round the room pulling a truck and ringing the bell twice each time he passed the toy, failed to find out about the buzzer. Learning during this "playful" phase, therefore, was largely accidental. If, during such play, the child chanced upon the lever movement which operated the buzzer, then a further period of exploration would ensue. Thus, playful behavior may actually *preclude* learning, in the sense of acquiring information from a novel or unfamiliar source. It is easy to see how this is so: on presentation of something new, something not encountered before, the child is *set* to investigate and find out about it. The orienting reaction, of course, is one of the most primitive and earliest manifest responses in our behavioral repertoire. Pavlov termed it the "what-is-it" reflex. New materials, objects, or toys are not involved in play until the child feels quite familiar with them. It is important to stress that this criterion is a subjective rather than an objective one—playful behavior emerges when the child *feels* he has learned all there is to know about an object, rather than when he *has* actually learned about it. Herein lies the danger of the premature appearance of symbolic play, for we should not expect learning necessarily to occur during such activity. The motivation for the behavior is clearly different—the child engages in fantasy or symbolic play because he chooses to, for his own enjoyment, and he seeks no other fulfillment.

As a result of these distinctive motivational states associated with specific and diversive exploration, we found that children would tolerate interruption of one but not the other. In other words, children did not seem to mind unduly if an adult interrupted when they were "playing," but did get annoyed if an attempt at intervention was made while they were exploring. It appears that exploration is an activity akin to problem solving, and arouses, in Berlyne's terms, *perceptual curiosity*, a state of drive or discomfort which can only be alleviated by specific exploration; during such exploration the child is likely to absorb the new information at a rate compatible with his cognitive capacity, and hence appears to resist any attempt to hasten or impede him. During playful activity, on the other hand, the primary motive being enjoyment, the child does not mind interruption.

As we are accustomed to refer to both these categories of behavior as "play," it becomes very difficult to communicate the significance and implications of the distinction between them. This difficulty led to an attempt to develop a taxonomy of play which would permit such distinctions to be made. But before outlining this scheme, another related series of studies needs to be described.

Since, by the age of three years, these two classes of behavior are clearly distinguishable, we were interested to know when, in development, they became discriminable from each other, and how early in life children were capable of symbolic play. Children were seen, together with their mothers, at six months, 12 months, and 24 months of age. At each session, after a period of play and acclimatization, each child was given a novel toy to explore, appropriate for its age. The child's behavior was videorecorded by one camera while its heart rate was telemetered and the paper trace recorded by another camera. The two pictures were then superimposed to give a composite picture of behavior with accompanying heart-rate changes (see Figure 2). We monitored heart rate because these measures have been shown to be particularly informative in the study of infant attention, and this supplementary information would make it easier to interpret behavior that was ambiguous.

When an individual is attentive to external sources of stimulation, heart rate decreases; when he is anxious or apprehensive, heart rate tends to increase. Apart from these phasic changes in heart rate associated with behavior there is yet another feature of cardiac function whose significance has only recently been noted, that is, heart rate *variability*. When a

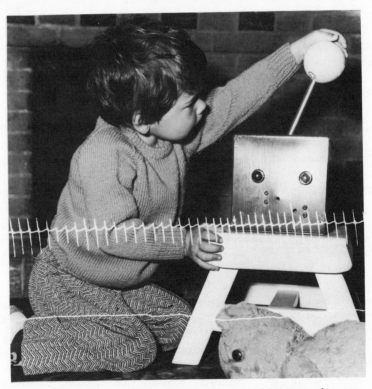

FIGURE 2. Composite picture showing behavior and heart-rate changes.

person is relaxed and lying or sitting quietly, the heart beats are not exactly regular, so that the interval between successive beats may not be the same. If the temporal intervals between beats are converted by some means into distance and written out on a paper trace (cardiotachograph) we have upward and downward deflections of the trace corresponding to acceleration and deceleration respectively, and a steady horizontal line in the case of an extremely stable and regular heart rate (see Figures 3 and 4). Thus the amount of "choppiness" in the cardiotachograph would indicate the degree of beat-to-beat fluctuation, referred to as *variability*. When an individual is engaged in mental activity, however, this variability is suppressed. This phenomenon has recently been made much use of in certain industrial operations and flight tasks in order to ascertain the "mental load" of the task (see Rolfe, 1973). The greater the mental effort involved, that is, the more difficult the task, the greater appears to be the suppression of variability.

We wondered, therefore, if this phenomenon also occurred in very young children and, if so, whether it could be used as another index to help distinguish between different behavioral categories. At six months and at 12 months of age the child's behavioral repertoire was rather limited, and we were unable to differentiate unambiguously between specific exploration and playful behavior. For instance, the infant might squeeze a squeaky toy while looking away, but with a very serious expression. By the age of two years, however, it was considerably easier

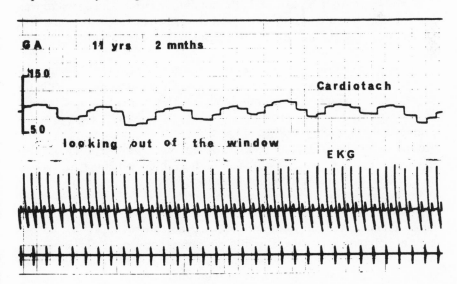

FIGURE 3. Example of cardiotachograph showing considerable variability while subject is relaxed.

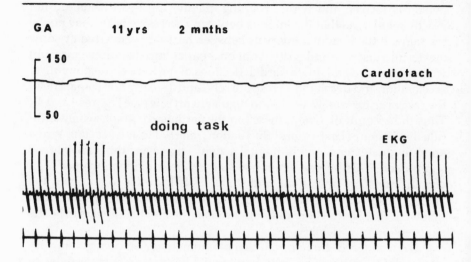

FIGURE 4. Example of cardiotachograph showing variability suppressed during a task.

to distinguish these behaviors. At this age the child was also given a problem to solve—a six-piece formboard. What is interesting is that every child appeared to know exactly what was expected of him: when the board was placed in front of him with the pieces around it, he immediately picked up a piece and attempted to insert it. The problem was tackled with great concentration, and never, except when a piece was successfully inserted or the puzzle completed, did the children smile or laugh during its execution.

There were thus three phases in the experiment: (1) the familiarization and *play* phase, when the child was given three toys to play with; (2) the *exploratory* phase, when a completely new toy was substituted for one of the familiar toys; (3) the *problem* phase. Behaviorally, the play and problem phases were readily distinguished: smiles and looking away or around or looking at mother were most infrequent during problem solving compared with play. During exploration, however, the expressions and general posture were very similar to those occurring during solving of the problem, but there were more instances of examination and visual inspection of the toy and parts of it during the former than during the latter. Thus, though the differentiation of problem-solving behavior from playful behavior was easy, the differentiation between exploration and problem solving was much less clear cut. Exploration and play, of course, differed in the many respects already enumerated.

Next, the heart-rate variability associated with these three phases was examined, and it was found that variability was greatest during play and least during problem solving (see Figure 5). Variability during exploration was less than during play, and was more similar to that during problem solving; in fact, in boys they were indistinguishable from each other. Girls and boys differed slightly in overall amount of variability, but the trend in each sex was the same.

These data from cardiovascular function therefore strengthened the interpretation that when a child is playing he is engaged in less mental effort, he is more relaxed, and less attentive to external sources of stimulation. By virtue of both behavioral indices and heart-rate measures, play activity is seen to differ distinctly from problem solving activity, and exploration, though clearly different from play in terms of heart rate, shares some similarities with the behavior. But all these behaviors are commonly referred to as play, in the circular manner that much of what children do is considered play—because children do it. It seemed that if we were not to be repeatedly confronted by incontrovertible clichés like "children learn through play" or "play is children's work," a more precise classification was imperative (Hutt, 1979).

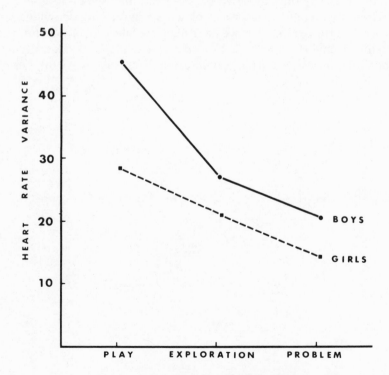

FIGURE 5. Heart rate variability during play, exploration, and problem-solving for girls and boys.

A TAXONOMY OF PLAY

There now seems to be ample evidence for distinguishing between two major subdivisions of all those intrinsically motivated, self-chosen activities we call play: *epistemic* behavior and *ludic* behavior, that is, behavior which is concerned with knowledge and information, and behavior which is playful. These two categories differ in very many respects, as we shall see, and they are similar to, but not identical with, specific and diversive exploration respectively, which were discussed earlier. These categories differ first in their focus of attention, epistemic behavior being cued by an external source of stimulation, whereas ludic behavior lacks such a specific focus. Second, though epistemic behaviors are relatively independent of mood state, ludic behavior is highly mood-dependent—the child plays because he wishes to and simply for the fun of it, and if he is anxious it is hardly reasonable to expect him to "have fun." Third, there are constraints imposed on epistemic behavior which stem from the nature of the focus of attention, whereas any constraints in ludic behavior are only those which the child imposes on himself.

These two major categories of play may be further subdivided (see Figure 6): on the extreme left we have most tasklike or worklike forms of epistemic behavior, namely, *problem-solving* activities—puzzles, jigsaws, formboards, mazes, etc. To a certain extent, the objective is inherent in

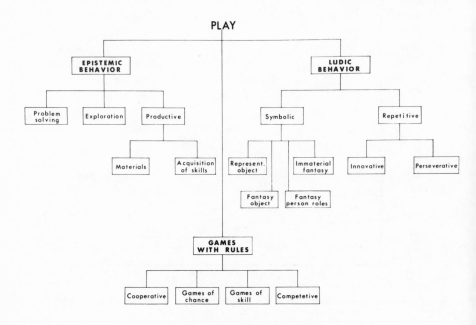

FIGURE 6. A taxonomy of play.

the task itself: the two-year old does not need to be told what to do with the formboard, for as it is placed before him he reaches out to pick up the pieces and promptly inserts them. The desire to achieve solution wholly constrains the child, and the particular behavior patterns shown are determined only by the nature of the problem. An equivalent of this category for the adult may be the solution of crosswords.

A second subdivision of epistemic activity whose objectives are only a little less explicit is that of *exploration* (specific): here again, the particular manipulatory movements depend on the object or material being explored, but the behavior will be recognized by its attentive features of inspection and investigation, and the other features already described as characteristic of specific exploration (Hutt, 1970).

The third subdivision of epistemic behavior we have termed *productive*, since it concerns those activities which are designed to effect a change, which alters the state of the material with which the child is engaged or the performance of the individual. This change is demonstrable whether it concerns actions or the substance acted on. Since there are these two types of processes involved, we may further subdivide the category accordingly: into those activities involving *materials*, such as sand, clay, paper, etc., and those involving *skills*. Thus, the child might make a bridge or castle with sand, a snake with plasticine, or a collage scene. In each case, the end product is implicit in the child's activity; in other words, although the end product may not be evident from the activities themselves, the child is nevertheless aware of the end to be achieved, and can usually make it explicit if requested to do so. With skills like riding a scooter or bicycle, throwing and catching balls, or skipping, the end state to be achieved is *competence*, and therefore demonstrably different from the initial state of incompetence.

In fact, most young children of about five do make this distinction between work and play. In general, those activities in which they feel constraints do constitute work, those they have fun doing constitute play. Epistemic behaviors which require effort, sustained attention, and persistence tend to be considered more like work, and therefore distinct from the more light-hearted, enjoyable, ludic behaviors. It is suggested that the distinction the children are making in this differentiation is between feeling constrained and feeling free.

Epistemic behavior is also capable of overriding particular mood states. Because of the external cueing of attention, even a shy and apprehensive child may be distracted by being made to solve a jigsaw puzzle. Ludic behavior, on the other hand, depending on interiorized imagery, is highly sensitive to mood states, and may only be elicited when the child feels relaxed and well.

Ludic behavior may be subdivided into two major categories—*symbolic* (or *fantasy*) play, and play which has a *repetitive* element.

Symbolic play may be further subdivided according to the focus of the fantasy. The pretense may concern some article or object, as when a stool serves as a hospital trolley or a plate as a steering wheel (*fantasy object*); or it may involve the child becoming another character (*fantasy person*) such as fireman, Dr. Who, doctor, etc.; or it may involve something entirely conjured out of the imagination with no material props at all (*immaterial fantasy*), as when a child takes Black Beauty for a walk. These categories of fantasy play were developed by Charmian Davie in a study of young children in their homes, and are defined principally in terms of the focus of the imagination or fantasy (Davie, Forrest, Hutt, Mason, Vincent, & Ward, 1975). We shall return to a further discussion of symbolic play after completion of the taxonomy.

Repetitive play may contain new features admixed with the repetition of certain patterns, as in the game where a child runs around the room ringing the bell of our novel toy each time he passes it, but each time doing so with a different part of his anatomy—palm, elbow, head, shoulder, and even foot. Again, a child may rehearse an acquired skill like catching a ball bounced off a wall, but may bounce off different parts of the wall—high, low, far left, far right, etc. Play that involves the repetition of certain actions but also introduces some novel elements may be called *innovative*, and in such play the child is consolidating some skill or knowledge while introducing some novelty to prevent the execution of such skill from becoming monotonous, as well as perhaps to extend "combination flexibility" (Bruner, 1976). Where actions are repeated without any novel features, they become *perseverative*. The most extreme examples of such activity are the sterotypies of autistic children, where the same sequence of actions is repeated in unvarying form over and over again (Hutt, S. J., & Hutt, C., 1968; Hutt, C., & Hutt, S. J., 1970). Although such extreme manifestations of perseverative behavior are rare in normal children, we may regard thumbsucking, rocking, or some such repetitive mannerism as falling in this category.

The categories of epistemic behavior are defined primarily in functional terms, whereas the categories of ludic behavior are defined more in morphological terms. These relative emphases are the inevitable consequence of the salient features of the behaviors involved: epistemic behaviors are distinguished by the salience of their objectives or goals, whereas what characterizes all ludic behavior is its repetition, its exaggeration, its lack of economy (Loizos, 1967), its galumphing quality (Miller, 1973), or its pretense.

This taxonomy accords well with distinctions that many other authors have attempted to draw. Bruner & Sherwood (1976) remark that

> the difference between play and work is that in the latter the objective is held
> invariant and the means are varied for achieving it. In play, an animal varies

both means and objectives, gaining a better conception of the possibilities of connections and consequences that can be stored as generative knowledge for the future. (p. 153)

Although one may have reservations as to how far such quasi-hypothetical activity could function as a generative store, the essential distinction parallels that made in the present taxonomy. Berlyne (1970) states:

Of these two forms of exploratory behaviour, (specific and diversive), the diversive form may have more affinities with autistic or free-associative thinking, but directed thinking and reasoning must be more closely related to specific exploration. Thus specific exploration and directed thinking are aimed at access to information that can relieve specific subjective uncertainties. Both can be regarded as means of relieving an aversive condition due to lack of information. Both seem to arise from the kinds of motivational condition that, in everyday parlance, we call "curiosity." (p. 967)

Indeed, the parallel between child's play and adult thought has been noted by Freud, by Piaget, and by Vygotsky.

Play enables the child to reexperience, to remold past impressions and events and their accompanying moods and emotions. *Playful repetition provides essential, possibly indispensible steps toward concept formation.* Freud defines thinking as test-acting (*Probehandeln*) carried out with a minimum of expenditure of energy. By pointing out the similarities between thought processes and direct action, by looking for their common denominator, we gain a better understanding. (Peller, 1971, p. 124)

The customary differentiation of thinking into directed or focussed thought and associative thought (reverie or reminiscence [Berlyne, 1965]) exactly complements the differentiation of play into epistemic and ludic behaviors. Directed thought and epistemic play are both externally cued, and thereby constrained by the specific demands of the situation, whereas associative thought and ludic play are spontaneous, unconstrained, and only occur in states of relaxation. The commonplace saying "I have no time to stop and think" refers to associative thinking, which is evidently dispensable during inclement circumstances. Similarly, ludic behavior, whether in animals or humans, only occurs in the absence of biological pressures. Whereas epistemic behavior is *obligatory* in some sense, ludic behavior is *optional*.

In outlining a temporal scheme of exploratory behavior, Nunnally and Lemond (1973) have paid special attention to the covert processes underlying specific exploration and the transition to diversive exploration (see Figure 7). Albeit a temporal sequence, this scheme applies remarkably well to the transition from epistemic to ludic behaviors in play too, and, moreover, suggests the operation of yet another dimension—the physiological one of *arousal*.

TIME ⟶

OBSERVED BEHAVIOR

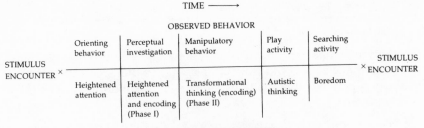

	Orienting behavior	Perceptual investigation	Manipulatory behavior	Play activity	Searching activity	
STIMULUS ENCOUNTER ×						× STIMULUS ENCOUNTER
	Heightened attention	Heightened attention and encoding (Phase I)	Transformational thinking (encoding) (Phase II)	Autistic thinking	Boredom	

PRESUMED COVERT PROCESSES

FIGURE 7. A temporal scheme of exploratory behavior.

Using the central tenets of Berlyne's theory (1960, 1967, 1969) we may now develop a model of play.

It was noted that both high- and low-arousal potential tend to be associated with elevations of arousal, and such conditions are mildly aversive. Under such conditions, the organism will engage in those responses which will result in a return to arousal tonus. Arousal potential is directly proportional to the intensity of a stimulus and its collative properties, and inversely proportional to time, or the duration of exposure to that source of stimulation. With continued exposure to a stimulus, its arousal potential wanes. Thus, combining Berlyne's (1967) adaptation

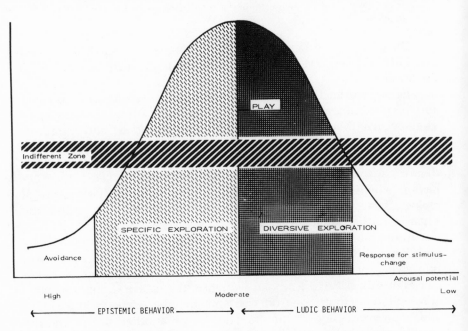

FIGURE 8. Relationships between hedonic tone and arousal potential.

of Wundt's curve relating hedonic tone to arousal potential and the scheme of Nunnally and Lemond we derive the relationships shown in Figure 8. When arousal potential is high, at extreme levels it may lead to avoidance responses; but as it decreases the individual engages in commerce with it in order to reduce uncertainty and cognitive conflict, that is, in those responses which may loosely be considered exploratory. As arousal potential reaches moderate proportions there is a tendency for productive and skilled activities to appear, since there is no longer the predominant need to reduce uncertainty. With this progressive decrease in arousal potential, affect becomes more positive and enjoyment becomes evident. As arousal potential continues to decrease, affect becomes neutral or minimally negative, and under these conditions repetitive activities are likely to be elicited. Finally, minimal levels of arousal potential are aversive, and the individual endeavours to optimise arousal by engaging in instrumental responses to obtain changes in stimulation.

There is yet another dimension of the model to be considered, and this concerns the degree of cortical control over subcortical centers. During most epistemic behavior the inhibitory influence of the cortex over the arousal system is operative. The cortical gating mechanisms (Sokolov, 1963) deal with the impact of stimuli, and enable appropriate responses to be deployed. In circumstances which elicit ludic behavior, however, the cortical inhibition of lower centers is relaxed, and we may consider the neocortical and subcortical systems to be disengaged or uncoupled, so to speak. A crude but helpful analogy may be that of a car in gear (epistemic behaviors), or in neutral with its engine idling (ludic behaviors— particularly *repetitive*) with the possibility of engaging gear should the need arise.

This model takes account of the characteristic of functional autonomy evident in much *perseverative* activity, as well as the phenomenon of stereotypy in autistic children (Hutt, S. J., & Hutt, C. 1968; Hutt, C., & Hutt, S. J., 1970). Furthermore, it is also able to encompass the changes in heart-rate variability during play (Hughes & Hutt, 1979), and during stereotypy in autistic children (Hutt, Forrest, & Richer, 1975): as cortical control becomes less rigorous, heart-rate variability increases. (It has already been suggested that corticofugal control is dampened in autistic children during performance of stereotyped activities [Hutt & Hutt, 1978].)

The present taxonomy appears to take account of the behavioral distinctions which characterize different forms of play. It has also made possible the development of a model which seeks to integrate data of different system levels, as well as to synthesize the observations and interpretations made of both animal and human behavior. It may be noted that in this taxonomy *games with rules* occupy a special position intermediate between epistemic and ludic behavior. This is because games have their own determinants and conventions, and are usually highly socially constrained, and often ritualized. Whether they classify as play at all depends on their context—for a professional footballer the game of football constitutes work, but it is play for the child on the street.

Finally, it should be pointed out that behaviors in the epistemic category may also be performed playfully, in which case the enactment takes on some of the attributes of ludic behavior. As Miller (1973) argues, "A child can use a tool or skill for clearly utilitarian purposes—or he can play with it" (p. 92), and as Piaget (1951) in a more general statement proclaims, "A schema is never essentially ludic or nonludic, and its character as play depends upon the context and on its actual functioning" (p. 90).

FUNCTIONS OF PLAY

All accounts of the functions of play must explain why play only occurs when the biological needs of the organism are satisfied and when no imperative demands occupy its attention. We saw that for Freud and Vygotsky play is a means of wish-fulfillment, of satisfying desires which in reality cannot be met.

Miller (1973) sees play as a motor or imaginative activity whose emphasis is on the process (the means) rather than the goal. It is "galumphing" rather than streamlined or economic behavior. He sees its function as the provision of opportunity for combinatorial freedom and for releasing behavior from the demands of goals:

> The organism that plays is more capable of coming up with novel behavior; the organism that is efficient and flexible is more adaptable than the one that is more efficient but unable to experiment with useless, "unproductive activities." (p. 75)

This distinction is one that Morris (1967) agreeably captures in contrasting the "opportunist" with the "specialist."

A function similar in nature to Miller's is also attributed to play by Sutton-Smith (1971) and Bruner (1976). Using the metaphor of systems theory, Fagen (1976) sees play as a test system rather than as a control system, the signals given and information obtained by each being quite distinct: "The function of play in model learning systems is best characterized as optimal generic learning by experimentation in a relaxed field" (p. 103).

Still with the metaphor of systems theory, Reynolds (1976) sees play as behavior functioning in the *simulative mode:*

> If we think of a system as operating in conjunction with other systems, so that its output serves as inputs to the others, then a system whose output is temporarily uncoupled from its normal input relations to other systems will be said to be functioning in the *simulative mode*. (p. 621)

Although uncoupled from its consequences, feedback to such a system is nevertheless intact. As Reynolds observes, a simulative mode is paradoxical: the system's operations should have their normal consequences, but such consequences must be made inconsequential. He regards the play system as a vehicle for transmission of information between the environment and the nonplay systems, since behavior patterns and sequences are transferred to "play control for simulative mode execution" and information relative to the nonplay systems is transferred. But herein lies another paradox: behavior executed in the simulative mode will only elicit information relevant to that mode, as with the metacommunicative signal of "this is not real threat" accompanying play threat (Bateson, 1956).

Moreover, none of these statements of the functions with which play has been invested has dealt with the awkward facts that play only occurs in certain exceptional circumstances, and that many animals and children do not play—in the ludic sense. In fact, in many subsistence economies play is a luxury, as it is to the ambitious company executive. Berlyne (1969) recalls the well-documented case of a Mexican peasant who had no time for play or leisure. What exactly are the disadvantages or deficits that may accrue from the lack of play? Play may indeed have some of the functions ascribed to it, but, if so, it is curious that they should occur largely as a matter of happenstance.

A rather different function to those outlined and one more akin to Berlyne's is given by Ellis (1973), namely, that of stimulus seeking. Ellis adopts the Hebbian position of regarding arousal as high during stimulation and low in its absence; consequently, his definition of play is "that behavior that is motivated by the need to elevate the level of arousal toward the optimal" (p. 110). Ellis draws the parallels between stimulus seeking and play:

> They occur when they are not preempted by the need to satisfy prepotent drives; they are accompanied by positive affect; they both involve exploration, investigation and manipulation of the environment or the symbolic representations of experience; and such stimulus-seeking and play behaviors that are observable are both emitted with high frequency by the young of a species. The similarities between them lead to the obvious question, "Are they not the same phenomenon?" The answer seems to be that play is clearly stimulus-seeking behavior, yet not all stimulus-seeking behavior is play. (p. 109)

The primary function ascribed to play in the present model is somewhat similar to that of Ellis but is directly derived from Berlyne's arousal formulations. In those animal species upon whom pressures for survival are not too great, among those animals with a protracted period of infancy and dependence, among domesticated animals from whom all pressures are removed, and chiefly among children, is the phenomenon of play most evident. In other words, in those circumstances when time and effort are not preempted by extrinsically motivated behavior. For such animals and individuals there must be some means of keeping neural centers alert and active. In the absence of such activity, which is maintained by patterned and varied stimulation, we know that the individual is likely to become drowsy and inattentive, his vigilance deteriorates, and eventually he may be overcome by sleep. If in fact the individual has had sufficient sleep, the conditions of stimulus deprivation are aversive (see Zubek, 1969), and all endeavors are made to increase stimulation and arousal potential. In normal circumstances people are not exposed to this degree of stimulus deprivation but may simply experience stimulus reduction, and it is then that they need recourse to alternative sources of stimulation. Whereupon behaviors which have no explicit purpose or goal but are within the organism's repertoire are utilized for this purpose. In any species there is a particular class of behaviors, intimately related to limbic system arousal (Routtenberg, 1968), which readily lend themselves for such use. In human adults, symbolic processes, that is, thoughts, fulfill this function adequately. In children, however, where symbolic representation is yet to become established, thought is overt and manifest as play. Thus, the primary function of play is to keep neural and behavioral systems primed and active in the absence of alternative stimulation. Since such behaviors have no explicitly utilitarian function, they are invested with properties which serve to distinguish them from more goal-directed behavior, properties such as exaggerations, galumphing, and caricatures. As a secondary consequence, play may indeed also result in the advantages described by Bruner, Miller, Reynolds, Sutton-Smith, and others. This statement of function accommodates the paradox that play or ludic behavior is extremely low in the motivational hierarchy.

POSTSCRIPT

To the reader of this chapter, the influence of Daniel Berlyne will be readily apparent. Our own studies of children's play, which began in 1963, were directly inspired by a reading of his seminal work *Conflict, Arousal and Curiosity*, and we have continued to be invigorated by his more recent writings. (It is perhaps slightly ironical that our studies should have gained sustenance, both theoretically and practically, from one who so strongly argued for the deletion of "play" from the vocabulary of psychology [Berlyne, 1969].) Although we have constantly been delighted by the originality and ingenuity of Berlyne's experiments, it is perhaps his theoretical writings which have had the greatest impact on our own research. Berlyne was a theoretician of enormous stature, able to integrate material from comparative, physiological, and human experimental psychology in an apparently effortless manner. Such syntheses, however, were not merely intellectually satisfying but always contained within them clear indications of what new avenues of research it would be most profitable to explore next. By focusing on the motivational and functional aspects of play, rather than solely on the morphological, we have made our model more amenable to attack and thereby to empirical investigation. We believe that this is a strategy of which Dan would have approved.

ACKNOWLEDGMENTS

In preparing this chapter the assistance of Mrs. Helen Foy and Mrs. Dorothy Masters has been indispensable. I am deeply grateful to them both.

SJH

REFERENCES

ALDIS, O. *Play fighting.* New York: Academic, 1975.

AITKEN, P. P., & HUTT, C. Do children find complex patterns interesting or pleasing? *Child Development,* 1974, *45,* 425–431.

AITKEN, P. P., & HUTT, C. The effects of stimulus incongruity upon children's attention, choice and expressed preference. *Journal of Experimental Child Psychology,* 1975, *19,* 79–87.

ARIES, P. *Centuries of childhood.* Harmondsworth: Penguin, 1973.

BARNES, G. W., & KISH, G. B. Reinforcing properties of the onset of auditory stimulation. *Journal of Experimental Psychology,* 1961, *62,* 164–170.

BATESON, G. The message "This is play." In B. Schaffner (Ed.), *Group processes.* New York: Josiah Macy Foundation, 1956.

BERLYNE, D. E. Novelty and curiosity as determinants of exploratory behaviour. *British Journal of Psychology,* 1950, *41,* 68–80.

BERLYNE, D. E. The arousal and satiation of perceptual curiosity in the rat. *Journal of Comparative and Physiological Psychology,* 1955, *48,* 238–246.

BERLYNE, D. E. *Conflict, arousal and curiosity.* New York: McGraw-Hill, 1960.

BERLYNE, D. E. Motivational problems raised by exploratory and epistemic behavior. In S. Koch (ed.), *Psychology: A study of science* (Vol. 5). New York: McGraw-Hill, 1963.

BERLYNE, D. E. *Structure and direction in thinking.* New York: Wiley, 1965.

BERLYNE, D. E. Curiosity and exploration. *Science,* 1966, *153,* 25–33.

BERLYNE, D. E. Arousal and reinforcement. In M. R. Jones (Ed.), *Nebraska symposium on motivation* (Vol. 15). Lincoln: University of Nebraska Press, 1967.

BERLYNE, D. E. Laughter, humor and play. In G. Lindzey & E. Aronson (Eds.), *Handbook of social psychology* (2nd ed.). New York: Addison-Wesley, 1969.

BERLYNE, D. E. Children's reasoning and thinking. In P. H. Mussen (Ed.), *Carmichael's manual of child psychology* (3rd ed., Vol. 1). New York: Wiley, 1970.

BERLYNE, D. E. *Aesthetics and psychobiology.* New York: Appleton-Century-Crofts, 1971.

BERLYNE. D. E. The vicissitudes of aplopathematic and thelematoscopic pneumatology (or, The hydrography of hedonism). In D. E. Berlyne & K. B. Madsen (Eds.), *Pleasure, reward, preference.* New York: Academic Press, 1973.

BERNSTEIN, B. *Class, codes and control* (Vol. 1): *Theoretical studies towards a sociology of language.* London: Routledge & Kegan Paul, 1971.

BERNSTEIN, I. S. Taboo or toy? In J. S. Bruner, A. Jolly, & K. Sylva (Eds.), *Play: Its role in development and evolution.* Harmondsworth: Penguin, 1976.

BERTRAND, M. The behavioral repertoire of the Stumptail Macaque. In J. S. Bruner, A. Jolly, & K. Sylva (Eds.), *Play: Its role in development and evolution.* Harmondsworth: Penguin, 1976.

BLURTON-JONES, N. An ethological study of some aspects of social behavior of children in nursery school. In D. Morris (Ed.), *Primate ethology.* London: Weidenfeld & Nicolson, 1967.

BOLLES, R. C. The usefulness of the drive concept. In M. R. Jones (Ed.), *Nebraska symposium on motivation* (Vol. 6). Lincoln: University of Nebraska Press, 1958.

BRUNER, J. S. Nature and uses of immaturity. In J. S. Bruner, A. Jolly, & K. Sylva (Eds.), *Play: Its role in development and evolution.* Harmondsworth: Penguin, 1976.

BRUNER, J. S., & SHERWOOD, V. Peekaboo and the learning of rule structures. In J. S. Bruner, A. Jolly, & K. Sylva (Eds.), *Play: Its role in development and evolution.* Harmondsworth: Penguin, 1976.

BUTLER, R. A. Discrimination learning by rhesus monkeys to auditory incentives. *Journal of Comparative and Physiological Psychology,* 1957, *50,* 239–241.

BUTLER, R. A., & ALEXANDER, H. M., Daily patterns of visual exploratory behavior in the monkey. *Journal of Comparative and Physiological Psychology,* 1955, *48,* 247–249.

BUTLER, R. A., & HARLOW, H. F. Persistence of visual exploration in monkeys. *Journal of Comparative and Physiological Psychology,* 1954, *47,* 258–263.

CAZDEN, C. B. Play with language and metalinguistic awareness: One dimension of language experience. *International Journal of Early Childhood,* 1974, *6,* 12–24.

DANSKY, J. L., & SILVERMAN, I. W. Effects of play on associative fluency in preschool children. *Developmental Psychology,* 1973, *9,* 38–43.

DAVIE, C., FORREST, B., HUTT, C., MASON, M., VINCENT, E., & WARD, T. *Play at home and at school.* Paper presented at the Third Biennial Congress of the International Society for the Study of Behavioral Development, Guildford, July 1975.

DEARDEN, R. F. The concept of play. In R. S. Peters (Ed.), *The concept of education.* London: Routledge & Kegan Paul, 1967.

DOLHINOW, P. J., & BISHOP, N. The development of motor skills and social relationships among primates through play. In J. P. Hill (Ed.), *Minnesota symposia on child psychology* (Vol. 4). Minneapolis: University of Minnesota Press, 1970.

EIFERMANN, R. R. *Determinants of children's game styles.* Jerusalem: Israel Academy of Sciences and Humanities, 1971.(a)

EIFERMANN, R. R. Social play in childhood. In R. E. Herron & B. Sutton-Smith (Eds.), *Child's play.* New York: Wiley, 1971.(b)

EIFERMANN, R. R. It's child's play. In E. Bower & L. M. Shears (Eds.), *Games in education and development.* Springfield, Ill.: Charles C. Thomas, 1972.

Eifermann, R. R. It's child's play. In J. S. Bruner, A. Jolly, & K. Sylva (Eds.), *Play: Its role in development and evolution*. Harmondsworth: Penguin, 1976.

Ellis, M. J. *Why people play*. Englewood Cliffs, N. J.: Prentice-Hall, 1973.

Fagen, R. Modelling how and why play works. In J. S. Bruner, A. Jolly, & K. Sylva (Eds.), *Play: Its role in development and evolution*. Harmondsworth: Penguin, 1976.

Fein, G. G. A transformational analysis of pretending. *Developmental Psychology*, 1975, *3*, 291–296.

Feitelson, D., & Ross, G. S. The neglected factor: Play. *Human Development*, 1973, *16*, 202–224.

Fowler, H. *Curiosity and exploratory behavior*. London: Macmillan, 1965.

Friedlander, B. S., McCarthy, J. J., & Soforenko, A. Z. Automated psychological evaluation with severely retarded institutionalized infants. *American Journal of Mental Deficiency*, 1967, *71*, 909–919.

Freyberg, J. T. Increasing the imaginative play of urban disdavantaged kindergarten children through systematic training. In J. L. Singer (Ed.), *The child's world of make-believe*. New York: Academic Press, 1973.

Garvey, C. Some properties of social play. *Merrill-Palmer Quarterly*, 1974, *20*, 163–180.

Garvey, C. Play with language. In B. Tizard & D. Harvey (Eds.), *Biology of play*. London: William Heinemann, 1977.

Glanzer, M. Stimulus satiation: An explanation of spontaneous alternation and related phenomena. *Psychological Review*, 1953, *60*, 257–268.

Glanzer, M. Curiosity, exploratory drive, and stimulus satiation. *Psychological Bulletin*, 1958, *55*, 302–315.

Gleitman, L. R., Gleitman, H., & Shipley, E. F. The emergence of the child as grammarian. *Cognition*, 1972, *1*, 137–164.

Goodson, B. D., & Greenfield, P. M. The search for structural principles in children's manipulative play: A parallel with linguistic development. *Child Development*, 1975, *46*, 734–746.

Greenfield, P. M., Nelson, K., & Saltzman, E. The development of rulebound strategies for manipulating seriated cups: A parallel between action and grammar. *Cognitive Psychology*, 1972, *3*, 291–310.

Harlow, H. F. Learning and satiation of response in intrinsically motivated complex puzzle performance by monkeys. *Journal of Comparative and Physiological Psychology*, 1950, *43*, 289–294.

Harlow, H. F. Mice, men, monkeys and motives. *Psychological Review*, 1953, *60*, 23–32.

Harlow, H. F., & Harlow, M. K. Social deprivation in monkeys. *Scientific American*, 1962, *207*, 136–138.

Harlow, H. F., & McClearn, G. E. Object discrimination learned by monkeys on the basis of manipulation motives. *Journal of Comparative and Physiological Psychology*, 1954, *47*, 73–76.

Harlow, H. F., Blazek, N. C., & McClearn, G. E. Manipulatory motivation in infant rhesus monkeys. *Journal of Comparative and Physiological Psychology*, 1956, *49*, 444-448.

Hebb, D. O. Drives and the C. N. S. (Conceptual Nervous System). *Psychological Review*, 1955, *62*, 243–254.

Held, R., & Hein, A. Movement-produced stimulation in the development of visually guided behavior. *Journal of Comparative and Physiological Psychology*, 1963, *56*, 872.

Horn, G. Neuronal mechanisms of habituation. *Nature*, 1967, *215*, 707–711.

Hugelin, A., & Bonvallet, M. Analyse des post-décharges réticulaires et corticales engendrées par des stimulations électriques réticulaires. *Journal de Physiologie et de Pathologie Générale*, 1957, *49*, 1225–1234.

Hughes, M. M., & Hutt, C. Heart-rate correlates of childhood activities: Play, exploration, problem-solving and daydreaming. *Biological Psychology*, 1979, *8*, 253–263.

HUTT, C. Exploration and play in children. In P. A. Jewell & C. Loizos (Eds.), *Play, exploration and territory in mammals: Symposia of the Zoological Society of London,* 1966, *18,* 61–68.

HUTT, C. Temporal effects on response decrement and stimulus satiation in exploration. *British Journal of Psychology,* 1967, *58,* 365–373.(a)

HUTT, C. *Exploring novelty.* Film, 16mm black & white. British Film Institute, 1967.(b)

HUTT, C. Effects of stimulus novelty on manipulatory exploration in an infant. *Journal of Child Psychology and Psychiatry,* 1967, *8,* 241–247.(c)

HUTT, C. Exploration, arousal and autism. *Psychologische Forschung,* 1969, *33,* 1–8.

HUTT, C. Specific and diversive exploration. In H. Reese & L. P. Lipsitt (Eds.), *Advances in child development and behavior* (Vol. 5). London: Academic Press, 1970.

HUTT, C. Degrees of novelty and their effects on children's attention and preference. *British Journal of Psychology,* 1975, *66,* 487–492.

HUTT, C. Exploration and play. In B. Sutton-Smith (Ed.), *Play and learning.* New York: Gardner Press, 1979.

HUTT, C., & HUTT, S. J. Stereotypies and their relation to arousal. In S. J. Hutt & C. Hutt (Eds.), *Behavior studies in psychiatry.* Oxford: Pergamon Press, 1970.

HUTT, C., & HUTT, S. J. Heart-rate variability: The adaptive consequences of individual differences and state changes. In N. Blurton-Jones & V. Reynolds (Eds.), *Human behavior and adaptation.* London: Taylor Francis, 1978.

HUTT, C., & McGREW, P. L. Do children really prefer complexity? *Psychonomic Science,* 1969, *17,* 113–114.

HUTT, C., FORREST, S. J., & RICHER, J. Cardiac arrhythmia and behavior in autistic children. *Acta Psychiatrica Scandinavica,* 1975, *51,* 361–372.

HUTT, C., FORREST, B., & NEWTON, J. The visual preferences of children. *Journal of Child Psychology and Psychiatry,* 1976, *17,* 63–68.

HUTT, S. J., & HUTT, C. Stereotypy, arousal and autism. *Human Development,* 1968, *11,* 277–286.

HUTT, S. J., HUTT, C., LEE, D., & OUNSTED, C. A behavioral and electroencephalographic study of autistic children. *Journal of Psychiatric Research,* 1965, *3,* 181–197.

KAVANAUGH, J. F., & MATTINGLY, I. G. (Eds.). Language by ear and by eye: The relationship between speech and reading. Cambridge: M. I. T. Press, 1972.

KISH, G. B. Learning when the onset of illumination is used as a reinforcing stimulus. *Journal of Comparative and Physiological Psychology,* 1955, *48,* 261–264.

KISH, G. B., & ANTONITIS, J. J. Unconditioned operant behavior in two homozygous strains of mice. *Journal of Genetic Psychology,* 1956, *88,* 121–124.

KLINGER, E. *Structure and functions of fantasy.* New York: Wiley, 1971.

KÖHLER, W. *The mentality of apes.* London: Kegan Paul, 1925.

LEUBA, C., & FRIEDLANDER, B. Z. Effects of controlled audiovisual reinforcement on infants' manipulative play in the home. *Journal of Experimental Child Psychology,* 1968, *6,* 87–99.

LOIZOS, C. Play behavior in higher primates: A review. In D. Morris (Ed.), *Primate ethology.* London: Weidenfeld & Nicholson, 1967.

MARSHALL, H., & HAHN, S. C. Experimental modification of dramatic play. *Journal of Personality and Social Psychology,* 1967, *5,* 119–122.

MENZEL, E. W. Spontaneous invention of ladders in a group of young chimpanzees. *Folia Primatologica,* 1972, *17,* 87–106.

MILLAR, S. *The psychology of play.* Harmondsworth: Penguin, 1968.

MILLER, S. N. Ends, means and galumphing: Some leitmotifs of play. *American Anthropologist,* 1973, *75,* 87–98.

MONTGOMERY, K. C. The relationship between exploratory behavior and spontaneous alteration in the white rat. *Journal of Comparative and Physiological Psychology,* 1951, *44,* 582–589.

Montgomery, K. C. Exploratory behavior as a function of "similarity" of stimulus situations. *Journal of Comparative and Physiological Psychology*, 1953, 46, 129–133.

Montgomery, K. C. The role of the exploratory drive in learning. *Journal of Comparative and Physiological Psychology*, 1954, 47, 60–64.

Moon, L. E., & Lodahl, T. M. The reinforcing effect of changes in illumination on lever-pressing in the monkey. *American Journal of Psychology*, 1956, 64, 288–290.

Morris, D. (Ed.). *Primate ethology*. London: Weidenfeld & Nicolson, 1967.

Müller-Schwarze, D. Ludic behavior in young mammals. In M. B. Sterman, D. J. McGinty, & A. M. Adinolfi (Eds.), *Brain development and behavior*. New York: Academic Press 1971.

Myers, A. K., & Miller, N. E. Failure to find a learned drive based on hunger: Evidence for learning motivated by "exploration." *Journal of Comparative and Physiological Psychology*, 1954, 47, 428–436.

Nissen, H. W., Chow, K. L., & Semmes, J. Effects of restricted opportunity for tactual, kinesthetic and manipulative experience on the behavior of the chimpanzee. *American Journal of Psychology*, 1951, 64, 485–507.

Nunnally, J. C., & Lemond, L. C. Exploratory behavior and human development. In H. W. Reese (Ed.), *Advances in child development and behavior* (Vol. 8), New York: Academic Press, 1973.

Nuttin, J. R. Pleasure and reward in human motivation and learning. In D. E. Berlyne & K. B. Madsen (Eds.), *Pleasure, reward, preference*. New York: Academic Press, 1973.

O'Connell, R. H. Trials with tedium and titillation. *Psychological Bulletin*, 1965, 63, 170–179.

Peller, L. E. Models of children's play. In R. E. Herron & B. Sutton-Smith (Eds.), *Child's play*. New York: Wiley, 1971.

Piaget, J. *The moral judgment of the child*. London: Kegan Paul, 1932.

Piaget, J. *Play, dreams and imitation in childhood*. London: Routledge & Kegan Paul, 1951.

Piaget, J. Response to Brian Sutton-Smith. *Psychological Review*, 1966, 73, 111–112.

Reynolds, P. C. Play, language and human evolution. In J. S. Bruner, A. Jolly, & K. Sylva (Eds.), *Play: Its role in development and evolution*. Harmondsworth: Penguin, 1976.

Rheingold, H. L., Stanley, W. C., & Doyle, G. A. Visual and auditory reinforcement of a manipulatory response in the young child. *Journal of Experimental Child Psychology*, 1964, 1, 316–326.

Rolfe, J. M. Introduction: Symposium on heart-rate variability. *Ergonomics*, 1973, 16, 1–3.

Rosen, C. E. The effects of sociodramatic play on problem-solving behavior among culturally disadvantaged preschool children. *Child Development*, 1974, 45, 920–927.

Routtenberg, A. The two-arousal hypothesis: Reticular formation and limbic system. *Psychological Review*, 1968, 75, 51–80.

Saltz, E., & Johnson, J. Training for thematic-fantasy play in culturally disadvantaged children: Preliminary results. *Journal of Educational Psychology*, 1974, 66, 623–630.

Schiller, P. H. Innate motor action as a basis of learning: Manipulative patterns in the chimpanzee. In C. H. Schiller (Ed.), *Instinctive behavior*. London: Methuen, 1957.

Scholtz, G. I. L., & Ellis, M. J. Repeated exposure to objects and peers in a play setting. *Journal of Experimental Child Psychology*, 1975, 19, 448–455.

Singer, J. L. *The child's world of make-believe*. New York: Academic Press, 1973.

Smilansky, S. *The effects of sociodramatic play on disadvantaged preschool children*. New York: Wiley, 1968.

Smith, P. K. Social and fantasy play in young children. In B. Tizard & D. Harvey (Eds.), *Biology of play*. London: William Heinemann, 1977.

Sokolov, E. N. Higher nervous functions: The orienting reflex. *Annual Review of Physiology*, 1963, 25, 545–580.

Sutton-Smith, B. Piaget on play: A critique. *Psychological Review*, 1966, 73, 104–110.

Sutton-Smith, B. The role of play in cognitive development. In R. E. Herron & B. Sutton-Smith (Eds.), *Child's play*. New York: Wiley, 1971.

SUTTON-SMITH, B., & ROSENBERG, B. G. Sixty years of historical change in the game preferences of Amnerican children. In R. E. Herron & B. Sutton-Smith (Eds.), *Child's play*. New York: Wiley, 1971.

SYMMES, D. Anxiety reduction and novelty as goals of visual exploration by monkeys. *Journal of Genetic Psychology*, 1959, *94*, 181–198.

THOMPSON, R. F., & SPENCER, W. A. Habituation: A model phenomenon for the study of neuronal substrates of behavior. *Psychological Review*, 1966, *73*, 16–43.

VAN LAWICK-GOODALL, J. The behavior of free-living chimpanzees in the Gombe Stream Reserve. *Animal Behavior Monographs*, 1968, *1*, 161–311.

VYGOTSKY, L. S. Play and its role in the mental development of the child. *Voprosy psikhologii*, 1966, *12*, 62–76. Translated in *Soviet Psychology*, 1967, *5*, 6–18.

WEIR, R. H. *Language in the crib*. The Hague: Mouton, 1962.

ZUBEK, J. P. (Ed.). *Sensory deprivation: 15 years of research*. New York: Appleton-Century-Crofts, 1969.

12

Intrinsic Motivation and Health

SALVATORE R. MADDI AND SUZANNE C. KOBASA

The concept of intrinsic motivation, championed by D. E. Berlyne, has by now taken root in psychology. Whether deprived of nutrients or not, both animals and humans will display considerable curiosity and play, and will actually work for no other reward than gaining information about the environment. Further, intrinsically motivated activities have proven to be especially satisfying, and without boredom or anxiety. Consistently with this, stimuli of a complex or changing nature attract more attention, and are considered more aesthetically pleasing.

Theories about the functional significance of intrinsically motivated behavior have contended that through curiosity, play, and an interest in complex, changing stimuli the organism gains valuable information about the environment. For example, in the study of the role of intrinsic motivation in learning, evidence is accumulating that more is learned faster when the subject's curiosity and playfulness are aroused. Other theorizing has emphasized the functional significance of intrinsic motivation as it leads to activities which are useful in future adaptation. Very possibly, intrinsic motivation is not only a source of pleasure and satisfaction with one's activities, but an important determinant of survival as well. The work to be presented here explores this second interpretation by asking whether intrinsic motivation is one factor keeping the person healthy despite stressful life events that would otherwise be debilitating.

STRESS AND ILLNESS

Over the past twenty-five years, a primarily medical literature has accumulated showing a positive relationship between stressful life events

---

SALVATORE R. MADDI AND SUZANNE C. KOBASA • Department of Behavioral Sciences, University of Chicago, Chicago, Illinois 60637. The research reported here has been supported in whole by NIMH grant number MH 28839.

and illness symptoms (e.g., Dohrenwend & Dohrenwend, 1974). These studies derive from Seyle's (1956) conceptualization of the *general adaptation syndrome* as a protective organismic response to stressors. In this formulation, individual stressors can accumulate to a degree sufficient to exhaust the adaptational capability of the organism, resulting in any of a wide range of symptoms or illnesses. The studies typically have a questionnaire-measure of life events (e.g., Holmes & Rahe, 1967) which includes the whole range from extreme, infrequent occurrences (e.g., death of a spouse) to ordinary, common ones (e.g., vacation). Usually, these events are quantified as to stressfulness by employing weights deriving from the consensus of large samples employing psychophysical scaling procedures. Also typical are questionnaire measures of symptomatology (e.g., Wyler, Masuda, & Holmes, 1968), which include a range from severe illnesses (e.g., heart disease) to common annoyances (e.g., headache). These symptoms are usually also quantified using psychophysically derived weights. There is regularly a low positive correlation between such measures of stressful life events and symptoms, regardless of which measure follows the other in the data-collection procedure.

The consistently weak magnitude of this relationship has not inhibited the generalization, reiterated not only in the journals but across the mass media as well, that stress debilitates and is therefore to be avoided. Individuals and organizations are taking steps, accordingly, to simplify and routinize life. Procedures for distracting oneself from pressures (e.g., using tranquilizers, meditating at one's desk) have never been more popular.

There can be little doubt that the blanket conclusion about the debilitating effects of stress is an overgeneralization. Not only is the typical correlation on the order of only 0.30, but the standard deviation of stressful life events and illness distributions is often eight times the mean. It stands to reason that there are many subjects who are not becoming ill even though their lives are quite stressful.

REMAINING HEALTHY DESPITE STRESS

What kinds of resistance resources would be likely to neutralize the otherwise debilitating effects of stressful life events? A plausible list would include constitutional strengths (e.g., little history of family illness), social supports (e.g., social contacts and status centrality), health practices (e.g., jogging), and personality dispositions.

How might these factors operate in keeping the person healthy during the encounter with stress? Constitutional strengths are important because the breakdown into illness envisioned by Selye and others occurs in "weak" organs and bodily systems once there has been adaptational exhaustion in the face of stressors. How much exhaustion is too much is a function of the strength of organs and bodily systems in this "weakest link" theory. The longer symptom emergence is delayed, the greater the likelihood that stressors will diminish and adaptational energy be restored. Similarly, health practices, if they are successful in strengthening organs and bodily systems, should delay the onset of symptoms.

In order to understand the supposed beneficial effects of social supports and personality dispositions, a more psychological approach to bodily functioning must be taken. It must be recognized that one reason why stressful life events are indeed stressful is that they cause the person experiencing them to worry, ruminate, become anxious, angry, or depressed, engage in criticism of self or others, lose interest in other things, deteriorate in ability to make decisions clearly, and remain awake at night. From a psychological viewpoint, these are the kinds of reactions that constitute progressive adaptational exhaustion.

Social supports can decrease the psychological debilitation of stressful life events by the reassurance that, whatever else happens, the person still has his place, and that it is a worthwhile place. However stressful life becomes, if you still have your friends and family to talk to and count on, if you still have a definite and admirable position in society, then you can face a lot more than if the social situation were otherwise. Social supports, if you have them, help you to keep stressful life events in perspective and, in that sense, minimize their debilitating effects.

Also operating at a psychological level, personality dispositions have both perceptual and response aspects. At the perceptual level, personality dispositions constitute bases for experiencing stimuli in a particular fashion, as having a particular meaning. At the response level, personality dispositions energize a particular set of activities experienced as appropriate given the particular perceptions that have occurred. This formulation of personality dispositions integrates the classical positions of Allport (1937) and Murray (1938) with the recent interactional emphasis of Mischel (1973).

What personality dispositions mitigate the otherwise debilitating effects of stressful life events? Specifically, those which have the perceptual effect of rendering the events not so terrible after all, and the response effect of instigating coping activities that involve interacting with and thereby transforming the events, rather than avoiding them. In this fashion, the stressful life event is first kept in perspective and then altered so as to be less stressful. Persons with personality dispositions of this sort possess a valuable aid in avoiding adaptational exhaustion. They should be able to remain healthy while experiencing events that would be debilitating for others without those personality dispositions.

PERSONALITY DISPOSITIONS IN INTRINSIC MOTIVATION

In the literature, intrinsic motivation tends to be discussed as a function of task characteristics. Thus, the complexity, difficulty, and interest value of tasks is regarded as provoking or discouraging intrinsically motivated performance. Other aspects of the environment, such as reinforcement extrinsic to the task, are also regarded as having an effect on intrinsic motivation. Empirical studies are almost exclusively experimental in design, with little attention expended on characteristics of subjects. Given the emphasis on variables such as complexity, difficulty, and interest value, it is particularly surprising to see so little consideration of subject variables as they may influence intrinsic motivation. What is optimally complex, difficult, or interesting for one subject may be overwhelming or boring for another. Even with the prevalence of an experimental methodology, one might have expected more of an emphasis on the interaction of subject and task characteristics in the explanation of intrinsic motivation.

Perhaps the absence of an interactional emphasis is one reason why the bustling activity in this research area has not lead to any consensus or accumulated sense of understanding. At the moment, there are several proposed explanations of intrinsic motivation, all heavily situational, and each with its proponents and some evidence to support it. According to one review (DeCharms & Muir, 1978), this problem derives from the insufficient theoretical elaboration of the various proposed explanations. Beyond the middle-level theorizing which characterizes the explanations is considerable similarity in underlying, implicit assumptions. Because these explanations are really more similar than different, there appears evidence for them all, and yet somehow nothing much seems to have been learned. Similarly, Csikszentmihalyi (1975) argues for more reliance on naturalistic observation of intrinsically motivated activities in everyday life, rather than rushing prematurely into the formulation of experiments, however clever and seemingly decisive they may be. This approach will inevitably involve consideration of individual differences and person variables.

The work reported on here attempts to correct the imbalance by emphasizing personality characteristics that could predispose persons to be intrinsically motivated in performance. This is not to say, however, that task characteristics will be overlooked completely. Indeed, an attempt will be made to demonstrate that events generally regarded as stressful (in the sense of disrupting life and requiring readjustment) will be less debilitating to persons predisposed toward intrinsic motivation than they are to others not so predisposed. The personality characteristics to be considered are *commitment, control,* and *challenge.*

The tendency toward *commitment to* (rather than alienation from) whatever one is doing or encounters is an important aspect of intrinsic motivation. It would be hard to imagine losing track of time and place through the intense involvement which appears basic to intrinsically motivated behavior (Csikszentmihalyi, 1975) if the person were predisposed to be detached and aloof from the environment and experience. It should be remembered that Calder and Staw (1975) have shown that the well-known effect of extrinsic reinforcement in decreasing intrinsically motivated performance only occurs when the task employed is regarded as interesting by the subjects, and therefore involves them. The personality characteristic of commitment should increase the number of tasks which appear interesting.

Further, the intrinsically motivated person feels in *control of* (rather than powerless toward) what is going on. This does not imply the naive expectation of complete determination of events and outcomes, so much as the perception of oneself as a definite influence through the exercise of imagination, knowledge, skill, and choice. Relevant to this dimension are findings (Greene, Sternberg, & Lepper, 1976) in which subjects were extrinsically reinforced for either their previously demonstrated preferred activity, least preferred activity, activity of their own choice, or (for control purposes) all of these activities. Contrary to the experimenters' expectation, results showed greatest undermining in performance of the chosen activity. This suggests that a sense of control (expressed in choice) is an important personality characteristic of intrinsically motivated behavior.

Finally, such behavior involves a sense of *challenge* (rather than threat) at the prospect of change and novelty. Csikszentmihalyi's (1975) subjects reported the experience of what we have called commitment and control specifically when involved in tasks a bit beyond their capabilities, such that change was more or less necessary and outcomes were somewhat unpredictable. These tasks involved a sense of excitement and challenge which deepened the intrinsically rewarding nature of performance of the task. The position taken here is that some persons are especially likely to have this experience because they are predisposed to feel stimulated and challenged by changes.

What is proposed here, in short, is that persons differ in (1) the ease with which they commit themselves to (or involve themselves in) tasks, (2) the likelihood that they will feel in control of (or able to influence) what happens, and (3) the vigor with which they feel challenged (or stimulated to strive and change) in what they do. Persons high on these aspects of intrinsic motivation may well feel more satisfied as they move through life's tasks, and gain more of the information and skills marking competence (White, 1960). As a special aspect of the survival value of their vigorous intrinsic motivation, they may well be able to tolerate more severely stressful life events than other persons without becoming ill.

The last statement should be amplified, as it constitutes the general hypothesis of the research reported below. If commitment, control, and challenge constitute personality dimensions enhancing resistance to stress, then they should influence both perceptions of and coping attempts toward events generally regarded as stressful. In this regard, commitment has the general perceptual effect of predisposing one to identify with and be curious about the events, things, and persons of one's environment. On the response, or coping, side, commitment predisposes one to approach and interact with aspects of the environment rather than be a passive observer. Consistent with this formulation are recent findings (Maddi, Hoover, & Kobasa, 1981) that persons with strong feelings of alienation explore a mock waiting room less than do their more committed counterparts. Through the commitment predisposition, one learns about the environment and practices one's adaptational skills in a manner that helps in maintaining a generally positive attitude toward stressful life events, should they occur.

Challenge mitigates the stressfulness of events by entailing the expectation that it is natural for change to take place and that changes provide an opportunity for personal growth. Thus, when events occur, they will tend to be perceived as positive challenges rather than as threats merely because they are changes requiring readjustment. In coping behaviors, challenge will lead to attempts to transform oneself and thereby grow rather than conserve and protect what one can of the former existence.

Control enhances stress resistance through the conviction that events generally arise out of and can be modified according to one's own influential nature. Perceptually, this increases the likelihood of experiencing as natural outgrowths of one's action, and therefore not foreign, unexpected, and overwhelming. In terms of coping, a sense of control leads to actions aimed at transforming events into something consistent with an ongoing life plan (Averill, 1973), and thereby less jarring.

For all these reasons, commitment, challenge, and control should have the effect of keeping persons healthy despite encounters with events generally regarded as stressful. In a relevant study, Kobasa (1979) found support for this hypothesis. Questionnaire measures of stressful life events and illness symptoms were obtained on a sample of business executives. As usual, these measures showed a low, but significant, positive correlation. Partitioning the distribution of scores on these two dimensions at the median, Kobasa constructed two groups of subjects. Both groups were high in stressful life events, but differed in that one group was high in symptomatology and the other group was low. Then these two groups were administered personality scales constructed to measure commitment, control, challenge, and several other dispositions. Through analysis of variance and discriminant function techniques, Kobasa showed that the High Stress/Low Illness group was stronger in measures of commitment, challenge, and control than the High Stress/ High Illness group. These results are enhanced by the fact that various demographic characteristics, such as socioeconomic level, failed to discriminate the groups.

In a similar though less extensive study, Johnson and Sarason (1978) obtained from their college-student subjects measures of stressful life events, symptomatology, and internal versus external locus of control. They demonstrated that subjects believing in an internal locus of control show a lower correlation between stressful life events and illness than do subjects believing that they are externally controlled. Although this study appears to indicate the importance of a sense of control as a resistance resource against stressful life events, caution should be exercised in reaching a conclusion. One problem is that the severity of stress associated with events was determined by each subject for his- or herself. It seems plausible that a person feeling externally controlled would, because of this, experience events as highly stressful in the sense of being changes requiring readjustment, and that the opposite should occur for subjects feeling an internal sense of control. If this is true, then the findings reported by Johnson and Sarason may be artifactual in the sense that measures of stressful life events and internal versus external locus of control, though purportedly different, are actually indexing the same thing.

Kobasa's study avoids this difficulty by using consensually derived weights in developing a stressful-life-events score. All the subject does is indicate whether the events have or have not occurred in a designated period of time. That the stressful-life-events score obtained in this study is conceptually expressive of the cultural level bodes well for its being considered different from personality scores, which express the individual level. Indeed, the modest average correlation between stressful life events and personality scores in this study lends empirical support to this contention.

But both studies suffer from yet another problem, namely, the retrospective nature of the design. In Kobasa's study, the personality data were collected shortly after the stress-and-illness data, and Johnson and

Sarason collected all measures at the same time. It could be argued, therefore, that the personality scores are little more than reflections of the concomitant state of affairs regarding illness, or even both illness and stressful life events. A person who is suffering with symptoms, and perhaps also from the burden of stressful life events, may well feel pessimistic enough to fill out personality questionnaires in a manner suggesting a settled sense of powerlessness, threat, and alienation. Such "situational" responses to personality questionnaires may not actually indicate the person's usual orientations. Although the studies discussed here are an intriguing and promising start, more compelling demonstrations are needed before it can be concluded that the interaction between stressful life events and personality dispositions has an influence upon symptomatology.

OVERVIEW OF A PROSPECTIVE STUDY

What is needed is a prospective study, in which personality dispositions are measured first and illness symptoms are measured later. With such a design, one could better evaluate the contention that personality dispositions influence health and illness. In what follows, we will describe such a study and report its results.

The subject pool for this study were the middle- and upper-level management personnel of a large utility company. At Time One, a composite questionnaire was mailed to all personnel, along with a letter soliciting cooperation and an informed consent form. Included in the questionnaire were measures of stressful life events and illness symptoms having taken place over the previous three years. The questionnaire was completed and returned to the University of Chicago by 86% of the subject pool.

At Time Two, approximately six months later, another composite questionnaire was mailed to 400 subjects selected at random from the pool of initial respondents. This questionnaire contained measures of the personality dispositions of commitment, challenge, control, and various demographic characteristics. This questionnaire was returned by 81% of the subjects. The mailings for Times Three and Four were separated from Time Two and each other by one-year intervals. The questionnaires for both Times Three and Four included the same measures of stressful life events and illness symptoms administered at Time One, but with the instruction to complete them for the preceding one-year period. The return rates for Times Three and Four were also quite high (80% and 78%, respectively). Deletion of incomplete protocols yielded a final sample of 259 subjects.

The effect of this design was to produce stressful-life-events and illness scores on the final sample for five consecutive years, and personality scores at the three-and-a-half-year period. This facilitates comparison of the relationship of personality scores to the other measures when those personality scores have a prospective as opposed to a retrospective status.

Measures of Stressful Life Events and Symptom Status

The measure of stress was an adaptation of the familiar Schedule of Life Events (Holmes & Rahe, 1967). The original Schedule lists numerous events, with their stressfulness determined by the method of psychophysical scaling: subjects were to determine for each event how much life readjustment it required on a scale from 0 to 100, in comparison with a standard item, "divorce," which was assigned a score of 50. A large, representative sample was selected for this task, and the mean of the judgments was taken as the stressfulness of each event. Deriving weights by consensus in this fashion constitutes a kind of cultural expression of stressfulness. This measure has consistently shown a low, positive correlation with measures of illness.

For purposes of this study, certain modifications were made in the Schedule of Life Events. In criticizing this test, investigators appear to agree on the problem of ambiguous items and the need to include items appropriate for the population being studied (e.g., Dohrenwend, Krasnoff, Askenasy, & Dohrenwend, 1978; Johnson & Sarason, 1978). Ambiguous items were deleted or replaced by less ambiguous versions (e.g., "change in financial condition" was changed to "improvement of financial condition" and "worsening of financial condition"). In a pilot study, some management personnel of the utility company not subsequently used as subjects were permitted to add to the Holmes and Rahe list events typical in their lives and to give them weights representing amount of readjustment required. Events mentioned frequently and weighted similarly were added. Some investigators (e.g., Johnson & Sarason, 1978) advocate replacement of the consensus weights for items with idiosyncratic, subjective weights. Other investigators (e.g., Dohrenwend et al., 1978) disagree strongly, considering subjective weights to represent a confusing combination of the results of environmental input, the stressed individual's personality and other predispositions, and his or her evaluation of the consequences of the event. We agree with this view, regarding it as more advantageous to determine the effects of culturally defined stressfulness of events separately from the idiosyncratic effects of personality dispositions on health and illness.

Symptomatology was measured through the Seriousness of Illness Survey (Wyler *et al.*, 1968), a self-report checklist of 126 commonly recognized physical and mental symptoms and diseases. In the development of this instrument, a general severity weight for each disorder was obtained by asking a large sample of physicians and lay persons to rate each of them. The ratings reflected prognosis, duration, threat to life, degree of disability, and degree of discomfort. A highly significant mean rank-order correlation was found between the medical and the lay samples, and a system of weights was accordingly constructed. This carefully developed scale of seriousness of illness has served as a frequent tool in stress-and-illness studies. For present purposes, several symptoms of obvious irrelevance to the male sample were deleted.

Measures of Personality Disposition

The personality dispositions of commitment, control, and challenge were each measured by two scales. In the case of commitment, the *alienation-from-self* and *alienation-from-work* scales of the Alienation Test (Maddi, Kobasa, & Hoover, 1979) were employed as negative indicators. High scores on alienation-from-self reflect a general absence of introspection on and understanding of one's own feelings and actions, whereas high alienation-from-work scores indicate detachment from that which one does to earn money and be a productive member of society. These scales have been shown to yield adequate internal consistency and stability, and to have reasonable construct validity (Maddi *et al.*, 1979). Each scale has 15 items which are rated by the subject in terms of his or her agreement with them.

The disposition of control was measured negatively by the *external locus-of-control scale* (Rotter, Seaman, & Liverant, 1962) and the *powerlessness* scale of the Alienation Test (Maddi *et al.*, 1979). The familiar locus-of-control scale consists of items presented in a forced-choice format. Considerable research has shown that this scale is a reliable and valid index of belief in whether one is controlled by external forces (e.g., Phares, 1976). Although newer, the powerlessness measure also appears to have reliability and validity (Maddi *et al.* 1979).

The challenge disposition was measured negatively by the *security* scale of the California Life Goals Evaluation Schedule (Hahn, 1966) and by the *cognitive structure* scale of the Personality Research Form (Jackson, 1974). Both scales have been used widely and appear to have adequate reliability and validity. The security scale measures the degree to which socioeconomic safety, stability, and predictability are deemed important. The emphasis of the cognitive structure scale is on inflexibility of cognitive categories and intolerance of ambiguity. The items of the former scale are answered "yes" or "no," whereas those of the latter scale involve a 0 to 4 rating.

Demographic Characteristics

Included in the initial questionnaire were items indexing age, education, job level, length of time in job level, religion, ethnicity, marital status, and various other demographic considerations.

RESULTS

Characteristics of the Final Sample

The final sample of 259 subjects on whom all data were available from the four testing sessions was predominantly Protestant, white, married, without close ethnic ties, and exclusively male. The sample ranged in age from 32 to 65 with a mean of 48, in job level from middle managers to officers, and in length of time at job level from less than one year to more than 20 years, with the majority having spent six to ten years at current job level. On these various characteristics, the final sample closely resembled the initial pool of all the management personnel at the utility company.

Characteristics of Stress and Illness

The correlation between stressful life events and illness on the subjects returning the questionnaire sent at Time One was 0.24. This finding is quite consistent with others in literature, as are the large standard deviations of the two distributions. Such results suggest the existence of sizable individual differences in the degree to which stressful life events are associated with illness symptoms. In the final sample of 259, the correlation between stressful life events and illness across the five years for which data are available is 0.23, indicating that this group is representative of the initial pool.

The mean score on the stressful-life-events measure of 886 for five years marks the initial pool as comparable to other groups reported on in the literature. The mean stress score corresponds to the occurrence of several significant events, such as job transfer and illness of family member, in the space of one year.

The mean illness score for the initial pool of 2,335 for five years is also comparable to results obtained with other groups of the sort mentioned above. This score amounts to the occurrence of a significant symptom (e.g., peptic ulcer) and several minor ones (e.g., flu) over the course of a year.

It also appears that stressful life events increased over the period of data collection, as can be seen in Figure 1. The increase is quite apparent over the first three years, and is somewhat obscured because of increased variability over the last two years. The results are similar for illness symptoms. The two peaks in the stress curve coincide with the institution of major policy changes by the company, namely, job evaluation (just how well is each manager doing) and salary adjustments. It is surprising that the curve should dip so much immediately following the peaks. Perhaps restraint on the part of the individuals and the organization following especially stressful times produces a period of relative placidity. It is certainly true that not only individual managers but the utility company as a whole were very much concerned about the possible adverse effects of the institution of job evaluations and salary changes.

In any event, the general increase in stressful life events and illness symptoms occurring from 1972 through 1977 indicates dramatically the limited utility of attempts to avoid stressful live events in order to remain healthy. In modern, industrialized societies such as our own, stress has been increasing and is likely to continue to do so. Avoidance is therefore unrealistic as a coping technique. Health may well be the prize of those whose personalities permit them not only to persist in the face of stressful life events, but actually to transform them to advantage.

Intercorrelations of Personality Measures

Table I shows the intercorrelations among the six personality scales mentioned before. In general, the relationships are substantial, suggesting the presence of an overall tendency toward intrinsic motivation. The results also permit an interpretation that commitment, control, and challenge are three components of intrinsic motivation. The two proposed measures of commitment, alienation from self and alienation from work, intercorrelate at 0.53, which is higher than the mean intercorrelation of each measure with the other four scales (0.39 and 0.33, respectively). Similarly, the intercorrelation of the two control measures, powerlessness and external locus of control, is 0.50, whereas the mean intercorrelation of each of these with the other four scales is lower (0.26 and 0.43, respectively). The situation regarding challenge is more complicated. The intercorrelation of the two challenge measures, security and cognitive

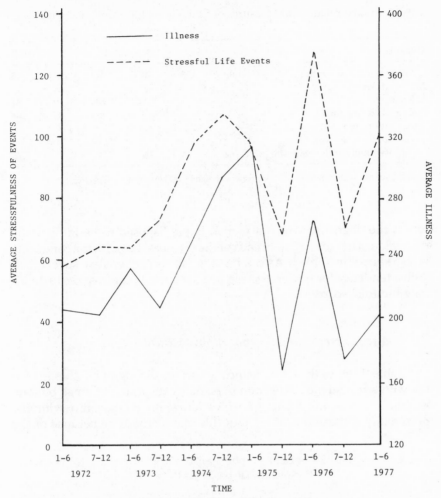

FIGURE 1. Stressful life events and illness over time.

structure, is 0.20, and the mean correlation of the latter with the other four scales is a lower 0.04. But the mean intercorrelation of cognitive structure with the other four scales is a slightly higher 0.24. Scrutiny of Table I shows that this is because cognitive structure shows a pattern of lower correlations with all the other measures. In general, however, it may be concluded that there are commitment, control, and challenge dispositions which are positively intercorrelated.

Z-scores for the six measures were computed, and subject scores were added across measures. The resulting composite score was taken to

TABLE I. Intercorrelations of Measures of Commitment, Control, and Challenge $(N = 259)^a$

Measures	1	2	3	4	5	6
1. External locus of control	1.00	.50	.17	.04	.38	.45
2. Powerlessness		1.00	.29	.02	.66	.74
3. Security			1.00	.20	.20	.31
4. Cognitive structure				1.00	.02	.06
5. Alienation from self					1.00	.53
6. Alienation from work						1.00
Intrinsic motivation composite	.64	.84	.56	.27	.72	.78

^{a}All product-moment correlations .17 or greater are significant beyond the .01 level.

reflect the degree to which a person is predisposed to be intrinsically motivated. The correlation of each of the six measures with the composite is also shown in Table I. As can be seen, all correlations are substantial, with a tendency for powerlessness and the alienation measures to dominate the total score.

Personality, Stress, and Demographic Characteristics

Table II shows the relationships of various demographic characteristics with stressful life events and personality dispositions. In all but one instance, the demographic variables show no relationship with the personality dispositions. Although this may perhaps be because of the

TABLE II. Relationships of Demographic Variables with Stressful Life Events and Personality Dispositions ($N = 259$)

Independent variables	Demographic characteristics			
	Age	Education	Job level	Time at level
External locus of control	.12	.02	.09	.11
Powerlessness	.02	.04	.04	.12
Cognitive structure	.09	−.10	−.04	.04
Security	.06	.04	−.07	.04
Alienation from self	−.07	.01	−.07	.07
Alienation from work	.05	−.02	−.06	.17^a
Composite	.07	−.01	−.02	.15^a
Stressful life events	−.20^b	−.01	−.08	−.11^a

^{a}Product-moment correlation significant at .05 level.
^{b}Product-moment correlation significant at .01 level.

relative homogeneity of the sample with regard to demographics, the results obtained do indicate that whatever effects of personality dispositions there may be on illness cannot readily be explained away as merely reflective of demographic considerations. The one exception to the general picture of absence of relationship is a modest correlation between amount of time a person spends at various job levels in the organization and his alienation from work. Such a finding is hardly surprising, and is too small to warrant reconsideration of the conclusion reached above. This finding is also reflected in the one modest correlation of the composite measure of tendency toward intrinsic motivation and demographic characteristics. Once again, this relationship is too modest to suggest that the composite score is largely an expression of time at job level.

The picture concerning relationships between stressful life events and demographic characteristics is a bit more complicated. Both age and time at job level show a modest but significant relationship with stressful life events. Although it can hardly be concluded that stressful life events index nothing other than age and time at job level, it may be useful to disentangle the effects of demographics from life events per se.

The Contribution of Intrinsic Motivation to Health

In evaluating the role of intrinsic motivation in health, several two-way analyses of variance were performed. In each, stressful life events and the composite measure of intrinsic motivation were the independent variables, with illness as the dependent variable. Both stressful-life-event and intrinsic-motivation distributions were split at the median to yield high and low categories, whereas the illness distribution was treated as continuous.

The first of these analyses utilized the data collected over the entire time of the study. Table III summarizes the results, which indicate that both main effects and the interaction are significant. Scrutiny of the cell means indicates that both main effects and interaction are interpretable. As has been found in so many studies before, stressful life events are associated with illness. But intrinsic motivation holds down the likelihood of illness. The significant interaction indicates that it is especially important to be high in intrinsic motivation if one is experiencing many and/or serious life events. But even when stress is relatively low, high intrinsic motivation means fewer symptoms.

Although these results are consistent with the hypothesis, the use of data from the entire period of the study means that the measure of intrinsic motivation is both retrospective and prospective with regard to illness, having been collected only once, at the three-and-a-half year

TABLE III. Effects of Stressful Life Events and Intrinsic Motivation on Illness Over Total Time Period

Classification	Mean	N	F	df	p
High stressful life events					
Low intrinsic motivation	3914.49	63			
High intrinsic motivation	2224.91	66			
Low stressful life events					
Low intrinsic motivation	1731.17	66			
High intrinsic motivation	1460.94	64			
Main effect: Stressful life events			20.23	1	.001
Main effect: Intrinsic motivation			8.93	1	.003
Interaction			4.71	1	.03

point. In contrast, illness and for that matter stressful-life-events measures were obtained for quarter-year intervals throughout the five-and-a-half-year period of the data collection. It is possible to evaluate whether intrinsic motivation has a prospective influence on, or is merely a retrospective reflection of, illness by repeating the kind of analysis of variance reported above with the data of portions rather than all of the time period of the study.

In the second analysis of variance, the first three-and-a-half years of data were employed. As the measure of intrinsic motivation occurred at the end of this period, this analysis may be regarded as retrospective with regard to the role of personality dispositions. Table IV summarizes the results of this analysis. Once again, the main effects of stressful life events and intrinsic motivation are significant, indicating that the former is associated with higher and the latter with lower levels of symptomatology. But the interaction is not significant. In general, these results are not so strong as those employing the data of the entire time period.

TABLE IV. Analysis of Variance on Illness Using a Concurrent Estimate of Stressful Life Events and a Retrospective Estimate of Intrinsic Motivation

Classification	Mean	N	F	df	p
High stressful life events					
Low intrinsic motivation	2446.38	68			
High intrinsic motivation	1822.87	62			
Low stressful life events					
Low intrinsic motivation	1446.41	61			
High intrinsic motivation	1004.24	68			
Main effect: Stressful life events			11.65	1	.001
Main effect: Intrinsic motivation			4.01	1	.046
Interaction			0.12	1	.73

The third analysis of variance employed the data of the final two years of data collection. As the personality testing took place at the beginning of this period, the measure of intrinsic motivation has a prospective status with regard to illness, which was estimated over the two years. The estimate of stressful life events employed was concurrent with illness, also having been collected over the entire two-year period. Table V summarizes the findings. As in the first analysis, this one shows that both main effects and the interaction are highly significant, and all are interpretable. There is a clear demonstration here that the tendency to be intrinsically motivated is a negative predictor of subsequent levels of symptomatology. Intrinsic motivation is especially important when one's life is highly stressed, but makes some contribution to health even when events are not particularly stressful. Interestingly, this prospective analysis yields much stronger results concerning the importance of intrinsic motivation than did the preceding analysis in which the estimate of intrinsic motivation had a retrospective status with regard to illness symptoms.

In the analysis just discussed, the estimate of stressful life events was concurrent with that of illness. The ultimate prospective test would involve an estimate of stressful life events that, together with the estimate of intrinsic motivation, is also prospective. The next analysis of variance accomplished this by employing an estimate of stressful life events from the first three-and-a-half years of data collection, the measure of intrinsic motivation which occurred at the end of this period, and an estimate of illness from the last two years of data collection. Table VI summarizes the findings of this analysis, yielding significant main effects and an interaction in the predicted direction that approaches significance. Once again, the main effects and interaction are interpretable. It would appear that the experience of stressful life events increases, and the tendency to be

TABLE V. Analysis of Variance on Illness Using a Prospective Estimate of Intrinsic Motivation and a Concurrent Estimate of Stressful Life Events

Classification	Mean	N	F	df	p
High stressful life events					
Low intrinsic motivation	1266.03	63			
High intrinsic motivation	522.23	66			
Low stressful life events					
Low intrinsic motivation	401.85	66			
High intrinsic motivation	352.98	64			
Main effect: Stressful life events			20.69	1	.001
Main effect: Intrinsic motivation			10.62	1	.001
Interaction			8.13	1	.005

TABLE VI. Analysis of Variance on Illness Using Prospective Estimates of Both Intrinsic Motivation and Stressful Life Events

Classification	Mean	N	F	df	p
High stressful life events					
Low intrinsic motivation	1079.82	68			
High intrinsic motivation	510.05	62			
Low stressful life events					
Low intrinsic motivation	538.64	61			
High intrinsic motivation	403.16	68			
Main effect: Stressful life events			7.17	1	.008
Main effect: Intrinsic motivation			8.58	1	.004
Interaction			3.24	1	.07

intrinsically motivated decreases, the likelihood of subsequent symptomatology. The effectiveness of intrinsic motivation as an illness-resistance resource is especially apparent when there is much stress in one's life.

The Relative Importance of Commitment, Control, and Challenge

Having demonstrated the importance of intrinsic motivation as an illness-resistance resource, it would be useful to determine the relative contribution of each of its components. For this purpose, a stepwise regression analysis of the six measures of commitment, control, and challenge on illness for the entire data-collection period was performed. In order to obtain a more complete picture, stressful life events and demographic characteristics were also included as independent variables. In this kind of analysis, each variable is purified of the effects of the other variables, thus permitting assessment of the relative contribution of variables to illness. Table VII shows that the overall R^2 of 0.219 yields an F of 6.31, significant beyond the 0.05 level. Not surprisingly, stressful life events make the largest contribution to illness scores. Among the demographic characteristics, time at job level and age make some contribution as well. Of the measures of intrinsic motivation, security and cognitive structure are the most important, although external locus of control also makes some contribution. The other personality variables do not appear to be important. It would appear that the challenge component of intrinsic motivation, as indexed by security and cognitive structure, is more influential as an illness-resistance resource than either commitment or control.

Table VII. Stepwise Regression of Stressful Life Events, Intrinsic
Motivation Variables, and Demographic Characteristics on Illness
($N = 259$)

Variable	R^2	Beta	df	F	p
Stressful life events	0.090	0.367		38.00	
Time at job level	0.144	0.148		4.51	
Security	0.181	0.182		8.86	
Cognitive structure	0.195	0.089		2.31	
Age	0.205	0.157		4.64	
External locus of control	0.212	0.088		1.74	
Job level	0.217	0.047		1.73	
Education	0.218	0.010		0.58	
Powerlessness	0.219	0.027		0.03	
Alienation from work	0.219	0.025		0.09	
Alienation from self	0.219	0.051		0.08	
Total	0.219		6,252	6.31	.05

Discussion and Conclusions

This study provides evidence that persons who are flexible, tolerant
of uncertainty, and untroubled by the need for socieconomic security are
especially resistant to the debilitating effects of stressful life events. These
persons remain healtheir than those whose ways of looking at experience
are more fixed and who seek socioeconomic reassurance. The orientation
identified with health may well express an underlying belief that life is by
its nature changeable, and that the changes provide a stimulating challenge rather than a dire threat.

This sense of challenge is reminiscent of Csikszentmihalyi's (1975)
finding that persons intrinsically motivated to perform tasks see them as
just difficult enough to provide stimulating obstacles without being either
overwhelming or boring. Although tasks can probably be found which
will produce this effect for many persons, it is also likely that some
persons are more predisposed to perceive a wide range of tasks as challenging. Apparently, it is this predisposition that has been measured in
this study. In that it should lead persons to be interested in tasks for the
satisfaction involved in performing them, it is justifiably considered an
aspect of intrinsic motivation.

The challenge disposition seems to guard health. This is a tangible
demonstration of the survival value of intrinsic motivation. Under-
standably, persons who are flexible and undisturbed by socioeconomic
risk will tend to react to changes, even those which have definitely

negative implications in their culture, as natural and as occasions for growth. In this fashion, stress reactions to such events are minimized or even avoided altogether through the process of perceiving events as not so terrible after all, and engaging in coping activities that further transform them into the stuff of growth. For example, if a person high in challenge loses his job, he may perceive it as an acceptable level of risk that he had always recognized when deciding to enter such an occupation, and cope with the loss by trying to learn how it happened, how it might be avoided in the future, and whether the readjustment required might be an occasion to reconsider occupational decisions for the better. All this may deplete adaptational energy (Seyle, 1956) a lot less than feeling threatened to one's core by being fired, and becoming obsessed endlessly about one's irremedial failings, the ending of opportunity, and how to pay the bills. Nor is it clear that regressive coping techniques, such as drinking more alcohol or denying one's doomsday thoughts, will help much, as they may have the paradoxical effect of prolonging the agony, since they are not really attempts to transform (and thereby end) the negative features of the event.

The connotation of persistence in the challenge disposition may seem inconsistent with experimental evidence in which intrinsically motivated behavior appears diminished by extrinsic reinforcement, whether negative or positive. From the experiments, one would think of intrinsic motivation as a gentle and easily disrupted thing, not persistent at all. This inconsistency can be resolved by recognizing that both situation and person factors must be considered. Situationally, it may be that some tasks can arouse intrinsic motivation in many persons. At the person level, a strong challenge disposition may arouse intrinsic motivation as well. One prediction following from these assumptions is that persons in whom the challenge disposition is strong should be able to resist the tendency of extrinsic reinforcement to disrupt intrinsically motivated behavior. Conversely, persons low in the challenge disposition will have little basis for persisting in intrinsically motivated behavior aroused by the task alone when other environmental factors have altered the task situation. This prediction should be tested by repeating the usual study in which extrinsic reinforcement is introduced after initial task performance, but with subjects who have been assessed beforehand for the challenge disposition. This proposal is quite in keeping with the modified experimental procedures now popular as a function of the interactional accord recently fashioned in psychology (Bowers, 1973).

Taking all the results of the study reported here into account, the status of the proposed commitment and control dispositions is equivocal. Although the measures of these dispositions dominated the composite intrinsic motivation score, they do not appear, taken singly, to have contributed much to the regression equation accounting for illness score.

One possibility is that the measures of these dispositions were less adequate than in the case of challenge. In this regard, it is interesting that three out of four measures that contributed least to the regression equation derive from one test, and are highly intercorrelated. Their empirical redundancy may be the problem. Another possibility, however, is something more like conceptual redundancy. It may be that the challenge disposition already includes within it the major implications of commitment and control. If this is so, then measures of the three dispositions would very likely overlap precisely in regard to the characteristics that would effect illness scores (assuming the conceptualization to be valid). In computing a stepwise regression, this problem would show up as a phenomenon where the first measure or two selected dominates the illness variance. Subsequent measures, being purified of the effects of previously selected measures, would have little to contribute. Certainly, it would be sensible to attempt more adequate measurement not only of commitment and control, but of challenge as well. After all, existing measures were selected for this study, rather than measures constructed to precise conceptual designs. But it should also be kept in mind that the challenge disposition may carry all the effective connotations of person-based intrinsic motivation.

Given the support for the challenge disposition, it should be considered further here. The next step is to gather empirical evidence regarding its antecedents and consequences. As to consequences, it is of importance to determine whether persons high in challenge do indeed engage in transformational coping when confronted with stressful events. Ideally, such persons could be observed actually dealing with stressful events. They should avoid regressive coping, such as trying not to think about the events, seeking reassurance rather than confrontational reactions from others, spending more time in entertaining activities, relying more on alcohol or tranquilizers. Such regressive coping may even extend to sleeping more and practicing meditation, though these two activities are more complex in their possible meanings. Meditation often involves a fairly radical change in life-style which amounts to dealing more straightforwardly and transformationally with one's problems. But when meditation truly involves making one's mind a blank and detaching oneself from practical pressures, then it is probably more regressive than anything else. In contrast, transformational coping involves learning more about the stressful events, considering not only the cons but also the pros that they constitute, seeking the complete and straightforward reactions of others rather than their reassurance, and attempting to incorporate what has happened into an existing or altered life plan. Persons high in the challenge disposition should engage in some combination of these, and also not spend more time entertaining or tranquilizing themselves.

The question of antecedents for challenge amounts to understanding how high and low levels of this disposition are learned. It seems plausible (Kobasa & Maddi, 1977) that children will emerge as high in challenge if the significant others in their lives (1) love and admire them as potentially independent persons (this is not the same as the blanket unconditional positive regard of Rogerians), (2) encourage a wide range of experiences and the formulation of cognitive differentiations among them (it has little effect to experience many things if all are loosely lumped together as similar), (3) impose reasonable goals and limits that can function as obstacles to be transformed, and (4) inculcate in various ways the view that life is naturally a changing and evolving thing.

Needless to say, considerable empirical work is necessary before this list of developmental considerations can be evaluated. Such study is urgent. If we can understand better how persons learn to be disposed toward intrinsic motivation, then we will have a powerful tool in aiding them to remain healthy in the encounter with stressful life events. As such events are likely to continue to increase in modern industrialized states (if not everywhere), encouraging intrinsic motivation seems a more realistic approach than the avoidance techniques of regressive coping.

ACKNOWLEDGMENT

We are grateful for the assistance given by Dr. Robert R. J. Hilker, Jr., and by Sheila Courington, Caren Gotlieb, Marlin Hoover, Stephen Kahn, and Tim Strauman.

REFERENCES

ALLPORT, G. W. *Personality: A psychological interpretation.* New York: Holt, 1937.

AVERILL, J. R. Personal control over aversive stimuli and its relationship to stress. *Psychological Bulletin*, 1973, *80*, 286–303.

BOWERS, K. S. Situationism in psychology: An analysis and a critique. *Psychological Review*, 1973, *80*, 307–336.

CALDER, B. J., & STAW, B. M. Self-perception of intrinsic and extrinsic motivation. *Journal of Personality and Social Psychology*, 1975, *31*, 599–605.

CSIKSZENTMIHALYI, M. *Beyond boredom and anxiety.* San Francisco: Jossey-Bass, 1975.

DECHARMS, R., & MUIR, M. S. Motivation: Social approaches. In M. R. Rosenberg & L. W. Porter (Eds.), *Annual Review of Psychology.* Palo Alto: Annual Reviews, 1978.

DOHRENWEND, B. S., & DOHRENWEND, B. P. (Eds.). *Stressful life events: Their nature and effects.* New York: Wiley, 1974.

DOHRENWEND, B. S., KRASNOFF, L., ASKENASY, A. R., & DOHRENWEND, B. P. Exemplification of a method for scaling life events: The PERI Life-Events Scale. Journal of Health and Social Behavior, 1978, *19*, 205–229.

GREENE, D., STERNBERG, B., & LEPPER, M. R. Overjustification in a token economy. *Journal of Personality and Social Psychology*, 1976, *34*, 1219–1234.

HAHN, M. E. *California life goals evaluation schedule*. Palo Alto: Western Psychological Services, 1966.

HOLMES, T. H., & RAHE, R. H. The social readjustment rating scale. *Journal of Psychosomatic Research*, 1967, 11, 213–218.

JACKSON, D. N. *Personality research form manual*. Goshen, N. Y.: Research Psychologists Press, 1974.

JOHNSON, J. H., & SARASON, I. G. Life stress, depression, and anxiety: Internal-external control as a moderator variable. *Journal of Psychosomatic Research*, 1978, 22, 205–208.

KOBASA, S. C. Stressful life events, personality and health: An inquiry into hardiness. *Journal of Personality and Social Psychology*, 1979, 37, 1–11.

KOBASA, S. C., & MADDI, S. R. Existential personality theory. In R. Corsini (Ed.), *Current personality theories*. Itasca, Ill.: Peacock, 1977.

MADDI, S. R., HOOVER, M., & KOBASA, S. C. Alienation and exploratory behavior. *Journal of Personality and Social Psychology*, 1981, in press.

MADDI, S. R., KOBASA, S. C., & HOOVER, M. An alienation test. *Journal of Humanistic Psychology*, 1979, 19, 73–76.

MISCHEL, W. Towards a cognitive social learning reconceptualization of personality. *Psychological Review*, 1973, 80, 252–283.

MURRAY, H. A. *Explorations in personality*. New York: Oxford University Press, 1938.

PHARES, E. J. *Locus of control in personality*. Morristown, N. J.: General Learning Press, 1976.

ROTTER, J. B., SEAMAN, M., & LIVERANT, S. Internal vs. external locus of control of reinforcement: A major variable in behavior theory. In N. F. Washburne (Ed.), *Decisions, values and groups*. London: Pergamon, 1962.

SEYLE, H. *The stress of life*. New York: McGraw-Hill, 1956.

WHITE, R. W. Competence and the psychosexual stages of development. In M. R. Jones (Ed.), *Nebraska symposium on motivation*. Lincoln: University of Nebraska Press, 1960.

WYLER, A. R., MASUDA, M., & HOLMES, T. H. Seriousness of Illness rating scale. *Journal of Psychosomatic Research*, 1968, 11, 363–375.

The Psychological Aesthetics of Narrative Forms

CHRISTY MOYNIHAN AND ALBERT MEHRABIAN

The study of aesthetic experience may be approached from a number of viewpoints. A work of art is composed of a myriad of elements, any one of which may be examined with respect to its impact on aesthetic preference. A painting may be analyzed in terms of color, form, or subject matter: a story or novel in terms of style, plot, theme, or point of view; a song in terms of melody, rhythm, or harmonal structure, and so forth. The multiplicity of elements in a work of art, as well as the diversity among different art forms, would seem to make it difficult to identify general principles underlying all aesthetic experience. Berlyne (1971, 1974), however, has constructed a general theory of psychological aesthetics which conceptualizes all aesthetic experience, whether in response to visual art, literature, or music, as a unitary phenomenon. This theory is based not on the kinds of elements in a work, but on the degree of interdependence among these elements.

THE INVERTED-U HYPOTHESIS

Berlyne contends that aesthetic pleasure or preference is primarily a response to the degree of structure or complexity in the work of art. He notes that aestheticians have often declared aesthetic pleasure to be the result of the balance or interplay between two opposing sets of variables: those, such as variety, novelty, and multiplicity, which reduce structure and increase complexity, and those, such as harmony, balance, or unity, which are attributes of ordered structure. Berlyne conceives of all these

CHRISTY MOYNIHAN AND ALBERT MEHRABIAN • Department of Psychology, University of California, Los Angeles, California 90024.

diverse variables as belonging to a single dimension of structural complexity, ranging from the extremely simple, or ordered, to the extremely complex, or unordered. Berlyne further defines these variables in terms of information theory (see Attneave, 1959; Cherry, 1966; Garner, 1962): complexity implies high uncertainty, whereas order indicates redundancy, with uncertainty and redundancy constituting opposite ends of the same continuum.

Complexity or uncertainty affects aesthetic pleasure through its effects on arousal. Basing his argument on physiological evidence concerning the relationships among exploratory drive, arousal, and pleasure, Berlyne (1960, 1971) hypothesized that pleasure is curvilinearly related to arousal, such that when arousal is low, stimuli which increase arousal are pleasurable. When arousal is high, however, stimuli which decrease arousal are pleasurable. Complex stimuli are arousal-heightening, whereas structured stimuli are arousal-moderating. Thus, pleasure is greatest at intermediate levels of arousal or complexity.

The relationships among arousal, uncertainty, and various measures of preference have been examined in studies concerned with diverse behaviors and situations. The hypothesized relationship between uncertainty level and arousal has received strong empirical support (Berlyne, 1960; deCharms, 1968; Fiske & Maddi, 1961). The hypothesized inverted-U relationship between uncertainty level, whether experimentally manipulated or subjectively rated, and measures indicative of pleasure or "hedonic value" (i.e., verbally expressed preference, evaluative judgments, or ratings of pleasingness and pleasure) has also been found in a number of studies (Berlyne, 1974; Crozier, 1974; Kammann, 1966; Munsinger and Kessen, 1964; Normore, 1974; Vitz, 1966a,b).

In other studies using the same or similar measures, however, pleasure was found to be either a monotonically increasing or a monotonically decreasing function of uncertainty level (Osborne & Farley, 1970; Walker, 1970). When other behaviors and other types of verbal ratings are examined, the results are even more complex. Rather than showing the inverted-U relationship that would be expected if these behaviors were direct functions of pleasure, the judged interestingness of the object, exploratory time (i.e., time spent looking at the object), and exploratory choice (i.e., choice of one object over another for further viewing) are almost always positively related to uncertainty level (Cantor, Cantor, & Ditrichs, 1963; Leckart and Bakan, 1965; Wohlwill, 1968). Although these variables tend to have strong relationships with uncertainty, they are also correlated with hedonic value, although to a lesser degree (Berlyne, 1974; Berlyne & Ogilvie, 1974; Crozier, 1974; Hare, 1974).

Studies which find a linear rather than an inverted-U relationship between hedonic value and uncertainty do not necessarily contradict

Berlyne's hypothesis. Such results could be caused by the failure to sample stimuli over a wide enough range in terms of uncertainty level, so that the obtained results reflect only the ascending or descending portion of the curvilinear function. Studies done by Mehrabian and his associates (Hines & Mehrabian, 1979; Mehrabian & Russell, 1974a; Mehrabian & West, 1977; Russell & Mehrabian, 1976, 1978) in the area of environmental psychology, however, indicate that other factors may affect the relationship between information rate and preference. This body of work, in addition, provides a framework for examining the joint influence of pleasure and uncertainty on behaviors relating to the evaluation of, preference for, and exploration of aesthetic objects.

THE PLEASURE × AROUSAL INTERACTION HYPOTHESIS

In the studies of Mehrabian and colleagues, approach toward or preference for an environment is hypothized to be mediated by the emotion-eliciting qualities of that environment. Three orthogonal dimensions, which are the fundamental components of all emotions, are distinguished. These are feelings of pleasure, arousal, and dominance, which correspond to the evaluative, activity, and potency dimensions of connotative meaning found by Osgood, Suci, and Tannenbaum (1957), as well as to dimensions of emotional experience obtained by other investigators (see Russell and Mehrabian, 1977). Thus, in contrast to Berlyne's work, within this framework pleasure and arousal are seen to be orthogonal dimensions of experience. In addition, preference for an environment, though partially determined by pleasure, is not totally identifiable with the pleasure induced by the environment.

A number of studies have examined approach toward environments for which the pleasure- and arousal-eliciting qualities were independently varied (Hines & Mehrabian, 1979; Mehrabian & Russell, 1974a; Russell & Mehrabian, 1976, 1978). These studies have generally shown that the inverted-U relationship between arousal and approach behavior occurs only for situations neutral in pleasantness. In pleasant situations, approach increases with arousal without a downward inflection point, whereas in unpleasant situations approach tends to decrease with arousal, although sometimes increasing for the highest levels of arousal. (This latter effect is interpreted as reflecting the learning and adaptive function which exploring unpleasant, arousing situations may have for the individual.) These studies have, in addition, consistently shown a significant main effect of pleasure, such that approach is always greater in more pleasant situations, regardless of the situation's arousing quality.

The pleasure–arousal interaction hypothesis has implications for a theory of aesthetic preference. Like Berlyne, Mehrabian and his associates postulate a direct relationship between uncertainty level, which they term information rate, and arousal (Mehrabian & Russell, 1974b). Since arousal and information rate are positively correlated, it follows from the pleasure–arousal hypothesis that (1) aesthetic preference is a positive correlate of the pleasantness of the aesthetic object, and (2) the pleasantness of the aesthetic object moderates the effects of information rate on aesthetic preference. In particular, a higher information rate should be tolerated for pleasant works than for unpleasant ones.

The pleasantness of an aesthetic object requires some comment at this point. That works of art, even nonrepresentational ones, have an emotional impact is well-established (see Child, 1969). Narrative and other representational works may depict certain situations which would produce unhappy, depressed, or otherwise unpleasant emotions in the individual if he were actually experiencing them—and may, in fact, produce similar though less powerful emotions in the reader of the work. Nonrepresentational art, such as music or abstract painting, also has been shown to have strong negative and positive effects on mood, through the use of color, tonal quality, and so forth (Hevner, 1937; Wexner, 1954).

Aestheticians distinguish between the formal qualities of a work and the mood or emotion induced by it. In a "truly" aesthetic response, aesthetic pleasure is seen to derive from these formal aspects, rather than from the mood produced by the content (Stolnitz, 1960). This may be true, however, only for a minority of readers, namely, those who, because of their training, have learned to subordinate their emotional response to an intellectual appreciation of the work.

AESTHETIC PREFERENCE, PLEASURE, AND INFORMATION RATE

The independent effects of pleasure and information rate on aesthetic preference have been examined in a preliminary investigation by Moynihan (1980). This study employed 45 short stories which represented a broad range of literature, including both traditional and more experimental works. An effort was made to sample stories representing many possible combinations of information rate and pleasantness.

Information rate was measured with a verbal report scale, consisting of adjective pairs in a semantic differential format. The adjective pairs used in the scale consisted of terms connoting simplicity or ordered structure on the one hand, and complexity or lack of structure on the other (e.g., single focus/multiple focus; sparse/dense; orchestrated/free-roaming; cohesive/diffuse). For each pair, the two terms were equated for the degree of pleasant or unpleasant connotation expressed by each term, thus ensuring the independence of the final information rate measure from judgments of pleasantness ($r = -0.19$). The final scale, consisting of 100 items, exhibited high internal consistency ($KR20 > 0.96$).

The pleasantness of stories was also assessed, using verbal reports based on adjective pairs in a semantic differential format. Readers were asked to rate their mood in response to a story using such items as "unhappy/happy," "gloomy/light-hearted," and "depressed/cheerful." The internal consistency of this six-item scale was 0.89.

Preference was measured on a sixteen-item Likert scale. Items assessed a variety of responses to stories including evaluative responses (e.g., "I didn't much care for this story"), degree of enjoyment or interest experienced while reading the story (e.g., "This story was so boring I couldn't help skimming most of it"), and desire for further exposure to the story or to similar ones (e.g., "I'd like to read other stories by the same author"). Internal consistency for this scale was 0.96.

In addition to the above variables, a measure of the reader's orientation toward literature was included. That individual differences have a strong effect on response to, and preference for, a work of art has long been recognized. Many investigators have, for example, found differences in aesthetic preferences of those with and those without formal training in art (e.g., Barron, 1953; Keston & Pinto, 1955; Valentine, 1962) and in particular in the preference for complexity in a work (e.g., Barron & Welsh, 1952; Munsinger & Kessen, 1964).

In addition to differences in formal training, individuals may vary in terms of their orientation or attitude toward art. The most influential movement in literary criticism of this century is formalist criticism (Scott, 1962; Stolnitz, 1960)—an approach which evaluates a literary work in terms of the formal relationships among its elements. Although persons taking such an academic approach to their general reading experience undoubtedly represent only a small portion of the reading population, their responses to art are of theoretical interest, because they demonstrate what is gained (or lost) through a deliberate and self-conscious analysis of art. The Formalism scale used in the study measured a subject's general orientation toward art, although it was recognized that persons can and do become more or less analytical in their approach to art under different circumstances. Subject-recruitment procedures used in Moynihan's study ensured that there was an adequate number of formalists in the sample for the purpose of statistical analysis.

Items measuring the following aspects of formalism were included in the scale ("+" and "−" indicate the direction in which the item was keyed): (1) interest in literature as an object of formal study ("I generally enjoy my English classes whether I get good grades in them or not" "+"); (2) acceptance, or at least tolerance, of a wide range of literature ("Even if a story seems pointless to me I usually try to finish it to see what the author was trying to accomplish" "+"); (3) tolerance for greater complexity in literature ("I could never like a poem I had to read five times before I could figure it out" "−"); (4) an interest in the formal aspects of literature ("Style is just window-dressing. I think the meaning of a novel is much more important" "−"); and (5) the adoption of a deliberate, analytical approach to literature ("I try to notice some of the techniques good writers use to make a particular effect" "+"). The internal consistency of this nineteen-item scale was 0.77.

In Moynihan's study, information rate, pleasure, and formalism were each found to affect preference, and, in addition, to interact in their effects on preference. Overall, pleasant stories were preferred to unpleasant ones, and formalists preferred stories more than nonformalists. With respect to information rate, preference was found to be a curvilinear function: preference was greatest at intermediate levels of information rate and least for very high or very low levels. The results of the study, thus, support Berlyne's inverted-U hypothesis, and demonstrate once again that aesthetic preference involves an optimum balance between complexity and order.

Pleasure

As in previous studies done within Mehrabian's framework, pleasure had a pronounced effect on preference, and, in fact, had a much greater main effect on preference than information rate. To ensure that the preference and pleasure scales were in fact measuring different dimensions, two validation scales were employed. The first assessed the happiness of the story's content (e.g., happy ending/unhappy ending; humorous/serious); the second assessed evaluative judgments of various aspects of the story, including its style, characters, dialogue, and subject matter (e.g., good dialogue/poor dialogue; well-written/poorly written). The pleasure scale was found to be highly correlated with the happiness of content dimension and not with the evaluative dimension, whereas the converse was true of the preference scale. Thus, although preference is affected by pleasure, the two are, in fact, distinct psychological entities.

Further study is required to determine what causes a story to be experienced as pleasurable or unpleasurable. Subject matter alone does not seem sufficient, since, for example, of two stories about murder one can be experienced as unpleasant and another as pleasant (e.g., Dostoevski's *Crime and Punishment* versus Agatha Christie's *Death on the Nile*). It is not the subject matter per se which makes a story pleasurable, but the point of view taken toward that subject matter. Pleasant stories may simply adopt a more positive outlook on life. In addition to content factors, however, stylistic factors may also affect pleasantness. Unpleasant stories may be sparser or more austere, less humorous or witty, have fewer embellishments of character and story, and, in general, show less concern for the psychic comfort of the reader.

The Pleasure × Information Rate Interaction

The necessity of making a conceptual distinction between preference and pleasure is further dictated by the fact that the relationship between information rate and preference is moderated by pleasure. As in previous studies which found an interaction between pleasure and arousal in determining preference (e.g., Hines & Mehrabian, 1979; Mehrabian & Russell, 1974a; Mehrabian & West, 1977; Russell & Mehrabian, 1976), an interaction between pleasure and information rate was found in Moynihan's study. This interaction is shown in Figure 1. As predicted, the relationship of preference to information rate had a higher point of inflection for higher levels of pleasure: For high pleasure, preference was an inverted-U function of information rate. For low pleasure, preference tended to decrease as information rate increased, remaining constant for low and moderate rates of information, and declining for high information.

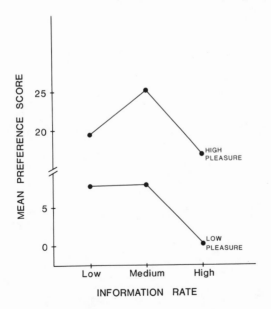

FIGURE 1. Mean preference scores as a function of pleasure and information rate.

Thus, although individuals try to achieve optimum rates of information in their environments and aesthetic experiences, this is not the only factor influencing their approach toward an aesthetic object. Any form of aesthetic activity, such as reading a story, is complex and may have many different and often conflicting functions. Aesthetic activity, on the one hand, is a cognitive process, often requiring intense mental effort. On the other hand, it is an entertainment, approached because it is fun. Aesthetic activity, thus, has elements of both *work* and *play*. It is likely that individuals try to achieve an optimum balance between these two functions, and that when the work and play functions become unbalanced in either direction, preference declines. The work versus play qualities of aesthetic activity are most likely affected both by information rate and by pleasantness: higher rates of information and lower degrees of pleasure make aesthetic activity more like work and less like play.

Although both the work and play functions of aesthetics affect all readers to some degree, the preferred balance may not be constant. Which of these functions is predominant at any given time depends on the characteristics of the story, the reader, and the situation in which the aesthetic experience takes place (Mehrabian, 1976). This was found to be the case in Moynihan's (1979) study. Figure 2 shows the relationship between pleasure and preference for formalists (i.e., those above the median on the Formalism scale) and for nonformalists (i.e., those below the median). As can be seen in Figure 2, although preference increases

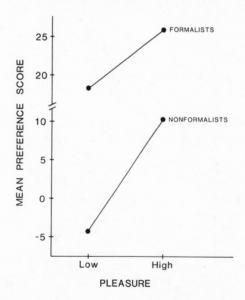

FIGURE 2. Mean preference scores as a function of formalism and pleasure.

with pleasure for both formalists and nonformalists, the rate of increase is more than twice as great for nonformalists as for formalists. Thus, although pleasure affects the preference of formalists, it affects them to a lesser degree than it does the preferences of nonformalists. It appears that formalists, with their interest in the analysis and intellectualization of aesthetic experience, are more oriented toward the work aspect of literature, whereas nonformalists are more oriented toward the entertainment or play aspect.

ASPECTS OF INFORMATION RATE IN NARRATIVE FORMS

In the analyses described above, as in most investigations in this field, the stimulus was defined in terms of its overall complexity or information rate. Although such an approach has proved fruitful, it overlooks certain aspects of the relationship between structure and aesthetic preference. An object may be composed of many different sets of elements, each varying in terms of information rate. Some sets may tend to unify a work, others to complicate it (see Arnheim, 1966, for a discussion of the coexisting elements in a landscape design which create "tension" as opposed to those which unify the design).

It is suggested that preference is greatest not when a work is intermediate in its degree of structure, but when the structure-inducing and structure-reducing elements of a work are both maximized. Berlyne (1971) noted the work of Eysenck (1942), who suggested that pleasure is a multiplicative function of order and complexity, being greatest when both are at a maximum. Based on a study by Hare (1974), however, Berlyne (1974) concluded that complexity and order are not two independent dimensions, but endpoints of a single continuum.

Narrative Structure

The present study, though characterizing stories in terms of overall information rate, also attempted to identify independent dimensions of information rate within a work. These dimensions were hypothesized to derive from the temporal organization of a narrative piece. These states were held to be psychologically meaningful in terms of the reader's attempts to structure a narrative: the degree of uncertainty created prior to the ending, the degree of surprise created by the ending, and the degree of resolution achieved by the ending.

Beginning with Aristotle, many scholars have noted that the sequence of events in a narrative is not arbitrary or random, but is instead conditional, proceeding in an organized fashion from the story's initial premises to its final conclusions (see Culler, 1975, for a review of investigations in the "grammar" of plot structure). Kermode (1967), Shklovsky (1965), and others have noted the importance of the ending in organizing a narrative and completing or resolving issues raised in the initial part of the work. These scholars contend that the need for resolution is a basic human requirement, and that lack of resolution in a narrative has a psychologically disturbing effect.

The sequence of events in a narrative is, thus, organized toward a specific end. Because that sequence necessarily unfolds over time, however, the reader cannot know the outcome of events prior to their occurrence. Uncertainty and surprise, therefore, become important components of the narrative experience. Uncertainty refers to the difficulty the reader has in predicting events prior to their occurrence, and surprise derives from the reader's failure to have predicted these events. Uncertainty, surprise, and resolution may all be conceptualized in terms of information rate. Events high in uncertainty or surprise have a high information rate. Resolution, on the other hand, since it has the effect of organizing and structuring the story, lowers the information rate.

The Psychological Effect of Uncertainty, Surprise, and Resolution

Rather than being a trivial or unfortunate side-effect of narrative structure, the creation of uncertainty and surprise is an important factor underlying narrative satisfaction. Although the aesthetic value of surprise in a narrative is commonly recognized (Abrams, 1971), that of uncertainty is often overlooked. As noted by Scholes (1974), however, the postponement of knowledge is almost the raison d'être of the narrative form:

> A story may be said to exist by virtue of starting actions and raising questions which it then refuses to complete for a certain period of time. A story consists of barriers to the completion of actions and various lures, feints, and equivocations which delay the answering of questions. (p. 154)

Barthes (1974) similarly refers to the role of "enigma" in narrative experience, noting its importance, not just in mystery novels, but as a basic structuring force in all narratives.

Reading a story, or experiencing any type of narrative, is partly a game, then, involving an interplay between the reader's guesses and the story's solutions. The interaction among uncertainty, surprise, and resolution affects the degree of satisfaction which a reader obtains from the narrative. Achieving resolution is paramount for the reader's satisfaction. Among stories which resolve, however, those which create greater uncertainty or lead to greater surprise should be enjoyed more. For stories which fail to resolve, the combination of high uncertainty followed by high surprise should be the least satisfying. Thus, preference is determined by two sets of elements: those which reduce order (uncertainty and surprise), and those which induce order (resolution), being greatest when both are at a maximum.

The Empirical Study of Narrative Structure

In Moynihan's study, the information rate of the story was measured on four different scales, all using an identical semantic differential format. (Note, the overall measure of information rate used in the analysis discussed above was the sum of all the individual information-rate measures.) Prior to the end of the story (which was defined as the final 25%) subjects were asked to rate the uncertainty of the story using adjective pairs such as "uncomplicated/complicated" and "constant/shifting." After finishing the story, subjects were asked to rate it in terms of its surprisingness (e.g., "predictable/unpredictable" and "anticipated/unforeseen") and its degree of resolution (e.g., "resolved/ambiguous" and "clear/veiled"). In addition, subjects were asked to assess the information rate of the story as a whole.

Uncertainty, surprise, and lack of resolution were all positively correlated and, in addition, were correlated with the measure of total information rate, indicating that it is indeed appropriate to conceptualize all as dimensions of information rate. In spite of this, however, the effects of these dimensions on preference were not the same. Although surprise and lack of resolution were positively correlated, lack of resolution was negatively correlated with preference, and surprise was positively correlated with preference. In addition, although uncertainty had a slightly negative effect on preference overall, when coupled with high surprise or high resolution, it had a greatly magnified positive effect on preference. Stories which combined high uncertainty with low surprise or low resolution, however, were the least preferred types of stories. Thus, high uncertainty intensifies the positive effect of high surprise and high resolution, but is detrimental with low surprise and low resolution.

Table I presents predicted preference scores (based on a multiple regression analysis of story ratings) for the eight possible combinations of uncertainty, surprise, and resolution. Combinations are listed in descending order of preference. As can be seen, the most highly preferred story is one which is surprising, resolved, and high in initial uncertainty. This was by far the most preferred type of story.

Among the next more preferred stories (rows 2 through 4, Table I),

TABLE I. Predicted Preference Scores for the Eight Combinations
of Uncertainty, Surprise, and Resolution[a]

Uncertainty	Surprise	Resolution	Preference
+	+	−	50
−	+	+	27
−	+	−	18
−	−	+	18
+	−	−	10
−	−	−	9
+	+	+	6
+	−	+	−34

[a] "+" indicates high uncertainty, high surprise, and lack of resolution. "−" indicates
low uncertainty, low surprise, and high resolution. Preference scores may range from
−64 to +64, with higher scores indicating greater preference. Obtained preference
scores had a mean of 13.0 and a standard deviation of 32.0.

formal perfection, in the sense of high resolution, is not necessarily the
most desirable quality. For these three types of story, two are low in
resolution. The main impression that emerges from an examination of
Table I is that some type of increase in information rate or arousal is
preferred at the end of the story. Although the most satisfactory way of
increasing arousal appears to be through surprise, readers seem to be
willing to settle for lack of resolution *if* the story is already low in initial
uncertainty. Lack of resolution appears to make an initially dull story
somewhat more interesting.

Stories which fail to provide any type of high arousal ending are
among the four types least preferred. In addition, stories with a uniform
rate of arousal throughout, whether uniformly low or uniformly high, are
among the three least preferred. The only type of story less preferred than
one uniform in arousal—and the only type to be rated negatively in terms
of preference—is one which is unsurprising, unresolved, and high in
initial uncertainty. From the reader's point of view, this combination
epitomizes everything that can go wrong with a story: it requires the
reader to sit through a confusing and unpredictable series of events, only
to come upon an ending which is not only unsurprising, but does nothing
to alleviate the confusion.

The Inverted-U Function and Narrative Structure

The curvilinear relationship of overall information rate to preference
can be explained in terms of the relationships among uncertainty, surprise, and resolution given in Table I. Since uncertainty, surprise, and

lack of resolution are all high in information rate, stories which are high on all three dimensions have the highest information rates overall. Stories which are low in uncertainty, surprise, and lack of resolution have the lowest information rates overall. As predicted by the inverted-U function, these stories are among the three least preferred types. Stories that are high on some dimensions, but low on others, that is, intermediate in information rate, tend to be more preferred. Thus, the inverted-U function between preference and overall information rate is the end product of a set of relations among information-increasing and information-decreasing forces in the work. Although the inverted-U function summarizes this set of relationships, it fails to reflect many of the dynamics underlying aesthetic preference.

SUMMARY AND CONCLUSIONS

The preliminary study discussed above examined the effect of information rate on preference within a framework which takes into account the intervening emotional state created by the work and differences in information rate provided by different sets of elements in the work. Berlyne's basic hypothesis—that preference is an inverted-U function of information rate—was supported. This relationship was shown, however, to be moderated by both of the above factors.

To say, for example, that individuals prefer intermediate levels of stimulation obscures certain aspects of the aesthetic phenomenon. Aesthetic experience, like any cognitive activity, is one not of passive reception, but of active construction. While reading a novel, watching a film, or engaging in any narrative activity, the viewer must attempt to structure the narrative as it unfolds. The interactions among uncertainty, surprise, and resolution found by Moynihan suggest that part of the satisfaction involved in the aesthetic experience derives from the structuring process itself, provided that the effort to structure the work is successful. Narrative experience, thus, has much in common with other game-like forms of entertainment.

The opposition between order-inducing and order-reducing elements in the work found by Moynihan reflects the opposition of the material to the reader's attempts to structure it. Maximum preference, therefore, occurs at the point where the mental efforts of the reader produce the best returns on the investment. Preference declines for stories which are too easy or too difficult to structure. It is possible that narrative literature and other narrative forms require more in the way of active, and often conscious, structuring processes than other art forms. It seems, nevertheless, that a similar dialectical process might underlie preference for other art forms. Mehrabian (1976), for example, points out the interplay in great poetry between complex symbolization and intense phonological regularities. In visual art, the order-inducing and order-reducing elements would, most likely, change from work to work. In some cases, for example, color could be used to unify a work, and in other cases to create disharmony.

Although aesthetic activity is a cognitive process, Moynihan's study also showed it to be, at heart, an emotional one. The emotion of pleasure, in particular, had a large impact on preference—larger, in fact, than that of information rate. Pleasure has long assumed a major role in theories of human behavior. It appears to be an important factor in aesthetic behavior as well. Although aestheticians recognize that art produces an emotional response, it is generally maintained that aesthetic preference should not derive from the perceiver's mood or emotional state. Preference instead should derive from a state of "aesthetic pleasure" produced by an appreciation of the formal beauty of the aesthetic object. The present study appears to demonstrate, however, that aesthetic activity is undertaken, not just for the sake of art, but also as a form of play or entertainment. Pleasure, thus, is a major factor, whether conscious or unconscious, in an individual's aesthetic preferences.

In Moynihan's study, high levels of pleasure were preferred to low levels for all rates of information. Pleasure affected even the preferences of formalists, a group of individuals oriented toward the appreciation of art for art's sake. Thus, there appears to be a limit to the degree to which one can be objective and analytical about one's aesthetic responses. Aesthetic experience is firmly rooted in psychobiological processes, and studies of aesthetic preference cannot ignore the pleasure-inducing, entertainment function which art has, not only for nonformalists, but for all readers. Since nonrepresentational art forms have also been found to produce an emotional response in the perceiver, pleasure should affect preference in a similar manner for visual art, music, and so forth.

Although aesthetic preference was affected by pleasure, it was also shown to be conceptually distinct from it. In addition to its entertainment or play function, art has a purely aesthetic or work function. These two functions, however, are somewhat in conflict, accounting for the fact that information rate affects preference differently at high and low levels of pleasure. In pleasant stories with moderate rates of information, the aesthetic and entertainment functions are most in balance, making these the most preferred type of story. Unpleasant, complex stories carry a doubly negative burden in terms of entertainment value, making them the least preferred of all types of story.

Engaging in any type of aesthetic activity occurs within the context of the individual's ongoing behavior, and implies a choice over other types of activities which the individual could engage in. It must, therefore, be asked what function this type of activity has for the organism. Aesthetic activity must ultimately be analyzed within a framework which considers both its similarities to and its differences from other playlike and worklike activities. A theory of aesthetic preference must examine why aesthetic activity is chosen over other types of play, and why certain types of aesthetic activity are chosen over others.

Within the framework presented by Mehrabian and his colleagues, behavior is seen as mediated by the individual's emotional state. Individuals change environments to change their emotional state and, in particular, to change their feelings of pleasure, dominance, and arousal. Moynihan's findings shed some light on the dynamics underlying aesthetic preference: people engage in aesthetic activity to increase their levels of pleasure and to achieve optimum levels of stimulation. The importance of pleasure in determining preference was shown to depend on the reader's orientation to literature. Similarly, the background emotional state from which the individual approaches the aesthetic activity should affect the salience of these two factors on preference.

Mehrabian (1976) discusses some of the determinants of preference in terms of the individual's general emotional state, immediate situation, and the pleasure- and arousal-eliciting qualities of different art forms and media. Classes of narrative may differ, for example, in terms of their typical rates of information. Genre works have a lower information rate overall, because they follow a more familiar pattern. In addition to information rate, other stylistic and content factors affect the arousingness of the work. For example, violence or action-oriented content, fast cutting in film, or an abrupt prose style are more arousing. Different media also differ in terms of their characteristic arousal-inducing qualities. Unlike McLuhan (1964), for example, Mehrabian hypothesizes movies to be a "hotter," that is, more arousing medium than television. This is due to the magnitude and salience of the visual stimuli, as well as the fact that viewing a movie takes place in public, rather than in a comfortable low-arousal home situation.

Individuals approaching an aesthetic activity from a low-pleasure state—either one of boredom (i.e., low pleasure, low arousal) or anxiety (i.e., low pleasure, high arousal)—will probably be strongly motivated by the pleasure or entertainment aspects of the work. These people are likely to seek out "escapist" fare in order to escape literally from an unpleasant emotional state, caused, for example, by a stressful day at work. Individuals already in a pleasant or at least neutral frame of mind might be more willing to respond to the formal qualities of a tragic, austere, or otherwise less pleasant work.

The rate of information preferred should also depend on the initial arousal state of the individual. Those in an anxious, high-arousal state should prefer lower information rates and generally less arousing forms of entertainment, preferring to stay at home and watch television or to read a favorite genre author. People in a low arousal state, such as boredom, will seek out higher arousal experiences, preferring to go out to a movie to watch an action-oriented feature. Other forms of arousing entertainment, such as those provided by amusement parks, might compete for their attention.

REFERENCES

ABRAMS, M. H. *A glossary of literary terms* (3rd ed.). New York: Holt, Rinehart & Winston, 1971.

ARNHEIM, R. *Toward a psychology of art: Collected Essays.* Berkeley: University of California Press, 1966.

ATTNEAVE, F. *Application of information theory to psychology: A summary of basic concepts, methods, and results.* New York: Holt, Rinehart, & Winston, 1959.

BARRON, F. Complexity–simplicity as a personality dimension. *Journal of Abnormal and Social Psychology,* 1953, *48,* 163–172.

BARRON, F., & WELSH, G. S. Artistic perception as a possible factor in personality style: Its measurement by a figure preference test. *Journal of Psychology,* 1952, *33,* 199–203.

BARTHES, R. *S/Z: An essay.* New York: Hill & Wang, 1974.

BERLYNE, D. E. *Conflict, arousal, and curiosity.* New York: McGraw-Hill, 1960.

BERLYNE, D. E. *Aesthetics and psychobiology.* New York: Appleton-Century-Crofts, 1971.

BERLYNE, D. E. (Ed.). *Studies in the new experimental aesthetics: Steps toward an objective psychology of aesthetic appreciation.* New York: Wiley, 1974.

BERLYNE, D. E., & OGILVIE, J. C. Dimensions of perceptions of paintings. In D. E. Berlyne (Ed.), *Studies in the new experimental aesthetics: Steps toward an objective psychology of aesthetic appreciation.* New York: Wiley, 1974.

CANTOR, G. N., CANTOR, J. H., & DITRICHS, R. Observing behavior in preschool children as a function of stimulus complexity. *Child Development,* 1963, *34,* 683–689.

CHERRY, C. *On human communication: A review, a survey, and a criticism.* Cambridge: M.I.T. Press, 1966.

CHILD, I. L. Esthetics. In G. Lindzey & E. Aronson (Eds.), *Handbook of social psychology* (2nd ed., Vol. III). Reading, Mass.: Addison-Wesley, 1969.

CROZIER, J. B. Verbal and exploratory responses to sound sequences varying in uncertainty level. In D. E. Berlyne (Ed.), *Studies in the new experimental aesthetics: Steps toward an objective psychology of aesthetic appreciation.* New York: Wiley, 1974.

CULLER, J. *Structuralist poetics: Structuralism, linguistics, and the study of literature.* Ithaca: Cornell University Press, 1975.

DE CHARMS, R. *Personal causation.* New York: Academic Press, 1968.

EYSENCK, H. J. The experimental study of "good Gestalt": A new approach. *Psychological Review,* 1942, *49,* 344–364.

FISKE, D. W., & MADDI, S. R. *Functions of varied experience.* Homewood, Ill,: Dorsey Press, 1961.

GARNER, W. R. *Uncertainty and structure as psychological concepts.* New York: Wiley, 1962.

HARE, F. G. Verbal responses to visual patterns varying in distributional redundancy and in variety. In D. E. Berlyne (Ed.), *Studies in the new experimental aesthetics: Steps toward an objective psychology of aesthetic appreciation.* New York: Wiley, 1974.

HEVNER, K. The affective value of pitch and tempo in music. *American Journal of Psychology,* 1937, *49,* 621–630.

HINES, M., & MEHRABIAN, A. Approach-avoidance behaviors as a function of pleasantness and arousing quality of settings and individual differences in stimulus screening. *Social Behavior and Personality,* 1979, *7,* 223–233.

KAMMANN, R. Verbal complexity and preferences in poetry. *Journal of Verbal Learning and Verbal Behavior,* 1966, *5,* 536–540.

KERMODE, F. *The sense of an ending: Studies in the theory of fiction.* New York: Oxford University Press, 1967.

KESTON, M. J., & PINTO, M. Possible factors influencing musical preference. *Journal of Genetic Psychology,* 1955, *86,* 101–113.

LECKART, B. T., & BAKAN, P. Complexity judgments of photographs and looking time. *Perceptual and Motor Skills,* 1965, *21,* 16–18.

McLUHAN, M. *Understanding media: The extensions of man.* New York: McGraw-Hill, 1964.

MEHRABIAN, A. *Public places and private spaces.* New York: Basic Books, 1976.

MEHRABIAN, A., & RUSSELL, J. A. *An approach to environmental psychology.* Cambridge: M.I.T. Press, 1974.(a)

MEHRABIAN, A., & RUSSELL, J. A. A verbal measure of information rate for studies in environmental psychology. *Environment and Behavior,* 1974, *6,* 233–252.(b)

MEHRABIAN, A., & WEST, S. Emotional impact of a task and its setting on work performance of screeners and nonscreeners. *Perceptual and Motor Skills,* 1977, *45,* 895–909.

MOYNIHAN, C. *Structuring processes and aesthetic preference in the experience of narrative forms.* Unpublished doctoral dissertation, University of California at Los Angeles, 1980.

MUNSINGER, H., & KESSEN, W. Uncertainty, structure and preference. *Psychological Monographs,* 1964, *78,* (9, Whole No. 586).

NORMORE, L. F. Verbal responses to visual sequences varying in uncertainty level. In D. E. Berlyne (Ed.), *Studies in the new experimental aesthetics: Steps toward an objective psychology of aesthetic appreciation.* New York: Wiley, 1974.

OSBORNE, J. W., & FARLEY, F. H. The relationship between aesthetic preference and visual complexity in abstract art. *Psychonomic Science,* 1970, *49,* 69–70.

OSGOOD, C. E., SUCI, G. J., & TANNENBAUM, P. H. *The measurement of meaning.* Urbana: University of Illinois Press, 1957.

RUSSELL, J. A., & MEHRABIAN, A. Some behavioral effects of the physical environment. In S. Wapner, S. Cohen, & B. Kaplan (Eds.), *Experiencing the environment.* New York: Plenum Press, 1976.

RUSSELL, J. A., & MEHRABIAN, A. Evidence for a three-factor theory of emotions. *Journal of Research in Personality,* 1977, *11,* 273–294.

RUSSELL, J. A., & MEHRABIAN, A. Approach-avoidance and affiliation as functions of the emotion-eliciting quality of an environment. *Environment and behavior,* 1978, *10,* 355–387.

SCHOLES, R. *Structuralism in literature: An Introduction.* New Haven: Yale University Press, 1974.

SCOTT, W. S. (Ed.) *Five Approaches of literary criticism: An arrangement of contemporary critical essays.* New York: Macmillan, 1962.

SHKLOVSKY, V. La construction de la nouvelle et du roman. In T. Todorov (Ed.), *Théorie de la littérature.* Paris: Seuil, 1965.

STOLNITZ, J. *Aesthetics and philosophy of art criticism: A critical introduction.* Boston: Houghton Mifflin, 1960.

VALENTINE, C. W. *The experimental psychology of beauty.* New York: Barnes & Noble, 1962.

VITZ, P. C. Affect as a function of stimulus variation. *Journal of Experimental Psychology*, 1966, 71, 74–79.(a)

VITZ, P. C. Preference for different amounts of visual complexity. *Behavioral Science*, 1966, 11, 105–114.(b)

WALKER, E. I. Complexity and preference in animals and men. *Annals of the New York Academy of Sciences*, 1970, 169, 619–652.

WEXNER, L. B. The degree to which colors (hues) are associated with mood tones. *Journal of Applied Psychology*, 1954, 38, 432–435.

WOHLWILL, J. F. Amount of stimulus exploration and preference as differential functions of stimulus complexity. *Perception and Psychophysics*, 1968, 4, 307–312.

14

A Conceptual Analysis of Exploratory Behavior

The "Specific-Diversive" Distinction Revisited

Joachim F. Wohlwill

Introduction

> Better go back now and start about my business. The trouble is that down the hill to the right I've caught sight of accented green roofs and curved gables painted jade green and vermilion. That must be Chinatown. Of course the thing to do is to take a turn through Chinatown on the way down toward the business district. I find myself walking along a narrow street in a jungle of Chinese lettering, interpreted here and there by signs announcing Chop Suey, Noodles, Genuine Chinese Store. There are ranks of curio stores, and I find myself studying windows full of Oriental goods with as much sober care as a small boy studying the window of a candy store. The street tempts you along. Beyond the curio shops there are drug stores, groceries giving out an old drenched smell like tea and camphor and lychee nuts, vegetable stores, shops of herb merchants that contain very much the same stock of goods as those Marco Polo saw with such wonder on his travels. In another window there are modern posters: raspberry-and-spinach-tinted plum-cheeked pin-up girls and stern lithographs of the Generalissimo; a few yellowing enlargements of photographs of eager-looking young broad-faced men in cadets' uniforms. The gilt lettering amuses the eye. The decorative scroll-work of dragons and lotus flowers leads you along. You forget the time wondering how to size up the smooth Chinese faces. At the end of the street I discover that an hour has passed and that I have been walking the wrong way all the time. (Dos Passos, 1944, p. 330)

This chapter is an inquiry into the nature of exploratory activity—the type of behavior so vividly described by Dos Passos in the preceding account of

Joachim F. Wohlwill • College of Human Development, Pennsylvania State University, University Park, Pennsylvania 16802.

his meanderings through San Francisco's Chinatown. Exploratory activity played a central role in Berlyne's empirical and theoretical work, and yet his treatment of exploration constitutes perhaps the least systematically worked-through aspect of his theory.

This observation applies in particular to one of the several distinctions among different forms of exploratory behavior that Berlyne proposed—that between "specific" and "diversive" exploration. After introducing it in his 1960 volume, *Conflict, Arousal and Curiosity*, Berlyne returned repeatedly to this distinction in his research and thinking (e.g., Berlyne, 1963, 1971), and it was taken over by diverse other workers in this area—including the writer—as well (Dent & Simmel, 1968; Hutt, 1970; Wohlwill, 1968; 1975a). This distinction, intended to differentiate between two different motivational bases for exploratory activity, was clearly of much importance to Berlyne (cf. Berlyne, 1971); yet it was not too clearly stated, and indeed was defined in uncharacteristically inconsistent terms by Berlyne. Thus, when he originally introduced it, in his 1960 volume, it was couched (p. 80) as a difference in the specificity of the object of the individual's exploratory activity, specific exploration being treated as *search* behavior (e.g., for a lost article, or a solution to a problem), whereas diversive exploration was less strongly directed activity designed to provide an increase in arousal when the organism is in a state of boredom. But in subsequent uses of the distinction by Berlyne himself, as well as by others who have taken it over, an important change has set in. Thus, in his 1971 volume, specific exploration is defined (p. 100) as activity in direct confrontation with a particular stimulus, designed to reduce conflict or uncertainty, and diversive exploration is defined as it was previously, that is, as activity aimed at seeking out stimuli characterized by some optimal level with respect to their collative properties, for the sake of dispelling boredom.

The shift in the conception of specific exploration, from activity in search of a particular stimulus to that which takes place in confrontation with a stimulus, has engendered a fair amount of confusion and lack of clarity. The reason is that it has introduced a confounding of two very different elements, one concerning the *object* of exploratory activity proper, undertaken in the absence of a stimulus, the other concerning the *properties of a stimulus* encountered by the individual, and inspected by that individual—to use Berlyne's apt term in his 1960 volume. Indeed, his distinction in that volume between "inspective" and "inquisitive" exploration, that is, between exploration elicited by a stimulus confronting the individual and that occurring for the purpose of bringing the individual into contact with some stimulus, or with stimulation more generally, gives explicit recognition to the importance of this differentiation. It is thus doubly puzzling that he should have seemingly lost sight of it in his subsequent writing.

This confounding has, unfortunately, come to characterize treatments of exploratory behavior more generally. Interest in this topic appears initially to have grown out of research at the animal level, and on maze behavior in the rat, in particular, which disclosed certain forms of seemingly random movement that could not be accounted for through the reduction of any primary drives. This led some investigators to postulate the existence of an exploratory drive, seemingly involving movement for its own sake, or more particularly for the sake of change in the environmental stimulation afforded the animal at a particular point. One manifestation of this "drive" was seen in the well-known tendency of rats in a maze to engage in alternation behavior between the two arms of a T- or Y-maze, presumably based on a bias towards *change* in stimulation. (See Fowler, 1965, for a thorough, as well as critical analysis of such accounts of exploratory behavior.)

Limited as these accounts were to the behavior of rats in mazes, intended to reveal the operation of "basic" principles of behavior as bequeathed by the controversy over Hullian versus Tolmanian learning theory, the larger ecological context and functional significance for such behavior was generally lost sight of. It was, however, captured most compellingly by Shillito (1963) in her account of exploratory behavior in the vole. Shillito recognized that exploratory activity occurs in both unfamiliar and familiar environments, though it may take somewhat different forms in each, and that it typically starts as seemingly spontaneous and possibly random-appearing behavior for the sake of "reconnaissance" of an unfamiliar environment, which may lead to a second phase of "investigation" if some unfamiliar stimulus is encountered. But Shillito called attention at the same time to the fact that exploratory behavior may be set off by the *absence* of a familiar, as well as the presence of an unfamiliar, stimulus. Particularly pertinent to Berlyne's specific-diversive distinction is her point that the animal needs to be in an "exploratory mood" before exploration, that is, investigation, of an unfamiliar object will occur.

Shillito's formulation fits quite readily Berlyne's initial definition of diversive exploration referred to above, conceived as activity directed at increasing level of arousal, in the absence of a stimulus demanding attention. Yet most subsequent discussions of exploratory activity in general, and of the specific-diversive distinction in particular, such as Berlyne's later treatments, as well as those by Hutt (1970), Nunnally and Lemond (1973), and Keller and Voss (1976), have started from the premise of activity elicited by a stimulus confronting the organism, and focused almost exclusive attention on the characteristics of the stimulus maximally conducive to the different kinds of exploratory activity.

EXPLORATORY ACTIVITY AS A PROCESS OVER TIME

The cases of Hutt's and Nunnally and Lemond's analyses of exploratory activity are particularly instructive, since both papers concern themselves with the temporal sequencing of different phases of such activity. In Hutt's presentation this is limited to the observation that diversive exploration had to follow the specific. That is, given a stimulus confronting the individual to begin with, uncertainty concerning it would have to be reduced before the individual would employ it to derive affective arousal from it—as seen in a child manipulating a new toy. Nunnally and Lemond go further in devising a schema to represent the temporal course of exploratory activity, as shown in Figure 1.

Note that Nunnally and Lemond, although starting with a "stimulus encounter" phase that initiates an extended chain of activity from orienting behavior to play, do provide for searching behavior activated by boredom as a phase presumably set off when their chain of stimulus-induced exploration, manipulation, and play has run its course, and the organism's arousal has dropped to a suboptimal level. Such searching activity then leads to a further stimulus encounter, setting off a new chain of exploratory behavior.

Thus, Nunnally and Lemond's schema is, appropriately, a cyclical one, and it would be quite legitimate to enter it at any point, including that of search activity aimed at bringing about an encounter with a stimulus. Yet these authors do not concern themselves with this phase, nor with the specific-diversive distinction, beyond citing it near the

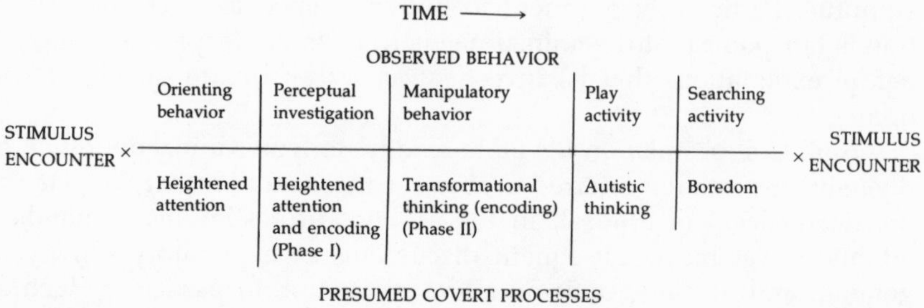

TIME ⟶

OBSERVED BEHAVIOR

STIMULUS ENCOUNTER ×	Orienting behavior	Perceptual investigation	Manipulatory behavior	Play activity	Searching activity	STIMULUS × ENCOUNTER
	Heightened attention	Heightened attention and encoding (Phase I)	Transformational thinking (encoding) (Phase II)	Autistic thinking	Boredom	

PRESUMED COVERT PROCESSES

FIGURE 1. Nunnally and Lemond's schematic representation of the temporal course of exploratory behavior. (From Nunnally and Lemond, 1973, p. 63. Reprinted by permission of Academic Press.)

beginning of their paper and noting its importance. Instead, they devote almost exclusive attention to the perceptual investigation phase, and to the role of Berlyne's collative properties in instigating such investigation, in adults as well as in children at different ages.

Four Cases of Exploratory Activity

A reformulation of Nunnally and Lemond's schema, starting from the point at which exploratory activity is instigated, involves more, however, than a mere shift of the starting point of the cycle. Several different situations arise, depending on the conditions under which the activity is initiated. There are, to begin with, the conditions that Berlyne originally, in his 1960 book, identified with specific and diversive exploration, respectively, in the sense of either a search for a specific stimulus, or the seeking out of stimulation, or stimulus change, for the sake of a change in arousal. And to these two we must add two additional ones. One of these we may call "vigilance," that is, a continuous perceptual scanning and frequently locomotor traversal of a given environment to minimize threats from unknown stimuli and facilitate appropriate action under potentially unstable environmental conditions. The case of the cop on his beat, or the lookout on a fire tower, would be instances in kind. And, finally, we have "specific" stimulus exploration in the sense Berlyne used the term in his later writings, that is, instigated by incidental encounter with a stimulus, and aimed at reducing uncertainty and curiosity. This type is illustrated in such diverse situations as looking at some interesting sight encountered along the roadside while driving, rushing to the window to investigate an apparent automobile accident, and, last but not least, taking part in a standard experiment on exploratory activity.

The four cases are represented in Table I, which indicates for each the implicit question, or mental set, instigating the original exploratory activity leading to some stimulus encounter, the question or other response at the moment of encounter, the character of the resulting exploration of the stimulus, and the likely phase of activity following stimulus exploration.

The following points are to be noted with respect to the formulation of exploratory activity in terms of the four cases outlined in Table 1:

1. Exploratory activity needs to be studied as a process structured over time. This point was already noted in connection with Nunnally and Lemond's schema, but emerges more sharply in the light of the vast differences in temporal patterning associated with the different cases.

2. The exploration of a stimulus in general (and in cases A, B, and C specifically) involves an *interaction* between given properties of the

TABLE I. Four Cases of Exploratory Behavior

Situation	Question or set instigating exploratory activity	Question or other response at moment of stimulus encounter	Character of exploration of stimulus	Poststimulus exploration phase	Example
A. Stimulus search	"Where is X?"	"Is this X?" (Or: "Eureka!")	Directed exclusively at stimulus identification	If $S = X$, search terminated; if $S \neq X$, search continued	Search for a person or a missing object
B. Vigilance	"Are there any A in this area?"	"Is this an A?"	Directed primarily at stimulus identification	If $S \in A$, appropriate action taken; $S \notin A$, exploration continued	Cop on his beat
C. Diversive exploration	"Let me find some S."	"Let's look at this S!" (Or: "Let's skip this one!")	If exploration occurs, mixture of inspective[a] and affective[a]	Manipulation or play, if appropriate to subject and object. Alternative: proceeding to encounter with further stimulus object, or source of stimulation	Sightseeing, window-shopping, visiting zoos, museums, etc.
D. Incidental stimulus encounter	None	"What is this S?"	Largely inspective[a], but may shift to affective[a] after curiosity has been satisfied	None	Looking at a sight along the highway while driving to work; looking at a stimulus in a stimulus-exploration experiment.

[a] For explanation, see text, pp. 351–353.

stimulus, and the set or goal of the individual's activity that produces the encounter with the stimulus. Such questions as what, if anything, the person is looking for, and how this sought-for stimulus compares to the one encountered, presumably affect the extent and nature of the exploration of the stimulus that will occur. The stimulus characteristics by themselves can determine exploration only in case D, where the stimulus is encountered incidentally, although they may on occasion come to *override* the influence of the person's set or goal, notably under case C. (For instance, a person twiddling the dials of the TV set in search of low-key entertainment may stay with a very different type of program, such as a horror movie, if curiosity is sufficiently aroused, as, for example, through the sight of some monster creature.) The same phenomenon may even occur under cases A and B—we may be detoured from our vigil, or search for a specific object, by some particularly intriguing sight or event (as befell the leading characters in Antonini's *L'Avventura*). There is, in fact, a name for occurrences of this type: serendipity.

3. By extension of the preceding point, the generic properties of the encountered stimulus play a differential role in the various prototype situations. In the case of A and B they are essentially irrelevant (apart from the possibility of "detouring" effects just cited). In case C, on the other hand, they will, in the first instance, affect the probability of a particular kind of stimulus being encountered, as well as the probability of such an encounter leading to exploration. Thus, a person in search of amusement is apt to pass by a bookstore or museum, without entering it and exploring its wares; similarly, the poster in the window of the tourist agency may be noticed with but a passing glance. Where the interaction of the person's set and the stimulus encountered is propitious, however, so that exploration of that stimulus ensues, the stimulus properties will obviously determine the extent and nature of the exploration that will occur. Yet even then it may not be some intermediate level of collative properties, as suggested by Berlyne in his conception of diversive behavior, that will determine such an exploration. Rather, it could be a stimulus high in collative properties, in which case it will arouse curiosity which will be reduced through specific exploration—that is, diversive exploration may, through an encounter with a suitable stimulus, result in specific exploration. Alternatively, such an encounter could involve a stimulus that is explored for reasons quite unrelated to its collative properties, such as a high-intensity stimulus, or one whose content or meaning provokes emotional arousal, as in the case of a stimulus with sexual connotations.

As for the last case, D, here we may expect the collative properties of the stimulus to play a primary, though not necessarily exclusive, role in determining exploration of an incidentally encountered stimulus.

SPECIFIC VERSUS DIVERSIVE EXPLORATION REEXAMINED

The formulation of exploratory activity given in Table I, along with the three preceding elucidatory comments, lead to a reassessment of Berlyne's differentiation between specific and diversive exploration. As noted previously, if we take his original definition, the distinction amounts to the differentiation between cases A (search for a specific stimulus) and C (seeking out of stimulation). The picture becomes more complex once we turn to his subsequent identification of specific exploration with that occurring on encounter with a specific stimulus, for the sake of curiosity reduction. The two types of exploration are now seen as complementary, rather than mutually exclusive, in two quite different senses. First of all, according to case C, it is diversive exploration that leads to stimulus encounters resulting in specific exploration. This point, which is nicely illustrated in the passage from Dos Passos quoted at the start of this paper, is significant, as it points to a process of seeking out of stimuli for the sake of the arousal of curiosity, which in turn is reduced through specific exploration. Berlyne considered this type of phenomenon only in the rather special case of the "arousal jag," that is, the seeking out of highly intensive levels of momentary stimulation, as in amusement-park rides and other forms of thrill seeking. What he does not seem to have considered—undoubtedly because of his failure to take the temporal course of exploratory activity into account—is that this cycle of successive raising and reducing of uncertainty is endemic to diversive exploration of many kinds, as in window-shopping, thumbing through a picture magazine, etc.

A second complementary relationship applies to the reduction of curiosity through "specific" exploration of a stimulus—henceforth to be referred to as "inspective" exploration, in accordance with Berlyne's own use of that term in his 1960 volume—and the arousal of affect derived from the stimulus. Although this affective response is certainly not to be equated to the diversive exploration that has brought the individual into contact with the stimulus, it does presumably represent the intended result of that activity, bearing in mind the definition of diversive exploration as directed at creating an optimally satisfying level of arousal. Indeed, in the comparatively rare instances in which Berlyne referred to diversive exploration in the context of an experiment, it is clear that he identified it operationally with the positive affect derived from the stimulus. But this point leads us to the much more intricate question of the operational differentiation between the inspective and the affective components of the stimulus exploration, both as Berlyne himself studied it, and as it might be approached on the basis of a reformulation of the two as complementary processes.

The "Specific-Diversive" Distinction in Berlyne's Research

Berlyne's own thinking on this issue emerges most directly from a study (Berlyne, 1963) that was explicity designed to provide a comparison between specific and diversive exploration. It utilized the "exploratory choice" method, in which subjects are presented with pairs of stimuli for a short time, and then asked which of the two they would rather look at again. The results, in most instances, depended on the amount of time the subject had to explore the pair of stimuli originally: following very brief exposure time (.5 sec) the more irregular stimulus (the one containing more heterogeneous elements, or a more irregular or asymmetrical pattern, etc.) was chosen for further viewing, whereas after a longer original period of explosure (4 sec) the tendency was in the opposite direction. These differences were actually far from consistent across the individual types of manipulations of irregularity used, and generally held true in only a relative sense (that is, in no case was there a reversal, from a clear preference for the more irregular stimulus under short exposure to a similarly unequivocal preference for the more regular stimulus under long exposure). Nevertheless, in the aggregate, the data do provide some support for the postulated difference between preferential choice occurring following adequate exploration of a stimulus, as compared with that to be expected after brief exposure, and thus before the uncertainty or conflict engendered by it has been fully resolved.

Berlyne identified this difference with that between the two modes of exploratory activity that he had distinguished earlier in his 1960 book, but already in his article he switched to the later conception of "specific" exploration, not as search behavior, but as activity elicited by the characteristics of a stimulus confronting the person. But the real question arising in regard to this study is the meaning of the choices occurring following longer exposure, and thus presumably after the perceptual curiosity aroused by the stimuli had been dissipated. On the one hand, Berlyne still interpreted this exploration as "diversive," in the same sense that he originally conceived of the term, that is, as exploration mediated by a desire for an optimal level of arousal. On the other hand, he considered this type of exploration as essential to aesthetic behavior, and in support of this view he cited results from a further study using the same stimuli employed in the main part, but involving ratings on two different scales, "interesting-uninteresting" and "pleasing-displeasing." For three of the types of manipulations of irregularity, the more irregular members of the stimulus pairs were rated as significantly more interesting (differences for the remaining pairs were nonsignificant, but in no case in a direction favoring the more regular stimulus). In contrast, for six of the eight types of stimulus pairs, the more regular stimulus was rated as more pleasing.

These differences are impressive, and undoubtedly significant for an understanding of exploratory choice and aesthetic preference and evaluation. But it is not clear that they provide a real test of the differences between the two types of exploratory activity that Berlyne intended to differentiate. In his introduction to the article, Berlyne suggested that the introduction of the choice element somehow changes the situation from "forced" to "free" exploration (in fact he related that differentiation to the one he had suggested originally between "inspective" and "inquisitive" exploration, depending on whether or not there is a stimulus confronting the subject). Yet the exploratory choice method can hardly be said to provide an analogue to "inquisitive" exploration, undertaken in search of a stimulus, in terms of the extent of the individual's control over the stimulus. The difference is basically equivalent to that between a "constructed response" format and a multiple-choice format for test items. Thus, the relevance to this case of the concept of "diversive" exploratory remains questionable. A fortiori, it is doubtful whether this latter type of activity, which appears appropriate to such behaviors as window-shopping or nightclubbing, is at all equivalent to that which is involved in response to works of art. Thus, the very adequacy of Berlyne's intent to construct a behavioral framework for an account of the aesthetic response is thrown into question.

But if this study is less than fully convincing as a demonstration of the "specific-diversive" distinction, the situation in this regard is thrown into utter confusion by the finding in a subsequent study (Berlyne & Crozier, 1971) that the controlling factor in the exploratory choice situation appears to be not so much the opportunity given the subject to dispel uncertainty or reduce curiosity in regard to a stimulus as simply the sheer level of stimulation to which he had been exposed just prior to being asked to choose between exposure to a more and a less complex stimulus. Berlyne and Crozier found that subjects displayed a strong preference to see the more complex stimulus of a pair when the pair was exposed over a long series of trials, so that curiosity could not have been a relevant factor, at least over the latter part of the series—providing only that prior to the exposure of each stimulus the subject experienced a brief period of complete darkness. Indeed, under these circumstances the preference for the complex stimulus held even for series of 50 trials of a single stimulus pair and a 5-sec exposure period of whichever stimulus the subject chose to expose on a given trial. On the other hand, in a condition affording a maximum of pre-choice stimulation (a different color slide of a tourist attraction shown on each trial), the preference for the more complex stimulus of the pair dropped to a chance level.

In their discussion of the results of this experiment, Berlyne and Crozier fail to address themselves to the implications of these results for the specific-diversive distinction, even though they refer to it at the outset, in connection with the 1963 study that served as the starting point for this later one. Clearly, the foundation on which the distinction was built has crumbled under the weight of the new evidence showing that stimulus characteristics such as high complexity, previously assumed to determine specific exploration, that is, motivated by perceptual curiosity, could function equally well in the service of diversive exploration, that is, motivated by the desire to raise arousal level to compensate for a preceding lack of stimulation.

An Alternative Conception: "Inspective" and "Affective" Exploration as Complementary Processes

Consider the case-D situation (cf. Table I), which corresponds to that represented by the typical experiment on voluntary exploration time, as well as by such everyday occurrences as being confronted, without the individual's seeking out any particular stimulus or type of stimulation, with some stimulus that evokes interest and curiosity. What is the nature of the exploratory activity that may be expected to occur, and how is that activity related to the characteristics of the stimulus, on the one hand, and to affective or evaluative responses of the individual on the other?

As far as the sheer amount of exploration, or attention to the stimulus (e.g., in the case of auditory stimuli) is concerned, we do have a fairly complete picture, from the work not only of Berlyne and his students and associates, but from others such as Hutt (1970), Nunnally and Lemond (1973) and Keller and Voss (1976), and overall it bears out the role of the collative properties emphasized by Berlyne, and the process of resolution of conflict and uncertainty that he regarded as basic. Yet the relationship between this process and that of aesthetic judgment and preference was not dealt with in wholly satisfactory fashion by Berlyne, even his 1971 volume ostensibly devoted to the behavioral basis of the aesthetic response. (As for the other investigators cited above, none professed an explicit interest in questions of aesthetics.)

The previously cited study by Berlyne and Crozier (1971) serves as a convenient starting point for examining this question more closely. For, as we saw, this study showed that subjects preferentially chose the more complex of a pair of stimuli, long after the uncertainty concerning it had been reduced, given a context of a relative absence of stimulation preceding the exposure to the stimulus as well (and perhaps also surrounding it, that is, the typical laboratory cubicle in which the experiment was carried out presumably served further to create a temporary condition of stimulus deprivation). We noted that this finding went against Berlyne's earlier notion of diversive exploration, as distinguished from specific. But, more positively, what does it tell us about the meaning of responses in this exploratory choice situation, and its relationship to aesthetic preference and judgment?

As a very partial answer to this question, consider a recently completed study of the author's (Wohlwill & Harris, 1980). In the main part of the study, college subjects were shown sets of slides depicting park scenes that had been scaled with respect to the congruity or fittingness between some man-made structure featured in the slide and the natural context surrounding it. These congruity values turned out to be very highly correlated (across slides) with a variety of evaluative ratings made by the subjects. This finding is not, however, of primary interest for us here, except insofar as it points to the contrast between *in*congruity, as a factor enhancing attention and amount of exploration—as found by Berlyne and Lawrence (1964), Nunnally, Faw, and Bashford (1969) and others—and the clear preference for *con*gruity where preferential or evaluative responses are concerned.

In a supplementary study, the same stimuli were presented to a new group of subjects for viewing, under voluntary exploration instructions: they were simply asked to look at each slide as many times as they wished, the slides being presented for ½-sec exposure periods. In this case the relative "popularity" of a slide, in terms of mean number of times the subjects exposed them to view, was quite uncorrelated with the fittingness measures, on the one hand, and with the evaluative ratings on the other. Significantly, the one verbal-rating measure that did show a moderate correlation (across slides) with the number-of-exposure measure was rated interestingness—a finding consonant with previous findings (e.g., Day, 1967) of the differentiation between pleasingness and interestingness. But a closer examination of the number-of-exposures data for each slide disclosed a marked tendency for these values to vary as a function of *either* of two variables: the novelty or complexity of the pictorial material in the slide, and the overall attractiveness of the slide (as determined from the evaluative ratings). Thus there were in fact two different kinds of slides that evoked a relatively large number of exposures: those that were in some way novel or complex, and those that were particularly satisfying aesthetically. It appears, then, that data on total amount of time spent exploring a stimulus, which is probably the single most widely used measure of exploratory behavior, may well confound what are in fact two distinct types of exploration: inspection for the sake of uncertainty or conflict reduction (motivated by perceptual curiosity), and contemplation, for the sake of enjoyment or pleasure. It seems likely that more fine-grained analysis of the mode of exploration occurring to these different types of stimuli would in fact differentiate between these two modes of exploration: the former would be expected to be much more mobile, involving a much more extensive form of scanning, than the latter.

It might be thought that in this result we have simply confirmed the distinction between specific and diversive exploration that has been the object of such intensive criticism in the preceding discussion. Indeed, the differentiation just presented does resemble closely Berlyne's distinction, but we are now in a position to reformulate it in somewhat different terms, that is, "inspective" versus "affective." This is to be preferred to "specific" versus "diversive," since we are clearly dealing with responses to specific stimuli in either case, namely, those presented to the subjects, while on the other side the affective exploration mode may be not so much directed at "diversion" (a term again most appropriately applied to stimulation-*seeking* activity) as to the maintenance of an optimal hedonic tone.

There are two further points to be made in this regard. First, we have already seen from the studies of Berlyne and Crozier and Wohlwill and Harris that the two modes of exploration cannot be differentiated operationally by recourse to amount of voluntary exploration for the first, as compared to some suitable preference response or affective judgment for the second. We are thus still in need of a valid and operationally feasible distinction between them at the response level. Second, though the stimulus correlates of inspective exploration seem by now firmly established, that is, the various collative properties, or the uncertainty or conflict generated by the stimulus, we are as yet far from understanding the stimulus determinants governing a mode of exploration directed at an affective response or determining aesthetic preference.[1]

This latter question, along with a further one, namely, the relationship between the two modes of exploration, may be taken as the central questions for psychological aesthetics; we will consider them presently. Before doing so, however, an examination of the first question, and of some operationally viable differentiation between these two modes, is in order.

Operationalizing the Inspective-Affective Conception

One issue needs to be confronted head-on in this regard: are we dealing with a dichotomy between two mutually exclusive modes, or rather with a continuum involving varying mixtures of the two? The latter

[1]This point is borne out by the fairly irregular and inconsistent relationships frequently obtained in studies of the relationship between complexity and preference (e.g., Day, 1967; Wohlwill, 1968), in comparison with the functions that relate complexity to looking time.

seems to be a more profitable way of looking at it: we may postulate a continuum running from a purely inspective orientation toward a stimulus at one extreme to a purely affective orientation at the other. The first might be exemplified by a pathologist examining a piece of tissue under a microscope, to determine the nature of the disease affecting it. The latter would be exemplified by a person gazing at a sunset at sea. Yet, customarily we may expect that any stimulus encountered by individuals, whether they be watching television, admiring some outdoor scenery, or visiting an art museum, will evoke some degree of exploration of both types. The particular mix will depend on two sets of factors. The first set relates to stimulus characteristics, that is, the relative amount of complexity, novelty, etc., for the individual, in comparison with its potential for arousing and maintaining hedonic tone (these two being considered as largely independent characteristics of the stimulus (cf. below). The second set relates to the individual's attitude or motivation in confronting the stimulus, that is, is it that of the investigator or explorer, intent on information, or is it that of the pleasure seeker, or the aesthete, aiming at a purely affective or hedonic experience? Here we have, of course, a restatement of the interaction principle noted earlier (p. 345, point 2).

Once this notion of a continuum, represented by the confluence of two separate factors, is accepted, several alternative approaches may be suggested for assessing the actual mode of exploration at play in some given situation, in terms of the relative potency of each factor. First of all, in the case of visual exploration, we may assume that there are differences in the pattern and perhaps sheer amount of scanning occurring as one moves from the inspective to the contemplative pole. Thus eye-movement records might well prove instructive. For instance, would the results obtained by Mackworth and Morandi (1967) and others, according to which "the gaze selects informative details within pictures" (to quote the title of the paper just cited), necessarily apply to less neutral, that is, more affectively toned pictorial material, or to subjects coming with less of an analytic, information-oriented set? It might well prove rewarding to reexamine the pioneering work of Buswell (1935) on eye-movement patterns in response to works of art, in the light of the preceding discussion.

Admittedly, the approach just suggested has several major limitations. First, it presupposes some fairly elaborate, refined apparatus for recording eye movements, and is thus largely limited to use under laboratory conditions, though not entirely—we have work such as Carr and Schissler's (1969) and Mourant and Rockwell's (1970) use of eye-movement recording with subjects driving or riding in an automobile. Second, it is confined to the visual modality, although it could well be adapted for use with kinesthetic stimuli. In fact, a differentiation between inspective exploration for information extraction and exploration for affective arousal would probably be even easier in this later modality, where manual exploration can be subjected to direct observation both quantitatively and qualitatively, as demonstrated in a previous developmental study by this writer (Wohlwill, 1975b). In the case of the auditory modality, on the other hand, there is of course no overtly observable exploratory activity to be measured; indeed, the very term "exploration" seems somehow unsuited to the time-bound character of auditory patterns (except, indirectly, via the use of musical scores, assuming a musically sophisticated individual).

A third problem with the above-mentioned approach is that it does not provide independent measures of the two factors presumed to be interacting in determining the place on the inspective-affective continuum corresponding to a specific instance of stimulus exploration, but simply assumes that their relative mix will be translated into differences in either amount or patterns of eye movements. It would be desirable to devise approaches that start from such independent measures, and express the resultant exploratory mode as a difference or ratio between the two.

Two possibilities suggest themselves in this regard. The first, again limited to the laboratory, is through the recording of EEG patterns, in conjunction with records of autonomic arousal. The problem with this approach is that, although EEG-derived measures have been shown to vary systematically with such collative properties as complexity and novelty (e.g., Berlyne & McDonnell, 1965; Gale, Christie, and Penfold, 1971), and thus appear to be correlated with inspective exploration, the relationship between autonomic arousal and stimulus-derived affect is much more uncertain. At least for stimuli within a normal range of intensity of arousal, such as represented by typical art or environmental stimuli, as opposed to those evoking sexual excitation, stress, fear, and similar responses, evidence of consistent autonomic responses reliably linked to affective reactions is not easy to find.[2] The fact, furthermore, that EEG may itself vary with hedonic tone, even overriding the effects of complexity (Gale, Bramley, Lucas, & Christie, 1972), as well as with stimuli equated with respect to information (Ulrich, 1981), suggests that much more fine-grained analysis of physiological data will be required before it can be used reliably for this purpose.

Finally, one might suggest a verbal measure, based on the difference between the ratings of a stimulus on a scale from interesting to uninteresting and those on a scale from attractive to unattractive, for instance. The

---

[2]Thus, Berlyne and Lawrence (1964) found that neither of two different GSR-derived measures of autonomic arousal differentiated stimuli varying in regularity, although the same set of stimuli yielded significant effects in terms of both looking time and rankings of preference.

premise here is that a stimulus rated as highly interesting is attended to primarily for the positive affect derived from it. Note that this conception leads further to a potential measure of the degree of differentiation between the two sets, either across a set of stimuli, or, more plausibly, across a set of subjects, in terms of the independence between the two sets of ratings, that is, the approach to a correlation of zero between them.

Schachtel's Allocentric and Autocentric Modes of Perception

For those familiar with the writings of Ernest Schachtel, and particularly with his book, *Metamorphosis*, the preceding distinction between the affective and the inspective modes of exploration will bring to mind the latter's differentiation between two modes of perception: the autocentric and the allocentric. According to Schachtel (1959), autocentric perception is directed primarily at pleasurable sensations, or at the arousal of positive affect. It is considered as the dominant mode in infancy, not only because instinctual gratification is the main goal of the young organism's behavior, but also because of the domination of the infant's perceptual world by the senses of smell, taste, and touch, all of which are considered to serve a predominantly affective rather than cognitive function. As the individual matures, the distance senses, vision and audition, come to displace the preceding ones, and with that shift comes a change toward the allocentric mode, directed at the extraction of information from the environment.

Schachtel did not, of course, consider these two modes as sharply dichotomous, nor the autocentric mode as the exclusive province of infancy, or of the proximal senses of touch, taste, and smell. In particular, he considered visual art and music as involving a synthesis of the allocentric and autocentric modes of perception in adults. The case of touch was noted, furthermore, as an intermediate one; though generally subordinate in seeing adults to sight and audition, and used by them primarily in an autocentric fashion, as in feeling a mohair coat, or the body of a sexual partner, it obviously has the potential for being used for purely information purposes, not only on the part of the blind, but, with some effort, by the ordinary adult (cf. Geldard, 1957).

Schachtel's theory served as the basis of a dissertation by Klein (1964), who derived from it the hypothesis that, for the analogue of the color versus form preference question in the domain of kinesthetic perception, there would be a progressive shift with age from a dominance of texture to choices based on shape. (Klein used a series of stimulus triads, such that one stimulus, the sample, always matched one of the remaining pair in terms of texture, and the other in terms of shape.) Not only was this hypothesis strongly confirmed over the age range from six to 14 years, but the differentiation between two modes of perception received additional support from the much more active and differentiated manner of exploring the stimuli on the part of the older subjects. In this respect the results bear a close resemblance to those of the author's found with purely voluntary-exploration instructions (Wohlwill, 1975b). Thus, as was noted already in that report, there is clearly a very close relationship between the autocentric-allocentric differentiation of Schachtel's and the differentiation between a curiosity-based information-extraction-directed mode of exploration, which we are calling "inspective," and an affectively oriented one.

The Interrelationship between Inspective and Affective Exploration

The differentiation that has been proposed between two modes of exploration, replacing the specific-diversive one of Berlyne's, may strike some as harking back to the cognition–conation dialetic that plagued early conceptions of human psychology and which have been largely discredited in contemporary psychology as simplistic and somehow Aristotelian in their postulation of two completely separate, independent processes. It is important to reiterate, therefore, that they are not so regarded here; not only does the notion of a variable running from one pole to another, even if based on a dual-process theory, argue against such a dichotomous conception, but no assumption whatsoever is made as to their independent functioning. In fact, it is the interaction between them that presents us with some of the most fascinating questions in the psychology of aesthetics, and of cognition and motivation more generally.

Berlyne concerned himself with this question, particularly in the volume of research, *The New Experimental Aesthetics*, that he edited near the end of his life (Berlyne, 1974). The concluding chapter contains a review of a large number of factor-analytic studies, both from his own laboratories and from other sources, including a listing of the major factors uncovered in the experimental-aesthetics literature, and their differential relationships to specified stimulus properties, notably complexity. Among these are hedonic tone and uncertainty, which generally emerge as orthogonal to one another. The latter factor, furthermore, consistently exhibits high loadings for scales of complexity, whether assessed through verbal ratings or independent measures of uncertainty; at the same time, it is strongly related to measures of amount of exploration. Relationships between complexity and hedonic tone, on the other hand, do not appear clearly in the findings, though on the basis of both theory and other research the relationship is assumed to be an inverted-U-shaped one.

This point relates, of course, to one of the signal limitations of factor analysis, that it is predicated on a linear model of relationships among variables, and thus could not reveal the type of inverted-U-shaped relationship with complexity that one might suspect exists. Furthermore, the question of the degree of interdependence of the factors is in part determined by the choice of the factorial model utilized to generate the factor matrix, and of the rotation of axes. And it is apparent that such factor-analysis data fail altogether to reveal the nature of the interaction among the processes assumed to underly the factors—in particular, the inspective and affective modes of exploration, which may be assumed to relate to the uncertainty and hedonic tone factors, respectively.

Consider, for instance, Berlyne's interpretation of loadings of exploration time on the hedonic tone factor found in several studies (e.g., Chapters 5 & 9 of the 1974 volume). In the aforementioned concluding chapter, Berlyne states that this finding "indicates that exploration time can be affected by hedonic tone when variations in complexity, uncertainty and information content are held constant" (p. 322). That conclusion, if valid, would surely require a reassessment of the significance of exploration time—reinforcing, in fact, the points made above in this regard. Indeed, the results obtained from the author's study with slides of park scenes, cited earlier, bear out this notion, since there appeared to be a group of slides that evoked above average numbers of exposures simply for their general attractiveness. And there is additional evidence of an association between looking time and liking, as illustrated in Day's (1966) finding that free-exploration times were higher for slides subsequently rated as "liked" than for those rated as "disliked." This relationship held for both the designs of the Barron–Welsh Art Scale and for stimuli taken from Berlyne's own work, though in the latter case the relationship was confounded by the role of complexity (the more complex designs were both looked at longer and more frequently rated as "liked").

Yet none of this evidence is adequate to establish Berlyne's above-cited postulate of an effect *of* hedonic tone *on* exploration time, since that postulate assumes, after all, a direction of causality from affect to exploration. However reasonable this interpretation may seem, the possibility should be considered that cause and effect may in fact be reversed: for certain kinds of pictorial material, at least, the longer the person views it, the more positively it may be evaluated. (Recall that evaluative judgments are typically obtained following an ample period of prior exploration, of the order of 8 to 10 sec in many instances.)

This is by no means a chicken-or-the-egg sort of argument, for it is amenable to empirical test. Such a test would require evidence on the changes in liking occurring as a function of exploration time. Revealing data on this point were obtained by Ertel (1973), who compared verbal ratings representing five factors (the basic three known from Osgood's research, along with clarity and balance) following both brief (.5 sec) and long (4 sec) exposures of designs presented in pairs; he further obtained exploratory choice data for the same pairs of stimuli after brief and long prior exposures. The resulting data gave some very suggestive indication of shifts occurring in evaluative responses as a function of exploration time. This point was revealed first of all indirectly in the fairly *low* correlation between the evaluative ratings obtained after the brief and long exposures; it was but .40, whereas for the other four dimensions the correlations ranged from .74 to .90. This finding suggests that different factors determine evaluation after brief as compared to after longer exposure times. More positively, however, when he examined the difference in evaluation between the two exposure times, Ertel obtained evidence that, the more a given stimulus gained in activity and balance from .5 to 4-sec exposures, the more it tended to gain in evaluation as well. This finding points to the operation of an attempt by the viewer to structure the stimulus, given sufficient time, so as to make it appear more balanced, and more active as well; where the stimuli permit such a change to occur, this process will in turn affect the viewer's evaluation of it, as well as his preference for it in the exploratory choice situation. For these choices likewise appeared to be determined by different factors following brief and long prior exposures. After .5 sec, the unbalanced member of the pair was generally chosen for further viewing, evidently because curiosity regarding it had not been dispelled. Following longer exposure, on the other hand, it was generally the stimulus rated as more pleasant that was preferred. This was sometimes the more balanced one and sometimes the (initially) less balanced one, depending on whether or not an increase in perceived balance had taken place.

Ertel's study, along with some others (e.g., Dorner & Vehrs, 1975) clearly bring out the role of organization factors in both aesthetic judgment and exploratory behavior, transcending the collative properties emphasized by Berlyne. As the author has more fully argued elsewhere (Wohlwill, 1980), the concept of uncertainty, and of collative properties based on uncertainty reduction, does not seem sufficient to do justice to aesthetic preference; an effective understanding of the latter will require that we come to grips with structural characteristics such as order, balance, unity, and the like that involve the pattern of relationships among the elements of a configuration, and with the individual's activity in structuring these relationships. Since it is clearly such structuring that occurs during the process of inspection of a stimulus, it is apparent that exploratory activity itself will be related to the opportunity for the perceiver to introduce order or detect patterning in the stimulus, and thus an account of such exploration will likewise demand attention to these structural qualities.

All of which lends further emphasis to the point already made repeatedly before, that inspective and affective exploration are by no means mutually exclusive, but are closely interdependent. To this writer, it is one of the primary challenges of experimental aesthetics to unravel these two intertwined processes, so as to arrive at a fuller understanding of their interplay.

CONCLUSION

To conclude this excursion into the domain of exploratory behavior, I should like to touch briefly on two quite different points.

The first is a methodological one, but considered in a rather broad sense. If we are to do justice to exploratory behavior in all its facets, as represented in Table I, and to the search or stimulation-seeking phase in particular, it is clearly essential that we study the individual as he or she is engaged in such behavior—that is, without predetermining the stimuli to which the person will attend. It seems that psychologists have felt uncomfortable about undertaking such study, in part, undoubtedly, because it involves giving up a degree of control over behavior that the presentation of a preprogrammed series of stimuli affords. Search behavior with a specific stimulus or category of stimuli as a predesignated target has been studied, to be sure, but only in the very limited context of search for particular letters or words in the context of a list or matrix of similar stimuli (e.g., Neisser, 1964). As for generalized stimulation seeking, it has not been subjected to empirical study at all, even though scales have been devised to measure the disposition of the individual to engage in such behavior, that is, as a dimension of individual differences (McCarroll, Mitchell, Carpenter, & Anderson, 1967; Zuckerman, 1974).

As a result, our picture of the course and determinants of this type of behavior is as yet most limited, and based almost entirely on work at the animal level, such as the study of environmental exploration in the vole by Shillito (1963) referred to earlier, as well as some limited work with infants, (e.g., Eckerman & Rheingold, 1974; Rheingold & Eckerman, 1970). The self-imposed restriction of investigators studying exploratory behavior to structured situations in which specific stimuli are presented to a subject not only has hampered our understanding of the first phase of exploratory behavior, but, by extension of categories of behavior based on free exploration and search, notably of play and creativity. This short-

coming becomes particularly noteworthy in the child-psychological literature, when attempts are made to provide an account of play in terms of
response to structured stimuli (cf. Hutt, 1970), since play, just as does
creative behavior, depends on the ability to construct and transform
objects, rather than to merely scan, manipulate, or contemplate them.
There is undoubtedly a strong component of free exploration and search
behavior to such activity. (Cf. Weisler and McCall, 1976, for a comparative
analysis of exploration and play.)

The temptation to stick to the study of exploration in the sense of
inspection of controlled stimuli confronting the subject has not only failed
to do justice to the phenomenon of diversive exploration (in the sense in
which Berlyne originally used the term), and of the motivational basis for
the instigation of exploratory activity, but has narrowed the choice of
behavioral measures to those having specific reference to an individual
stimulus, such as looking time, evaluative ratings, etc. If exploration in its
initial phase, that is, in search of a stimulus or of stimulation (case C,
Table I), is to be included in our investigation of exploration, we clearly
need to broaden our approach at the behavioral level as well. Among
behavioral measures that may be suggested for a more comprehensive
attack on exploratory behavior are the choice of strategies of exploration,
persistence of exploratory activity, and perhaps above all behavior on
confrontation with a particular stimulus. Here the question changes from
that of the choice between looking at one stimulus or another, or the
decision as to when to stop inspecting a given stimulus in order to
proceed to the next, to the prior question of what stimuli elicit an approach response for the purpose of investigation, and how such confrontation responses relate to the specificity or generality of the individual's
exploratory set, etc. Observational studies, along the lines of the behavioral ecologist's approach, of such activities as window-shopping,
behavior of museum visitors, etc., appear to be called for, and indeed a
beginning toward research of this type has already been made (cf.
Bechtel, 1970; Melton, 1972).

The second and final comment concerns the interplay between inspective and affective exploration, and its relevance for aesthetic appreciation, and for education in the arts. The central question here is: to what
extent does the extraction of information concerning an aesthetic
stimulus modify the affective response to that stimulus, and how is such
change related to the stimulus properties of the stimulus? A very partial
answer was already seen in the aforementioned study by Ertel (1973),
which showed that a complex, "unbalanced" design could gain in pleasingness through sustained exploration, to the extent that the viewer was
able to increase the sense of balance conveyed by the configuration,
presumably by more effectively discerning the structural patterns con-

tained within the configuration. The enterprise of art education, aiming to increase the person's sensitivity to the structural properties of a work of art, would seem to be predicated on the operation of such a process. It clearly deserves much more explicit attention on the part of workers in the field of experimental aesthetics, not only because of its evident significance for aesthetic training and education, but for basic theoretical reasons. For the gain in hedonic tone deriving from the imposition of structure on a complex configuration is not readily deduced either from notions of "specific" exploration such as Berlyne's, based on the reduction of conflict aroused by collative properties, or from the conception of some unrelated activity of "diversive" exploration directed at the attainment or maintenance of some optimal level of arousal. And, going even beyond the realm of art to that of geographic exploration, or scientific discovery, surely the affective response obtained from such discovery requires likewise a considerable broadening of our understanding of the interaction between our two postulated modes of exploration.

Lest the preceding comments be read as advocating an overly intellectualizing approach to the domain of art, it is well to remind ourselves, finally, that a strong affective response to an aesthetic object, such as pure enjoyment, can and frequently does occur in the absence of sustained inspective activity aimed at information extraction, configurational structuring, or the like. We need but think of the reveler in "mood music" literally soaking in the aural stimulation emanating from the stereo set, with the lights turned off, and in a virtual state of trance. Perhaps, then, there are different modes of affective exploration, further complicating our already labyrinthine analysis of exploratory activity. Thus our exploratory foray into the world of exploration has left us with yet another question, another source of uncertainty, for the future to resolve. Those steeped in Berlyne's thought will, hopefully, be inspired to further investigative effort by such an inconclusive conclusion.

REFERENCES

BECHTEL, R. B. Human movement and architecture. In H. M. Proshansky, W. H. Ittleson, & L. G. Rivlin (Eds.), *Environmental psychology: Man and his physical setting*. New York: Holt, Rinehart & Winston, 1970.

BERLYNE, D. E. *Conflict, arousal and curiosity*. New York: McGraw-Hill, 1960.

BERLYNE, D. E. Complexity and incongruity variables as determinants of exploratory choice and evaluative ratings. *Canadian Journal of Psychology*, 1963, 17, 274–290.

BERLYNE, D. E. *Aesthetics and psychobiology*. New York: Appleton-Century-Crofts, 1971.

BERLYNE, D. E. (Ed.). *Studies in the new experimental aesthetics*. Washington, D.C.: Hemisphere Publishing, 1974.

BERLYNE, D. E., & CROZIER, J. B. Effects of complexity and prechoice stimulation on exploratory choice. *Perception and Psychophysics*, 1971, 10, 242–246.

BERLYNE, D. E., & LAWRENCE, G. H. Effects of complexity and incongruity variables on GSR, exploratory behavior, and verbally expressed preference. *Journal of General Psychology*, 1964, *71*, 21–45.

BERLYNE, D. E., & MCDONNELL, P. Effects of stimulus complexity and incongruity on duration of EEG desynchronization. *Electroencephalography and Clinical Neurophysiology*, 1965, *18*, 156–161.

BUSWELL, G. T. *How people look at pictures*. Chicago: University of Chicago Press, 1935.

CARR, S., & SCHISSLER, D. The city as a trip: Perceptual selection and memory in the view from the road. *Environment and Behavior*, 1969, *1*, 7–35.

DAY, H. Looking time as a function of stimulus variables and individual differences. *Perceptual and Motor Skills*, 1966, *22*, 423–428.

DAY, H. Evaluations of subjective complexity, pleasingness and interestingness for a series of random polygons varying in complexity. *Perception and Psychophysics*, 1967, *2*, 281–286.

DENT, O. B., & SIMMEL, E. Preference for complex stimuli as an index of diversive exploration. *Perceptual and Motor Skills*, 1968, *26*, 896–898.

DORNER, D., & VEHRS, W. Asthetische Befriedigung und Unbestimmtheitsreduktion. *Psychologische Forschung*, 1975, *38*, 1–14.

DOS PASSOS, J. San Francisco looks west. *Harper's Magazine*, March 1944, *188*, 328–338.

ECKERMAN, C. O., & RHEINGOLD, H. L. Infants' exploratory responses to toys and people. *Developmental Psychology*, 1974, *10*, 255–259.

ERTEL, S. Exploratory choice and verbal judgment. In D. E. Berlyne & K. B. Madsen (Eds.), *Pleasure, reward and preference*. New York: Academic, Press, 1973.

FOWLER, H. *Curiosity and exploratory behavior*. New York: Macmillan, 1965.

GALE, A., CHRISTIE, B., & PENFOLD, V. Stimulus complexity and the occipital EEG. *British Journal of Psychology*, 1971, *62*, 527–531.

GALE, A., BRAMLEY, P., LUCAS, B., & CHRISTIE, B. Differential effect of visual and auditory complexity on the EEG: Negative hedonic value as a crucial variable? *Psychonomic Science*, 1972, *17*, 21–24.

GELDARD, F. A. Adventures in tactile literacy. *American Psychologist*, 1957, *12*, 115–124.

HUTT, C. Specific and diversive exploration. In H. W. Reese & L. P. Lipsitt (Eds.), *Advances in child development and behavior* (Vol. 5). New York: Academic Press, 1970.

KELLER, H., & VOSS, H. G. *Neugierde und Exploration*. Stuttgart: Kohlhammer, 1976.

KLEIN, S. D. *A developmental study of tactual perception*. Unpublished doctoral dissertation, Clark University, 1963. *Dissertation Abstracts*, 1964, *24*, 2977.

MACWORTH, N. H., & MORANDI, A. J. The gaze selects informative details within pictures. *Perception and Psychophysics*, 1967, *2*, 547–552.

MCCARROLL, J. E., MITCHELL, K. M., CARPENTER, R. J., & ANDERSON, J. P. Analysis of three stimulation-seeking scales. *Psychological Reports*, 1967, *21*, 853–865.

MELTON, A. W. Visitor behavior in museums: Some early research in environmental design. *Human Factors*, 1972, *14*, 393–403.

MOURANT, R. R., & ROCKWELL, T. H. Mapping eye-movement patterns to the visual scene in driving: An exploratory study. *Human Factors*, 1970, *12*, 81–87.

NEISSER, U. Visual search. *Scientific American*, 1964, *210*(6), 94–102.

NUNNALLY, J. C., & LEMOND, C. Exploratory behavior and human development. In H. W. Reese (Ed.), *Child development and behavior* (Vol. 8). New York: Academic Press, 1973.

NUNNALLY, J. C., FAW, T. T., & BASHFORD, M. B. Effect of degrees of incongruity on visual fixations in children and adults. *Journal of Experimental Psychology*, 1969, *81*, 360–364.

RHEINGOLD, H. L., & ECKERMAN, C. O. The infant separates himself from his mother. *Science*, 1970, *168*, 78–83.

SCHACHTEL, E. G. *Metamorphosis: On the development of affect, perception, attention and memory*. New York: Basic Books, 1959.

SHILLITO, E. E. Exploratory behavior in the short-tailed vole *Microtus agrestis*. *Behaviour,* 1963, *21,* 145–154.

ULRICH, R. Some psychophysiological effects of nature versus urban scenes. *Environment and Behavior,* 1981, *13* (in press).

WEISLER, A., & McCALL, R. B. Exploration and play: Resume and redirection. *American Psychologist,* 1976, *31,* 492–508.

WOHLWILL, J. F. Amount of stimulus exploration and preference as differential functions of stimulus complexity. *Perception and Psychophysics,* 1968, *4,* 307–312.

WOHLWILL, J. F. Children's responses to meaningful pictures varying in diversity: exploration time vs. preference. *Journal of Experimental Child Psychology,* 1975, *20,* 341–351.(a)

WOHLWILL, J. F. Children's voluntary exploration and preference for tactually presented nonsense shapes differing in complexity. *Journal of Experimental Child Psychology,* 1975, *20,* 159–167.(b)

WOHLWILL, J. F. The place of order and uncertainty in art and environmental aesthetics. *Motivation and Emotion,* 1980, *4,* 133–142.

WOHLWILL, J. F., & HARRIS, G. Responses to congruity or contrast for man-made features in natural-recreation settings. *Leisure Sciences,* 1980, *3,* 349–365.

ZUCKERMAN, M. The sensation-seeking motive. In B. Maher (Ed.), *Progress in experimental personality research* (Vol. 7). New York: Academic Press, 1974.

15

Ambiguity, Complexity, and Preference for Works of Art

RICHARD M. NICKI

According to Berlyne (1971), collative variables, such as ambiguity and complexity, are characterized by uncertainty and have the power to heighten indices of arousal in an individual through the generation of response conflict. Exploratory behavior, in general, and aesthetic behavior, in particular, are looked upon as being determined to a significant degree through this process. Over the past 25 years, many experimental findings have been reported in support of this point of view.

The purpose of this chapter is to review a number of experiments I have done in collaboration with my students and colleagues demonstrating the relevance of these variables to preference for (1) Cubist works of art and (2) nonrepresentational works of art. The former directly stemmed from work as a doctoral student in Daniel Berlyne's laboratory in the 1960s. The latter was influenced importantly but less directly by his theoretical writings and experimental work.

In the 1960s, a series of experiments (Nicki, 1967, 1970) was undertaken which later were to prove to have a bearing on why people appreciate Cubist paintings. However, at that time, they were run to attempt to resolve a controversy between two rival explanations of the motivational basis of exploratory behavior in general. Fowler (1965), consistent with Koch (1956, 1961), had formulated an "incentive-motivational" model where motivation was defined in terms of the length of deprivation of stimulus change, and incentive in terms of the magnitude of the change in stimulation that the organism experienced on emitting an exploratory response for novel stimuli. On the other hand, Berlyne (1960) had attempted to account for exploratory behavior by

RICHARD M. NICKI • Department of Psychology, University of New Brunswick, Fredericton, New Brunswick E3B 5L4, Canada.

categorizing it in two ways: diversive exploration, and specific exploration. The former had an incentive–drive motivational basis similar to Fowler's (1965) model. The latter was occasioned by the exposure of the organism to novel, ambiguous, complex, surprising, or incongruous stimuli, and was reduced by the removal of these stimulus characteristics rather than by stimulus change alone.

Generally, undergraduate university subjects were first presented with a blurred slide of an everyday object, and then permitted by means of choosing the appropriate key to see either a clear version of the blurred object or a comparable but unrelated clear picture. As indicated in Figure 1, keypresses that obtained related clear pictures increased in frequency over trials. The function resembled a learning curve, adding strength to Berlyne's (1960) point of view that collative stimuli, such as novelty, ambiguity, etc., generate a kind of drive state, perceptual curiosity, or response conflict, which, when reduced, should result in learning of an instrumental response. That response conflict and not blurredness alone was necessary to achieve this effect was affirmed by the finding that, when response conflict was removed by presenting a clear version of the blurred object prior to the presentation of the later, the effect vanished. A further experiment indicated that increases in keypresses which obtained clear versions of blurred objects were found only with slides of an intermediate degree of blur, as indicated in Figure 2. This was consistent with the results of a fourth experiment which revealed that subjective uncertainty, an information-theory measure based on the number of guesses

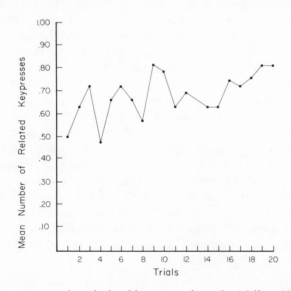

FIGURE 1. Mean number of related keypresses for each trial (from Nicki, 1970).

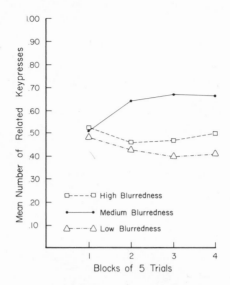

FIGURE 2. Mean number of related keypresses for each block of five trials for each degree of blurredness (from Nicki, 1970).

regarding the identity of the blurred objects and the relative subjective estimate of certainty of each guess, to be an inverted-U-shaped function of blurredness (see Figure 3). That is, subjective uncertainty, a concept sharing some of the attributes of response conflict, was looked upon as maximally energizing instrumental responses that made objects of an intermediate degree of blur clear. All this, of course, was contrary to Fowler's (1965) position, and supportive of Berlyne's (1960) interpretation of the motivational basis of exploratory behavior.

Subsequently, Berlyne and Borsa (1968) provided evidence that objects blurred to an intermediate degree evoked longer EEG desychronization than did their clear versions in the sequence, blurred slide–clear slide, but not in the sequence clear slide–blurred slide. This result was replicated by Nicki and Shea (1970), and, in addition, it was shown that, in the two-choice situation, keypresses that obtained clear versions of medium blurred slides were negatively related to the viewing duration of the blurred slide. Likewise, the rate of EEG desynchronization, as well as the rate of subjective uncertainty, were found to decrease with viewing duration (see Figure 4). The similar function for all three dependent variables furnished further support for the claim that an instrumental response such as keypressing was energized to the extent that subjective uncertainty, that is, response conflict or beta activity, was present at the emission of the response. For longer durations, energization of keypresses decreased because of the lessening of response conflict or the

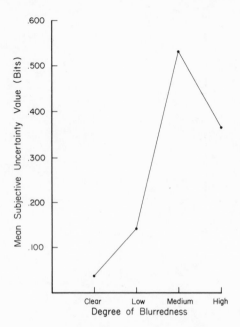

FIGURE 3. Mean subjective uncertainty value (bits) for each degree of blurredness (from Nicki, 1970).

orientation reaction brought about by the extinction of guessing, since guessing in almost all cases would be incorrect (see Nicki and Shea, 1970), and not result in uncertainty reduction.

In short, the above experiments had shown that, with artificially generated stimuli such as blurred slides of objects, that is, a source of ambiguity, subjects would learn an instrumental response to bring about the reduction of the uncertainty, response conflict, or arousal generated by the blurred object. Furthermore, the strength of response or degree of learning would be commensurate with the amount of uncertainty, response conflict, or arousal present when the response was occasioned. The question now arises: What is the relevance of these findings to one's appreciating Cubist paintings?

The usual approach in attempting to answer such a query is to present an argument in an analogue fashion. That is, it might be pointed out that blurred objects and Cubist paintings are equivalent to some degree because both are ambiguous stimuli. In accord with this, Berlyne (1971) and such aestheticians as Rosenblum (1960) have asserted that Cubist works of art exemplify ambiguity, which seems to be reasonable on an experiential level. Second, one might claim that people appreciate or look at Cubist painting to some extent at least because of the amount of ambiguity which characterizes it. Furthermore, behavior that leads to the

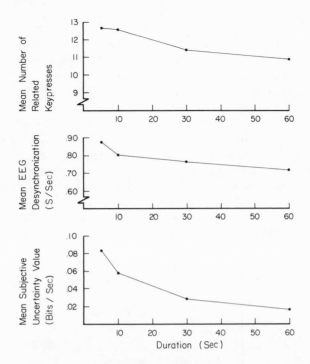

FIGURE 4. The relationships of subjective uncertainty/sec, EEG desynchronization/sec (blurred slides, blurred-clear order), and related choices to viewing duration (from Nicki & Shea, 1970).

reduction of this ambiguity or uncertainty, such as perhaps looking at the title of the painting, asking someone about the nature of the painting and receiving an answer, inspecting the painting more closely, etc., should have a higher probability of occurring in the future. This line of argument seems reasonable, but would be less conjectural and more convincing if such equivalencies between behavior directed toward blurred objects and Cubist paintings could be experimentally established.

This was the aim of a second series of experiments (Lee, 1972; Nicki & Lee, 1977) which were patterned on those of Wohlwill (1968), who used nonrepresentational works of art as stimuli. Generally, these experiments involved undergraduate university subjects keypressing for 1-sec exposures of early Cubist paintings of previously determined uncertainty values. Twenty paintings had been chosen, so as to provide a fairly broad range of ambiguity; the early Cubist works, mainly Braque and Picasso, afforded such a selection while, at the same time, minimizing large variations in color and general style.

Ambiguity values expressed in terms of information theory of the Cubist paintings had been determined using a technique devised by

Laffal (1955) to quantify the capacity of words to generate different free associates. Similar applications had been reported by Driscoll and Lanzetta (1964) and Nicki and Shea (1971). On the basis of this technique, half the slides could be roughly categorized as generating few guesses that were different from one another regarding the identity of the main object or person in the painting (low uncertainty); the other half could be looked upon as generating many different guesses (high uncertainty). The mean number of 1-sec exposures for low-and high-uncertainty paintings is given in Figure 5. Inspection of this figure would indicate that subjects keypressed more often to view high-uncertainty paintings than low-uncertainty ones. This would be in accord with Berlyne's notion of the operation of an arousal boost mechanism of reward or hedonic value, that is, moderate increases in response conflict or arousal are reinforcing. However, the differences were *not* statistically significant ones. These

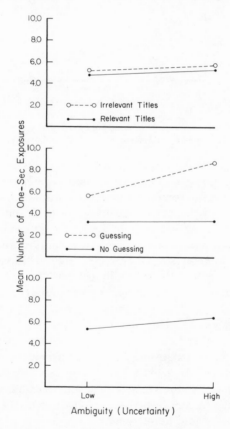

FIGURE 5. Mean number of 1-sec exposures for low- and high-uncertainty slides: no-guessing condition; guessing and no-guessing conditions; relevant and irrelevant titles.

results were not unanticipated, since Lee (1972) with a different but comparable set of Cubist paintings had found a similar (and insignificant) trend. Furthermore, even within a set of paintings which displayed little variation in the use of color and general style, there might be other, unspecified and uncontrolled sources of attractiveness which may have swamped any effect of ambiguity. Therefore, another experiment employing a larger number of subjects might have run to put this conjecture to the test. However, a second alternative would be to use the same set of paintings and approximately the same number of subjects in a situation where the effect of ambiguity might be magnified by varying the instructional set given the subjects. The latter approach was the one followed in experiment 2 of the series, where half the subjects were instructed to guess the identity of the main object or person in the slide and the other half were given no special instruction (as in the first experiment). The results are given in Figure 5; an analysis of variance revealed significant effects of uncertainty, guessing, and a significant interaction. These results were congruent with Berlyne's (1971) point of view, since guessing overall should have produced more response conflict and greater investigatory behavior; therefore, any difference between the number of exposures to low- and high-uncertainty paintings should have been augmented in the guessing condition. Consistent with this interpretation, Godkewitsch (1972) found a manipulation of an expectancy effect to enhance the funniness ratings of adjective–noun pairs varying in semantic distance (uncertainty).

In order to provide further support for the above, a third experiment was undertaken, involving a different manipulation of uncertainty than guessing, that perhaps more closely resembled the every-day life situation. The instructions were similar to those in the above experiments, except that no mention of guessing was made. Half the low-uncertainty slides had a title which corresponded to a fair extent to the content of the painting projected underneath; for the other half, the title only remotely pertained to the painting's content. The same conditions prevailed in the case of the high-uncertainty paintings. All titles were derived from responses given by subjects who had been involved in the initial determination of the uncertainty values of the paintings using Laffal's (1955) technique.

The mean number of exposures for low- and high-uncertainty paintings associated with relevant and irrelevant titles is given in Figure 5. An analysis of variance revealed only significant effects of titles and uncertainty. The results are consistent with those above and Berlyne's (1971) viewpoint, in that paintings with irrelevant titles represent situations of higher uncertainty (arousal, response conflict) than those with relevant titles, and as a consequence are viewed more often. Second, the presence of *any* title presumably creates an expectancy which has a consequence similar to that of requesting subjects to guess, that is, high-uncertainty paintings were viewed more often than low-uncertainty ones. Incidentally, therefore, it appears that the title of a particular work of art is of more than minor significance, since it is a variable affecting viewing behavior.

In sum, the above group of experiments has demonstrated that viewing behavior of Cubist paintings is determined to some extent by the uncertainty of the paintings expressed in information-theory terms, and by expectancy. It is argued that Cubist paintings and blurred slides are similar, in that both may be characterized by uncertainty, and both have the power to induce response conflict or arousal.

In order to establish this correspondence more closely, further data from the last of the above group of experiments may be cited which resulted from an additional requirement for subjects at the completion of the experiment to recall the titles of the paintings when the latter were presented to them for eight sec each. The mean number of relevant and irrelevant titles recalled for low- and high-uncertainty slides is given in Figure 6. That is, an analysis of variance indicated that subjects recalled

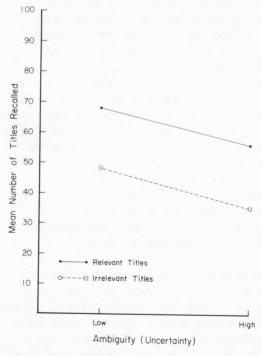

FIGURE 6. Mean number of relevant and irrelevant titles recalled for low- and high-uncertainty slides.

titles associated with low-uncertainty paintings more so than with high-uncertainty paintings; second, subjects recalled relevant titles to a greater degree than irrelevant ones. These findings may be explained, according to Berlyne (1971), in that titles associated with low-uncertainty paintings, and relevant titles, both represent instances where uncertainty has been aroused and maximally reduced, thus presumably facilitating correct recall. Furthermore, these results were congruent with those of Berlyne and Normore (1972), who found incidental recall of items shown in the order blurred object–related clear object to be superior to those in the order clear object–blurred object, or of double clear objects.

An additional study (Nicki, Forestell, & Short, 1977) exploring this parallel between ambiguity of artificially generated stimuli and actual works of art involved six "impossible" figures such as, three-stick clevis, continuous flight of stairs; six "ambiguous" figures, such as rabbit-duck, man-girl; and six portions of drawings by M.C. Escher. These kinds of stimuli appeared appropriate because of their capacity to induce response conflict on an experiential level, and were supported by the findings of Fischer (1967). In addition, psychologists at least from the time of Koffka have been interested in perceptual phenomena associated with such stimuli, and Escher, himself, appears to have been influenced by the writings of the Gestalt school (Teuber, 1974).

Specifically, undergraduate subjects were permitted to keypress for 1-sec views of the three types of stimuli under two conditions, unaltered and altered. The former were tracings of the three types of stimuli; the latter were tracings that were changed so as to diminish uncertainty or response conflict associated with the stimuli. Examples are given in Figure 7. Half the subjects saw the unaltered picture first and then the altered version; the reverse was true for the other half. The mean number of 1-sec exposures for each type of stimulus in the unaltered and altered conditions is shown in Figure 8. The number of exposures to unaltered stimuli was significantly greater than to altered ones. Furthermore, the number of exposures significantly increased for unaltered stimuli over the three types of stimuli while remaining fairly constant for altered ones. Again, these results are comparable with Berlyne's (1971) position that moderate increases in arousal have greater reward value, since it seems reasonable to assume that unaltered pictures should possess greater collative value (conflict, arousal) than altered ones. Likewise, "impossible" figures, at least, may have occasioned maximal viewing because of the enhancement of response conflict owing to their being more predominantly three-dimensional. The mean number of exposures for unaltered and altered slides in the orders unaltered-altered and altered-unaltered is given in Figure 9. The significant interaction was anticipated, since the uncertainty value of an unaltered stimulus should diminish

FIGURE 7. Examples of stimuli.

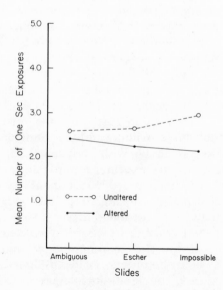

FIGURE 8. Mean number of 1-sec exposures for each type of slide and condition.

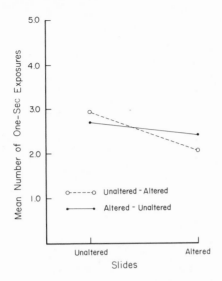

FIGURE 9. Mean number of 1-sec exposures for unaltered and altered slides in the orders: unaltered-altered, altered-unaltered.

when preceded by an altered version, in much the same way as the uncertainty value of a blurred slide lessens when preceded by a related clear one (Berlyne & Borsa, 1968; Nicki, 1970). In short, these results represented a further development in the correspondence of effects derived from different sources of ambiguity: artificially generated stimuli, and works of art.

Similar work with checkerboardlike patterns and non-representational works of art has also extended over a number of years. The first study (Nicki, 1972) dealt only with artificially generated stimuli —checkerboardlike patterns modelled on those used by Dorfman (1965). In Experiment 1, undergraduate subjects were given the choice of viewing, for 7 sec, patterns of either low (4 bits) or medium (36 bits) complexity, medium or high (900 bits) complexity, or low or high complexity. The results are given in Figure 10. That is, subjects preferred medium to low complexity, and medium to high complexity; no preference was shown between low and high complex patterns. These results were consistent with those of Sales (1968) with rats and checkerboard patterns, Munsinger and Kessen (1964) with humans and asymmetrical polygons, and Dorfman (1965) with humans and checkerboardlike patterns. In addition, the data appeared to be in agreement with Berlyne's (1971) position concerning the reward value of a moderate degree of arousal. Experiment 2 was undertaken to investigate the relationship between arousal and the range of complexity chosen in Experiment 1, and simply involved under-

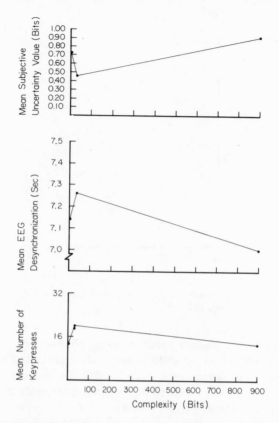

FIGURE 10. The relationships of subjective complexity, EEG desynchronization, and preference to pattern complexity (from Nicki, 1972).

graduate subjects being exposed to each of the patterns in the series for 7 sec while their EEGs were being recorded. As indicated in Figure 10, EEG desynchronization was revealed to be an inverted-U-shaped function of complexity, which was consistent with Rietveld, Tordoir, Hagenouw, Lubbers, and Spoor (1967), who found an inverted-U-shaped relationship between parameters of the visually evoked potential and checkerboard pattern complexity.

These results indicated that preference for complexity was not only a consequence of the amount of arousal potential in the pattern, but was greatest for stimuli that caused *maximal* arousal. Of course, these data would still be consistent with Berlyne's (1971) position, if it were assumed that the maximal amount of arousal associated with an intermediate degree of complexity represented in absolute terms only a moderate increase in the subject's level of arousal. Experiment 3 was run to ascertain more clearly the source of arousal. Since, according to Berlyne's (1971) position, complex stimuli should arouse one because of their capacity to induce response conflict, the aim of Experiment 3 was to measure this potential employing an information-theory-based technique similar to that used by Nicki (1970) with blurred slides. That is, undergraduate subjects were shown each slide for 20 sec, and instructed to utter all the names of objects that the pattern reminded them of during this period (and, if necessary, during a subsequent time when a blank slide was on the screen). In addition, subjects were to provide an estimate of how strongly the patterns reminded them of each object. These data were converted into a measure, subjective complexity, and are shown in Figure 10. Inspection of this figure reveals subjective complexity to a U-shaped function of objective complexity (a significant bitonic component of trend at $p < .01$), which, at least at first glance, seems to be contrary to what one would have predicted from the results relating subjective uncertainty and blurredness. An attempt to resolve this apparent disparity involved citing a finding of Berlyne (1957) which demonstrated response conflict to cause longer reaction times. That is, when two or more responses are instigated simultaneously, the consequence may be a delay or even an omission of an overt response, a phenomenon often noted by clinicians. This would mean that subjective complexity as a measure would be looked upon as being inversely related to a covert process, response conflict. Differences between the relationships of subjective complexity, subjective uncertainty, and the energization of behavior may be the product of different task demands (see Nicki, 1972).

The sequel to the above work with complexity exemplified by artificially generated checkerboardlike patterns involved two studies concerned with nonrepresentational works of art. Experiment 1 of the first study (Nicki & Moss, 1975) had undergraduate subjects keypressing for 1-sec views of 18 slides of paintings by such artists as Albers, Dove, Rothko, Vasarely, Riopelle, etc., and, later on, rating the paintings with respect to "pleasingness" and "interestingness." Three measures of painting complexity were used: judged complexity, based on judgments dealing with variation regarding color, shape, etc. and modelled on Wohlwill's (1968) measure; redundancy, pertaining to the number of different elements and the irregularity of their arrangement, and derived from a suggestion by Moles (1968) and the use of a similar technique with verbal material by Taylor (1953), Kamman (1966), and Evans (1970); and subjective complexity, as above. Only the mean number of exposures as a function of judged complexity is given in Figure 11, since, generally, an analysis of variance revealed all three independent variables, judged complexity, redundancy, and subjective complexity, to have a similar significant effect on all three dependent variables—number of exposures,

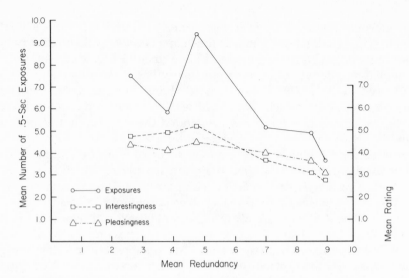

FIGURE 11. Mean number of .5-sec exposures and ratings of interestingness and pleasingness as a function of judged complexity (from Nicki & Moss, 1975).

ratings of interestingness, and ratings of pleasingness. In all cases, there were significant linear components of trend.

Generally, these results were similar to those of Wohlwill (1968) and those above (Nicki, 1970) with Cubist paintings as stimuli. That is, in an open-ended situation where subjects are permitted to view stimuli for as long as they want, viewing duration increased as uncertainty increased. These results were in accord with those of Jones, Wilkinson, and Braden (1961) with artificially generated stimuli, and also with those of Experiment 1 (above), which found preference to be an inverted-U-shaped function of checkerboardlike-pattern complexity with a fixed viewing duration of short length. That is, with increased exposure time or experience, findings by Munsinger and Kessen (1964), Brennan, Ames, and Moore (1966), and Vitz (1966), for example, indicate that preference is for higher degrees of complexity (or uncertainty).

More specifically, a problem regarding interpretation does arise on consideration of the finding that all three dependent response measures *increased* with increases in subjective complexity. That is, in the experiments above with checkerboardlike patterns, subjective complexity was found to be *inversely* related to arousal. Yet, according to Berlyne's (1971) position, ratings of interestingness and pleasingness should *increase* with increases in the arousal potential of patterns. An additional study (Nicki & Gale, 1977) below had a direct bearing on this dilemma.

The purpose of the second experiment of this study was to investigate the relationship between the three measures of complexity and

performance on a new task *not* involving preference, in order independently to test the validity of these measures, and perhaps discover
whether there are any differences among them in their representation of
complexity. Briefly, matte photographs were taken of the art slides,
mounted on thin cardboard and cut into four equal pieces. The subject's
job was to reconstruct each painting as quickly as possible. If the above
measures of complexity are valid ones, then the time taken to reconstruct
the paintings correctly should vary with the degree of complexity present. That is, in order to put the pieces of each painting together properly,
the subject must attend to the elements that comprise it, and longer
completion times should occur when elements are more numerous and/or
more diversely arranged. The findings are presented in Figure 12.

All three measures had a significant effect on completion time, as
well as significant linear components of trend. However, the linear component represented the largest source of variability in the case of only two
measures, judged complexity and redundancy. For subjective complexity
an inverted-U-shaped function best characterized its relationship to
completion time. One interpretation of these results might be that only
two of the above measures of complexity are valid ones, that is, preference and completion time vary in the same predominantly linear fashion
with them. However, another possibility is that there are two factors
responsible for the successful and rapid completion of the puzzle-
paintings—perceptual complexity, as measured by the number of

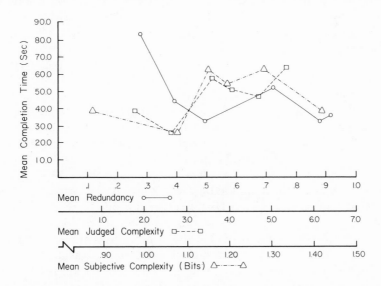

FIGURE 12. Mean completion time of puzzle-paintings as a function of three measures of
complexity (from Nicki & Moss, 1975).

stimulus elements and degree of irregularity in their arrangement *per se*, and cognitive complexity, involving the cognitive labels or associations evoked by the array of elements. An additional assumption would be that correct completion of puzzle-paintings is facilitated either by high or low values of response conflict, that is, low or high value of subjective complexity. Unfortunately, the basis for such an assumption is not an obvious one.

The second study (Nicki & Gale, 1977) had the aim of investigating the relationship between the complexity of the paintings used above and physiological arousal as measured by alpha abundance, that is, integrated output of alpha activity, an inverse measure of arousal. The discovery of a large *positive* correlation between judged complexity and subjective complexity by Nicki and Moss (1975), and the previous finding that subjective complexity and arousal are *inversely* related (Nicki, 1972), would lead to the prediction that, for a viewing time of fixed, relatively short duration, arousal should *decrease* as complexity, that is, judged complexity, $(redundancy)^{-1}$, increases.

The subject population sampled was somewhat broader than in previous experiments, and consisted of townspeople as well as students from the University of Wales Institute of Science and Technology. The stimuli were grouped into three levels of complexity on the basis of the redundancy measure used above. Each slide was presented to a subject for 27 sec; the subject's task was merely to relax and look at each slide. Immediately after seeing all the paintings, subjects were again shown the slides, and required to rate each one for complexity, pleasingness, and interestingness. Since previous research by Gale, Spratt, Christie, and Smallbone (1975) had revealed different results from bandwidths within the alpha range, EEG abundance values for gross alpha (8.0–13.0 Hz), low alpha (8.5–10.5 Hz) and high alpha (10.5–12.5 Hz) were scrutinized. These are plotted in Figure 13. The relationships between both gross alpha and low alpha and alpha abundance were found to be significantly increasing monotonic ones, which is in accord with the prediction above.

At least at first glance, these results appeared to be incompatible with those of Gale, Christie, and Penfold (1971), who found alpha abundance to decrease with increasing number of squares of checkerboardlike patterns. However, as mentioned above, Rietveld *et al.* (1967) and Nicki (1972) had found an inverted-U-shaped relationship between arousal and complexity. Thus, the results of this experiment would be compatible with the above if the range of objective complexity sampled in the paintings were restricted to intermediate to high levels. A casual examination of both the checkerboardlike patterns used by Nicki (1972) and the paintings supports this supposition; furthermore, an unpublished experiment which involved undergraduates at the University of Bristol rating

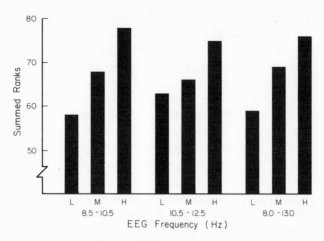

FIGURE 13. Summed ranks of EEG abundance values for each frequency bandwidth and for each level of complexity (redundancy measure) (from Nicki & Gale, 1977).

both kinds of stimuli with regard to complexity provided some corroboration.

Ratings of interestingness and pleasingness were found to be significantly correlated with redundancy and judged complexity (Wales). Furthermore, judgments of complexity by Welsh subjects were highly correlated with those by Canadian subjects, $r = .73, p < .01$. These results are congruent with those reported above (Nicki & Moss, 1975), and suggest that judgments of complexity of nonrepresentational works of art can be made fairly easily and consistently across related cultural groups. However, they are problematical in that ratings of interestingness and pleasingness increase with *increasing* complexity but *decreasing* values of arousal. A possible solution might be that judgments of interestingness and pleasingness depend on factors other than arousal, for example, social learning. A less drastic alternative would be that such verbal ratings are determined by the arousal *potential* of stimuli patterns, rather than the immediate value of arousal experienced by the organism. Both positions would probably require a revamping of Berlyne's (1971) viewpoint of ratings of interestingness and pleasingness being related to different neurological reward mechanisms. More empirical work needs to be done investigating the relationships among these variables in order to resolve this question more adequately.

In conclusion, these studies have followed along the two pathways of empirical investigation of aesthetics inaugurated by Fechner in the nineteenth century, one involving measures of preference for artificially generated stimuli, and the other, actual works of art (see Berlyne, 1971).

382 CHAPTER 15

They have been guided by the theoretical framework of D. E. Berlyne and his experimental findings. The fruitfulness of this approach involving an explanation of the results of experiments with blurred objects, Cubist paintings, checkerboardlike patterns, and nonrepresentational works of art using such concepts as ambiguity, complexity, uncertainty, and arousal is of course left to the judgment of the reader. Daniel Berlyne, scientist par excellence, would have had it no other way.

References

BERLYNE, D. E. Conflict and choice time. *British Journal of Psychology*, 1957, *48*, 106–118.

BERLYNE, D. E. *Conflict, arousal, and curiosity.* New York: McGraw-Hill, 1960.

BERLYNE, D. E. *Aesthetics and psychobiology.* New York: Appleton-Century-Crofts, 1971.

BERLYNE, D. E., & BORSA, D. M. Uncertainty and the orientation reaction. *Perception and Psychophysics*, 1968, *3*, 77–79.

BERLYNE, D. E., & NORMORE, L. F. Effects of prior uncertainty on incidental free recall. *Journal of Experimental Psychology*, 1972, *96*, 43–48.

BRENNAN, W. M., AMES, E. W., & MOORE, R. W. *Science*, 1966, *151*, 354–356.

DORFMAN, D. D. Esthetic preference as a function of pattern information. *Psychonomic Science*, 1965, *3*, 85–86.

DRISCOLL, J. M., & LANZETTA, J T. Effects of problem uncertainty and prior arousal on pre-decisional information search. *Psychological Reports*, 1964, *14*, 975–988.

EVANS, D. R. Conceptual complexity, arousal, and epistemic behavior. *Canadian Journal of Psychology*, 1970, *24*, 249–260.

FISHER, G. H. Measuring ambiguity. *American Journal of Psychology*, 1967, *80*, 541–577.

FOWLER, H. *Curiosity and exploratory behavior.* New York: Macmillan, 1965.

GALE, A., CHRISTIE, B., & PENFOLD, V. Stimulus complexity and the occipital EEG. *British Journal of Psychology*, 1971, *62*, 527–531.

GALE, A., SPRATT, G., CHRISTIE, B., & SMALLBONE, A. Stimulus complexity, EEG abundance gradients, and detection efficiency in a visual recognition task. *British Journal of Psychology*, 1975, *66*, 289–298.

GODKEWITSCH, M. The relationship between arousal potential and funniness of jokes. In J. H. Goldstein & P. E. McGhee (Eds.), *The psychology of humor.* New York: Academic Press, 1972.

JONES, A., WILKINSON, H. J., & BRADEN, I. Information deprivation as a motivational variable. *Journal of Experimental Psychology*, 1961, *62*, 126–137.

KAMMAN, R. Verbal complexity and preferences in poetry. *Journal of Verbal Learning and Verbal Behavior*, 1966, *5*, 536–540.

KOCH, S. Behavior as "intrinsically" regulated: Work notes towards a pretheory of phenomena called "motivational". In M. R. Jones (Ed.), *Current theory and research in motivation* (Vol. 4). Lincoln: University of Nebraska Press, 1956.

KOCH, S. Psychological science versus the science–humanism antimony: Intimations of a significant science of man. *American Psychologist*, 1961, *16*, 629–639.

LAFFAL, J. Response faults in word association as a function of response entropy. *Journal of Abnormal and Social Psychology*, 1955, *50*, 265–270.

LEE, P. L. *Ambiguity and preference in Cubist paintings.* Unpublished master's dissertation, University of New Brunswick, 1972.

MOLES, A. *Information theory and perception.* Urbana: University of Illinois Press, 1968.

MUNSINGER, H., & KESSEN, W. Uncertainty, structure, and preference. *Psychological Monographs*, 1964, *78* (9, Whole No. 586).

NICKI, R. M. *The reinforcing effect of uncertainty reduction on a human operant.* Unpublished doctoral dissertation, University of Toronto, 1967.

NICKI, R. M. The reinforcing effect of uncertainty reduction on a human operant. *Canadian Journal of Psychology*, 1970, *24*, 389–400.

NICKI, R. M. Arousal increment and degree of complexity as incentive. *British Journal of Psychology*, 1972, *63*, 165–171.

NICKI, R. M., & GALE, A. EEG, measures of complexity, and preference for nonrepresentational works of art. *Perception*, 1977, *6*, 281–286.

NICKI, R. M., & LEE, P. L. *Ambiguity (uncertainty) and preference for Cubist works of art.* Paper given at the Annual Meeting of the Eastern Psychological Association, Boston, April 1977.

NICKI, R. M., & MOSS, V. Preference for nonrepresentational art as a function of various measures of complexity. *Canadian Journal of Psychology*, 1975, *29*, 237–249.

NICKI, R. M., & SHEA, J. F. Subjective uncertainty, the orientation reaction, and the reinforcement of an instrumental response. *Perception and Psychophysics*, 1970, *7*, 374–376.

NICKI, R. M., & SHEA, J. F. Learning, curiosity, and social group membership. *Journal of Experimental Child Psychology*, 1971, *11*, 124–132.

NICKI, R. M., FORSTELL, P., & SHORT, P. *Uncertainty and preference for "ambiguous" figures, "impossible" figures and the drawings of M. C. Escher.* Paper given at the Annual Meeting of the Canadian Psychological Association, Vancouver, June 1977.

RIETVELD, W. J., TORDOIR, W. R., HAGENOUW, J. R., LUBBERS, J. A., & SPOOR, T. A. Visual evoked responses to blank and checkerboard patterned flashes. *Acta Physiologica et Pharmacologica Neerlandica*, 1967, *14*, 259–285.

ROSENBLUM, R. *Cubism and twentieth-century art.* New York: Abrams, 1960.

SALES, S. M. Stimulus complexity as a determinant of approach behavior and inspection time in the hooded rat. *Canadian Journal of Psychology*, 1968, *22*, 11–17.

TAYLOR, W. L. "Cloze procedure": a new tool for measuring readability. *Journalism Quarterly*, 1953, *30*, 415–433.

TEUBER, M. L. Sources of ambiguity in the prints of Maurits C. Escher. *Scientific American*, 1974, *231*, 90–104.

VITZ, P. C. Preference for different amounts of visual complexity. *Behavioral Science*, 1966, *11*, 105–114.

WOHLWILL, J. F. Amount of stimulus exploration and preference as differential functions of stimulus complexity. *Perception and Psychophysics*, 1968, *4*, 307–312.

16

About the Role of Visual Exploration in Aesthetics

FRANÇOIS MOLNAR

> Scientific inquiry must always seek to measure as precisely and reliably as possible any phenomenon that can exist in different amounts or to different extents. This is because information is maximized when numbers or their equivalents can be assigned to phenomena and because only then can mathematical functions, reflective of causal and other relations, be used to express the concomitant variations and interpredictabilities that link phenomena. (Berlyne, 1978, pp. 129–130)

INTRODUCTION

Descartes is probably the first known person to recognize the importance of eye movements in vision and visual perception, although Leonardo da Vinci may have recognized this before him.

The French painter and scholar Roger de Piles, probably under the influence of Descartes, demonstrated the role of eye movements in the appreciation of paintings. It was some 200 years later that the opthalmologist Javal discovered the fact that when we are reading, our eyes do not move in a continuous way but make a lot of fast and short jumps, called *saccades*.[1] The eyes stop only three or four times for each line, depending on the reading capacity of the subject and the difficulty of the text.

---

[1]"While the term is widely used by specialists, the fact that nonspecialists are generally unacquainted with it points to the desirability of using the more straightforward term "jump" from English rather than this obscure French word, which means to jerk on the reins of a horse" (Gaarder, 1975).

FRANÇOIS MOLNAR • Institut d'Esthétique et des Sciences de l'Art, Université de Paris, 75015 Paris, France.

With the work of Javal, a long series of research began concerning eye movements in reading and other visual tasks. This research produced important results but still left many questions unanswered. In fact, we do not know whether the extent of the saccades depends on the physical feature of the stimulation, on linguistic data, or on both. Reading is only one of the aspects of vision where the study of eye movements is fruitful. Almost all visual activity requires eye movements, so eye-movement study can produce valuable information about underlying mechanisms of vision, form perception, visual communication, etc. In addition, attention and eye movements are closely related. The study of eye movements can give us useful information concerning attention. Some recent work even shows a correlation between higher mental activity (e.g., learning, thinking, problem solving) and eye movements. We encounter eye movement study in nearly every field of scientific psychology. Consequently, the number of such studies have been steadily increasing in the last two or three decades.

Strangely enough, there are only a very few recent works on eye movements connected with empirical aesthetics. Nevertheless, as soon as Javal's findings were known, aestheticians understood that eye movements could be a tool of great utility for their work. In fact, they stated that when the eye explores a form or an object, the characteristics of the eye movements must be the same as those of the form or object. This means that a jagged form should be seen by jagged eye movements and a harmonious one by harmonious movements. It is a philosophical argument for the defense of dogmatic assertions concerning the beauty of curved lines. The muscles of the eye are so placed that one might expect a kind of pull, since the three pairs of muscles in each eye are not arranged symmetrically, hence, it was easy to argue that the eye moves more naturally and easily in a curve, and so one finds greater pleasure in looking at curved lines rather than straight ones.

But aestheticians soon became disappointed. At the beginning of our century, Stratton (1902) instructed his subjects to look at curved lines while he photographed their eye movements with a camera. He found that the eye does not follow the line of a "pleasing curve" at all. Indeed, our eyes do not follow the borders of an object point by point in a harmonious way, even if the object is harmonious. The findings of Javal showed clearly that our eyes move in jumps or jerks from one point to another in an apparently random manner without following the exact borders. So, the most beautiful object, or the most harmonious one, will not be explored by harmonious or beautiful eye movements. After a few fruitless attempts in this domain, Gibson (1950) could affirm that eye movements are more or less random and that if there is some relationship between eye movement and the picture composition, it has not yet been demonstrated.

New investigations have been started in different directions, but without real aesthetic aims. Most of the results concerning aesthetics and eye movement are produced by non-aesthetic-oriented research. For instance, Yarbus's work (1967) on the exploration of a picture under various instructions concerns, without a doubt, aesthetics. However, the aim of his research was not an aesthetic one. Buswell's (1935) problem, how people look at pictures, was a problem of perception, producing, nevertheless, important data for aesthetics. More closely related to aesthetics, but perhaps less useful for real aesthetic research, are the works of other investigators, like Brandt (1945), who found some rules of eye movement in advertisement and graphic design. Other scientific workers found valuable data concerning aesthetics in studying eye movements under such various perceptual tasks as searching and detecting. Most of the research in eye movements, functional fovea, and more generally on seeing conducted by Hochberg (1968) was possibly more useful for aesthetic purposes than the aesthetically oriented work of Brandt. In the same way, the studies by Hochberg and Brooks (1963) on perceptual problems, such as right–left preference of the eyes, were also of an aesthetic concern.

We already have a sufficient amount of knowledge about eye movements and their mechanisms to be able to begin a serious search on the role of eye movements in aesthetics based on a more global aesthetic hypothesis. One cannot claim that a harmonious picture will be explored by means of harmonious eye movements, but one can say that eye movements are related to aesthetic feeling via visual perception, or, at least, that they may be considered in some way as indices of what happens in the brain during aesthetic contemplation.

The problems raised by eye movements in connection with aesthetic behavior are very complex, very rich, and very large. It is impossible to examine all these problems here even briefly, so I must limit myself to one or two important ones. One of them is a purely motivational problem. I shall try to examine whether there is a visual-exploration specific to aesthetics. The second one is indirectly related to motivation and raises the question whether complexity is related to eye movement.

INFLUENCE OF AESTHETIC MOTIVATION ON VISUAL EXPLORATION

We have to examine first the differences between the modalities of exploration under aesthetic and non-aesthetic conditions, if such differences do exist. Yarbus (1967) has convincingly demonstrated the role of instruction in eye-movement strategy. He showed pictures to subjects under different instructions. The subjects looked mostly at the clothing of the represented persons and at the furniture when they were asked to estimate material circumstances of the represented families. More fixations went toward the face when they were asked to determine the age of the persons. If the subjects were asked to remember something, some detail of the picture, they obviously looked at this detail. There is nothing astonishing in Yarbus's findings. If I am asked to look at an object, I will look at it. But what happens if the curiosity of the subject is guided by aesthetic motivations? Will the movements of his eyes be different than eye movements under ordinary conditions?

Two obstacles arise here: (1) It is impossible to produce a real aesthetic attitude in the laboratory or in any other artificial condition. Aesthetic emotions are essentially private. Strange interventions, such as the presence of the experimenter or even of scientific instruments, can destroy all aesthetic feeling. (2) We do not possess any reliable sign that is able to indicate the aesthetic attitude of the subject. One cannot trust a response which is only verbal and based on introspection.

Global Study of Visual Exploration

Nevertheless, in an experiment not yet published, we tried to obtain some information concerning this problem. We projected eight classical pictures (from Rembrandt to Chirico) to volunteer subjects who were fine-art students at the university. Nine subjects were female and seven were male, with ages ranging from 18 to 26. Half of them were instructed to attend closely because after projection, they would be questioned about what they saw in the pictures (semantic group). The other students were instructed to look at the pictures attentively, because they would be interrogated about aesthetic qualities of the pictures (aesthetic group). Their eye movements were registered by the method of corneal reflexion (Young, 1962), combined with a videotape recording. This procedure permits the obtaining of a picture of the stimulus on the screen of a videomonitor together with the position of the eye. Results were collected and treated manually and occasionally introduced into a computer by means of a light pen on a CRT screen (IBM 2250). In this investigation, we are interested first in the global character of the exploration, such as the mean duration of the fixations and the mean length of the saccades. The results obtained are quite interesting.

The histogram in Figure 1 shows the distribution of the durations of fixations in percentages.

First we notice that the duration of fixation in the "aesthetic" situation (Fig. 1A) has an outline radically different than the outline of the semantic group (Fig. 1B). In particular, we find a greater number of

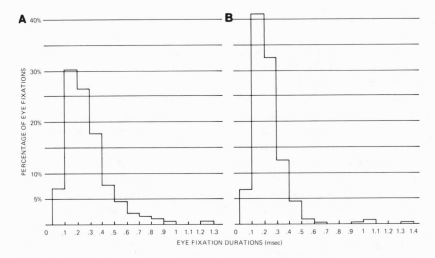

FIGURE 1. Distribution of durations of fixations grouped in classes of 100 msec: (A) aesthetic group; (B) semantic group.

fixations longer than 300 ms in the aesthetic group. Thus, the exploration of the aesthetic group is slower than the exploration of the semantic one. We can observe this difference between the two types of exploration at the level of mean duration of fixation. The mean for the semantic group is 315 ms and is significantly different from the mean of the aesthetic group: 365 ms ($p < .01$). This difference still holds if we compare the duration of fixation, following Jeannerod (1967), in three classes: less than 100 ms, less than 300 ms, and more than 300 ms ($100 < 300 < ...$) (see Table I).

Concerning the spatial aspect of exploration, the results are less interesting. If we arrange the lengths of saccades by degrees in the same way that we did for the times, we cannot find any difference between the two groups. Nothing is astonishing about this. The two parameters, spatial and temporal, are two different functions and are linked to different psychological mechanisms. The temporal one depends principally on the level of interest and motivation, the spatial depends especially on the stimulation. If there are four targets in a visual field, the length of sac-

TABLE I. Frequency of the Different Durations of Fixation of the Aesthetic and of the Semantic Groups

	100<	300<	300>	Total
Aesthetic	33	280	199	512
Semantic	32	329	90	451

cades will depend, in large part, on the objective distance between the targets.

Nevertheless, our finding seems proof that aesthetic motivation involves slower visual exploration. Can we be sure that this is true? Indeed, our results are clear. But, on the other hand, it is well known that all secondary tasks given to the subject while reading slow down the eye movements. If we ask the subjects to solve some arithmetical problems, even very simple ones, the rate of eye displacement becomes immediately slower. This is similar in aesthetically directed picture exploration. Here, the aesthetic task committed to the subject is very difficult. Our post-experimental interview indicates this. All the subjects declare that they had more problems with the aesthetic task than with the semantic task. It may be that it is the cognitive difficulty of making aesthetic judgments that reduces the speed of exploration.

Thus, studying the global form of the exploration, we cannot find convincing proof of the influence of aesthetic motivation on visual scanning. A detailed study of eye movements should be more instructive.

Study of Scannpath

It would be interesting, of course, from a motivationally oriented point of view, to examine the contents of the individual fixations. In other words, which part of the picture catches the eye, and which part the subject actually sees. Kolers (1973, 1976), based on the results of Yarbus (1967) and Buswell (1935), thinks that the eye seeks the region of semantically rich information. This is the opinion of Gould (1973), Loftus (1974), and almost all psychologists concerned with this problem.

There is much experimental evidence that the eye fixes principally on the information part of the picture. But the term *information* is very ambiguous. The specialists employ it in a quite different sense than does common use. Shannon and Weaver (1962) insist on the fact that this special sense "must not be confused with its ordinary usage. In particular, *information* must not be confused with meaning" (p. 99). If we find many fixations on any part of the picture, we cannot be sure that it is a region full of semantic information. There are numerous other perceptual variables that intervene in the strategy of exploration that can be named, legitimately, *information.* Can we hope that in aesthetic attitude the subject will attend, with his eyes, the part which is rich with *aesthetic* information? I think so. But we cannot actually demonstrate it. The difficulty has been due largely to the lack of apparatus and techniques for processing the large volume of data concerning eye movements by aesthetic exploration. (For instance, our recording technique does not permit great preci-

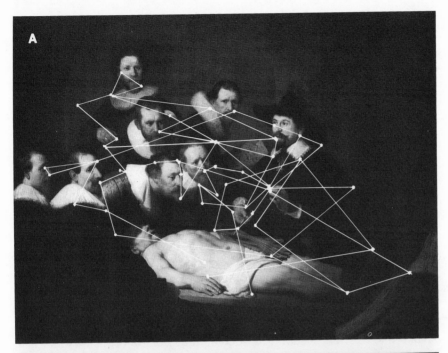

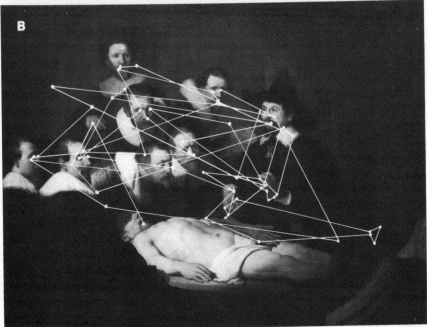

Figure 2. Graph of 60 fixations of 2 subjects: (A) aesthetic group; (B) semantic group.

sion. The precision is about ± 1–1.5 degrees, but the precision of the eye is much less, about ± 2 degrees.)

Figure 2 (A & B) shows the first 60 fixations made by two subjects, one (A) from the aesthetic group and the other (B) from the semantic, looking at the same picture. Indeed, there is little difference between the two explorations. The part of the picture most often looked at was nearly identical in both recordings. Most of the fixations in both pictures correspond with the heads, and sometimes the hands, of the persons. Therefore, they are highly correlated with the parts that are full of semantic information and are also at the same time, from a sensory point of view, the most important—the most attractive for the eyes. The most explored part of the image is the center, where there is most semantic information. Yet, it is well known, and Kaufman and Richards (1969) have shown, that the center of gravity in a picture is explored much more than the other parts, probably because of the physiological constitution of the visual system.[2] We cannot know whether this part of the picture was chosen because of its semantic information or because of a function of its formal qualities. The greatest merit of Rembrandt is that he could combine all informative parts of the picture and manage to have the formal qualities (luminescence, color, contrast) in the same places simultaneously. We shall see in the next section that such a utilization of formal qualities is a requirement for all good composition. In a good composition there will be a good correspondence between formal qualities and semantic information. We shall also see that there are certain types of exploration that cannot correspond with good composition. For instance, we can imagine a set of elements disposed in such a way that all the parts attract the eyes with the same force. Such a picture probably destroys all aesthetic feeling. Therefore, we cannot decide, after our experimental results, if a specific aesthetic scanning, a specific visual exploration corresponding to the aesthetic attitude, does exist.

Various Types of Visual Exploration

One of the fundamental hypotheses on which the psychobiology of art of Berlyne (1971) is based is the existence of two types of exploratory behavior, *specific* and *diversive*, which obey distinct motivations; the aim of specific exploration is knowledge, whereas diversive exploration seems to lack any goal except entertainment or amusement. Berlyne thought that both kinds of exploration are prominent constituents of aesthetic

[2]Here we meet some difficulties. The center of gravity is defined mathematically as $\Sigma \mu_i x_i$, where all x_i are the elements for the picture, given by their coordinates, and all μ_i are the weight associated to x_i. But how can we determine the perceptual weight of an element?

behavior. Of course, both are influenced by collative properties of a stimulus. Nevertheless, it seems that diversive exploration, thanks to moderate arousal increments, is more closely related to pleasingness and, consequently, to the aesthetic.

Berlyne also divided exploratory behavior into three categories according to their modalities. The first is the orientating response: the *receptor adjustment*, as he termed it later, consisting of changing position or orientation of the sense organs. Hence, eye movement is a typical example of the orientating reponse.

If eye movement may be considered a kind of exploratory behavior, and if Berlyne's distinction between two types of exploratory behavior is well founded, it is reasonable to expect that there would be two types of visual exploration with parameter differences. Actually, several authors state that there are two kinds of eye-movement patterns when we look at a complex scene. The first few eye movements made while looking at a picture are long in extent, and the fixations between the two movements are short in duration. A few moments later, fixations become longer and the saccades smaller. It seems that the eye surveys the totality of the stimulus before examining the details. Hochberg (1976) summarized the situation by a diagram (Figure 3), using the data of Antes (1974). We can see in Figure 3 that fixations become progressively longer in duration and closer in space. Note that the curve represents the mean square of the mean of 20 subjects. In any case, it is undeniable that the first fixations have other temporal and spatial parameters than later fixations will have; even the change in parameters is not so regular as in the curves of Antes.

Can we assume that at the beginning of the visual exploration it is the epistemic curiosity that directs the gaze, and that once curiosity is satisfied by enough knowledge, the exploration becomes diversive? In a

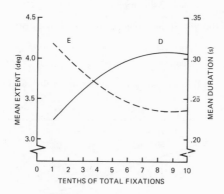

FIGURE 3. Hochberg's representation of the change in duration and in length of fixations. (After Hochberg, 1976, data by Antes.)

recent experiment we tried to obtain data in this field (Molnar, 1977). Eye movements of six subjects (art students at the university) were recorded, using two classical works of Rembrandt, "Dr. Tulp's Anatomy Lesson" and "The Drapers' Union," as stimuli. The subjects saw each picture for five minutes, which is an unusually long time in eye-movement experiments. The eye made over 1,000 movements during this time; in fact, we stopped counting after 1,000 movements.

As we are used to doing, we first studied two principal parameters of exploration: the length of saccades, and the time of pauses. There were many individual differences between the subjects, but, for our purposes here, we can confound the individual results and calculate the means. We studied the fixations 10 by 10 and at the beginning even, 5 by 5. That is to say, we took the average of 5 or 10 fixations. Table II shows the first 10 fixations (1–10) and the last ten fixations (990–1,000).

We found the classical results; the duration of the first 10 fixations is much shorter than that of the last 10. We then tried to study this finding in a more detailed way. We examined the statistical relations between the average of the second, third, and fourth groups of 5 fixations. Afterward, we compared the first 10 fixations with the second 10. Finally, we compared the mean of the first 5 fixations with that of the first 20. The results of all these comparisons are reported in Table II.

Note that this table shows a break in the curve between the fifth and the tenth fixation, which is much stronger than Antes thought. The

TABLE II. Comparative Data of the Temporal Aspect of Visual Exploration.

A. Comparison of duration of the first 10 and the last 10 fixations:

First 10 fixations	280 msec
Last 10 fixations	370 msec

B. Mean duration of the first 20 fixations grouped by classes of 5:

Fixation	5	10	15	20
msec	245	315	350	320

C. Comparison of the first 5 fixations with the second, third, and fourth 5 fixations:[a]

	5	10	15	20
5		$t = 3.18$ $p = .01$	$t = 2.1$ $p = .025$	$t = 2.9$ $p = .01$
10			ns	ns
15				ns
20				

[a]We consider these statistics as purely indicatives.

velocity of exploration does not reduce progressively as it does in the experiment of Antes (1974) but suddenly, somewhere between the fifth and the tenth fixation. Surprisingly enough, we find in this situation the magic number 7 ± 2 of Miller (1956).

Now, if we observe what happens further, we may observe a second change in the temporal pattern of exploration. Between the 300th and the 600th fixation, say after about 1.5–2 min of gazing, depending on subject and stimulus, we find another significant increase in the duration of the pauses. The mean duration of fixation between the 50th and the 300th glance is equal to 320 msec, which differs significantly from the mean duration of the glances between the 750th and the 1,000th, which is of 370 msec.

Similarly to the temporal aspect of scanning, we can observe some important changes in its spatial aspect, too, but with the contrary algebraic sign. The few first movements are very large in extent, depending, naturally, on the composition of the stimulus, that is to say, on the arrangement of the targets, those elements which catch the eye. The size of the displacements becomes shorter after a few fixations. The spatial aspect of this type of exploration is very characteristic. It is built principally by sequences of short eye movements, interrupted at almost irregular intervals by longer saccades which carry the eye to a distant part of the stimulus; the eyes move first to a point of fixation, then, having examined the neighboring area sufficiently, the eyes move on to another area. Finally, we may distinguish another style of exploration, which differs from the preceeding one principally in the extent and the frequency of the long saccades.

Epistemic and Diversive Exploration

So, we may establish the existence of three types of visual exploration, with different temporal and spatial characteristics. The first type of exploration is formed by the first few saccades, which are long in extent and fast in time. This way of exploration corresponds to the activity of overseeing and is probably of biological necessity. The second has shorter displacements, with pauses long enough to permit a beginning of perceptual identification. The spatial aspect of this kind of exploration is characterized by relatively short saccades, interrupted by long eye movements at irregular intervals. In the third kind of exploration, there are even longer pauses between the saccades. The spatial aspect of this exploration is roughly like the aspect of the preceding one. Nevertheless, the period of interruption of the short saccades by long ones seems to be smaller and more regular. The long saccades become shorter, the interruptions are more frequent.

This organization suits well Berlyne's theory concerning the two types of exploration. Of course, except for the first five or six fixations, which may be considered as a kind of particular specific exploration, guided by the physical forces of the stimulus, we found the two types of exploration. Our first, and principally our second type of exploration, should correspond to Berlyne's specific exploration for which the motivation is curiosity. In this case, the eye obeys the force coming chiefly from the part of the picture where semantic information is accumulated. Our third type of exploration should be connected with what Berlyne called diversive exploration. Epistemic curiosity having been satisfied, it is again the physical stimulation, the collative forces, which should guide the exploration.

We are not sure that this finding is strong enough to justify definitively Berlyne's hypothesis concerning diversive and epistemic exploration, but it is certainly new experimental evidence to support it.

COMPLEXITY AND EYE MOVEMENTS

Speaking about collative variables, Berlyne (1960) wrote: "Complexity is without any doubt the most impalpable of the four elusive concepts that we are attempting to delimit" (p. 38). He added: "It is however possible to enumerate some of the most obvious properties on which the complexity ascribed to a pattern will depend." Berlyne defines these properties as the number of distinguishing elements, their dissimilarity, and the degree of their unity.

The mathematician Birkhoff (1932), who was one of the first to use the notion of complexity in aesthetics, defines complexity in elementary geometrical terms as the size of angles, the number of sides, the number of sequences, etc. Birkhoff thought that he had found experimental support for his theory. But a few years later, another investigator (Davis, 1936) failed to find experimental evidence for Birkhoff's theory. "In making empirical tests, the formula cannot be accepted directly" (p. 239), affirmed Davis. Nevertheless, the notion of complexity remains in the literature. With the development of information theory in psychology, Attneave (1957) gave experimental proof that it is the independent turns, the contour, the presence or absence of symmetry, and the mean difference between the angles of successive turns in the contour which define the complexity. It is thus possible that Birkhoff was right from a certain point of view. Among the physical features of a complex stimulus are found the number and size of angles and many other elements already mentioned by Birkhoff. However, from the point of view of perception, these physical elements are not sufficient to explain perceived complexity. Psychological factors, such as knowledge, familiarity, and affectivity, are all factors that could change one's perception of complexity. The city of Venice seems complex on a first day's visit, but this impression wears off after walking around for a few days.

Measurement of Complexity

How can we describe complexity—first objective complexity, and then subjective complexity—if we really can legitimately speak of objective and subjective complexity? In fact, it is after the success of information theory that the concept of complexity took an important place in the vocabulary of modern psychology. Following Shannon, it was Attneave (1953) and Hochberg and McAlister (1953) who first began to use the term "complexity" in psychology. We must note, nevertheless, that simplicity, the opposite of complexity, was one of the most important concepts in a Gestalt theory, described as one of the most important components of the good form. So, when Hochberg tried to approach figural goodness by a quantitative method (Hochberg & McAlister, 1953), the notion of complexity was almost at his disposal. In the same period, Moles wrote a book (published only in 1958) about aesthetics and information theory in which he clearly used the notion of complexity in aesthetics. Berlyne (1957) also started to speak about complexity as one of the important collative variables in aesthetics. But the questions remain open: How to measure complexity and, if that is not possible, how at least to describe it.

As far as an artificial stimulus is concerned, there is no problem. A scientist is always free to define his independent variables as he decides on the condition that he makes his definition explicit. "Il suffit d'avertir," said Pascal. We learned from Attneave and Arnoult (1956) to make a random pattern with statistically defined physical characteristics. Experimenters deployed considerable energy to find relations between well-defined artificial stimuli and judged complexity. "Rated complexity" said Berlyne (1978, p. 126) "has been found to increase with the number of independently chosen elements in a pattern (Attneave, 1957; Day, 1967; Berlyne, 1974), the number of attributes distinguishing elements (Berlyne, 1972a,b,c), the number of forms that each attribute can take (Crozier, 1974; Berlyne, 1974) and the number of attribute distinguishing elements (Berlyne, 1971)."

Statistical Method

But what about complexity of natural stimuli, or all the stimulations in which the experimenter has no possibility of modifying the physical elements? No doubt, the psychologist can require the subject to rate stimuli for complexity on a 7-, 9-, 11-, or n-point scale. But how can we decide which parts, which features of the stimulus, make this stimulus complex? In other words, how can we describe the complexity of a natural stimulus? It is possible, in the case of the very simple stimulus, to count the number of elements or to evaluate the symmetry or other qualities of the stimulus. But this kind of measurement cannot be used generally. A technique better adapted for this task would be the well-known "chessboard method," in which a grid divides the image into a large number of small squares easily submitted to statistical analysis. Since this method is often used, we must briefly examine it. Maser, in his study *Numerische Ästhetik* (1971), gives an example of informational aesthetic measurement: a comparison of aesthetic value in three Rembrandt drawings, each of a young girl. To measure the aesthetic mass of these drawings, the author divides the drawing into a large number of little squares, using the chessboard method. It is obvious that the sequences will be different grays, depending on the tonality of the image. Then he classifies the different grays according to their intensity, going from black to white, in eleven different divisions from 0 to 10. Then he counts how many are in each class, that is, he establishes the frequency of each class of gray. This lets him estimate the entropy following the classical formula.

In dividing the picture, Maser has artificially made a discrete set from a continuous one. He has obtained countable elements like letters in a written text or words of spoken language.[3] But the discrete elements in language are almost "natural," and Maser's divisions are artificial. Maser's division would be arbitrary even if the squares were as small as points in a photogravure. However, this is not the case, as they measure 1cm^2. To cut up a picture naturally into discrete elements, they would have to be as small as the receiving cells in the retina, which would be the size of about a *micron*. This, of course, is impossible.

Some of these problems can be solved with modern techniques. Harmon and Knowlton (1969) built a picture-processing system able to break down the images into discrete elements as small as desired. Then the images are classified according to their luminous intensity or their spectral composition in as many classes; all this is done with specific physical measurements. From these measurements one can regroup the elements and make transformations and permutations. One can even transform the sequences by replacing the spatial distances by temporal distances and calculate the spatial autocorrelation. But this transformation into temporal sequences will always be arbitrary in relation to the ones actually perceived. All the problems created by temporal aspects in

[3]As far as a printed text is concerned, the cutup is natural. In the case of handwriting, there are some problems.

visual perception have not been solved yet. Nevertheless, Maser's technique using drawing without color is good enough to give quite useful results.

In an experiment (Molnar, 1966), we tried the same method to obtain a break down of the colors in a Cézanne painting. For technical reasons, we cut up reproductions of the Cézanne into 1,200 little squares and asked the subjects to classify them according to their color in as many classes as necessary. The results were deplorable. Cézanne's chromatic richness was reduced to an average of eight or nine classes. The little squares, which seemed to be wonderfully colored, once moved out of their place, became gray, dull, and lusterless. The color of a small surface evidently depends on the colors surrounding it. In addition, we met here a classical psychophysical problem, how to classify a stimulus on one dimension, which has two, and even three dimensions. It does not appear that psychophysics can formulate a definitive answer to this question, but, regardless of these problems, which are but secondary from our point of view, the greatest difficulty related to this method is that of transforming a spatial whole into a temporal sequence.

When the statistician counts the occurrence frequency of a certain letter or word in a text, or of a note in a musical score, he has a well-defined temporal order; he can study the probability of one letter's preceding another. It seems that it is the conditional probability of the succession of elements that is the most characteristic of a work, a style, or a school. This method is unusable in the study of paintings. In the case of a visual stimulus, detaching the elements from the whole, categorically separating one element from another, and then establishing an order which allows one to affirm that one element precedes or succeeds another, is a procedure which does not take into account man's perceptual mechanism. It is altogether arbitrary to divide an image into parts, for instance, beginning at the top on the left and finishing at the bottom on the right.

Discretization by the Eye

It is useless to wish to break down the visual world into elements, since it has already been done. The visual world is essentially discrete; its continuity is a psychological illusion. In some still unknown way our visual system fills in or supplements the discrete input to create the subjective sense of continuity (Kolers, 1973).

In his theory of phase sequences, Hebb (1949) convincingly demonstrated that visual perception is built up not only from successive views of given objects or scenes, but from previous discrete experiences as well. The process of intermittancy (gateing process) in perception also intervenes at a higher level. It is obvious that the brain operates by picking up sensory information at different points and different times. No doubt, "the visual system is a discontinuous processing system, where discontinuities are usually marked by the occurrence of 'jumping eye,' " as it is pointed out by Gaarder (1975, p. 63). Eye movements transfer pictures, a spatial phenomenon, to a sequence of temporal events.

So, we do not need a method to transform continuous space into a set of discrete temporal events. The visual world is digitalized by nature. Under these conditions, we could imagine that we have only to observe the eye movements and count the saccades with their spatial coordinates to obtain a first-order statistical description of a picture. We could then observe and compute the successive displacements of the eye, looking for the predecessor or the successor of all fixations. We could thus make second-, third-, and nth-order statistics. In this way, we could treat the information content of the picture in a manner very similar to Shannon's. Now the measurement of information content also measures the amount of complexity, because information in a Shannonian sense and complexity are closely linked.

Unfortunately, the problem is not so simple. It has already been stated that we know, at least since the work of Buswell (1935), that eye movements are not necessary for perception (Molnar, 1974). But eye movements are not completely determined either. The eye does not explore the same picture in exactly the same way twice. This is quite natural. The exploratory pattern depends on both the stimulus and the subject. Not one of the models proposed to explain scanning strategy can forget that subjective psychological forces intervene strongly in the exploration, and that these subjective forces are in constant motion, in constant evolution. In the model proposed by Hochberg (1970), "cognitive exploration" principally obeys these subjective psychological forces, whereas the "peripheric exploration" depends chiefly on the physical forces of the stimulus connected to the receiving physiological system. It is possible, to some extent, to foresee the structures of the peripheric exploration, but those of the cognitive exploration are nearly unpredictable. A certain amount of controversy surrounds this question. Noton and Stark (1971a,b) affirm that subjects always explore the same picture with almost identical eye fixations even within several-days interval, but the same picture will be explored by two subjects in a different way. Mackworth and Morandi (1967) think that all subjects gaze at the more informative part of the picture, that is, that different subjects' eye movements are somehow similar; whereas Gibson (1950) claims that eye movements are absolutely unpredictable.

As far as individual differences in the exploration are concerned, the authors agree. It is generally accepted that there are "enormous" individual differences. Buswell (1935), for instance, plotted the first three fixations on a picture made by 40 persons. The fixations are very widely dispersed. But it is hazardous to consider the very first fixations. The first two or three fixations, in the experimental conditions of Buswell, seem to be really random. Rather, we recorded the first 10 eye movements of 10 subjects looking at Manet's "Olympia" (Figure 4).

Looking at Figure 4, we may say that the individual differences are not so enormous as was generally supposed. We can find many sequences of 3, 4, and sometimes 5 fixations that are nearly identical for several subjects. In any case, there is much more agreement among different fixations made by different people than we can expect by pure chance. In addition, two points of fixation within an angle of two degrees may be confused (Jernigan, 1975). Of course, as we have already said, the spatial precision of eye movements is mediocre. The accuracy of the saccade depends on its magnitude. If the saccade fails to bring the target on the fovea, it will be followed by a correctional saccade. Weber and Daroff (1972) show that for a displacement of 10 degrees we can expect an error of 1.5 degrees in almost a quarter of the cases, and that with a displacement of 50 degrees the probability to over- or undershoot is nearly 50%. We will therefore never know for certain if two neighboring fixations correspond to one or two targets, but we can estimate this probability. Under such

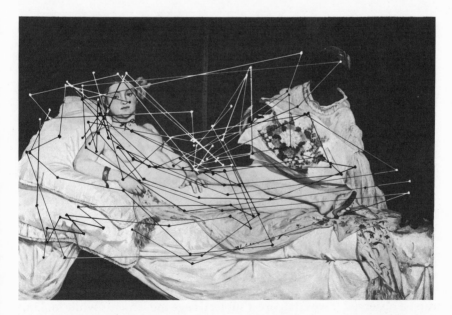

FIGURE 4. Graph of the first 10 eye movements of 10 subjects looking at Manet's "Olympia."

conditions, if we do statistics on identical sequences of fixations, by confounding the fixation points within a circle with a visual radius of 1 degree, we can sometimes find quite good interindividual agreement. This permits the development of statistics on the frequency of fixations. Even more important, after sufficiently long observation, we can do statistics on the succession of fixations. The precision of all these statistics depends on the precision of the observation and on that of the counting. This precision is mediocre, because of the nature of the phenomenon observed and the difficulty of the observation. Thus, if we cannot describe a spatial pattern of exploration in a determinist way, we can describe it in a probabilist way. All these statistics can be easily transformed into probability. If we are not able to predict with precision the individual fixations, hopefully we can determine the probability that a target has to be fixed. Furthermore, these statistics help us to estimate all the parameters necessary for the calculation of Shannonian information contained in the image and to measure its complexity by using the method proposed by information theory. The measurement obtained in this way may be considered as the expression of both objective and subjective complexity.

Before pursuing our inquiry into this problem, it would be interesting to examine briefly some concrete problems concerning relations between complexity and eye movements.

Visual Mechanism and Complexity

It is possible to measure the complexity of a picture directly by a visual mechanism without speaking of probability or the concept of information. Berlyne (1958, 1971) and Day (1966, 1968) presented pairs of pictures of varied complexity to subjects. In each case, one of the members of the pair was complex and the other relatively less so. It was found that the subjects tended to spend more time looking at the complex than at the less complex member of the pair. However, this interest in the complexity has a limit and explains the famous inverted U-shaped curve of the Berlyne school (Day, 1965).

In a way more closely related to eye movements, we tried to show (Molnar, 1974) that there are some relationships between eye movements and certain stylistic aspects of the picture. The classical works of art of the Renaissance, for instance, are explored by large and slow eye movements, whereas Baroque painting, much more dense, much more animated, involves small and quick eye movements. The same phenomenon can be observed if we compare a subject's eye movements while looking at a picture by Vasarely and a painting by Mondrian; the Vasarely will be explored much more quickly. Some of the differences in any individual subject can be very important, whereas with other subjects the differences are less so. Some slow subjects explore Baroque-style paintings more slowly than rapid subjects explore paintings in a classical style. But each subject explores Baroque work more rapidly than classical. Therefore, despite individual differences, we calculated the averages of two types of exploration. If one considers the mean time of the fixations to be indicative of the speed of the exploration, one notices a difference of about 60 msec between the two averages (Figure 5).

We asked a group of "experts" (three painters, three aesthetes, and three art critics) to classify all the pictures which were used in our experiment according to their complexity. The experts executed this task without difficulty. The interindividual agreement was very good. In general, the Baroque pictures were judged much more complex than the classical ones. Pollock's or Vasarely's paintings were judged more complex than Mondrian's. It seems that there is a good correlation between the speed of exploration and judged complexity, as well as between the length of saccades and complexity. These experimental results are in good agreement with the theoretical considerations. If the number of possible targets is big enough—as is the case in general in Baroque paintings, which are often very dense—the distance between the targets is reduced. It seems that the eyes tend to choose the nearer target for fixation. In a Rubens or in a Vasarely, the probability of short saccades is very great because of the closeness of targets. There are more difficulties in explaining why the fixation time grows shorter in Baroque pictures which are judged complex

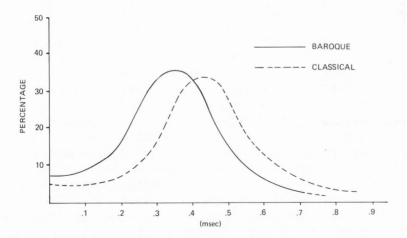

Figure 5. Distribution of the durations of fixations on a classical picture (Titian's "Venus") and on a baroque picture (Tintoretto's "Origin of the Milky Way").

by the experts. Of course, it may seem paradoxical that the time of fixation becomes shorter as the perceptual task becomes more difficult. The paradox disappears if we consider that the aim of eye movements is not only the identification of the object appearing on the fovea, but also the estimation of the peripheric elements (Jannerod, 1967). In fact, there are, in general, two forces determining eye movements. One is cognitive and the other is peripheral, as Hochberg underlines. In a Baroque painting, a lot of details attract the gaze simultaneously. Many targets in the periphery may shorten the fixation time. On the contrary, a picture of classical style has, in general, fewer elements. That is, the distance between the elements is greater, and the subject's eye is less solicited. This is especially obvious when one compares a baroque, a Vasarely, and a classical Mondrian. When we count the angles and line intersections that attract the eye in a Mondrian painting, we find hardly more than a dozen, whereas in a Vasarely such elements exist by the hundreds.

With this brief examination of some experimental facts, we may return to a more theoretical preoccupation.

Graph Theory Applied to Visual Aesthetics

In the visual field there are a set of fixation points, visual targets, which are or are not related by eye movements. (The eye goes from one point to another.) Berge (1967) defines the graphs as "un ensemble X et une application de Γ de X dans X; le couple $C = (X,\Gamma)$ constitue un graphe." We can agree that this definition is well suited to visual exploration. The set of X could be constituted by all the possible points of fixation and the function Γ by the eye movements. Graphically, two points representing two possible targets are connected by a line only if the eye goes from one to the other. In this way, it is possible to establish the graph of the exploration of a picture by joining with a line all points that are visually connected. This graph, like all graphs, has an associated matrix. Since, in theory, each possible fixation point can be related to all the others, this matrix will be a square matrix in which the joining of two points is represented by the number 1 and the nonjoining by a zero.

We cannot survey or even enumerate all the positive aspects of the introduction of graph theory in the field of visual aesthetics; we would only like to examine a few, which seem to us to be the most important.

1. For thousands of years paintings have been discussed in geometrical terms. According to our knowledge of the mechanism of vision and that of eye movements, it is not even certain that geometry is adequate for analyzing a picture. For instance, the geometric center of a picture is its middle, or, if we wish to use a sophisticated method of calculation, its

center of gravity. However, the perceptive center of a picture rarely corresponds to its middle or to its center of gravity. In addition, there are sometimes two or even more than two centers, which in classical geometry would be impossible.

2. The Euclidian distance does not measure the real perceived length between two points inside the picture. The spectator does not necessarily perceive all the details in the immediate neighborhood of his fixation point. His attention may be drawn by an element farther away toward the periphery. Therefore, from the point of view of perception, the Euclidian distance is not the most significant. The distance in visual perception would be measured more accurately by the length of eye movements, and even more precisely by the number of fixations that the subject makes in going from one point to another. For example, let us look at Hokusai's painting "The Wave" (Figure 6). Between the first fixation and the boat, the Euclidian distance is quite small; to get to it, one needs 9 fixations.

Similarly, to measure the distance inside a graph one counts the number of arcs to be crossed to go from one point to another. Apparently we had better modify our old conception of geometry in painting and replace it by graph theory.

3. The use of graph theory in the study of the pattern of exploration

FIGURE 6. Successive fixations of the eyes looking at Hokusai's "The Wave" (after Buswell, 1935). The first 8 fixations are connected by thick lines.

has another—and perhaps more important—advantage. In the optics of graph theory we consider the fixations as the summits of the graph and the eye movements between two summits as arcs, as we have already said. So, theoretically, we can trace the graph of the exploration of a painting. To this graph there can be associated a matrix. We cannot foresee with precision where the eye will be the next time, but, as we have said, we can estimate it with a good probability. That means that in an associate matrix the connection between two points will not be expressed by 0 or by 1, but by a number somewhere between 0 and 1 (stochastic matrix).

We can, in addition, formulate the hypothesis that exploration by eye movements is Markovian, that is to say, that all individual fixations depend only on the preceding ones. This hypothesis is strong, especially when we consider its limitation as far as semantically guided exploration is concerned.

We can reasonably assume that, during the exploratory period (the "second" type according to our terminology and "specific" or "epistemic" according to Berlyne), it is cognitive curiosity, the semantic interest, which guides the eye. This curiosity depends largely on what one is looking at. This dependence, however, is not immediate; the 250–400 msec, corresponding to the length of a fixation, are obviously not enough (1) to prepare the next saccade, (2) to identify completely what one is looking at, and (3) to compare the present visual content with information already registered. The eye is faster than thought. It is therefore difficult to admit, during the second exploratory period, that the process is Markovian.

On the other hand, during the exploratory period of the first type, during the first 5 or 6 fixations (that is, during the first 2 sec of contemplation) we can admit the Markovian restriction. The first foxation on a painting is made at random; it depends on the position of the body, the head, and the eye of the spectator when the stimulus appears. Once the stimulus is centered on the fovea, the next 5 or 6 fixations will be guided by the arrangement of the physical features of the painting. During this period, just before the first perceptual identification of the stimulus, cognitive forces hardly intervene. The eye movement depends on the distribution of the targets projected on the retina. Each displacement radically changes this disposition in relation to the retina and the fovea. Consequently, we can say that during this short period the fixations depend on the preceding ones. We tried to show above (Molnar, 1977) that the pattern of succession of eye movements during visual exploration, called diversive by Berlyne and the third type of exploration by ourselves, looks, in some respects, like the pattern which we called the first type.

There are many arguments to credit this statement. First, there is plain common sense. Once epistemic curiosity is satisfied, there is no longer any reason to look for significant elements. The exploration will be conducted by physical forces of stimulation, associated with the physiological mechanism of vision, in exactly the same manner as in the first period of exploration, when epistemic curiosity did not yet intervene. Second, we have a lot of experimental evidence to support our hypothesis. We found that in the third type of exploration the eye movements become slower and their temporal and spatial aspects more regular. Obviously, there were no important problems disturbing the exploration program, which seemed to be guided by the joint forces belonging both to the oculomotor mechanism of the subject and to the physical characteristics of the stimulus. In particular, it is remarkable that the long saccades which shift the gaze to another region of the stimulus are regular and moderately extended (about 5 or 7 degrees). Of course, according to our hypothesis, they are not provoked by unexpected changes of attention, as they are in the case of epistemic exploration. These movements are related to the eye movements which we call elsewhere (Molnar, 1977) "supervisor eye movements," that intervene at regular periods in ordinary exploration as a biological necessity.

So we can admit, at least as an hypothesis, that the pattern of eye movements during diversive exploration is stochastic and Markovian, as we have suggested several times since 1966. The stochastic and Markovian character of the exploration graph (we can speak interchangeably of graphs or matrices, for they are two expressions of the same thing) implies two consequences particularly important for scientific aesthetics. Actually, we can determine with a good probability the succession of the points of fixation. In this manner, we can describe in a natural way the probabilistic structure of a picture in terms of second- or third-order statistics, whereas classical methods, such as the chessboard, only allow us to treat images in terms of first-order statistics. Now, according to the recent research done by Julesz (1975), the second- (and third-) order statistics seem to be very important in visual perception, and, as we have already underlined above, the most adequate description of a picture might be made by second- (and perhaps third-) order statistics.

Some of Markov's processes have a particular property, very important in communication theory, which we hope will be profitable to scientific aesthetics. This particular property is *ergodicity*. Although a complex mathematical definition of an ergodic process is in some way involved, the general idea is simple. In an ergodic process, every sequence produced by the process is the same as far as the statistical property is concerned. So, the ergodic property means statistical homogeneity. Still more important is the fact that all ergodic processes have a final equilibrium; that is, that such a system, in a shorter or longer time, after several transition states, reaches a final state where it will stay *ad infinitum*. From our specific point of view, this signifies that, if the visual exploration of a picture is ergodic—which it is in theory (although not always in practice[4])—the eyes of the spectator begin to move over the picture in a random way, guided by different forces. However, after a variable period of time, the gaze settles on a determined average path and continues to follow this path (with some deviation) during the whole time it is viewing the picture.

If we admit that the exploration of a picture is Markovian, we can assert that a good composition must be ergodic. Indeed, besides the ergodic modality a Markovian process may be either decomposable (reducible), or periodic. The decomposable modality signifies, from our perspective, that the exploration will be limited to a single part of the picture. In the case of the periodic modality, the spectator's eye will oscillate between two distinct elements of a picture; as soon as the gaze alights on the first element, it is immediately attracted to the other one. Obviously, both modalities reflect bad compositions. The only structure for a good composition is the ergodic one.

But we can go further. It was said that an ergodic system reached a final equilibrium, a stationary state, after a certain period of time, after more or less but a finite number of transitions. Knowing the transition-probability matrix, it is possible to calculate the form of the final equilibrium and the number of steps necessary to reach it. These two data should be considered as characteristic of the quality of a pictural composition; the fewer the transitions necessary to reach the equilibrium state, the higher the quality of the composition. It is, of course, obvious that a composition, made with forms that render difficult the passage to certain areas of the picture, will reach a final equilibrium only after a long period of exploration; in other words, after a great number of transitions, if it can still reach this equilibrium. In any case, this equilibrium will not be satisfactory. In the same way, if the composition of a picture is such that two different details catch the gaze alternatively, the final equilibrium, once reached, will have a form forbidding the aesthetically satisfying contemplation of the picture. A good composition, on the contrary, reaches, after a relatively few number of transitory states, a final equilibrium, and the form of this equilibrium will be such that all the important parts of the picture will be successively explored following a strict hierarchic probability. To avoid all misapprehension, we have to point out that the number of transitions, which is one of the variables of which we propose to measure the compo-

---

[4] In theory, the eye can go from any single point to any other one. But in practice, this liberty is restrained by psychological and physiological factors.

sition quality, is a mathematical fiction, an *index*. This index does not correspond to the time that is spent by a real subject's eye to reach the final equilibrium. The theory postulates that the transition of the states of each element intervenes simultaneously. In fact, this seldom happens in nature, and in visual exploration this simultaneity is impossible. However, this restriction does not diminish the utility of this method of measurement.

Naturally, we tried several times to demonstrate experimentally the validity of these propositions. Unfortunately, it is extremely difficult and also very expensive to carry out exact experimentation in this field. The principal difficulty consists in obtaining a valid transition-probability matrix; that is, in obtaining a set of transition probabilities after the recording of an important number of the subject's eye movements done in constant conditions. In spite of the difficulties, we think that we accomplished this task with an acceptable precision.

We could not hope to establish second-order statistics on all individual eye movement. We could not count the predecessors of every fixation point. That would have been a very difficult task, and, in addition, probably useless. Because of the already-mentioned inaccuracy of the eye, all fixations are not necessarily meaningful. To simplify our task and to reduce the difficulty, we treated a certain number of fixations together. We determined, by means of first-order statistics obtained by the recording of very large number of eye movements, the density of distribution of the fixations on the picture. We next chose a few, say 6 or 8, areas which received the most fixations. Then we counted the successive displacements from one area to another. The frequency of these displacements was transformed into probability. Figure 7 shows the partition of one of the favorite stimuli of our laboratory, Manet's "Olympia."

The matrix of transition probability, established after more than 3,000 fixations, is as follows:

	1	2	3	4	5	6
1	.3	.3	.2	0	0	.2
2	.2	.3	.2	.1	0	.2
3	.1	.2	.1	.3	.1	.2
4	.1	0	.2	.3	.1	.3
5	0	.2	.1	.1	0	.4
6	.2	.2	.1	.1	0	.4

This matrix signifies that, if the eye is directed to Area 1, the probability that the next fixation will be in Area 2 is .3, in Area 3 is .2, etc. It is important to notice that this average stochastic structure of the picture is nearly identical to the structure obtained after the exploration of every

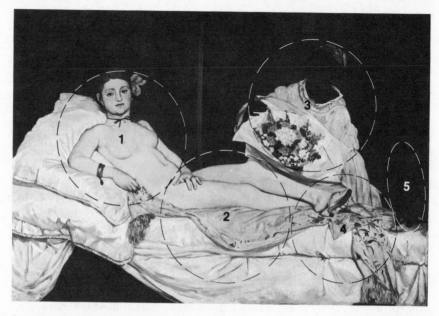

FIGURE 7. Schema of a partition of Manet's "Olympia" in 5 areas. (The 6th area is the complement, the rest of the picture.)

individual subject. Hence, in contrast to detailed fixation-by-fixation treatment of exploration, there are no differences among subjects in the statistical structure of visual exploration.

The exploration of "Olympia," whose matrix of transition probability is reproduced, reaches this final equilibrium in a very short time. After less than 25 iterations, a stable state is obtained that can be expressed by the following vector:

$$
\begin{array}{cccccc}
1 & 2 & 3 & 4 & 5 & 6 \\
(0.181, & 0.211, & 0.153, & 0.140, & 0.036, & 0.276)
\end{array}
$$

We can see that the most explored area is, and remains henceforth, Area 2. Twenty-one percent of the fixations go to this region. The next is Area 1, around the head of Olympia, followed by Areas 3, 4, and 5. No. 5 designates the part, little explored, corresponding to the cat, that we have included for semantic reasons only.

Another comparable painting, the "Venus from Urbino" by Titian, gives a better result. The final equilibrium in this picture is reached after less than 20 iterations, and the form of this equilibrium is better. Of course, in Titian's painting, there is no such area as that of the cat, so weakly explored in the Manet.

All pictures are not so perfect from this point of view. There is another great work of art which we very often use for experimentation, the famous painting by Titian, "Sacred Love and Earthly Love." With difficulty, this painting reaches a final balance, after a long period of exploration. Let us examine the graph corresponding to the transition probability of this painting. After a long observation (Figure 8) we can state that there are no saccades (at least not statistically important ones) going from one person to the other. All joining between the two people goes through a fixation on the central part of the picture, and the probability of the passage is weak. Under these conditions, the final equilibrium is reached only after a long set of transitions (about twice the number that was necessary in the case of Manet's "Olympia"). So we can say that, from this aspect, this painting is badly composed. If we suppress the central "figurine," we demolish the unity of the picture. This work of Titian ceases to be a whole, and, at the same time, the graph of exploration is no longer ergodic.

FIGURE 8. Titian's "Sacred Love and Earthly Love."

CONCLUSION

This review of the role of eye movements in aesthetics does not need any conclusion. In our opinion, a review does not have to have one. But, having committed the unpardonable mistake (whether out of inadvertence or habit) of starting this article with an introduction, we are now forced to end it with a conclusion. *"Logic obliges."* So, as a conclusion, we will continue the quotation of Berlyne's posthumus paper, of which the first part figures *in exergue* at the head of this chapter.

> But as far as the collative stimulus properties are concerned, measurement is a more pressing need than in many other fields of psychology, because the nature, and even the direction, of their motivational effects can depend very delicately on the precise degree to which they are present. (1978, p. 130)

We hope that the few propositions contained in this text will help to carry out Berlyne's wish.

REFERENCES

ANTES, J. R. The time course of picture viewing. *Journal of Experimental Psychology*, 1974, 103, 62–70.

ATTNEAVE, F. Psychological probability as a function of experienced frequency. *Journal of Experimental Psychology* 1953, 46, 81–86.

ATTNEAVE, F. Physical determinants of the judged complexity of shapes. *Journal of Experimental Psychology* 1957, 53, 221–227.

ATTNEAVE, F., & ARNOULT, M. D. The quantitative study of shape and pattern perception. *Psychological Bulletin* 1956, 53, 452–471.

BERGE, C. *Théorie des graphes et ses applications.* Paris: Dunod, 1967.

BERLYNE, D. E. Uncertainty and conflict: A point of contact between information-theory and behavior-theory concept. *Psychological Review* 1957, 64, 329–339.

BERLYNE, D. E. The influence of complexity and novelty in visual figures on orienting responses. *Journal of Experimental Psychology* 1958, 55, 289–296.

BERLYNE, D. E. *Conflict, arousal and curiosity.* New York: McGraw-Hill, 1960.

BERLYNE, D. E. *Aesthetics and psychobiology.* New York: Appleton-Century-Crofts, 1971.

BERLYNE, D. E. Uniformity in variety: Extension to three elements visual patterns and to non-verbal measures. *Canadian Journal of Psychology,* 1972, 26, 277–291.(a)

BERLYNE, D. E. Ends and means of experimental aesthetics. *Canadian Journal of Psychology,* 1972, 26, 303–325.(b)

BERLYNE, D. E. Experimental aesthetics. In P.C. Dodwell (Ed.), *New horizons in psychology.* London: Penguin, 1972.(c)

BERLYNE, D. E. The new experimental aesthetics. In D.E. Berlyne, (Ed.), *Studies in the new experimental aesthetics.* Washington, D.C.: Hemisphere Publishing, 1974.

BERLYNE, D. E. Curiosity and learning. *Motivation and Emotion,* 1978, 2, 2.

BIRKHOFF, G. D. *Aesthetic measure.* Cambridge: Harvard University Press, 1932.

BRANDT, H. F. *The psychology of seeing.* New York: Philosophical Library, 1945.

BUSWELL, G. T. *How people look at pictures.* Chicago: University of Chicago Press, 1935.

CROZIER, J. B. Verbal and exploratory responses to sound sequences varying in uncertainty level. In D.E. Berlyne, (Ed.), *Studies in the new experimental aesthetics.* Washington, D.C.: Hemisphere Publishing, 1974.

DAVIS, R. C. An evaluation and test of Birkhoff aesthetic measure formula. *Journal of Genetic Psychology,* 1936, 15, 231–241.

DAY, H. I. *Exploratory behaviour as a function of individual differences and level of arousal.* Doctoral dissertation, University of Toronto, 1965.

DAY, H. I. Looking time as a function of stimulus variables and individual differences. *Perceptual and Motor Skills,* 1966, 22, 423–428.

DAY, H. I. Evaluations of subjective complexity pleasingness and interestingness for a series of random polygons varying in complexity. *Perception and Psychophysics,* 1967, 2, 281–286.

DAY, H. I. The importance of symmetry and complexity in the evaluation of complexity, interest and pleasingness. *Psychonomic Science,* 1968, 10, 339–340.

GAARDER, K. R. *Eye movements, vision and behavior.* Washington, D.C.: Hemisphere Publishing, 1975.

GIBSON, J. J. *The perception of the visual world.* Boston: Houghton Mifflin, 1950.

GOULD, J. D. Eye movements during visual search and memory search. *Journal of Experimental Psychology*, 1973, *98*, 184–195.

HARMON, L. D., & KNOWLTON, K. C. Picture processing by computer. *Science*, 1969, *164*, 67–77.

HEBB, D. O. *The organization of behavior.* New York: Wiley, 1949.

HOCHBERG, J. In the mind's eye. In R. N. Haber, (Ed.), *Contemporary theory and research in visual perception.* New York: Holt, Rinehart, & Winston, 1968.

HOCHBERG, J. Components of literacy: Speculation and exploratory research. In H. Levin & J.P. Williams (Eds.), *Basic study on reading.* New York: Basic Books, 1970.

HOCHBERG, J. Toward a speech-plan eye-movement model of reading. In R.A. Monty & J.W. Senders (Eds.), *Eye movements and psychological processes.* New York: Wiley, 1976.

HOCHBERG, J., & BROOKS, V. Geometrical vs. directional factors in the prediction of attention distribution. *American Psychologist*, 1963, *7*, 437–441.

HOCHBERG, J., & MCALISTER, E. A quantitative approach for figural "goodness". *Journal of Experimental Psychology*, 1953, *46*, 361–364.

JEANNEROD, M. Déplacements et fixations du regard dans l'exploration libre d'une scène visuelle. *Vision Research*, 1967, *8*, 81–97.

JERNIGAN, M. E. *Eye movement analysis in plotting the visual field.* Doctoral dissertation, M.I.T., 1975.

JULESZ, B. Experiments in the visual perception of texture. *Scientific American*, 1975, *232*, 4.

KAUFMAN, L., & RICHARDS, W. Spontaneous fixation tendencies for visual forms. *Perception and Psychophysics*, 1969, *5*, 85–88.

KOLERS, P. A. Some modes of representation. In P. Pliner, L. Krames, T. Alloway (Eds.), *Communication and affect.* New York: Science Press, 1973.

KOLERS, P. A. Buswell's discoveries. In R.A. Monty, J.W. Senders (Eds.), *Eye movements and psychological processes.* New York: Wiley, 1976.

LOFTUS, G. R. Acquisition in information from rapidly presented verbal and non-verbal stimuli. *Memory and Cognition*, 1974, *2*, 545–548.

MACKWORTH, N. H., & MORANDI, A. Y. The gaze selects informative details within pictures. *Perception and Psychophysics*, 1967, *2*(11)547–552.

MASER, S. *Numerische Ästhetik.* Stuttgart-Bern: Karl Kräme Verlag, 1971.

MILLER, G. A. The magical number seven, plus or minus two: Some limits on our capacity for processing information. *Psychological Review*, 1956, *63*, 81–87.

MOLES, A. A. *Théorie de l-information et perception esthétique.* Paris: Flammarion, 1958.

MOLNAR, F. Das problem der Zeit in der experimentallen bildenden Kunst. In H. Hacke & K. Staudt (Eds.), *Drei Probleme aus dem Bereich der Informationsästhetik.* München: Staudt, 1966.

MOLNAR, F. *Perception visuelle de l'unité.* Thesis, University of Nanterre, 1974.

MOLNAR, F. La composition picturale et la théorie des graphes. In *Actes du VIIème Congrès International d'Esthétique*, 1972, Bucarest: Editura Academia, 1977.

MOLNAR, F. *Movements des yeux et l'hypothèse des explorations épistémiques et diversives.* Nice: Journal National de la Société Française de Psychologie, 1977.

NOTON, D., & STARK, L. Scanpaths in eye movements during pattern perception. *Science*, 1971, *171*, 308–311.(a)

NOTON, D., & STARK, L. Eye movements and visual perception. *Scientific American*, 1971, 244(6)34–53.(b)

STRATTON, G. M. Symmetry, linear illusions and the movements of the eyes. *Psychological Review*, 1906, *13*, 82–96.

WEBER, R. B., & DAROFF, R. B. Corrective movements following refixation saccades. *Vision Research*, 1972, *12*, 467–475.

YARBUS, A. L. *Eye movements and vision.* New York: Plenum Press, 1967.

YOUNG, L. R. *Eye movements.* Doctoral dissertation, M.I.T., 1962.

Bases of Transcultural Agreement in Response to Art

Irvin L. Child

Early and Extreme Views

In the early days of experimental aesthetics, agreement among different persons in affective response to stimuli was often attributed to a very simple form of intrinsic motivation. If a particular color or shape was generally liked or disliked, this fact was attributed to human nature—that is, people were assumed to share, simply as human beings, inborn dispositions to like or dislike particular stimuli or particular positions along sensory dimensions. The graduate students in psychology, who were often each others' subjects in those days, were thought of as representative of humankind. The intrinsic pleasure or displeasure of their sensory experience was a consequence of the universal human nature they shared. Until the most recent decades, experimental aesthetics did not greatly advance beyond this simplistic approach.

Meanwhile, social psychology and anthropology influenced general opinion about the sources of affective response. This influence was toward a position of complete cultural relativism, implying a total rejection of intrinsic motivation as used or implied in aesthetic theory. Found in its extremest form more often in outsiders influenced by the social sciences, rather than in social scientists themselves, this position held that the apparent satisfaction people find in artistic and other stimuli has nothing to do with the immediate realities of their interaction with the stimuli. It originates only in their training in, or acceptance of, customs of their group about what stimuli they should find pleasant or unpleasant, commendable or deplorable. The motivations and gratifications lie solely in a

Irvin L. Child • Department of Psychology, Yale University, New Haven, Connecticut 06520.

person's interactions with his social group, not at all in his interactions with the apparent stimuli to aesthetic enjoyment.

In view of its association with these extreme positions, it is not surprising that the early research both in experimental aesthetics and in social psychology, using stimuli that were works of art or simple analogs of works of art, disappointed the hopes of those who looked to this research for illumination of human artistic activities and experience.

The resurgence of experimental aesthetics in recent decades has occurred in the context of a much more mature psychology and social science. Intrinsic motivation can now readily be seen not to imply uniform motivation, and variability of response to art can be seen not to imply absence of intrinsic motivation. The extreme complexity of human interaction with art can be recognized without our having to abandon hope that a scientific approach can help in understanding it. In this paper, I should like to sketch out some of what a scientific approach might contribute to understanding agreement across cultural boundaries in response to art. I shall gather together some evidence that there are transcultural agreements, and then consider—for the most part speculatively—the varied bases for these agreements.

WHY CONCENTRATE ON VISUAL ART?

Research comparing response to art and related stimuli across cultural boundaries is almost entirely confined to visual art and its components or simple analogs. (A striking exception is the French versus Japanese comparison, by Francès and Tamba, 1973, of liking for traditional Japanese music.) Yet the theoretical interests leading to this research extend far byond visual art; all the arts seem pertinent to the underlying questions about aesthetic enjoyment. Why the restriction?

Aesthetically relevant research on components or simple analogs of the arts could be conducted on sounds, movements, words, etc., and some has been. There seems no theoretical or practical reason that research on colors and forms should take complete priority over that on the elements of other arts. But in studying response to works of art themselves, very compelling practical reasons have led to predominant attention to visual art. In working with a homogeneous group of persons in his own society, the researcher is able to obtain information about their response to visual art enormously more speedily than about their response to the other arts. Works which to be apprehended must be performed or reproduced through time, as in music and drama, create for the researcher difficulties beyond enumeration here.

The visual arts have especially tempted researchers for another reason which is partly illusory. More than any of the other arts, the visual arts seem to present a clear objective stimulus to be entered into the paradigms of psychological research. A painting, a statue, a building, appears to be a thing. In real life its stimulus potentialities vary considerably as reflections of light on the painting change, as the person walks around the statue, as he explores the inner regions of the building. These complicating variations are commonly removed in research by using a photograph instead of the real object. Though this step lessens the relevance to art as ordinarily experienced, it facilitates comparison of individuals and groups.

In research comparing response to works of art in very different cultures, additional reasons have strengthened the bias toward studying visual art. Poetry is obviously impossible for this purpose, unless the poem is first radically transformed by translation. The meaning of a piece of music is widely thought to depend on familiarity with the musical tradition from which it stems. Practical difficulties of producing the appropriate stimuli in the field are also greater for most of the nonvisual arts.

The research has mostly been restricted to visual art, then; but it has been done with a hope that it is applicable in important ways to the other arts as well. The obvious difficulties with studying the other arts should alert us, however, to the possibility that subtle difficulties of similar character may confront the student of response to visual art. Extreme statements have been made about cultural variation in visual perception. We do not need to accept such exaggerations in order to recognize that there is great variation in what is experienced when different people look at the same painting. I. A. Richards (1929) could easily demonstrate a parallel point about lyric poetry, perhaps helped by the fact that poems and their explications are expressed in the same medium. Variations in the grasp of visual art, even in a group as homogeneous as Richards used, might be equally dramatic, but we do not know. This is the reason I say that the advantage of studying visual arts may be partly illusory. When it comes to comparing vastly different groups, we probably lack even good methods for making adequate comparisons of their experiences in observing a work of visual art. Research comparing preferences across cultural boundaries has usually included no attempt to compare the experiences on which the preferences are based. One of Berlyne's last papers (1976) provides a notable exception. He used multidimensional scaling procedures to compare perception of paintings by different groups, whose preferences were also studied. He found differences among the groups in those aspects of pictorial perception which could be assessed in this way.

At the same time, his findings are reassuring about the extent of similarity in picture perception between, at the extreme, Canadian university students and illiterate villagers in India.

Despite this basic gap, the research on aesthetic response has proceeded. The difficulties restrict the confidence we can have in the generalizations we arrive at, but, in my opinion, they do not justify abandoning pursuit of this imperfect but fascinating inquiry.

A PROCEDURE TO BE USED

One of the most dependable impacts of quantitative data about aesthetics is the demonstration that agreement is probabilistic rather than absolute, and may be indisputably present even where not at all obvious. Early studies of the "golden proportion" did not find uniform agreement on one most pleasing shape of rectangles, but they completely refuted any notion that pleasingness of different shapes was completely unpredictable. The lesson that consensus is imperfect but real has been reinforced over and over.

I shall take an example from research with visual art. To do so I need to introduce first a kind of stimulus material used in several studies I shall refer to later in the paper also. The material consists of a number of pairs of works of art, reproduced sometimes as photographic prints and sometimes as projected slides, according to the availability of equipment and electrical power and whether people are taking part individually or in groups. Each pair consists of two works of similar type or subject matter, often also of similar style, selected so that one work is much better aesthetically, in the opinion of the selector and of other artistically knowledgeable persons to whose judgment the pairs were submitted. In research using this material, a person is asked to indicate, for each pair shown to him, which work he likes better (or, in some research, which he considers to be the better work of art).

When a group of people have responded to a set of these pairs, adequate characterization of the group's response seems to require considering two different aspects:

1. How frequently do their choices correspond to the judgments of aesthetic value on which the formation of the pairs was based? I will cite later some facts that emerge from this aspect of the outcome.

2. What is the pattern of their choices, as they vary from one pair to another? In the set of pairs shown to a group, the percentage choosing the work intended to be aesthetically superior could theoretically vary all the way from 100 for some pairs down to 0% for some at the other extreme.

What the particular group agrees on can be represented by a set of numbers, one number for each pair, indicating the degree of unanimity with which the group's preference corresponds to, or disagrees with, the opinion of experts about aesthetic quality. In a large group, complete unanimity in either direction is very rare, of course. But the way the pairs are spread out by these numbers, from rather general disagreement with expert choice to rather general agreement with expert choice, is highly consistent for the group. (If anyone felt a need to ask whether there is statistically significant evidence of consistency, a characteristic answer, for a set of 80 pairs and a group of 75 persons, is that the evidence of consistency is significant at the level indicated by a p of about 10^{-14}. In each of four school groups tested by Duffy, 1977, for instance, averaging 75 persons, the alpha coefficient for item discrimination approximated .90.)

It is this second aspect of the aesthetic choices of a group that I want to draw on here to answer the question, "How much agreement?" The pattern of one group's preferences may be compared with the pattern of another group's preferences, to test how closely the differentiation one group makes among the pairs agrees with the differentiation another group makes among the same pairs. The agreement need not have anything to do with the "aesthetic value" that experts might consider to vary between the two pictures in a pair; the direction in which expert judgment distinguishes the two pictures may simply provide a constant reference frame, so that the difference between 30% agreement on one pair and 70% agreement on another has some meaning, instead of being purely arbitrary.

IS THERE TRANSCULTURAL AGREEMENT?

The materials I have described in the preceding section had by 1968 been used by field-workers in a number of groups in several different cultural settings. The groups were drawn mainly from four somewhat distinctive regions: the United States, Puerto Rico, Ecuador and Peru, and Japan. Very small samples were also studied in Egypt and in India (11 and 7 persons, respectively). The particular set of pairs used varied from one setting to another, but with overlap of anywhere from 28 to 96 pairs. A report by Child, Iwao, Briddell, Fintzelberg, García, Hetata, Most, Ning, and Sewall (1968) presented the intergroup comparisons that could be made from the data accumulated up to that time.

The outcome was a great preponderance of positive correlations. For any two groups in the same general region, the correlations between their responses to overlapping pairs were always positive, with no exceptions whatever, even though cultural diversity within a region was sometimes very considerable. More important, however, are the correlations between groups in different regions. I have summarized the relevant facts from the report cited, and present them in Table I. The correlations between groups in different regions averaged +.295, and 92.5% of the correlations were positive, indicating a strong tendency toward agreement rather than disagreement. The consistency with which any two groups tended to agree rather than to disagree is particularly striking in view of the small size of some of the groups, which would have permitted a certain number of negative correlations to emerge through sampling error even if the true relationship were uniformly positive. Though the average group consisted of 58 persons, 16 groups (including all those outside Japan and the United States) contained 25 or fewer persons. For none of the regions did the percentage of positive correlations with groups in other regions fall below 81, and five of the six regions had over 90% positive correlations.

The average agreement between groups, by the measure used here, is not very large; but the tendency toward agreement rather than disagreement is overwhelming. For simpler analogs of visual art, similar conclusions are reached (though with different indices of agreement) in research by Eysenck and Iwawaki (1971), Soueif and Eysenck (1972), Berlyne, Robbins, and Thompson (1974), and Berlyne (1975). The one available study of responses to music (Francès and Tamba, 1973) suggests that for music transcultural agreement may not be so general, though it is not completely absent.

What are the sources of such agreement? There is no way to be certain about the sources for these particular bodies of data. But speculations about possible sources may point toward limited conclusions from present knowledge, and possible questions to be pursued in the future.

TABLE I. Similarity of Aesthetic Response between Groups in Different Cultural Regions

Region	Number of groups	Number of correlations with groups in other regions	Mean of all correlations with groups in other regions	Percentage of these correlations found to be positive
United States	16	304	+0.32	90.8%
Japan	7	196	+0.22	81.6%
Ecuador and Peru	6	174	+0.27	92.5%
Puerto Rico	4	124	+0.39	91.9%
Egypt	1	34	+0.35	97.1%
India	1	34	+0.24	93.9%

CULTURAL TRANSMISSION AS A SOURCE OF AGREEMENT

Between different groups, one source of resemblance in the pattern of their preferences is found in a shared past. The culture of one group might have influenced the culture of which the other group is a representative, or the two groups might have derived from a common cultural background.

For the importance of this source I can cite evidence, if evidence be needed, from the body of data I have already drawn on in the previous section. Within each of four regions, preferences were assessed for several groups—from four up to sixteen. The sharing of history would seem in a general way to be closer within any of these regions than it is between them. The influence of cultural transmission might be manifested, therefore, in a tendency for groups to have more similar preferences if they are in the same region than if they are in different regions. I have already indicated that this tendency is present; all correlations between groups within a region are positive, whereas some of the correlations across regions are negative. The tendency is also exhibited in the mean of various sets of correlations. The United States groups have a mean correlation with each other of +.55, whereas in Table I they were shown to have a mean correlation with groups in other regions of only +.32. For the Japanese groups, the corresponding figures are +.51 and +.22; for the groups in Ecuador and Peru, +.33 and +.27; and for the Puerto Rican groups, +.61 and +.39. Clearly, when the question is tested in this way with these data, the preferences of groups with more of a common history show more resemblance than do the preferences of groups with less of a common history.

Could all of the resemblance *across* regions also have been brought about by shared aspects of history, perhaps as one aspect of the diffusion throughout the world of modern international culture? I have no conclusive evidence to offer against that possibility. But there is no evidence in its favor, either. To the extent that appeal to other possible sources of agreement has special plausibility, that appeal may justifiably take some precedence over the rather empty claim of passive historicity as ubiquitous influence. But we should be alert to the possible role of broad transcultural diffusion.

DIRECT GENETIC INFLUENCE ON PREFERENCE AGREEMENT

Normal human beings might be so constituted biologically that regardless of their environment—provided only there be an environment that permits survival and growth—they will exhibit preferential liking or disliking of various stimuli.

It is easy to suppose this true of some smells. We may all have strong olfactory likes and dislikes that are peculiar to us or to our social group, but it is hard to resist the supposition that some are inherited uniformities. The case seems strong for a survival value, in the evolution of our species, of aversion responses to smells which often signal danger, and of attraction to other smells, most notably, those which are associated with food and other desiderata. If mutations have at times created or strengthened such response tendencies, therefore, we should expect them to become eventually a part of the species endowment. Whether, in fact, this has occurred remains, so far as I know, to receive adequate test in the future.

In another sensory mode, that of taste, for the dimension of intensity the a priori case seems even stronger; surely the aversion to intense acidity, for example, must be universal and genetically determined. The same claim seems reasonable for attraction to moderate sweetness and saltiness. (See Moskowitz, 1978, pp. 174–177, for relevant evidence based on neonatal preferences.)

Aversion to extremely high intensity in other modalities, too, may be genetically determined. But is anything else about the modalities of greatest aesthetic interest—sight and hearing—likely to be determined genetically in a simple and uniform way? For dimensions such as hue and saturation (and even brightness within a restricted range) it seems hard to make any a priori case. For visual and auditory patterns that might serve as a releaser stimuli—an expression and yell of rage, gestures of attack, a smile, a babyish form—the predictable responses may be generally evoked if the patterns arise in a realistic situation. But if the same patterns occur in play or in art, the response may be very different. The meaning the person finds in the total situation mediates the actualization or non-actualization of the possibly innate response tendency. The tendency to respond in a predetermined way may be aroused by the releaser stimulus, but between the tendency and conscious awareness or overt action lie many opportunities for modification or replacement by other tendencies.

Direct genetic influences may also determine individual differences in preference, and thus create transcultural agreement between particular individuals. Of special importance, if they occur, may be genetic differences betweem male and female that could be directly responsible for widespread agreement among men in different cultures, or among women. Though our knowledge is very fragmentary, sex differences in aesthetic preference seem to me more likely to be traced to complex processes in which hereditary endowment is only one element.

Uniformities of Experience as a Source of Preference Agreement

Transcultural similarities in preference may arise in uniformities of experience. The widespread liking for sky blue may, in societies that share it, grow from its association with pleasant days free from rain or snow. If this be true, predictions about variation follow; sky blue should be less liked in dry regions for whose inhabitants freedom from rain is a source of suffering. Of various specific hypotheses about simple environmental sources of transcultural aesthetic agreement, a number might like this one be capable of verification because they would also predict transcultural differences and hence a correlation between environmental conditions and an aspect of aesthetic response. Other specific hypotheses might refer to truly universal implications of the environment for aesthetic response, and for these no such critical test seems to be available.

The trace left by uniformities of experience may appear as potentialities to be appealed to, rather than preferences inevitably present. The fact that every human being has once been a small child cared for by powerful adults may leave a propensity toward imaging a powerful caretaker, toward objectifying that image in art, and toward preferring this art over art lacking any reference to emotionally significant uniformities of experience. C. G. Jung (cf. Philipson, 1963) has argued for the importance of propensities such as this, and has given them the name *archetypes*. Jung seems often to think of them as inborn; similarities in our ancestors' experience through generations led eventually, he supposes, to the biological inheritance of appropriate cognitive tendencies. Jung probably exaggerated the role of heredity, and seemed little concerned with whether his expectations were reasonable in the light of biological knowledge of how traits get established genetically. The majority of psychologists, on the other hand, may well have unduly belittled the possible role of heredity. Even if archetypes are found to have their origins to an important degree in genetic endowment, however, they are likely to be strengthened and modified in individual experience.

A powerful source of agreement between certain persons in two different cultural groups may lie in a particular uniformity of experience: exposure to standards of art preference in expert circles, where these standards are closely similar in the two cultural groups. Such a source would still leave open the question of why art experts in the two cultural settings evaluated art in the same way. But it is useful to note that the psychological processes leading to an identical transcultural agreement can be quite different for different groups—in this instance, for leaders and followers in the intracultural development and diffusion of norms.

DEVELOPMENTAL SEQUENCES IN THE INDIVIDUAL

I have considered so far three sources of transcultural agreement that may reasonably be thought of abstractly as simple and direct influences on preference. Cultural diffusion, biological heredity, and various environmental factors may be imagined as producing a more-or-less uniform effect on preference wherever they occur. Of course, these influences are not generally going to be operating in such splendid isolation as theory may envisage. But a somewhat oversimplified theory about them may not lead us badly astray.

We come now to some influences on preference whose operation seems bound to be more subtle and complex, because of the obvious importance of developmental changes in the life history of the individual. Eventually, perhaps, we may need to recognize the importance of developmental changes even for the seemingly simpler phenomena. For these more complex influences, the importance of development is already clear.

I am using *development* here to mean changes emerging in the individual through complex processes in which genetic and environmental influences interact. The concept of *development* implies no special priority for genetic influences, as is often mistakenly thought; indeed, it is based on a denial that isolated consideration of purely genetic or of purely environmental influences can carry us very far. The state of the individual at any point in time, which has resulted from complex interactive processes in the past, will generally have features that need to be taken into account in predicting future development.

Some General Characteristics of Early Years

Preferential reactions to art are apparent at an early age, and may yield transcultural agreement. Child and Iwao (1977) provide some information on this with the kind of materials I have described above. They used 27 pairs of works of art, selected on the basis of the preferences of school children in the United States. In some pairs, the work judged better by experts was preferred by school children, in some the other work was preferred; in some pairs the same picture was chosen throughout the school years, whereas in others the choice (or whether there was any decided choice) varied systematically with age. The school data had been gathered in the classroom, with each child recording his response to pairs of projected slides. Child and Iwao extended this information downward in age, by individual interviews with younger children who were confronted with photographic prints mounted in an album. In general, the preferences of children in the lowest school grades were confirmed for children five or four years old, and with fair regularity even for the youngest children interviewed, those three years old or a few months below three. Most of the preferences were shared by the samples of children studied in two countries, Japan and the United States.

What young children prefer in art, in these two national samples, could be characterized by relating their preferences to the features that distinguish the two works in the pairs offered for choice. The outcome here is subject to considerable sampling error, because there were only 27 pairs, and only 13 in color. What it indicates is that young children tend to choose pictures that are clear, happy, suggestive of abundance, and colorful (with varied hues, and high saturation predominating).

One aspect of this childhood-preference pattern, the special liking for highly saturated colors, is confirmed by studies in which children were asked to choose merely between two color samples. Child, Hansen, and Hornbeck (1968) found a maximum preference for more saturated colors in about the fourth grade (i.e., children about nine years old). The tendency for relatively young children to like strongly saturated colors has also been found in Vietnam (unpublished data of Kastl and Child, 1968). So far as we know, it has not yet been looked for elsewhere.

The suggestion that I should extract from these findings is that young children tend to like visual stimuli that are attention-getting and reassuring. These formulations may suggest extrapolations that could be tested, predictions about children's likes in music, literature, and drama, for example. Behind these visual preferences may lie features of the general developmental status of young children, a need for strong stimulation and a need to be reassured by symbols of security and happiness. If these are usual characteristics of children over some considerable span of ages in the United States and Japan, perhaps they are attributable to uniformities of development to be found in all societies. But these characteristics may apply only to development in societies where—as in the American and Japanese urban groups we tested—children do not have to work for their living. However broad the generalization, these features of childhood do not seem likely to be attributable in any simple way to either biological or social determinants; they seem rather to emerge from the interaction of the child's small size and his maturational status with the role expectations and provisions resulting from the pattern of family life and economy.

Predictions might also be ventured about other categories of persons; adults in chronic situations that produce a need for reassurance or for strong stimulation might tend to share the preferences of young children.

These extrapolations to other developmental statuses are also potentially applicable to transcultural agreements.

Development toward Distinctively Aesthetic Values

As children grow into adolescence and adulthood, do their preferences in art change in the direction of increasing resemblance to the preferences or judgments of artists and other experts? Is there movement, that is, toward greater aesthetic sensitivity or interest, and is this a potential source of transcultural agreement?

Several sets of data, obtained through use of the materials I have described, indicate that there is an average change in that direction. Child (1968), surveying school populations in the state of Connecticut, found that through the primary-school years (ages about 6 to 11) average agreement with expert response was about 40%, but that in the following six years of secondary school average agreement rose steadily to about 50%. Data obtained by Duffy (1978) in schools in the states of Rhode Island and Connecticut confirm this upward movement, and so do data obtained by Child (1971) in the state of West Virginia. The only data yet available for secondary-school comparisons in other countries are those obtained by Haritos-Fatouros and Child (1977) in Salonika, Greece; a sample of boys in the final year of secondary school averaged 50% agreement with expert response, and a comparable sample four years younger averaged 41% agreement.

These changes with age might be ascribed simply to gradual assumption of adult standards current in the society in which a person is developing; similarities of age change in different societies would then be attributed to similarities of adult standards. There is a real difficulty here, in that the responses of experts are probably not those of the general adult population. The changes in the direction of expert evaluation would probably have to be seen as the adoption of standards of a specialized group within the adult population, rather than of the adult population as a whole.

In understanding this age change, it is important to note that it is a change in average response. It is based on averaging groups of persons at each age. The groups at different ages are not the same people, so we have no way of tracing the change in individuals, determining how many are changing, and in which directions. The general finding of change is also based on averaging the outcome for various pairs of works of art. Only in the West Virginia study (Child, 1971) and in Child and Iwao (1977) are data reported separately for distinct groups of pairs. It is clear from these two sources that the changes with age are very consistently different for various sets of pairs. On some pairs the movement is toward increased agreement with expert evaluation, but on some it is exactly the opposite. The movement is not just toward adopting expert standards, then; some of it may be, but a great deal of the movement—and perhaps all of it—must be traced to other processes.

Of these other processes, one that I have stressed because of its special interest for aesthetic theory is an autonomous development in some individuals of increasing interest in kinds of art which happen also to interest artists and others devoted to art. The evidence that such a process occurs is indirect. It consists primarily of the well-established finding that preferences agreeing with expert judgment are correlated with certain personality characteristics, plus the fact that these characteristics are ones that should favor the development from within of the kinds of preferences that experts express. The pattern of personality characteristics I refer to includes independence of judgment, liking for cognitive challenge, complexity, novelty, and tolerance of unrealistic experience. This general pattern, first noted in American college students (Child, 1965), has been found also in American secondary-school pupils (Child, 1971; Child & Iwao, 1968), and in university students in Japan (Child & Iwao, 1968), Pakistan (Anwar & Child, 1972), and Greece (Haritos-Fatouros & Child, 1977). These personality characteristics are ones that would favor independent exploration of the visual environment, and spontaneous enjoyment of what is challenging, complex, novel, and somewhat unrealistic. To prefer art which offers this enjoyment would often mean preferring art liked by artists and other experts, whose preferences may likewise be based partly on independent discovery.

According to the self-descriptions that participants in our research supply in their questionnaire responses, these personality characteristics become decidedly stronger through the secondary-school years. In two cultural settings where a whole school population or a representative sample answered our questionnaires, scores were consistently higher in the last year of secondary school than they were in an earlier year. One was West Virginia (Child, 1971); the other was Salonika, Greece (Haritos-Fatouros & Child, 1977). These changes were large. Averaging various groups in West Virginia, the increase in percentage answering the average questionnaire item in the direction correlated with aesthetic orientation increased from 51% in the seventh grade to 64% in the twelfth grade. In Salonika the corresponding change was from 42% in the eighth grade to 55% in the twelfth grade. More than just the steady pressure of these traits, in persons who share them to a high degree, may thus be involved in the change toward aesthetically oriented preferences; there is also an acceleration of the pressure as the traits are strengthened.

In each of the cultural settings in which we have worked, perhaps a large enough fraction of the population has these personal characteristics that may lead to aesthetic sensitivity, so that development of aesthetic sensitivity in those individuals accounts for the change with age in average response to our pairs. Perhaps, too, the movement of the average is at the same time being pushed in the same direction by individuals who, regardless of their personal motivations for developing an aesthetic interest, are learning what sort of art is esteemed by experts and are basing their preferences on that knowledge. I have no way of confidently distinguishing the effects of these two processes, and stress the developmental one because I think that emphasis heuristically more valuable, pointing to processes more distinctively relevant to the understanding of art and likely to be overlooked by people little acquainted with art.

Alternative Sequences of Development

If development of some individuals in each culture toward distinctively aesthetic values is one basis for transcultural agreement among adults, it is not the only developmental sequence that may underlie such agreement. For other sequences, the presently available evidence is more indirect, and even conjectural. But one sequence needs especially to be noted, because it calls attention to the fact that transcultural agreement does not necessarily have anything to do with aesthetic appreciation as that is understood and practiced by persons with a specialized interest in art.

In studying French children's explanations of their likes and dislikes of pictures, Machotka (1963) and Francès and Voillaume (1964) both found that, with increasing age, at least up to the age of 11 and perhaps beyond, children increasingly base their preferences on representational realism. In an extensive study of the preferences of American school children with the paired slides I have described, findings obtained by Child and Schwartz (unpublished manuscript, 1980) suggest progressive differentiation of groups with age. Separately for each grade in elementary school and for each grade in secondary school, we selected children high and low in overall tendency for their preferences to agree with expert evaluation of aesthetic merit. For the group high in aesthetic sensitivity by this criterion, preferences were correlated with realism much less in secondary school than in elementary school. For the group low in aesthetic sensitivity, the shift was in the opposite direction; preferences were correlated with realism more highly in secondary school. These opposite movements were substantial and highly significant—from .41 to .24 in the high scorers of primary and secondary schools respectively, from .37 to

.48 in the low scorers, with each correlation being based on hundreds of items.

At the same time that some individuals are developing toward the specialized interests of aesthetic involvement with art, others—and they may well be the majority—are developing toward decisive preference for realistic visual representation. In many specific instances of responding to art, the two bases for choice will clash, but in others they may lead to the same preference; the two bases, though negatively correlated, are by no means completely incompatible with each other.

Features of human development that are irrelevant to aesthetic orientation, then, may be responsible for any tendency toward agreement between groups of different cultural origin who do not show marked agreement with expert standards. The instance I have been able to cite presumably is related to the increase in objectivity which is part of general intellectual development (cf. the interpretation in Piagetian terms advanced by Machotka, 1963). Other features of development found in widely varying cultures might produce other instances of agreement in response to art, again perhaps essentially orthogonal to distinctively aesthetic interests in art.

DEVELOPMENTAL SEQUENCES AT THE SOCIAL LEVEL

As an art develops through time in a particular society, it may undergo progressive change which seems comparable to autogenous developmental change in an individual. Historical accounts of style in the various arts have often been directed at delineating steady sequences of change in the art produced, presumably often accompanied by changes in preferences. An account of special interest to psychologists, because of its attempts at psychological interpretation of the stylistic sequence, is provided by Peckham (1965).

Psychologists are inclined to want more definite evidence than can be provided by typical historical studies, for even the very existence of progressive changes in style. Martindale (1975) has brought the methodological equipment of modern psychology to bear on this problem. With thoroughly objective techniques he has shown very clearly the reality of progressive sequences of stylistic development in English and French poetry. What he shows is not mere change, but a regular change that progresses, in which each step follows from the former in a predictable manner. The particular development he traces is toward increasingly regressive imagery, and he interprets it as an expression of the need in a poetic tradition for steady production of novelty. The movement through time of a specific cultural tradition is thus shown as having a kind of internal dynamism, parallel on the social level to the dynamism of successive equilibrations in the intellectual development of the individual as portrayed by Piaget.

Now, for my purposes here, these studies add one more potential source of transcultural agreement: the fact that the artistic tradition in two cultures under comparison happens to be, at the time for which the comparison is made, at a similar point in parallel sequences of stylistic development. To the extent that the people sampled in each cultural setting are involved in the stylistic development and reflect it in their responses to art, agreement of those responses between the two samples may be time-dependent, a special product of the coincidence of the two historical movements.

It also follows, of course, that transcultural disagreement can be brought about by a lack of synchrony in parallel developments in different cultures. Were responses to art completely dominated by the features most subject to historical changes of the sort traced by Martindale, moreover, all transcultural agreement might be a by-product of synchrony in stylistic changes. This does not seem likely. But synchrony of autogenous development is one possible source of agreement to be kept in mind, and asynchrony of autogenous development is a possible obscuring factor that may reduce the amount of transcultural agreement below what it would otherwise be.

CONCLUSION

Transcultural agreement in response to art needs to be considered in a context of intracultural disagreement. Differences among members of another society may be closely parallel, and may influence response to art in much the same way. Transcultural agreement will in that event be much greater, and its sources will become evident when comparable individuals in the two societies are looked at. Transcultural agreement in this refined sense may be present to a high degree, regardless of whether average preferences in one society agree with average preferences in the other.

Exploration of transcultural agreement and disagreement in response to art has, then, no simple bearing on the old nativist versus environmentalist controversy. But it holds great promise for our understanding of the complex processes by which people arrive at evaluations of art.

REFERENCES

ANWAR, M. P., & CHILD, I. L. Personality and esthetic sensitivity in an Islamic culture. *Journal of Social Psychology*, 1972, 87, 21–28.

BERLYNE, D. E. Extension to Indian subjects of a study of exploratory and verbal responses to visual patterns. *Journal of Cross-Cultural Psychology*, 1975, 6, 316–330.

BERLYNE, D. E. Similarity and preference judgments of Indian and Canadian subjects exposed to Western paintings. *International Journal of Psychology*, 1976, 11, 43–55.

BERLYNE, D. E., ROBBINS, M. C., & THOMPSON, R. A cross-cultural study of exploratory and verbal responses to visual patterns varying in complexity. In D. E. Berlyne (Ed.), *Studies in the new experimental aesthetics*. Washington, D.C.: Hemisphere Publishing, 1974.

CHILD, I. L. Personality correlates of esthetic judgment in college students. *Journal of Personality*, 1965, 33, 476–511.

CHILD, I. L. Développement psychologique et préférences esthétiques. *Sciences de l'Art*, 1968, 5, 10–20.

CHILD, I. L. Assessment of affective responses conducive to esthetic sensitivity. Final Report, January 1971, of Project No. 9–0029, Bureau of Research, Office of Education, U.S. Department of Health, Education, & Welfare. (Obtainable from author.)

CHILD, I. L., & IWAO, S. Personality and esthetic sensitivity: Extension of findings to younger age and to different culture. *Journal of Personality and Social Psychology*, 1968, 8, 308–312.

CHILD, I. L., & IWAO, S. Young children's preferential responses to visual art. *Scientific Aesthetics*, 1977, 1, 291–304.

CHILD, I. L., & SCHWARTZ, R. S. Growing up to art. Unpublished manuscript, 1980.

CHILD, I. L., HANSEN, J. A., & HORNBECK, F. W. Age and sex differences in children's color preferences. *Child Development*, 1968, 39, 237–247.

CHILD, I. L., IWAO, S., BRIDDELL, D., FINTZELBERG, N., GARCIA, M., HETATA, F., MOST, S., NING, L., & SEWALL, S. Art preferences in culturally varying groups. Final Report, August 1968, of Project No. 7–8638, Bureau of Research, Office of Education, U.S. Department of Health, Eduation, & Welfare. (Obtainable from senior author.)

DUFFY, R. A. *An analysis of aesthetic sensitivity, creativity, artistic potential, visual-haptic aptitude, cognitive style, personality, and demographic variables in grades four, six, eight, and ten.* Unpublished doctoral dissertation, University of Connecticut, 1977.

DUFFY, R. A. Personal communication, 1978.

EYSENCK, H. J., & IWAWAKI, S. Cultural relativity in aesthetic judgments: An empirical study. *Perceptual and Motor Skills*, 1971, 32, 817–818.

FRANCÈS, R., & TAMBA, A. Etude interculturelle des préférences musicales. *International Journal of Psychology*, 1973, 8, 95–108.

FRANCÈS, R., & VOILLAUME, H. Une composante du jugement pictural: La fidélité da la représentation. *Psychologie Française*, 1964, 9, 241–256.

HARITOS-FATOUROS, M., & CHILD, I. L. Transcultural similarity in personal significance of esthetic interests. *Journal of Cross-Cultural Psychology*, 1977, 8, 285–298.

KASTL, A. J., & CHILD, I. L. Comparison of color preferences in Vietnam and the United States. *Proceedings of the 76th Annual Convention of the American Psychological Association*, 1968, 437–438.

MACHOTKA, P. Le développement des critères esthétiques chez l'enfant. *Enfance*, 1963, 16, 357–379.

MARTINDALE, C. *Romantic progression: The psychology of literary history.* Washington, D.C.: Hemisphere Publishing, 1975.

MOSKOWITZ, H. R. Taste and food technology: Acceptability, aesthetics, and preference. In E. C. Carterette & M. P. Friedman (Eds.), *Handbook of perception* (Vol. VIA): *Tasting and smelling.* New York: Academic, 1978.

PECKHAM, M. *Man's rage for chaos*. Philadelphia: Chilton, 1965.

PHILIPSON, M. *Outline of a Jungian aesthetics*. Evanston, Ill.: Northwestern University Press, 1963.

RICHARDS, I. A. *Practical criticism*. London: Kegan Paul, Trench & Trübner, 1929.

SOUEIF, M. I., & EYSENCK, H. J. Factors in the determination of preference judgments for polygonal figures: A comparative study. *International Journal of Psychology*, 1972, 7, 145–153.

18

Information Theory and Melodic Perception

In Search of the Aesthetic Engram

J. B. Crozier

THE PROBLEM OF AESTHETIC PERCEPTION

The material to be presented in this chapter addresses a number of academically disparate but conceptually related concerns. This, of course, is not an unusual circumstance for research in the area of intrinsic motivation; however, in order to facilitate presentation of the material, two principle themes will be developed. The first theme is the role of form and structure in aesthetic perception, and the contribution of information-theoretic approaches to our comprehension of these concepts. The second theme is the role of melody in music perception, and the contribution of the research in this area to a psychology of music in particular, and a psychology of art in general.

Turning first to the issue of form and structure in perception, we can begin by noting that an axiom of psychological research in the arts is that response to art is not random. Proceeding on this principle, researchers for some decades now have investigated the dimensionality underlying aesthetic experience and expression. However, the evidence in support of common modes of perception generalizable across subjects and objects has proved equivocal, and in consequence many have questioned the soundness of this axiom.

Of course, one of the difficulties in evaluating the literature on this topic is the absence of a methodology which adequately considers the interactive nature of aesthetic object and aesthetic response. Most of the

J. B. CROZIER • Department of Psychology, Glendon College, York University, Toronto, Ontario M4N 3M6, Canada.

various techniques employed have been based on data derived from aesthetic responses, and the resulting typologies have often obscured as much as clarified the issues at hand. And though recent procedures, based largely on nonparametric multidimensional scaling principles, have answered some of the technical limitations of the earlier work, they still have not overcome the limitations inherent in considering principally the response side of the aesthetic equation.

To be fair, it should be acknowledged that the aesthetic stimulus has not been totally ignored. For example, categorization in terms of schools, or historic style, has been one of the most common approaches to selecting and editing material for presentation to subjects. Such an approach results in a largely qualitative consideration of extant artistic material, and this would seem, at first blush, to contribute to the credibility of any project. But, as many a researcher has discovered, the main difficulty with this approach lies in determining exactly what one has presented to one's subjects. Not only do art works vary in an historic framework, but also appreciators vary in their prior exposure and comprehension of art forms. And so, though there is a vigorous research tradition using formally composed artistic materials, these materials have introduced an element which has, simply by its presence, often frustrated the search for a common perceptual theme.

But before concluding that the axiom of a shared aesthetic perceptual domain is unsound, perhaps we should be certain that our classification of the aesthetic object is based on adequate principles. What this seems to require is something more detailed than a subjective classification of the artistic domain: something which will provide an *a priori* analysis of the stimulus characteristics—the structure—on which aesthetic responses ultimately depend. This type of analysis, in combination with the analysis of subjects' responses afforded by current multivariate techniques, would seem to provide the interactive approach demanded by the problem.

THE INFORMATION-THEORY APPROACH

Although a number of approaches toward quantitative analysis of stimulus properties have been suggested, perhaps none has generated more reaction than information theory. From its genesis in the writings of Shannon and Weaver (1949), its principles were soon transcribed into a behavioral science context in now classic treatises by authors such as Hochberg (1953), Attneave (1954), and Garner (1962). Portrayed in these accounts was an approach that afforded an analysis of terms such as "structure" which was compelling in its elegance and power. However, as practise followed theory, it became apparent that this conceptual tool did have its limitations. The area of visual art proved particularly problematic (see Green & Courtis, 1966), and, as a result of these initial difficulties, the early enthusiasm toward information theory was soon qualified.

In retrospect, this appears unfortunate, for many of the initial applications, especially those in the visual arts, did not meet the basic assumptions of this approach. Where these assumptions were reasonably met— assumptions regarding stochasticity, ergodicity, and stationarity—the initial results were promising. In the area of music, the pioneering applications were particularly fruitful, establishing the conceptual affinity between this art form and information-theoretic analysis.

This is not that surprising when one recognizes that many of the basic information-theory concepts already have their analogues in traditional music analysis. For example, the analysis of music as a stochastic process is readily identifiable with the aleatoric, or so-called *chance*, music tradition. The composition of melodies in a manner expressible in terms of probability or chance is also a well-established tradition in Western music, dating back to the turn-of-the-century serial technique of the composer Arnold Schoenberg. This technique, centering on the equal occurrence of pitches in the chromatic scale, was not very well received, and even today the results outpace the ears of many listeners. But this reaction has not prevented the further development of these serial techniques by contemporary composers, and as a result the vocabulary, if not the practise, of serial composition has become an accepted part of musical life.

The first step in joining this minority tradition in music to information-theory concepts occurred through the descriptive analysis of extant musical materials in communication-system terms (see Cohen, 1962; Pinkerton, 1956). This procedure soon led to the composition—or, if one prefers, the construction—of melodic materials using information-theory principles (see Vitz, 1966). In order to apply these principles to melodic construction, one must be able to specify the number of possible tones which can occur, and the rules for each and every tone's occurrence. When these two constraints are specifiable, then one can summarize the structural properties of a given melodic sequence in terms of its average information content.

Here is a simple illustration to show this analysis in action. The tune to be analyzed, if it can be called such, will consist of the tones *doh* and *ray* repeated at equal durations such that there will be an equal number of *dohs* and *rays* over time. Stated most simply, our example consists of two tones sounding equally often. Applying the formulas of information theory, we are able to state that the average information in our example is 1.00 binary unit, or one "bit," for each tone which sounds.

The potential usefulness of this analysis is, hopefully, self-evident. By employing this theory, any melody can be objectively analyzed, and have its structure expressed in terms of an easily grasped index. This index, called bits per tone, or *uncertainty* per tone, can range from 0.0, which presumably represents one continuous, unchanging pitch, to values up to 15.00 or so, which represent tone rows of incredible range and variety. In illustration, the rock-and-roll tune "Hound Dog" has an uncertainty value of 1.73 bits per tone, whereas the tune "Don't be Cruel" has a value of 2.32 bits per tone (from Cohen, 1962).

INITIAL RESEARCH

In the initial research of this project, undertaken largely in collaboration with the late D. E. Berlyne, melodic sequences were constructed using an algorithm based on information-theory principles. Tones were drawn in succession from a specific set of tones, each tone being a particular pitch, duration, and loudness combination. By drawing tones in an equiprobable fashion without regard to intercorrelations between tones, six melodic sequences ranging in average information content, or uncertainty, from 1.0 to 9.17 bits per tone were constructed. Using this material, the interaction of melodic structure and listeners' perceptions was studied, using both verbal rating scales and nonverbal exploratory responses.

This initial research, which is reported in Crozier (1974), supported the conjunction of information-theoretic stimulus analysis and multivariate-response analysis. Listeners' common perceptual typology, which was reliably related to the uncertainty of the tone sequences, was interpretable in terms of two underlying and orthogonal dimensions. The first dimension was a monotonic, linear function of uncertainty, and represented judgments of complexity, variation, and so on. As such, it was seen as reflecting the formal, structural, technical aspects of melodic-sequence perception, and was referred to as the *activity* dimension. The second dimension was a bitonic, curvilinear function of uncertainty, and represented judgments of goodness, pleasingness, melodiousness, and so on. As such, it was seen as reflecting affective, evaluative aspects of melodic-sequence perception, and was referred to as the *evaluative* dimension.

In identifying these two dimensions, they were related to a large body of literature seeing response to music as an interaction of two perceptual processes. Writings ranging from Copland's *What to Listen for in Music* through Leonard Meyer's *Emotion and Meaning in Music* to Zink's article "Is the Music Really Sad?" all speak of two dimensions, albeit using a variety of terms. Whether it be called a "sheerly musical plane" (from Copland) or an "intellectual response" (from Meyer), phrases are used by these authors which seem to denote comprehension of the formal structural aspects of the flow of sound, and seem to have much in common with our *activity* dimension. And whether it be called "the sensuous and expressive plane" (from Copland) or "the affective response" (from Meyer), phrases are used which seem to denote comprehension of the properties found in our *evaluative* dimension.

Support for a two-dimensional model of aesthetic perception has not been limited only to the musical sphere. In aesthetic theorizing in general, writers in a number of settings have focussed on the interplay of two counterbalancing factors. This literature, which is reviewed in detail in Berlyne (1971, pp. 124–130), has to date lacked a sufficient empirical base, but this limitation will no doubt be addressed as research proceeds in a variety of aesthetic contexts.

CURRENT RESEARCH CONCERNS

Following these initial experiments, this research with melodic sequences has pursued two major concerns. First, the limitations of information theory in analyzing melodic structure have been explored by introducing qualitative features of familiar music which fall outside the theory's analysis. For example, the tempered scale and metric rhythm are obvious characteristics of Western music which are unaccounted for in the uncertainty measure. These characteristics were introduced by constructing melodic sequences featuring pitches based on tempered tuning and durations which produced a semblance of metrical rhythm. The effects of these properties were assessed by comparing melodic sequences with these cultural properties with sequences violating such cultural expectations.

Although the exact role that the above qualitative features might play in melodic perception was not very clear, one possibility did stand out. Given that reactions to these qualitative features were encompassed within a two-factor *activity:evaluation* model, it was thought that the qualitative features should affect only the *evaluative* dimension. That is, melodic sequences of identical uncertainty level incorporating the culturally expected should be found more musical, beautiful, and so on than those violating these expectations. However, the *activity* dimension should remain unaffected by this property, as the melodic sequences at a given uncertainty level would not differ in structure—that is, the quantitative aspects captured by information theory, such as the numbers of pitches, durations, and loudnesses, would be identical. The above predictions were confirmed in subsequent research (see Crozier, 1974), with cultural features affecting only *evaluative* judgments.

In the present article, a somewhat more subtle property falling outside the scope of information theory is considered, this being the degree of repetition of tones in melodic sequences of like uncertainty level. A nursery rhyme such as "Row, Row, Row your Boat" nicely illustrates this property, for the tones associated with the words "row" and "merrily" involve a repetition not found with the other tones in the rhyme. This property was introduced into the melodic sequences by constructing sequences at the same uncertainty level which incorporated relatively high and low levels of tone repetition. These melodic sequences, which were called the "high" and "low" repetition sequences respectively, were used in the second experiment reported in this chapter. Complete details of their construction, including their analysis in probability-matrix terms, are given later.

The second major concern pursued in recent research has been the systematic introduction of information-theory concepts to the construction and analysis of melodic sequences. Noting the parallelism between many information theory and musical-composition concepts, this effort has been directed at progressively examining the properties attributed to natural melodies through information-theory procedures. In this way, it was hoped that the conceptual properties of importance to melodic perception, and indeed possibly to aesthetic perception in its broadest sense, could be established.

In the two sets of experiments reported in this chapter, a seemingly important property of musical composition—redundancy—was explored. As considered by musicians, redundancy refers to the unequal frequency with which tones of the chromatic scale appear in music. This fact is recognized in musical analysis by the names given to the tones, the most frequent tones of a key signature being called the tonic and dominant, and the least frequent not having any particular names at all.

From an information-theory perspective, redundancy occurs in a symbol system whenever the symbols occur in differing degrees. There are two principle ways in which redundancy is seen to operate. The first is when some events (in this case the tones in our melodic sequences) are more likely to occur than others. This condition has been given a variety of names, but here we shall refer to it as "distributional redundancy" (from Garner, 1962). The second way in which redundancy has been introduced is when certain combinations or successions of events are more probable than others. This property has been referred to as "correlational redundancy" by Garner and others.

Regardless of which way redundancy is manipulated, it has been seen as a central aspect of higher-order stimulus organization. In illustration, Garner (1962) has elaborated on a line of inquiry initiated by Hochberg and McAlister (1953) and by Attneave (1954) equating redundancy with classic Gestalt notions such as "Prägnanz" (Koffka, 1940). More recently, writers such as Moles (1958) and Frank (1959) have identified uncertainty and redundancy with earlier notions such as Birkoff's (1933) mathematical theory centering on "complexity" and "order" respectively. In the process, these authors, representing what Berlyne (1971) has called the Franco-German school of information aestheticians, have also advanced particular roles for both distributional and correlational redundancy in aesthetic perception.

From the Franco-German perspective, distributional redundancy has been seen to contribute to aesthetic structure by making some elements more "striking" (auffällig) than others, owing to the unequal presentation values of events. The effect of correlational redundancy is a bit more complex, depending on the perception of "supersigns" through the recognition of interdependencies among elements. This recognition is seen as reducing the influx of information, thus affecting reactions to the aesthetic stimulus.

In the experiments to be reported, the uncertainty of the melodic sequences employed was manipulated both by changes in the size of the set of tones which could occur (a property referred to here as "variability"), and by changes in the level of redundancy within a given variability level. Adhering to a research strategy of extending the underlying structural model in a conceptually progressive fashion, the first set of experiments featured variations in distributional redundancy, and the second set featured variations in correlational redundancy. In passing, it can be noted that this progressive extension in the sequences' statistical properties was possible only through the use of a small computer (PDP 8/S), which permitted the extension in the compositional algorithm demanded by the redundancy concept.

Considering listeners' responses to our melodic material, previous experimental and theoretical work suggested two alternate ways in which redundancy could affect the dependent responses. Approaches which have seen redundancy not only as a quantitative feature affecting uncertainty value, but also as a qualitative feature affecting higher-order stimulus organization, would lead one to expect redundancy and variability differentially to affect the dependent measures. This expectation, which finds its theoretical underpinnings in positions allocating a special role to redundancy, can also be related to the distinction which this project has drawn between qualitative and quantitative stimulus manipulations. As described earlier, the effects of qualitative manipulations have been confined to our evaluative dimension, whereas quantitative manipulations have been reflected in both dimensions. Given the possibly hybrid nature of redundancy as both a qualitative and a quantitative stimulus property, it may be that its effect will fall, in part, outside the uncertainty measure; and thus it will be only partially accounted for by an information-theory analysis.

In opposition to the above predictions, the previous results of this project, as well as a great deal of other research (Berlyne, 1971), suggested that uncertainty alone might be the primary determinant of aesthetic appreciation. Given the exact correspondence previously found between objective and subjective uncertainty, it seemed conceivable that the dependent measures might reflect uncertainty, however it was varied. In other words, both variability and redundancy might work through their contribution to uncertainty, and manipulation of either might be directly related to the overall uncertainty level at any given time.

DISTRIBUTIONAL-REDUNDANCY EXPERIMENT

A series of three studies was carried out. In the first study, listeners judged the melodic sequences on four verbal rating scales, these being *simple:complex, uninteresting:interesting, displeasing:pleasing,* and *disorderly: orderly.* These four scales have been extensively used in previous research involving both auditory and visual stimuli, and here our concern was to establish the effects of variability and distributional redundancy on these verbal judgments.

In earlier research with zero-redundancy melodic sequences, complexity and interestingness have typically been monotonic and close to linear functions of uncertainty, and have proved to be critical variables in defining the activity dimension described earlier. Pleasingness has typically been bitonic in nature, increasing and then levelling off, and possibly decreasing as uncertainty increased. Judgments on this scale have been associated with the *evaluative* factor in melodic perception, and so served as a marker for this second dimension. Judgments of melodic sequences on the final scale, *disorderly:orderly,* were introduced into this project for the first time here, so no previous response pattern had been established. However, it was expected that judgments on this scale would be instructive in separating the effects of redundancy from those of variability.

In the second and third studies of experiment 1, the dependent variables were nonverbal measures of exposure to the melodic sequences, the two standard exposure measures used being listening time and exploratory choice. In previous research using zero-redundancy sequences, the group pattern of exploratory responses to sequences has fallen somewhere between the monotonic function predicted if listening time and choice were determined by *activity* alone, and the bitonic function predicted if they were determined by *evaluation* alone. Whether this two-factor account of these nonverbal behaviors would still hold when redundancy was also a factor was not apparent, especially in view of the absence of previous empirical data here.

The Distributional-Redundancy Melodic Sequences

Twelve melodic sequences in all were constructed, representing four different variability levels and three different redundancy levels. Table I presents the number of pitches, durations, and loudnesses at the four variability levels. The uncertainty value of each of the 12 sequences is also given. This information value, expressed in terms of bits per tone, was calculated using the standard formula for H or U. (For particular details of the computations involved, the interested reader is referred to Shannon, 1949, page 14).

The specific pitches given in Table I represented an expansion of the F major scale across uncertainty levels. The durations were integer multiples of each other, a property which resulted in an underlying metrical pulse or rhythm. The specific millisecond values were also chosen in such a way that the mean duration of a tone for all twelve sequences was 500 millisec. Loudness levels one, two, three, and four were 70 db, 75 db, 80 db, and 85 db, respectively, at 1,000 Hz. Specific loudness levels across the range of 65 to 1,760 Hz used in these sequences were calculated from a loudness function which approximated that of traditional sources such as Robinson and Dadson (1956).

Table II presents the distributional-redundancy values used to determine the relative probabilities of specific pitch, duration, and loudness values at each redundancy level. In the case of the zero redundancy level, the elements of each of the six sets of probabilities were equiprobable. In the case of low and high redundancy levels, certain elements of each set were more probable than others in that specific set. The particular probabilities given were chosen in order to introduce 12.5% and 25% redundancy, respectively, at the low and high redundancy levels.

In order to keep specific elements at a probability level which made their sampling a reasonable possibility, it was decided that the lowest probability of occurrence of any element in a set would be 0.01. Because of this minimum sampling constraint, it was not possible to introduce redundancy levels of 12.5% into the set involving 33 elements, or 25% into the sets involving 11 and 33 elements. As a result, the highest redundancy levels realized for stimulus-variability level four were 9.5% and 15.8%.

In constructing the sequences, the three lists defining the pitch, duration, and loudness values for a given sequence were sampled independently of each other. Thus, correlational redundancy was not a vari-

TABLE I. Summary of the Variability Characteristics of the Melodic Sequences

Stimulus variability level	Total number of possible tones	Pitches (Hz)	Durations (msec)	Loudness levels[a]	Uncertainty per tone (in bits)		
					Zero redundancy	Low redundancy	High redundancy
1	2	349 (F) 392 (G)	500	3	1.00	.88	.75
2	16	plus 440 (A) 523 (C)	333 667	2 3	4.00	3.50	3.00
3	132	plus 175 (F) 220 (A) 262 (C) 294 (D) 466 (B♭) 587 (D) 698 (F)	200 400 600 800	1 2 3	7.04	6.17	5.54
4	1056	plus 65 (C) 73 (D) 87 (F) 98 (G) 110 (A)	40 81 162 323 485	1 2 3 4	10.00	9.06	8.42

117	(B♭)	646
131	(C)	970
147	(D)	1293
165	(E)	
196	(G)	
233	(B♭)	
330	(E)	
659	(E)	
784	(G)	
880	(A)	
932	(B♭)	
1,047	(C)	
1,175	(D)	
1,319	(E)	
1,397	(F)	
1,568	(G)	
1,760	(A)	

[a]Level 1 = 70 db at 1000 Hz; level 2 = 75 db at 1000 Hz; level 3 = 80 db at 1000 Hz; level 4 = 85 db at 1000 Hz.

TABLE II. Summary of the Distributional Characteristics of the Melodic Sequences

Set of probabilities	Pitch Elements (Hz)	Duration Elements (msec)	Loudness elements	Distributional probability of element occurring		
				Zero redundancy	Low redundancy	High redundancy
SET 1 = 2 ELEMENTS	349	333	2	.50	.705	.786
	392	667	3	.50	.295	.214
SET 2 = 3 ELEMENTS			1	.333	.445	.482
			2	.333	.110	.036
			3	.333	.445	.482
SET 3 = 4 ELEMENTS	349	200	1	.250	.107	.055
	392	400	2	.250	.393	.445
	440	600	3	.250	.393	.445
	523	800	4	.250	.107	.055
SET 4 = 8 ELEMENTS		40		.125	.040	.011
		81		.125	.040	.011
		162		.125	.210	.239
		323		.125	.210	.239
		485		.125	.210	.239
		646		.125	.210	.239
		920		.125	.040	.011
		1293		.125	.040	.011
SET 5 = 11 ELEMENTS	175			.0909	.020	.010
	220			.0909	.020	.010
	262			.0909	.020	.010
	294			.0909	.150	.158
	349			.0909	.150	.158
	392			.0909	.150	.158
	440			.0909	.150	.158
	466			.0909	.150	.158
	523			.0909	.150	.158
	587			.0909	.020	.010
	698			.0909	.020	.010

SET 6 =
33 ELEMENTS

Frequency			
65	.030	.010	.010
73	.030	.010	.010
87	.030	.010	.010
98	.030	.010	.010
110	.030	.010	.010
117	.030	.010	.010
131	.030	.010	.010
147	.030	.010	.010
165	.030	.052	.052
175	.030	.052	.052
196	.030	.052	.052
220	.030	.052	.052
233	.030	.052	.052
262	.030	.052	.052
294	.030	.052	.052
330	.030	.052	.052
349	.030	.052	.052
392	.030	.052	.052
440	.030	.052	.052
466	.030	.052	.052
523	.030	.052	.052
587	.030	.052	.052
659	.030	.052	.052
698	.030	.052	.052
784	.030	.010	.010
880	.030	.010	.010
932	.030	.010	.010
1047	.030	.010	.010
1175	.030	.010	.010
1319	.030	.010	.010
1397	.030	.010	.010
1568	.030	.010	.010
1760	.030	.010	.010

able systematically incorporated into this first set of sequences. Thirty minute audiotapes of each sequence were recorded, and these tapes were used to conduct the experiments.

Experiment 1: Verbal Rating-Scale Study

Subjects and Design

Forty-eight University of Toronto students participated in this study. Twenty-four were enrolled in an introductory psychology course, and 24 were enrolled in a music summer extension program.

The 12 melodic sequences and four rating scales were treated as within −S factors. Thus, each subject rated all 12 sequences on all four rating scales, making a total of 48 responses. The 12 sequences were rotated against the four scales, so that a subject judged all 12 sequences against one specific rating scale at a time. The order of presentation for the sequences was based upon a 12 × 12 balanced Latin square derived from an algorithm by Williams (1949).

All 24 possible permutations of the four rating scales were used. Two permutated orders were randomly assigned to each row of the 12 × 12 sequence square, and two subjects were randomly assigned to each of these 24 permutated orders. Subjects rated all 12 sequences on one specific rating scale, and then proceeded to rerate the 12 sequences on a second rating scale, and so on. On completion of a given rating scale, the 12 × 12 stimulus-presentation square for a subsequent scale was obtained by a one-step cyclic permutation of the square (see Winer, 1971).

Procedure

Each subject was seated at a table and fitted with high-fidelity headphones. The subject was then given a copy of the instructions to read and simultaneously heard a prerecording of the instructions through the headphones. The instructions began by stating that "the purpose of this study is to obtain your judgments of a number of tone sequences by having you judge them on a series of descriptive scales." This was followed by an explanation of how the sequences and rating scales would be presented, and detailed instructions on how to use the rating scales.

Following the instructions, a 20-sec excerpt of each sequence was presented according to the balanced design, and each sequence presentation was followed by a ten-sec silence, during which the subject recorded his judgment. At the end of each presentation of the 12 sequences, the experimenter entered the room, collected the subject's response sheet, and gave the subject a new sheet on which to judge the next presentation of the 12 sequences. Each response sheet bore 12 reproductions of a given rating scale using standard semantic differential format.

Experiment 1: Listening-Time Study

Subjects and Design

Twenty-four subjects were recruited from students enrolled in the summer session at the University of Toronto. Subjects were paid $2.00 for their participation. The 12 tone sequences were presented to each subject, using the 12 × 12 balanced Latin square employed with the rating scales to determine the presentation order. Two subjects were assigned to each row of the square, and the subject's listening times were recorded in seconds.

Procedure

Each subject was seated in a comfortable lounge-type chair and fitted with headphones. The subject was told that he was "to listen to 12 sequences, each sequence consisting of a number of single, consecutive tones . . . any one of the 12 sequences will continue for as long as you wish to listen to it. Whenever you want to go on to the next sequence, just press the button on the box in front of you and this will cause the next sequence to begin . . . this is not a tonal memory test and it will not be necessary for you to recall any specific sequence or to memorize details of the sequences."

Experiment 1: Exploratory Choice Study

Subjects and Design

Twenty-four undergraduates enrolled in an introductory psychology course voluntarily participated in the study. Each subject received all possible pairings of the 12 sequences, but not both orders (a–b and b–a) within each pair. Thus, each subject received 66 paired presentations of the 12 sequences and 11 presentations of each specific sequence. The order of presentation of the 66 pairs was derived from an algorithm advanced by Ross (1934), which controlled for space and time errors, regular repetition, and spacing between pairs involving the same sequence. Twelve balanced orders were generated, and two subjects were arbitrarily assigned to each of these orders.

Procedure

Each of the 66 paired presentations consisted of a 10-sec sample of a sound sequence; 2 sec of silence; 10 sec of a second sequence, followed by a further 10-sec continuation of whichever sequence the subject chose to hear. As in the previous experiments, subjects were fitted with head-phones and told that "your task is to choose the first or the second sequence of the two sequences in each pair for 10 seconds further listen-ing." The subjects were given no explicit criteria whatever on which to base their choice, and indicated their choice by pressing one of two buttons which were clearly marked "First" and "Second."

Experiment 1: Results

With the exception of the exploratory-choice results, the data were analyzed by analysis of variance. For this analysis, a standard 12 rows (subjects) × 12 columns (periods) × 12 treatments (sequences) summary table was adopted (see Winer, 1971, page 696). The treatment variable, which represented the 12 levels of melodic-sequence uncertainty, was further broken down into its orthogonal components, variability, and redundancy and their interaction. In the case of the exploratory-choice data, a non-parametric analysis of variance by ranks was carried out, and so only the main effects were analyzable.

From the overall patterns of statistical significance of the treatment variable, which are summarized in Table III, it is evident that uncertainty, as determined largely by variability, has been the principle factor under-lying listeners' responses. Redundancy has been of significance only in the case of complexity, orderliness, and interestingness judgments, and in no instance has there been a significant redundancy × variability interaction.

Turning to the individual rating scales, judgments of complexity and orderliness were both monotonic, and close to linear, functions of uncer-tainty. Trend analyses indicated that 99% of the uncertainty sum of squares for complexity and 95% of the uncertainty sum of squares for orderliness were accounted for by the linear-trend component. Plotting these two effects (see Figure 1, upper panel), it can be seen that variability and redundancy have both contributed to the overall uncertainty effect, as expected. As variability has increased, complexity and disorderliness have increased, and as redundancy has increased, complexity and disor-derliness have decreased.

Judgments of pleasingness, which are plotted in Figure 1, middle panel, showed an increase and then a leveling off and possibly decline

TABLE III. Summary of Patterns of Statistical Significance: Experiment 1

Source of variance	Semantic differential scales					
	Simple: complex	Disorderly: orderly	Displeasing: pleasing	Uninteresting: interesting	Listening time	Exploratory choice
Uncertainty (11 df)	a	a	a	a	a	a
Variability (V) (3 df)	a	a	a	a	a	a
Redundancy (R) (2 df)	a	a		b		
V × R (6 df)						N/A

$^a p < .01.$
$^b p < .05.$
N/A = not applicable.

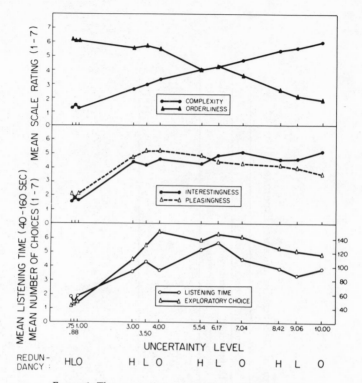

FIGURE 1. The uncertainty main effects: Experiment 1.

across uncertainty levels. Only the variability factor was significant within uncertainty, indicating that redundancy has not been an evident factor in determining this "r-shaped" function. Judgments of interestingness, which are plotted in the same panel, showed the not atypical balance between complexity on the one hand and pleasingness on the other. The result is an "r-shaped" function which, owing to the leveling off of responses at upper uncertainty levels, resulted in only a marginally significant redundancy effect. However, in spite of the curvilinearity present, the trend within the variability main effect was clearly monotonic, with interestingness increasing across the four variability levels.

The two nonverbal dependent measures, which are plotted in Figure 1, lower panel, both revealed that exposure to the melodic sequences increased up to an uncertainty level in the range of 4.0 to 6.17 bits/tone, and possibly declined beyond this level. Further analysis of the listening-time trend using Duncan's new multiple range test indicated that the extremes of uncertainty were listened to significantly less than the intermediate levels ($\alpha = 0.05$), and that the lowest levels of uncertainty were also listened to significantly less than the highest levels ($\alpha = 0.05$). In light of these differences, it was felt that the trend was better described as "r-shaped" rather than "inverted-U-shaped." As was the case with pleasingness, distributional redundancy showed no significant effects on listening time and choice.

Experiment 1: Discussion

As in previous work with zero-redundancy sequences, our dependent variables have formed two classes. The first class has been monotonically related and the second nonmonotonically related to uncertainty level. Ratings on *simple:complex, uninteresting:interesting,* and *disorderly:orderly* scales have belonged to the former class, and pleasingness ratings, listening time, and exploratory choice have belonged to the latter class.

The effects of redundancy on the three variables that were monotonically related to uncertainty were statistically significant. The influence of a decrease in redundancy on these variables was in the same direction as that of an increase in variability. So, it would seem that redundancy and variability have acted on them through their effects on uncertainty.

As far as the three variables nonmonotonically related to uncertainty are concerned, the effect of redundancy was not significant. This is what one would expect if the curves relating these variables to uncertainty are inverted-U-shaped, so that increases in uncertainty, whether owing to a decrease in redundancy or to some other manipulation, would sometimes raise and sometimes lower the value of a dependent variable, depending on which sector of the curve one is dealing with. But in the two cases where parametric analysis of variance was possible, the interaction between redundancy and variability was not significant. So, in the face of these results, we have no clear evidence that redundancy affected these variables, and must conclude that they depended primarily on variability.

However, the significant effects of redundancy on rated complexity, interestingness, and orderliness demonstrate that the distributional redundancy effect has been detected by listeners. And even though distributional redundancy has not resulted in statistically significant effects in terms of rated pleasingness, listening time, and choice, the trend present does suggest that any role that redundancy might play resembles the effects of changes in overall uncertainty level. Whether the melodic structure was changed through variability or redundancy, the resultant uncertainty value was apparently the index of overriding import.

Of course, this conclusion is not without qualification, for undoubtedly the results would have been more convincing had the redundancy manipulation been more powerful. On the practical side, the relatively restricted range of redundancy employed—zero to only 25%—is an obvious limitation. Taking this into account, it could be argued that redundancy would have affected all the dependent measures if higher levels had been used.

On the theoretical side, information-theory principles would suggest that, though distributional redundancy is important, of even more importance here is correlational redundancy. As previously discussed, the effect of correlational is more complex than that of distributional redundancy, involving the perceptual grouping of tones into "supersigns," and thus the reduction of the subjective uncertainty of the aesthetic stimulus. In consequence, correlational redundancy would prove a more powerful manipulation, and would provide a more convincing test of redundancy's significance to melodic perception, and indeed possibly to aesthetic perception in general.

CORRELATIONAL-REDUNDANCY EXPERIMENT

The second set of studies to be reported addressed the above issues through the use of melodic sequences incorporating high levels of correlational redundancy. In contrast to the previous sequences, this time the low and high redundancy levels were set at 25% and 50%, respectively, and first-order correlational properties were introduced. In order to maximize comparability with the previous experiments, the same dependent measures, and similar experimental designs and statistical analyses, were used.

The Correlational-Redundancy Melodic Sequences

The correlational-redundancy sequences, as before representing four variability levels and three redundancy levels, were based on the same numbers of pitches, durations, and loudnesses as given in Table I. Because of the increase in low and high redundancy levels from 12.5 to 25% and from 25 to 50% respectively, the uncertainty per tone values for the sequences were as follows:

	Correlational-Redundancy Level		
	Zero	Low	High
1. Variability Level 1	1.00	.75	.50
2. Variability Level 2	4.00	3.00	2.00
3. Variability Level 3	7.04	5.25	3.50
4. Variability Level 4	10.00	7.50	5.00

In Table IV, the correlational-redundancy values used to determine the first-order probability of specific pitch, duration, and loudness combinations are given. In the case of the zero redundancy level, all combinations occurred with equal probability. However, in the low and high

TABLE IV. Summary of the Correlational Characteristics of the Melodic Sequences

Sets of probabilities	Correlational probability of element occurring		
	Zero redundancy	Low redundancy	High redundancy
Set 1 = 2 elements (2 × 2)	.50 | .50 .50 | .50	.786 | .214 .214 | .786	.89 | .11 .11 | .89
Set 2 = 3 elements (3 × 3)	.33 | .33 | .33 .33 | .33 | .33 .33 | .33 | .33	.696 | .152 | .152 .152 | .696 | .152 .152 | .152 | .696	.84 | .08 | .08 .08 | .84 | .08 .08 | .08 | .84
Set 3 = 4 elements (4 × 4)	All matrix entries =.25	Major diagonal =.64 All other entries =.12	Major diagonal =.80 All other entries =.067
Set 4 = 8 elements (8 × 8)	All matrix entries =.125	Major diagonal =.552 All other entries =.064	Major diagonal =.753 All other entries =.035
Set 5 = 11 elements (11 × 11)	All matrix entries =.0909	Major Diagonal =.520 All other entries =.048	Major diagonal =.731 All other entries =.0268
Set 6 = 33 elements (33 × 33)	All matrix entries =.0303	Major diagonal =.43 All other entries =.018	Major diagonal =.677 All other entries =.010

redundancy levels, certain combinations were more probable than others in the specific set. Of the numerous rationales which could have been used to determine this property, two were chosen. Thus, in contrast to the distributional-redundancy set of sequences, there were two melodic sequences at each of the twelve variability × redundancy levels, resulting in 24 sequences in all.

The rationale used for the first set of 12 sequences, which is the one entered in Table IV, consisted of increasing the probability that elements (i.e., specific pitches, durations, or loudnesses) would fall on the major diagonal of the relevant correlational-probability matrix. In illustration, the matrix for the tone sequence incorporating two elements gave a higher probability to the pitch 349 Hz, the duration 33 msec and loudness level two being followed by themselves than by the pitch 392 Hz, duration 667 msec or loudness level three. Likewise, pitch 392 Hz, duration 667 msec and loudness level three were more likely to be followed by themselves than by the other pitch, duration, and loudness in the two-element set. The result of this rationale was readily perceptible upon listening, the effect being to maximize the probability that tones would be consecutively repeated. For this reason, the 12 tone sequences constructed in this fashion were referred to as the "high-repetition" or "on-diagonal" tone sequences. In probability-matrix terms, redundancy has been introduced by increasing the probability of occurrence of major diagonal elements, with a matching decrease in the probability of all other matrix entries.

The second set of 12 sequences employed a correlational probability matrix rationale which, in contrast to the one used in the first set, maximized the probability that tones would not immediately follow each other. This was accomplished by assigning the entries to the low- and high-redundancy matrices such that the high probability element did not fall on the major diagonal. Rather, it took any other row-column position, with the further constraint that once a row-column position was occupied by the high-probability event, it could not be so occupied again.

This rationale can be simply illustrated by reference to the 4 × 4 matrix for tone sequences incorporating four elements. Using only the low-redundancy matrix for our illustration, it can be seen that example A below represents a distribution possible under the sampling rationale outlined above, and example B represents a distribution violating both the major diagonal and repetition of rows-columns constraints.

Example A (meets sampling rationale)				Example B (violates sampling rationale)			
.12	.12	.64	.12	.12	.12	.64	.12
.12	.12	.12	.64	.12	.12	.12	.64
.64	.12	.12	.12	.12	.12	.64	.12
.12	.64	.12	.12	.64	.12	.12	.12

The resultant set of 12-tone sequences, which will be referred to as the "low-repetition" or "off-diagonal" set, differed from the first set only on this dimension of tone repetition. In terms of all other properties— variability, redundancy, and tone elements—the two sets were identical. As in the first experiment, the 24 sequences were generated using a PDP 8/S computer to monitor a Wavetek wave-form synthesizer. Thirty-minute audio tapes of each sequence were recorded, and these tapes were used to conduct the experiment. Three studies were carried out, the first obtaining ratings of the melodic sequences on the four verbal rating scales used previously, and the second and third obtaining subjects' listening times and paired comparison choices.

Experiment 2: Verbal Rating-Scale Study

Subjects, Design, and Procedure

Twenty-four University of Toronto students enrolled in an introductory psychology course volunteered to participate in the study. Their participation qualified them for extra credits toward their final course grade.

The rating scales were treated as within-subject factors, with subjects judging either the off-diagonal or the on-diagonal set of tone sequences on all four scales. The twelve sequences were rotated against the four scales, so that a subject judged all 12 sequences against one specific rating scale at a time. The presentation order for the sequences was based on the 12 × 12 balanced Latin square used in the first experiment.

Two subjects—one judging the on-diagonal set and the other the off-diagonal set of sequences—were randomly assigned to each row of the 12 × 12 sequence-presentation square. Twelve of the 24 possible permutations of the four rating scales were used, and these were assigned in arbitrary fashion, one to each of the 12 rows of the sequence-presentation square. The experimental setting and procedure were identical to that used with the distributional-redundancy sequences.

Experiment 2: Listening-Time Study

Subjects, Design, and Procedure

Twenty-four undergraduates volunteered to participate in the study, in order to earn credits for their introductory psychology program. As in the rating-scale study, the subjects were divided into two equal groups, one group listening to the on-diagonal and the other to the off-diagonal set of melodic sequences. The sequence-presentation order for the two groups was determined by the 12 × 12 balanced Latin square used in the previous study. One subject from each group was assigned to each row of the Latin square, and the subjects' listening times were recorded. The procedure was identical to that employed with the distributional-redundancy sequences.

Experiment 2: Exploratory-Choice Study

Subjects, Design, and Procedure

Twenty-four undergraduates enrolled in an introductory psychology course voluntarily participated in this study. As in the previous two experiments, the on- and off-diagonal variable was treated as a between-subjects factor, with 12 subjects choosing from the on-diagonal set, and 12 from the off-diagonal set. Aside from this division, all other aspects of the design and procedure were identical to those described earlier and used with the distributional-redundancy sequences.

Experiment 2: Results

The listeners' responses were analyzed using an analysis of variance conceptually similar to that of the previous experiment. The major difference was that one further factor was present in the analysis, this being the low: high repetition variable. As before, the exploratory-choice results were analyzed using a nonparametric analysis of variance by ranks.

The patterns of statistical significance, which are summarized in Table V, showed the overall uncertainty effect that has typified this project so far. Looking at the breakdown of uncertainty into variability and redundancy, it is apparent that redundancy as well as variability has now proved to be a consistent contributor to the uncertainty main effect. Notably, though, redundancy and variability have functioned in relative independence of each other, as evidenced by the absence of significant redundancy × variability interaction effects.

The significance of this fact became evident upon examining the response trends across melodic uncertainty, for these trends were marked by "sawtooth" oscillations which also reflected themselves in significant higher-order trend components. This pattern of responding was owing to the fact that ordering the melodic sequences by uncertainty did not also rank them by redundancy within successive variability levels. This lack of correspondence between uncertainty order and variability × redundancy ranking only occurred in this final set of sequences because of the expansion of redundancy to 50%, as this expansion produced an overlap of redundancy across adjacent variability levels.

By reorganizing the data according to redundancy within variability levels, results readily comparable to those of the previous experiment emerged. As in Experiment 1, judgments of complexity and orderliness were monotonic functions of redundancy within variability (see Figure 2, upper panel), with both variability and redundancy main effects contributing to this trend. Also as before, judgments of pleasingness and interestingness, plotted in the middle panel of Figure 2, showed the initial increase and decline which has typified these measures. However, they both also showed the effect of the more powerful redundancy manipulation, this being a decrease in pleasingness and interestingness as redundancy increased. This effect, which has somewhat moderated by variability level four, is particularly notable at the lower variability levels.

The two measures of exposure, listening time and exploratory choice, both reached a unimodal peak at midrange sequence complexity levels (see Figure 2, lower panel). Redundancy was again a more prominent factor here than in Experiment 1, with listeners' choices tending to favor lower redundancy sequences.

The low:high repetition or off:on diagonal variable produced reason-

TABLE V. Summary of Patterns of Statistical Significance: Experiment 2

Source of variance	Semantic differential scales				Listening time	Exploratory choice
	Simple: complex	Disorderly: orderly	Displeasing: pleasing	Uninteresting: interesting		
Uncertainty (U) (11 df)	a	a	a	a	a	a
Variability (V) (3 df)	a	a	a	a	a	a
Redundancy (R) (2 df)	a	b	a	a		a
V × R (6 df)			b			N/A
Diagonal (D) (1 df)			a		b	N/A
D × V (3 df)			a	b	b	N/A
D × U (11 df)					a	N/A

[a] $p < .01$.
[b] $p < .05$.
N/A = not applicable.

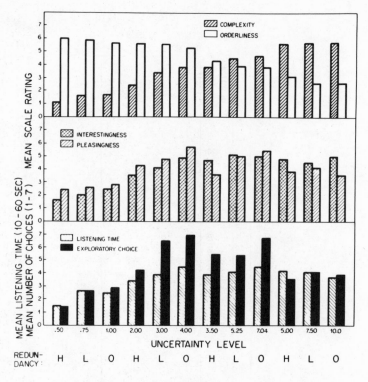

FIGURE 2. The uncertainty main effects: Experiment 2.

ably clear effects on the dependent measures. In terms of verbal responding, the listeners found the high repetition of material to be more pleasing at the two lowest variability levels, and the low repetition to be more pleasing at the two highest variability levels. But, aside from also finding that the high repetition sequences were somewhat more interesting at low variability levels, there were no other significant effects of diagonality on verbal judgments. In the case of listening time, the one nonverbal measure assessing the diagonality variable, the high repetition sequences were listened to for greater lengths of time than the low repetition across the midrange of uncertainty, with convergence occurring at the two extremes.

Experiment 2: Discussion

On the whole, the results of Experiment 2 do seem to represent the expected extension of Experiment 1. As on previous occasions, the dependent measures have formed two classes, one showing a monotonic and the other a bitonic relationship to the independent variable. And, as predicted, the extension of the melodic sequence algorithm to include both higher levels of redundancy and the conceptually more powerful correlational redundancy has clearly been evidenced in the presence of significant redundancy effects on all but one of the dependent measures. Of course, what part of this result reflects the increase in redundancy to 50%, and what part reflects the introduction of first-order correlation properties, is not distinguishable, as these two factors have been simultaneously varied.

In spite of this confounding, the failure of the uncertainty measure to underlie the grouping of the dependent measures into monotonic and bitonic functions is suggestive of the changes in subjective uncertainty which have been attributed to the correlational manipulation. However, as our analysis has shown, this first failure of uncertainty to capture and summarize melodic structure was owing to the overlap of redundancy values across neighbouring variability levels which resulted from increasing redundancy to 50%. (For the reader who may still have concerns on this point, the exact nature of this overlap can be ascertained by reordering the abscissa of Figure 2 by ascending uncertainty levels rather than by redundancy nested within variability.) But even though this failure of uncertainty to summarize the combined effects of redundancy and variability is readily explainable, it still represents a qualification of the information-theoretic approach. For these data would suggest that informational analysis is logically constrained to a defined set of symbols, and cannot be used in order to order overlapping symbol sets conceptually. This conclusion, though not a prohibitive restriction, does somewhat qualify the use of uncertainty as an index of melodic form and structure.

As the patterns of significance in Table V indicate, the effects of the low:high repetition variable have been largely confined to pleasingness ratings and to listening times. This is in keeping with the results found with previously introduced qualitative variables such as Western scale tuning and metrical rhythms. These variables affected only the dependent measures which have been curvilinear in nature, and have been associated with an *evaluative* dimension of aesthetic response.

The evidence for effects of the low:high repetition factor on the linear measures associated with an *activity* dimension has been of quite limited strength and prominence, and suggests that the earlier restriction of qualitative effects to evaluative responses does not require reconsideration at this point. Although establishing the robustness of this particular *activity:evaluation* distinction will certainly demand further experimentation, the information-theoretic analysis has reasonably encompassed the repetition variable within a two-factor model.

CONCLUDING COMMENTS

The composer Schoenberg (1950), in what was hopefully a satirical vein, prophesized that

> one day the children's children of our psychologists and psychoanalysts will have deciphered the language of music. Woe, then, to the incautious who thought his innermost secrets carefully hidden and who must now allow tactless men to besmirch his most personal possessions with their own impurities. Woe, then, to Beethoven, Brahms, and Schumann and all other "Unknown" composers, when they fall into such hands—these men who used their human right of free speech only in order to conceal their true thoughts! Is the right to keep silent not worthy of protection? (p. 209)

Although indeed this chapter has been concerned with deciphering the language of music, it is doubtful that the results of research such as this will lead to the exposé so dramatically predicted above. Based as it is on an analysis of music as part of a larger phenomenon of human communication, the informational approach used here has addressed the analysis of form and structure more than the analysis of content. And, as this project has shown, even this conservative analysis does have its logical limitations.

But these limitations should not be taken as a basis for the total dismissal of approaches such as this. As was argued earlier, a quantitative analysis of the aesthetic stimulus seems an essential prerequisite to any typology of aesthetic response. Its absence, though often expedient, must surely hinder as much as help the search for common modes of perception.

That limitations will be placed on any quantitative analysis is perhaps inevitable, especially as the analysis is extended to encompass more and more of the properties found in an art form. However, these limitations alone will not defeat its utility in considering the dynamic interaction of aesthetic stimulus and response. Space does not permit the exploration of this further, except to note that multivariate analysis of the data in this chapter did reveal two perceptual dimensions underlying listeners' paired-comparison choices. As in earlier research, these dimensions were interpretable in terms of the uncertainty of the melodic sequences, with the first dimension bearing a linear relationship and the second a curvilinear relationship to stimulus-uncertainty levels.

And so, though the information-theoretic approach may not have ended the search for the aesthetic engram, in the case of the premier temporal art form it still remains as an approach of compelling power and singular scope.

REFERENCES

ATTNEAVE, F. Some informational aspects of visual perception. *Psychological Review*, 1954, 61, 183–193.

BERLYNE, D. E. *Aesthetics and psychobiology*. New York: Appleton-Century-Crofts, 1971.

BIRKOFF, G. D. *Aesthetic measure*. Cambridge: Harvard University Press, 1933.

COHEN, J. E. Information theory and music. *Behavioral Science*, 1962, 7, 137–163.

COPLAND, A. *What to listen for in music*. New York: McGraw-Hill, 1939.

CROZIER, J. B. Verbal and exploratory responses to sound sequences varying in uncertainty level. In D. E. Berlyne (Ed.), *Studies in the new experimental aesthetics*. Washington D.C.: Hemisphere Publishing, 1974.

FRANK, H. *Grundlagenprobleme der Informationsaesthetik und erste Anwendung auf die mime pure*. Quickborn: Schnelle, 1959.

GARNER, W. R. *Uncertainty and structure as psychological concepts*. New York: Wiley, 1962.

GREEN, R. T., & COURTIS, M. C. Information theory and figure perception: The metaphor that failed. *Acta Psychologica*, 1966, 25, 12–35.

HOCHBERG, J., & MCALISTER, E. A quantitative approach to figural "goodness." *Journal of Experimental Psychology*, 1953, 46, 361–364.

KOFFKA, K. Problems in the psychology of art. In *Art: A Byrn Mawr symposium*. Lancaster, Pa.: Lancaster Press, 1940.

MEYER, L. B. *Emotion and meaning in music*. Chicago: University of Chicago Press, 1956.

MOLES, A. Information theory and esthetic perception (J. Cohen trans.). Urbana: University of Illinois Press, 1966. (Originally published, Paris: Flammarion, 1958.)

PINKERTON, R. C. Information theory and melody. *Scientific American*, 1956, 194, 77–86.

ROBINSON, D. W., & DADSON, R. S. A redetermination of the equal loudness relations for pure tones. *British Journal of Applied Physics*, 1956, 7, 166–181.

ROSS, R. T. Optimum orders for the presentation of pairs in the method of paired comparisons. *Journal of Educational Psychology*, 1934, 25, 375–382.

SCHOENBERG, A. *Style and idea*. New York: Philosophical Library, 1950.

SHANNON, C. E., & WEAVER, W. *Mathematical theory of communication*. Urbana: University of Illinois Press, 1949.

VITZ, P. C. Affect as a function of stimulus variation. *Journal of Experimental Psychology*, 1966, 71, 74–79.

WILLIAMS, E. J. Experimental designs balanced for the estimation of residual effects of treatments. *Australian Journal of Scientific Research*, 1949, 2, 149–168.

WINER, B. J. *Statistical principles in experimental design*. New York: McGraw-Hill, 1971.

ZINK, S. Is the music really sad? *Journal of Aesthetics*, 1960, 19, 197–207.

19

Toward an Integrated Theory of Aesthetic Perception in the Visual Arts

GERALD C. CUPCHIK AND R. WALTER HEINRICHS

INTRODUCTION

Consider the following scenario: A spectator is standing in front of a painting in an art gallery, he moves up close to the canvas, and then retreats several paces, finally, shaking his head as if to indicate displeasure, he moves on to the next painting. This episode appears simple to us, and its explanation seems obvious. Yet, on further examination, we recognize that this simplicity is deceptive. We have only observed the behavioral manifestations of an aesthetic encounter. As soon as we seek answers to such questions as what specific properties of this painting led to an unfavorable reaction, and what processes transpired in the viewer's mind to produce displeasure, we have entered a realm full of complexity and uncertainty. In this chapter, we shall move beyond obvious and superficial analyses of aesthetic experience, and begin to consider the multifaceted nature of artistic perception in depth.

The psychologist who seeks to illuminate the aesthetic episode utilizes his understanding of human thought, emotion, and behavior to provide causal explanations. He is not, however, alone in this endeavor. The art historian and the psychoanalyst are equally concerned with aesthetic issues. The visual qualities of a painting, the influence of the artist's personality in determining style and imagery, and the reactions of the spectator are essential components of all three approaches. There is, indeed, a vast psychoanalytic literature on the subject of creativity and aesthetic perception (Freud, 1932; Kris, 1952; Pfister 1913, 1923; Rank, 1907). In addition, art historians from Vasari (1568) to Kenneth Clark

GERALD C. CUPCHIK • Division of Life Sciences, Scarborough College, University of Toronto, Toronto, Ontario M1C 1A4, Canada. R. WALTER HEINRICHS • Department of Psychology, University of Toronto, Toronto, Ontario M5S 1A1, Canada.

(1939) have been concerned with related topics, not to mention the contributions from philosophy (Read, 1949). Is there anything unique about the approach of the experimental psychologist, and what does he have to offer that the others do not?

This question is in itself a complex issue. We cannot simply invoke the image of the experimental aesthetician donning the mantle of science, since the psychoanalyst also aspires to this role. The characteristics which distinguish the experimental psychologist from his colleagues in aesthetics may relate more to the methods he employs in gathering knowledge and the qualifications he places on the goals of inquiry than to the actual subject matter under analysis. It is more a matter of perspective and methodology which separates his efforts from those of the art historian and the psychoanalyst.

These differences and similarities may be clarified by examining Table I. As we scan over the subject matter of the three approaches, we

TABLE I. A Comparision of Art History, Psychoanalysis, and Experimental Aesthetics

	Art history	Psychoanalysis	Experimental aesthetics
Subject matter	Artistic style & content cultural determinants of style; stylistic variations within artist's lifetime, and among artists; biography of artist.	Similar to art history but in addition, focuses on artist's and viewer's associations to work. More concerned with unconscious influences on perception–creation.	Similar subject matter but translated into informational properties. Sometimes with nonartistic visual patterns as well.
Goals	Understanding the components of effective and ineffective art work; seeks to account for stylistic evolution, and idiosyncracies of artistic expression.	Similar to art history but places the role of personality in a preeminent position, seeks an understanding of creative motivation, and nature of aesthetic pleasure.	Primary concern is with finding consistent, objective tendencies in aesthetic perception. Again, the goals are different primarily because there is an emphasis on structure.
Methods	Historical postdictive logical analyses. Use of biographical and autobiographical accounts. Some use of color and compositional theory in visual analysis of paintings.	Uses art-historical methods and data from clinical interviews. Employs free association, dream analysis, etc. as a way of dissecting personality constitutents of art.	Experimental creation of an aesthetic episode. Quantitative methods and statistical techniques, mechanical measuring devices, and subject sampling.

notice only minor differences. The experimental aesthetician is perhaps more concerned with informational elements, but much of this resides in his concept of what constitutes information (Moles, 1966). The subject matter is identical, but he chooses to interpret it in a highly structured manner. With respect to goals, clearly all three approaches are interested in providing explanations of aesthetics. They are concerned with detecting structure and consistency among visual properties, and with perceptual reactions to these properties.

However, the experimental aesthetician is also concerned with prediction, with the establishment of universal principles which are testable, and with a communication model of aesthetic perception. The art historian is more interested in the contributions of sociocultural dynamics to aesthetic style, and the psychoanalyst tends to emphasize his interest in the personality of both artist and viewer as his ultimate goal. The most definitive differences occur when we consider the methods each approach brings to bear on their clearly overlapping goals. Both art history and psychoanalysis use postdictive, historical forms of analysis to create inferences about aesthetic processes. The data of the analyst are primarily clinical or biographical, and his methods incline toward naturalistic observations. The art historian, for his part, uses similar methods, albeit not in a clinical context, and relies somewhat more on cultural and social documentation to support his assertions. The experimental aesthetician is unique in that he employs experimental, quantitative hypothesis-testing techniques. He is much less concerned with historical antecedents, and much more interested in the present interaction between art and viewer. This methodology embodies his concern with the stability of findings and their universality. Moreover, he, in effect, recreates an aesthetic episode in his laboratory and manipulates various potential influences on perception to arrive at sound explanations. He seeks, ultimately, to demonstrate the validity of his constructs by predicting aesthetic behaviors and processes.

In general, then, the experimental aesthetician is distinguished more by the methods he utilizes than the questions he asks, although his techniques clearly influence the interpretations he is willing to make concerning aesthetic phenomena. With respect to this methodological distinction, it is important to note that experimentation in psychology has occasioned a considerable amount of criticism (Rosenthal, 1966; Silverman, 1977). This criticism has centered on arguments that experimental paradigms do not accurately reflect the conditions which exist in the everyday world; they are seen as artificial, contrived, and limited in terms of generalizability. There is, however, good reason to believe that, though experimental aesthetics employs similar methods, it does not find its results so questionable. This is owing to the fact that the laboratory very effectively reflects the situation which the viewer encounters in an art gallery. Aestheticians as early as Fechner (1801–1887) indicated a sensitivity to this problem. Fechner (1876) actually conducted experiments in an art gallery. However, as we have suggested, this extra step is probably no longer necessary, because the environment of an art gallery is so similar to that of the aesthetician's laboratory. Both are generally sparse, neutral environments which focus attention on the aesthetic object rather than the surroundings. As modern art has become more conceptual and experimental itself, we often find the viewer engaged actively in manipulating the object as an integral part of the aesthetic experience.

Having detoured through these initial problems of definition, delineation, and validity, it is now possible to articulate the interests of the experimental aesthetician in a more comprehensive manner. The psychologist must first of all provide a coherent and universal account of the aesthetic object. This account must reveal how a work of art differs from the many kinds of stimuli which are encountered in everyday life. Some very valuable work in this regard has already been accomplished by Moles (1966) and Berlyne (1960, 1971, 1974). Furthermore, the psychologist may wish to explore the relationship of the artist to his own creation. Such an exploration may probe the family constellation of the artist, and search for dynamics which may have influenced his development. This approach gave impetus to an experimental study of the perception of Impressionist style (Cupchik, 1976) conducted in our own laboratory.

However, the most important and potentially fruitful avenue of inquiry is probably the interactional processes which operate within the aesthetic episode itself. In this case, the problem lies in determining how the spectator invests his experience of the aesthetic object with meaning. This entails, in turn, an examination of the process of aesthetic perception, and hence presupposes a theoretical framework which does justice to the aesthetic object. Several related questions may be posed. What happens during the initial moments that the spectator views a painting? How does his perception unfold as a function of viewing time? Furthermore, how do the properties of the aesthetic object influence his experience? Although the formulation of such questions is not unique to the experimental aesthetician, the broad array of powerful methodological tools which he has at his command, and his concern with recreating the aesthetic episode, allow him to explore previously obscure problems and provide answers which reflect his unique perspective.

An attempt will be made in this chapter to develop a coherent account of the structure of an aesthetic object, and to examine the interaction of such an object with a spectator. In a sense, this interaction forms the viewer's link with the absent creator. The aesthetic object incorporates the artist's visual language, his structuring of its informationl components, and the levels of meaning which such a structuring creates. The viewer must, in a way, experience the artist's own vision if aesthetic communication is to occur. Although part of this vision is idiosyncratic, personal, and inaccessible, we must assume that a large portion of it is amenable to the spectator's interpretive skills.

DANIEL BERLYNE AND THE NEW EXPERIMENTAL AESTHETICS

The experimental approach to psychological aesthetics has enjoyed a resurgence during the past 20 years. A key figure during this period of development has been Daniel E. Berlyne (1924–1976) of the University of Toronto, whose contributions encompassed both theoretical and empirical aspects of aesthetics (1960, 1971, 1974). Berlyne followed in the footsteps of Gustav Fechner, the father of empirical aesthetics, in his search for the determinants of aesthetic pleasure and displeasure. He was convinced that motivational or hedonic effects were determined by certain properties of pictures and patterns. The problem held a special fascination for him because these properties could evoke profound reactions even though they had no apparent connection to the requirements of survival. Berlyne's approach was psychological (1971) and avoided evaluation, the description language of art historians, and the interpretive constructs of psychoanalysts.

Readers who are familiar with Berlyne's work as a whole know that his research was founded on an interest in curiosity and exploratory behavior in general. Those who know only of his work in aesthetics may be surprised to learn that it originated in what might be termed, for want of a better label, the study of animal aesthetics. In his first book, *Conflict, Arousal, and Curiosity,* he admonished behavioral researchers for concentrating on "response selection" while treating the stimulus setting in a simplistic manner. Berlyne argued that animals in their natural surroundings are "inundated with an endless variety of stimuli coming from all directions" (1960, p. 7). The problem of stimulus selection in a complex environment became central to Berlyne. In his book *Aesthetics and Psychobiology,* the "complex environment" became the aesthetic episode and the work of art became the visual stimulus in question. His goal was to characterize those properties of the stimulus which could account for its motivational effects on the spectator.

Following an information-theory approach, Berlyne focused his attention on the general structure of the stimulus. This reflected the long standing tradition of identifying "beauty" with harmonious qualities of the aesthetic object. The phrase "unity in diversity" has traditionally been used to account for the beauty and evocative power of the work of art. Berlyne (1971, 1974) applied the same information-theory vocabulary to both works of art and visual patterns. He conceived of the work of art as an "assemblage of elements" comprising dots or dabs of color which had a particular structure. Qualities such as complexity, uncertainty, novelty, and surprisingness were viewed as being responsible for the aesthetic effects of the work. These "collative variables" resulted from the viewer's examination of similarities and differences between elements within the stimulus (complexity), and also between the elements of the stimulus and the spectator's previous experience (novelty) or expectations (surprisingness). Aesthetic pleasure was a direct function of the spectator's ability to organize or interpret the uncertainty or originality in the work.

Berlyne (1971) described the four specific kinds of information which could be conveyed by paintings or stimulus patterns: semantic, expressive, cultural, and syntactic. Semantic information denotes external objects and pertains to realism and representation. The remaining three sources all transmit "aesthetic information," and reflect: (1) psychological processes within the artist (expressive information); (2) social norms (cultural information); and (3) the relations among elements or distributions of elements in space (syntactic information). The four kinds of information were treated as independent and in competition "for the limited capacity of the channel linking them with the work" (1974, p. 6). This analysis was comprehensive in the sense that both semantic and aesthetic information could be analyzed in terms of collative properties (Moles, 1966).

Berlyne's work also reflected a strict behaviorist approach to aesthetics. The behaviorist viewpoint required that he focus on aesthetic behavior and mediating physiological structures to the exclusion of mentation, experience, and subjective interpretation. At one level, he was concerned with the relationship between particular collative properties and exploratory behavior. For example, a subject would be presented with two stimuli varying along a particular dimension such as complexity, and Berlyne would ask the subject to select one or the other for a second viewing period (exploratory-choice paradigm). At another level, Berlyne considered the role of physiological structures in shaping exploratory behavior. He theorized about locations and processes within the brain which could produce aesthetic pain or pleasure, and used brain-wave activity as an index of attention during exploration. During the later phases of his work, he used multidimensional scaling techniques in an effort to detect the dominant stylistic properties of paintings, and was preparing to follow this up with an investigation of visual tracking shortly before his untimely death.

CRITIQUE OF BERLYNE'S APPROACH

The wedding of information theory and behavioristic concepts has certainly advanced psychological aesthetics by affording a rigorous grasp of the aesthetic stimulus. However, it is essential to recognize that aesthetic communication involves not only the properties of the aesthetic object, but also the decoding and interpretive skills of the spectator. As Moles (1966) has stated, "Communication is dependent on the common knowledge shared by the transmitter and receptor" (p. 55). The spectator must possess "perceptual sensibilities" (Hester, 1975) and a repertoire of semantic and aesthetic knowledge, which enables him to determine the originality of the message. If we presuppose that aesthetic communication occurs through the medium of structured quanta of visual elements, we are immediately faced with the corollary of this assumption, namely, that aesthetic phenomena constitute a kind of language (Goodman, 1968). The ability to comprehend this language must necessarily be predicated on the viewer's ability to detect and decode its visual configurations. This process is not necessarily restricted to aesthetic perception. Indeed, as Kolers (1979) has shown with respect to reading, the perceiver's pattern-analyzing skills are of paramount importance in facilitating comprehension. This research underscores the notion of an active rather than passive recipient of aesthetic information.

When the experimental aesthetician adopts the viewpoint that the spectator is essentially passive in relation to the environment, then his psychological formulations become correspondingly restricted in focus. This, in turn, has implications for our understanding of aesthetics.

The notion of passivity in relation to an active environment corresponds to the principle that the environment controls behavior. This idea forms an integral part of the behavioristic tradition which permeates Berlyne's work. In order to arrive at a critical evaluation of his approach, we must examine those junctions at which the behaviorist paradigm limits, rather than enhances, our understanding of art.

To a certain extent, Berlyne (1960) was himself aware of the restrictions of classical Hullian behaviorism. He could not have even approached aesthetics without the notion of intrinsic, as opposed to extrinsic, motivation. Yet, despite this departure, many essential characteristics of radical behaviorism were preserved and integrated into the new experimental aesthetics.

Behaviorism, as its name implies, is essentially concerned with observable behavior (Watson, 1924). Unobservable processes such as subjective experience, acts of mind, and the derivation of meaning are suspect. Aesthetic behavior is seen as a consequence of stimulus characteristics which induce given responses. Alternately, these responses are mediated by the nervous system of the aesthetic viewer. This gives rise to two forms of reductionism. One is concerned with reducing aesthetic phenomena to specifiable stimulus–response contingencies, and the other with reducing aesthetic motivation to biological processes.

These tenets are highly visible in Berlyne's work. His early (1960) use of the term "collative variables" reflected a sensitivity to problems of internal processing and the spectator's interaction with the stimulus. However, he later abandoned this term, and introduced the concept of "collative properties" (Berlyne, 1971, 1974), thus transferring attention to qualities embedded within the stimulus patterns. This may be attributable in part to his conviction, based on his own research, that objective variables and subjective variables are highly correlated. A firm grasp of the external stimulus should be sufficient to account for internal states (Berlyne, 1974). In addition, he believed that the act of collation or comparison occurred in the nervous system along with processes such as adaptation (1971, p. 106). Clearly, the thematic touchstones of behaviorism are all present: operationalism, external control, and biological reductionism. In addition, we notice that he has approached aesthetics as a detached "third person." The aesthetician's scientific value is seen in direct relation to the extent to which he remains an outsider, isolated from both the artist–creator's perspective and the experiences of the viewer.

What are the limitations imposed by approaching the aesthetic viewer as an organism which reacts to art as a function of the stimulus properties of a given work? For one thing, it tells us very little about the emotional forces which are inspired by art, and which interact during the viewing process. Constructs such as "arousal" or a pleasure–displeasure dichotomy hardly bridge this gap adequately. Furthermore, the dynamics which produce meaning in art cannot be accounted for. The richness of the viewer as a conscious, reflective psychological being has been sacrificed in favour of the efficiency of approaching him as essentially a pleasure-seeking biological organism. Why do some of us find the simplicity of oriental watercolors as moving as the "complexity" of Baroque painting? Why do we find evocations of the tragic in life so compelling, and why are some artists, such as Rembrandt, so successful in communicating it?

Part of the reason for these omissions lies in the fact that the reductionist approach, concerned with dividing and subdividing phenomena into components, cannot furnish us with a paradigm for integration. The complexity of sensory, affective, and cognitive interactions defies, indeed contradicts, the efforts of the aesthetician whose primary concern is with simplification and atomization. In addition, adopting the behaviorist perspective makes it extremely difficult to study the artist–creator himself. Clearly, the artist is not "passive." He is an actor in the aesthetic event, who creates visual stimuli for his own purposes, and not simply in response to the environment. It is not surprising, therefore, that Berlyne had very little to say about creativity and the action-oriented behavior of the artist.

The second major component of Berlyne's aesthetic psychobiology involves the adaptation of information theory to behavioral processes. As has been suggested, treating an aesthetic object as an "assemblage of elements" makes it easier to quantify the problem. It also enables the researcher to pursue a "synthetic" approach (Berlyne, 1974). This involves the construction of artificial stimulus materials in which particular variables, such as complexity, are manipulated. However, the application of a mechanical model of communication (Shannon & Weaver, 1949) to aesthetics entails a paradigm which does violence to the very phenomenon it seeks to illuminate.

Consider, for example, the implications of describing a work of art as a closed system in which four sources of information (semantic, expressive, cultural, and syntactic) compete for "the limited capacity of the channel linking them with the work" (Berlyne, 1974, p. 6). The notion of "competition" anthropomorphizes information and attributes intentional action to theoretical constructs. It may not be inappropriate to remind ourselves that the artist, *not* information treated as an abstract commodity, is the active part of the creative process. Interestingly, this injection of human qualities into the objective world may have resulted from the attempt to deprive the human spectator of his cognitive flexibility. The perceptual plasticity denied the viewer resurfaced in the form of "bits" of information which compete for the attention of the passive viewer.

A further objection to Berlyne's adaptation of information theory rests in his conceptual isolation of "elements" of a work of art. Surely, this is more appropriate to synthetic or artificial materials than genuine works. Analyzing the locations of these elements in a work of art from a probabilistic standpoint is also problematic. The idea that dots of color have a certain "uncertainty" of appearing next to each other reflects the opinion of a detached "third person." This person, the experimental aesthetician, is removed from the very processes he is describing, and makes his inferences after the fact. Is he justified in imposing such a framework on aesthetic perception and creativity? The application of outline and color by the artist achieves its impact through the complex visual effects which are evoked. Furthermore, these effects take place within the context of the work as a whole. It is this holistic phenomenon, rather than the perception of discrete "elements," which typifies visual art. The relationships of these elements to one another are at least partly controlled by the guiding visual idea of the artist during creation. Hence, we are again faced with a perspective which cannot account for integrated, coordinated, holistic creation and perception.

The various perspectives concerning the appropriate way to conceptualize a work of art have deep roots in established intellectual traditions. English empiricist philosophers such as John Locke and David Hume maintained that all knowledge was ultimately derived from sensory experience. The contents of the mind could be analyzed into independent units which were related through associations in time or space, or through similarity. The German rationalists took issue with this highly atomistic view, and instead emphasized the unity and active nature of the mind. This difference between a passive and an active conception of the mind has come down to us in the form of the content-versus-act controversy (Boring, 1950). Clearly, this dualism has left its mark on psychological aesthetics. Either we approach the problem from a third-person perspective and see the paintings in terms of objectively isolated contents, or we assume that the painting is the intentional product of the artist's actions and reflects his unique understanding and vision. The same argument may be extended to the processes whereby the perceiver perceives meaning in a work of art. Both pragmatics and intellectual predilections govern whether one adopts an atomistic or a holistic approach to aesthetics.

It is interesting to consider Berlyne's approach within the context of what contemporary information theorists have to say about some of these issues. Although European writers such as Frank (1959), Gunzenhäuser (1962) and Ertel (1974) employ information theory in perceptual analysis, they have also been sensitive to the problem of stimulus processing by the subject. Ertel, a German aesthetician, has addressed himself directly to the issue of collative properties and aesthetic perception. He demonstrated in his research that the phenomenal qualities of an aesthetic object can change during the process of perception. For example, the amount of "balance," "activity," or "pleasantness" changes with increased viewing time. Research from our own laboratory has produced similar conclusions (Cupchik & Berlyne, 1979). Ertel (1974) advised researchers against treating visual qualities as "quasi-objective, invariant attributes" (p. 106). An overemphasis on the stimulus effects of the physical environment may lead scholars "to regard figural properties of the visual world as parameters of the geometric world, without noticing that the source is perception" (p. 126). The essence of this criticism is that aesthetic perception is a *process*, and the judgments of the subject reflect the interaction of stimulus parameters with the subject's own constructive efforts at structuring and giving meaning to the stimulus. Hence, Berlyne may have unnecessarily reified information theory in his efforts to objectify aesthetic behavior.

In summary, Berlyne's integration of information theory and behavioristic concepts has revitalized psychological aesthetics and made meaningful research possible. This integration is useful because it can be used to describe the process of communication between a work of art and a spectator. The psychologist can now accurately specify the communication situation (Step A) and the repertoire required to interpret the aesthetic message (Step B) (Moles, 1966). However, the formal and quantitative application of information theory (Step C) requires a statistical determination of "the probabilities of occurrence (expectancy) of each element of the repertoire" (Moles, 1966, p. 55). This atomistic treatment of the aesthetic message may be more appropriate for the analysis of musical forms, the elements (notes) of which are discrete, and unfold temporally. The notion that dabs of color have a quantifiable uncertainty of appearing next to each other (Berlyne, 1971) does not reflect the structure and creative origin of the work. Moles himself acknowledges that information as a quantity is different and independent from the meaning of a work of art.

We have articulated some of Berlyne's fundamental assumptions and their limitations with respect to aesthetics. This critical examination suggests that his approach may have introduced an element of artificiality into the study of aesthetic communication. In essence, our critique reflects the difference between an emphasis on the contents which accrue during the aesthetic episode, and an emphasis on the synthetic role of the intellect and the influence of emotion. It has also been noted that an information-theory orientation need not incorporate all the assumptions of behaviorism. It is not necessary to stress the stimulus in isolation, at the expense of the processing characteristics of the spectator.

Finally, it should be said that the work which lies before us is largely the product of a rich dialogue between Berlyne's natural-science view and our own more phenomenological orientation. It is a tribute to his scholarship that we now possess the conceptual tools to build on the foundations he erected.

The Process of Aesthetic Perception

In what remains we are going to examine the aesthetic episode in great depth. Our overriding goal is to develop a framework for a theory of aesthetic perception. This framework incorporates both a structural analysis of the aesthetic object and an account of the processes which underlie its perception and interpretation by the spectator. Structurally speaking, the work of art consists of basic materials such as paint and canvas, whose organization conveys an aesthetic message. We discuss the stylistic, contentual, and collative components, drawing on the work of Berlyne and others to integrate them. Aesthetic perception is contrasted with pragmatic and mundane perception in everyday life. The complex temporal aspects of aesthetic perception are then discussed in such a manner as to develop a harmony between information and phenomenological approaches. Our hope is that this synthesis will encourage developments along a course which Berlyne helped to chart.

THE STRUCTURE OF THE WORK OF ART

The work of art occasions a unique and indirect encounter between the spectator and the artist, who would otherwise never meet. From the artist's viewpoint, the work embodies his perceptions, beliefs, feelings, stylistic innovations, etc. From the viewpoint of the spectator, the artist's visual statement provides a rich source of stimulation appealing to mankind's higher faculties. However, the power of the work may not be fully realized unless the spectator is able to interpret and understand it. From a historical perspective, we have evidence of the problems which arise when communication is unsuccessful. Spectators have always rejected stylistic innovations which they were unable to "see" and understand, as in the case of French Impressionist painting. Fortunately, artists have faith in the sincerity and integrity of their innovations, and display remarkable resilience when faced with hostile criticism. Picasso is reported to have responded to a complaint that his portrait of Gertrude Stein did not look like her by tersely stating: "No matter, it will" (cited in Goodman, 1968, p. 33).

The work of art itself comprises an arrangement of material elements such as canvas or wood, oil or acrylic paint, etc., which define its medium and its basic physical qualities. The pattern or configuration of these material elements then determines the structure of the work. Moles (1966) has elegantly argued that a work of art can simultaneously embody qualitatively independent levels of organization superimposed upon each other. Each level conveys its own unique message and possesses specific rules of organization. The two major levels of organization described both by Berlyne (1971, 1974) and Moles (1966) are the semantic and the aesthetic. Before considering these levels in greater detail, it should be noted that the notion of qualitatively independent domains of organization has gained acceptance among information theorists, who deal not only in pictorial but also in written material (Craik & Lockhart, 1972; Sutherland, 1972).

Goodman (1968) offers a simple and clear account of the semantic information which may be contained within a picture. "The plain fact is that a picture, to represent an object, must be a symbol for it, stand for it, refer to it. . . . Denotation is the core of representation and is independent of resemblance" (p. 5). Similarly, Werner and Kaplan (1963) argue that symbolic relations are isolated by an "intentional act of denotative reference . . . which culminates in one entity being 'taken' to designate another" (p. 21). In short, the domain of semantic information has a practical utility and informs about the external world (Berlyne, 1971; Moles, 1966). The semantic domain also encompasses those special techniques which delineate objects and define dimensions such as perspective and equilibrium (Moles, 1966). These techniques are essentially geometrical, as opposed to expressive (Werner & Kaplan, 1963).

Aesthetic information, on the other hand, includes the expressive organization of physical and sensory aspects of a work of art, which does not serve to denote objects. This category of information is very broad indeed, defining the style of a painting through the selection of particular colors, brush-stroke techniques, or ways of connecting forms. According to Moles (1966), aesthetic information (1) is specific to the channel transmitting it (e.g., a painting versus a symphony); (2) determines "internal states" including emotions and sensory reactions; (3) is not translatable (e.g., a symphony cannot replace an animated cartoon); and (4) is uniquely personal. The term used by Berlyne (1971) which most closely approximates these ideas is "syntactic information."

The work of art differs radically from everyday pictures and signs, in that aesthetic information is equal in value and importance to semantic information. In fact, in certain styles of art, semantic information is virtually nonexistent (e.g., the work of Jackson Pollock). The effects of works of art on the spectator can therefore be determined by (1) the independent effects of the semantic and aesthetic domains, and (2) the interactional effects of these domains. Effects which primarily originate from the semantic domain are diverse, ranging from classicism to superrealism and surrealism. Uniquely aesthetic effects encompass a variety of styles, including, for example, American color-field painting of the 1950s, and hard-edge painting. The special interactions which can occur between semantic and aesthetic information have been discussed with reference to French Impressionist painting (Cupchik, 1976). In Monet's work, for example, color bridges the gap between the two domains. It can serve to create light and sensory effects in the aesthetic domain, while at the same time denoting an object by falling within a particular shape or outline. In general, blurring the boundaries between the semantic and the aesthetic domains serves to seize the appearance of reality (Wölfflin, 1915), and adds a temporal dimension by suggesting an interaction of the object with its setting.

Semantic and aesthetic information give a work of art its unique character and meaning. They do not however, account for the special appeal and intrinsic value associated with a work of art. This appeal has instead been attributed to a more general quality of the work. Terms like originality, novelty, and unexpectedness have been used to describe the quality which shapes aesthetic appeal. Collectively, these variables contribute to *uncertainty*, and this collative property affects aesthetic behavior and response (Berlyne, 1971, 1974). Moles (1966, p. 134) has shown that uncertainty (or complexity) can be evaluated separately for both the semantic and the aesthetic domains. Berlyne (1971, 1974) has argued that, in general, spectators prefer intermediate levels of uncertainty in an exploratory-choice task. Recalling our earlier critique of Berlyne's theory, it is important to remember that uncertainty does not merely reside in the work. Instead, it represents an interaction of the structure of the work and the interpretive skills of the spectator. In sum, an evaluation of the originality of the work of art can best be performed by experts who are familiar with the range and history of art. The preferences of a particular spectator should be seen in the light of the objective originality of the painting as well as his own needs, visual sensibilities, and personal history.

A few final words should be offered about the extrinsic value of a work of art. As an independent physical object, it bridges the gap in time between creation and aesthetic episodes. Its material existence is of course threatened by the ravages of time (Dufrenne, 1973) and historical events, as any art historian or restorer will attest. The work of art may also sometimes serve purposes which could hardly be considered aesthetic in nature. A painting, for example, may be used to obtain information about the physical appearance of historical personages (Dufrenne, 1973) and customs of a particular period in history. It may also remain forgotten in a vault accruing monetary value amidst a large uncatalogued collection. Finally, as an instance of modern vulgarity, consider the purchase of a work of art because it matches the color of a living room wall. The artist who is dependent for his livelihood on the capricious wishes of the collector may choose to overlook these peccadillos. Such diverse and sometimes less than noble functions reflect the extrinsic or instrumental value of art objects.

PERCEIVING THE WORK OF ART

The attitude which a spectator assumes toward a work of art differs fundamentally from that which he adopts during his mundane daily activities. Everyday perception tends to be extrinsically and pragmatically oriented, concerned with achieving of goals. In contrast, aesthetic perception tends to reflect an intrinsically motivated search for stimulation

(Berlyne, 1974). This implies that the spectator engages in the aesthetic episode for its own immediate experiential or reward value. Moles (1966) argues that extrinsically and intrinsically oriented motives correspond to semantic and aesthetic information, respectively. A similar notion of contrasting viewpoints is also revealed in the work of Gestalt-oriented psychologists such as Arnheim (1971) and Werner and Kaplan (1963). They argue that expressive or physiognomic perception (associated with intrinsic motivation and aesthetic information) actually develops chronologically before geometrical-technical perception (associated with extrinsic motivation and semantic information). However, our scientifically oriented education, Arnheim (1971) suggests, devalues and suppresses physiognomic or expressive perception. A practically oriented society may prefer that people react mechanically to the signs and signals around them, rather than "know" the world at its expressive level (Werner & Kaplan, 1963). The adopting of an expressive or aesthetic viewpoint, therefore, requires an ability to shift away from society's pragmatic attitude.

The psychological aestheticians face a challenge when describing the processes which underlie the spectator's encounter with a work of art. They generally agree that the spectator adopts a special viewpoint or set when engaged in aesthetic perception. However, fundamental conceptual differences do exist concerning the underlying processes. Behaviorally oriented aestheticians like Berlyne described the spectator as *reacting* to the work of art. Berlyne (1974) cites the results from a variety of factor-analytic studies, involving both visual and musical material, which suggest two dimensions of reaction: Uncertainty (e.g., simple-complex) and Hedonic Tone (e.g., displeasing-pleasing). Uncertainty judgments tend to increase monotonically as a function of the objective complexity of the stimulus. Hedonic Tone judgments are represented by an inverted U-shaped curve, suggesting an interaction between the properties of the stimulus and an organizational process in the spectator.

A phenomenologically oriented approach maintains that the spectator does not merely *react* to a work of art but rather *interacts* with it. The spectator brings to the aesthetic episode skills of visual sensibility (Hester, 1975), needs, moods, feelings, expectations, etc. which shape his examination and experience of the work of art. Dufrenne (1973) acknowledges the role of the spectator when he states that the work of art is transformed into an "aesthetic object" during the process of aesthetic perception. We want further to state that the spectator responds to the aesthetic object at many levels simultaneously, including the sensory-physiological, cognitive-intellectual, emotional, etc. The integration of these many levels reflects the meanings of the aesthetic object for the spectator at a particular moment. Thus set, context, and individual differences among spectators may eventuate in very different "reactions" along the uncertainty or hedonic-tone factors for the very same aesthetic materials.

STAGES OF PERCEPTION

We have drawn attention to some of the shortcomings implicit in the marriage of information theory and behaviorism. Moreover, we have suggested that what is missing is a phenomenological paradigm for integration which can account for the origins and development of meaning in art. The notion that perception unfolds over time and passes through successive stages of processing is a natural way to begin our task.

A surprising amount of agreement has been shown concerning the time course of perception in general, and aesthetic perception in particular. Experimentalists and phenomenologists have independently arrived at a description of three distinct stages. Berlyne (1971) cited early tachistoscopic research which suggested that the perception of patterns proceeds through a series of stages. During the first stage, only general structural qualities, such as size or extent, are discussed. The second stage involves identifying the stimulus as a member of a particular class of objects. The third stage results in the discrimination of specific details.

Information theorists have similarly distinguished three stages in the perception of written materials, each of which involves unique processing operations (Craik & Lockhart, 1972; Lockhart, Craik, & Jacoby, 1976). The preliminary stage involves an analysis of physical and sensory properties of the stimulus such as lines, angles, or brightness. The remaining two stages involve progressively more semantic and cognitive analyses. A second stage leads to the recognition or labeling of stimulus content by matching it "against stored abstractions from past learning" (Craik & Lockhart, 1972, p. 675). The third and "deepest" of the "levels of processing" involves elaboration and enrichment owing to the incorporation of associations or images from the individual's memory which were triggered by the stimulus.

The French phenomenologist Michel Dufrenne (1973), who follows in the tradition of Merleau-Ponty, has also delineated three qualitatively different stages of aesthetic perception. The first stage of perception, *presence,* involves a global and prereflective awareness of the sensuous qualities of the aesthetic object. The second stage, *representation* and *imagination,* leads to the distinguishing and identification of objects and events. The third stage involves *reflection* and *feeling.* It is at this level that the spectator understands and empathizes with the inherent expressive qualities of the work. The later stages provide a basis for the *depth* of the spectator's reaction to the work. The similarity of the stages described by the phenomenologists and the experimentalists offers convergent evidence for the existence of three stages of perception.

Some differences between the approaches of information theorists involved in memory research (e.g., Craik & Lockhart, 1972) and psychological aestheticians should, however, be noted. Information theorists emphasize the practical or instrumental value of perception. Hence, they maintain that the "transient products" of preliminary physical or sensory analyses may be discarded in favor of the results of "deeper" semantic analyses (Craik & Lockhart, 1972). They also argue (Lockhart, Craik, & Jacoby, 1976) that a person is consciously aware of only that level of analysis which receives attention and extensive processing. From the perspective of psychological aesthetics, all levels of processing, including sensory and semantic analyses, are of equal importance. Further, the aesthetic set of the spectator sensitizes him to all levels of analysis. These "levels" may be processed simultaneously or in parallel. This implies that the aesthetic set involves a broader mode of attention, which can grasp interactions among the levels.

Consider the following example in light of these criticisms. Two individuals are about to enter an art gallery which is hosting an exhibition of Impressionist paintings. One of these spectators knows very little about art and has never experienced the work of Monet and his contemporaries in any intensive way. The other person is a devoted admirer of this school of painting, and is well informed concerning its fundamental attributes and subject matter. The information theorists and psychologists who adopt Berlyne's perspective would have us believe that both these individuals would pass through the same three stages of perception, and in the same sequence. Perhaps they would allow for the fact that the expert spectator might traverse them more quickly; but that is all.

Yet, it seems unlikely that speed of processing is the only difference. The expert possesses an aesthetic set which is already highly tuned to the sensory and physical qualities of Impressionism. Moreover, he may also already possess many memories and attendant emotions derived from past exposure. Thus, is there any reason to believe that he needs to go through stages at all? On the other hand, his interest in Impressionism may be based *solely* on an appreciation of its physical and sensory qualities. He does not need to proceed to any other stages, since this is the effective locus of what Impressionism means to him. In this case, the first stage could in effect represent a consolidation of attributes from the various "stages." The viewer may never have negotiated his way through them sequentially. In contrast, we may consider the novice spectator. Perhaps his aesthetic set constrains him to search only for semantic content, and for the "realistic" qualities of painting. He does not enter the first stage, which is sensory and physical, other than in the sense that he must register the paintings in his visual system. The syntactic qualities are bypassed in his search for quality of realistic representation. In addition, the works evoke no memories or associations, since he simply considers the paintings in the same way as one would view a pleasant postcard.

When stages become interchangeable, when one stage is not a consolidation of its predecessor, or when a given stage may be unnecessary owing to aesthetic set, we are left with a series of processes which cannot be understood as "stages" in any accepted sense.

Of foremost importance in our discussion, then, is the principle of aesthetic set, and the plasticity of perception itself. Depending on his skills, the spectator may analyze and act on perceptions in various ways. The modes of viewing which he adopts may be subject to spontaneous revision. The situational context which the viewer finds himself in, and his frame of mind, are crucial contributors to the fluidity of his perception.

The initial perception of physical and sensory properties in an aesthetic object may provide a background or horizon against which the recognized elements are perceived. As the examination of the object proceeds, all levels can simultaneously contribute to the aesthetic experience. The "stages" of perception may simply be components of aesthetic perception, with little inherent organizational quality. Thus, what we must now do is take the components of the sequential, stage-oriented approach and restructure them in such a way as to allow for the plasticity of perception, change over time, and the concept of meaning as a holistic, context-bound process.

Imagine a graph, such as the one depicted in Figure 1, which has three axes corresponding to three-dimensional space. We have labeled these axes in accordance with Dufrenne's (1973) tripartite division of

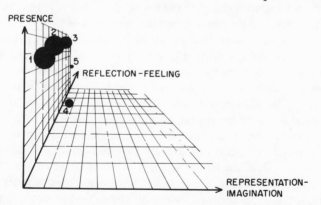

FIGURE 1. Aesthetic experience in three dimensions over a series of psychological moments. (Based on Dufrenne, 1973.)

aesthetic perception. Each of these axes represents continua of psychological *salience* for the spectator, with the arrows indicating directions of increasing magnitude. The result is a three-dimensional structure with points in the space representing various possible combinations of the three continua in terms of relative magnitude.

Now suppose that we brought a spectator into our laboratory and presented him with a slide of a Rembrandt painting. Furthermore, suppose that at any given moment we could stop the viewing process, and elicit from the viewer what was foremost in his mind as he viewed the painting. Our scales would naturally have been devised in such a way as to tap into Dufrenne's (1973) three-factor typology. The result of our inquiry would be a composite measure reflecting the relative weight or importance which each of the three factors has in determining the make-up of the viewer's perception. Then, by using coordinates on the graph, we could plot the location of this psychological moment in the space. We have chosen dots of decreasing size as a means of indicating position on the receding third dimension (reflection and feeling). In general, the size of the dots indicates the relative importance of this dimension's contribution to the viewer's psychological moment.

Having plotted this initial point, we could elect to make another measurement to see whether his perception had changed over time. By performing this testing successively over a certain span of time, we could visually represent the course or evolution of the viewer's aesthetic perceptions. On the graph (Figure 1) the earliest measurement is indicated by the number 1, and so on. This series of progressively plotted points has a number of theoretical implications which are intriguing from a psychological point of view. We are going to suggest that, at the time when measurement is made, the previously plotted points form a horizon, context, or, in Gestalt terms, "ground" against which the most recently measured psychological moment is perceived. The relative contributions of the three factors to this "ground" effect are determined by their magnitude on the dimensions, and by their proximity in time to the final perception. Ultimately, a time-series or path analysis may enable us to examine trends and constraints in the course of aesthetic perception.

Thus, in Figure 1, the first percept (1) with a high value on *presence*, and low values on the other dimensions, would form the context within which the second percept (2) is interpreted. This figure-ground kind of analysis could be carried out at any point in the series. It allows us to see not only how perception changes over time, but also the possible influence of earlier percepts on later ones.

Let us return to our previous example which involved a novice viewer and an expert entering an exhibition of Impressionist painting. We have suggested the crucial role in aesthetic perception played by the perceptual set of the viewer. Our novice spectator (see Figure 2A) has adopted essentially a pragmatic set. He is searching for quality of reproduction; his criterion for "good" art depends heavily on how photographic it appears to him. Thus, the first measurement which we might obtain from him (1) would represent a percept which is high on the Representation–Imagination dimension ($R–I$), with moderate input from Presence (P), and very little from Reflection and Feelings ($R–F$). As he probes the work before him in terms of his personal criterion, we make another measurement (2). As we continue to make periodic measurements over time, it becomes clear that his perceptions are relatively static. His rigid set and quality criterion constrain the evolution of his perceptions and create the clustering effect of Figure 2A. Our final measure (5) indicates a high loading on both the P and $R–F$ dimensions. This appears curious to us until we inquire as to his final verdict on the painting. He tells us that he finds the blurring of outline and exhuberant coloration frustrating, since it obscures the subject matter of the painting. In light of his aesthetic set and the sequence of his perceptions, this now makes sense to us. He found the Impressionist stylistic conventions obstructing and confining, rather than evocative and expressive.

Our expert viewer presents a somewhat different picture (see Figure 2B). He has seen many similar exhibitions in the past and is a devotee of the Impressionist masters. Accordingly, his perceptual set is highly attuned to the characteristic properties of the paintings before him. Our first measurement (1) places him high on both the P and $R–F$ dimensions. The sensory qualities of the works fill his vision, and he responds in an emotional, pleasurable manner. Over time, we see that he begins to probe detail and subject matter more closely, but the high loadings in the P and $R–F$ dimensions remain. They form the context within which his perception evolves.

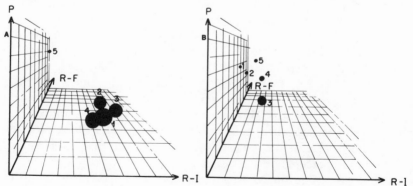

FIGURE 2. A hypothetical comparison of the aesthetic experience of novice (A) and expert (B) spectators in response to an Impressionist painting.

What are the benefits of our scheme, and how are they superior to other conceptualizations? For one thing, it is uniquely sensitive to individual differences and the unfolding of perception over time. It also allows us to infer the contextual significance which earlier percepts have on later ones, and how placement in the space depends on aesthetic set. Our model accounts for the fact that an expert could move almost instantaneously from sensory phases in perception to reflection and feeling. In contrast, Craik and Lockhart (1972) would predict a uniform progression from dimension P to dimension $R–I$ to dimension $R–F$, with no input from other dimensions, few individual differences, and little in the way of contextual effects. Our essential objection to this approach is that it imposes a rigid processing sequence which does not do justice to the plasticity of human perception.

Clearly, this outline is not as comprehensive as one would like. Moreover, it is no easy matter to conceptualize in four dimensions. The tentative nature of our model is, however, a problem which further theoretical articulation and progressive experimentation should help resolve.

The strength of the model is that it does justice to the fluid, multifaceted nature of aesthetic perception. It allows us a glimpse of how reactions develop as a function of time and salient perceptual components. We have not sacrificed what is fruitful in earlier appoaches (Berlyne, 1971, 1974; Dufrenne, 1973; Moles, 1966), but have integrated past work with phenomenology, and with developments in cognitive psychology. Hopefully, the future will provide us with an indication of our model's empirical validity.

CONCLUSIONS

In this chapter, we have striven to develop an appreciation of the new experimental aesthetics, its brief past and promising future. Hopefully, its unique place within psychology, as well as its differentiation from other disciplines which are concerned with aesthetics, has become apparent.

The work of Daniel E. Berlyne is, and will remain, a cornerstone of experimental aesthetics. His integration of behavioral theory, information theory, and intrinsic motivation provided the impetus necessary for progress in this complex field. However, as is customary in science, any given theoretical approach only represents an approximation to the hidden nature of the phenomena we seek to uncover. We have, accordingly, pointed out the junctures where previous efforts have been inadequate.

No doubt our own attempts at understanding will prove similarly vulnerable to critical evaluation.

Finally, we have presented the beginnings of a model of aesthetic perception which seeks to consolidate past research with our expectations for progress in the field. We have endeavoured to structure this model in such a way as to do justice to the nature of aesthetic perception, its depth and richness. Much work remains to be done. A sensitive methodology and much theoretical elaboration are required to explore the psychological moment and the unfolding of aesthetic perception.

ACKNOWLEDGMENTS

The authors wish to express their appreciation to Dr. Felix Klajner of the University of Toronto and Dr. Constantine X. Poulos of the Addiction Research Foundation for their most helpful comments about the manuscript.

REFERENCES

ARNHEIM, R. *Art and visual perception.* Berkeley: University of California Press, 1971.
BERLYNE, D. E. *Conflict, arousal, and curiosity.* New York: McGraw-Hill, 1960.
BERLYNE, D. E. *Aesthetics and psychobiology.* New York: Appleton-Century-Crofts, 1971.
BERLYNE, D. E. *Studies in the new experimental aesthetics: Steps toward an objective psychology of aesthetic appreciation.* Washington, D.C.: Hemisphere Publishing, 1974.
BORING, E. G. *A history of experimental psychology.* New York: Appleton-Century-Crofts, 1950.
CLARK, K. E. *Leonardo da Vinci: An account of his life and development.* Cambridge, England: Cambridge University Press, 1939.
CRAIK, F. I. M., & LOCKHART, R. S. Levels of processing: A framework for memory research. *Journal of Verbal Learning and Verbal Behaviour,* 1972, *2,* 671–684.
CUPCHIK, G. C. Perspectives théoriques et empiriques sur la peintures impressioniste. *Bulletin de Psychologie,* 1976, *36,* 720–729.
CUPCHIK, G. C., & BERLYNE, D. E. The perception of collative properties in visual stimuli. *Scandinavian Journal of Psychology,* 1979, *20,* 93–104.
DUFRENNE, M. *The phenomenology of aesthetic perception.* Evanston: Northwestern University Press, 1973.
ERTEL, S. Exploratory choice and verbal judgement. In D. E. Berlyne & K. B. Madsen (Eds.), *Pleasure, reward, preference.* New York: Academic, 1974.
FECHNER, G. T. *Vorschule der Aesthetik.* Leipzig: Breitkopf & Haertel, 1876.
FRANK, H. *Grundlagenprobleme der Informations-Ästhetik und erste Anwendung auf die Mime pure.* Quickborn: Schnelle, 1959.
FREUD, S. *Leonardo da Vinci* (Trans. A. A. Brill). New York: Dodd, Mead, 1932. (Originally published, 1910.)
GOODMAN, N. *Languages of art.* New York: Bobbs-Merrill, 1968.
GUNZENHÄUSER, R. *Ästhetisches Mass und ästhetische Information.* Quickborn: Schnelle, 1962.
HESTER, M. Sensibility and visual acts. *American Philosophical Quarterly,* 1975, *12,* 299–308.

Kolers, P. A. Reading and knowing. *Canadian Journal of Psychology*, 1979, *33*, 106–117.

Kris, E. *Psychoanalytic explorations in art*. New York: International Universities Press, 1952.

Lockhart, R. S., Craik, F. I. M., & Jacoby, L. L. Depth of processing in recognition and recall: Some aspects of a general memory system. In J. Brown (Ed.), *Recognition and recall*. London: Wiley, 1976.

Moles, A. *Information theory and aesthetic perception*. Urbana: University of Illinois Press, 1966.

Pfister, O. Die Entstehung der künstlerischen Inspiration. *Imago*, 1913, *II*, 481–512.

Pfister, O. *Expressionism in art: Its psychological and biological basis* (Trans. B. Low & M. A. Meugge). New York: Dutton, 1923.

Rank, O. *Der Künstler: Ansätze zu einer sexual Psychologie*. Wien: H. Heller, 1907.

Read, H. *The meaning of art*. Hammondsworth, Middlesex: Penguin Books, 1949. (Originally published, 1931.)

Rosenthal, R. *Experimenter effects in behavioral research*. New York: Appleton-Century-Crofts, 1966.

Shannon, C. E., & Weaver, W. *Mathematical theory of communication*. Urbana: University of Illinois Press, 1949.

Silverman, I. *The human subject in the psychological laboratory*. New York: Pergamon, 1977.

Sutherland, N. S. Object perception. In E. C. Carterette & M. P. Friedman (Eds.), *Handbook of perception* (Vol. 3). New York: Academic, 1972.

Vasari, G. *Lives of the artists*. Hammondsworth, Middlesex: Penguin Books, 1965. (Originally published, 1568.)

Watson, J. B. *Psychology from the standpoint of a behaviorist*. Philadelphia: Lippincott, 1924.

Werner, H., & Kaplan, B. *Symbol formation*. New York: Wiley, 1963.

Wölfflin, H. *Principles of art history*. New York: Dover, 1950. (*Kunstgeschichtliche Grundbegriffe*. Munich: Bruckmann, 1915.)

20

Recent Developments in Experimental Aesthetics

A Summary of Berlyne Laboratory Research Activities, 1974–1977

The D. E. Berlyne Laboratory of Aplopathematic and Thelematoscopic Pneumatology at the University of Toronto was, for a relatively brief period, the most active North American center for experimental aesthetics research. This chapter will outline and summarize some of the recent work by lab members, focusing on the period between the publication of our *Studies in the New Experimental Aesthetics* (Berlyne, 1974) and the closing of the lab in August 1977.

The chapter is divided into three sections. In the first, the objectives and assumptions of our research will be presented, as will our two research approaches. The second section will consider in some detail several of our research projects. The third section will consist of an annotated bibliography of articles and papers written by lab members, covering activities since our 1974 book.

OBJECTIVES, ASSUMPTIONS, AND APPROACHES

As a group, we were working on the development of an empirically based taxonomy of aesthetic stimuli, a classification scheme based on the perceptual judgments of ordinary subjects. Our assumption was that a

FRANCIS G. HARE • Department of Psychology, Ryerson Polytechnical Institute, Toronto, Ontario M5B 1E8, Canada. Former director of the Berlyne Laboratory and research associate to Dr. D.E. Berlyne.

knowledge of the perceptually salient attributes of aesthetic stimuli was the first step in an analysis of the determinants of hedonic value and the role of hedonic value in the determination of behavior.

Another guiding assumption was that responses to aesthetic stimuli such as paintings were not basically different from other kinds of behavior. We defined aesthetic stimuli as works of art or components of such works. We used real music and synthetically generated tone sequences and chords, real paintings and synthetically generated visual patterns, sculpture, architecture, and, in an interesting tie-in with the interpersonal-attraction literature, photographs of human faces. We defined aesthetic behavior to include a wide variety of verbal and nonverbal responses, thus permitting analysis of the interrelationships of various responses considered indicative of "pleasure," "choice," or "preference." By broadly defining aesthetic stimuli and aesthetic behavior and by considering aesthetic behavior to be common and normal rather than unique, we hoped to help coax experimental aesthetics (one of the very few centenarians in psychology) back into the mainstream by underlining its close relationships with other areas, such as perception, motivation, individual differences, scaling theory, and social psychology.

Two terms were used in our 1974 book to describe our approaches to experimental aesthetics. These terms, *synthetic* and *analytic*, define the two complementary research strategies we have followed. Following a synthetic approach, one tests hypotheses about the effects of some particular stimulus variable. Stimuli are chosen or generated to represent different levels of that variable. Stimulus interrelationships are clearly defined. Hevner's (e.g., 1937) series of studies investigating the effects of musical mode, melodic line, rhythmic motion, dissonance, pitch, and tempo would be considered synthetic research, as would Crozier's (1974) work on the relationship between stimulus complexity and judgments of pleasingness.

One difficulty with the synthetic approach is that a very large number of stimulus attributes could be defined for any aesthetic medium. Considerable research time, effort, and money could conceivably go into the investigation of some attribute that contributes only minimally to the determination of responses to, for example, music. We therefore assume that those attributes that dominate perception of the stimulus material are the ones most likely to play a part in determining aesthetic behavior. The analytic approach takes as its starting point the attempt to discover attributes that are predominant in subjects' perception of the stimulus material.

Until very recently, following an analytic approach meant factor analyzing a large number of responses to the stimuli in an effort to find common threads in subjects' characterizations of the stimulus material. Sticking with examples drawn from research using musical stimuli,

Gundlach (1935) and Henkin (1955) illustrate the analytic approach. The major problem with the factor-analytic technique as used in this kind of research is that it is necessary for the researcher to provide the words used by the subjects in their characterizations of the material. The danger is that one factor may be overemphasized and another ignored as the result of an investigator's predilection for certain scales or adjectives at the expense of others.

In order to overcome the limitations of the factor-analytic technique and realize the aims of the analytic approach, we turned to multi-dimensional-similarity scaling. Imagine music excerpts floating in a room, floating subject to one constrain: similar excerpts float close together, and the more dissimilar two excerpts were, the further apart they would be. If you were to walk from one end of this room to the other, sampling excerpts along the way, you would have an arrangement of the stimuli along a dimension of similarity. The data base for this stimulus configuration is subjects' pairwise judgments of interstimulus similarity. If ten stimuli are used there are 45 nonredundant pairings of the stimuli. For each stimulus pairing the subject is asked to indicate on a seven-point scale the similarity between the two members of the pair. It is important to note that similarity is left undefined. This is consistent with the goal of deriving or discovering, rather than defining, the dominant attributes of the stimulus material.

Having derived an n-dimensional similarity space, one then must interpret these dimensions. This is done by scaling the stimuli in terms of a variety of specific attributes and then correlating stimulus values on each of those scales with stimulus values on the similarity dimensions. A high correlation indicates that the attribute in question is at least related to something that subjects took into account when judging similarity. To complete this outline it should be noted that the analytic approach complements the synthetic in that these derived and interpreted dimensions of similarity represent variables that are assumed to be important determinants of aesthetic behavior. The precise effects of these variables may be investigated following the synthetic approach. Two studies reported in the next section (Hare, 1977, 1978; see Annotated Bibliography) in fact demonstrate this complementarity of approaches, with the perceptually dominant dimensions of music being identified in an analytic study, and variables associated with the dimensions being manipulated in a later synthetic study.

RECENT RESEARCH

Seven analytic and three synthetic research projects will be presented in this section, categorized according to medium.

Painting

Berlyne Dimensions of Perception of Exotic and Pre-Renaissance Paintings

This project (1975) is a sequel to the Berlyne and Ogilvie (1974) research using Western Renaissance and post-Renaissance paintings. That study was the first lab project to use the multidimensional-similarity scaling technique with similarity an undefined concept. Results had indicated the usefulness of the approach and that subjects not only had little difficulty making the similarity judgments but also tended to agree in their judgments. The research also supported the idea that perceptually dominant attributes enter into the determination of aesthetic behavior.

This second project extended the range of stimulus material in order to address the question of whether the results of the first study were general, or whether they applied only to the particular set of paintings. Twenty paintings were used, sampling non-Western art and Western pre-Renaissance art. In the first experiment, subjects made judgments of interstimulus similarity for each of the 190 possible nonredundant pairings of the 20 stimuli. These responses were then analyzed using the INDSCAL—individual differences multidimensional similarity scaling technique—(Carroll, 1972; Wish & Carroll, 1974). A three-dimensional solution was accepted, in accordance with criteria suggested by Shepard (1972) and Wish and Carroll (1974).

In order to interpret these dimensions of unidentified similarity, two more experiments were conducted. In these experiments, subjects scaled the paintings in terms of various attributes, using descriptive, affective, and stylistic rating scales. These scales, and factors derived from an intercorrelation of the scales, were then correlated with the similarity dimensions. A high product–moment correlation of stimulus values on a scale with stimulus values on a dimension strongly suggests that the attribute is either perceptually salient or strongly related to some other attribute that is.

Identification of the similarity dimensions presented some problems, because correlations of scales and factors with the dimensions, though significant, were relatively weak. Tentative identification of the dimensions was made, with the second dimension being related to Uncertainty, a factor derived from clarity, order, and balance rating scales, and the third dimension related to Arousal, a factor derived from interest and potency rating scales. The first dimension could not be interpreted.

Subjects in the final experiment of this study made pairwise preference judgments indicating which of two stimuli thay preferred and the degree to which one was preferred over the other. The former data were analyzed using MDPREF (Chang & Carroll, 1968), a multidimensional preference scaling technique, and the latter data were treated as representing the preference distance between the two members of each pair. These data were analyzed using the INDSCAL procedure. These spaces were then related to the similarity space. A modest degree of relationship was found, indicating that, to a certain extent, the perceptually dominant dimensions also underlie preference judgments.

Berlyne: Similarity and Preference Judgments of Indian and Canadian Subjects Exposed to Western Paintings

This analytic project (1976) followed essentially the same procedures as outlined in the first project. The subject population was expanded rather dramatically as undergraduate psychology students at the University of Toronto were joined on our data sheets by Indian students and villagers. Western Renaissance and post-Renaissance paintings were used. Two types of similarity spaces were derived from subjects' judgments of interstimulus similarities. The first type was subgroup-specific. A similarity space was derived for each of the three subgroups of subjects, based on the similarity judgments of that group. The second type was a joint analysis, including the judgments of all subjects. The data of all subjects can be accommodated within a single similarity space, but the separate spaces show that the groups emphasize attributes to differing degrees. Berlyne's report of the research contains the warning that firm conclusions about cultural differences in perception and aesthetic behavior may not be drawn on the basis of this relatively small-scale project. The results, on the other hand, suggest quite strongly that the multi-dimensional-similarity scaling procedures are applicable in other societies, and could represent a useful method for cross-cultural research.

Berlyne: Extension to Indian Subjects of a Study of Exploratory and Verbal Responses to Visual Patterns

This synthetic research project (1975) continues the cross-cultural investigation of the effects of stimulus complexity. The previous study (Berlyne, Robbins, & Thompson, 1974) compared the reactions of Canadian and Ugandan subjects. The question was whether the findings common to the Ugandan and Canadian subjects would reappear with Indian subjects. Subjects were told to look at the stimuli "for as long as you wish," and their time was recorded. The subject was then requested to rate some of the stimuli on seven-point scales which in this study took the form of ladders, a more familiar device for the subjects. Results in all three subject groups support the importance of factors related to Osgood's (Osgood, Suci, & Tannenbaum, 1957) evaluative and activity dimensions.

Music

Hare: Dimensions of Music Perception

This research was the first extension of the analytic approach into musical stimulus material. Sixteen 10-sec excerpts of recorded music composed between 1700 and 1900 were used.

In the first experiment, musically naive and musically sophisticated subjects made judgments of interstimulus similarity, and the data were submitted to the INDSCAL individual differences scaling procedure. In the joint analysis for the two subgroups, a three-dimensional solution was most appropriate. Of the three dimensions, the first was clearly dominant and common to the two subgroups. The naive and sophisticated subjects were differentiated in terms of the importance attached to the other two dimensions, with the second being more important for the former and the third more important for the latter. This differentiation was supported by separate analyses for the two groups. Two-dimensional solutions were most appropriate in each of the separate analyses, and these dimensions corresponded to the dimensions of the joint analysis.

Two more experiments were conducted in order to interpret the similarity dimensions. In these experiments, subjects performed descriptive, affective, and stylistic scalings of the stimuli. Stimulus values on these scales were then correlated with stimulus values on the dimensions of similarity. Several correlations were quite high, and clearly suggested interpretations of the dimensions. The first dimension, dominant and common to the two subject groups, was interpreted as Tempo/Playfulness, related to judgments of tempo, degree of staccato, amount of activity, degree of playfulness, complexity, and subjective alertness. The second dimension was more important to the naive subjects than to the sophisticated, and was interpreted as Potency, related to judgments of powerfulness and subjective tension. The third dimension was more important to the sophisticated subjects, and was related to date of composition and the extent of the composer's divergence from rules of composition.

In other experiments the dominant Tempo/Playfulness dimension proved to be an important determinant of exploration time, exploratory choice, and preference judgments.

Berlyne: Dimensions of Perception of Exotic and Folk Music

This analytic project (1977) is a replication of Hare's work, except that non-Western music and distinctive Western folk music are used in place of Western "classical" music. In the similarity-scaling experiment, a two-dimensional solution was considered most appropriate. No differences were found between musically naive and musically sophisticated subjects. The two dimensions were interpreted through descriptive, affective, and stylistic scalings of the stimuli. One dimension was related to the strangeness of the music, with Russian and Hungarian folk music at the more familiar end and Far Eastern and African music at the less familiar end. The other dimension was very similar to that found by Hare with western music. It was correlated with a factor derived from tempo, activity, alertness, and playfulness scales.

Subjects also did exploratory-choice, listening-time and preference-judgment tasks. Choice and preference judgments were influenced by the attributes underlying both similarity dimensions, whereas listening time was influenced only by the strangeness of the music.

Hare: Exploring the Perceptually Dominant Dimensions of Music

This synthetic project (1978) was undertaken in order to follow up on some of the hypotheses suggested by Hare's analytic music research and by the theorizing of Kreitler and Kreitler (1972). Stimulus complexity, perceived playfulness and feelings of tension have been identified as important determinants of responses to music. This research was designed to identify the stimulus determinants of complexity, playfulness, and tension. Synthetic musical stimuli were generated, and two experiments were conducted. In the first experiment, tone-presentation rate and stimulus uncertainty were varied. Subjective tension (consistent with the Kreitlers' hypothesis) was a function of presentation rate. Judged complexity was found to be a function of information-transmission rate, calculated by multiplying uncertainty (bits per tone) by tempo (tones per unit time). In the second experiment, presentation rate and degree of staccato were varied. Each of the variables was independently sufficient to produce variations in judged playfulness.

Maher: "Need for Resolution" Ratings for Harmonic Musical Intervals

Maher's synthetic study (1976) was prompted by the observation that the Western musicological literature and the Indian musicological literature do not agree on the emotional concomitants of certain tonal dyads or musical intervals. This led into a consideration of musical dissonance and the possibility of cultural influence on the perception of dissonance. Maher argued that consonance and dissonance are more nearly equivalent to the terms restfulness and restlessness than to the more usual terms pleasant and unpleasant.

Tonal dyads were generated and presented to Indian and Canadian subjects, who rated them on a seven-point Restful–Restless scale. The scale was in English for the Canadian subjects, and Marathi for the Indian subjects. Results supported a cultural theory of musical consonance, rather than a universal, physiologically based (e.g., critical-band) theory.

Architecture and the Built Environment

Oostendorp and Berlyne: Dimensions in the Perception of Architecture

This project (1978) extends the stimulus range in analytic studies to include slides of buildings representing major architectural styles. The four main dimensions in the perception of architecture were identified as design clarity, hedonic tone/arousal, stimulus uncertainty, and familiarity. Several nonverbal measures of exploratory behavior were obtained as part of this project. These were interrelated and related to the perceptual dimensions. Perceptual curiosity induced by the unusualness or interestingness of the building promotes exploratory behavior, as do buildings verbally rated as beautiful or pleasing. These Hedonic Tone/Arousal and Familiarity dimensions also entered into the determination of verbally expressed preference judgments.

Oostendorp: The Identification and Interpretation of Dimensions Underlying Aesthetic Behavior in the Daily Urban Environment

This analytic study (1978) of the urban environment used techniques and procedures outlined in the previous projects on music and paintings, with several notable modifications. In the first place, a new multi-dimensional-similarity scaling model was used in addition to the usual model, and the results of the two procedures were compared. In the second place, Oostendorp investigated the effects of familiarity with an environment on the perception of that environment. A third objective was to compare responses to color slides of the area with responses made while present in the area. A fourth point involved the comparison of two areas, one modern and suburban, the other containing a mixture of new and old buildings and located in the heart of town. Related to this fourth point was the fifth concern, reflecting a somewhat different orientation in

Oostendorp's work as compared with earlier projects. An attempt was made to identify particular types of aesthetic behavior associated with given environments. For example, the aesthetic behavior in the modern area was identified as Contemplation, related to descriptive activities. In the mixed area, the dominant dimension was related to an Originality versus Banality dimension, suggested by some environmental asetheticians as being a major determinant of aesthetic value. A second dimension in the mixed area was associated with potency and feelings of alertness, and was related to affective responses.

Human Faces and Interpersonal Attraction

Milord: Aesthetic Aspects of Faces

This last analytic project (1978) extended our stimulus range to cover human faces as aesthetic stimuli and as cues to interpersonal interactions. Milord briefly argues that the kind of work we do, using multi-dimensional-similarity scaling methods in order to establish perceptual spaces based on the data of individual subjects, is consistent with the aims of phenomenological psychology, an argument that deserves further development.

Milord used the usual techniques and procedures, except that in his first series of experiments he selected faces categorized according to race, sex, age and expression. In his second series of experiments he did away with these obvious criteria for judgment and used faces that were of white college-age males and were virtually expressionless. Various verbal and nonverbal responses to the stimuli were obtained in addition to similarity scalings. Results supported some earlier research on the important aspects of faces, and added others that grow out of this consideration of the face as an aesthetic stimulus. In other words, faces function in much the same way as music, painting, and architecture, with aspects that arouse curiosity and interest and encourage exploration; but because they are faces of human beings, there is an added dimension of the possibility of social interaction.

ANNOTATED BIBLIOGRAPHY

BERLYNE, D. E. Dimensions of perception of exotic and pre-Renaissance paintings. *Canadian Journal of Psychology*, 1975, 29, 151–173.

Twenty non-Western and pre-Renaissance Western paintings were used. A similarity space was derived from subjects' judgments of interstimulus similarity. Dimensions were interpreted through descriptive, affective, and stylistic ratings. A preference space was derived from pairwise preference judgments. Relationships between the similarity and preference spaces were discussed.

BERLYNE, D. E. Extension to Indian subjects of a study of exploratory and verbal responses to visual patterns. *Journal of Cross-Cultural Psychology*, 1975, *6*, 316–330.

A cross-cultural experiment using synthetic stimuli representing a complexity variable. Dependent measures were looking time, verbal-descriptive and affective scaling, and pairwise preference judgments. The issue of cross-cultural validation of experimental aesthetics findings is discussed.

BERLYNE, D. E. Similarity and preference judgments of Indian and Canadian subjects exposed to Western paintings. *International Journal of Psychology*, 1976, *11*, 43–55.

A cross-cultural analytic project using 10 Western post-Renaissance paintings. Indian students, Indian village residents, and Canadian students made pairwise judgments of interstimulus similarity. A similarity space was derived from these data. Canadian students also rated the paintings on a variety of descriptive, affective, and stylistic scales in order to interpret the dimensions. Other Canadian students made pairwise similarity judgments with respect to various specific attributes of the paintings. A final group of Indian students, Indian villagers, and Canadian students made pairwise preference judgments. Results were compared and discussed, with special attention paid to the importance of cross-cultural research.

BERLYNE, D. E. The affective significance of uncertainty. In G. Serban (Ed.), *Psychopathology of human adaptation*. New York: Plenum, 1976.

This theoretical paper discusses subjective uncertainty as a source of affect, various determinants of uncertainty, the motivational properties of uncertainty reduction, and the role of uncertainty in aesthetic behavior.

BERLYNE, D. E. The new experimental aesthetics and the problem of classifying works of art. *Scientific Aesthetics*, 1976, *1*, 85–106.

The synthetic and analytic approaches to experimental aesthetics are outlined, and an overview of several lab-research projects is presented.

BERLYNE, D. E. *The new experimental aesthetics and environmental psychology*. Paper read at the seventh annual conference of the Environmental Design Research Association, Vancouver, B. C., May 26, 1976.

Relations between Experimental Aesthetics and Environmental Psychology are outlined, as are common methodological issues. The Oostendorp and Berlyne research project is presented.

BERLYNE, D. E. Psychological aesthetics, speculative and scientific. *Leonardo*, 1977, *10*, 56–58.

Opening address to the VIth International Symposium of Empirical Aesthetics, Paris, July 1976.
The differences between nomothetic and idiographic investigations are outlined, and each is related to a type of psychological aesthetics.

BERLYNE, D. E. Dimensions of perception of exotic and folk music. *Scientific Aesthetics*, 1977, *1*, 257–270.

An extension of the Hare (1975, 1977) research project using non-Western music and distinctive Western folk music. A similarity space was derived from subjects' judgments of interstimulus similarity, and the dimensions were interpreted through descriptive, affective, and stylistic scalings of the stimuli. Nonverbal responses were also obtained, as were pairwise preference judgments. Results were compared with those of Hare.

BERLYNE, D. E. Psychological aesthetics. In H. C. Triandis (Ed.), *Handbook of cross-cultural psychology* (Vol. 3). Boston: Allyn & Bacon, 1980.

A wide-ranging examination of issues in psychological aesthetics, with particular emphasis on the effects of one's culture. The importance of cross-cultural research is stressed. Synthetic and analytic research projects are outlined and discussed.

GODKEWITSCH, M. The "golden section": An artifact of stimulus range and measure of preference. *American Journal of Psychology*, 1974, *87*, 269–277.

Examines the literature on the importance of the "golden section" in architecture and visual art, and hypothesizes that the golden-section effects are best explained as an artifact of the way research has been conducted. An experiment is performed supporting this hypothesis.

HARE, F. G. The identification of dimensions underlying verbal and exploratory responses to music through multidimensional scaling. Unpublished doctoral dissertation, University of Toronto, 1975.

Extended the Berlyne and Ogilvie (1974) research with paintings to cover a new type of stimulus material. Sixteen brief excerpts of European tonal music composed between 1700 and 1900 were used. Earlier research on the effects of music and musical stimuli was reviewed, with the studies categorized as either synthetic or analytic. Experiments include the derivation and interpretation of a similarity space, and verbal and nonverbal indications of choice or preference.

HARE, F. G. Dimensions of Music perception. *Scientific Aesthetics*, 1977, 1, 271–290.

Briefer, less technical, and more readily available version of the doctoral dissertation listed above. Analytic research using music excerpts.

HARE, F. G. *Exploring the perceptually dominant dimensions of music.* Paper presented at the 86th Annual Convention of the American Psychological Association, Toronto, September 1, 1978. Symposium: Musical and Extramusical Determinants of Reactions to Musical Materials.

Synthetic project following up on some of the research directions suggested by the analytic project listed above. Musical determinants of subjective tension are investigated, and implications for music therapy are considered. Complexity is shown to be determined by information-transmission rate, combining tempo and stimulus uncertainty. The "playfulness" of a piece of music, an important attribute in subjects' perception of interstimulus similarity in Hare's analytic research, was demonstrated to be a function of information-transmission rate and a staccato-legato variable.

MAHER, T. F. "Need for resolution" ratings for harmonic musical intervals. *Journal of Cross-Cultural Psychology*, 1976, 7, 259–276.

A cross-cultural synthetic research project, inspired by a discrepancy in the Indian and Western musicological literatures with regard to the effects of certain tonal dyads. The concept of musical consonance is examined, and cultural influences in music perception are discussed.

MAHER, T. F., & BERLYNE, D. E. Verbal and exploratory responses to melodic sine-wave musical intervals. Unpublished M.A. thesis, University of Toronto, 1975.

Synthetic research on the effects of melodic musical intervals in which component tones are successively sounded. Assumptions underlying theories of musical consonance are questioned.

MILORD, J. T. Aesthetic aspects of faces: A (somewhat) phenomenological analysis using multidimensional scaling methods. *Journal of Personality and Social Psychology*, 1978, *36*, 205–216.

Points out that multidimensional-similarity scaling is useful in phenomenological investigations. Milord reports an analytic research project using photographs of human faces as stimuli. Similarity spaces are derived and interpreted and related to measures of preference or choice. Results were in some ways similar to those found with other aesthetic stimuli, with interpersonal implications of faces adding a new element.

OOSTENDORP, A. *The identification and interpretation of dimensions underlying aesthetic behaviour in the daily urban environment.* Unpublished doctoral dissertation, University of Toronto, 1978.

An analytic study designed to discover the relationships between the physical characteristics of specific urban areas and aesthetic behaviour in those settings. Two different areas of Toronto were used. One area was modern, suburban, with office buildings. The other area contained a mixture of older and modern buildings. Two multidimensional-similarity scaling techniques were used and compared and their dominant dimensions interpreted as representing types of aesthetic behavior associated with the buildings of the two settings.

OOSTENDORP, A., & BERLYNE, D. E. Dimensions in the perception of architecture. I. Identification and interpretation of the dimensions of similarity. II. Measures of exploratory behavior. III. Multidimensional preference scaling. *Scandinavian Journal of Psychology*, 1978, *19*, 73–82; 83–89; 145–150.

This analytic research project extends the range of stimulus material to include architecture. Twenty stimulus slides were used, representing major architectural styles. A similarity space was derived from pairwise judgments of interstimulus similarity. The space was interpreted through descriptive, affective, stylistic, and technical scalings of the stimuli. Verbal and nonverbal measures of choice or preference were interrelated, and related to the perceptual dimensions.

REFERENCES

BERLYNE, D. E. *Studies in the new experimental aesthetics.* Washington, D.C.: Hemisphere, 1974.

BERLYNE, D. E., & OGILVIE, J. C. Dimensions of perception of paintings. In D. E. Berlyne (Ed.), *Studies in the new experimental aesthetics.* Washington, D.C.: Hemisphere, 1974.

BERLYNE, D. E., ROBBINS, M. C., & THOMPSON, R. A cross-cultural study of exploratory and verbal responses to visual patterns varying in complexity. In D. E. Berlyne (Ed.), *Studies in the new experimental aesthetics.* Washington, D.C.: Hemisphere, 1974.

CARROLL, J. D. Individual differences in multidimensional scaling. In R. N. Shepard, A. K. Romney, & S. Nerlove (Eds.), *Multidimensional scaling: Theory and applications in the behavioral sciences* (Vol. I). New York: Seminar Press, 1972.

CHANG, J. J., & CARROLL, J. D. *How to use MDPREF, a computer program for multidimensional analysis of preference data.* Unpublished report, Bell Telephone Laboratories, 1968.

CROZIER, J. B. Verbal and exploratory responses to sound sequences varying in uncertainty level. In D. E. Berlyne (Ed.), *Studies in the new experimental aesthetics.* Washington, D.C.: Hemisphere, 1974.

GUNDLACH, R. H. Factors determining the characterization of musical phrases. *American Journal of Psychology,* 1935, *47,* 624–643.

HENKIN, R. I. A factorial study of the components of music. *Journal of Psychology,* 1955, *39,* 161–181.

HEVNER, K. The affective value of pitch and tempo in music. *American Journal of Psychology,* ·1937, *49,* 621–630.

KREITLER, H., & KREITLER, S. *Psychology of the arts.* Durham: Duke University Press, 1972.

OSGOOD, C. E., SUCI, G. J., & TANNENBAUM, P. H. *The measurement of meaning.* Urbana: University of Illinois Press, 1957.

SHEPARD, R. N. Introduction to R. N. Shepard, A. K. Romney, & S. Nerlove (Eds.), *Multidimensional scaling: Theory and applications in the behavioral sciences* (Vol I). New York: Seminar Press, 1972.

WISH, M., & CARROLL, J. D. Applications of individual differences scaling to studies of human perception and judgment. In E. C. Carterette & M. P. Friedman (Eds.), *Handbook of perception* (Vol. II): *Psychophysical judgment and measurement.* New York: Academic, 1974.

Index